When Russia Learned to Read

WHEN RUSSIA LEARNED TO READ

Literacy and Popular Literature, 1861-1917

JEFFREY BROOKS

Princeton University Press

Princeton, New Jersey

Published by Princeton University Press, 41 William Street,
Princeton, New Jersey 08540
In the United Kingdom: Princeton University Press,
Guildford, Surrey

Library of Congress Cataloging in Publication Data will
be found on the last printed page of this book

First Princeton Paperback printing, 1988

Publication of this book has been aided by a grant from the
Publications Program of the National Endowment for the
Humanities, an independent Federal agency

This book has been composed in Linotron Sabon type

Clothbound editions of Princeton University Press books
are printed on acid-free paper, and binding materials
are chosen for strength and durability. Paperbacks,
although satisfactory for personal collections, are not
usually suitable for library rebinding

Printed in the United States of America by Princeton
University Press, Princeton, New Jersey

CONTENTS

ILLUSTRATIONS

TABLES

ACKNOWLEDGMENTS

I ACKNOWLEDGE with great pleasure the assistance of friends and colleagues and the support of various institutions.

Karen McConnell Brooks helped with the book from start to finish, and I thank her. Richard Hellie was unsparing of his time and considerable energy in making suggestions from the moment I arrived at the University of Chicago; I am also grateful to him for seeing merit in this project at a very early stage. Jean Laves Hellie gave me the benefit of her perceptive criticism many times. Norman Naimark and Christina Lodder both read the manuscript carefully and made copious suggestions. Arcadius Kahan and Eric Kollman shared their ideas and time with me; I am sorry I cannot share the final product with them. William Mills Todd, Neil Harris, Arthur Mann, Vladimir Shlapentokh, Wendy Griswold, Sergei Ignashev, Tsuyoshi Hasegawa, Milton Ehre, Richard Stites, Ralph Fisher, and Daniel Field all took time to read and comment on my lengthy text. My anonymous reviewers at Princeton University Press made a number of suggestions, most of which I followed. Alfred J. Rieber shared his ideas about my chapter on success. David Joravsky commented on several chapters I presented as papers, one of which I presented at the Northwestern University Center for the Interdisciplinary Study of Science and Technology. I benefited from comments received at the University of Chicago workshops in the History of Education, the Sociology of Culture, and International History; I thank John Craig, Wendy Griswold, and Akira Iriye for their help in this regard. Peter Kenez shared parts of his forthcoming study of literacy and propaganda in Soviet Russia with me. William Todd permitted me to read his forthcoming study of literature and society in early nineteenth-century Russia. I also learned much from the work of A. V. Blium. James Krukones sent me his dissertation about *Selskii vestnik*, and I gained much from reading it.

I would like to thank my teachers at Stanford University, Terence Emmons, Wayne Vucinich, Donald Fanger, and Ivo Lederer. Although this book did not grow out of my dissertation, my interest in the subject began in the latter period of my graduate studies. William Heywood and my other colleagues at Cornell College, where I began the book, encouraged my efforts.

I also benefited from the lively intellectual atmosphere at the University of Chicago, and from interaction with my colleagues in the History Department. D. Gale Johnson and Theodore W. Schultz of the Department of Economics are not aware of their contribution to this project, but their teaching and writing about the process of growth in rural economies enriched my thinking about changes taking place in Russia in this period.

Several research trips to the Soviet Union were made possible by support from the International Research and Exchange Board and Fulbright-Hays. A grant from the National Endowment for the Humanities made it possible for me to rethink and expand the project at an early stage. Several summer sojourns at the University of Illinois summer workshop in Urbana were also of great help, as was a summer session I spent at the City University of New York studying literary modernism on an NEH summer grant.

My work profited from the resources of many libraries and from the help of librarians. I am particularly grateful to Vaclav Laska at the University of Chicago, his assistant Halyna Pankiw, and the library staff who succeeded in obtaining microfilm copies of many of the popular works I discuss in this book. Without their help this would have been a very different study. I am also grateful to the staffs of the Saltykov-Shchedrin Public Library in Leningrad, the Lenin Library in Moscow, and the Manuscript Section of that library, the Slavic and University Libraries of Helsinki, the New York Public Library, the University of Illinois Library at Urbana, the Cleveland Public Library, and my home library at the University of Chicago. Marianna Tax Choldin and the library staff at Urbana helped me a great deal. I was also helped by my student assistants, Louise McReynolds and Dmitry Shlapentokh. I received technical assistance from Keith Reynolds, George Fowler, and Ed Covington-East. I am grateful to Gail Filion Ullman and Alice Calaprice at Princeton University Press for their help. I thank Cambridge University Press for permission to use material from my essay in *The Zemstvo in Russia* (1982), edited by Terence Emmons and Wayne Vucinich.

I dedicate the book to my parents, Judith and Joseph Follmann, and to the memory of my father, Jerome Brooks.

INTRODUCTION

Russia sees her salvation not in mysticism, nor asceticism, nor pietism, but in the successes of civilization, enlightenment and humanity. What she needs is not sermons (she has heard enough of them!) or prayers (she has repeated them too often!), but the awakening in the people of a sense of their human dignity lost for so many centuries amid the dirt and refuse; she needs rights and laws conforming not with the preaching of the church but with common sense and justice, and their strictest possible observance. Instead she presents the dire spectacle of a country where men traffic in men, without even having the excuse so insidiously exploited by the American plantation owners who claim that the Negro is not a man; a country where people call themselves not by names but by sobriquets, such as Vanka, Vaska, Steshka, Palashka; a country where there are not only no guarantees for individuality, honor and property, but even no police order, and where there are nothing but vast corporations of official thieves and robbers of various descriptions.
  —Vissarion Belinsky, Letter to N. Gogol, July 3, 1847

A POPULAR culture based on common literacy arose in Russia from 1861 to 1917; this is the story of that unique form of expression, of its genesis and function in the changing world of the common reader. The thinking of ordinary people is part of Russia's history, and popular literary culture contains many clues to the character of Russian culture as a whole. We know much about the rich, creative world of educated Russia, but little about the imagination and intellect of the rest of Russian society.

Russia became more modern in the last half century of the old regime, and the attitudes of those who experienced and contributed to this modernity changed accordingly. Emancipation, urbanization, and industrial growth meant new opportunities for many people born into the lower classes. The gradual erosion of premodern social and legal constraints, including the division of the population into corporate groups such as gentry, clergy, merchants, lower middle class (*meshchanstvo*), and peasants, signaled the birth of a more fluid society. The dreams of Belinsky and other Westernized intellectuals that the common people might one day gain the freedom and personal dignity to fulfill their individual aspirations gained plausibility.

xiii

The external signs of a great shift in popular thinking were many. New tools, implements, and paraphernalia appeared among the lower classes throughout Russia, and they were purchased by people who sought a better way of life. The iron plows and harrows, threshers and other mechanical aids in agriculture, tin roofs and brick stoves, suits and long dresses of machine-made cloth, as well as caps, leather footwear, vests, and other products of the factory were all signs of tastes and higher incomes.[1] Contemporary photographers illustrated these external changes with pictures of young peasants or workers in Western clothes and leather boots standing beside old men in traditional Russian dress.

Changes in the inner world of the same people, at least those who were literate, are evident in the literature that they purchased and read. When the lower classes learned to read, they turned from their oral heritage to the printed word, and new types of publications appeared to serve their needs. These ephemeral texts had little lasting literary value, but they meant something to the people who purchased them, and they remain a revealing artifact of their imaginative lives.

The study of popular reading material leads beyond the lower-class milieu. The Russian educated elite shared a common national experience with their more humble compatriots, and themes and issues that captivated intellectuals and writers frequently appeared in the popular literature, albeit simplified and compressed.

Most of the people who read the new popular literature were peasants or former peasants. The first section of this book is about their literacy, their efforts to acquire it, and how they made use of it. My principal intent here is not to explain the spread of literacy and schooling, but to show how the printed word entered the experience and imagination of ordinary people.

Literacy can be measured or defined by census data, the ability to sign one's name, tests of competency, various concepts of functionality, and other criteria.[2] The term is used throughout this book, however, in the sense the common people of Russia understood it at the time. To them literacy was a form of higher learning, a science (*nauka*), but it was also a skill their children could acquire quickly during a couple of winters of formal or informal schooling. The popular understanding of what literacy meant was bound up with a sense of its worth. People became literate because they valued it, and when they sacrificed to gain literacy for themselves or their children, they expected future rewards. In this respect people chose to make an investment in themselves or their children by becoming literate. This understanding of literacy is consistent with the approach to education developed by economists in recent years.[3]

Peasants' determination to acquire literacy led them to organize private schools of their own and to influence the content and duration of instruction at public and Church institutions. Primary schooling became widely available in the late nineteenth and early twentieth centuries, and before World War I the majority of peasant children were likely to attend school, but attendance never became compulsory. Therefore most children stayed for no more than a year or two, only long enough to attain the rudimentary literacy they or their parents valued. Because children spent so little time in school, the effect of schooling was more limited in Russia than in the more advanced nations of Western Europe and the United States. For that reason, the kind of literature read by Russian pupils and adults after they finished formal schooling was particularly important in forming new values and in improving reading skills.

Literacy meant reading. Writers, publishers, and distributors inspired by both ideological and commercial motives sought to provide the new readers with something to read. State and Church officials, philanthropists, educators, and political activists of all sorts put their ideologies into print and tried to spread their particular messages. Commercial publishing houses also went into action, but their objective was profit. The transformation of popular values owes something to both ideological and commercial publications. The popular commercial publications, however, are our best clues to the kinds of thinking the readers found most intelligible and appealing. The connection between the noncommercial publishers and their intended audience was always tenuous. The commercial publishers, on the other hand, had links with readers as solid as the rubles, or more appropriately, the kopecks, that changed hands in exchange for their wares.

The new popular culture was embodied primarily in the commercially printed materials that circulated among the lower classes, and this is the subject of the second section of the book. The growth of literacy, rising consumer income, and improvements in technology facilitated a rapid expansion of commercial publishing, and fortunes were made by entrepreneurs able to take advantage of the new opportunities. The success of individual publishers and authors usually depended on satisfying consumers more effectively than their competitors could. Firms that identified the demands of the new reading public flourished, and those that did not vanished or diminished in size.

The evolution of popular taste in reading is revealed by changes in the availability of different types of publications over time. The commercial firms produced a wide variety of reading matter ranging from song books and saints' lives to instructional tracts and even agronomical pamphlets; but the works that eventually captured the popular imagination most effectively were those of fiction. Commercially produced popular fiction became the predominant form of reading matter sold to the common people during the late nineteenth century. By commercial popular fiction I mean those works that have formulaic qualities,[4] even though during this period the formulas were still emerging in Russia. Genuinely popular works of belles lettres, such as fiction by Maxim Gorky, Leonid Andreev, or Leo Tolstoy, are not considered under this rubric. Works of known and respected authors that reached the widest audiences were generally more expensive than the cheap commercialized fiction, and in the occasional instances when they were not, there was often some sort of subsidy involved. Popular works of belles lettres usually reached the common reader only through the mediation of educational and philanthropic institutions.

The materials produced by the commercial firms were, in my opinion, a genuine manifestation of consumer sovereignty. Objections can be raised to this view, but I do not feel that they are borne out by the evidence from the Russian experience. It has been argued that popular literature is only a form of amusement, and that the authors represent no one but themselves. Marxist critics argue that the literature signifies a spurious system of values imposed upon the common people by a bourgeoisie.[5] The existence of the tsarist censorship may seem an additional barrier between the readers' demand and the printed word.[6] The study of popular publishing in Russia, however, shows the unusually close ties between the industry and its lower-class audience, and the popular commercial authors revealed their genuine independence from the censor in many ways. The continuity in popular publishing, the selectivity of the popular writers in choosing what to write about and what to ignore, and the divergence between the themes of popular commercial literature and those of the sponsored materials all illustrate the writers' sensitivity to their readers.

The public for the rudimentary popular literature that existed at the outset of the period included many readers who were not of lower-class origins, but the composition of the audience soon changed, and a new reading public of peasants, former peasants, and nonpeasant lower-class city folk became the popular writers' main clientele after the emancipation. These people were semiliterate even in the Russian context, and they were also poor, but this did not mean they were not demanding readers. The popular writers had to create a product with a powerful appeal in order to induce their audience to purchase it.

Russian popular fiction reflected both the backwardness of Russia and the country's rapid growth. The popular writers were often former peasants who shared the social backgrounds of their readers, and they had few predecessors on whom to draw. The educational level of the readers was too low for authors to borrow extensively from Russian belles lettres, although they took what they could. They had neither the time nor the learning to incorporate the literary traditions of educated Russia into their work in the way that, for example, American popular writers used the novels of James Fenimore Cooper. Nor were they able until the early twentieth century to appropriate much from the popular literatures of the more advanced societies of Western Europe and America, whose literatures were too sophisticated for Russian readers. The writers could draw on the familiar oral heritage, but they had to modify it to suit the modern tastes of their readers. The literature they created under these conditions was particularly close to the interests and concerns of their audience.

Such popular fiction reached its readers in different packages, and the form of delivery is important for understanding how it was read. The four most successful forms of popular fiction are discussed in Chapters 3 and 4 of this book. These publications include: (1) the single booklets (*lubochnaia literatura*) that were marketed by peddlers throughout the nineteenth and early twentieth centuries and took their name from the popular prints (*lubki, lubok*) that were the first printed material to reach the common people; (2) the serialized novels published in cheap newspapers beginning in the 1880s; (3) the short detective stories and mammoth adventure novels that often had Western heroes, both widely sold in installments (*vypuski*) after the Revolution of 1905; and (4) the women's novels that won a large and diverse audience during the same period.

These forms of popular fiction had their own peculiarities. The most important differences were between the separate booklets of the lubok, among which the readers could choose and read at their leisure, and the serials that demanded steady commitment to one particular story or type of story over a period of time. Like the humble English chapbooks they resembled, the lubok booklets served to initiate lower-class readers into the imaginative world of the printed word. The readers of these texts could move gradually at their own pace from traditional religious works and folkloric tales to more modern titles. All were available in the same format from the same peddlers. The reader of newspapers or serials, in contrast, had to follow the pace of reading set down in a series of texts. The serials allowed a more sustained contact between writers and readers. Writers could take their readers more closely in hand, and therefore depart further from the terrain of the familiar to build up exotic and remote fictional environments.

The literature of the lubok was most successful with peasant readers. The serials, which required daily or at least regular distribution, were more suited to an urban lower-class audience. The audiences were not clearly divided, however, since peasants moved to the cities and workers took serials to the countryside. These lubok tales are of particular importance because through them we can trace shifts in popular taste over a long period. The changing content of the lubok fiction is evident from a sample of two thousand titles and six thousand editions listed in pre-revolutionary and Soviet catalogues. I categorized these stories on the basis of their titles, which were usually long enough to reveal something of their subject, as in the case of *Grandma Marfa or a Prayer to God and a Service to the Tsar are Never in Vain* (1899) and *The Bandit Churkin or the Bloody Retribution* (1885). This rough ad hoc categorization includes genres such as popular historical fiction, romance, humor, folklore, and chivalrous tales, but also thematic groupings such as instructive stories and tales about bandits, merchants, travel, and war. The benefit of this approach is that it allows us to see the gradual evolution of the content of available reading materials over the whole period.

More than a survey of titles is required to identify patterns of popular thought, and Chapters 5 through 8 concern four themes from the literature. These include freedom and rebellion, national identity and the image of foreigners, science and superstition, and success and social mobility. They were chosen because they are prominent in the fiction and important in marking the evolution of popular thought, but they are also the main categories of popular fiction that have been studied elsewhere, particularly in the United States. As we trace the unfolding of these themes in the lubok tales and other forms of popular fiction, we can compare Russian attitudes and values with those expressed in the contemporary Western European and American literatures. A limited comparison of these popular literatures with the Russian is one of the objectives of the book.

The study of the development of these themes reveals the tension and movement in Russian popular culture between modernity and tradition. When we read this literature we witness the appearance of more secular, rational, and cosmopolitan attitudes, an increased sense of individuality, and a growing belief in the ability of individuals to influence the course of their lives through their own initiative and talents. The spread of these attitudes represents the belated entry of the ideas of the enlightenment and industrial Europe into the Russian popular milieu in a modified and simplified form, just as they had earlier penetrated the world of educated Russia. There is also, however, a very Russian aspect to this transformation. The passive obedience to authority, close identification with the tsar and Orthodox Church, xenophobia, superstition, fatalism, and humility that were the hallmarks of the Russian traditional mind gave way to new but still characteristically Russian ideas and attitudes. For example, national pride based on images of the Russian land and the expanse of the empire supplanted the earlier loyalty to tsar and Church. In the portrayal of the foreigner from the West, admiration and respect replaced mockery and contempt. The idea of freedom eventually came to resemble that expressed in Western European and American popular fiction. So did that of success, as the image of rural happiness gave way to dreams of wealth and fame in the city, and social mobility rather than prosperity within one's corporate or class group became an ideal.

Commercial popular literature did not exist in a vacuum. The attitudes of the rest of Russian society to these changes influenced the future course of this popular modernity, and the educated and semieducated responses to commercial popular literature are the subjects of Chapter 9 of this book. Critics, educators, political activists, and others interested in the common people worried about the influence of this literature and the meaning of its popularity. Their complaints about the commercial media illuminate the areas in which the emergent popular culture of the common people diverged most sharply from the values that the upper classes preferred them to hold.

Educated Russians competing for influence in the popular milieu produced their own reading materials, and I briefly and selectively consider these insofar as they also illustrate the contrast between the two cultures. The treatment of social mobility provides the most striking dichotomy between the sponsored and commercial products. Despite disagreements among themselves about other things, all the educated sponsors, in their literature, generally urged peasants and workers to accept their class identity, while the popular commercial literature was filled with glossy but not entirely fanciful dreams of individual mobility. The radical publicists exhorted the common people to struggle collectively for a better world, whereas those on the right warned them to accept their lot.

The new popular culture also met hostility further down the social scale in the large and rapidly expanding middle strata of upwardly mobile people of common origins. The beliefs and attitudes of these people were of great importance in determining the direction of Russian social development, particularly after the October Revolution, when they put their class credentials to good use. Some among them, chiefly the primary schoolteachers and those who identified themselves as "the intelligentsia from the people," had very definite views about what a culture based on common literacy should contain. I briefly discuss their perspective on the new popular culture in Chapter 9 of this book, because their hostility toward the values expressed in popular commercial literature was ultimately of great importance in determining its fate.

When we enter the territory of the lubok tale, the newspaper serial, the Russian detective story, and the women's novel, we stand on largely unexplored literary and historical ground.[7] Prerevolutionary popular commercial literature was banned soon after the October Revolution by Bolshevik educators and administrators who found it lacking in the proper didactic quality and the required message. Existing stocks of literature were destroyed. What survived the ravages of the revolutionary decade remained locked in Soviet libraries, and these materials have been even more difficult for Russian scholars to obtain than early Soviet newspapers filled with pictures of Trotsky and other dethroned revolutionary heroes. A few scholars have recently begun to describe this fiction, but the time when its content is integrated into the study of Russian history and literature in the Soviet Union is still far in the future. The hostility felt by Bolshevik revolutionaries for this literature has survived them.

Yet this popular literature can be the basis for a major reformulation of our views of modern Russian culture and literature. It lacks the profundity and originality of belles lettres, but this becomes a virtue when we seek to contrast one civilization with another. The Russian popular writers turned out crude and repetitive tales, but so did those of other lands, and a comparison of these small fictions yields a different kind of information than the study of works of world literature. The minds that expose themselves to us in popular literature are ordinary rather than extraordinary, and we encounter attitudes and values familiar to a multitude rather than to an elite. Russian prerevolutionary popular fiction is a unique source for including Russia in cross-cultural comparisons because it is equivalent to popular commercial literatures elsewhere, and in contrast to later Soviet publications that were produced under very different conditions.

Historians of exotic areas can serve as interpreters who try to explain how other societies differ from their own. This is my objective when I contrast Russian popular literature with that published in the United States, England, and France during the same period. Russia differed from these countries, and a comparison of these literatures illuminates that difference.

Russian belles lettres was not only part of the larger circle of Russian intellectual life, but it also belonged to a cultural system that included popular literature. Great themes of Russian belles lettres, such as crime and punishment and Russia's relationship with the West unfold on the small stage of popular fiction in ways that resolve seeming ambiguities, and the marionette-like heroes of the little literature have much to tell us about the world they share with their betters.

The distinctiveness of Russian popular literature reveals large patterns of Russian social and literary thought. Just as it is now difficult to conceptualize aspects of American civilization without reference to the popular images of success and the frontier, so our sense of the grand themes of Russian civilization can be much enriched by drawing out the parallels between popular notions and those developed in the high culture. This book is intended to provide a foundation for such new departures. It is not a study of Russian belles lettres with reference to popular themes, nor could it be, for the task at hand had to come first. Only occasional references are made to correspondences between the two, but this should heighten rather than obscure their importance.

The reader of this book takes part in an exploration of the minds of ordinary people at a crucial juncture in world history—when Russia approached and then turned away from the kind of market economy and the pluralism and democracy that were developing in Western Europe and North America. The pattern of modernization and Westernization in prerevolutionary Russia is familiar, but the changes in popular attitudes that accompanied it are not. The discovery of how rapidly the literate common people abandoned the mental architecture of the old regime and how quickly they absorbed values appropriate to the industrializing world around them leads to a new perspective on the Russian Revolution. It appears likely that the aspirations of many of the literate common people were individual rather than collective by the early twentieth century. They strove for personal success within the market economy rather than for a class victory over the prerevolutionary social order. The demand for social justice formed in these terms meant a just reward for talent, initiative, and virtue, rather than social equality. However, there is also evidence of a growing spirit of rebelliousness, and the breakdown of authoritarian ideas, which is revealed in the literature, probably cleared the way for the fall of the old regime. But a reading of this literature also suggests that few among the newly literate readers of popular fiction shared the ideals or the ideology of the Bolshevik revolutionaries.

We can learn much about the process of development and social change from the prerevolutionary Russian experience with literacy and the printed word. An extraordinary psychological metamorphosis took place among ordinary people in the last half century of the old regime. Not only did they seek and obtain literacy without compulsion, but they began to look at themselves and the world around them differently. Attitudes and beliefs that might have slowed economic development weakened, and the role of the commercial media in this process was very great. The kinds of commercialized reading materials that pedagogues and other educated Russians thought were pernicious proved to be full of useful information. In this respect, the Russian case can serve as a lesson for our own time. Those who argue that the path to modernity can be smoothed in developing countries through state control over the circulation of the printed word can learn from the Russian experience. Pre-revolutionary Russian peasants and other ordinary people entered a very diverse literary marketplace as consumers, and the evidence suggests that they spent their hard-earned money in a way that not only brought benefit to themselves, but also added to the modernity of their society.

I discuss the popular literary sources on which this book is based in a bibliographic essay, and there the interested reader will find tables showing the samples on which I base my conclusions. There is also a bibliography that contains a full listing of the popular literature I read, and its locations.

When Russia Learned to Read

I

USES OF LITERACY

A PARISH priest in the south of Russia at the time of the emancipation of the serfs in 1861 decided to bring literacy to his parishioners. He picked out thirty boys and began their instruction. When the parents realized, however, that the schooling was not compulsory, they ordered their children home, and the experiment in primary education came to an end. "Not only did the peasants not see any material benefit from the teaching of their children," wrote the disappointed priest to a clerical magazine, "but they saw this as a loss of needed work time and turned to me with the request that I assign their childen a salary for attending school, even though it be not large."[1] The priest refused. With this proposal, he complained, they "decisively crushed every inclination and love I had for the matter."

He had reason to be shocked. Educated Russians who differed about much else thought of literacy as a gift the peasants would be eager to receive. Literacy, they felt, would bring with it a multiplicity of benefits ranging from increased economic well-being to spiritual health. These hopes were not immediately fulfilled, and most peasants were indifferent to literacy at the time of the emancipation. For literacy to become a valued skill among peasants, Russia had to change, and the thinking of rural people had to change as well.

Change came during the last half century of the old regime. A growing number of ordinary people discovered the usefulness of literacy, and they made the effort to obtain it for themselves and their children. These are the people with whom this study is concerned. They constituted the bulk of the new audience for popular literature, and this literature bore the imprint of their experience. They sought literacy while others did not because they were living their lives differently, and they had different hopes and expectations. Their attitudes toward the printed word and toward popular literature—their ways of reading and their choice of reading materials—were influenced by their more general experiences with literacy in daily life. Their daily uses of literacy constituted the foundation on which the popular literacy of prerevolutionary Russia developed.

3

Literacy rates rose from 21 percent of the population of the Russian Empire in 1897, according to the census of that year,[2] to an estimated 40 percent on the eve of World War I.[3] Literacy among new recruits in the army rose from 21 percent in 1874, the first year of the new national service army, to 68 percent in 1913.[4] Although literacy among the rural population was low—no more than perhaps 6 percent in the 1860s and 25 percent in the 1910s[5]—male literacy was high throughout the industrialized provinces of central Russia. According to the 1897 census, male literacy outside the cities was over 70 percent in Moscow Province and nearly 68 percent in nearby Vladimir.[6] Literacy was also particularly high among the young, and the 1920 census showed that among children aged twelve to sixteen in European Russia, 71 percent of the boys and 52 percent of the girls were literate.[7] This was the last generation to pass through the prerevolutionary schools. Because of the predominance of the rural population in the total, rural literacy was roughly the same.

Illiteracy in Russia, as elsewhere in the world, was most prevalent among the peasants. Russian peasants decided to seek literacy for themselves or their children on the basis of their own perceptions of its economic and cultural value. The tsarist government influenced the preconditions for their choice, however, in a series of administrative policies that gradually freed them from long-established legal restraints on their independence and initiative. These policies began with the reform of the economic and legal status of the state or nonseignorial peasants in 1837, continued through the emancipation of the serfs and the establishment of local government in the 1860s, and concluded with the attempt in the early twentieth century to dismantle the peasant communes and encourage the formation of a class of independent small farmers. As a result of these changes, literacy gained value for individuals and also for communities, which needed literate intermediaries to deal with government authorities.

Administrative Uses of Literacy

The reorganization of rural Russia during the reign of Nicholas I (1825-55) paved the way for the emancipation of 1861 and had important implications for the growth of literacy. The reforms were carried out between 1837 and 1858 under the authority of P. D. Kiselev.[8] Their purpose was to reduce the economically unproductive restrictions on the lives of the state peasants, who in 1833 comprised a third of Russia's rural population. Kiselev offered the peasants new opportunities, and required them to select officials from among themselves. Peasant communities were introduced into a new circle of legal and economic relations in which written documents gained increased importance. Measures instituted to allow peasants to move from populated districts to unoccupied state lands, to make use of state forests, to colonize sparsely settled areas, and to leave rural Russia for the expanding cities provided the literate with additional opportunities and advantages. Peasant communes were allowed to establish capital funds for investment and emergency loans, and literacy was a useful skill for those who managed the fund and those who borrowed from it. Illiterate peasants kept records of these loans on a notched stick called a *birka*, but the literate had the advantage of being able to check and keep such records with accuracy.

More important in increasing the value of literacy was the rural administration organized under the reforms. There was a village elder, who was elected by village heads of households; a *volost* or canton elder, who was chosen by village elders; and a clerk, who was hired by the canton. The canton elder was involved in a considerable amount of paperwork, and the canton clerk was a salaried official whose main function was to carry out official correspondence. Although elections were often controlled by local gentry or state authorities, peasant officials played a role in the legal and economic affairs of their villages, and literacy was of advantage to them. If they were illiterate, village elders had to give written assent to official decisions with some kind of a mark.

The new responsibilities of the peasant commune, the *mir*, included matters of personal concern to every villager, and the way these responsibilities were carried out depended on the written word. The peasant community acted through the gathering of heads of households, who presented official documents to the *mir*, and its decision was recorded in writing. If no literate peasant was available, the record of the decision was made by someone from outside the village, usually a canton clerk or a police official. The lists of potential army recruits and tax records were also verified at the meetings, but only the literate could ascertain if they had been cheated.

Just as the Kiselev reforms gave literacy additional value for state peasants, the emancipation in 1861 of the gentry serfs had a similar but more powerful effect on the rest of the peasantry. The emancipation thrust the printed word into the villages—first with the physical presence of the Emancipation Proclamation of February 19 and of the emancipation statutes; then in the form of the various written and legal documents that the former serfs had to sign both with their former owners and with the state; and finally in the mass of documents and forms that characterized the administrative order established among the former serfs in 1861 and expanded to include the rest of peasant Russia in 1866.

The emancipation was enacted with the secret printing of the proclamation of February 19 and the 1861 legal statutes.[9] The bulky statutes were issued in 68,454 complete copies, and in 20,658 copies with local provisions for a single area, but the Emancipation Proclamation itself was printed separately in 280,000 copies. This short proclamation was read in the churches of Moscow and St. Petersburg on March 5, and within a few weeks it was read in most of the churches of rural Russia. The 280,000 copies were not sufficient, however, and provincial authorities ordered additional printings.[10] The proclamation announced in stilted language the main conditions of the emancipation: the peasants would be given their personal freedom in two years, and, although they would receive land, they would have to pay for it. The proclamation was thus a piece of printed paper that had important bearing on the peasants' future.

The authorities did everything possible to make the peasants respect this paper and to have the proclamation strike them with the force of liturgy. The date, a Sunday during Lent, the church setting, and the prayers that accompanied the event all combined to serve this purpose. The peasants' experience with public readings had been only religious—the reading of the Holy Scripture by the priests and the professional psalm readings at funerals—but this was a different kind of reading. Instead of spiritual guidance the peasants needed specific practical information from the readers of the proclamation. They needed to know whether they still had to work for their gentry owners, to pay them traditional dues, and to obey them. Their demand for answers to these questions pushed them to press against the curtain of their illiteracy and make the effort to see beyond it.

Peasants sought additional explanations of the text because they had already forgotten what they heard because they did not understand it, because they mistrusted gentry readers, or because they doubted the legitimacy of the proclamation itself. The idea of paid readers was already well established in rural Russia, since peasants were accustomed to pay for readings over the dead. Official accounts relate that they turned to retired clerks, psalm readers, priests, and other literate inhabitants of the countryside for additional readings of the proclamation.[11] In Smolensk Province, according to one account, a retired noncommissioned officer collected three to five kopecks from every listener, though sometimes he did not charge for his services.[12] A contemporary painting, "Reading the Manifesto," by G. G. Miasoedov shows peasant men of various ages gathered closely around a small boy who has a copy of the proclamation in his hands.[13]

The second stage of the emancipation came about with the appointment of local peace arbitrators who supervised the legal agreements between peasants and former owners regarding the size and location of the peasants' allotments, and arbitrated the rent to be paid for them until the plots were purchased. The allotment deeds required the peasants' signatures, and they again sought out literate people for advice. In a petition to the tsar a peasant explained that an unknown person—in fact, the peace arbitrator—had come from a nearby town, gathered them together, and demanded their signatures on "documents unknown to them."[14] The peasants thus asked for the documents so that their own literate could read them. The drawing up of the deeds was followed by the more lengthy process of making decisions on the redemption or purchase of allotments by the peasants—a process that took over two decades and also stimulated a demand for literacy.

The third stage in the emancipation was the establishment of local organs of self-government among the peasantry. Two levels of peasant government were created, as with the Kiselev reforms: first, the village commune with its regular meeting of heads of households and its elected elder; and second, the canton administration, consisting of a gathering of village elders, a canton elder elected by them, his assistants, a canton clerk hired by the elder, and a separate canton court of rotating judges, chosen by the canton gathering and empowered to adjudicate minor crimes. The canton administration became a center of literacy in the countryside.

The canton elder was the chief administrative official among the peasants. He was subordinate to officials from the nobility and the police, but he and his clerk had power over the peasants in their district. The canton administration linked rural Russia with the state bureaucracy. It interpreted laws sent down from above and applied them to village life, as the gentry serf owners had done previously, and it was a clearinghouse for all documents, tax records, recruitment lists, and for the internal passports needed by peasants who wished to leave the canton. Since the bureaucratic paperwork of the canton was usually beyond the comprehension of the village elders who made up the canton assembly, canton administration usually fell into the hands of the more educated canton clerks and elders. As the paperwork expanded, the clerk employed assistants, and the influence of the canton government grew.

Changes in the economy of rural Russia and the legal and administrative reforms brought the villagers before the canton government with increasing frequency. Arguments between landlords and peasants about allotments, rents, water rights, and the use of forests and meadows were aired at the canton, as were disputes about taxes and redemption payments. A priest wrote to a Church magazine in 1862 that the canton

7

government gave every peasant a lesson in the usefulness of literacy and derided the use of the old counting stick, the *birka*.[15] "The literate person does not pay money [at the canton]," explained a peasant from Orel in the 1880s. "He is more likely to receive some himself."[16] Even though clerks were often disliked, schoolteachers observed that peasants sent their children to school in the late nineteenth century in the hope that they would become canton clerks.[17]

The creation of the zemstvos in 1864, the new all-class institutions of local government, also had implications for the development of literacy. The zemstvos were dominated by the gentry, and their taxing power and executive authority were limited; their role in education and public health, however, made them a force for rural development. They were composed of provincial and *uezd* (district) assemblies of elected representatives, and each assembly had its own executive board. The zemstvos created opportunities for the more knowledgeable villagers to acquire useful information about agriculture, public health, and other subjects of interest. They were also a source of employment and occasionally provided other benefits to those who were alert and energetic enough to take advantage of them.

The demand for literacy encouraged by the Kiselev reforms, the emancipation, and the zemstvos was a function of the collective needs of the peasant communes as well as of the individual needs of the peasant families. The communes needed literate intermediaries to interpret and evaluate the legal documents sent to them by the canton and the state administration. Local government correspondents in Saratov at the beginning of the twentieth century observed that the literate were interpreting documents and giving advice at communal gatherings,[18] and it was in reference to such uses that peasants sometimes referred to literacy as a "trade" (*remeslo*). The literate could assist the illiterate and do them small favors on many occasions, but the patriarchal structure of village authority within the commune limited the power of the young literate men to advising their elders.

The Stolypin agrarian reforms of 1906 and 1910 weakened the communal land tenure system and patriarchal authority throughout Russia, and made it easier for peasants to leave the commune by selling their land, by consolidating it into a separate holding, or by establishing an independent farmstead. Peasants who left their communes had less need for the applications of literacy specific to collective life, especially the administrative applications. Some peasants commented that literacy was not useful on an isolated farmstead, and some educated observers felt that literacy gained significance for peasants only in a community environment, where it was certainly easier to attain.[19]

Those who expressed these views did not take into account the changed economic life of peasants who became independent cultivators. The general effect of the Stolypin reforms was probably similar to that of the emancipation. The establishment of separate holdings and farmsteads, and the settling of disputes between those who wished to divide and those who did not depended on written documents. Literacy had value not only for the more active peasants who left the communes, but also for those who sought to maintain them. The Stolypin reforms intensified the division that was taking place in rural Russia between those who were able to farm productively and those who were not, and in this way they probably heightened the economic value of literacy, as had the emancipation a half century earlier.

Economic Uses of Literacy

Historically, literacy has spread with industrialization, and this was the case in Russia. The rural reforms that brought the peasants increased independence also opened the way to new opportunities within the expanding market economy. Peasants had little incentive for personal development under the serf system, and because of the restrictions on their mobility, literacy had limited economic value for them. Even state peasants, who were not dependent on the whims of individual gentry owners, were bound to the land and to regular labor duties on it. Peasant literacy had pecuniary value before the emancipation, but primarily to serf owners. An exasperated rural priest wrote to a Church magazine soon after the emancipation, explaining why the peasants in his parish had previously shown no interest in learning to read. " 'What's literacy to us,' they usually said.[20] 'Although you know how to seize the stars in the sky, you'll go out on corvée labor all the same, and on corvée everyone is equal.' " This forced equality disappeared gradually after the emancipation.

Students of contemporary agricultural development observe that the value of literacy is reduced in traditional agricultural systems, where changes in productive techniques are slow to come, but that it increases as the pace of technological change picks up.[21] Until the Stolypin reforms of the early twentieth century, most Russian peasants were locked into the relatively static three-field system by the practice of communal land tenure and by the commune's authority, which was sanctioned in the emancipation legislation. Educated activists concerned with rural development at the beginning of the twentieth century thought that by ac-

9

quiring literacy, peasants would change their attitudes toward most issues, including rural development.

There is little evidence, however, that literacy alone was sufficient in dispelling superstition, or that it had much practical value in raising the technical level of agriculture in places where the commune still functioned. When questioned about the usefulness of literacy in the 1880s, peasants replied with reference to economic applications related to their involvement in the market. In a predominantly agricultural district in Orel Province, peasants indicated that literacy was useful for recording items that were loaded in a cart, for counting money received, and for borrowing and lending.[22] An observer of peasants in eastern Siberia in the late nineteenth century noted similarly that peasants used literacy for the narrow practical purpose of signing agreements.[23]

The Stolypin reforms made it possible for the more active peasants to establish themselves outside the authority of the commune where they could use more modern methods of farming and improve and expand their holdings. For these peasants, who were able to take advantage of technical improvements and who benefited from learning about them, the ability to read was of some value. Agronomical information ranging from tracts on beekeeping to designs for better chicken coops was being made available to those farmers who could make use of them in the late nineteenth and early twentieth centuries. The more prosperous and energetic peasants who modernized separate holdings were envied, hated, and mistrusted by the other peasants, but they also represented a standard of success. "The farmer is being born and the peasant is dying," wrote an activist in the cooperative movement in 1912.[24] To these peasants literacy may have had some value.

Home Production and Handicrafts

Peasants who did not become small farmers had three main alternatives to a dependence on established traditional agriculture: cottage industry, off-farm labor, and resettlement in a more promising locale. Literacy was more valuable to those who sought these opportunities than to those who remained in traditional agriculture. Some became *kustari*, the home-based peasant craftsmen, who, with the help of their families, produced sheepskin coats, woolen goods, bast sandals, agricultural implements, furniture, barrels, wheels, musical instruments, clay toys, icons, and much else needed by the people of rural and urban Russia. Among them were autonomous producers who turned readily available local materials into goods they sold in nearby markets and cities and to local customers.

Others depended on middlemen who sold to a larger market and supplied them with raw materials on credit.

Estimates of the number of craft workers in the early twentieth century vary enormously. One cautious calculation, based on zemstvo data, put the number in the forty zemstvo provinces at 1,800,000, but this is probably low.[25] Craft work was primarily winter work, but it provided peasants with a substantial portion of their total income.

Literacy was of obvious use to craft workers. They were perpetually buying and selling, and counting what they owed and were owed. "The peasants of our locale, who are constantly involved in the lively trading life of the well-known settlement of Rogachev," wrote a schoolteacher in reply to a turn-of-the-century zemstvo survey, "recognize and feel the need for literacy."[26] Others replying to the same survey noted the necessity of account keeping for all such peasants.

The literate craft workers were also able to use their skills when they bought materials and when they sold their products. Even those who marketed their products through middlemen, however, were likely to confront a situation in which the literate had the edge. Literacy was probably least useful to craftsmen whose entrepreneurial opportunities were the most restricted—for example, those who worked for someone or who had a contractual relationship with middlemen and had little opportunity to bargain. Literacy among craft workers was not much over 30 percent in the late nineteenth century, though it was higher among those who worked more independently, such as toy makers and icon painters.[27] Those who attended school or an apprentice program, according to one study, were more interested in getting established as independent craftsmen, and they had a better chance of doing so.[28]

Off-Farm Labor

Approximately twelve million people legally designated as peasants were living outside their native provinces or districts in 1897, according to census data.[29] The legal designation of peasant also included many who were second or even third generation urban inhabitants. Two-thirds of these mobile peasants lived in the countryside, but movement meant a break with traditional patterns of life for all except perhaps those who married into a neighboring county. Those who left their villages in search of seasonal or permanent work, the migrant and off-farm workers or *otkhodniki* (literally, those who go away), were likely to find literacy useful in locating work and in bargaining for wages. Like the craft workers, they were primarily peasants who chose not to depend entirely on their farm holdings for subsistence, and many of them also came from the densely populated areas of central Russia.

Two principal types of workers left their homes in rural Russia: the farm laborers and those who found employment in cities, factory districts, or on the railroads. Many agricultural laborers found temporary employment on large commercial farms in southern Russia, where tobacco and sugar beets were profitably grown. As many as a million migrant farm workers labored in the twelve provinces of southern Russia alone by the late nineteenth century, and an estimated four million were scattered throughout the fifty provinces of European Russia by the outbreak of World War I.[30]

The wages of agricultural workers were low, the labor was seasonal and uncertain, and the availability of jobs depended on the size of the crop. Literacy would have helped these migrants locate work and avoid disastrous mistakes, but migrant farm work was probably not an occupation in which literacy was of particularly high benefit. More likely, it was an inducement for workers to seek other employment after a stint as migratory farm laborers.

City Life

Cities were an important market for peasant labor, and literacy and school attendance among peasants increased with their proximity to a city.[31] The influx of peasants into Russian cities continued unabated throughout most of the postemancipation period, and became a flood in the early years of the twentieth century.[32] Cities not only provided temporary and permanent employment, they were also a place in which local peasants found opportunities to trade and make small purchases. Many villages had customary relationships with the cities near them, and such contacts encouraged literacy. The city with its shop signs and street names, window displays and price tags, newspapers and kiosks, announcements and bookstalls exhibited the written word to all who walked its streets. Peasants found employment in cities not only as industrial workers, but also as day laborers, servants, shop assistants, and odd jobbers of various sorts. More Russians were employed in 1897 in trade, private service, restaurants, and as day laborers than in industry.[33]

The literate had advantages at many levels of urban employment, and they were more likely to migrate to cities than the illiterate, even though cities attracted both.[34] The comments collected by zemstvo investigators in Moscow Province illustrate this: "The peasants' striving for literacy is stimulated by the fact that literate people are mostly required in workshops of tradesmen, factories, offices, and so forth." "The local popu-

lation dreams of work in a shop; there the work is clean and easy."
"Now the illiterate is the same as a blind man; he has nowhere to go
and no value; they do not take illiterates in the trades."[35]

According to an 1896 study, literacy was high among people employed
as stevedores (54 percent), day laborers (59 percent), urban coachmen
(84 percent), sausage makers (85 percent), bakers (86 percent), and in
restaurant service (90 percent), the common occupations for peasant
migrants, including children who were often apprenticed to shops and
restaurants.[36] Shop assistants in Odessa at the turn of the century earned
wages that were usually not much higher than those of factory workers,
but such work had great attractiveness for peasant children and their
parents.[37] "I want to be a shop assistant," remarked a peasant schoolboy,
"because I do not like to walk in the mud. I want to be like those people
who are cleanly dressed and work as shop assistants."[38]

Although boys were sometimes sent to school in the hope that they
would get such a job, girls were sometimes kept home on the assumption
they would not. "Why should girls study? They are not going to sit in a
shop," remarked a Moscow peasant.[39] "Why should I teach a girl to read
and write?" queried another. "She won't be a soldier, she won't be a
shop assistant, and a peasant woman has no time to busy herself with
reading books the way the lords do."[40] The most common nonagricultural
employment for women was that of servant. There were 1.2 million
women in service in 1897, and the literacy rate among them was 23
percent.[41] Clearly literacy was not a prerequisite for such employment,
but it may have brought higher wages or a more pleasant position.

The servants, waiters, coachmen, doormen, janitors, and others oc-
cupying the lower levels of the service sector constituted a particularly
influential group of city inhabitants from the standpoint of popular literacy. Many retained close ties with their rural relatives, although their
work put them into contact with more educated people. They could see
for themselves the benefits of literacy under such circumstances, and
reading could bring them both amusement and material advantage.

One of the first literary descriptions of the Russian common reader is
Nikolai Gogol's mocking portrayal of Chichikov's servant, Petrushka, in
the second chapter of *Dead Souls*. Petrushka, who likes to read while
lying down, consumes whatever is at hand, regardless of content. A prayer
book or a primer, it is all the same to him. What he likes is "the process
of reading itself." He may want to ape the gentry, but he is a reader
nevertheless, and when the Petrushkas ceased to be serfs, had some money
in their pockets, and began to read books of their own, their taste was
quickly discovered by commercial publishers. In fact, the editors of the
first cheap newspapers published in Russian cities were quick to identify
the serving people as an audience worthy of special attention.

Factory Work

Factory work was perhaps not so attractive to peasant men as work in a shop, or as a waiter or a servant, but many of them chose to do it, and in this group literacy was sometimes associated with higher wages.[42] There were 2.6 million workers in industry, transport, and trade in 1897, 85 percent of whom were men, and a majority (53 percent) were literate.[43]

The lives of many peasant migrants included a shorter or longer sojourn in the city, often followed by a return to the countryside prompted by old age, illness, or personal preference.[44] Such workers retained unbroken ties with rural life. They often left wives and children in villages, and frequently went back to visit, sent letters, and sometimes took over the family land when the head of the village household died. "The peasants leave our village for work in factories in St. Petersburg, where they live for three or four years because it is a long way. Peasants of other villages go off as carpenters, but they return home in winter," wrote a correspondent to N. A. Rubakin, adding that peasants who had learned to read but never left the village often forgot "their science."[45]

The factory was often a literate environment that left its mark on those exposed to it. Not only did many employers value literacy, but so did the workers themselves, who were occasionally willing to pay a comrade to entertain them by reading a book. "Learning that I read well, the factory workers began to get chapbooks for me to read, while they themselves listened," reminisced the lubok writer Ivan Ivin in the late nineteenth century.[46] Maxim Gorky had much the same experience.

Railroads

The peasants who went to work on the railroads, like those who came to the cities, entered an environment in which literacy had a multiplicity of uses. The railroad station was as much a center of literate activity as the factory or, for that matter, the city. The difference was that the railroads extended deeper into rural Russia. The demand for workers in construction and in the operation of the lines brought a new kind of labor market and a new sense of the value of literacy to many regions. The railroads were one industrial undertaking in which it was difficult to do without literate workers, even at the lowest levels. Section chiefs were required to be literate, and when foremen were chosen from among the workers on the lines, preference was given to those who were literate.[47] The first railroad opened in 1837, and the lines from St. Petersburg to Moscow began to function in 1851. Mileage of common carrier lines grew from 11,000 in 1874 to 43,900 in 1913.[48]

Workers were recruited both from villages near construction sites and from villages farther out, but once hired, they followed the tracks. Initially, many would combine their work with farming in their villages, returning home for the growing season, but the long distances gradually made this practice unattractive. The repair crews that worked along the lines, however, were primarily local peasants hired on a daily basis. There were almost 190,000 day laborers on the lines in 1905, and they comprised about a quarter of all railroad workers and employees.[49]

Railroads brought the logic and illogic of industrial society to rural Russia, and neither was comprehensible without an understanding of the written word. Illiteracy suddenly became a disadvantage and even a hazard, as the appearance of the railroad lines affected landownership, and the needs of railroad employees and passengers disrupted local prices, trade patterns, and peasant customs, creating opportunities for some and difficulties for others.

An observer during World War I described what happened when a railroad station was constructed a decade earlier on a strip of infertile land between two villages in Moscow Province. Near the building site a commercial settlement sprang up, and by the time of the war there were stone buildings, granaries, shops, a school, a post office, a church, bars, and teahouses. Here "life always boiled," as he put it, and the settlement was soon crowded with "people who are sharp and resourceful, our own type of Americans, Americans in the Russian manner, to be sure."[50] Besides the energetic and ambitious Russian "Americans" who were drawn to this site of activity, there were those who found themselves confused and bewildered by the new developments. Anton Chekhov, in his story "The Criminal," describes a peasant accused of causing a train wreck by taking a bolt from the rails to use as a fishing sinker. The man is unable to understand how he caused the wreck, since he and his friends had taken many other bolts without causing any obvious harm in the past.

Migration

Migration to distant Siberia, the steppe regions of Central Asia and the Caucasus, and to the Russian Far East involved great risk and hardship for Russian peasants, but large numbers chose to make the move anyway. It was an incalculably more difficult choice than seeking work in a city. Land hunger took the peasants to Siberia, but the move often created new problems. One of the best-informed of the prerevolutionary investigators, A. A. Kaufman, argued that Russian peasants had a better chance to make the transition to more modern methods of farming in their own villages than in the Siberian taiga or the Kirgiz steppe, where conditions were unfamiliar to them.[51]

Government authorities responsible for overseeing the migration attributed it to a variety of causes, including the crop failure at the beginning of the 1890s and the general changes in Russian agriculture, as well as political events in Russia and the Far East and the Stolypin agrarian reforms. Migration was, in the words of an observer, "the safety valve" that "averted poverty and catastrophe."[52] A group of local government specialists who studied the settling of the Russian Far East suggested, on the other hand, that peasant settlers, particularly the early ones, went in search of a better life and religious freedom.[53]

Literacy is not discussed in the volumes of the official series *The Migration and Settlement of Lands Beyond the Urals* (1910-15), but the story of its importance is revealed in various comments about the difficulties in providing the settlers with information, and also in the photographs scattered throughout the text. According to government data, 300,000 settlers migrated from European Russia to the lands beyond the Urals from 1861 to 1885, 1.5 million from 1885 to 1905, and 2.5 million from 1906 to 1910.[54] Most of them went to Siberia, but the steppe region and the Far East gained in importance in the twentieth century. They came primarily from the densely populated and long-cultivated lands of the black-soil region. Out of the approximately four million who made the trip, some 450,000 straggled back to European Russia.

Literacy was likely to be advantageous to the Russian migrants in all phases of their endeavor, whose success or failure depended to a large measure on their own personal qualities, first as migrants and later as independent farmers or in other occupations. The freedom in the new areas relative to the environment of their home villages may have meant greater opportunity to those with initiative and energy.[55]

The migrant settlers were largely on their own until substantial government assistance became available in the early 1890s. As Kaufman put it, "These were settler pioneers," who "put their hopes only in God and themselves."[56] The early settlers had to plan ahead for their survival and to work out their own routes, and the risks of going astray were likely to be greater for the illiterates. The value of literacy increased later on, when reading and writing meant improved access to government assistance.

One of the main tasks of the Migration Bureau, which was established in 1896 to organize and support the migration, was to acquaint prospective settlers with living conditions in the new regions, and to advise them about what was available and what help they could expect. The Migration Bureau published substantial guides in the early twentieth century that sold for under ten kopecks and contained information about the soil, climate, flora, inhabitants, size and locations of parcels of land, post and telegraph addresses, government offices, and the rights of inhabitants in different regions.[57] Such publications came complete with sample petitions needed to gain permission to move and for receiving parcels in the new territories. Settlement offices in European Russia had window displays to show the parcels of land available in different regions, but more information was provided when the prospective settlers were already en route, generally in Cheliabinsk.

The literate must have led the illiterate in all stages of the migration. Those responsible for the resettlement in different regions complained that the migrants showed "a herd instinct," and when one group rejected a location, other groups followed.[58] Once the settlers reached their chosen region they had to exchange their migrants' documents for a paper that gave them the right to a certain piece of land. A picture of a resettlement area in the Tobolsk region shows a man in uniform sitting at a tiny makeshift desk before a small cottage.[59] A hundred or so settlers are gathered around, one of them holding a piece of paper in his hand. Other photographs in the official volumes on the migration tell a similar story.[60] In one, the Migrants' Barracks Building of the Cheliabinsk Migration Point in 1908 is shown as a large wooden building with a signboard in front. On the board are tacked many small pieces of paper. Do they advertise available parcels? Or different regions? They are too small to read. Beside them stand four peasant women and a girl. In another, taken in Irkutsk in 1914, the prospective settlers stand in line for the kitchen. Over them looms a gigantic sign, "For the Settlers," but the smaller letters are illegible. Perhaps this sign also tells of available tracts of land, as did the one that was photographed a year earlier at Cheliabinsk, which read: "For the Settlers; there are available. . . ." Other signs captured in photos identify resettlement reception points, cafeterias, various shops for food stuffs and agricultural implements, and the points at which information was available.

The decision to go, the trip itself, and the conditions of resettlement led to a division between those who were able to adapt to the new conditions and those who were not. Kaufman commented that throughout the Russian Far East the ordinary peasant was not like Saltykov-Shchedrin's passive *muzhik*, who obediently assumed a subservient position and fed the two generals marooned on an island.[61] The successful Far Eastern settlers, in the words of one local *intelligent*, represented a completely unique type of Amur peasant, "a former peasant, a real American," who was "completely unlike the rather inert Russian peasant who so thoroughly knows his place as a muzhik."[62]

The process of migration and settlement encouraged the formation of communities of active people who were less bound to tradition than the peasantry of European Russia, not only in the new lands but also along the routes of the migration, where new commercial centers sprang up. In one of these centers, Blagoveshchensk, a city in the Amur, at the beginning of the twentieth century, a typist charged a ruble or two a page for copying with a "Remington," and a literate clerk could not be hired for less than 75 to 80 rubles a month, two to four times the wage of a primary teacher in European Russia.[63] Boom towns dotted the new territories, and a lore grew up around them. There were tales of sudden wealth from gold in the Amur and Siberia, and from treasure in Central Asia. The great migration was of enormous interest to the literate, and tales of sudden wealth in remote regions of the empire eventually found their way into popular literature. However, it was not necessary to be literate to migrate successfully, and most peasants who migrated could not read.[64]

Military Service

The possibility of military service rather than the blandishments of civilian life encouraged many common people to seek literacy for themselves and their children in the nineteenth and early twentieth centuries. Russian military authorities did not have the foresight to make the army an effective instrument of literacy; but in response to changing technical requirements, they eventually moved in this direction.

The prereform army was as backward as the rest of Russian society. At a time when Western military leaders were adopting new weapons and learning to use the telegraph and railroad, the Russian military clung to familiar practices. In many respects, the Russian generals had little choice, given the educational level of their soldiers and the technical base from which they operated. The pre-emancipation army was a force of former serfs who were freed to become soldiers but could not enjoy their freedom until they had completed their twenty-five-year period of service. The call-up age ranged from twenty to thirty-five, and the average number of yearly conscripts was only 80,000 before the Crimean War.[65] Since only a few were needed to serve, the chances of being chosen were slight, and ordinary people did not plan on military service. The civilian thus did not expect to share in whatever benefits literacy had for the soldier.

When peasants were taken into the army, they were often forgotten by their villages, and families considered them gone forever. The military was, in this respect, an institution separate from the rest of society. Such an army had many advantages for the tsarist regime, but by the middle of the nineteenth century it was becoming an anachronism.

The first step in creating a modern army in Russia was the formation of a reserve. The term of service was reduced in the 1830s, and demobilized soldiers formed the core of the reserve. This meant that more old soldiers, some of whom were literate, trickled back into rural society. By 1853 the reserve force created from these retired soldiers reached 200,000 men. Literacy among them was higher than among the rest of the population, though probably lower than 20 percent.[66]

The nearly lifelong conscription was replaced with six years of active duty for the lower classes following the general reform of the army in 1874. The peasant commune ceased to be responsible for providing a quota of recruits, and military service became obligatory for all twenty-year-olds. The yearly contingent taken into active service was set at 27 percent to 30 percent of the entire age group, with the rest going into the reserves.[67] The choice was made by lot, and the hiring of substitutes became illegal.

When military service became a common experience, whatever value literacy had for the soldier became relevant to the civilian who had not yet served. At the same time, military leaders were becoming increasingly aware of the need for more literate soldiers. In the first half of the nineteenth century, these leaders had, for the most part, considered literacy unnecessary or even undesirable for the common soldier. "They looked upon the literate soldier as fit only for the office, and did not consider this condition even of slight use at the front," wrote one military man in 1870.[68] At a time when Western European military instructors were using military manuals to teach literate soldiers, Russian noncommissioned officers themselves were often unable to read, and lacked, in the words of one military observer, "literacy, this first weapon for intellectual development, . . . the necessary condition to place the noncommissioned officer above the rank and file."[69] Provisions were made in the early nineteenth century to train soldiers to do office work, and schools were established for soldiers' children, who constituted a special social class until the emancipation. With these measures the issue rested until the Russian defeat in the Crimean War.

The first change in army policy toward literacy came in 1855, when schools were established to spread literacy among the lower ranks, particularly among the noncommissioned officers, but these efforts did not bring significant results. A more decisive step was taken in 1867, with the order that "the study of reading is to be considered compulsory for all the lower ranks in general, but only the more successful are to study writing and the beginning fundamentals of arithmetic."[70] Although literacy was made obligatory for all the rank-and-file soldiers, there was little formal organization of instruction. Money was allotted, and books and materials were purchased; but these actions produced limited results, since many of the teachers came from among the noncommissioned officers and the more literate rank and file, and were themselves scarcely able to read and write.

The new military statute of 1874 gave literacy a boost by providing a four-year term of active service for those who finished primary school and received an examination certificate, whereas less educated soldiers still served six years. The 1867 order on literacy was revised in 1875. Literacy remained obligatory, but only for the new recruits, and the emphasis shifted from all the rank and file to those who would attend company schools (about one quarter of the total), and then to those who would be trained as noncommissioned officers. The company schools and the scaled-down army literacy program continued to function until the 1890s, when most courses of this sort were abolished.

The term of service was reduced to five years in 1888, and the value of a school certificate as a means to a shorter stint declined. The value of the certificate had to be weighed against the cost to parents of sending their children to school for the whole three-year period, and only a small percentage of the parents thought it worth the price.[71] The shorter term of service for those with the school certificate was abolished in 1906. This ended the curious situation in which the Russian government, with one of the least literate populations in Europe to draw upon for its armed forces, probably increased the proportion of the illiterate among the lower ranks by making the illiterate serve longer.

The 1874 army reform required drastic changes in the whole process of teaching soldiers and noncommissioned officers their business. Earlier, the army authorities could count on the influence of the experienced soldiers and the long term of service generally to turn the promising conscript into a sergeant major, and the ordinary one into a credible soldier. With the shorter term of service, they found themselves with a serious pedagogical problem. The material they had to convey was more complicated and technical, but the time available for instruction was much reduced. The ordinary soldiers had formerly been trained in small groups by soldier "uncles." Such instructors could no longer be relied upon; the "uncles" had to be replaced by literate teachers.

Literacy eased the life of the common soldier as well. When training became more complicated and service manuals more common, literacy became increasingly helpful in the performance of regular tasks, in learning rules and regulations, and in securing soft duty posts. Literacy was higher in the more technically advanced units. At the time of World War I, literate recruits were more likely to go into the engineer corps, into air, automobile, railroad, and convoy troops, and into the artillery, the navy, and even the cavalry, whereas the illiterates usually ended up in the infantry.[72] For noncommissioned officers literacy became essential.

Graduates of the company schools in 1874 were supposed "to be able to read printed books and manuscripts, to pronounce each word unhurriedly, distinctly, and correctly, and to communicate the meaning of what was read."[73] A similar definition of acceptable literacy was in use at the company schools in 1892. The literate were expected to be able to read aloud, and to understand "a small excerpt on a subject accessible to their comprehension," to copy and take dictation, and to perform the four arithmetic processes.[74] The noncommissioned officer "should know how to entrench, to use local topography for defensive positions, and to read a map. Obviously all this knowledge is more easily acquired by an educated, or at least literate man."[75] A lieutenant remarked in the same year that, although the company commanders had to send literate soldiers to be instructed as noncommissioned officers, the experienced commanders kept back the best men for themselves, to be trained in the company as sergeant majors or other similar ranks.[76]

The need to have literate noncommissioned officers and common soldiers to convey messages, keep records, manage supplies, and write orders and reports was obvious, but some officers were ambivalent about the idea of a literate common soldier. They felt that the literate soldiers were less reliable politically than illiterates. "One rarely meets a literate and completely moral new recruit," a captain complained in a prominent military journal in 1886.[77] Two years earlier the same officer described the literate mischief-maker as someone who knows how to flatter the noncommissioned officers and how to get in their good graces.[78] The same "mischief-makers," however, brought the printed word to the barracks. Some read by their own gas lamps after compulsory lights out, and a company commander described small groups that gathered around someone reading "a monotonous popular tale."[79] A sailor who was enthusiastic about reading described how books went from hand to hand "like hot cakes" among his comrades.[80]

The value of literacy in the military was made relevant to civilians in peacetime by the possibility of conscription, and it became increasingly so in wartime as the likelihood of service rose. During the Crimean War of 1853-56, the Russo-Turkish War of 1877-78, the Russo-Japanese War of 1904-1905, and World War I, new recruits entered the armed forces and became acquainted with the demands of military life. The reformed army, with its shorter term of service and its large reserve, was more closely linked with civilian Russia than was the old serf army. When the new army went to war, reserves were mobilized and tours of duty of soldiers already in uniform were extended. The new mobilization procedures touched the civilian population more directly than did the old, and during the Russo-Turkish War, and particularly during the wars of the early twentieth century, peasants sought information about the conflicts.

Schoolteachers and government officials who investigated conditions in the villages often commented on the peasants' understanding of the value of literacy when serving in the armed forces. The establishment of universal military obligation made the "tangible advantage of education felt at once," explained a commentator in a pedagogical magazine in 1874.[81] Potential soldiers were influenced not only by the benefits of literacy, but also by "the knowledge of the discomforts that threaten the illiterate soldier," as one observer delicately put it.[82] In the blunter words of a peasant, "Among the soldiers the illiterate is a doomed man."[83] As the number of illiterate recruits declined, the unlettered were left to suffer embarrassment and humiliation.

Returning soldiers became propagandists for literacy in their villages, impressing on their fellow peasants the idea that this was a necessary skill for each recruit, and sometimes offering to impart it to them for a price. An experienced pedagogue explained in 1890 that the peasant who returned to the village after military service was a very different man from the one who left. Compared to his fellows, he had seen life beyond the village, had read a few books, and had attained "external polish" and "bearing." To the peasants, he had become a "mental person," and was treated with respect.[84]

Religious Uses of Literacy

Reading was often a religious experience for the ordinary people. The book was a religious symbol, and the process of reading had religious connotations. The religious associations with literacy came from generally shared traditions and usages that went back to the beginnings of historical time in Russia, when the first written words were the Scriptures and the readers were Orthodox priests. Most writing was considered religious in the early years of Russian Christianity, and the literate person was a link with enlightenment and, hence, salvation.

The local church stood out as a bookish territory within the circle of every villager's experience. There were books in the church, and the clergy read from them. Selected laymen participated in the service; they sang and read or recited from memory in the *kliros*, or choir. The author of a religious primer published in 1880 explained: "In former times all Christian men and women in the church knew how to sing and sang church songs. . . . But afterwards, when the numbers of prayers increased, not all believing laymen took part in the singing, and then those readers and singers chosen from the laymen began to sing and read."[85]

The tradition of memorizing religious texts made it possible for those who could not read to participate in the services; but literacy, especially that of children, was nevertheless highly prized. A priest from Voronezh wrote in a church magazine a year after the emancipation: "Our people love church singing. The literate and the illiterate love to stand in the kliros. Sometimes they know whole canons by memory—for example, the Easter canon—and standing in the kliros, they join in singing with pleasure. The junior deacon cannot do a peasant a greater favor than to allow his son to read through the Lord's Prayer in the presence of the whole church, and to stand in the kliros and sing along with him."[86]

The religious prestige of literacy was a boon to priests and school-teachers, and they made use of it when they could. "Look at that inexpressible joy, at that delight that shows among the peasants when they see that their children, relatives, or friends are taking part in the church singing. Then they begin to regard the school with more sympathy, since they see that it is of use to the children, and educates them in a spirit of Christian piety," wrote a commentator in an article published in 1903.[87] "Thank God our school board is now supplying the zemstvo schools with the Book of Hours and the Psalter," wrote a teacher to a pedagogical journal in 1890. "This gives us the opportunity to make the children read in turn at matins in the church, and in this way to elevate the importance of the school in the eyes of society."[88]

The religious functions of literacy outside the church service were also compelling. The priests and teachers of religion who hailed the usefulness of literacy inside the church sometimes promised peasants that reading the Scriptures would bring them closer to God outside of it. In this opinion they followed the early Russian clergy who promoted the reading of the Scriptures as self-help for salvation. "Take up literacy," exhorted one priest in 1867, "in order to see the contemporary light of the Scriptures, the light of the Orthodox faith, in this world."[89] The reason to attend school, according to the 1880 religious primer cited earlier, was not only to learn to read and write, but also "to know and love God correctly."[90]

Religious texts were read individually and in groups. The books were obtained from the local church, from schools, and from the byways of the trade networks that covered rural Russia. For the peasants, being able to read religious works had practical utility for improving one's life on earth and assuring a place in heaven. "Books of spiritual content are preferred, and they are read by all during Lent and constantly by the old, because they desire salvation," wrote a correspondent of the educator and bibliophile, N. A. Rubakin.[91] Such readings were often done in groups. "It is not a rarity now [1896] on a summer holiday to see a group of old men and women, and sometimes adolescents, sitting in the street, on the *zavalinkas* [the earth mounds along the outer walls of the peasant cottages], listening to a reader, a youngster, reading the Holy Gospels taken from school or some other religious book," wrote a pedagogical journalist.[92]

People could learn to read Church Slavonic, the language of the Scriptures, religious texts, and the church service without reading modern secular Russian. This suggests that Russia had a tradition of "restricted literacy"—that is, a literacy whose use was narrowly limited to a well-defined purpose.[93] In fact, Russia differed from societies that had a separate religious language, such as the non-Arab Islamic societies, in which Arabic was the language of the holy book. Church Slavonic and contemporary secular Russian were similar enough so that those who could read Church Slavonic could easily learn to read modern Russian if they wished. Reading the old script in which Church Slavonic was written required special instruction, however. Most schools taught the children to read old and new texts, and they were usually able to learn to read Church Slavonic without much difficulty. Russian editions of the Bible did not become widely available until the 1860s and 1870s, although translations were made in 1817-23, the last years of Alexander I's reign, and editions of the Psalter and the Gospels were distributed then. The extensive circulation of the Scriptures in Russian translation came in the late nineteenth century, when various religious and philanthropic societies, most notably the British and Foreign Bible Society, sold and gave away millions of copies. The vernacular religious literature of saints' lives and the Psalter and the Gospels also became more widely available in the last third of the nineteenth century.

Peasants especially favored reading the saints' lives and the Psalter, for such reading was thought to bring them practical benefits. In the words of one Church publicist, church educators liked the saints' lives because they contained "practical images of holiness and piety."[94] The Psalter was the most widely owned book in the countryside; it was read over the deceased, was used to teach children to read, and it was considered salutary to have one in the house. "In the understanding of our people, literacy without being able to read from the Psalter is not complete literacy," explained a teacher in 1894.[95] The peasant who could read the Psalter could avoid paying a professional reader to do so when there was a death in the family. "We heard praise from the fathers for Ivan, who read the Psalter over the deceased grandfather," said a pedagogue in the early twentieth century.[96] The Psalter had other uses. Peasants in Moscow Province in the late nineteenth century thought that the person who read the Psalter forty times would be forgiven some of his sins, and on occasion they used it to identify a thief.[97] The Psalter perhaps lost some of its primacy in the early twentieth century when children learned to read mostly from schoolbooks in secular schools. A priest complained in 1912, perhaps with some justice, that there were fewer and fewer old village Psalter readers.[98]

The religious meaning of literacy was nourished by dissident sectarian movements as well as by the Orthodox, and the peasants' enthusiasm for the Scriptures in the second half of the nineteenth century was as likely to signal the peasants' break with the Orthodox Church as their involvement in it. The majority of the dissidents were either Old Believers, who denied the modern Russian Church in favor of an idealized ancient one, or were members of what were called "rationalistic sects," whose practices were frequently akin to those of Western Protestants.

The rationalistic sects claimed the right to interpret the Scriptures for themselves. One historian of their movement has dubbed them proponents of "free faith," as contrasted with the Old Believers who followed the old faith.[99] For them, as for the priestless Old Believers, the church was the community of the faithful, and responsibility for salvation rested with the individual believers. The Scriptures became central to their understanding of salvation, and faith in the Bible led some dissidents toward literacy and away from the tradition of oral memorizing.

Literacy was also important to Old Believers because they treasured the old uncorrected books of liturgy, which predated the Nikonian Church reforms of the seventeenth century. The preservation of the old ways and the old writings was crucial to the movement, and only the literate could distinguish between the true and false texts. This tended to make Old Believer communities dependent on the literate among them, and the Old Belief very nearly became a religion of antiquarian books. The police and the Orthodox Church eagerly impounded and sometimes destroyed Old Believer books, but a substantial trade in the forbidden books was carried on at fairs and at markets. In his autobiography, Maxim Gorky describes the lively under-the-counter sale of Old Believer books and manuscripts in the late nineteenth century at the Nizhnii Novgorod Fair, and he comments on the reverence with which Old Believer peasants regarded even the new editions of the Scriptures.[100]

The Old Believer tradition was an argumentative one, and disputes over the Scriptures and doctrine among themselves and with Orthodox opponents were part of the daily life of Old Believers. The Old Believer activists were called *nachetchiki* (masters of Scripture) and were experts on the pre-Nikonian texts and the Scriptures. An observer of one such Old Believer stalwart among the Ural Cossacks commended his "great erudition in Holy Scripture" and his ability to argue.[101]

The active search for religious truth and the defense of it is what distinguished the Old Believers from the Orthodox peasants, who passively accepted the teachings of the Church in the person of the priest. The fervor with which the Old Believers professed their faith convinced many observers that they were much more literate than their Orthodox fellows; indeed, literacy was significantly higher among Old Believers than among the Orthodox, perhaps by as much as a third.[102] As N. I. Kostomarov explained in a nineteenth-century essay: "The Russian peasant received his own kind of education in the schism, worked out his own sort of culture, and more willingly acquired literacy."[103]

Among the rationalistic sects, such as the Molokane (milk drinkers) and the Baptists, believers read because the Scriptures were their source of faith. Like Western European Protestants, theirs was a religion of the book. "From early years they accustom themselves to discuss the Gospels, to be aware of their beliefs, to interpret them in their lives," wrote an observer of the Molokane in 1870.[104] The Baptists showed similar concern. "We spent our free time in reading the New Testament and in prayers," wrote one Baptist. "Our children also loved holy reading and prayer; they did not run about the streets, did not make mischief, and did not curse."[105] Collections of spiritual verse circulated among these groups, and the reading of Scripture and hymn singing were common. For such people literacy was an indispensable part of religious life.

Religious dissidence was a mass phenomenon among the peasantry at the time of the emancipation, and the numbers of Old Believers and rationalistic sectarians increased steadily throughout the nineteenth and early twentieth centuries. The persecution of the dissidents and the establishment of churches with Old Believer rites within the Orthodox Church hierarchy make the determination of their actual numbers difficult: estimates range from no more than one or two million to twenty million.[106] Regardless of the figure, however, the dissidents caused many ordinary people of Russia to think more consciously about religion and exerted an influence in favor of literacy far beyond their own communities and households.

Religious dissidence was one way in which peasants adapted their religious beliefs to the social and cultural changes around them. The dissidents' strict piety, their praying habits, and their reading of the Scriptures made them appear pious to many observers. Eager to spread their faith, even at serious personal risk, literate Old Believers and members of the rationalistic sects carried on religious propaganda among the peasantry, often as freelance schoolteachers, and stimulated as well as satisfied a demand for literacy. A contemporary observer commented in 1865 on the activity of Old Believer elders and their female "agents," who were not only literate but also well-read: "Their influence on the people has greatly increased because, in the face of the awakening craving for literacy everywhere, these women were ready teachers who did not demand monetary rewards and taught in the spirit of the people."[107] The persecution of the dissidents, and the destruction of their monasteries and prayer houses, which continued with only a few interruptions throughout most of the nineteenth and early twentieth centuries, scattered individual devotees and spread their teaching.

Not only did the dissidents have a more conscious and thought-out religion, but they often also lived less traditional economic lives, with some achieving notable prosperity. The role of Protestantism in stimulating and sustaining literacy and capitalism in Western Europe and Colonial America is familiar. Likewise, Russian religious dissidence was a catalyst for entrepreneurship and capital formation.[108] Russian dissidents often showed initiative and enterprise even when they remained peasants. They stimulated the thinking of the Orthodox common people about literacy and its implications, and about the possibilities for a more prosperous life. The government and the Orthodox Church responded not only by regulation and persecution, but also by competition, an energetic policy of counter propaganda, and ultimately an officially sponsored Church school system.

Secular Cultural Uses

People used their literacy not only for occupational or monetary reward, but also for pleasure, to satisfy their curiosity, and to exchange greetings. Reading for pleasure and information was often a social process for the Russians, and they frequently read aloud, allowing the illiterate to share the experience. "The stories that are read are often passed on from one person to another orally," wrote a correspondent of N. A. Rubakin in the late 1880s. "Not infrequently one hears a bookish story from the mouth of an illiterate."[109]

Literacy also meant access to that particularly modern package of information and entertainment, the daily newspaper, and newspaper reading became a regular practice among many ordinary people in the late nineteenth and early twentieth centuries. After the lower classes of the cities became accustomed to reading the press, newspapers began to trickle into the countryside. They were often sources of extraordinary information for the common reader, and enabled him to learn about the wider world around him. The self-taught poet and songwriter M. I. Ozhegov wrote to Rubakin in 1893 that the peasants of his village were interested in reading newspapers only when there was something about how "some city is swallowed up by the earth or consumed by fire."[110] "Only the news of the evils of the day or about the birth of a dog with twenty heads," he continued, "can reach our peasants through newspapers, and in such instances, they talk about it until another similarly unusual event occurs."

The most unusual events from the standpoint of the ordinary people were not dogs with twenty heads, but wars and revolutions. These events were a spur to reading and were topics about which the literate were constantly called on to inform the illiterate. The populist writer Gleb Uspenskii provides a good description of the mobilization for the Russo-Turkish War of 1877-78 in his *Village Notebook*: The canton clerk received the mobilization order, and the canton elder was summoned. The village elders were also sent for, and they in turn brought the peasants who were subject to recall. The future soldiers' questions about where they were going were not answered. There was no explanation of the official paper ordering the mobilization, and no one could clarify the situation.[111]

The situation soon changed, however. Newspapers became available in the cities and were read by workers in their cafeterias and taverns, and peasants who came to the cities to trade brought home single issues, as did migrant workers. Contemporary periodicals described peasants meeting at canton centers to listen to readings of the war news.[112] A mass of cheap booklets and printed sheets on the war and on related subjects appeared in the cities with tributes to the heroism of the Russian troops and caricatures of the Turks. Some of these materials were also observed circulating in the countryside.[113]

The mobilization of reserves and horses for the war with Japan and for World War I created a similar demand for information among peasants and the lower classes in the cities, but only the literate were able to obtain it. Newspaper reading became common in rural Russia during and after the Russo-Japanese War of 1904-1905. Many observers described the peasants' eagerness for news of the conflict, the demand for newspapers in the villages, and the gathering of peasants to hear the news read aloud, either by literate peasants or by others.[114] A self-taught peasant from Tver wrote to N. A. Rubakin in early 1905: "Until the war our peasants read no newspapers and considered this an unnecessary and superfluous matter," but the war changed that and the peasants began to read them.[115] A second informant of Rubakin reported that "a whole crowd of peasants gathered on the porch of a village shop to listen to a reading of war news."[116] A report in the Moscow daily *Rus* (Russia) described peasants obtaining newspapers from priests and railroad workers at a nearby station, and then gathering in the homes of the literate for readings.[117]

The revolution of 1905 was also of compelling interest. A correspondent of Rubakin's, a local activist in the agrarian Socialist Revolutionary Party, described events in Ekaterinoslav in southern Russia. After the railroad and postal strike of 1905, "when we did not receive the newspapers we subscribed to and began to read the local revolutionary newspapers and leaflets, which appeared in abundance, . . . then eyes were opened among the peasants, and they and we saw that the peasants and workers are the most offended and oppressed and most unhappy people in Russia."[118] In the fall of 1906, he continued, a circle of politicized peasants began gathering in a cottage to read and discuss books and newspapers.

World War I and the revolutions of 1917 provoked a similar response, and group readings were held much more widely. One journalist described the excitement about the war: "Never yet has interest in the printed word been as great in the village as it is now, according to general testimony. They say that in some villages every shred of printed paper is read, even if it is only package wrapping. Sometimes they send special couriers fifteen to twenty miles to the district centers for fresh newspapers. Afterward, they discuss in common the newspaper they have read together."[119] A study of 110 villages in Voronezh Province in the first year of the war revealed that newspapers were read in most villages and that one quarter of the villages had regular subscribers.[120]

Interest in the war widened the horizons of the literate and illiterate alike. Among the illiterate it encouraged contact with the literate and sometimes it sparked an interest in learning to read. A fortunate consequence of the war was, in the words of one correspondent, that "it called forth interest in foreign peoples and countries, and increased the demand for books on history and geography."[121] According to another observer, a new profession appeared at this time—that of newspaper reader. "A thoroughly literate person without any definite profession reads the newspapers to those who wish it for an insignificant fee."[122] Many reports indicated that adult peasants sought literacy, bought primers, and even attempted to go to school.[123]

Last, but far from least, among the uses of literacy was the reading of secular works by ordinary people who sought entertainment and enrichment in their lives. The lubok author I. S. Ivin (Kassirov) wrote in one of his several autobiographies that, to a newly literate peasant youngster, the reading of a secular tale seemed to open the door to "an enchanted region."[124] Because more and more inexpensive secular reading material became available in the late nineteenth and early twentieth centuries from both commercial and subsidized presses, literacy gained an increased value.

Group readings were common in rural Russia during the nineteenth century, as peasants sought to amuse themselves on long winter evenings. "Sometimes they [the peasants] gather in a house and one reads and the others listen," wrote a correspondent to Rubakin.[125] Readings took place in peasant houses, factories, inns and taverns, and even in the streets, as well as within the family circle. "You go along the street and what do you see," wrote an observer in the 1800s. "Now in one cottage and then in another, a little lamp burns on the table (we have kerosene lamps, which thanks to the nearness of the city—15-16 kilometers—have become the predominant means of domestic lighting), and at the table an adolescent boy or girl sits reading a book, and all the family members listen. Neighbors also come by to hear a bit."[126]

Group readings allowed illiterate parents to benefit from the literacy of their children. "They, the children, read a little to us and tell us how the fox cheated the rooster, and we laugh a lot with them," commented a peasant in Orel Province in the late 1880s.[127] According to an observer in central Russia, readings were popular at Easter, when it was considered a sin to sing.[128] A schoolteacher wrote of a former house serf: "As soon as the long fall and winter evenings begin, he manages to obtain a book from somewhere and gathers listeners, who are primarily workmen, at his house."[129]

What preconceptions did the common people of Russia bring to the texts they read? Concerned intellectuals involved in popular education made systematic attempts to answer this question in the last decades of the old regime, and their efforts provide us with the materials to clarify the character of the reading experience.[130] A. S. Prugavin, a journalist and scholar with a populist bias, produced questionnaires in 1888 and 1891 that circulated widely in rural Russia. N. A. Rubakin, a part-time Socialist Revolutionary whose many activities included self-education columns in newspapers, issued a similar survey in 1889 and collected information on this subject well into the twentieth century.[131] S. A. Rappoport, who wrote under the pseudonym of An-skii, lived among miners and peasants, and commented extensively on his experience of reading to them and discussing their reading with them. L. M. Kleinbort, a Social Democratic journalist, explored the question of popular reading from the standpoint of factory workers. Kh. D. Alchevskaia, a Sunday school teacher in Kharkov with a moderate political perspective, carried out an extensive investigation of taste in reading. She organized a group of activists to study responses to particular texts at a number of schools in her area, and they published a three-volume compendium titled *What to Read to the People* (1884, 1889, 1910). Early Soviet educators continued this tradition of studying the reader, and some of their first results serve as a final commentary on the prerevolutionary popular experience with the printed word.[132]

There were few disagreements about the peasant reader among prerevolutionary investigators. Prugavin, Rubakin, Rappoport, Alchevskaia, Kleinbort, and many others came to similar conclusions. Peasants read to be instructed. For them the very process of reading was salutary. The book was useful because it was a means to save one's soul and to improve one's life. The model for the book was the saint's life, the most popular of the commercial religious publications. As pupils who finished the primary schools of the St. Petersburg school district replied to a survey in the early 1880s, religious books were read because they "turn thoughts to the creator of all good," and "they help one to avoid evil."[133] The book was therefore functional and not a luxury. It was something to be used, and the physical pronunciation of the word was often what counted. "For the old lovers of godly soul-saving reading, comprehension played almost no role," observed an investigator on the eve of the Bolshevik Revolution.[134]

The power of the book was demonic as well as divine. The nineteenth-century village was a milieu from which demons, sprites, and witches were never entirely absent—a world in which Christianity was tempered with pagan survivals. In this realm of "double faith," as one experienced schoolteacher described it, repeating the complaints of early Russian churchmen, the book was sometimes infused with supernatural properties.[135] A commentator in a pedagogical journal of 1887 noted that the peasants believed in the existence of books that had "everything" in them.[136] A teacher wrote to the same periodical three years later that "six people asked me where they could get books on black magic."[137] The association of books and readers with magic is a common phenomenon in traditional societies, and bookish sorcerers could also be found in nineteenth-century France.[138] As secular reading became predominant, the book lost something of its mystery for peasants.

Because books were held in such high esteem, their content was supposed to be serious and true, and this judgment extended to secular as well as religious reading. All those who studied peasant attitudes toward reading came to this conclusion. In the words of Rappoport, for the peasants "Printed means it is true, printed means it is just."[139]

Although Soviet investigators who studied popular reading after the Revolution were bound by different biases and often operated under stiff constraints, they confirmed the findings of their prerevolutionary predecessors. N. D. Rybnikov and others who studied the results of a survey of 11,200 Red Army soldiers in 1920 and 1921 concluded that Rubakin and Rappoport were essentially right about the peasants' religious approach to reading. Peasants wanted practical advice about "how to live" from books, and they were more interested in religious questions than their urban comrades.[140] Another Soviet investigator summed up the first decade of Soviet study of peasant readers with the same conclusion: "From books they demand not only practical instruction—so to speak, advice—but they demand some moral influence as well."[141] The model of the saint's life is called to mind by a comment of one of the most perceptive early Soviet investigators, M. I. Slukhovskii. After studying a wide range of materials he concluded, "The literate peasant 'reader' seeks the description of heroic lives in belles lettres."[142] This did not mean that the peasants read only religious works; by the end of the nineteenth century their reading was primarily secular. What it does mean is that they transposed the habits of reading associated with religious materials to secular texts.

The peasants tended traditionally to divide all books into two categories, the godly and the humorous. The Scriptures were the model for the first sort of text, and the frivolous fairy tale the exemplar of the second. The fairy tale was ungodly, untrue, useless, amusing, and uninstructive. The true religious book had the opposite qualities. Even with the coaching of Sunday school teachers, Alchevskaia's pupils sometimes reacted negatively to fairy tales. "There is nothing serious in them," said one pupil; "it is a fairy tale and nothing more," observed another.[143]

As peasant readers accepted commercial popular fiction, the traditional dichotomy between the secular and the religious weakened, and their approach to the printed word became more complex. Although some prerevolutionary observers believed that peasants considered all popular fiction to be as useless as fairy tales, there is reason to conclude that only stories lacking a certain level of realism were relegated to the realm of useless fantasy. The commercial authors created fiction that contained enough didacticism and verisimilitude to suit their audience. Secular works were often taken to be as noteworthy as religious ones. A peasant replied to a survey conducted during World War I that he liked "books about Jesus Christ, how they tortured him, and about Kuzma Kriuchkov

[A Russian war hero], how he chopped up the Germans."[144] Peasants found apparent falsehood in fiction and not secularism itself suspect. As Slukhovskii concludes in his study of Soviet peasant readers, the peasants rejected utopian literature because "they speak out against anything in a story that is unlike the truth."[145] Other Soviet investigators came to similar conclusions. According to a study of peasant youth at the end of the 1920s, the peasants enjoyed romantic adventures so long as they did not "leave the limits of the real."[146]

The blurring of the line between religious and secular works helps to explain the degree of success enjoyed by educated activists in presenting selections from nineteenth-century Russian literature to peasant readers in instructional situations and public readings. Prerevolutionary and some Soviet investigators agreed that peasants were willing to accept the works of classical Russian writers as useful reading. Leo Tolstoy was the favorite author of the Red Army soldiers who were surveyed in 1920 and 1921 because "he writes truthfully," "as a teacher."[147] Rappoport made a most cogent case for the view that peasants could accept the nineteenth-century Russian classics as a third type of book, which was true to life. As a populist, however, he believed that peasants should have their own special reading material.

The study of lower-class urban readers was complicated by the investigators' attempts to contrast peasant and worker readers, an approach likely to heighten their biases. Nevertheless, the agreement between prerevolutionary and Soviet investigators is striking.[148] Although the difference between peasant and worker readers can hardly have been as sharp as investigators suggest, it is reasonable to believe that the general outlines of their comparison are valid. Workers were found to be more secular readers than their rural cousins. They read more, more regularly, and more widely, and investigators attributed this to the fact that their horizons, experiences, and opportunities were greater. More important, they were not as apt to demand didacticism of literature, and they did not require as clear a message as did the peasants. This meant that they were more willing to read light fiction.

Rappoport stressed that workers like to lose themselves in adventure stories as an escape for their uninspired lives, whereas the peasants wanted to read about subjects closer to their interests. The validity of this observation is open to dispute in view of his populist bias, but workers did seem to have a less purposive understanding of the function of the printed word. L. M. Kleinbort found breadth in the workers' reading that was absent among the peasantry.[149] Soviet investigators confirmed this insight when they found that workers were more interested in reading about foreign places and that they even liked translations of foreign works.[150] These observations are borne out by the contrast between the content of the literature of the lubok, which had a large rural audience, and that of the newspaper serials, detective stories, and installment novels, which attracted a more urban readership.

Workers also differed from peasants, according to some observers, in their respect and admiration for the authors of the books they read.[151] Whereas the book was frequently an anonymous instrument of enlightenment to peasant readers, workers saw it as the product of someone's creativity, effort, and ambition. Popular authors of belles lettres were portrayed as celebrities in the cheap newspapers and magazines that were more likely to be read by city people than by peasants. For both workers and peasants, however, the printed word retained something of its original religious significance, which enhanced the power of the printed word, and the idea of spiritual self-perfection was translated into a quest for personal self-improvement in the secular texts.

The belief that the printed word is a means to attain power over oneself and one's environment was at the heart of the demand for literacy in Russia. Growing numbers of ordinary people took the trouble to learn to read before the October Revolution because they became aware of the practical and cultural uses of literacy in their daily lives.

II

PRIMARY SCHOOLING

POPULAR education in Russia was rudimentary, but the school figured prominently in the lives of the literate. In many rural communities, the schoolteacher was the only secular authority on the printed word, and the school the only place where a substantial quantity of nonreligious books was available. The teaching curriculum and the observable effects of instruction on the pupils added to the meaning of literacy in the popular milieu. Educators, government and Church officials, and others sought to use schools to disseminate the values they considered appropriate for the common person. Although the representatives of officialdom could determine formal school programs, often they were less influential than the teachers and parents, who were personally involved in the life of the individual schools.[1]

The quality of popular literacy depended on local involvement in schooling, and the willingness of parents to send their children to school was influenced by the accessibility and kind of instruction provided. The predominant influence of the local community on the content of primary schooling was inherent in the evolving structure of the rural primary school system, through which the vast majority of Russian school children passed. Since compulsory primary schooling was never instituted, school attendance depended on the parents' willingness to invest in their children's future, and therefore on a belief in the ability of people to improve the quality of their lives with acquired skills.

The establishment of a comprehensive network of primary schools in which the children of peasants and lower-class city residents could learn to read was the essential prerequisite for the appearance of a mass audience for the popular commercial literature that was detested by teachers and educators, as well as for the semiofficial people's literature they sponsored as an alternative. But the limited character of primary schooling, restricted largely to a year or two of instruction, gave school children relatively little opportunity to acquire general information in the schoolhouse. As a result, popular literature had a greater importance as a source of information in Russia than elsewhere in Europe, where primary schooling lasted longer and government control over curricula was more effective.

The schooling of the common people took place, for the most part, where they were—in the countryside. Migrants to cities usually did not leave their home villages until they were already past school age, and many of those working in cities left wives and children at home in the countryside. City children were more likely than rural children to attend school, but it was in the rural schools that the majority of common people learned to read. Some adult education was available in Russian cities as well, but it was primarily for those who were already literate or semiliterate.

The development of primary schooling in Russia, as in Western Europe, depended on an interplay of private and public initiative. Schools were founded in rural Russia between the emancipation and the October Revolution by activists in the new zemstvo institutions of local government, the Orthodox Church, the Ministry of Education, and the peasants themselves. The competition among various funding authorities led to increased expenditures for schooling. Although the content of instruction differed in different types of schools, the influence of the local communities was paramount.

Peasant Schools of Literacy

Peasant communities exerted the dominant influence on schooling in the first decades after the emancipation, and the peasant schools of literacy (*shkoly gramoty*) reflected the popular demand for education. Schools of this type appeared throughout Russia in the postemancipation period; although no firm figures exist on the numbers of such schools before 1894, one estimate indicates there were from 15,000 to 20,000 in the 1880s, with 300,000 to 400,000 pupils.[2] Peasants established these schools when and where they sought literacy. They paid voluntarily for instruction they valued, and their children attended willingly, insofar as the family means and the wishes of the parents permitted. The teachers were paid a wage that reflected both the value placed by the peasants on instruction and the availability of instructors; they sought to satisfy their clientele, and the peasants were active in assuring that they got what they paid for. If the arrangement was not satisfactory for parent and teacher alike, either party could easily terminate it.

The literacy schools differed from one another in external format, but invariably depended on peasant demand and initiative. Sometimes a literate outsider was hired to teach the children for a single winter, at other times a literate villager would teach his neighbors' children in his own cottage, and in some cases peasants joined together to found a more permanent school in a separate building. The simplest arrangement was a temporary teacher from outside the village. In such cases, peasants provided room, board, and sometimes payment in kind in addition to a small salary during the period of instruction, and sent the tutor on his way when the job was done. One such teacher, who subsequently got a secondary education and a zemstvo school post, described in a letter to a pedagogical magazine how he left his village to seek work in the famine winter of 1891-92 and was taken in by a prosperous peasant who offered him room and board in exchange for teaching his son.[3] The wandering teachers resembled migrant laborers in their search for work outside the village. Their position was therefore equivalent to that of a hired worker of the commune, and their status correspondingly low.

Literate villagers who instructed the children of fellow peasants were socially superior to the itinerant teacher. The former were usually members of the commune, and the school functioned like a cottage industry within the village. "These schools exist like the tailors' and joiners' workshops," wrote Leo Tolstoy in 1862. "The people even regard them in the same way, and the teachers use the same methods."[4] A literacy school teacher from Riazan wrote in a letter to N. A. Rubakin how he learned to read from his father, a Crimean War veteran, and in 1879, at the age of ten, before he even knew how to write, began giving reading lessons in his native village.[5]

Schools with special buildings involved the participation of a group of peasants or of a whole commune. The schools administered by peasant communes were not formally considered literacy schools, and were listed separately in official statistics. The commune schools were similar to literacy schools in that local peasant control over them was substantial, and they were sometimes developed on peasant initiative. But unlike the literacy schools, they were supervised by the Ministry of Education, and they were larger and often more permanent.

Religious dissidence was an important spur to private primary instruction in rural Russia throughout the nineteenth and early twentieth centuries, and such astute contemporary students of popular education as A. S. Prugavin and N. V. Chekhov believed that the teachers in these schools were often Old Believers and other sectarians.[6] The complaints of conservative and clerical observers support this view. A commentator in a moderate clerical publication bemoaned the ubiquitous influence of Old Believer and sectarian *nachetchiki* over the Orthodox peasants: "The teachers in the village are often diverse literate people, nachetchiki from the schismatics or some wandering pilgrims with perverted religious no-

37

tions, who are honored in popular belief as people of strict piety and learning."[7]

The schools established through the peasants' own initiatives were often a step toward more formal schooling, and the zemstvos and clerical authorities took over many of them when they formed their own school systems. The legal standing of the peasant schools was insecure until the early 1890s, when they were placed under Church authority. Most of them were either closed or turned into regular Church schools a decade and a half later in conjunction with plans for the standardization of instruction. The changing structure of rural primary schooling in Russia is shown in Table 1. Variations in the categorization of schools reduce the accuracy of the figures, but they clearly reflect the growth of the zemstvo, Ministry, and Church schools, as well as the decline of the independent peasant schools (the literacy schools and the commune schools).

Zemstvo Schools

The zemstvo activists set the standard in Russian primary instruction, and the zemstvo school became the model for the Russian public school despite the weaknesses of the zemstvos themselves. Education was among the nonobligatory responsibilities of the zemstvos, but the legal arrangements for schooling were such that zemstvo authorities shared jurisdiction with the Ministry of Education.[8] The 1864 statute on primary schools divided the economic and pedagogical supervision of schooling by grant-

TABLE 1. Number of Rural Primary Schools

Year	Zemstvo	Commune	Church	Literacy	Ministry	Other	Total
1879-84*	9,108	?	4,213	?	?	?	22,770
1894	13,129	8,014	11,197	16,799	964	4,333	54,436
1911	27,944	11,051	31,202	4,291	5,752	9,478	89,718
1914	44,879	4,893	34,341	2,171	21,996	?	108,280

* Figures for 1879-84 include only European Russia. All figures are for rural schools except in the case of the 1914 Church schools, where the figure is for one-class schools, which were almost all rural.
Sources: Statisticheskii vremennik Rossiiskoi Imperii, series iii, vol. 1 (St. Petersburg, 1884), pp. 290-95; Nachal'noe narodnoe obrazovanie v Rossii, ed. G. A. Fal'bork and V. Charnoluskii (St. Petersburg, 1900), 2:x,368; Odnodnevnaia perepis' nachal'nykh shkol Rossiiskoi Imperii proizvedennaia 18 ianvaria 1911 goda, vol. 16, part 2 (Petrograd, 1916), pp. 2-3, 19-20; Nachal'nye uchilishcha vedomstva Ministerstva narodnogo prosveshcheniia v 1914 godu (Petrograd, 1916), pp. 76-77; Istoricheskii ocherk razvitiia tserkovnykh shkol za istekshee dvadtsatipiatiletie (1884-1909) (St. Petersburg, 1909), appendix, pp. 14-15; Tserkovnye shkoly Rossiiskoi Imperii za 1914 god (Petrograd, 1916), p. 33.

ing financial jurisdiction to the institutions that funded schools, and allowing the provincial and district school boards to supervise instruction. The zemstvo representatives were in a minority on the boards, and the Ministry of Education was granted additional powers in the school statute ten years later.

Baron N. A. Korf, a visionary educator, sketched out the model for the zemstvo school in his widely acclaimed handbook, *The Russian Primary School*, which appeared soon after the 1864 statute.[9] He advocated a regular school with a qualified and properly paid teacher, a three-year program of instruction, an adequate building, and a secure source of financial support and enthusiasm from the peasant commune. To attain this ideal, zemstvo educators supported already-existing peasant and commune schools and founded new ones where local support was sufficient. They attempted to raise standards in the peasant schools by rewarding the best teachers, paying salaries to teachers, and providing teaching materials.

As the number of schools founded by the zemstvo in zemstvo provinces increased, the balance of funding shifted until the zemstvos provided primary funding, and the communes contributed supplementary support. By 1883, 40 percent of the schools in the sixty provinces of European Russia were supported predominantly by the zemstvos.[10] The peasant communes, however, continued to make substantial nonmonetary contributions, including provision and maintenance of a building and custodian, fuel for heat and light, land for the school, and contributions in kind toward support of the teacher. According to the historian of the zemstvos, Boris Veselovskii, the zemstvo school expenditures did not equal the total communal contribution until 1889.[11]

Toward the end of the century, the emphasis of zemstvo educators was increasingly on the establishment of proper zemstvo schools that met the standards defined by educators such as Baron Korf. Zemstvo teachers were accountable to the zemstvos and to other school board representatives, as well as to Ministry of Education inspectors. The zemstvos were often too remote to supervise the teachers effectively or to give them much day-to-day encouragement.

Government officials and members of the school board also supervised the teachers when they could. They exercised their authority through occasional unannounced visits to the schools, as did the official school inspectors. The effectiveness of this kind of surveillance was limited by the infrequency of inspection of remote rural schools, however, and the surprise calls, according to comments in school journals, succeeded only in frightening the teachers and disrupting classes. Administrative control was more effective in the Ministry schools, which were fewer in number, more accessible and whose teachers were either part of the civil service hierarchy or hoped to be.

District and provincial zemstvos established and funded an extensive network of schools, but the zemstvo educators never gained complete control over their school system. They were hampered by the laws governing education, and by the limitations of the zemstvos, which never became fully representative and always suffered from a lack of local executive authority. Zemstvo educators managed their school systems through a variety of ad hoc administrative mechanisms, special boards, bureaus, and commissions, but the pattern of zemstvo school management remained an uneven one. When plans were laid for universal primary education with substantial state funding, zemstvo educators found themselves outmaneuvered by Ministry of Education officials.

Church Parish Schools

Schools sponsored by the Orthodox Church, like those of the peasants, existed long before the emancipation. In the pre-emancipation Church school, a priest taught on a voluntary basis, and instruction was free of charge. The priest-teacher was a mentor to the pupils, whose attendance was also voluntary. Instruction took place in the church, and was inseparable from church functions. The pupils learned to read religious books, and were able to participate in the service. By the middle of the nineteenth century very few of these schools remained, but they revived suddenly with the approach of the emancipation. By 1865, at the peak of the revival, there were over 21,000 schools with more than 400,000 pupils, according to the Synod.[12] The ideologue of the Church schools, S. A. Rachinskii, hoped for a rebirth of the kind of schooling that would enliven parish priests and refresh and purify religious understanding among the common people. "In the parish school," he wrote, "the priest does not appear as a hired teacher, but as the executor of his real duties toward his flock."[13] Rachinskii's hope, however, was not fulfilled.

Church authorities supervised their schools through parish priests and diocesan school boards, and still later through district school boards, and diocesan and district school inspectors. Although the Church system did not suffer from the bifurcation of authority in the zemstvo system, Church officials still had difficulties maintaining local control. The parish priest could observe the school, and the Church had some advantage in monitoring school quality, but, as was the case with the zemstvo schools, the parents of the school children were most important to the teacher. How to involve local people in the life of the school was one of the most common topics of discussion when teachers got together to discuss professional concerns. Teachers needed a steady supply of pupils as well as fuel and maintenance.

Lacking formal funding, the makeshift and haphazard Church schools of the 1860s disappeared rapidly, as priests and other clerical employees discovered that they had neither time nor inclination to supplement regular parish duties with voluntary teaching. But Rachinskii's dream was not abandoned, and he and other clerical educators had the opportunity to realize it partially in the 1880s and 1890s when new laws encouraged the Church to become active again in primary education. Two-year schools were established in 1884, and various arrangements were made to provide for staffing and funding. Diocesan school councils were set up to oversee the schools, and a school council under the Synod managed the entire system. The Church bureaucracy responsible for primary schooling expanded, until by the middle of the 1890s there were diocesan school councils in many district capitals, over sixty diocesan school observers, and many more local inspectors.[14] With state support, the Church parish schools, originally designed as a cheap alternative to zemstvo schools, were continually upgraded. In 1903 they were officially recognized as three-year institutions on a par with the zemstvo institutions.

State Schools

The Ministry of Education was granted only limited responsibility for primary schooling in the zemstvo provinces under the 1864 law, but it retained authority elsewhere in the empire. Ministry officials continued to administer schools that they and other government departments had managed before the emancipation with compulsory contributions from peasant communes; but many of these schools failed after the emancipation, when peasant support became voluntary. The Ministry also retained authority over the commune schools in the non-zemstvo provinces. There was some interest in establishing a Ministry-dominated primary educational system throughout the zemstvo provinces in the early 1870s, but within a decade high officials turned instead to the Church as the institution most capable of supplanting the zemstvos in school management. Commune schools remained significant, however, and even with the expansion of the Church system, the Ministry retained its own schools. At the time of the 1911 school census there were nearly 6,000 rural Ministry schools, and the role of the Ministry in primary education expanded rapidly in the early twentieth century. By 1914 the Ministry counted 22,000 rural schools under its exclusive control.

In conjunction with plans for the establishment of universal primary education, Ministry officials claimed authority over both the zemstvo and Church school systems in the last decade of the old regime. A Ministry plan containing guidelines for universal primary education was presented to the Second State Duma, Russia's new parliament, on February 20, 1907. The plans called for one teacher per fifty children, one school within two miles of each village, a four-year course, and a state subsidy of from 360 to 390 rubles for each satisfactory school. This law was not passed, but the Ministry began to dispense funds according to it, and most district and provincial zemstvos, as well as city governments, began submitting plans for opening new schools and upgrading existing ones. Both Church and zemstvo school administrators hurried to qualify as many of their schools as possible for state funds, abandoning some marginal schools in the process.

Expenditures of the Ministry rose rapidly until they rivaled the educational budgets of the zemstvos, and officials of the Ministry claimed increased authority over all schools, arguing that since the Ministry subsidized the schools, they should be under its authority. The reentry of state authorities into the field of primary education was in many respects a consequence of the decision to provide universal primary education on a systematic scale, and was perhaps even a necessary condition for the rapid expansion of the school system in the absence of an effective nationwide system of local government. Although the plans to make primary schooling available to every village were only incompletely realized by the time the autocracy fell, the provision of state funds led to more and better schools. The shift from private to public schooling, funded by the zemstvos, the Orthodox Church, and the state, encouraged school attendance by reducing the direct cost of schooling for parents.

School Attendance

The real measure of the prerevolutionary educational system was the number of children educated and the quality of the schooling they received. Progress toward universal primary education in the last years of the old regime was usually gauged by the percentage of the school-age population (8-11 years or 7-14 years) in school at any one time, and by the ratio of pupils to teachers. By the 8 to 11-year standard, nearly half of the school-age population appeared deprived of schooling. The number of teachers would have had to have approximately doubled in order for all school-age children to be taught in classes with fifty pupils per teacher, the Ministry norm for class size. Ministry of Education officials calculated that as of January 1915, only 58 percent of all 8 to 11-year-olds were in school in European Russia, and only 70 percent of the necessary teachers were available. The figures for the empire as a whole were 51 percent and 61 percent, respectively.[15]

The assumption that every child would attend for four years, however, was an unrealistic one, since parents could not be compelled to send their children to school, nor to keep them there for the full course. Most children attended school for fewer than four years, and the supply of teachers relative to requirements based on actual patterns of school attendance in 1911 appears not to have been as deficient as the Ministry officials had calculated. If all the children had attended for the full four years, a fifty-place school could have served 12.5 new entrants each year. Under the prevailing school-leaving rate, the same school could serve 20.7 entrants each year. Under these conditions, the number of teachers necessary for the 3.8 million potential school entrants (one-quarter of all 8 to 11-year-olds in the Russian Empire in 1911) was 183,575, just barely less than the 186,859 teachers actually employed, and not the 305,075 calculated by the Ministry.[16] The actual ratio of pupils to teachers was 41, rather than 50, and under these conditions, 223,529 teachers would have been required for all children to start school and remain in class according to the 1911 pattern of attendance. This would have required a 20 percent increase over the number of teachers actually employed, and in European Russia the increase would have been much less: only 5 percent, rather than the 43 percent suggested by the Ministry figures.

Certainly there were many deficiencies in the primary school system, but lack of teachers and schools may not have been the main obstacle to increased primary education. More important may have been the parents' perception that a more limited course of instruction than that favored by the Ministry was adequate for their children. As the Moscow zemstvo economist P. Vikhliaev commented at the first all-zemstvo congress on the statistics of popular education in 1913, "It is hardly possible to consider establishing universal primary education if a significant proportion of the pupils leave school before completing the course."[17]

The proportion of children who attended school at some time in their childhood can be seen in the school attendance patterns reported in the 1911 school census.[18] From these attendance patterns one can calculate the probabilities that a child would attend school for a given number of years in the Russian Empire (see Table 2). As these figures suggest, the probability that a child attended school for at least one year was 70 percent, rather than the 50 percent implied by assuming that all children stayed for the full four years.

The availability of schooling and the value of literacy were not all that

TABLE 2. Estimated Likelihood that a Child 7-11 Will Attend
Each School Year

Year of School Attendance	Boys	Girls	Both
1	87.8	52.4	70.0
2	72.0	41.4	56.7
3	38.5	8.0	23.6
4	18.6	5.4	12.2
5	6.1	1.8	4.0

Source: *Odnodnevnaia perepis' nachal'nykh shkol Rossiiskoi Imperii 18 ianvaria 1911 goda*, no. 16, part 2, pp. 22-23, 103-104.

parents took into consideration when deciding whether and for how long to send their children to school. They also had to weigh the sacrifices that schooling entailed. A major cost for parents was the loss of the children's labor from the household economy. "When the school, in the opinion of the peasants, tears their little workers from the family, the peasants see the school as their enemy," wrote one of the participants in the local committee on agricultural production from Arkhangelsk Province in 1903.[19]

Peasant farmers, craft workers, migrants, and various types of urban workers faced different sacrifices and costs, which undoubtedly influenced their decisions about their children's schooling. For farmers, the size of the landholding and the number of boys in the family were important in determining the value of the labor of a single boy. Peasants with large holdings were often wealthy enough to hire a replacement for a son at school, and peasants with small holdings and many sons did not need the labor of all their progeny.[20] For most peasants who worked the land, however, schooling could not be allowed to interrupt peak seasonal labor needs. "I happened to discover the main reason that above all keeps local people from sending their children to school," wrote a priest at the time of the emancipation. "They are afraid to lose the working time of their helpers in field work. During plowing, sowing, haying, and so forth, the boys' hands are of great service to them, although at other times their help is almost entirely unneeded."[21] This priest arranged his class schedule to fit the farm work seasons, and the school was successful.

In rural Russia, as elsewhere in the world, the seasonality of agricultural labor determined the length of the school year. When the school and farm schedules did not quite mesh, tension between parents and teachers arose. Even in the twentieth century, teachers sometimes had to bargain with or cajole parents, who wanted an extra hand for spring planting, to leave their children in school until the final exams.[22] Attendance fluctuated with the rhythm of the peasant economy, and teachers often had difficulty in retaining pupils once they had been withdrawn for seasonal tasks.

Changes in the rural economy in the late nineteenth and early twentieth centuries affected the indirect or opportunity costs of education, i.e., the foregone value of the work that the children might have performed inside or outside the home economy had they not attended school. Peasants who left the commune after the Stolypin reforms of 1906 and 1910 were more likely to use education to improve their agriculture than were peasants living within the traditional commune; but they were also frequently farther from schools and more dependent on the labor of their children. Tasks that were generally divided by the commune among all the children of the village, such as tending animals, had to be performed by fewer children if other households left the commune. "Because of this," remarked one observer, "the school-aged and even preschool children of the isolated farmers are busy working almost the whole year round."[23] However, as the size of peasant allotments shrank throughout the late nineteenth and early twentieth centuries, the productivity of peasant family labor also declined, and so did the inducement to keep a child out of school.

Girls were much less likely than boys to be sent to school, and this reflected in part the lower value of literacy for them. The opportunity cost of the girls' time may also have been higher, though this may not have been the case in families with many girls. The work of boys was mainly seasonal, but the housework performed by girls was not; thus it was difficult for parents to lose a daughter's labor. One investigator in the 1890s commented: "Once the girl bears some responsibility in the home—for example, looking after her brothers and sisters or weaving and spinning—then one must state the bitter truth; it is a rare mother who will allow her daughter to study."[24] A peasant described the work that awaited his daughter: "In the future she will be occupied from morning till evening with various heavy tasks equal to those of men, in the field, the forest, and garden, and also at home, where her work will be no lighter. She ought to prepare the family breakfast, dinner, and supper, tend the cow, look after the children, bathe the whole family, and keep them in clothes."[25] Because of these conditions, girls were often kept at home while their brothers went off to school.

The economies of the craft workers and others who had productive enterprises within the household involved the whole family, and their children were also often kept home from school. Zemstvo studies showed that the employment of children in home production reduced school

45

attendance.[26] "Despite all my persuasion, the parents will not agree to send the girls to school," complained a clerical schoolteacher in 1862. "They keep them beside them for constant help in cotton spinning, the sole means of winter support for many peasants."[27]

Factory workers faced different problems in deciding whether or not to send their children to school. Until legislation banned child labor for those under the age of twelve, first in 1882, then more effectively in 1890, children could and did work in industry.[28] Once the opportunities for factory work were reduced, schooling for boys required less of a financial sacrifice for the family. However, as in villages, girls contributed to the upkeep of the home, and parents who could not forfeit this aid kept their daughters at home. When women worked outside the home, the housework performed by girls was even more important,[29] and schools took on the added function of day-care centers for school-aged children.

Regardless of parental occupation, poverty kept children home from school. According to a study conducted in 1893 by the statistical bureau of the Moscow zemstvo, poverty was the reason most often given for a child's nonattendance of school. Sometimes a lack of proper clothing, shoes, or lodging was the decisive issue if the school was far from home. Nearly 30 percent of those who missed school did so because they had to work or live outside the area.[30]

The Schoolteachers

The content and the effectiveness of schooling depended in part on the teachers, and the quality of the teachers depended on the salaries schools could pay. Salaries differed significantly by type of school. The average pay of teachers in 1911 in city schools was 528 rubles per year for men, and 447 rubles for women. In rural schools, the average for both men and women was 340 rubles. Estimates of average yearly salaries of workers in European Russia on the eve of World War I ranged from 200 to 300 rubles, but skilled workers in some industries earned much more.[31] Teachers often received housing and other benefits in addition to salary. State schools provided the best remuneration, with zemstvo, commune, parish, and literacy schools following in that order. Zemstvo teachers received on average of 285 rubles a year in 1894 and about 380 rubles in 1911. In contrast, literacy school teachers were paid only 23 rubles in 1894; in 1911, men were paid 82 rubles and women 131 rubles.[32]

The training of teachers in the different schools also varied sharply. The proportion of teachers having had only a primary education was much higher in literacy, commune, and parish schools than in zemstvo and Ministry of Education schools.[33] Teachers' wages generally reflected training, and where pay was low, teacher turnover was high. In 1911 teachers stayed from five to seven years in literacy and parish schools, six to ten years in commune and zemstvo schools, and slightly longer in some government schools.

School Curriculum

Teachers were required to conform to certain general curriculum guidelines. Educators, state and Church officials, and others who worked to develop the school network tried to specify how literacy should be taught and what materials should be used. They drew up curricula and wrote textbooks, which impart something about the school systems, though the question of what was actually taught and learned is much more complex. However, it is clear that reading was given priority, followed by arithmetic and writing.

Different types of schools offered different official curricula, but religion is conspicuously present in all of them. The state and Church officials who designed the programs considered religion the foundation of the Russian state system. This intent was expressed in the 1864 and 1874 rules for secular schools, in which the stated purpose of schooling was to "uphold religious and moral understanding in the people, and spread useful primary knowledge," and also in the 1884 rules for parish schools, according to which the purpose of schooling was similarly "to uphold the teachings of the Orthodox faith and Christian morality in the people, and to impart useful information."[34] Teachers spent a significant amount of time teaching Church Slavonic, which meant reading the Gospels and sometimes also the Psalter and the Book of Hours in old Russian, even though special religious instructors, usually priests, came into the schools several times a week to teach religion.

The literacy schools, by their very remoteness, escaped some of the curricular requirements of the more established schools, and they had no formal program until they came under the administration of the Church in 1891. What was taught in these schools reflected the values of the parents and children, and the religious connotations of literacy were much in evidence, but not to the exclusion of the secular. Modern Russian language and arithmetic were taught in most of these schools in addition to religious subjects, according to a late nineteenth-century survey of 446 schools in Tver Province.[35] The religious overtones of literacy were implicit in the words used by villagers to describe instructors in

47

literacy schools. The men were often called mentors (*nastavniki*) and the women either nuns (*chernichki*) or lay sisters (*devushki-kleinitsy*).

How much children actually learned in the literacy schools is unclear, but one suspects that there were some long-term benefits. The children, or at least their parents, were usually well motivated, since they paid voluntarily and only as long as they were satisfied with the results. The children were taught what the parents most wished them to learn. The Old Believer schools reinforced the piety of the pupils, but did not necessarily cut the children off from other peasants. Many Orthodox peasants were probably drawn to the dissident schools, and the Orthodox illiterate had to rely on the more literate dissidents when occasions demanded reading or writing. One late nineteenth-century observer commented: "Receiving a sufficiently adequate bookish education in their families and schools, the schismatics go out into life with an independent and strengthened religious conviction that allows them to repel the attempts of missionaries to convert them."[36]

There was no official program for the basic three-year primary schools of the zemstvos and the Ministry, the so-called one-class schools that comprised the great majority of all schools until 1897. The authors of the 1864 statute specified only that instructors should include the three R's, plus religion, Church Slavonic, and church singing, where possible. A suggested program published in 1885 recommended attention to religion and grammar. In the mandatory program issued in 1897, religion and Church Slavonic were prominent (9 out of 24 hours per week), but reading and writing (10 hours) and arithmetic (5 hours) were allotted the bulk of the day.[37] Some zemstvos managed to add natural science, history, and geography to the primary school program by adding a year of instruction to the three-year program or by establishing four- or five-year "two-class schools" in the late nineteenth or early twentieth century. These subjects were also taught at the two-class Ministry schools.

Religion was more important in the Church schools than in those of the zemstvo. According to the 1896 parish school curriculum, the weekly program included fifteen lessons in religious subjects and only sixteen in secular ones.[38] This ratio was not altered significantly when the course program of the Church schools was extended to three years in 1903. Geography, natural history (instead of natural science), drafting, and drawing featured in the program of the two-class Church schools.

The official curriculum was no more than a suggested outline of material, and teachers themselves decided what they would teach. In making their choices, they responded to the demands of parents, the zemstvos, school boards, Church or state school inspectors, and examiners who tested children at the completion of the course. Zemstvo educators and interested pedagogues in the late nineteenth and early twentieth centuries conducted a number of studies of pupils who had finished the zemstvo course five or ten years previously.[39] Often the proportion of primary school graduates who were willing to be tested was as high as half of the total. The results in almost every case showed that religion and reading were the subjects best retained by former pupils. Arithmetic was next, and writing, which was learned last, was usually the most easily forgotten. Instruction in writing stressed spelling, penmanship, and grammar rules, and pupils who did not obtain office jobs were unlikely to have much use for this training. Even the skill of fine handwriting declined in value as typewriters came into use around the turn of the century. And "A knowledge of grammar," as a school inspector in the late nineteenth century observed, "flies from the head of the primary school pupil soon after he finishes the course."[40]

Instruction in arithmetic may not have been adequate because the teaching materials and the subject as taught were far from the daily experiences of peasant children. Observers complained that exercises in texts featured couriers galloping between Moscow and St. Petersburg, or the volume of water in an ornamental fishpond. These kinds of problems did not engage the children, and it was also difficult for them to memorize tables. Pupils tested some years after leaving school were less adept at solving the academic exercises of the class program than when they were in school, but were quicker and more able to solve arithmetic problems related to their daily lives, suggesting that the skills taught in class did serve them in later life.

Religion was stressed in the official curricula of all schools. "The law of God," as religion was called, was taught by outside instructors, most of whom were priests. There were 76,000 such instructors in 1911, and they gave approximately ten lessons a week in each of the one-class schools.[41] According to observers, however, these priest-teachers paid little attention to methodology, and usually lectured all three levels of the one-room schools together, so that the second- and third-year pupils heard the same lectures as the year before.[42] Perhaps not surprisingly, teachers identified religion and Church Slavonic as the subjects least liked by the pupils.[43] Despite the weakness in religious instruction, religion was important in the school experience, largely because parents of peasant children looked more favorably upon schooling that included such instruction.

The ordinary school day in rural Russia began with the reading and singing of morning prayers before the lighted icon lamp, and ended with evening prayers.[44] The Gospels were usually read from a book that had facing Russian and Church Slavonic texts, and on holidays and Sundays pupils often attended the liturgy with their teachers. Favored pupils could participate in the service. During Lent, if the church was not far away, pupils went to services with the teacher on Wednesdays and Fridays and then returned to class after church. Teachers and school boards considered religious participation a simple way of increasing community support for the school, and some zemstvos made church singing a compulsory subject. A teacher who had organized a school choir urged the teaching of singing, noting that "the peasants tried to send their children to the school one after the next in hope that they would end up in the choir."[45]

Although teachers were more inclined to secular views in the early twentieth century, there is little reason to suppose that religious instruction declined very much in the schools. It had the support of Church and state administrators, as well as zemstvo representatives and board members. The general 1911 Zemstvo congress on primary education, attended by over four hundred delegates, passed a resolution that primary schooling ought, among other things, to develop religious feeling, and "foster a striving to put the principles of the teaching of the Gospels into practice."[46] The examiners of primary school graduates in the late nineteenth and early twentieth centuries found that former pupils remembered the meaning of the symbols of the faith, the ten commandments, and stories from the Old and New Testaments, as well as the prayers they had memorized in school. Some were also able to explain the service and the significance of the most important holidays.[47]

Pupils, teachers, and parents agreed that reading was the core of the primary school curriculum. It was taught predominantly by two methods: the older letter recognition technique and the newer sounding-out method. With the latter, pupils immediately began practicing the pronunciation of different combinations of letters rather than the names of the individual letters. A parish teacher commented after learning the new method, "I joyfully meet the children because I know that now I will not torment them with the ABC book, but I will teach them to read and write within two months."[48] The sounding-out method gained acceptance in the middle of the nineteenth century, and was endorsed by Korf and other pedagogues who shaped the zemstvo schools.

Teachers distinguished between reading aloud, which was called "mechanical reading" by some pedagogues, and reading for comprehension.[49] Since reading aloud was so valued for religious functions, the ability to read to gain information could have been slighted if it had not been particularly stressed by teachers. A commentator in the clerical-school journal suggested that teachers stress proper pronunciation, fluency, and comprehension.[50] To practice the quick translation of letter combinations into sound, the commentator urged choral reading. For comprehension, pupils were to read a text, and then "give an account of what they read."

Russian educators were confident that they could teach pupils to read within one or two semesters. Baron Korf expected his pupils to be able to read and write at the end of the first year, and an educator speaking in 1911 suggested that most pupils could begin to read in a couple of months.[51] These optimistic expectations about the time necessary to teach a child to read were probably not far off the mark.

The regularity of Russian spelling facilitated rapid instruction in reading, and the level of much of the commercially published popular reading matter was suitably low. The decision of parents and children to restrict school attendance to a year or two implied that a useful facility could be attained in this short period. The sustained growth of the commercial publishing industry also lends credence to this view.

Textbooks

The school primers were often the first secular texts children encountered in school, and the authors had great hopes for affecting the children's thinking. The limits on what could and could not be said were set by the censors, and educational authorities tried to promote a conservative viewpoint, but liberal and even radical authors managed on occasion to convey their messages. Baron Korf explained in his widely used handbook that the school's task was "not to train tradesmen and farmers, but to develop people."[52]

Liberal pedagogues who influenced the early zemstvo schools tried to encourage children to think about the world in scientific and rational, although not irreligious, terms. K. D. Ushinskii, who authored the Russian equivalent of America's *McGuffy Reader, Children's World,* explained in the preface to the first edition of his reader that he wished to provide positive information to encourage the child to think logically, and for this reason he chose to emphasize natural science, for "the logic of nature is the most worthy and useful logic for children."[53]

The authors interpreted their tasks differently, but most were eager to tell their readers how to live, and in doing so they reiterated, albeit in muffled tones, the intellectual arguments of their day. Ushinskii shared with other early authors a benign view of rural Russia. His reader is sprinkled with references to the riches of nature, God's gifts, and social duty. The seasons change, and

". . . the merciful creator opens wide his generous hand to all, . . . and the pleasant sounds of the scythe and happy songs are heard far and wide. . . . The peasant is not afraid of work; he was nurtured on work. Secondly, he knows that summer work will feed him the whole year, and that it is necessary to use the fine weather when God gives it—he cannot do without grain. Thirdly, the peasant feels that by his labor he feeds not only his family, but the whole world, including me and you and dressed-up folks."[54]

Ushinskii tried to convey to peasant children an appreciation for the work that awaited them as a "holy duty" of service to God and society. His primer, *The Native Word*, was simpler than the reader, but contained elements of the same ideas. In one tale, a poor peasant rescues a rich man and receives a piece of gold in reward. He eventually loses it, but finds that a peasant has enough happiness without gold.

Conservative textbook authors also included the natural world and teachings about social relations in their readers, but they stressed religious themes and lessons. A. Baranov was one of the most successful of the conservative authors, and his name became associated with the style of the conservative texts. A critic said of him, ". . . when they want to point to academic scholasticism, to murderously dead language, to ignorance of child psychology, or to tendentiousness, they usually just say, 'It is like Baranov.' "[55] Baranov's book of readings appeared in its seventy-second edition in 1915, and contained a series of fables and poems glorifying life in the countryside and warning against venturing outside it.[56] The pupils read of a peasant boy who went to the city as an apprentice, was tempted by wealth to steal, and ended up passing through his own village in chains, begging for bread. N. Bunakov, whose primer appeared in its hundredth edition in 1916, also moralized about the God-given pleasures of rural life, and the wealth available to those who could appreciate the free gifts of God.[57]

The image of the village as a joyful place faded in the late nineteenth century, as educated Russians became more aware of rural poverty, particularly after the horrible famine in the early 1890s. Conservative authors joined their progressive colleagues in an effort to present a more realistic picture of life in the countryside. So zealous and effective were their attempts that by 1913 observers began reporting that the texts depressed the school children: "They assiduously note the sad phenomena of peasant life that each peasant tries to brush aside."[58] Instead of the joy of the turn of the seasons, children read of "grief and need, poverty and distress" of village life.[59] D. I. Tikhomirov's *Vernal Sprouts* sold more than a million copies by 1911, and contained an illustrated story about two ragged beggar children.[60] I. I. Gorbunov-Posadov, a follower of Tolstoy and an active proponent of progressive pedagogical ideas, also felt duty-bound to inform children about the unpleasantness in store for them. In his *Little Red Sun*, a popular primer and reader in the early twentieth century, stories about peasant life showed drudgery, sadness, and death, and the happiness was at best bittersweet, as when a child thought of a grandmother who was old and sick, and then died, but was sweetly remembered.[61]

Conservative and nonconservative authors alike confronted a dilemma at this time. They felt obligated to portray the distressing features of rural life, but they did not want to encourage peasants to leave their villages. Until the Stolypin reforms there were legal barriers to permanent resettlement, although many peasants moved anyway. Moreover, the authors worried about the country's food supply, and they often felt that life in the countryside was morally superior to that in the cities. As a result they tended to include along with bleak pictures of rural life the message that there is no place like home.[62]

The treatment of religion in the texts changed dramatically over the period, as even conservative authors began to see Russian national identity in secular rather than religious terms. Most authors of the 1860s, 1870s, and 1880s showed their readers the guiding hand of providence at work in nature, history, and geography. Religion and nationality were interwoven, as in Bunakov's popular primer: "Our fatherland is Russia. We are Russian people. There are many cities, towns, villages, and settlements of all sorts in Russia. There are churches in the cities and villages. The church is the house of God."[63]

By the early twentieth century, the use of religion by writers of all political persuasions had both changed and diminished. In conservative Tikhomirov's *Vernal Sprouts*, religious stories and materials are few, and the blending of religion and nationality of early works here has been replaced by an amalgam of culture and nationality. Pushkin, Gogol, and Nekrasov are hailed together with Peter the Great as heroes of Russia's past. The writers are presented for emulation, and their works as examples of honorable service to the country: "Loving the simple people, Pushkin pitied them with all his soul, grieved at their difficult fate, and ardently wished for the liberation of the peasants and for enlightened freedom in his whole native land."[64] Whereas in the older texts God blessed the peasants' labor directly, in the newer ones, such as Tikhomirov's, the writers intercede for him. When the plowman labors peacefully in his field, it is not God who smiles on him, but Nekrasov, who "invokes the blessing of God on his labors."

More liberal authors also used literary and historical figures to develop a new sense of national identity, but in addition they often presented a secular humanism with an emphasis on science. When Baron Korf's textbook *Our Friend* was revised in 1908 after his death, the new authors replaced many of the descriptive passages about nature with geography, history, and excerpts from the works of classical Russian writers. The religious tone of the original work was retained, but secular rationality was emphasized. Both the original and the revised versions contained the passage: "Our lives are in God's hands, but God gave us reason so that we would know to avoid threats and dangers to our health." The revised text continued: "How much is each of us responsible to ponder the way he lives so as not to disgrace the name of man."[65]

Liberal writers such as V. and E. Vakhterov were eager to spread scientific understanding and dispel superstition. Their popular early twentieth-century reader, *The World in Stories for Children*, included sections on natural science entitled "The Great Inventor" and "The Benefactor of Man," in which the subjects are not God and Jesus, but James Watt and Louis Pasteur.[66] The Vakhterovs expressed the optimism of belief in the progress of science and the triumph of man over nature: "We can believe that our lives will become still better. Not in vain did the poet say, 'There are many great forces on earth, but there is nothing stronger in nature than man.' "[67] Their secular enthusiasm was in sharp contrast to the religious lesson of the conservative Baranov: "Knowing the limitlessness of the world, we recognize our insignificance and know the greatness of the Creator of the world, His wisdom, all powerfulness, and endless benevolence toward us."[68]

The impact of the changing texts on the children is difficult if not impossible to discern, but one thing is certain: the texts played their part in communicating a great lesson of schooling—namely, that the printed word is a source of information and wisdom rivaling and sometimes surpassing the community elders and the family.

Effects of Schooling

The effect of schooling on children's attitudes was limited but significant. It had more to do with the process of attending school, of recognizing the teacher as an authority figure, and of being introduced to an alternative set of expectations and aspirations than with the content of the primers and readers. Children who attended two or three years of school were unlikely to retain much of the content of the texts, though they did retain the skills learned therefrom. The importance of schooling was primarily the mastery of skills, and only secondarily of information. In addition, the very experience of going to school took the child out of the routine of lower-class urban or rural life. As one worker subsequently recalled, "At home was constant cursing, arguments, but then came at last the school, my consolation, and my life went differently."[69] For others, the experience was just the reverse, and "after the freedom and expansiveness of the street, the school atmosphere began to suffocate me," recalled another worker.[70] School attendance and class work imposed an unfamiliar discipline on the children, and teachers frequently commented on the difficulties of accustoming new pupils to the classroom regimen—even just getting them to sit still.[71]

How closed the circle of a lower-class child's daily experience was is evident from several studies of entering pupils.[72] Of the city children, almost all did domestic tasks, such as carrying water, washing, and looking after other children. Most appeared to have little positive contact with adults, and had learned what they knew in the streets. Over half the children did not know that they lived in the city of Moscow; to questions about their domicile, they would reply, "I do not live in a city. I live on Ostozhenka [a street]." About one-fifth of the children did not know the name of their street. Since the school texts included lengthy descriptions of the flora and fauna of Russia, the teachers wanted to know what the children knew about nature. Roughly four-fifths had been to the countryside, usually to visit relatives, and most could tentatively identify common farm and forest animals.

The rural children in general found the process of being questioned about what they knew unfamiliar, and had difficulty understanding questions and formulating answers. Most had a very vague understanding of their names and where they lived. About four-fifths knew their first names, and a slightly smaller proportion knew their village, but only half knew their patronymics and family names, and fewer still knew in which canton they lived. Most children could count to ten or twenty. Many were familiar with money, but some knew only copper money. Some knew measures of distance and depth. They knew names of the common animals, but often only in their local dialects.

Children arrived at school with a stock of oral lore, including folk tales, songs, and riddles. According to the teachers, they also brought superstitions to which they clung firmly. Most common were beliefs about graveyards and corpses, and a fear of the dead, as well as a faith in omens, the evil eye, house and wood sprites, and mysterious phenomena. A teacher observed in the Church school magazine that although children usually knew a few prayers from their parents and had a vague idea of the existence of God, they often thought he was the image in the icon, the priest, or St. Nicholas the miracle worker.[73]

What new information and changed attitudes did the children acquire in the course of their schooling? When seeking an answer to this question, Russian educators showed the same concern as the textbook authors about the unwillingness of peasant children to remain peasants. Not surprisingly, the results of one study suggest that few peasant school children were satisfied with peasant life. Nearly half of the rural children questioned in an early twentieth century survey wanted to pursue an "educated profession," which usually meant teaching, clerical work, or, for some, the creative arts.[74] Only 2 percent of the boys and 1 percent of the girls wanted to follow in the footsteps of their parents in the village.

The children's eagerness to lead lives different from those of their parents was an important development in prerevolutionary Russia. Many of those expressing a wish to leave the village in fact remained, but the widespread desire to escape from the peasantry was often commented on unfavorably by teachers and educated observers. The fact that parents sometimes abetted their children in aspiring beyond their origins further exasperated those teachers and educators who wanted to see an educated peasantry that remained on the land. These parents were stigmatized by teachers as "careerist-parents," who wanted to make their children into "respectable folks," who would "forcibly tear them from the plow," and for whom even the prospect of a teaching position in a parish literacy school was sometimes not good enough.[75] One such parent held his own with an unsympathetic interlocutor, and expressed the hope that his son could find a modest salaried position that would be more "peaceful" and "cleaner" than farm work.[76]

Some observers complained that children who had been to school were less willing than their uneducated peers to work hard and put up with the deprivation of rural and lower-class urban life. "Those finishing the course are ashamed of labor," a teacher commented about city children in the 1890s. "They consider themselves educated, and want some kind of gentry job."[77]

Educators already worried about the effects of education on attitudes toward work and occupational choice were outraged at its apparent influence on taste in clothing and personal appearance. There were repeated complaints that the newly educated gave up their humble peasant garb for an outlandish foppishness and dandyism. A correspondent for a clerical journal in 1904 reported the return to a village of a fellow "wearing a short coat, a fantastic shirt, dashing cocked hat, and boots with rubber bottoms—all that could separate him from the crowd of simple 'grey' villagers. They look on him as a marvel. The village beauties make up to him. The school boys run after him as after a miracle."[78]

The imaginative dress served to fulfill fantasies of class, and was evidence of the general and not very structured reorientation in the thinking of ordinary people. One consequence of the new ideas and aspirations was a decline in the prestige of traditional rural authorities, the priests and elders. As children were increasingly taught from the new, more secular readers and primers, the old style Psalter readers disappeared from the countryside. A priest complained in 1912 that although the new readers could read competently from both secular and sacred books, they did not show the same love and reverence for what they read as had the village readers of the "old school."[79] The popular image of the literate person had changed. The old readers of Scripture were replaced not only by former pupils, but by schoolteachers, medical assistants, and agronomists. As peasants saw their children struggling with school texts or heard them read aloud for entertainment, and as exposure to secular books increased, the printed word, formerly associated with the Holy Bible and Word of God, lost some of its aura of mystery. Although the new readers may not have been the pioneers of enlightenment in the village that some educators envisioned, they were more likely to turn to a new cheap almanac to answer a question, instead of quoting Scripture.

Most teachers reported not surprisingly that schooling increased the children's curiosity about the world and reduced their superstition and prejudice, according to a study in 1909-10.[80] N. V. Chekhov summed up the comments of teachers who replied to his 1909 survey: "The children are more sensible than the others. They are not oppressed by their own ignorance. There is not that submissiveness to old traditions among them, and they are less indifferent to their social and personal needs."[81] The teachers' responses probably reflected not only their observations, but also their hopes about the effects of schooling. Teachers and educators of late nineteenth-century Russia shared with missionaries and modernizers in other places and times the hope that schooling would improve basic hygiene and agricultural practices and make the village a healthier and more prosperous place to live.[82]

Schooling may have led to changed relations between the sexes. Coeducational primary instruction challenged the patriarchal separation of the sexes and the subordinate position of women and girls. The mingling of girls and boys at school took place at a time when new employment opportunities were changing traditional relationships between lower-class men and women. One of the few investigators to study this issue reported at the 1914-15 congress on education that after experiencing coeducational classes, boys were more willing to recognize girls as capable and able, and girls lost some of their passivity and subservience.[83]

An important consequence of the new attitudes and behavior associated with schooling was that the wisdom and authority of the village elders and household heads was challenged. Educated observers reported growing rivalry and strife between generations—in particular, between illiterate old men and former schoolboys. According to a study of the area around Voronezh at the turn of the century, almost all opponents of schooling were men over the age of fifty.[84] Initially the educated observers seemed to sympathize with the literate young people, and blamed the domination and ignorance of the old for the failure of young men to introduce reforms in farming techniques. After the Revolution of 1905, the Stolypin reforms, and other changes in the countryside in the early twentieth century, when the balance shifted in favor of the young, however, many observers described the breakdown in rural order and the loss of respect for the old people and old ways. The shaken authority of the family, the church, the village elders, and the land captain were lamented. "The young fellows and adolescents frequently shout at their elders and even beat them. . . . Parents have evidently lost all authority over their children, and do not have the strength to stop the disgraceful things that are happening."[85]

Primary school opened up a new intellectual world for some pupils. Among the subscribers to the relatively sophisticated popular science magazine for the new "intelligentsia from the people," *Vestnik znaniia* (Herald of Learning), in the early twentieth century were many who had no more than primary schooling. Twenty percent of the 678 readers who replied to the editors' survey described their education as limited to a rural primary school, a parish school, or simply a primary school.[86] Another 15 percent had attended a city school. More than half of those who indicated they had attended only a rural primary school informed the editors that they currently held white-collar jobs as local administrators, bookkeepers, businessmen, telegraph and railroad employees, or schoolteachers. The proportion of white-collar employees was even higher among those who had attended an urban school.

Opportunities were likely to be more circumscribed for the less talented and energetic. The literacy gained in two or three years of schooling was a very blunt tool, insufficient to reshape the entire world of its possessors. Rapid industrialization, the expansion of commercial relations, and the Stolypin agrarian reforms opened new opportunities for those capable of taking advantage of them. The less capable and ambitious, however, were still likely to find themselves in a world to which passivity and fatalism seemed an appropriate response. The use of literacy did not necessarily conquer fatalism and usher in a spirit of self-directed optimistic ambition, but it introduced a tension and questioning of the traditional peasant's acceptance of his life. The tension between accepting or making one's fate was expressed in the popular commercial literature widely read by the newly literate and in the literature created for the common reader by educated activists.

III

THE LITERATURE OF

THE LUBOK

THE USE of literacy led the literate toward involvement in more modern sectors of Russian life, and their thinking changed accordingly. As they developed new values, new ways of looking at themselves and the world around them, and new patterns of thought and imagination, the literate sought to orient themselves by reference to the printed word. The increasing numbers of literate people became a more attractive market for commercial suppliers of popular literature, and the quantity of books and pamphlets circulating in villages and among lower-class urban residents grew. There was a tremendous upsurge in publishing for the common people in the last half century of the old regime. The expansion came at a time when technological improvements had significantly lowered the costs of printing and distribution, but the electronic media had not yet begun to rival the printed word.

The development of the popular commercial publishing industry in Russia was remarkable in several respects. Expansion took place rapidly, and the educational level of the country as a whole was so low that this industry, like many others in Russia, was staffed by people who were often of peasant or lower-class origins. The popular commercial writers were therefore more familiar with the world of their readers than with the literature and learning of educated Russia. Since they had limited access to literary models from belles lettres, and since there was little existing popular literature appropriate for their readers, they drew largely on folklore and on their own experiences.

The people who succeeded in this industry had entrepreneurial skills of risk taking, organization, and openness to technological change, rather than loyalty to traditional values and time-tested commercial practices. They infused the popular commercial literature that they created and distributed with something of their own values, energy, and initiative. Such a literature was likely to appeal to ordinary people who had hopes, made attempts, and sometimes succeeded to move out of the familiar circle of a traditional agrarian order.

When it became evident that increasing numbers of common people were learning to read, the question of what they would read was of interest not only to the commercial suppliers of popular literature, but to many others as well. Educated Russians who thought about the issue of popular literacy were unanimous in the view that the question of what kind of literature reached the common people was of utmost importance. Representatives of the Church and state and people of more liberal or radical persuasions did not always agree on the choice of material appropriate for the common people. Their ideas on these matters produced another body of books and pamphlets for the common people in addition to the commercial works themselves. The efforts of the commercial publishers, state and Church propagandists, and enlightenment activists to reach "the reader from the people" made popular literacy a major cultural issue of late tsarist Russia as well as a thriving commercial enterprise. The question of what common people should read, and to what extent their own preferences should be respected, reemerged after the October Revolution, when the Bolsheviks formulated Soviet cultural policy.

Thus the expansion of the reading public was paralleled by an equally rapid growth in the quantity and variety of printed materials available. There was a perceptible increase in the number of titles published in the Russian Empire in the first half of the nineteenth century, but the real expansion began after 1850 and continued until war and revolution brought a precipitous decline in publishing, as in much else. The number of titles published is given in Table 3, which shows that the number of copies published nearly doubled between 1887 and 1895, and more than tripled between 1895 and 1914. The increase in publications intended primarily for the common reader, and generally called "people's books," was even sharper, as shown in Table 4. The number of copies of these works grew nine times between 1887 and 1912, rising from approximately 12 percent of all works published to about 21 percent.

Many of the school and children's books were also intended for common readers. In 1912 the average price per copy for all of these works was 21 kopecks, well below the ruble or ruble and a half charged for works intended for the educated reader. The average size of editions was 11,000 copies. There were several other categories of publications that at one time or another included substantial numbers of books likely to reach common readers. From the late 1880s to the early twentieth century, religious works intended for the lower classes were separately classified, and in 1901, according to one calculation, there were over 16 million copies of religious books published in editions averaging 13,500.[1] Many works published for the military, as well as some scientific and technical literature, were also intended for a popular audience. In addition

TABLE 3. Titles Published in the Russian Empire, 1825-1918

	All Languages	Russian	No. of Copies
1825	583	323	
1845	864		
1850	696		
1855	1,239		
1860	2,085		
1887	7,366	5,442	24,403,242
1895	11,548	8,728	42,987,707
1901		10,318	
1908	23,852		75,868,320
1912	34,630		133,561,886
1914	32,338		130,167,102
1916	18,174		109,148,721
1918	6,052		77,743,937

Sources: M. V. Muratov, *Knizhnoe delo v Rossii v XIX i XX v.* (Moscow-Leningrad, 1931), pp. 203-205; L. Muzi and V. Leman, "Knigoizdatel'stva v Rossii za 1908-25," *Krasnaia pechat'*, nos. 17-18 (1926), pp. 49-52.

TABLE 4. Books for the Common Reader, 1887-1914

	1887	1901	1910	1912	1914
People's books					
Titles	336	457	1521*	2,394*	2,028*
Copies**	3,050	8,779	17,527	28,866	21,018
Schoolbooks					
Titles	512	647	1,673	2,006	1,841
Copies**	3,632	6,595	18,483	18,270	16,937
Children's books					
Titles	105	427	1,031	1,117	1,197
Copies**	346	3,244	4,930	5,929	6,676
Almanacs					
Titles		288	299	215	
Copies**			10,556	13,686	10,007

* Includes people's books and detective stories.
** In thousands.
Sources: *Proizvedeniia pechati vyshedshie v Rossii v 1910* (St. Petersburg, 1911), for 1912, 1913, 1914, 1915.

there were propagandistic publications issued on special occasions, such as the hundredth anniversary of Napoleon's ill-fated invasion of Russia, and the 300-year anniversary of the founding of the Romanov dynasty in 1913.

Publications for the common reader were largely of two sorts, the commercial works published for profit and those materials sponsored by educators, propagandists, and others interested in promoting a message among the lower classes. Those who produced the sponsored materials hoped to drive their rivals from the marketplace with a better and cheaper product, but the common people in Russia showed a preference for a variety of commercial publications.

The quantity of commercial publications for the common reader is not easy to determine from the aggregate publishing figures. According to one estimate, commercial publications accounted for roughly 60 percent of all "people's books" in 1892 and 1894.[2] Approximately the same proportion is suggested by the figures available for 1910, when the thirteen major commercial publishers produced 9.8 million copies of people's books out of a total of 14.9 million copies.[3] Official figures for the earlier period suggest that sponsored noncommercial works constituted a higher proportion of the works for the common readers.[4]

The path to the new readers was blazed long before the printed book had a large readership by those who produced and distributed popular prints and manuscript works in the countryside. The popular commercial literature that developed in the nineteenth and early twentieth centuries depended on several generations of facile authors, largely of peasant and petty bourgeois origins. Their talents and energies were channeled by a few entrepreneurial publishers, some of whose lives were rags-to-riches sagas that rivaled anything their authors were able to concoct. The enterprising publishers relied on large numbers of city hawkers and rural colporteurs to carry their goods to remote corners of urban and rural Russia, and to report back on the preferences of customers. Authors, publishers, and distributors were thus all involved in the commercial effort to produce a literature that satisfied the demands of the common reader.

The Popular Lubok Prints

The staple of lower class reading for most of the nineteenth century was the chapbooklike publications distributed by colporteurs and called *lubochnaia literatura*, after the popular prints (*lubki*, sing. *lubok*) that the peddlers also sold. The term "literature of the lubok" was used to describe a wide variety of popular publications, but I use it only to refer to the booklets sold by peddlers, since the peddlers also sold the prints, and the prints and booklets were often on the same subjects.

The lubki were lively illustrations similar to European broadsides. They had short texts, usually at the bottom of the picture, and were often the first printed materials to enter the homes of the common people. Their circulation prepared the way for the book. Explanations of the origins of the term *lubok* are varied. The early student of the question, N. Snegirev, startled educated society in the early 1820s by pronouncing the lubok worthy of intelligent investigation, an opinion shared by Alexander Pushkin but few others.[5] Snegirev suggested that the word was taken from *lub*, the inner bark of the linden tree, which was at one time made into a crude paper, was later used to make the wood blocks for the prints, and from which the itinerant peddlers made the baskets for their wares. The pictures may also have been called lubki because they were at one time cut and printed on Lubianka Street in Moscow. According to D. Rovinskii, the lubok collector and author of the most complete study of the subject, the term did not come into use to describe the prints until the first half of the nineteenth century.[6] The adjective *lubochnyi* was used in the first half of the nineteenth century to describe things that were badly or hastily constructed, and there were *lubochnye* homes, furniture, and goods, as well as illustrations.[7] N. I. Pastukhov, the author of one of the classics of late nineteenth-century popular literature, described the Rogozhskaia district of Moscow in the 1870s as "known for its post houses, with their ramshackle (*lubochnye*) sheds."[8] It was perhaps to avoid this use of the word that Rovinskii, in his classic study, called the prints simply "people's pictures."

At different times, according to I. D. Golyshev, the peasant scholar and lithographer to whom we are indebted for much of our information about the production and distribution of the lubki, the pictures were also called *Suzdalskie*, because at one time the print sellers' villages were located in the district of Suzdal; *friazhskie* and German sheets, because some were of foreign origin; *bogatyri*, because they often showed knights, tsars, and military heroes; *konnitsy*, because many of the knights were on horseback; and *prazdniki*, because many were images of saints or other religious figures.[9]

The lubki were traditionally printed either from wood blocks or copper plates. The earliest paper icons and secular prints date from the beginning of the seventeenth century, soon after the establishment of printing in Russia, when early book illustrators used their art to create single pictures on separate sheets. Originally produced primarily on religious subjects for a largely upper-class audience, the lubki soon began to circulate more widely, and by the eighteenth century they adorned the walls of some of the humbler inhabitants of the cities as well.

The lubki soon lost favor with the upper classes. The rich and well-born developed more refined tastes in illustration during the second half of the eighteenth century as Peter the Great's policy of importing Western culture was taken up by his successors. They learned to scorn the lubki, which began a long descent to lower levels of Russian society, first finding favor among the middle classes of the cities, then with the serving people and tradesmen, and finally, in the early nineteenth century, with the peasantry in the countryside.

As the audience grew more humble, the prints became more simplified and satirical, and the messages cruder and more direct.[10] Parables on daily life, fictional characters familiar from folklore, jokes, and well-known historical scenes became the standard repertoire of the lubok publishers. Snegirev grouped the illustrations around five subjects in the 1870s: religious and moral, philosophical commentaries on the trials of daily life, judicial topics and illustrations of punishments, wars and past events, and symbolic or poetical scenes from legend or folklore.[11] A catalogue of almost all lubki published in 1893 shows that religious pictures comprised about half of the total, and were, for the most part, pictures of the Holy Family, the Savior, and scenes from the history of the church and the lives of saints. Nearly a third of the secular prints were texts of songs and pictures from various literary works. Portraits of the tsar and the imperial family, satirical pictures, hunting scenes (often very bloody), and pictures of various beauties were also important.[12]

The prints were changed to suit the tastes of more sophisticated consumers in the last decade or two of the old regime. Typical of some of the lubki in the last half of the nineteenth century were illustrations of popular fairy tales, examples for moral instruction, and military pictures from the Crimean War, the Russo-Turkish War, and later from the war with Japan and World War I. New subjects touching the lives of the common people, from railroads to city slickers appeared in the later prints. According to the early twentieth-century art historian A. A. Fedorov-Davydov, the process of secularization of the lubok can be traced back as far as the seventeenth and eighteenth centuries. A comparison of the prints published by the firm of I. D. Sytin in 1889 and twenty years later, in 1909, shows a decline in the number of prints on religious subjects, and an increase in those with secular themes.[13]

Both secular and spiritual authorities looked on the lubok with suspicion at various times during the seventeenth and eighteenth centuries, but their attempts to prohibit the prints were not successful. The Patriarch Ioakim attempted to end the printing and sale of paper icons in 1764, complaining that "any ignoramus cuts on boards and prints on paper corrupt icons of the Savior and the Mother of God, and the saints."[14] Effective censorship was established only in 1839, and in 1851 all hitherto uncensored wood blocks and plates were ordered destroyed by the authorities. "So ended the uncensored people's pictures," recounted Rovinskii.[15]

This destruction was not the end of the lubok, however. Publishers of the prints continued to issue traditional pictures, updated versions of older themes, and new images that captured contemporary interests of the lower-class lubok purchasers. The folkloric, religious, and literary subjects that had characterized the uncensored lubki remained the hallmark of the prints in the second half of the nineteenth century.

The first lubki done on copper plates were the work of typography pupils who used state-owned machines that were at their disposal. In the second half of the eighteenth century, silversmiths who lived in the village of Izmailov, near Moscow, did the engraving, and the pictures were printed at two factories in Moscow. One of the factories was located on Spasskaia Street, a place later associated with lubok literature. At the end of the eighteenth century and the beginning of the nineteenth, small printers who owned their own typographies took over the production of lubki. Some of the printers were located in Moscow, and others were in the neighboring province of Vladimir.

Lithography appeared in Russia in the 1820s, and was rapidly applied with great success to the printing of lubki. The gradual replacement of the old boards and copper plates with lithographic stone improved the quality and increased the quantity of prints that could be produced from a single engraving, but production of the prints still retained a handicraft character.[16] The lithographed pictures were usually hand colored in villages near the presses. According to Golyshev, one thousand self-trained peasant women were employed in the 1860s to hand color the prints in the village of Nikolskoe, eight miles from Moscow.[17] The prints were usually dabbed with a combination of the vegetable dyes the women mixed themselves, and the primitive appearance of many lubki owed much to this process, especially to the rapidity with which the women worked. After coloring, the prints were sold throughout Russia by wandering peddlers or colporteurs known as *ofeni* (singular *ofenia*).

When lithography stones were replaced with zinc plates in the second half of the nineteenth century, the production of people's pictures gradually merged with the manufacture of people's books. The introduction of the cheaper and lighter zinc plates, as well as improvements in ink and varnish and the use of steam presses, made the multicolored chromolithograph an item of mass consumption throughout the industrial world in the last few decades of the nineteenth century.[18] Innovations in the development of photolithography and new types of paper and ink further lowered the costs of printing pictures in the last quarter of the century. Book publishers took over the printing of lubki, and some of them, such as the young entrepreneur I. D. Sytin, who later became the largest publisher in Russia, did away with the crude system of village hand coloring.

The lubki of the late nineteenth century were printed by book publishers, submitted to the censor together with book texts, and often colored at the city presses. They continued to pass through the traditional distribution network of colporteurs, who either came to the city publishing houses to pick up their wares or purchased them at fairs from representatives of the city houses. The lubki retained their place in the daily life of the common people, and many peasant cottages were decorated with a selection of the prints.

The purchasers of lubki in the late nineteenth century could usually find an illustration of a hero or heroine from a favorite story. Alternatively, they could choose a book that elaborated on the adventures and romance suggested by a prized lubok. In order to facilitate the association of the prints and booklets, the pictures on the covers of the books were often brightly colored prints similar to the lubki. The intermingling of the various traditions and images of the lubki with the rapidly changing world of popular book publishing was described graphically in an apparently autobiographical novel, *Bookmen* by M. Chernokov, about the world of the popular publishers, which appeared in 1933:

Balakan went up to the counter. Reams of pictures in various formats and content lay there smelling of dyes. The first to meet Balakan's eye were the "Saints." "Look Pavel, what beauties! These are the god of the muzhik, and, my heavens, you won't find one muzhik with such a satisfied and full-blooded face. And Tsars? Wonder of nature! They are all shine and sparkle. How can one not love them? Here are 'The Stages of Human Life,' drawn undoubtedly by a janitor. There is some kind of bloody battle—in a word, everything is here. There are the little icons—also a fast-selling item. And now, let's have a look at the books. *Weeping About Sin*, a book for the beginning reader, after which you will not want to read. And here is *How to Get Rich*, a book written by a person who did not have even a kopeck, but wanted to have a lot. There is 'Queen Margo' and 'Ensign Swordbelt,' books of dream interpretation, and all kinds of secrets— everything that the poor mind of the simple person cannot absorb."[19]

The lubki slowly lost their place in the lives of the common people in the early twentieth century, as a different popular imagery became available in illustrated periodicals, photographs, and silent films. At the same time, the lubki themselves lost some of their traditional aspects. The introduction of chromolithography in the 1880s made the process of hand coloring by village craftsmen obsolete. The spread of small rural shops reduced the role of colporteurs, whose sales techniques gave the lubki some of their meaning. As early as 1891 one observer noted, "In many homes where in the past there were abundant colored lubok pictures, they are now replaced by the premiums [pictures given as premiums] of *Niva* (Grainfield), *Nov* (Virgin Soil), *Razvlechenie* (Entertainment), and other illustrated and humorous magazines."[20]

The Literature of the Lubok

The widespread distribution of lubok prints among the common people was followed during the second half of the nineteenth century by the publication of printed material for a similar audience. Innovative publishers and authors who tried to satisfy popular demands learned by trial and error in the period after the emancipation what kinds of books appealed to the lower-class reader, and they were cautious about departing from what they found to be profitable. The publishers chose materials from among the established religious texts, from folklore, and from the medieval and early modern literary traditions. Sometimes they used traditional stories as they found them, but more often they hired writers to update and modernize them. They also used the handful of late eighteenth- and early nineteenth-century works that had found favor with a predominantly urban lower-class reading public at that time. In addition, and perhaps most interesting, were the titles developed when the demand of the lower-class reader was already well known.

The available selection became increasingly secular in the second half of the nineteenth century as the popular narrative accounts of saints' lives gave way to imaginative fiction in much the same way as the subjects of the lubok prints were secularized. "Spiritual books are the advance detachment of the army of books," wrote N. A. Rubakin in 1903. "The readers of these books are on the very periphery of the circle of readers. . . . Once the spiritual books do their job, they are very quickly replaced by the secular ones."[21]

Secularization proceeded even more rapidly in commercial publishing than in schooling between the early 1890s and World War I. In 1894, the 4.1 million copies of religious works published commercially for the lower class readers constituted nearly half of the commercially published people's books. In 1910, 5 million copies of all types of religious works were reported by all publishers. The thirteen major publishers, who were responsible for two-thirds of all the people's literature published in 1910, reported less than a million copies of religious works. A sample of all titles published by commercial firms in 1912 shows that religious texts constituted only 11 percent of the total number of copies, compared to 64 percent for fiction.[22] The decline in commercial religious publications for the people was also evident in I. D. Sytin's catalogue. The quantity of religious books shrank from 39 percent of all the titles he listed under the heading of "people's books" in 1900 to only 26 percent of those listed in the 1915 catalogue.

The commercially published religious works were primarily saints' lives and morally instructive tracts by obscure authors. They constituted a forthright expression of popular piety in print, sometimes to the chagrin of Church authorities. The decision of commercial publishers to reduce the proportion of religious works represents an evaluation of popular demand based on decades of commercial experience. The Church and state, however, continued to supply large numbers of religious works irrespective of market trends, and therefore the decline of religious reading may have been somewhat less precipitous than the commercial figures suggest.

Secular Lubok Literature

Authors of secular lubok literature treated a wide variety of subjects over the course of the nineteenth and early twentieth centuries, and the changing trends in types of booklets and stories give an indication of changes in popular taste. The number of editions in which a work was published is a relatively accurate guide to popularity, since lubok publishers tended to print editions of a standard size and to reprint popular titles as frequently as every year or two rather than attempting to estimate future demand. Press runs of 6,000 to 12,000 copies were common in the late 1880s and early 1890s, and of 12,000 to 25,000 copies in the early twentieth century.

The majority of secular works were on four main subjects until the 1870s: stories derived from folklore, chivalrous tales, instructive works, and tales about merchants. These can be considered in the traditional subjects of lubok literature. Works in these categories comprised as much as 60 percent of all titles in the 1860s, but their relative popularity declined steadily thereafter, until they comprised about 40 percent of the market in the 1890s and only 20 percent in the 1910s.

A second group of stories maintained a relatively constant market share throughout the century. These included war and travel stories, humorous tales, and nonmilitary historical accounts. Stories of this type constituted about a quarter of all titles throughout the nineteenth and early twentieth centuries.

New subjects that gained popularity in lubok literature in the last decade or two before the Bolshevik Revolution constitute a third grouping of stories about banditry, crime, science, romance, and an admixture of crime and romance. They comprised less than 16 percent of all titles until the 1890s, but by the 1900s their share had risen to 40 percent.

Of the early lubok stories, those based on folklore or on late eighteenth-century archaic tales of chivalry were by far the most numerous. Folkloric subjects alone comprised about 40 percent of all editions in the 1850s, and then gradually declined to only about 10 percent in the decade following 1909. Folkloric subjects are perhaps the most shadowy category of lubok literature. Many of the works were children's stories, intended particularly for the new schoolchildren of lower classes. Sometimes publishers or authors lifted whole texts from scholarly editions of folklore, fairy tales, or the heroic epic poems called *byliny*. At other times they rewrote them to suit their own understanding of what would best appeal to their audience. Among the most popular titles were *Ilia Muromets, The Little Hump-Backed Horse, Ivan the Knight, The Lion Who Raised the Tsar's Son,* and finally *The Story of Ivan the Tsar's Son, the Firebird, and the Grey Wolf.*

Works on subjects from the oral tradition were most closely identified with the lubok prints, and there were many pictures of Ivan the Tsar's son riding the grey wolf, caged firebird in hand, accompanied by Elena the Fair, and of Ilia Muromets battling his fantastic enemy, Solovei the Bandit, who was half bird and half man. Folkloric subjects were often revised for chapbook editions, and lubok authors sought to make the familiar tales more realistic and credible to the contemporary audience.

One example of a folk tale that was radically revised in a lubok edition was the story *Ivan the Knight, His Fair Spouse Svetlana, and the Evil Wizard Karachun,* which was published over fifty-five times during the nineteenth and early twentieth centuries.[23] The version I will discuss here was published in 1900 in Kiev by T. A. Gubanov, one of the major lubok publishers. The subject of the story is almost identical to that of the folk tale of the frog-princess, which appears in the standard late nineteenth-century collection of A. N. Afanasev in three variants.[24]

In each of the three versions of Afanasev's collection, a tsar has three sons of the same age and orders them to shoot arrows to determine who their brides would be. The arrows of the first two sons land beside the beautiful daughters of respectable citizens—in various versions, a general, a prince, a merchant, and a boyar—but Ivan Tsarevich's arrow falls in a swamp and is picked up by a frog. Ivan is distressed. In two versions of the story he wonders, "How can I marry a frog?" but in each case he submits to his "fate": in one version he decides that there is nothing to do but marry the frog, and in the other two the tsar orders him to do

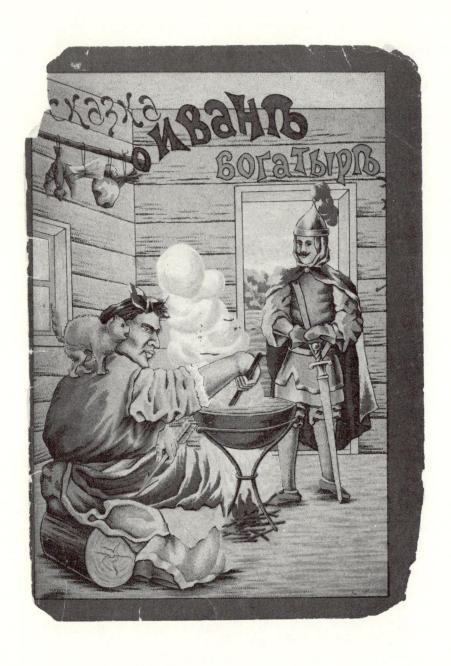

FIG. 1. *The Tale of Ivan the Knight, His Fair Spouse Svetlana, and the Evil Wizard Karachun* (Kiev: Gubanov, 1900).

70

so, saying, "Know that such is your fate." He is promptly married at court to the frog in all versions of the tale.

For the chapbook authors, a story about a forced marriage to an unpleasantly disguised princess required a different explanation of motivation and of the rationality of Ivan's action. The anonymous chapbook author confronted difficulties from the first line of the story, not only in the location of the tale, but in explaining how a father might have three sons exactly the same age. The story begins: "In a certain kingdom, not in our state, lived and flourished a certain grandee whose name was Dobromysl. He lived in pagan times when people had several dozen wives." Dobromysl, however, had only three, and on the extraordinary occasion of the simultaneous birth of three sons he had a great celebration. When his sons grew up he ordered them to shoot their arrows "so that you will know your fate." The arrows of the first two fell to daughters of other grandees, but Ivan's arrow disappeared. He hunted far and wide, and eventually found himself lost in a bog. In the middle of the bog was a small hut. He knocked on the door. "For a long time no one answered him, and our knight had already begun to lose patience when suddenly a decrepit old woman appeared on the threshold. Looking at her, Ivan took fright. In her hands the old woman held his arrow."

The fairy tale situation has become a more realistic one, and the wonder of the fairy tale has been replaced by the suspenseful chain of the written narrative, in which the imagination of the reader is prompted and cued by the writer. The more rational and self-conscious Ivan of the chapbook knows that he is in a fix from which he must and can extricate himself. "Is this old mushroom really to be my wife?" he asks. The answer is clearly no. He sits down and suddenly the interior of the hut changes into the parlor of a luxurious residence. He is given a fine dinner and settles into a soft armchair, but when he asks to leave, the old woman tells him to stay because "fate herself has ordered you to have me as your wife." But fate means nothing to the modern Ivan, who suggests she must be joking. "You can count more than two hundred years and are looking into the grave, but I am barely twenty-two," he complains. She is not willing to rely on fate either, and says bluntly, "If you do not marry me you will perish in the marsh." His efforts to outwit her and escape fail, so he agrees to marry her, although the reader knows this is only an expedient. Then she appears in her true beauty as a young woman, but Ivan learns that in order to break the spell she must be presented at court as his bride in the form of the old woman.

When Ivan comes before his father bride in hand, the discussion is the opposite of that in the folk tale. Instead of a father ordering a son to marry an unsuitable bride who turns out to be suitable, the son insists and the father protests. Fate is no longer an adequate justification for unacceptable behavior, and the son knows better than the father. Ivan's father complains that the bride looks like a grandmother, but he agrees to the marriage when he concludes that Ivan has been bewitched.

The lubok and folk versions of the tale are closer together in the subsequent development of the theme. As the rival wives perform tasks for the father, Ivan breaks a prohibition, the enchanted beauty is spirited away, and Ivan then rescues her from a faraway land. Some differences remain, however. The lubok version is more concrete and realistic. More important is the casual way in which the lubok author dispenses with the crucial moral element in the fairy tale. The frog-princess is able to escape from the spell in the fairy tale only when a prince will marry her of his own free will. Good comes of voluntary acceptance of an unpleasant fate. In the chapbook version she is able to gain the necessary promise by force and guile, and the prince agrees to marry her only when the alternative is death in the marsh. Even so, one senses that he kept his promise only because he had learned of her true nature.

Similarly revised versions of familiar folk and fairy tales provoked one of the more perceptive investigators of lubok literature to complain of how "a short, alive, expressive, and dramatic folk story is turned into the wishy-washy rhetoric of the lubok author."[25] Although the changes the authors made did not win the approbation of the critics, they were important in satisfying the readers and showed the difference in tastes between the audiences for popular fiction and for folklore.

Not all fairy tales in the lubok versions were so meaningfully transformed. The story of Vasilisa the Beautiful, one of the series of tales in which the fantastic witch Baba Iaga appears, turned up as *The Merchant's Daughter* in a 1915 lubok edition published by I. D. Sytin, but the story was not greatly changed. The author of the lubok edition gives more concrete details and clarifies motivations. Although there is even a reference to sending Vasilisa to school, the integrity of the tale is preserved. Vasilisa successfully avoids the machinations of an evil stepmother by being kind and listening to a doll given her by her dying mother. She fulfills the stepmother's request to get fire from the witch Baba Iaga, and the stepmother is burned to a crisp when Vasilisa gives her what she requested. Vasilisa's goodness brings doom to her enemies.[26]

Lubok authors also drew on Russia's epic folk poems, the byliny, and sometimes they used scholarly versions with few modifications. The story of the adventures of Ilia Muromets was published under the name of one of the best-known lubok authors, but it differs little in most respects from the standard texts of the byliny.[27]

The only written materials that rivaled oral culture in the popular milieu before the arrival of lubok literature were the works from the medieval and early modern literary tradition that were primarily available in manuscripts. The compendiums contained laboriously copied selections from the Chronicles, the lives of saints, the Psalter, the Book of Hours, and secular tales widely known and respected among the common people. Among the works of the old tradition still extant in the eighteenth and nineteenth centuries were "The Story of the Kingdom of Kazan," versions of Milton's "Paradise Lost," and satirical tales from the Petrine era, such as "The Story of the Russian Sailor Vasilii Kariotskii."

The secular manuscript works that most captivated the common readers were the chivalric tales, whose popularity became so great and lasting that their names became practically synonymous with lubok literature itself. These stories were known in other variants in many countries. Five of these tales that were particularly popular concerned the adventures of Bova Korolevich, Eruslan Lazarevich, Frantsyl Ventsian, Milord Georg, and Guak. Their names suggest their non-Russian origins—Bova, Frantsyl, Guak, and Milord from the West, and Eruslan from the East. Judging from the textual history of Bova and Eruslan, the stories reached Russia in the seventeenth century in oral and manuscript versions, and dispersed rapidly as folk tales, in handwritten copies, and, since the end of the eighteenth century, in printed editions.[28] Well known among the educated reading public, the stories were circulating in rural Russia by the end of the eighteenth century.[29] With a gloss of Christianity, the addition of the conventions of Russian folk tales, and a dusting with familiar touches from the byliny, the texts were rapidly adapted to suit a Russian audience. The stories were frequently printed in the first half of the nineteenth century, and rewritten after the emancipation, when the new lower-class reading public had taken shape as a well-defined market. In that form they attained wide popularity, and remained a staple of popular reading until the Bolsheviks took power.

The five tales had between six and eight hundred separate printings.[30] Bova and Eruslan appeared each in over two hundred separate editions. The five tales together comprise approximately 15 percent of all lubok editions published from the early nineteenth century through the 1880s, but their share of the popular market declined sharply—to 9 percent in the 1890s and to only 5 percent in the 1910s.

These tales retained their archaic flavor, and their continued success puzzled educated observers. Heroes of the stories were the subjects of folk tales,[31] and the very titles bespoke a link to folklore and to a premodern literary tradition. The heroes' attributes were listed and their consorts identified. Titles such as *The Tale of the Strong and Glorious Champion Eruslan Lazarevich and his Beautiful Wife Anastasia* (1904),

FIG. 2. *The Story of the English Milord Georg* (Moscow: Konovalov, 1914).

and *The Tale of the Glorious, Brave, and Unbeatable Champion Bova Korolevich and About his Beautiful Wife the Princess Druzhevna* (1916) were typical. The stories took place in vague or improbable locations, concretizations of "in a faraway kingdom, in a faraway land" of the fairy tales. Bova wanders from a city called Anton to Armenia. Frantsyl begins in "the Spanish Kingdom," but travels to Turkey and Persia, and Guak proceeds from his home in "the Kingdom of American Florida," to "the Amazonian Kingdom." Most of the action consists of heroic contests between valiant knights and their supernatural opponents, except in the story of Milord Georg, in which the subject is courtly love.

The adventures of Bova set the standard for the chivalric tale. Driven out of his own kingdom of Anton by his mother and her evil lover, the murderer of his father, Bova wanders the world, proves courageous in contests with such fantastic adversaries as the centaur, wins a princess and a new kingdom, and returns to avenge his father's death. Stories of this type were revised to suit more modern tastes and values in much the same way as the fairy tales, and although in eighteenth-century versions Bova repays his mother's treachery by burying her alive, by the late nineteenth century he accepts her sincere repentance, and she lives to a ripe old age.[32]

Educated critics used *The English Milord* as a symbol of all that they found pernicious in the literature of the lubok. The story is about a lord out on a hunt who loses his party and finds himself mysteriously before the Marquise Frederika Louisa Brandenburg. The Marquise is in her palace in the forest, with sixteen lovely handmaidens at her side. As soon as she announces her love for him, Milord forgets his betrothed and swears to be true to the lovely Marquise. The two are then separated, and in the longer versions of the story, Milord has a number of additional amorous adventures before being reunited with the Marquise.[33] In the short versions, Milord's only impropriety is the betrayal of his betrothed.[34] Traces of the early origins of this tale appear even in the short versions, and Milord appeals to Diana, goddess of the hunt, when he gets lost in the forest.

Although these chivalrous tales seemed no more than gibberish to most educated readers, each one contained a simple story, usually about the relations between the sexes. Such tales were passed from generation to generation, and the heroes were familiar to new readers. The theme of courtship and marital strife may have had a special meaning to young readers at a time when families were increasingly disrupted by migration and the search for work outside the village.

By the early twentieth century the traditional forms of lubok fiction were so familiar to lower-class readers that they could be parodied in

Fig. 3. *The Story of Frantsyl Ventsian and the Beautiful Queen Rentsyvena* (Moscow: Sytin, 1915).

more modern stories. *The Glorious Knight Antipka* was an anonymous story published by Sytin in 1914 that echoed the chivalrous tales in its title and folk tales in its structure.[35] In a fictitious village named Babino [from *baba*, peasant woman], located beyond valleys and mountains, a crotchety misogynist gets his due. The village ladies trick him into thinking that the local beauty is pining for his love. He learns his lesson and gives up his "war against women," an unexpected ending for a story set in as paternalistic a society as that of rural Russia.

The instructive stories were those with advice or admonitions in the titles. Although these tales comprised a small but relatively stable percentage of all titles throughout the period, their greatest importance was in the years 1820-49, during which they accounted for 6 percent of all works. Typical of the stories of this sort was *Grandma Marfa, or A Prayer to God and a Service to the Tsar Are Never in Vain*. In a version of this story by the popular lubok author V. A. Lunin, who wrote under the pseudonym of Kukel, Marfa is a kindly old lady who raises two orphan peasant children after their mother dies.[36] Common also in this subject grouping were cautionary tales, such as *The Best Medicine for Drunkenness* by Misha Evstigneev.

The stories of travel, humor, war, and historical subjects contain much more new information about daily life than do the folkloric or chivalric tales, and the content of the stories published in the postemancipation period usually reflects the interests of the new lower-class reading public. Travel stories, those in which a place of interest or a voyage is indicated in the title, and which account for 3 to 5 percent of all titles over the whole period, are an excellent example. One such story is *The New Voyage on the Bast Machine: A Thousand Versts for One Ruble*, which went through at least seventeen editions between 1870 and 1903.[37] The story begins, "What kind of a thing is the bast machine?" and the answer is, "Poor folks who cannot afford to stay in the capital or travel by the Nikolaev railroad put on bast boots when they get beyond the Neva embankment, and complete a journey of about a thousand versts and more on a ruble or less." Shalaev, the author of the booklet, was also its first publisher. He addresses his reader as "my good penniless chap." The story is about a young migrant's homeward journey in the company of a dozen comrades, each with no more than a ruble. They hop trains, sell their city clothes, and beg for handouts. The hero arrives home like a prodigal, happy to be back at work in the fields and glad to be rid of city life. "Laziness is the mother of all sins," concludes Shalaev, wishing all peasant migrants a safe return to their villages.

Popular authors used humor to comment on a variety of current themes, and such stories were usually identified in the title as "a merry

FIG. 4. *The Glorious Knight Antipka. A Humorous Story from Village Life* (Moscow: Sytin, 1914).

tale." These stories ranged from relatively early sketches, such as Misha Evstigneev's *The Barber, a Merry Story* (1882), in which an insolvent customer offers his moustache in payment, only to find that the barber demands half of it one week and half the next, to comments on the battle between the sexes, such as Valentin Volgin's *The Foolish Heart, a Merry Story* (1896), which illustrates a less than positive attitude toward women. There were also stories in which the railroad features prominently, such as Misha Evstigneev's *The Third-Class Railway Coach* (1868) and *The Railroad Conductor* (1869).

The war stories by commercial authors were usually more imaginative than official propaganda, but otherwise they were similar. Commercial publishers produced such works during various conflicts, and during peacetime they generated stories about soldiering to satisfy the widespread curiosity about the soldier's life. Among the war stories were sketches such as *The Russian Sword Moves on the Turkish Checkerboard* (1878), the title of which is a pun on the word for sword and checker (*shashka*), and *The Glorious Feat of the Don Cossack Kuzma Kriuchkov* (1914). *The Soldier Iashka* (1868) is a peacetime story about a young good-for-nothing orphan whose guardian uncle gets fed up with him and sends him off into the army.[38]

Among the nonmilitary historical subjects, the story of Ermak, the conqueror of Siberia, was told most often. Stories about historical rebels and bandits were also common. Peter the Great was the second most popular figure in historical fiction, and he was the subject of a wide variety of stories, in which he often appears as a just tsar who is close to the common people. *Anecdotes and Legends about Peter the Great, the First Emperor of the Russian Land and about His Love for the State* is a paean to Peter's wisdom in founding St. Petersburg, his diligence and energy, and his "steadfastness in the faith."[39] *The Legend of How the Soldier Saved Peter the Great* is one of the oldest of the Peter stories. It went through at least thirty-four editions from the time when it was first published in the 1840s until the end of the old regime.[40] Peter is typically presented in this tale as a Westernized gentleman, but also as a good comrade who does not recognize class distinctions.

The last group of subjects—the stories about banditry and crime, science and superstition, and romance—were most popular in the last decade or two of tsarist rule. The novelty of these tales for peasants and former peasants was often very great. Among the stories categorized as romance, for example, were many tales about changing relations between the sexes, such as Lunin's tale *The Fancy Wife* (1901), about a man who makes good but goes astray in his choice of a spouse.[41] Another is *The Factory Beauty* (1897), also by Lunin, in which an enterprising schoolteacher gets the girl of his dreams.[42] The authors of such stories described relations between the sexes in a world in which the traditional paternalistic values were contested.

The Authors

Who wrote these stories? The answer bears directly on the question of whether lubok literature was inspired by its lower-class audience or was merely a degraded and diminished version of high culture. The stories were not written by ordinary peasants or workers, but the available evidence suggests that many of the authors were of peasant origins and grew up within the bounds of lower-class life. Their social class explains in part why neither they nor their works were ever considered legitimate by educated Russians. The air of disrepute that clung to the lubok stories separated their authors from both the creators of belles lettres and from the writers who produced the sponsored literature intended for lower-class readers. The lubok authors were well aware of their position on the fringe of the literary world, but they also made a special claim to speak for and to a popular audience.

Matvei Komarov was the author of the enormously popular chivalry tale, *Milord Georg*, as well as of several picaresque novels on subjects including the renowned desperado, Vanka Kain. Komarov was acclaimed by the critic Victor Shklovskii in the 1920s as one of the founders of the Russian novel.[43] The anonymous author of another of the popular chivalry tales, *The Adventures of Fransyl Ventsian*, which also appeared in one hundred editions, was reputed to be a house serf.

The origins of most lubok authors of the early nineteenth century are obscure. Writers such as Alexander Anfimovich Orlov (1790?-1840), Vasilii F. Potapov, V. Ia. Shmitanovskii, and Petr Petrovich Tatarinov (d. 1858) seem to have lived among the lower middle classes of the cities, and they wrote about characters and scenes from this world. Their stories include folk tales and historical novels, and humorous and instructive yarns about the adventures of merchants and their sons. Of these earlier writers, most is known about Orlov. He was the son of a sexton and attended the university, but he lived a precarious and poverty-stricken life on the edge of respectable literary circles. As for the other lubok writers of this early period, only their works remain our witnesses.

More information is available about several lubok authors of the second half of the nineteenth century, the period when lubok literature became firmly established as lower-class reading. The lubok writers of the first half of the nineteenth century were usually considered too insignificant to merit much attention from their contemporaries, and the memory of and interest in the authors of the early twentieth century vanished with the Bolshevik Revolution, which left little time for this kind of nostalgia. We know something about Mikhail Evstigneev, who wrote perhaps one hundred stories from the 1850s to the end of the century, and was known to a whole generation of lower-class, predominantly urban readers. "I read the empty little books of Misha Evstigneev, paying a kopeck to read each, but they did not give me any satisfaction," wrote Maxim Gorky, who preferred more sophisticated adventure stories and historical novels.[44]

Although best remembered for his humorous works, Evstigneev wrote on a wide variety of themes. One of his earliest pieces was *The Panorama of the Second-Hand Market*, a humorous sketch he co-authored in 1858 with an older lubok writer named A. Nesterov.[45] The piece begins with a description of the Sunday sellers who unburden themselves of various pieces of junk they have found on the street or in the garbage. Evstigneev pays homage to a predecessor, for among the junk he finds "*Fomushka in Piter* and other tales of the late Tatarinov that are greasy and tattered from zealous reading." Typical of the humorous works of Evstigneev were *A Third-Class Railway Coach—Merry Scenes* (1868), containing humorous descriptions of the passengers, and *The Art of Living Off Someone Else in Moscow* (1868).[46] Evstigneev also wrote such tales as *The Daring Bandit* (1869), about a desperado named Smelchak who becomes the benefactor of a poor peasant and his son and is repaid for his efforts with treachery.[47]

Evstigneev was an unsuccessful student at Moscow University in the 1860s, and he turned to writing and to drink after failing at a number of professions. He was known as "the scholar" in the world of cheap publishing, a reputation due less to his education than to his ability to churn out books on subjects such as medical advice.[48]

Another popular author of the 1870s was Vladimir Suvorov, a lubok historian, who often rewrote stories by writers such as M. I. Zagoskin but also produced works himself, such as *How Man and Woman Loved in Olden Times or Death from Melancholy—A Historical Novel from the Time of the War between the Russians and the Germans* (1880) and *Essays on the History of the Russo-Turkish War* (1877), with "sketches and biographies of the Russian heroes of this struggle."[49] A retired officer who went about in a ragged army great coat and a uniform cap with a red band, Suvorov was known as "the colonel."[50] Both Suvorov and the more prolific Evstigneev were *raznochintsy*, or people of diverse ranks who were neither gentry nor peasants. Prugavin considered them members of the older generation of lubok authors when he studied the subject in the late 1880s.

The writers who began work during or after the Russo-Turkish War of 1877-78 were pioneers in satisfying a predominantly peasant readership, and at least six of them were former peasants themselves.[51] We have enough information about two of these authors, Ivan Semenovich Ivin (1858-1918 or 1921) and Matvei Ivanovich Ozhegov (1860-1933), to consider the questions of how they regarded their professions, and to what extent they shared in the experience of lower-class Russians.[52]

Both Ivin and Ozhegov were rural children of the era of the emancipation, but they had very different experiences and perspectives. Ivin, who wrote under the name Kassirov, was one of the most prolific lubok authors and published from the late 1870s until the turn of the century. He was the only chapbook author to attract the notice of educated Russia. He began earlier and published more widely than did Ozhegov, who was predominantly a songwriter. Ivin began his career with patriotic poems in the periodicals and miscellanies that flourished briefly during the Russo-Turkish War. His "Songs of a Warrior," a poem in which he writes of his journey to "fierce battle" in a "remote region" appeared in *A Humorous Album with Caricatures* (1878).[53] His first story, *The Adventures of a Common Russian Soldier Returning from the War* (1878), was about a homeward-bound soldier who is tricked out of his money by a beautiful woman and is left drunk in a field.[54]

Ivin produced a prodigious number of works in a career that lasted into the twentieth century. He wrote or rewrote traditional fairy tales and chivalric novels, historical works, adventure stories, and tales intended to dispel superstition as well as tracts on religious themes. Among his secular works were such stories as *The Enchanted Castle or the Unhappy Princess, a Tale for the People* (1889), *The Witch or a Terrible Night on the Other Side of the Dnieper* (1894), and *A Popular Account of a Captive of the Circassians* (1892). His religious works included *Understanding the Church of Christ, Life Beyond the Grave, The City of Jerusalem,* and *The Life of Jesus.* In a letter to Rubakin, he identified these works as "among my most successful and best loved by the people."[55] His writings remained popular until the Bolshevik Revolution, and from 1908 through 1916 more than thirty of his stories were in print.

According to an autobiography he sent to Rubakin in 1892—one of several he wrote—Ivin was the son of a literate serf. His father worked before the emancipation as a cashier on the Moscow estate of Count Uvarov, a well-known archeologist. From that time on the family was known as the "Kassirovs," and Ivin took the name as his pseudonym.[56]

His native village was forty miles from the nearest railroad station, and, according to his account, had neither factories, craft workers, nor Old Believers. (Rubakin queried his correspondents about these things in order to understand better the factors affecting rural literacy.) The village was not, however, untouched by modern life. Ivin explained that "the young people of our locale almost all live in Moscow at factories and plants."

The young Ivin received his first instruction in reading from his father, but he was also taught at a church and attended a secular school for seven and a half months. Like many who had only a little instruction, he considered himself an autodidact, and shrugged off the idea that he had been to school at all: "One could say that I learned to read by myself."[57] In 1888, at the age of thirty, he took and passed the certifying exam for rural schoolteachers, though he never used the credential. While still a boy he left his village with his father, worked at various factories, one in the south and several in Moscow, and was then apprenticed to the Goper factory in Moscow to learn a trade. Early in his career as a worker, he became a reader for other workers. At that time he felt the desire "to write something of this sort" himself, and at the age of 14 began to write poems. Within a year or two he became acquainted with the then well-known and respected peasant autodidact writer I. Z. Surikov, who happened to live in his neighborhood in Moscow. Surikov encouraged him to continue writing and to read.

Fed up with what he considered an unsuitable factory career, Ivin convinced his father to let him return to their home village and see the Countess Uvarov about opportunities to continue his education. She discouraged him at first, because he had not even finished primary school. Nevertheless, after seeing some of his poems, she decided to help him enter a teacher's seminary, in which he could have studied for four years. Unfortunately, he was by this time nineteen years old, and too old to be accepted into the program. "I was very sad," he explained, "and I wrote the poem 'The Path to Learning.' " He bought himself a primer, began to study, and sent poems to several popular magazines. A few were accepted. He became acquainted with lubok publishing and began to write for the lubok firms as well as for popular humor magazines.[58] In 1882 his father died and he married, apparently taking over the family land. By the late 1880s, Ivin was well established as a prolific lubok writer. He spent his winters in Moscow and his summers on his land in the village. In 1892 he wrote to Rubakin to explain that he would spend the whole winter in Moscow after he worked his fields.[59]

Ozhegov wrote songs rather than fiction. His first poem appeared in a Moscow illustrated paper in 1890, and his first book, *Songs and Verses*, was issued in 1891 by a little-known publisher in 20,000 copies.[60] A shorter version, entitled *Field and Village*, appeared in 6,000 copies. Two years later, E. A. Gubanov, a successful lubok publisher, brought out three of his songbooks: *Brave Sorrow, The Herdsman*, and *The New Songbook*. Ten thousand copies of each were sold in a year. Ozhegov's verses were also used as texts for lubok prints. He continued to publish, and the first volume, entitled *My Life and Songs for the People*, of a projected five-volume series appeared in 1901. Some of his songs were widely sung during his lifetime and a few are still popular and anthologized. Ozhegov was active in the Revolution of 1905, and he cooperated with the Soviet government after 1917. He is now recognized officially in the Soviet Union as a legitimate cultural figure, unlike the other lubok writers.

Ozhegov was born in 1860 in the countryside. His parents were illiterate Orthodox state peasants, and his father was a village carpenter. Like Ivin, Ozhegov was drawn into the off-farm work force at a young age. He learned to read from an older brother. He also had Old Believer teachers, and they strongly influenced his development. He wrote his first verses in the Old Slavonic letters used by the Old Believers in their verses and canons. Later he wrote poems directed against the Old Believers. After learning to read informally, he attended a zemstvo school for two winters and learned to write and do arithmetic. He was then apprenticed to a traveling bookbinder, whose main customers were Old Believers. Later, when he was fourteen, he was apprenticed to a merchant in a neighboring district, and served as an occasional coachman and janitor. He also traveled for this merchant, selling petty goods at fairs and markets. At sixteen he joined a party of neighbors who went to Perm Province to work on the railroad.

Ozhegov went home, took the school exam, and when he returned to the railroad, it was as a foreman. He did not stay at this job, however, and he eventually went back to his village. At age twenty-two he married a peasant girl, traded in grain, managed a tavern for a merchant, and then headed for the Siberian gold fields "to seek happiness." There he prospected for himself and worked for others, but had no great luck. He returned home and did field work, but soon after he went off again with his neighbors to work on the railroad, this time on the Ural line. Finally, at age twenty-five in 1885, Ozhegov went to Moscow "to seek adventures," leaving his wife and family in the village. He worked as a waiter, janitor, newspaper seller, and even as some kind of commercial reporter; but he again returned home penniless, though satisfied at having seen Moscow. As he explained in his autobiographical preface to *My Life and*

Songs for the People, "I was in tatters, like a beggar, but I already knew the capital. I had read newspapers."

He was granted a new passport only on the condition, set down by the village elder, that he not abandon his wife and child again. They all went to Moscow together, and he and his wife worked at a series of jobs. He kept a newsstand, and she took over his old newspaper delivery route. He obtained a position with the Moscow-Kursk Railway in 1893, his first in a variety of office jobs at the station, and then, after passing several exams, he worked as a telegraph operator. He advanced rapidly in his new profession, and by 1897 he was a cashier, with an annual salary of 600 rubles, plus an apartment allowance of 150 rubles, twice the average earnings of a primary schoolteacher.

Ozhegov's successful career was soon interrupted, however. He returned triumphantly to his village in the late 1890s; but in 1901 he moved to Orel, which is located to the south of Moscow on the Oka River, and worked as an assistant cashier. According to a later Soviet account, he turned up as a railroad employee in Iaroslavl in 1905, where he sat on the revolutionary strike committee as the representative of the switchmen and watchmen.[61] According to this source, he was imprisoned in Iaroslavl prison, but returned to his railroad work, which he continued until 1921, when old age forced him to abandon his post. His situation may have taken a turn for the worse after 1905, and it is possible that he was unemployed.[62] He published some poems in local periodicals in Iaroslavl, but the optimistic tone of his earlier writings had vanished.[63] Whether or not he greeted Soviet power with enthusiasm is unknown, but he did live long enough to hail the collectivization of his village in 1930 with a laudatory poem. His seventieth birthday was celebrated officially with an article in *Literaturnaia gazeta* (The Literary Newspaper), now the official organ of the Writers' Union.

Ivin and Ozhegov shared with other people of peasant origin many of the conflicting and troubling pressures of their times. They may have escaped from their class, but they were deeply marked by its worries and concerns. When they wrote about social mobility and whether or not a person could and should make his way up in the world, they wrote from experience. Ivin and Ozhegov were writers with similar backgrounds, but they projected very different personae. They had different ideas about what it meant to be a writer, and, in particular, a writer from the people, but they shared a belief in the worth and distinctiveness of popular literature.

Ivin was influenced during the 1880s by Leo Tolstoy and the populists who dominated the thinking of that period. He was then eager to display his peasant credentials, and in his first letter to Rubakin at the beginning of the 1890s, he wrote, "I am a self-taught writer (*pisatel'-samouchka*), a peasant agriculturalist. I live permanently in the village and I work the land with my own hands, along with other peasants."[64] He explained that although he had corresponded with Prugavin, and knew that Prugavin had written about him, he had not read Prugavin's work, since he rarely read the expensive magazines in which Prugavin's articles were printed. He also mentioned that he was acquainted with Tolstoy and with S. T. Semenov, Tolstoy's peasant protégé whose work was published by Posrednik, the firm organized by Tolstoy and some of his followers to produce good reading material for the people. Similarly, in a letter to Rubakin, Ivin agreed to send a list of what was in his library, but explained, "The list will not be very long."[65]

Ivin voiced his distaste for urban life in his 1893 collection of poems entitled *Songs of the Motherland*. The first poem he wrote, "The Worker," is a gloomy commentary on proletarian life. So is "Lathe-Operator," another poem about a young apprentice who leaves the countryside. "Unhappy are his parents, his family, his father and mother! Why did they give up their son to be apprenticed to the lathe operator? Here he learned to work, but also to debauch himself."[66] He depicted the rural world as a place where "the laborer is childishly pure and forthright in spirit." Even when he found the village poor and grey and its inhabitants ignorant and superstitious, he still looked to the countryside: "I would like to remain in my remote village to breathe the air of the fields all my life," he wrote.[67]

Ivin's peasantism was conservative, and he was an enthusiastic supporter of the autocracy and the Orthodox faith. He began to write during the Russo-Turkish War of 1877-78, and he swelled with pride at the Russian victory. "Thanks to you, our powerful tsar, from all humble Russians," he wrote in 1878. Three years later he expressed his grief when Alexander II was assassinated: "The tsar was good and just. In Russian hearts he lives."[68]

When Rubakin, who was a Socialist revolutionary, urged him to look critically on Russian society, Ivin replied that Russia needed to unite behind the tsar and the Orthodox Church. Otherwise, he warned, catastrophe threatened as it had when the Tatars invaded, "destroying cities and towns to their foundations, burning all the manuscript books, and bringing coarse dissension and ashes to Russia."[69]

Ivin initially charmed Rubakin, who was excited to find a bona fide peasant writer, and he had made a similar impression on Leo Tolstoy a few years earlier. "After dinner, Ivin," Tolstoy wrote in his diary for 1889. "He is writing a life of Christ. A remarkable man."[70] Tolstoy's enthusiasm faded rapidly, however, and a month later he wrote of a

Gospel-reading session with Ivin: "His summary very much displeased me." Ivin, to Tolstoy's disgust, refused to give up the Orthodox Church: "Ivin sticks with Orthodoxy all the time." Ivin may also have offended Tolstoy with his coarseness. Tolstoy remarked on Ivin's confidences about his private life, and about drunkenness and debauchery. Ivin presented his view of his meetings with Tolstoy in one of the autobiographies he sent to Rubakin. He met Tolstoy, "at last," in the 1880s, he wrote, but he was unwilling to submit to the dictates of the great writer. "He wanted to see in me the angel of his 'teaching,' " he wrote, "and he set me to reading his 'Gospels,' *In What Is My Faith*, and other prohibited things, but I did not agree with them very much, and even rejected his argument."[71] Nevertheless, Ivin was very flattered to note that Tolstoy had praised one of his stories. He sent it to Posrednik, the publishing house with which Tolstoy was involved, but the censor rejected the story.

Ivin had a very clear sense of himself as a peasant writer whose position differed from that of educated writers and authors of sponsored works for the people. This was not an intentional separation from educated Russians, but a very real division that he had learned to appreciate. He had tried to get Rubakin's assistance in publishing some of his patriotic songs and poems of social commentary in the magazines read by educated people. Rubakin's reply is not preserved, but Ivin's work did not appear in the "thick" journals. He did succeed, however, in publishing a defense of lubok literature in the conservative thick journal *Russkoe obozrenie* (Russian Survey), but he signed the piece only as "the peasant Ivin." "One can say straight out," he wrote, "that the peasant who has read more than a thousand books of the intelligentsia carries away much less social and historical, and especially moral and religious, understanding than if he reads only one hundred books of lubok publishers."[72] He claimed that he was correcting and improving lubok literature, even though he received only a pittance for his writings, because he wanted "as little rubbish as possible communicated to the people."[73]

When Rubakin wrote to Ivin of the writer's social responsibility to inform his readers about the world, Ivin answered, in effect, that Rubakin was in no position to tell him what to write. "No," Ivin replied, "art demands most of all freedom for its inspiration."[74] Ivin was hypersensitive to the suggestion that an educated person should tell him what to write, but he himself shared the view that literature should promote social progress. In "The Path to Learning," the poem he wrote in despair when he found he was too old to get into the teacher-training institute, he wrote that he wanted to "[gain] knowledge by a feat of labor, in order afterwards to share this knowledge with the muzhiks," and "to go to my native countryside and sow knowledge among the people."[75] Ivin also wrote of the need to dispel superstition, but warned that peasants often did not understand scientific explanations.[76] "If you explain electricity to the muzhik," he wrote to Rubakin, "and that lightning is an electric spark, he only replies, 'Ah, what a clever thing.' "

Ivin expressed in his writing the conflict between personal initiative and fate that he experienced in his life, and he saw the conflict as a source of his artistic inspiration. "Yes, fate binds me, does not allow me to spread my wings," he wrote in one poem.[77]

Like Ivin, Ozhegov was proud and pleased to be able to present himself as a peasant writer to educated Russians of populist sympathy. "Living at home in the village as an ordinary member of peasant society, and at the same time an inquisitive *samouchka* (autodidact)" was the way he described himself in his first letter to Rubakin. He was, in his own view, a person craving enlightenment and general knowledge for his people, "one who fully recognizes the usefulness of all possible fields of science and labor for the good of the fatherland and the universal welfare, or more truly, for the simple worker."[78] He was also apparently influenced by Tolstoyan ideas of religion and dreamed of the spread of "popular universal learning in the spirit of the Gospels." Like Ivin, Ozhegov also had little use for educated writers who wrote about the common people "without knowing the reality of popular life."[79] He expressed his belief in the importance of writers like himself, who were "familiar with the laboring life of the peasantry." Ivin and Ozhegov met at this time, and Ivin described him in a letter to Rubakin as "a rather interesting person, but little educated, and not developed."[80] Ivin wrote that he introduced Ozhegov to the lubok publisher Gubanov to help Ozhegov earn some money.

Ozhegov was more optimistic than Ivin that personal initiative could conquer fate, and he cited his own story as an example in the autobiography he published in his volume of poems and songs, *My Life and Songs for the People* (1901). Ozhegov spoke as a peasant who had improved his lot and had attained the position of a prosperous railroad employee and popular song writer. Ozhegov's story, except for his literary activity, must have been similar to that of many ordinary people. He began it with a preface in which he thanked family, relatives, friends, employers, publishers, and other self-taught writers who had urged him to publish his autobiography.[81] He signed the preface simply "author." He made clear that the subject of the book was "the path of my life to light and freedom," and though he explained that his progress was not complete, the tone of the entire work was buoyant, self-congratulatory, and optimistic. "With the development of my literacy, my consciousness of my human worth grew, and my forces were strengthened for the struggle with an unattractive life in general, and for my existence in particular."

Ozhegov understood his struggle for upward mobility in an individual context in which will, talent, and opportunity were all turned to personal advantage. "I decided to be the master of my situation. I began to protest against the usual mode of personal and social life with all the force and means that I was given at birth, and I began to perfect myself and to improve." He turned to songs and singing not only because they were familiar to him from childhood, but also because he saw in them a way to protest "against my fate, against my bitter lot." Despite his belief in the power of personal initiative, Ozhegov had a sense that his path as a writer had, to some degree, been determined. "I go where God calls," he wrote in his autobiography.

Much of the autobiography concerned employment and salary. Typical of the pride with which he regarded each salary increase or opportunity was his description of the offer of 17 rubles a month to manage the apartment house in which he lived. "A more favorable opportunity," he wrote, "gave me the possibility of declining this honor." The opportunity was the job at the Moscow-Kursk railroad station, which promised to lead to apparently secure middle-class employment.

Ozhegov's consciousness of his separation from his native fields and community was strongly expressed in his autobiography. The theme of separation from the community, of being an outsider, so important in modern belles lettres, recurred frequently in the lubok literature. In Ozhegov's autobiography, as in many of the lubok stories, a triumphant return to the village resolved the tension of the separation, even if the protagonist chose not to remain in the village. The village represented continuity of place, and of a community where the protagonist had a rightful position, in case he failed in his efforts to make his mark in the larger world. For the successful, the trip back to the native village was a measure of how far one had gone and how much was achieved. The return validated the success, and the accomplishments were not fully real until recognized by the native village. The detailed descriptions of triumphant homecomings communicate the depth of emotion that this theme sounded in the writers and readers.

The culmination of Ozhegov's success story, although not his career, was his return to his native village. "Need and deprivation did not distress me," he wrote, "as much as the humiliations, insults, and the separation from home." The idea of returning home was constantly with Ozhegov, even though home held little attraction and few opportunities. His boss granted him a month off, and, leaving his wife and an elder son in the city, he set off with his two younger children for the village. He rode free of charge on the railroad, as an employee. On the steamship he heard sailors singing his songs. His brother greeted him at the dock and took him to a triumphant reception in the village, where he met "poor relatives who needed urgent help" in the form of material aid and advice, and neighbors who complained about their "fate." He remarked on the need for more schools and on the poverty of the village, and left. The whole village saw him off, with crowds equal to those at "the wildest holiday." Having described the triumphant return home, he concluded the account of his life with mention of other self-taught writers, and appended, "I firmly believe in my calling."

Ozhegov's optimism was captured in his songs and poems. "Faith in the heavens, in providence" is combined with the promise of a "new life," to be achieved by honest labor, by suffering, and by a determination to escape from the traditional constraints of peasant life. Ozhegov initially shared Ivin's patriotism and perhaps even some of his religiosity. Among the undated poems he sent to Rubakin were prayers for his mother and a song "For the Tsar," which began "For the tsar, for Orthodox Russia, for Great Russia."[82] The song contained plaintive lines about painful separation from home, and imprecations against rich peasant money-lenders or kulaks.

Ozhegov's success and prosperity proved short-lived. When he lost his job after the 1905 Revolution, his perceptions of his position changed, and he echoed Ivin on the cruel fate of the autodidact writer from the people. In a manuscript dated 1912 entitled "Our Fate, Self-Education, Literature, the People, and the Intelligentsia in a Contemporary Perspective," Ozhegov wrote of his disappointment, his resentment, and his awareness of the limits to upward mobility and the bonds of class.[83] Perhaps he had abandoned his career as a songwriter to pursue the will-o'-the-wisp of literary respectability, or perhaps his disappointment was the result of his inability to find suitable employment. Whatever the cause, his resentment was directed against educated Russia. He argued that because of their experience and closeness to the people, the self-taught writers had a special claim to speak for the peasantry, but, whereas all publications were open to the educated authors who regarded the peasants "with cold haughtiness," the writers from the people were limited to tiny brochures and miscellanies, "which we publish with our last kopecks, taken from our half-starved families."

He also returned in this essay to the theme of city and country. For the autodidact poet, the countryside was "as stuffy as a deep dark forest to wild flowers," but the alternative was also intolerable, because of the "ignorance, the barbarism, the philistinism, the hard-hearted kulakism of that milieu that surrounds us in the cities and the towns."

Ivin and Ozhegov, as seen through their letters and autobiographies, lived the effort to escape from their origins and achieve mobility—one of the major themes in lubok literature. The similarity between their lives and their writings and the appeal of their works to readers link the writers to their audience, and give justification to their claim to speak for the people. They were both conscious of their identity as writers from the people, and both had a sense of mission. Undoubtedly other popular writers shared these feelings; but there were probably also those who conformed in part to the educated Russians' stereotype of the lubok writer, sitting in the corner of a tavern in greasy clothes, turning out rhymes for rubles without a thought for the enlightening mission of literature.

The lubok authors, who wrote in the early twentieth century, showed a sense of mission similar to that of Ivin and Ozhegov, but their horizons were wider. Unfortunately, we know nothing of their lives. A prolific author such as V. A. Lunin, who used the pseudonym of Kukel, wrote frequently about foreign places. He may have hinted that his origins were among the poor gentry when he referred to "the good old time" when "our grandfathers lived on their estates."[84] His stories usually featured lower-class protagonists, and his consciousness of his role as a writer for the people showed clearly. Other writers from this period may have recalled their personal trials when they chose pseudonyms such as that of A. V. Prokhorov, who wrote under the name of Andre Tiazhelois-pytannyi ("hard knocks").

The last two generations of lubok writers revealed their concerns and values through their published stories, as well as through autobiographies, letters, and pseudonyms. The messages conveyed in these different forms are consistent enough to give a firm impression of their sense of themselves as writers. They took their writing seriously, and they were concerned about the issue of upward mobility particularly as it applied to their own careers. A number of recent critics have discussed the ways in which the reader's presence is implied in a text.[85] The lubok writers also conveyed their conception of their readers. They spoke to people who shared their values, but did not have their knowledge or experience in the world. Their writings implied that authors and readers shared experience with ambition, success, disappointment, and injustice. Both writers and readers sympathized with insulted virtue, thwarted efforts, and blocked talent.

The Publishers

The writers, if they did not publish their own works, had to find publishers, and the lubok publishers were the entrepreneurs of the business. The development of popular publishing was slow in the first half of the nineteenth century, and a small number of publishers, primarily family firms, produced a limited number of books and prints for a restricted audience.[86] From the 1860s on, however, lubok publishing became a booming enterprise. New publishing houses sprang up, fortunes were made in people's books and lubok prints, competition became sharp, and a wide field opened for entrepreneurial activity. More than a hundred lubok publishers operated in the last forty years of the nineteenth century.[87] The industry became more organized and more professional. The family houses became joint stock companies, and by the end of the nineteenth century publishing for the lower-class market was big business. In the early twentieth century, popular publishing spread beyond the capitals, and provincial firms entered the competition for the common reader, producing new types of printed material and periodicals that rivaled the traditional lubok prints and booklets.

The expansion of popular publishing depended to a great extent on technical improvements in printing that made the product cheaper to produce. Lithography and the engine press (*skoropechatnyi stan*) were introduced into Russia after the Napoleonic War and came into use in the first half of the century.[88] The number of lithographies and printing houses increased steadily between 1830 and 1860, but more rapidly thereafter.[89] The demand for printed materials of all sorts—not only books and periodicals, but also products for commerce, such as advertisements, posters, tickets, notices, and bureaucratic papers—grew enormously with increased literacy. The pace of technical change continued to be rapid in the 1860s and 1870s, as hand-driven presses were rapidly replaced by powered machines, and new and cheaper presses were developed. The first rotary presses were introduced in the 1870s and came into general use in the following decade. Advances were also made in the binding of books and pamphlets, and many publishers, instead of having books bound in binderies or by the readers, began to do their own binding in-house, thus completing the process of book production in one enterprise. A further advance came in the early twentieth century, when typesetting machines came into use.

The centers of the new popular publishing industry were first St. Petersburg, then Moscow, and later, to a lesser degree, Kiev. The St. Petersburg publishers predominated in the pre-emancipation period, when most readers of unsophisticated publications were middling or lower-class city folk, and the St. Petersburg firms continued to direct their products toward these audiences. The Moscow presses gained on their St. Petersburg rivals after the emancipation by publishing for a largely lower-class readership in the cities and in the countryside, the group also favored by the popular publishing industry in Kiev.

St. Petersburg publishing was concentrated in an area of small shops and antiquarian and second-hand bookstores known as Apraksin Market. One memoirist recalled it at the height of its bustle and glory, before the emancipation, as a place where everything but wine and vodka could be purchased.[90] Soldiers' buttons, clothes, portraits, picture frames, cloth, dishes, soup, and books were all for sale, and the market was the delight of bibliophiles, book browsers, and anyone interested in a bargain. The district was destroyed by fire in 1862, however, and many of the publishing firms never recovered their former glory.

One of the earliest of the St. Petersburg publishers was Vasilii Vasilevich Kholmushin. According to one contemporary observer, he began spreading his books out on a bast mat as early as the 1830s.[91] By the 1850s he had a substantial shop. His merchandise included Synod publications, saints' lives, and other spiritual books, as well as books about fortunetelling, guides to letter writing, songbooks, and lubok novels. He often sold to traders, who, in turn, retailed his books at stalls and shops in the immediate neighborhood along the Nevskii Prospect, and in provincial cities. When Kholmushin and his son died in the early 1870s, the business went to a distant relative, Vasilii Gavrilovich Shataev. Shataev, who later published the popular story, *The Bast Machine or 1,000 Versts for One Ruble*, sold crockery until he became the elder Kholmushin's protégé. Kholmushin had encouraged him to go into publishing, lent him money, and left him the shop.[92] Shataev dealt primarily in religious works, but he also sold songbooks, stories, and manuscripts by unknown authors. He in turn, left the business to a nephew of Kholmushin, A. A. Kholmushin, who continued to publish a variety of works into the early twentieth century, though by this time the firm was barely viable as a publishing house.[93] It maintained a precarious existence during the last years of the old regime selling classics of Russian belles lettres and adventure stories. A catalogue from this time includes *The Loves of Stenka Razin* (10 kopecks), *The King of the Detectives, Nat Pinkerton* (1.25 rubles), and *Petersburg Slums* (10 kopecks), as well as works by Gogol, Tolstoy, and Andreev, and primers in Latin, English, French, and German.[94]

Another late nineteenth-century publisher from the Apraksin Market was T. Kuzin, who, according to a statement on the back flap of a book issued in 1890, sought to provide readers with the best works of authors familiar to "enthusiasts of light reading in our capitals."[95] His 1889 catalogue included expensive works of military history, books of advice to newly married women, and handbooks of medical cures, as well as such bloody tales as *A Novel from the Lives of the Moscow Thieves and Thugs* by I. A. Chmyrev (35 kopecks) and *The Black Grave or A Bloody*

Star (35 kopecks). The cheapest booklets in this 1889 catalogue were the chivalric adventures of Milord Georg, Frantsyl, and a few other lubok classics priced at ten kopecks, but these works were absent from the 1916 catalogue.

The decline of the popular publishing industry in St. Petersburg was paralleled by the rise of the Moscow firms. By the late nineteenth century, Moscow was the hub of a thriving and diverse publishing industry, and St. Petersburg was hardly more than a provincial market. The average size of an edition published by the St. Petersburg firms was 6,000 copies in the early 1890s, compared with 12,000 for their rivals in Moscow.[96] The difference between the publishers of the two cities was not only one of scale. The Petersburg firms, unlike their Moscow rivals, did not produce lubok prints, nor did they issue in large quantities the very cheapest kind of books, the *listovki* (one sheets), which were printed on one printer's sheet (a signature) and usually folded into thirty-two pages. Also, many of the Moscow publishing houses were founded by people of peasant origins, in contrast to the older, more conservative family firms of St. Petersburg.

Popular book publishing in Moscow was centered in an area known as the Nikolskii Market, and for this reason popular commercial literature was sometimes identified as "Nikolskii." (The former Nikolskaia Street is now October 25th Street, between Red Square and Dzerzhinskii Square.) One contemporary later described the market as follows: "The book trade of the Nikolskii publishers and used book sellers was spread out along the whole of Nikolskaia Street, but the concentration was around Vladimir Proezd, near the Vladimir Church and the Trinity Fields, and it was located in tiny shops, by the gates of merchant townhouses, and along the low city walls."[97]

The Moscow publishers most similar to Kuzin and Kholmushin were D. I. Presnov, A. M. Zemskii, and S. Leukhin, who had their greatest sucess in the late 1880s and early 1890s. When Leukhin died in 1898, the book publishers' journal praised him in an obituary as unique among the cheap publishers in that he employed educated writers, such as one former philologist, D. I. Milchevskii.[98] Eight years earlier, however, the magazine had been less laudatory, and, following the conservative newspaper *Novoe vremia* (New Times), accused Leukhin of using a whole bag of tricks and ruses to dupe naive provincial customers. Leukhin was said to sell unoriginal and often deceptive works for prices as high as 5 and 6 rubles. One of his tricks was to find Nikolskaia Street authors with famous names and issue their collected works, as he did with one aspiring writer whose surname happened to be Pushkin. Among the works he published were various books of medical advice and prophecy, such as

The Stimulus of Pleasure and *The Telescope of Life and Death for All Those Who Wish to Know Whether or Not Their Lives Will Soon Come to an End.*[99]

Zemskii published similar works. He also wrote poems, and included them in collections of the works of Russia's great poets. In one collection, *The Three Greatest and Most Significant of all Russian Poets*, he included his own "intimate and love verses" together with the poems of Pushkin, Lermontov, and Koltsov.[100] Presnov, who had a bookstore that dated from the 1840s, flourished for a while with the same sorts of goods. Publishers such as Presnov, Zemskii, and Leukhin, who often priced their works quite high, were moving against the current of popular publishing. Profits by this time were made by efficient mass publication of cheap works attuned to the popular taste. Some book peddlers in Saratov remarked in the early 1890s that the products of Leukhin and Zemskii were "store goods" and too expensive to merit being hauled around the countryside.[101]

Prugavin called these publishers the purveyors of a "lackeys' literature," by which, as a populist, he meant a literature of the street, rather than of the village.[102] Among these publishers could also be included Manukhin, who issued some of the works of Misha Evstigneev, and whose house failed in the late 1880s. The line between the rural and urban lower-class reader was not so sharply drawn, however, and some of the publications of these firms, together with those of the St. Petersburg publishers, also found a popular readership.

Many publishers in Moscow produced cheap popular literature during the last third of the nineteenth century. The most important were Sharapov, Morozov, Abramov, Gubanov, and also I. D. Sytin, who soon left his lubok colleagues far behind and became the largest publisher in Russia, not only of popular materials, but also of serious books. The publishers' personal stories are as important as those of the writers in allowing us to understand the world in which the popular literature of nineteenth- and early twentieth-century Russia was created. They had a real appreciation of the demands and interests of the common reader, and perhaps that is why they were so successful.

P. N. Sharapov, who was something of an anomaly, was the earliest of the publishers about whom we have some information. He was primarily a fur trader but inherited a small publishing house from his brother. I. D. Sytin, who began to work for Sharapov as a boy of fourteen in 1866, remembered peasant peddlers coming into the shop to trade dried mushrooms and homespun for books and pictures.[103] The volume of trade did not exceed 18,000 rubles a year, and the inventory consisted of 120 lubok booklets and a few primers.[104] Sharapov himself was an old-fashioned merchant who leaned toward the Old Belief, valuing religious books and having a good understanding of their value to the peasants. But he was no entrepreneur. He was pleased that Sytin expanded his business, but refused to go along with the proposal that they form a company with outside capital. "I do not have time for that. I will quietly carry on my business."[105] Instead, Sharapov loaned Sytin 5,000 rubles to start his own firm. Sharapov did not have peasant roots, but his religious beliefs tied him to old-Russian culture and premodern spiritual values. In his choice of texts, he preferred that which was familiar in Russian culture, rather than that which was changing.

Other publishers, however, had peasant origins, and their experiences were not so different from those of Ivin and Ozhegov. I. A. Morozov, one of the first lubok publishers, began publishing the lubok prints in the 1850s.[106] Born into a poor peasant family in Tver Province, he spent all his childhood and youth at home, never attended school, and went to Moscow to seek his fortune as a young man in bast boots with 20 kopecks in his pocket. He fashioned a tray out of the ever-useful linden bark, bought some green onions, and went into business as a street peddler. From onions he switched to sausage, and then to hot rolls. Soon after that, he began to produce pictures on linden bark, and the sale of these went so well that it soon became his sole business. Somehow, in the meantime, he taught himself to read a little and to sign his name.

When the Crimean War broke out, Morozov was ready to satisfy the sudden surge in the demand for books and prints. His business boomed, and he began to publish tales, guides to fortunetelling, and saints' lives, as well as pictures. By the 1870s, the peasant from Tver had become a proper Moscow merchant with a large stone house, a lithographic plant, and a bookstore. Even after he lost his sight, he still had someone read lubok publications to him to keep up with his business. When he died, his sons took over the firm, but they did not prosper. Morozov's publications were characterized in the early 1890s by the Moscow Literacy Committee, a philanthropic educational organization, as heavily weighted toward didactic works, but the 1880 catalogue showed fewer religious texts than secular ones. Among the latter the stories of the indefatigable Misha Evstigneev featured prominently.[107] One contemporary described Morozov in his last years as "a semiliterate old man in a cap," and related how after returning from a pilgrimage to Jerusalem, Morozov commissioned a lubok print of himself seated beneath the Oak of Abraham,[108] where the patriarch Abraham is supposed to have entertained the Holy Trinity. This was a favorite site for Orthodox pilgrims and was the theme of Andrei Rublev's famous painting.

E. A. Gubanov's story is similar to Morozov's, but he proved himself a more modern publisher, capable of expanding his business to keep pace with a rapidly growing and changing demand. Gubanov was a peasant from Tula Province and began his career as a horse doctor. He then became a traveling peddler and sold books and prints throughout Russia.[109] After accumulating some savings, he decided to open his own shop in Moscow and to publish books and pictures for the people. According to Prugavin, Gubanov's literacy was limited to the ability to sign his name; but this was almost certainly an understatement, since people who can sign can usually read as well.

The peasant from Tula prospered in his chosen profession. He purchased a shop with a press in 1881, and was soon publishing a wide variety of religious and secular material. By the early 1890s he had shops in five cities, including Moscow and Kazan, and a bit later he opened a separate publishing house in Kiev. He drew on his firsthand knowledge of the way peddlers sold books in the countryside, and he took advantage of his familiarity with the peddlers from his native district in Tula Province. His Moscow press ceased to function in the early twentieth century, but the publishing house in Kiev remained an important source of popular reading material until the Bolshevik Revolution.

Prugavin tells little about A. Abramov except that his nickname was *Zhulik*, which means cheat. He had the reputation of being the stingiest of the cheap publishers, and was not averse to pirating a book if he thought it would sell.[110] Abramov was also one of the more successful of the lubok publishers in the late nineteenth century. In the 1880s his trade turnover reached 200,000 rubles, compared to 25,000 for Morozov's firm.[111]

The story of popular publishing and, in fact, all publishing in Russia, is inextricably linked with I. D. Sytin, whose life is one of the great entrepreneurial success stories of prerevolutionary Russia. Sytin's career did not differ markedly at the outset from that of the other Nikolskaia Street publishers, except in scale. The man who became the largest publisher in Russia catapulted himself from a provincial backwater in Kostroma Province, where the possibilities for advancement seemed limited, into the industrial and urban life of Moscow. Like his fellow publishers, many of whom he drove out of business, he knew the common people because he grew up among them.[112]

Sytin was born at the beginning of the 1850s in a canton center in Kostroma Province. His father was a state peasant employed as the clerk of the canton. Sytin went to school in the canton building, learned the Psalter and the Book of Hours by heart, and grew up surrounded by the elite of peasant society. In 1863 his father moved to another job as a clerk in the just-founded local zemstvo in the city of Galich. His salary was 22 rubles a month. The young Sytin was soon sent out with his uncle to find work at the Nizhnii Novgorod Fair, and after a second stint, his impressed employer agreed to find him a more promising and permanent position in Moscow with a friend in the fur trade, P. N. Sharapov.

The promised position did not materialize, but Sharapov also ran a publishing house and a bookstore. Sytin's career began at the age of fourteen in 1866, at Sharapov's, cleaning boots, running errands, and doing odd jobs at the shop. Four years later he received his first salary, 5 rubles a month, and he was soon sent out to the Nizhnii Novgorod Fair as a helper to one of Sharapov's employees. According to Sytin's account, this was his great opportunity. Bored with the slow pace of business, he stopped a passing peasant at the fair and asked him if he would like to sell religious prints. The peasant, an illiterate "grey muzhik" who worked as a water seller, agreed, and Sytin gave him 50 kopecks worth of prints as a start. The venture proved successful for the peasant and for young Sytin. Uncle Iakov, the water seller, returned several times during the fair, and at the end of it brought a friend with him, a veteran named Leontii from the army of Nicholas I. Together they purchased more than 30 rubles worth of prints to sell in the villages in the winter. Through them, Sytin's trade spread. In the course of five years, Iakov and Leontii brought more than one hundred men into the lubok trade, and under Sytin's management, Sharapov's trade at the fair reached 100,000 rubles.

As Sytin became more successful, he won Sharapov's favor. Relations between the two were old-fashioned and paternalistic. Sytin lived in Sharapov's house, went to church with him, and asked his permission when he wanted to stay out late. He also asked Sharapov's permission to marry. Sharapov had become wealthy and had no children, and promised to leave the shop to Sytin. When Sytin married, he wanted to branch out on his own, and he bought a lithograph plant for which Sharapov stood security. The year was 1877, the beginning of the Russo-Turkish War. Sytin described this second step in his march toward success: "On the day of the declaration of the war, in April 1877, I ran to Kuznetskii Most, bought a map of Bessarabia and Rumania, and ordered a craftsman to copy overnight the part of the map with the name of the place where our troops crossed the Prut. At five in the morning the map was ready for printing. It appeared with the caption: 'For newspaper readers. An aid,' and it sold out immediately." The map was changed to follow the advancing Russian troops, and for three months Sytin worked alone, selling his product.

After this initial triumph, Sytin expanded his offerings, hired capable draftsmen, and demanded high-quality work. He received a medal at the

1882 exhibition of "people's pictures." In January 1883, Sytin began to trade on his own, and a year later he opened a small shop by the Ilinskii Gate, near what is now Dzerzhinskaia Square. He organized a stock company with three other investors with a total capital of 75,000 rubles. His own business was worth 36,000 rubles at that time. The trade turn-over of the business rose rapidly from 200,000 rubles in 1883 to 585,000 in 1893, and to 1.8 million in 1903, 3.5 million in 1908, and 8 million in 1913.[113] During World War I, sales increased still further, reaching 13 million rubles in 1915. By 1909 the company was publishing 37 percent of all religious and moralistic works and other kinds of books for the popular readership in the Empire.[114]

Sytin was distinguished from his competitors by his success in estab-lishing his firm in the two rival marketplaces, the popular commercial arena with its distinct outlets and the educational market, in which the decision about what to purchase was made by pedagogues and educators. Almost as soon as he had begun to publish on his own, Sytin was ap-proached by Tolstoy's friend and follower, V. Chertkov, who suggested that he cooperate with Tolstoy and issue works by respectable authors for the common reader and price them no higher than the ordinary chapbooks. Sytin agreed, and a very profitable partnership, the firm Pos-rednik (Intermediary), was born. Publishing such texts as Tolstoy's own stories, Sytin was able to win for himself a respectability in society without ceasing to issue the lubok works on which his early success depended.

Sytin outpaced his commercial rivals by issuing works of superior quality for lower prices. According to book peddlers in Saratov in the early 1890s, Sytin had "better and cleaner paper, pictures, and covers than the other lubok publishers."[115] Sytin's works also sold for less. Previously lubki had been sold to peddlers for 2.25 rubles per hundred, but Sytin charged only 90 kopecks, which caused a major change in the popular market. Sytin also reduced book prices. In 1888 he was selling thirty-two-page books (one signature or one printer's sheet) for 1.25 rubles per hundred, and two-signature books went for 2.50 rubles.[116] By contrast, the heirs of his former boss in 1887 offered the one-signature books for 2.40 per hundred, and the two-signature books for five ru-bles.[117] By 1900, Sytin was selling the one-sheets for 70 kopecks, and the two-sheets for 1.70 rubles per hundred.[118] By that time other pub-lishers had become competitive.[119] Sytin lowered his prices in the last few years before World War I, and forced his main competitor, E. I. Konovalova, who apparently took over her husband's firm, to sell out to him in 1913.[120] In 1916 he bought the prestigious A. F. Marx Com-pany, which published the popular illustrated magazine *Niva* (Grainfield). By this time Sytin's firm had so nearly monopolized the trade in lubok-type booklets and prints that there was only one weak competitor who displayed printed material at the 1915 Nizhnii Novgorod Fair.[121]

The lubok publishers often dealt with their authors face to face, and the directness of the relationship helps to explain the eclectic and spontaneous qualities of lubok literature. The going payment to a writer for a one-sheet text was 3 to 4 rubles in the late 1880s and early 1890s, and, once sold, the author lost all rights to the work. A prolific author of the full-sized stories of 108 pages such as Ivin or Lunin, who produced nearly one hundred tales in a decade, might earn as much as 200 rubles a year, the salary of an unskilled worker. According to some accounts, publishers had their own stables of writers; but some writers published with a variety of firms, and sometimes sold the same work to different publishers.

The relationship between publisher and author seems to have been an adversary one in which there was a great deal of bargaining. According to one contemporary, the sale of manuscripts in Moscow took place in a tavern not too far from Nikolskaia Street, where "the publishers tried every means to fool the purveyors of this literature, and these, for their part, excelled in duping the merchant publishers."[122] Authors not only tried to resell their own work, but they pirated works of other authors, sometimes doing no more than copying the text and signing their names to it. Ivin is said to have claimed on one occasion that the work of copying the text plus the price of paper alone entitled him to the 3 or 4 rubles his publishers paid.[123]

His observation may not have been far from the mark. The self-educated scholar and publisher of people's prints, I. A. Golyshev, complained in the late 1880s that the chapbook authors were paid so little that they were hardly compensated for the "mechanical labor of writing," let alone pen, ink, and paper.[124] The writers had to submit their own works to the censors—spiritual and secular—depending on whether or not the work was religious, before selling them to a publisher. After the effort of acquiring the censor's approval, most writers wanted to sell quickly, and this strengthened the bargaining position of the publishers. According to Sveshnikov, a perceptive observer of the chapbook publishing scene, Shataev, the St. Petersburg publisher, decided whether or not to accept a work largely on the basis of its title. He would argue with the author about whether "this piece will go," but he read slowly and had difficulty deciphering a strange hand.[125] As a result of the strong position of the publishers and the competition from other writers, the "three kopeck literati," as they were sometimes called, did not get rich on their writings. They retained their lower-class status and lived a precarious hand-to-mouth existence in which they were continually reminded of the experience and interests of their readers.

The Distributors

The publishers of popular printed material retained close contact with their potential customers. Due to the slow development of retailing in the book business, the dearth of small local shops at which books might be sold, and the importance of periodic fairs and markets, publishers had to organize their own retailing to a greater extent than in other industries. The big publishers of books for the common people made arrangements with provincial retailers, who met them in Moscow or St. Petersburg. But more important, they developed close relations with a mass of large- and small-scale peddlers who carried their goods on foot and in horse-drawn carts in cities and in rural areas.

The city trade in lubok-type publications was much older than the rural distribution by colporteurs. Ivan Zabelin dated the sale of manuscripts and printed sheets, some of them Old Believer texts, at the Spasskii Gate as early as the seventeenth century.[126] Despite attempts by the government to prevent the sales, the trade continued, and printed secular and religious works were exchanged at this spot in the nineteenth century. Lubok works were also sold at the city markets. In Moscow, the most important were those at the Sukharevaia Tower and the Smolenskii Market, which, in the words of an observer in 1860, were the two main bazaars for all that was "false, tinted, patched, disguised."[127] The same observer described a display of books ranging from classics to lubok works, and recounted how a cleanly dressed young fellow was tricked into paying a ruble for a copy of the lubok chivalry tale *Guak*.

The sellers at these markets were usually peddlers from city shops or people who accumulated a stock of works in their homes and came out to sell at the Sunday markets. The Sukharevskii Market was the scene of a booming trade in used books and magazines of all sorts in the early twentieth century, and there educated shoppers mingled with the semi-literate, all eagerly engrossed in the perusal of the wares of the many stalls.[128] In St. Petersburg, most of Liteinyi Prospect and some of the streets branching off it were lined with bookshops and stalls of various sorts.[129] Books were also sold in such places at the Tolchevskii Second-Hand Market, at other markets in the city, and on the Field of Mars, where booksellers spread out their wares on bast mats in the appropriate season.[130]

Popular literature appeared not only at markets and bazaars, but also in taverns, on street corners, and on display boxes and baskets of the itinerant peddlers.[131] "Not very long ago," wrote an observer soon after the October Revolution, "it was possible to see in the doorways of large houses improvised bookshops where the little lubok publications were visible in all the colors of the rainbow."[132] In Moscow, itinerant sellers were sometimes called pharisees, a slang expression for people who had neither determined occupation nor place of residence, but lived a transient life selling books and pictures at drinking establishments and post houses.[133] On market days, peasants came into the city to trade, and after they had sold their products, they dispersed to teahouses and taverns. There they were met by the pharisees, who had goods from Sytin or other lubok publishers from Nikolskaia Street, and moved from table to table offering the customers their products. One pharisee told A. A. Bakhtiarov, the prerevolutionary historian of publishing, in the late 1880s that he visited fifty taverns a day, sold mostly almanacs, which he bought for half a kopeck and sold for one, and that he earned 25 kopecks a day and 50 on holidays.[134] Prugavin also described the pharisees gathering outside the shops of the lubok publishers, and, in his estimate, the number of street peddlers ran into the hundreds.[135]

The most numerous rural peddlers were called *ofeni* (sing. *ofenia*), a name that was derived, according to some accounts, from their presumed Greek origins or involvement in Greek trade, after the city of Athens (*Afiny, Afinei, ofeni*). According to other explanations, the traders originally came from the city of Ofena in Hungary.[136] The wandering peddlers who sold books, prints, and other goods were also called *khodebshchiki* (walkers), if they went on foot; *korobeiniki*, after the baskets in which they carried their goods; *kartinshchiki*, if they sold primarily pictures; and *mazyki* or *bogomaskateli*, if icons were their main items of trade.

There were wandering peddlers in Russia long before books and prints were in popular demand. Many of the peddlers who sold books on rural routes came from villages in several districts of Vladimir, Moscow, and Tula provinces.[137] Moscow and Vladimir were provinces in which much of the population was engaged in nonagricultural work, and the peddlers lived in and around trading and industrial settlements, but Tula was largely agricultural. Vladimir was considered the classical province of the peddlers, and there peddlers were concentrated in the vicinity of three large trading villages that were renowned centers of icon painting: Mstera, Kholui, and Palekh. (Palekh is today a center of folk and souvenir illustration.)

Palekh was already a center of icon painting at the end of the eighteenth century. By the time of the emancipation, most of the active inhabitants were engaged in this craft, and in a single year 440,000 boards were brought into the village to be painted.[138] Icon painting was also done in the village of Kholui as early as the seventeenth century, and by the late eighteenth century the village had become a major trading point for grain and other goods. By the middle of the nineteenth century, periodic fairs were held at which books and lubok prints were sold, along with textiles, fur, grain, and other products. By 1897 there were over two thousand inhabitants in the settlement, and over two million icons were being produced each year, predominantly for the peasant market.

Mstera was an important trading town by the beginning of the eighteenth century, with 182 houses, 57 shops, and a tavern, and it became a center of icon production by the early nineteenth century.[139] Lithographed lubok prints were also produced in the town in substantial quantities until competition from book publishers in the capitals proved too great toward the end of the nineteenth century. Other types of market production also developed in the nineteenth century, including textiles, market gardening, barge building, carpentry, and potash and tallow production. By 1897 Mstera was a town with over four thousand inhabitants, and the site of periodic fairs at which books and prints were sold. "The inhabitants of Mstera are only peasants in name," wrote Prugavin. "In essence these are real city folk."[140]

Located near the three towns were the large factory villages of Ivanovo-Voznesensk and Shuia, both rapidly developing centers of textile production. Most of the peddlers did not live within the villages of Palekh, Kholui, and Mstera, but around them, within easy reach of the markets and shops of the icon trade. Some of these traveling Vladimir salesmen who settled in Siberia, according to one memoirist, organized a substantial company to trade in needles, kerchiefs, and other cheap goods, as well as lubok booklets. One young Vladimirite, he recalled, was a clever fellow, "with an eloquence irresistible to the village ladies."[141]

The Tula peddlers lived in a settlement in a district in which the main occupation of the population was horse doctoring. The horse doctors from this district traveled throughout Russia plying their trade, leaving in the fall and returning in the spring. Sometime in the late eighteenth or nineteenth century, they began to carry books and prints as a light and profitable supplement to their main occupation. Selling these goods in the villages they passed through proved so profitable that some gave up their original occupations and became bookselling peddlers exclusively. The most famous and successful of the Tula peddlers were the Gubanov brothers, who gave up horse doctoring for book and print selling, and then went into publishing.

The Moscow peddlers were often called *kartinshchiki*, or picture sellers, although they also sold books and other goods. Their main trade was in and around Moscow, where they got their goods, and they did not venture too far afield. Other peddlers, who engaged in itinerant bookselling were from Nizhnii Novgorod, Riazan, Iaroslavl, and other provinces.

Estimates of the number of peddlers vary. There were probably more than five thousand at the time of the emancipation, and according to one study, two thousand in a single district of the province of Vladimir in 1902.[142] Prugavin calculated that the successful publisher I. D. Sytin had as many as two thousand purchasers among peddlers and owners of bookstores in the early 1890s.[143]

The peddlers sold all sorts of other products besides books and prints, including calico, icons and crosses, wooden dishes, thimbles, mirrors, ribbons, lace, buttons, combs, envelopes and paper, and a whole range of shiny trinkets.[144] There were rich peddlers who traveled with horses, carts, and assistants, whose investment and turnover ranged into the thousands of rubles; but there were also poor peddlers who set off by themselves, often pulling a sledge or a cart with a small stock of goods worth as little as 50 to 100 rubles. The most expensive goods were the icons, which sometimes comprised two-thirds of the total value of a peddler's inventory. Most of the peddlers were poor. According to a study of the Vladimir zemstvo in the early twentieth century, half of the peddlers had no capital and worked for a boss.[145] Assistants of the more prosperous peddlers, according to Rubakin, were paid less than 100 rubles a season, plus boots.[146]

Credit was an important part of the peddler's business. Rather than buying their inventory outright, even the more prosperous peddlers had credit relations with the publishers. Credit for six months, credit with an interest charge, and credit for all goods with return of unsold wares were some of the arrangements the peddlers made with their suppliers. Publishers were dependent on the peddlers, at least until the late nineteenth century, and were willing to accept the risk that credit for itinerant peddlers entailed.

Many peddlers went to Moscow to Nikolskaia Street to deal directly with the publishers and select the books and pictures they thought would sell. Publishers wooed the peddlers by various means. At Konovalova's, they were given a glass of vodka as well as a hospitable greeting. At Sytin's they got 20 kopecks for a lunch at the firm's expense.[147]

Fairs played an important, although declining, role in Russian commerce in the late nineteenth and early twentieth centuries, and the peddlers sometimes replenished their inventories at the fairs. The most important of the fairs was the yearly Nizhnii Novgorod Fair, at which a substantial quantity of goods—primarily textiles, but also books and prints—changed hands. Here Sytin's boss, Sharapov, had made his fortune in furs, and Sytin himself got his start at the fair by establishing his own network of loyal peddlers. The great fair remained a significant point in the wholesale book trade up to World War I, although by then

Sytin had driven out his competitors. Fairs were also held in Vladimir Province, where many peddlers lived, and five fairs a year were held in the village of Kholui.[148] In the late 1850s, according to A. I. Golyshev, six wholesale booksellers displayed their wares at the Kholui Fair, though the number declined later, as more peddlers got their goods in Moscow.[149] Peddlers would often take goods on credit at the Kholui Fair, with the promise to repay the publishers later at the Nizhnii Novgorod Fair, or at one of the many fairs in the Ukraine. Some book publishers sent their representatives from fair to fair, selling goods to peddlers in each place and to whoever else would buy. The sale of lubok prints and booklets was a familiar feature of every fair. As one observer recalled during World War I, "The fair and the lubok were so closely identified that it was difficult to imagine one without the other."[150] Maxim Gorky described a fair in the Ukraine in 1897 at which a peasant from the province of Iaroslavl, who also sold soap, combs, and knives, offered him, in addition to saints' lives and secular lubok works, "the very entertaining story of the death of Mr. Ivan Ilich, a work by Count Tolstoy."[151]

The peddlers traveled considerable distances, generally in search of areas in which the harvest had been good and the peasants had money to spare. Books and pictures were not high on the peasants' lists of priorities, and in poor years few were purchased in the countryside.

Books were very profitable for the peddlers. Their profits from booklet and picture sales were one hundred percent in the 1890s, according to estimates of A. S. Prugavin.[152] An investigator for the Vladimir provincial zemstvo suggested in 1900 that the figure could be as high as 300 or 400 percent for small booklets, and 100 percent for almanacs and copies of the Gospels.[153] According to the same source, printed material constituted no more than a sixth of the peddlers' business, and even less in the case of the more prosperous traders. Icons were the most important article, accounting for 80 to 90 percent of the peddlers' earnings.

The free movement of the peddlers often depended on the local police and other provincial authorities. Until 1865 peddlers could trade without special licenses; but in that year, according to the new censorship statutes, they had to obtain permission to trade from the local police in each district in which they operated.[154] These rules were relaxed, at least in theory, in 1881 by a ruling of the Main Administration for Press Affairs, according to which the peddlers could get a permit from the governor of the province in which they lived, instead of having to obtain a new permit in each area where they sold. This led to new difficulties for the peddlers, since they were often ill-equipped to secure such permits. There were, in addition, special rules for the sale of books on railways, and permission from the gendarmes rather than the local police was required.

For trading within cities, there were different requirements. The peddlers had been hounded by the police in the 1850s, when they were suspected of spreading sectarian and Old Believer materials, and this happened again in the early 1870s, when the radical movement to spread propaganda among the peasants led to increased police vigilance. Whether or not the regulations and police surveillance actually dissuaded many peddlers from trading in their accustomed way is a matter of conjecture.

Throughout the second half of the nineteenth century, there was a gradual decentralization of the book trade, a development that was probably of more significance for the peddlers than were the governmental efforts to regulate them. Large firms began to establish provincial shops and supply houses, from which they sold both wholesale and retail. At the same time, books and newspapers appeared among the goods sold at the increasing numbers of local general stores that were sprinkled throughout rural Russia.[155]

The provincial bookshops served the peddlers en route as well as the local urban residents. The rural general stores, in contrast, were in direct competition with the peddlers and were more numerous than the bookstores. A commentator on the Vladimir book trade in the early twentieth century wrote, "There is hardly a shopkeeper who does not have twenty to thirty one-sheet books—tales and saints' lives, together with the indispensable goods of the village shops."[156] This meant that the peddlers had to concentrate their efforts farther from the areas in which the retail trade was well developed, so they went to Siberia, the Caucasus, and the far south. The peddlers also faced increased competition from schools, churches, and other sources of sponsored publications. Moreover, the consumers themselves became more mobile. As a politicized worker wrote to Rubakin in 1909, "Good books enter the village not from the book market, but from city workers or those who go off for a month or two to work in the city."[157] Some peddlers settled down in the early twentieth century and opened shops and stands in towns and market villages.[158]

The disappearance of the itinerant peddler may have been more apparent than real, however. Observers sounded their funeral dirge throughout the nineteenth century. K. Tikhonravov, who studied the Vladimir peddlers in the late 1850s, suggested that the late eighteenth and early nineteenth centuries had been the peak period of the peddling trade.[159] Golyshev argued that the statutes of 1865, which required registration in each locale, caused a decline in peddling during the 1870s, and Sytin said that the 1881 clarification of the ruling had a similar effect during the 1880s.[160] Nevertheless, the number of permits issued to peddlers throughout the empire, including those who did not sell books, remained relatively constant from 1870 to 1912. There were roughly 25,000 permits given out yearly to traders who traveled on foot or with horses and carts. About a quarter of these were half-year rather than full-year permits.[161] Peddlers of books and pictures traveled both on foot and with various means of conveyance. About 5 percent of the permits were granted in Vladimir, Moscow, and Tula provinces. The permits were held by petty traders who did not sell books as well as peddlers who did. In addition, not all peddlers took out permits themselves; some traded under the permits of their bosses. The profession of itinerant peddling continued to be practiced throughout the late nineteenth and early twentieth centuries, and it was not an immediate casualty of the gradually expanding and articulated network of retail enterprises.

The peddlers lent a special character to the rural trade in popular printed material. The kindhearted and wise Uncle Iakov, whose praises were sung by the poet N. A. Nekrasov, may not have been the typical peddler, but these wandering bookmen were likely to have possessed much of his stamina and rambunctiousness. The peddlers were bearers of news in the villages they visited. Some peasants resented their worldliness and their willingness to outsmart the unwary customer, and they were known in some quarters as tricksters and fakers; but they were also sellers of serious religious materials as well as light literature, and this probably earned them some respect. They had to be resourceful and quick-witted to survive in their occupation. They had their own slang and a system of marks, so that the illiterate peddlers could identify prices.

Contemporary descriptions of the peddlers in action point up their importance as promoters of the printed word and as people who brought a bit of excitement into the world of the village. The populist writer A. Engelgart described a lubok peddler selling pictures such as "The Storming of Kars," "The Taking of Plevna," and "The Marvelous Dinner of General Skobelev under Enemy Fire" at the time of the 1877-78 Russo-Turkish War.[162] "This is Skobelev—the general who took Plevna," the peddler said. "Here Skobelev himself sits and points out to the soldiers how they will most rapidly enter the gates of Plevna. There you see the gates; there, our soldiers are running." This particular peddler confused the Russian and Turkish flags, and when Engelgart suggested he was mistaken, the peddler argued that the one with the eagle must be Turkish, because "on the Russian flag there would be a cross."

Rubakin described one peddler near Kiev selling a book with a picture on the cover of a crocodile threatening a girl.[163] " 'Yes, you have a look,' the peddler cried, poking the phlegmatic Ukrainian peasant in the nose with the book. 'This is the kind of thing that exists on earth. Start reading and you won't stop.' " In the preface to his fictionalized biography of Sytin, Konstantin Konichev remembered the peddler who regularly visited his village on the banks of the Kubenskoe Lake in Vologda Province before the Revolution, selling not only lubok literature to peasants, but also more serious books to the school teacher. Pronia, "who arrived with his wooden trunk attached to a hand sled," knew which peasants wanted secular tales, and who wanted saints' lives or other religious texts. He also visited the school with "fat" books—that is, thick or serious—purchased with silver rather than with 5-kopeck pieces, and brought Sytin's catalogues for the teachers.[164] After he had done his business and held court, Pronia settled down for the night in the place of honor in one of the peasant cottages on the raised platform over the stove. These traveling bookmen were active agents in widening the frontiers of the printed word in rural Russia, and their arguing and sales pitches helped convince new readers that books were important.

During the mid-1920s, when the peddlers and lubok literature had both vanished from the countryside and printed materials were very scarce, some readers and correspondents of the Soviet newspaper for the peasants, *Krestianskaia gazeta* (The Peasant Newspaper), reminisced fondly about the prerevolutionary peddlers. "These book carriers went through the villages and settlements," recalled one reader, "crying out under the windows of the peasant cottages, 'Books, pictures, don't you need some?' "[165] When the peddler spread out his books in the village or market square, remembered a correspondent from Ivanovo-Voznesensk, "A large crowd of children, older fellows, and even girls surrounded him, hung around beside him for almost the whole day, and bought what was interesting."[166]

The literature of the lubok was the first and most primitive type of Russian popular literature, and it was the material basis for common literacy. In the sacks of the colporteurs could be found the first printed words purchased by semiliterate former schoolchildren, their parents, and other new readers. Parents probably purchased these booklets with literacy in mind, as one Soviet newspaper correspondent recalled in 1922: "Father bought me the tale *About Eruslan Lazerevich*, so that I would not forget how to read, and mother exchanged eggs for *Bova Korolevich*."[167]

These lubok tales were read many times before they were passed on to neighbors or used as cigarette papers, and they certainly affected the thinking of their readers. Still more revolutionary in its impact on the common reader, however, was the periodical, which is discussed in the next chapter.

IV

PERIODICALS,

INSTALLMENT ADVENTURES,

AND POTBOILERS

INEXPENSIVE illustrated magazines and daily newspapers gained a wide readership in the last few decades of the old regime. In the early twentieth century, serialized novels appeared. These were sold in as many as a hundred separate parts that consisted of only ten or twenty pages each. There were also detective serials devoted to the continuing adventures of one or another dramatic hero. Similar to these publications were popular multivolume women's novels—melodramatic potboilers that attracted readers of different social classes.

These new materials differed in several important respects from the older lubok literature. First, and most important, they appealed to those of more modern, cosmopolitan, urban, and secular interests. The authors assumed their readers to be sophisticated and curious not only about contemporary Russian life but also about life abroad, international events, science and technology, and the latest fads. Second, periodical publications required regular reading and continual access to a market. Whereas the lubok tales could be read on an occasional or haphazard basis, the new literature could not. Periodical publications had to be purchased as they appeared, and their authors often assumed a continuing familiarity with current events. Not many issues could be missed by a reader if he followed a serialized plot.

The audience was also different. The new publications appealed to a more diverse group than the lower-class readership of the lubok stories. Members of the middle class as well as educated readers were familiar with the heroes and adventures of the new periodical literature. In this respect, the popular periodicals constituted a step toward a more unified literary culture. Some of the adventure stories and potboilers were so popular that when the silent film industry began to develop, the heroes and heroines were brought to the screen and the authors of this literature found new careers as film writers.

Although the new literature of the cheap newspapers, the serialized adventure story and the potboiler, differed in many ways from the more folkloric lubok tales, the publishing industry that produced it was similar. Here, too, the publishers, editors, and writers were often of lower-class origin, and their enterprises rested on rapidly increasing common literacy.

The new popular fiction was sold at newsstands, kiosks, and bookstores, and the expansion of the distribution networks was a necessary condition for its success. Newspaper kiosks multiplied in the late nineteenth century. By 1913 the conservative newspaper publisher A. S. Suvorin's company managed 600 railroad kiosks and over 1,000 other newsstands.[1] Another 100 to 130 kiosks in the provinces were run by a rival consortium of liberal publishers.[2] The number of bookshops and other types of distribution points also increased. There were only 63 bookstores in the country in 1864, but 611 in 1874, 1,725 in 1893-94, and 3,000 in 1903, according to the bookseller's weekly *Knizhnyi vestnik* (Book Herald).[3] The bookstores were concentrated in the largest cities. In 1890, according to N. A. Rubakin, Moscow had the greatest number of bookshops, with 205, followed by St. Petersburg, with 142, then Warsaw (137), Odessa (68), Tiflis (63), Riga (46), Saratov (42), Kiev (38), and Kharkov (23).[4] By 1906, there were 584 shops, kiosks, and stalls in Moscow where primarily printed material was sold and 378 in St. Petersburg in 1907.[5] Printed material was also sold through other outlets. In St. Petersburg, there were 237 additional shops and stalls where the merchandise included some printed materials.[6] Periodicals and other cheap reading matter were commonly sold in bars and tea houses, and on street corners and in doorways. Beggars in Moscow were reported to offer passersby copies of the boulevard newspaper *Gazeta kopeika* (The Kopeck Newspaper) in exchange for a handout.[7]

Publishers and distributors of the new cheap literature sought buyers through advertising and promotional gimmicks new to the book trade. The content of bookstore windows changed from a bland row of titles in plain covers that had been agreeable and familiar to the regular customer to a colorful display of eye-catching bindings and covers designed to attract the casual passerby.[8] One contemporary observer remarked in 1911 that only the specialized bookshops, catering to a limited circle of "serious" readers, displayed their wares in a way that resembled the earlier store windows.[9]

Changes in the censorship rules and declining costs in printing technology, in addition to increasing popular literacy, encouraged the phenomenal growth of a new mass literature. Censorship eased in 1865, when the new rules provided for an end to prepublication censorship for the periodicals of editors in good standing, and prepublication censorship was abolished for everyone in 1905. Authority over the press gradually shifted from the censors to the courts.[10] Selective censorship and the threat of punishment of editors who published objectionable material was the government's response to the increased quantity of popular literature after 1905, but it did not impede the expansion of the industry as much as prepublication censorship of each piece would have. The cost of subscriptions fell in the last two decades of the nineteenth century as technological improvements and an increasing volume of production brought down the price of publication. Simultaneously, publishers relied increasingly on retail sales of single copies instead of subscriptions. Purchasers no longer had to pay the price of a three-month or six-month subscription. This was true not only for newspapers, but also for illustrated weeklies, which were sold increasingly in single issues in the early twentieth century.[11] The rapid expansion in the publication of periodicals is evident from the numbers of periodicals appearing in the half century after the emancipation.

The number and diversity of periodicals increased rapidly in the pre-emancipation era, as shown in Table 5. The increase in the number of daily newspapers was very great after 1905, as shown in Table 6. The growth in magazine publishing was also rapid.

Illustrated Weekly Magazines

The pioneer in reaching a wide and diverse reading public in the nineteenth and early twentieth centuries was the so-called "thin magazine," the illustrated weekly that was contrasted with the more serious and ideologically focused monthly "thick journals" intended for the educated reader. The thin magazines flourished in the last quarter of the nineteenth century, and provided a source of light reading, serious fiction, and news for a diverse group of readers, including provincial gentry as well as village schoolteachers and parish clergy. For these readers they served as the forerunner of a daily newspaper. The illustrated weeklies' role changed somewhat in the early twentieth century, when some of these publications were no longer sold by subscription, but were peddled instead on urban street corners and at kiosks. The illustrated weeklies then became popular reading for the urban lower classes.

Three of the most successful of the thin magazines were *Niva* (Grainfield, 1870-1917), *Rodina* (Motherland, 1883-1917), and *Ogonek* (Little Light, 1899-1918). *Niva* was the model for the others and was founded in 1870 by A. F. Marx. Although it soon broke all circulation records

TABLE 5. Russian-Language Periodicals, 1860-1900

Year	Daily Biweekly, or More	Weekly, or 2-4 Times a Month	Monthly, or 3-12 Times a Year	Occasional (Fewer Than 3 Yearly)	Total
1860	16	92	58	4	170
1870	79	121	92	43	335
1880	126	154	135	70	485
1890	152	202	174	139	667
1900	151	181	161	113	606

Source: Data are calculated from material in N. M. Lisovskii, *Russkaia periodicheskaia pechat', 1703-1900* (Petrograd, 1915), Tables 1-11.

TABLE 6. Newspapers and Weeklies in All Languages, 1908-15

Year	Twice Daily	Daily	2,3,4 Times Weekly	Weekly	Total
1908	7	433	179	585	1,204
1910	6	506	202	633	1,347
1914	12	824	240	691	1,767
1915	10	584	176	512	1,282

Sources: *Vystavka proizvedenii pechati za 1908 god, ustroennaia Glavnym upravleniem po delam pechati v S. Peterburge s 9 maia po 9 iiulia 1909 goda* (St. Petersburg, 1909), p. 48; *Statistika proizvedenii pechati v Rossii v 1910 g.* (St. Petersburg, 1911). Volumes for 1914 and 1915 appeared in 1915 and 1916.

in Russian periodical publishing, *Niva* retained the respect of educated Russians, who regarded it as a useful vehicle for spreading enlightenment.

A. F. Marx was a German who came to Russia soon after the emancipation to work in the foreign department of the Wolf Bookstore, one of the best bookshops in St. Petersburg. Presumably Wolf recruited him. Marx had the acumen to perceive that Russia lacked moderately priced magazines of general interest. He intended *Niva* to be a politically neutral family magazine, but the periodical soon outgrew its original purpose and became an ambitious vehicle for the dissemination of good literature and news in the provinces.[12] It was read by an audience that extended from primary schoolteachers, rural parish priests, and the urban middle class to the gentry. Used copies filtered down to a lower audience.

Large colored prints offered as a bonus in the early years of publication were an important inducement to subscribe. These were generally in a respectable and very traditional style. In 1883 and 1886 readers were offered pictures by K. E. Makovskii, "The Guslar Player" and "Grandma's Fairy Tale." In 1888 the choice was "A Winter Evening in the

Environs of St. Petersburg" by Professor Iu. Klever, a member of the Imperial Academy of Art. Additional premiums were gradually added to *Niva's* offerings. After 1891 subscribers could receive a popular science and literature supplement of twelve issues annually, as well as a children's section. The collected works of classical Russian writers became the most important premium by the end of the century.

The emphasis on the classics was consistent with a general appreciation of these works and their authors as symbols of Russian national pride.[13] By 1912 *Niva* subscribers had received much of the best in Russian literature, including the works of Gogol, Lermontov, Goncharov, Dostoevsky, Turgenev, Leskov, Chekhov, and others. "Are these not the brightest stars of our literary firmament? The glory and pride of Russia?" asked the editors in a 1912 advertisement.[14] Despite the apparent triumph of literary modernism among educated Russians, the editors of *Niva* affirmed their loyalty to the "noble legacy of the Russian word," the classics.

Niva was a large publication almost the size of a tabloid newspaper. A typical issue in 1900, at the peak of its success, ran as many as twenty-four pages. A year's subscription sold for 5.50 rubles without delivery in St. Petersburg, where the magazine was published, or for 7.10 rubles anywhere in the empire.[15] Serial fiction by respected writers made up the bulk of the text in each issue. There were also short accounts of events at home and abroad, ethnographic essays, and notes on developments in science and technology. The emphasis on the Russianness of its offerings was characteristic of *Niva*, and this was evident early in the magazine's career. In 1889, for example, Marx informed his readers that *Niva* was a "Russian family magazine" that would contain all that was new and important in "Russian literature, Russian science, and Russian art."[16] News of Western Europe was also promised, but in contrast to the thick journals, such as *Vestnik Evropy* (Herald of Europe), news and cultural developments of foreign countries were of secondary importance.

The *Niva* formula was very successful. Circulation soared beyond anything hitherto known in Russia, from 9,000 copies in the first year of its publication to over 200,000 in the early twentieth century.[17] Its 1890 circulation of 120,000 was double that of its closest competitors, including newspapers.[18] Only in the early twentieth century did *Niva* begin to lose ground to other periodicals.

When *Niva* was purchased by Sytin in 1916, it was in financial trouble despite its large circulation.[19] Although it faltered, it had a major impact on Russian cultural life. As V. I. Nemirovich-Danchenko, a frequent contributor of popular adventure stories and the brother of the famous theater director, observed in his 1921 memoirs, "No minister of public education in Russia did as much to spread the really beautiful works of

Russian literature among the people as Marx."[20] In some respects, the publishers of all the thin magazines shared in this achievement.

Niva lost its preeminence in the early twentieth century when innovative publishers developed new types of weekly publications that appealed to a wider audience. A. A. Kaspari, the founder of *Rodina*, was particularly successful in reaching new readers. *Rodina* was founded as a monthly in 1879, a decade after *Niva*, but it became a weekly in 1883. The initial statement of the editor put the magazine firmly in the tradition of the didactic publications for the people. According to the editorial in the first issue, *Rodina* was to be a magazine for "our younger brother—the thinking and developed common person." The purpose was to enlighten those "who previously did not have the means or the method to enrich themselves with knowledge, moral ideals, and the rules of a reasoned society."[21] Its success was due to the genius of Kaspari, a former typography apprentice, a truly "self-made man" in the words of the author of an obituary.[22]

The reading public for *Niva*, Kaspari explained in a speech near the end of his career, was "the first, second, and even, let's say, the third class of the secondary institution."[23] The upper levels of the secondary institutions could read, in his view, the thick journals, such as *Russkoe bogatstvo* (Russian Wealth). No publication was intended exclusively for those with a university education because "it is impossible to publish a magazine for a handful of people." *Rodina* was intended as "a preparatory magazine," from which the reader could move to *Niva*, or to *Russkoe bogatstvo* and other "secondary magazines." It served "the most illiterate public," and Kaspari explained that he began by providing his semiliterate readers with lubok-type illustrations and old-fashioned stories well grounded in morality. The main task, as he saw it, was not to frighten off the new readers by offering works that were too difficult for them.

One of *Rodina's* contributors, A. Zarin, wrote in his obituary of Kaspari that the editor had the genius to seek out "the grey subscriber" and to make *Rodina* "a transitional step from lubok books to literary reading."[24] The difference between *Rodina* and *Niva* was significant. Kaspari offered works by classical Russian writers such as Tolstoy and Aksakov as premiums, but he also gave his readers classics of popular literature, including the works of V. Krestovskii, author of *The Petersburg Slums*, and translations of Ponson du Terrail (1829-71), who wrote the remarkable French serial novel *Rocambole*. Kaspari had supplements on fashion, subjects for children, and humor, as well as designs for woodcarving and needlework and a survey of current events.

Despite the initial didactic intentions of its editor, *Rodina* lacked the enlightenment emphasis of *Niva* in the early twentieth century. The serial fiction was by writers who had less claim to literary respectability but were more popular, such as L. Charskaia whose romance, "The Power of the Earth," was published in 1913. Instead of the puzzles and word games that appeared in *Niva* there were often crude jokes and cartoons. *Rodina*, unlike *Niva*, continued to depend on bonus prints to attract readers. Also unlike *Niva*, the pictures offered as premiums to *Rodina* subscribers were not reprints of works of recognized artists, but instead were anonymous illustrations of sentimental subjects. In 1913 subscribers received "The Charms of Love," showing a bashful young couple blushing at each other in a garden, and "Grandpa's Joy," a picture of an old man being drawn into a children's game.

Ogonek was the most successful of the three thin magazines in the last years before the Revolution. It was a small magazine, and the price in 1908 was 2 rubles including delivery, less than a third of the cost of *Niva* and less than half that of *Rodina*. *Ogonek* was offered as a supplement to the successful newspaper *Birzhevie vedomosti* (Bourse Gazette). The chief editor, S. M. Propper, promised in its first issue in 1908 that *Ogonek* was a new "foreign type of publication," a novelty in Russia. Each issue was to be self-contained. There would be no serial fiction, and readers would not have to "await the continuation or the end" of a story, or confuse the plot because they missed an issue. This last promise was not kept, but *Ogonek* did emerge as a new type of magazine with an emphasis on news. As the editors explained in an advertisement in 1912, in *Ogonek*, "All the events of the day are reflected as in a mirror" (no. 52, 1912). The circulation of *Ogonek*, according to the editors' claims, reached 150,000 in 1910, 300,000 in 1912, and 700,000 in 1914, bettering all periodicals in Russia, including the most successful daily newspapers.[25]

Fiction, photos, and illustrations made up much of *Ogonek*, as they did other thin magazines, but the fiction in *Ogonek* was spicier and livelier than that of *Niva*, and so were the news stories. There were short tales of crime and adventure, train robberies, harem escapes, and airplane escapades, but also romantic women's stories. Among the news stories were crimes, such as "A Mysterious Case of Poisoning," complete with photos of the victim and the accused (no. 29, 1910); surveys of the St. Petersburg underworld; balloon races and sports events; and coverage of advances in technology and wonders of science and nature, ranging from modern dairy farming (no. 39, 1909) to medical discoveries and natural "wonders," such as a bearded girl (no. 1, 1911) and a two-headed calf (no. 38, 1909). The editors of *Ogonek* did not share the educational focus of *Niva*, but they participated in the general celebration of the nineteenth-century classical Russian writers all the same. On the twenty-fifth anniversary of Turgenev's death, the writer was remembered in a series of laudatory articles, and Tolstoy's eightieth birthday and his subsequent death were also the occasion for extensive critical tributes. Important art exhibitions, such as the 1913 World of Art Exhibition (no. 2, 1913), were also covered.

The fine line that the editors of the magazine drew between sensational journalism and respectability was shown in a hoax they perpetrated on their readers in 1908. The readers' reaction to it suggests that the editors overestimated their audience's sophistication, even though they correctly gauged its preferences. In 1908 a flood of cheap detective stories engulfed the popular book market, outselling magazines and newspapers at kiosks and winning the sharp condemnation of serious journalists and educators. The *Ogonek* editors published several unexceptional detective stories in their first few issues. Then in the twelfth issue, they began a series entitled "The Adventures of Sherlock Holmes in Russia," which they claimed to have received from an anonymous correspondent (no. 12, 1908). The first adventure took place in Moscow. Then the detective moved to more exotic locations in Odessa and Baku. The stories lacked the analytical allure of the Conan Doyle originals, but the style and content were consistent with the other detective adventure stories then popular in Russia. In Odessa, Holmes and Watson solve the case of a baffling theft that occurred during the Revolution of 1905. In Baku, they brave a sea of burning oil to foil an apparent anarchist plot. The tales had an odd twist, however. In one, Watson provides the brain power but Holmes gets the credit. In the other, captured anarchists turn out to be famous detectives of international renown, who, like Holmes and Watson, are seeking the reward for solving the case.

The tales were a spoof, but a curious one. Within a month of the last of the Holmes stories, the magazine printed a telegram purportedly from Holmes, demanding that the anonymous author of the *Ogonek* stories identify himself. The heading read "The Case of the Magazine *Ogonek* and Sherlock Holmes." Beneath it was a note from the editors explaining that until receiving the telegram they had been convinced that Conan Doyle's Holmes was "the purest fantasy" (no. 24, 1908). They challenged the real Holmes to solve the riddle of the anonymous author. In subsequent issues, Holmes comes to St. Petersburg, visits the *Ogonek* offices, and even appeals to the Russian police to punish the editors for slandering him. The editor of *Ogonek*, S. M. Propper, ended the spoof with a note, explaining that because of the pernicious effect of the detective craze on readers of all ages, he had decided to combat "the microbe Sherlokiad" (no. 24, 1908). The note was not sufficient for *Ogonek* readers, some of whom were by now convinced that Sherlock Holmes was in fact a real person. The editors felt compelled to explain to their readers more explicitly several issues later that the hero of Conan Doyle's stories was "a detective Sherlock Holmes who never existed" (no. 30, 1908).

The confusion about Holmes showed the low educational level of *Ogonek's* readers and is evidence of the importance of such magazines in raising it. Not to know that Holmes was a fictional character at a time when hundreds of thousands of copies of stories about Holmes were circulating in Russia showed a naive confusion between fact and fiction. The misapprehension was also suggestive of the eagerness of lower class readers to accept everything that was printed as true. Popular writers of periodical fiction often capitalized on this tendency and proclaimed that their heroes were in fact real people. Interestingly, serious authors at this time were also experimenting with mixing fact and fiction, and writers such as F. Sologub began to include sections from newspaper stories in their novels.

There were also thin magazines in which news and fiction were not stressed. There were also periodicals, such as Sytin's *Vokrug sveta* (Around the World) and P. P. Soikin's *Priroda i liudi* (Nature and People), which emphasized adventure and popular science. When Sytin bought *Vokrug sveta* in 1891, the circulation was only 4,500, but by 1893 it had risen to 15,000, and by 1898 to 42,000.[26] Readers of *Vokrug sveta* were regularly treated to features such as "legends and myths of various peoples," "scientific expeditions and geographic discoveries," "biographies of important travelers and explorers," "the starry heavens and their marvels," and "people of science, arts, and literature."

P. P. Soikin (1862-1938), the publisher of *Priroda i liudi*, was of lower-class origins, but he attended the classical gymnasium in St. Petersburg and later took a course in bookkeeping.[27] His magazine was similar to *Vokrug sveta*. It had an adventure supplement, in which readers could find novels by H. G. Wells, Conan Doyle, and Jack London, as well as works by some Russian writers of adventure stories, such as N. N. Breshko-Breshkovskii.[28]

The proliferation of weekly and monthly magazines, some of which were priced within the reach of the working class and more prosperous peasant readers, brought the printed word to new and ever-wider circles of readers on a regular basis. This task was fulfilled more successfully by the new inexpensive daily newspapers.

Popular Daily Newspapers

The growing success of the thin magazines and weeklies paralleled that of the daily newspapers. To contemporary observers it appeared that the newspaper would put the traditional thick journals out of business and cut into the market for the newer, more popular magazines, but in fact the magazines and newspapers were more symbiotic than competitive.

The newspapers stimulated readers' appetites for the offerings of the thin magazines. More importantly, they reached a lower-class audience for whom lubok literature was still the staple fare.

Among the new types of newspapers that appeared in the last third of the nineteenth century were some that contemporaries identified as "the street press," "the little press," or less sympathetically as "boulevard papers" and "yellow journalism."[29] These newspapers were intended for a wide urban audience, and they contained far more coverage of the grim and sordid aspects of city life, crime, scandal, and misfortune than did the more respectable newspapers. The most important publications of this type in the late nineteenth century included *Svet* (Light), *Petersburgskii listok* (The Petersburg Sheet), *Moskovskii listok* (The Moscow Sheet), and, in the early twentieth century, the *Gazeta kopeika* (The Kopeck Newspaper) of St. Petersburg, which was the first newspaper to sell for only one kopeck and soon served as a model for similar publications in other cities.

Censorship and the poverty of potential readers prevented newspaper publishers from finding a dependable lower-class audience until the late nineteenth or early twentieth century. Ordinary people were often unable to pay the subscription price, and even if they could afford it, they were seldom willing to pay a year or half a year in advance. In addition, postal delivery was uncertain in the villages of rural Russia. Therefore the expansion of the popular press depended on sales at newspaper stands and kiosks and by peddlers. According to a 1915 study by the Moscow provincial zemstvo, 87 percent of the correspondents in villages of the province indicated that newspapers were obtained locally not by subscription, but from newspapers sellers, in towns, and at railroad stations.[30] As a result, until the very last few years of the old regime, the publishers of most newspapers thought primarily of a reliable and relatively prosperous middle and upper class audience when they designed features, arranged news, and set their prices. This was true even for very popular publications, such as I. D. Sytin's *Russkoe slovo*, which reached a circulation of 759,000 copies in 1916.[31]

There were a few papers, however, that showed signs of being designed with significantly more attention to the tastes of the common reader. One paper of this sort in the late nineteenth century was *Moskovskii listok*, which was a pioneer in the exploration of popular taste in the newspaper medium. *Moskovskii listok* was neither the cheapest nor the most popular newspaper in the late nineteenth century. The St. Petersburg daily *Svet* (Light) sold for less and probably reached more readers, but *Moskovskii listok* typified a new kind of popular journalism. Moreover, the editor, Nikolai Ivanovich Pastukhov (1822-1911), played a central role in the development of popular fiction. In his newspaper, he created "the first model of the Moscow street press," observed one commentator in a thick magazine at the time of his death.[32]

Like so many other leading figures in the business of Russian publishing, Pastukhov was a self-made man, who was known and, to a certain extent, admired as such by his contemporaries. On his death, a laudatory journalist in the reactionary newspaper *Moskovskie vedomosti* (Moscow Herald) wrote that with "natural talent, persistent labor, and Russian gumption it is possible to raise oneself from the lower strata."[33] Pastukhov's parents were lower-class people of insubstantial means who lived in the district town of Gzhatsk in Smolensk Province where he was born. Pastukhov had little or no primary education, but he made his way in Gzhatsk and eventually purchased a small shop.[34] He became dissatisfied with small-town life, and he set out for Moscow on the eve of the emancipation of the serfs. In the capital, he sold liquor as a wholesaler before the establishment of the state liquor monopoly.[35] His trade must have flourished, because he soon purchased a beer hall on Arbat Square, a neighborhood legendary for conviviality and good fellowship.

Despite his apparent early success, life may have been a struggle for the young Pastukhov. He published a small book of verses in 1862 as well as a short comedy about a drinking establishment. The verses suggest that he shared the experiences of many of his successful contemporaries in his endeavor to make his way in the world. Among his verses are not only wry comments on drinking and friendship, but also observations on loneliness, poverty, and insecurity. "In a foreign place he lives like an orphan, with a cheerless soul," reads a line in "A Black Day."[36] In "On the Boulevard," the poet is actually sitting in the street, "without a kopeck in my pocket," wondering where he can spend the night, and contemplating suicide.[37] Even love seems gloomy and implausible and he decides not to approach a pretty girl, out of fear of children and family life.[38] Later Pastukhov repeatedly bought all the copies he could locate of this apparently embarrassing debut, but some survived, and Anton Chekhov was said to have prized one.[39]

Pastukhov's path to journalism is explained in various ways. In one account, Pastukhov became friendly with a newspaper editor.[40] V. A. Giliarovskii, a fellow journalist, an employee of *Moskovskii listok*, and later a well-known Soviet memoirist, gives a more lively and detailed explanation. According to Giliarovskii, who sometimes errs on the side of a good story, Pastukhov took several poor students under his wing. Two of them who frequented his beer hall worked as journalists. In their company Pastukhov began to turn his information about city life into press commentaries.[41] The students corrected his work, submitted it under their own names, and taught Pastukhov the tricks of the reporter's trade. When they finished their studies, they left and started their careers.

Pastukhov then operated on his own and eventually became "the most popular reporter in Moscow" for his coverage of street life and the doings of Moscow merchants and businessmen.[42] "He remained semiliterate to the end of his life, but he had no equal in getting the news," recalled Giliarovskii.[43] In his first years in journalism, Pastukhov worked for *Sovremennye izvestiia* (Contemporary News) and *Russkie vedomosti* (Russian Herald). He became one of a small group of a new type of Russian journalists—news gatherers for a city desk and observers of the seemingly trivial minutiae of urban life. Alexander Chekhov, the journalist and brother of the writer, described the excitement and ephemeral character of the new journalism with the observation that the successful reporter had "to be first everywhere."[44] Pastukhov was more than just a news gatherer, however: he made news into drama. In what was becoming an age of advertising, he became the P. T. Barnum of Russian journalism. Like the famous American showman, museum magnate, and circus impresario, Pastukhov was a great self-promoter. He identified himself with the pieces he wrote, and he had a sixth sense for the point at which the seemingly outrageous became compulsively interesting. He himself became the subject of rumor and scandal, and his notoriety served well in selling newspapers.

He wrote under the name of *Staryi Znakomyi* (Old Acquaintance), which he reportedly acquired while passing through a particularly dangerous neighborhood on his way to one of his investigations. A gang of cutthroats stopped his coach, and when they peered inside, Pastukhov exclaimed, "Don't you recognize one of your own, fellows!"[45] One of the robbers looked at him and replied, "Yes, he's an old acquaintance," and they sent him on his way unharmed.

After Pastukhov established his own newspaper, he continued the practice of putting himself in the news. When his newspaper was in its heyday he ate and held court during the day at the Moscow Grand Hotel, which was given the highest rating in the 1914 Baedeker guide to Russia and was located on what is now Revolution Square, beside the Lenin Museum. In the evenings, he retired to a drinking establishment called *Iar* (The Ravine) in Petrovskii Park, where, according to an 1890 advertisement in *Moskovskii listok* (no. 214), the drinker could expect to be entertained by seven ladies "in luxurious Arab costumes, performing the national dances of African tribes" and "the favorite dance of the harem." With the profits from his newspaper, Pastukhov bought a splendid dacha outside Moscow, where he comported in summer like an old-fashioned gentry lord, and even sponsored a theater on his grounds.[46]

Characteristic of the aura that Pastukhov created around himself and his newspaper were his feuds with some circus celebrities. When the owner of the Solomonskii Circus failed to give Pastukhov a favored seat, the editor warned readers that it was dangerous to attend the shows because "bricks fall on the heads of the audience."[47] He also declared war on a clown named Anatoly Durov, and Durov pursued the campaign in the ring. The climax came at a performance attended by Pastukhov. The clown appeared outfitted as a pig and performed a scene called "The Swine Reader." The pig sat in an easy chair and was brought a pile of newspapers. The scene that followed is best related by Anton Chekhov in a humorous feuilleton at the time: "As they presented the newspapers one after another to the pig, she turned away from them with indignation and grunted contemptuously. At first, they thought pigs can't stand publications in general, but when they raised *Moskovskii listok* to her eyes, she grunted joyfully, twirled her tail, stuck her snout in the newspaper, running it along the lines with a squeal."[48] The public, which eagerly read *Moskovskii listok*, as Chekhov observed, did not take offense but was delighted and sent the pig off with applause. Pastukhov walked out of the performance, and, according to the memoirist Shevliakov, he ceased to attack Durov in his newspaper.[49] After this incident, Pastukhov was caricatured in the humorous magazine *Razvlechenie* (Entertainment). Pastukhov, shown lying drunk in the street, is poked by a pig. "Don't bother me or I will denounce you," was the caption.[50]

Even tragedy, when it touched Pastukhov, became the subject of exaggerated rumors. Pastukhov was a passionate fisherman, and he was involved in either a hunting or fishing accident in which he shot and killed a peasant boy. As Giliarovskii recalls the incident, Pastukhov shot at some peasant boys who were disturbing his fishing when the accident occurred.[51] The bereaved mother, according to this account, then called on God to avenge her, and soon thereafter both of Pastukhov's children died. Shevliakov, a more prosaic source, claims that Pastukhov shot at what he thought was a rabbit, paid the boy's family several thousand rubles after the accident, built a stone chapel in the village, and thought no more about it until the boy's father came to him a year later—with the offer of a second son at half the price.[52]

Pastukhov specialized in a kind of boisterous and personal journalism in which he could trade on his renown. An 1879 collection of articles, published under the pseudonym of "Old Acquaintance," contained sketches of the inhabitants of the Rogozhskii quarter of the city where merchants and their sons liked to go drinking, also a favorite subject of lubok writers of the mid-nineteenth century.[53] One sketch featured a clever barber, who, when he tired of cutting hair, arranged a funeral for himself so that his wife could collect condolences from a rich customer.

Pastukhov had an eye for talent, and he was willing to pay well for it. When V. M. Doroshevich, one of the most promising young reporters of the day, left his post at a rival paper, Pastukhov offered him an enormous bonus.[54] Doroshevich accepted, but soon moved on to a more promising position. Pastukhov assembled a group of effective reporters and feuilleton writers. Their stories and his own about crime, city low life, and the scandalous and often ridiculous activities of prominent businessmen and merchants gave Pastukhov's paper its unique character. "A Robbery in the Street" (no. 335), "Murder in a Shoe Shop" (no. 331), "A Bloody Drama in the City of Bogorodsk" (no. 349), and regular reports from the Moscow circuit court were characteristic stories in 1882, the second year of publication. Columns such as "Moscow by Day and Night" and "Along Streets and Lanes" provided curious readers with tantalizing details about life among the rougher elements of the city population, such as the nightly trials of strength and the fights among local strongmen in the shadows of textile and sugar factories in a working-class district (no. 333, 1882). Important events of the day were also reported, and one worker subsequently recalled hearing an account read aloud of the riot that took place when gifts were distributed at Nicholas II's coronation.[55]

Pastukhov's paper occasionally had a democratic flavor, but he stood firmly for order and authority. His good connections with powerful officials explain his success in getting permission to publish in 1881, the year Alexander II was assassinated. Yet the energetic poor boy from small-town central Russia, who lived like a proper lord when he made his fortune, may well have felt jealousy and resentment toward those who seemed to gain effortlessly by birth what he worked so hard to achieve. The paper provided the forum in which he could express his contradictory feelings about the poor, the dangerous classes, the orderly working people, and about those in authority and the rich who did not behave the way he thought they ought to. *Moskovskii listok* ran a story in 1882 about an imbroglio between a landowner and local peasants in which the peasants were treated sympathetically (no. 14), and a feature about "a certain Vasilii Markovich" who was too cheap to heat his factory properly, so that his workers continually had to stop work and warm themselves up (no. 81). In the popular column "Advice and Answers," Pastukhov ridiculed prominent businessmen who did not pay their debts, were intemperate, or were otherwise engaged in raucous behavior.

The lower classes did not always have Pastukhov's sympathy, however. In 1891, for example, the paper's New Year feuilleton warned against coachmen and servants who came to the capital only to rob their employers, and complained about factory workers "who have gotten completely out of hand" (no. 1, 1891). "They work when they want to, and when they go out on a spree they are completely unmanageable. Punish him with a fine and he will be impertinent and will lodge a complaint against you either with the local justice or the factory inspector, or both."

Pastukhov liked to intercede personally in the affairs of prominent businessmen. It was the business community in the widest sense—not only employers but also white-collar employees and service people—with whom he apparently felt the most affinity. One journalist recalled an incident in which the son of a candy manufacturer came to Pastukhov when his father refused to approve his marriage. Pastukhov published a note about the candy manufacturer in his column, and the stern father quickly gave the young couple his blessing.[56]

Pastukhov's politics were on the right, and anti-Semitism was part of his stock in trade. "A spider of a Jew" and "this rascal of Jerusalem" were among his choice phrases (no. 8, 1882). In an 1882 Easter editorial, Pastukhov condoned pogroms in the Ukraine as the expression of "the people's insistent demand to escape from the presence of the Jewish tribe, which is so antipathetic to them" (no. 86, 1882). The editors of *Moskovskii listok* welcomed Jewish leaders' interest in emigration: "The time has come to quit the country they have exploited for so long." Anti-Semitic articles appeared regularly throughout the 1890s, including one about the murder of a child by a Jewish woman in Poland. When it subsequently emerged that the woman was not Jewish, the paper published a retraction of sorts, and informed readers that the murderess was "not this time a Jewess" (nos. 41 and 42, 1890). According to a memoir, one of Pastukhov's rivals, the editor of the paper *Novosti dnia* (News of the Day) was a Jew, and Pastukhov chided reporters he knew who worked "for the Yids."[57] Pastukhov's overt anti-Semitism, his chumminess with police authorities, and the prominence he gave to rumor and scandal led educated Russians to condemn the paper as disreputable.

The Bandit Churkin

Pastukhov's most remarkable feat was to write an enormous feuilleton novel entitled *The Bandit Churkin*, which ran serially in *Moskovskii listok* from January 29, 1882, until the spring of 1885 and added greatly to the paper's popularity. According to Giliarovskii's account, Pastukhov called him into his office one day at the beginning of the 1880s and showed him a big packet of paper with "The Case of the Bandit Churkin" written on the official blue cover.[58] Pastukhov told him that his friend, a police superintendent, had secretly given him all the material and correspondence related to the case, and that he planned to write a novel about the bandit.

The police report provided the skeletal plot and cast of characters he needed to begin the Churkin story. The task of filling in the details of Churkin's adventures and embellishing the episodes required an imaginative feat as well as the skills of the sensational journalist. Pastukhov proved capable of both. He began the first episode with "Muscovites have undoubtedly heard of the celebrated bandit Vasilii Churkin, who in his time spread panicky fear with his daring raids, brigandage, and robbery against the inhabitants of the district of Bogorodsk and the neighboring districts of Vladimir, Riazan, and other provinces."[59] In the course of the novel, Churkin travels from the district of Bogorodsk in Moscow Province to western Siberia and then home again, plundering and murdering along the way, until he meets his accidental death from a falling oak branch in his native forest.

Although Churkin was no Robin Hood, the novel was popular among lower-class readers and was viewed with suspicion by the authorities. Influential people in the real world of Russian officialdom decided in early 1885 that the bandit Churkin had reigned long enough over the imaginations of the lower-class inhabitants of the city, and they informed Pastukhov accordingly. Giliarovskii reports that it was Prince V. A. Dolgorukov, the all-powerful governor general and "boss" of the city, who announced the bandit's death sentence to Pastukhov and threatened to close the paper if he did not comply. Pastukhov was given one issue in which to end the story. "Strangle him or drown him!" Dolgorukov ordered.[60]

According to Shevliakov, it was Pastukhov's old boss M. N. Katkov, the well-connected and influential editor of the conservative *Moskovskie vedomosti* (Moscow Herald), who heard rumors that the novel was infecting "the imagination and spirit of the insufficiently cultured class of people." Katkov called Pastukhov into his office, according to this account, asked him where Churkin was, and upon learning that he was in a forest, suggested that he be struck dead by an oak branch.[61] In fact, dissatisfaction with the novel, probably because of its violence, had reached the highest levels of the tsarist administration. Writing in *Moskovskie vedomosti* in 1884, Katkov observed that Pastukhov had been given a harsh sentence in a libel case because his publication was considered harmful rather than beneficial and constructive.[62] In February 1885 the influential procurator of the Holy Synod, K. P. Pobedonostsev, wrote to the chief censor, suggesting that it might be worthwhile for him "to think about ways of limiting the spread of such publications and their public sale."[63] Whatever the cause, the novel did end precipitously, with a spectacular storm and a plunging oak branch. The dead bandit had eluded human judgment, Pastukhov concluded, but not divine.

Tsarist authorities were not mistaken about the novel's popularity. Churkin was the sensation of the day, a swashbuckling hero for some, a foil and butt of jokes for others. Discoursing on the pride and surliness of Moscow water carriers, Anton Chekhov suggested, "Had the bandit Churkin not been a bandit, he would have been a Moscow water carrier."[64] Chivalrous tales of knights and James Fenimore Cooper's novels of America had gone out of fashion, Chekhov pointed out in another 1885 article; instead Churkin was read, and children wanted to play bandits. In some cases, Chekhov complained, childish banditry went beyond play, and a couple of Moscow boys rented a horse and murdered a peasant. "The young Churkins" ended up in prison.[65] Churkin even replaced "Sharik" and "Zhuchka" as the most popular nickname for stray dogs. There was also a song about Churkin, called "About the Bandit Churkin," based on a translation of the ballad "Burial of a Bandit" by the German poet Ferdinand Freiligrath (1810-76).[66] The song, entitled "The Burial of Churkin," appears in a 1936 Soviet collection, *Russian Ballads*, with a note explaining that the song was popular in the 1880s.[67]

Until the fatal oak branch fell, Churkin worked faithfully for his creator, Pastukhov, and the circulation of the newspaper soared. "I remember that the novel was printed on certain days," recalled the memoirist Ivan Belousov, "and on those days the circulation of the paper rose very high. . . . Workmen pooled their kopecks and bought the paper, which cost 3 kopecks."[68] Shevliakov recalled that once the novel caught on, the newspaper hawkers stopped janitors, cooks, coachmen, and others who hitherto had not read any newspaper."[69]

The Churkin serial resembled many other bandit stories that had great appeal to lower-class readers in the late nineteenth and early twentieth centuries. There was a whole series of Churkin stories in lubok editions, including *The Daring Bandit Churkin* and *The Wife of the Bandit Churkin*, among others.[70] Ivin produced two Churkin titles, *The Bandit Churkin or the Bloody Retribution* (Moscow, 1885), which also appeared as *The Wife of the Criminal*, and *The Bandit Churkin a Prisoner of the Circassians* (Moscow, 1885).

The Other *Moskovskii listok* Novelists

On the days when Churkin did not appear, and after his demise, other novels filled the columns for serial fiction in *Moskovskii listok*. Among the more successful novelists was I. I. Miasnitskii (I. I. Baryshev), whose fiction on a variety of subjects sold very well at Moscow bookstores and particularly at Suvorin's railroad newspaper stands. According to Giliarovskii, the Miasnitskii novels were also the main reason for the success of the K. T. Soldatenkov book publishers.[71] Rudnikovskii (M. N. Bylov) was another standby on the newspaper, and he captivated readers with such stories as "Innocent Blood" (no. 360, 1890) and "Without Kith or Kin" (no. 213, 1891), which is about a poor orphan girl. He also wrote columns of social commentary such as "For Bread" (no. 274, 1891), about a hungry peasant couple who come to the city to get bread from their son during the 1891 famine. A third feuilletonist was A. I. Sokolova, who wrote under the pseudonym Sinee Domino (Blue Domino). Her tales of a life of luxury and crime were a regular feature on Tuesdays and Fridays. She was a major figure in the journalistic world and worked on a number of different papers, not only *Moskovskii listok* and its rivals, but also the highly respected *Istoricheskii vestnik* (Historical Messenger). She was of gentry origins and had a stormy life. According to Giliarovskii, she was the unacknowledged mother of the star journalist Doroshevich.[72]

The most resourceful and persistent *Moskovskii listok* novelist, however, was Aleksei Mikhailovich Pazukhin (1851-1919), a one-time schoolteacher from Iaroslavl, whose younger brother wrote lubok tales. According to Giliarovskii, Pazukhin came to the editorial offices of *Moskovskii listok* with a manuscript. Pastukhov suspected that he had purloined the text from someone else and made him write a story then and there in the office.[73] Pazukhin wrote "The Arrival of the Rural Schoolteacher," which passed muster and was printed in the paper. He went on to write dozens of novels, sketches, and scenarios. Sometimes he had two going simultaneously.

"The Arrival of the Rural Schoolteacher" is clearly autobiographical and is a reminder of how close many of the authors were to the world of their readers. The story begins with the teacher arriving in a hay cart in his new village during a holiday when all the villagers are off drinking. Curious villagers soon surround the teacher's cart. "He felt very awkward among this crowd of fathers and brothers of his future pupils."[74] He is led off in search of the elder to a drinking establishment, where, in a small room with lubki on the walls, he drinks tea and answers the peasants' hostile queries. Drunks test his knowledge with questions such as: "What will happen if the whale-fish on which the earth rests [a popular superstition] turns over?" When the teacher's answer fails to satisfy, he is ridiculed for wearing glasses and for not having been to the capital. The conversation takes a still worse turn when the teacher admits he is of peasant and not of clerical origins. "What kind of science can he teach if he is a peasant himself?" the drunken peasants ask. The meeting with the canton elder and clerk caps his humiliation. When they learn that he is a peasant and therefore subject to corporal punishment at the canton court, they invite him to witness three whippings "for entertainment."

Pazukhin had his own following among *Moskovskii listok* readers, and some readers only bought editions that included his fiction.[75] Giliarovskii recounted that subscribers sometimes came into the office and asked for a half-year subscription "to Pazukhin."[76] Anton Chekhov, in a letter to his brother Alexander, described Pazukhin as "the nursling of *Moskovskii listok*," and expressed the fear that if Alexander worked for Pastukhov, he would be sullied himself by association: "Muscovites, reading my surname and not thinking of my brother, will associate me with Pazukhin and company."[77]

Pazukhin's career lasted from the Russo-Turkish War to 1917, when he published what was probably his last novel, *Around the Throne*. During the 1880s and 1890s, when *Moskovskii listok* was most successful, Pazukhin wrote novels of romantic entanglements in which the main question was whether or not the heroes and heroines could marry each other and live happily ever after. He also wrote novels of crime and wrongdoing, in which the culprits tried to cover their guilt.

One of Pazukhin's most engaging romantic serials was "Velvet Ladies," which began to appear early in the winter of 1893. Tania, a poor seamstress from a prosperous family that has fallen into penury, watches elegant coaches in the street and dreams of luxury. Her good aunt warns her about the fate awaiting poor girls who allow rich admirers to dress them in velvet, but Tania takes a job in a restaurant chorus and becomes the mistress of a married nobleman. He keeps her generously and conceals the relationship by finding her a prospective bridegroom, a Jewish cafe singer, who is one of his protégés. Her former boyfriend, an honest worker, has taken to drink in sorrow. A religious elder and family friend of her paramour convinces Tania to abandon the nobleman and the cafe singer, and arranges a good job for her previous boyfriend. They are reunited and start anew, "far from the noisy life of the capital and its temptations" (no. 363). The nobleman returns to his wife in a repentant mood.

Pazukhin's crime stories, like those written by his contemporaries, usually began with a secret wrongdoing, a murder or a theft that eventually came to light, bringing the perpetrator grief and punishment. For example, "The Millionaire's Daughter," which began to appear in 1893 (no. 151), opens on a scene in an inn, where a merchant is hiring a peasant to assassinate his brother, so that an inheritance need not be shared. Romance destroys the evil plot, and in the end the lovers marry and the guilty are punished. Readers could find confirmation of the adage "crime does not pay" in these stories, but they also had the thrill of following a tangled plot. Both of these aspects of the feuilleton novel proved immensely satisfying to large numbers of readers throughout nineteenth-century Europe.

Readers of *Moskovskii listok*

Who read Pastukhov's paper? Observers saw it as a bourgeois and petit bourgeois paper, even though factory workers and day laborers were seen reading it, particularly while the Churkin epic was serialized. In the 1880s, *Moskovskii listok* had some popularity in the countryside and factory villages surrounding Moscow. Only 350 peasants in Moscow province had subscriptions to periodicals in the early 1880s, according to a study by the provincial zemstvo, and *Moskovskii listok* led the list with 44.[78] Half of the subscriptions were by the owners of taverns and teahouses, and the rest from predominantly prosperous peasants engaged in trade or handicrafts.[79] Pastukhov himself apparently thought of clerks, shopkeepers, and servants as his main audience. He was reported to have returned manuscripts submitted by established writers with the observation, "Maybe the article is good, but my janitors and shopkeepers won't go for it."[80] Clerks in Moscow grocery and flour shops considered *Moskovskii listok* their favorite paper, according to a study published in 1906, and they preferred the chronicle of events and the "bottom" section—that is, the lower half of the paper where the serialized novels appeared.[81] Store clerks worked long hours, took their meals at the shops, and spent the day looking out into the streets, and the diverting fiction, rumors, and scandals found in the paper appealed to them. The more prosperous shop and business employees, on the contrary, according to the same study, preferred a more serious publication, such as Sytin's *Russkoe slovo* or one of the other papers more to the taste of educated readers.[82]

Pastukhov's contemporaries confirmed that the paper appealed to the less cultured merchants, businessmen, shopkeepers, and serving people. In columns such as "Advice and Answers," as well as in the rest of the paper, the readers from these groups were informed that it was their publication, and that the editors were concerned primarily with their taste. Under the heading "A Day in the Life of a Poor Man," which appeared in 1882 (no. 22), the readers found not a description of peasant poverty or the urban unemployed, but rather the story of a sixty-year-old clerk, a widower, who received a miserly salary and lived in cramped quarters with his son, a student at the gymnasium. Surveys of city life invariably began with the merchants (*kuptsy*) (no. 9, 1890), and touched the working people secondarily. The social events covered, such as "The Calico Ball" (no. 17), were usually events for the business community. Stories and sketches similarly often began "In a merchant's house," as did a sketch by I. Miasnitskii, "Toward Evening in Fall" (no. 293, 1890). Stories such as "Vaska and Vasilevich" (no. 11, 1882), about a rich but illiterate miller who is fleeced by a clever sharper he hired to teach him to read and write, appealed to the fears and suspicions of the small merchants, though their servants and workers were undoubtedly interested too. Such was also the case with many of the paper's novels in which the crucial distinction was between legitimate and ill-gotten wealth. So many of these morality plays centered on fears, transgressions, and sins of the commercial community that it is difficult not to recognize these people as the anticipated readers of the newspaper, even though it was read by a wider audience.

The readers of *Moskovskii listok* were, in a very modest but still significant way, a new kind of reading public. The paper appealed both to lower-class readers and their employers. Unlike late nineteenth-century *lubochnaia literatura*, and some of the periodicals that followed *Moskovskii listok* that drew readers primarily from among the lower classes, Pastukhov's paper succeeded for a time by reporting entertainingly about events of common interest to people of different classes employed in the same sector of the urban economy.

Moskovskii listok reached its peak of popularity in the 1880s and 1890s, prompting Pastukhov to become one of the first editors to purchase a rotary press in Moscow.[83] Giliarovskii estimated the circulation in 1885 to have been 40,000 and, according to the Soviet historian B. I. Esin, *Moskovskii listok* was still doing well, with a circulation of 30,000 to 40,000, at the end of the 1890s.[84]

The paper did not keep up with the changing times, however, and in 1910 the circulation had risen to only 45,000.[85] When Pastukhov began publishing there were too few literate readers from the lower class to support a daily newspaper devoted primarily to their interests. He identified a particular urban audience among the middle and lower classes, and the key to his success was his appeal to the interests of this larger group. His strategy became outmoded during the late nineteenth and early twentieth centuries, as the numbers of lower-class newspaper readers increased and the interests of all newspaper readers broadened. New national newspapers that appealed to all classes gained a wide readership at this time and so did inexpensive periodicals designed for the common reader.

The tsarist government had a part in the decline of Pastukhov's fortunes. When the authorities forced him to abandon the enormously popular Churkin epic, they halted the expansion of the paper at a time during which its popularity was increasing with a rapidly expanding reading public in Moscow. Official intervention also cut short his scandalously successful "Advice and Answers" column in which he had sniped at businessmen and merchants to the glee of his readers.[86] Whether such interference made a fundamental difference in the fortunes of the paper is difficult to say. The journalist A. R. Kugel, in his 1923 memoir on the press, suggests that the circulation of the paper fell—despite a variety of gimmicks including Pastukhov's visit to the Paris World's Fair—because the editors did not satisfy the readers' demand for some kind of "cultural minimum."[87] As Pastukhov "floundered," in the words of Kugel, he put his hopes in his son, Victor, who was provided with money to establish a new illustrated weekly. But Victor Pastukhov became ill and died, and the project was abandoned sometime in 1902 or 1903.

The Kopeck Newspapers

The editors of the kopeck newspapers of the early twentieth century borrowed and improved upon Pastukhov's journalistic formula, but they also learned something from the success of Marx and the illustrated weeklies. They made their newspapers inexpensive, displayed serial fiction prominently, and paid lavish attention to crime, scandal, and human-interest stories. They allotted space to national and international news, however, and they claimed an educational role. They also adopted a liberal political position.

The St. Petersburg *Gazeta kopeika* (1908-17) was a four- to six-page daily tabloid designed and priced to capture the interest of the new common reader. The appearance of the first issue, in the words of a commentator writing on the paper's fifth anniversary, marked "the birth of a new popular press, which soon created its own reader."[88] The principal editor and publisher of the paper, Mikhail Borisovich Gorodetskii (1866-1918), was an entrepreneur of humble origins, as were Pastukhov, Sytin, and other successful publishing magnates. He was born to a "poor family," according to the author of an obituary,[89] in the small town of Gorlovka in Donetsk Province. Unlike the other entrepreneurial publishers, Gorodetskii was Jewish.[90] He attended primary school and worked in the local coal mines. While still an adolescent, he turned up in Rostov jobless and penniless, and supported himself selling newspapers. There he attracted the attention of Rosenstein, the editor of the Rostov paper *Priazovskii krai* (Azov Region), who found a place for him at the press. He worked as an apprentice typesetter but showed talent and an interest in journalism and became a reporter. After perhaps a decade in Rostov he moved, in the middle of the 1890s at the age of thirty, to St. Petersburg. There he worked first for the thick journal, *Syn otechestva* (Son of the Fatherland) and then for the newspaper *Novosti* (News).

In 1908, after editing and publishing several newspapers in the capital, he began to put out *Gazeta kopeika* together with two partners. One partner, Vladimir Aleksandrovich Anzimirov (1859-1920), held populist sympathies, and he published a fictional memoir about the radical circles of the 1870s.[91] Anzimirov ceased to be involved with the kopeck newspapers after 1909 and began to put out a weekly newspaper for peasants.[92]

The St. Petersburg *Gazeta kopeika* was an enormous success. Circulation rose from 11,000 copies in the first few days of publication in 1908 to 150,000 in 1909.[93] By 1910 peak circulation reached 250,000 copies, according to a publicity flyer issued by the publishers, and that was the average size of an edition in June of 1913.[94] Circulation continued to grow until World War I, when, according to some sources, it leveled off.[95] The newspaper's success up to World War I paralleled that of the other mass circulation newspapers in the country, including Sytin's more respectable and more expensive *Russkoe slovo*, which sold for more than twice the price of the *Kopeika*. Sytin's newspaper, which had a more national and diverse readership, surpassed the *Kopeika* in 1912, and by early 1917 its circulation rose to 600,000 to 700,000 copies a day.[96] Sytin's great success with his newspaper came during World War I, when the paper became very nationalistic. Its circulation may have owed something to subsidized distribution among soldiers, which was not as common with Gorodetskii's kopeck newspaper.[97]

As the enterprise of Gorodetskii and his friends flourished, Gorodetskii branched out into other publications, and *Kopeika* became a joint stock company in 1913. One of his most interesting projects was the firm Contemporary Lubok, which issued propaganda posters by K. Malevich and other important artists during World War I.[98] The poet Vladimir Mayakovsky wrote captions for the pictures and drew a few illustrations on his own.

The independent Moscow edition of the *Kopeika*, which soon separated from its parent publication, was almost as successful as the St. Petersburg edition, despite competition from Sytin's more established newspaper. Circulation of the Moscow kopeck paper reached 60,000 in the first year of publication and 150,000 copies by 1912.[99] The name of the Moscow paper was changed in 1910 to *Trudovaia kopeika* (Working Kopeck), and a weekly Monday supplement was issued under the paper's old name. The success of the Moscow edition was short lived, however.

The government closed the newspaper in May 1912 because of an article written by Anzimirov, who was sentenced to a year in prison.[100]

The editors of the kopeck newspapers offered their readers a variety of supplements, depending on how much they paid. There were several kopeck magazines, as well as almanacs, a series of kopeck novels, and publications for homemakers and about health. The circulation of the most successful supplement, the magazine *Vsemirnaia panorama* (Universal Panorama), reached 350,000 copies by 1909.[101]

The editors of the kopeck newspapers of the capitals presented their paper to their readers and potential subscribers as a politically "progressive" and culturally informative newspaper, as well as a comprehensive and accessible source of world news. They took care, however, to dissociate themselves from the radical left. What Russia needed, the editors avowed in the first issue, was action "to heal the severe wounds of the past and to create the new, beautiful, and just world about which the late Chekhov and humanity's best minds have dreamed."

The St. Petersburg *Kopeika's* editors congratulated themselves in the June 19, 1910, issue on the second anniversary of their paper for awakening interest in social questions, in civic problems, and in bright ideals. The newspaper was "the heart of social conscience," the editors affirmed.

One expression of the social goals of the editors of the *Kopeika* was their advocacy of tolerance toward national minorities, an issue that was often a litmus paper of political position in tsarist Russia. "Russia is the same motherland for the non-Russian and non-Orthodox population of the empire as for the Great Russians," the editors explained in a 1910 editorial (no. 540). "To exclude them from the common Russian family, which would entail a knowing curtailment of rights," they continued, "is unjust and also foolish."

During the notorious trial of the Jew Mendel Beilis for ritual murder, the editors of the St. Petersburg paper allied themselves with those who supported Beilis's innocence. When the not-guilty verdict was announced, they hailed it as a vindication of the ordinary Russian citizens who had sat as jurors and upheld the truth despite the efforts of the authorities to sway them.[102] Coverage of Central Asians was less balanced. Unflattering stereotypes of various nationalities, particularly Tatars but also occasionally Jews and Poles, could be found in stories and novels.

The editors of the kopeck newspapers conceived of their papers as instruments for cultural enlightenment among the common people. As the editors of the Moscow *Kopeika* explained in a 1910 editorial, the newspaper "serves primarily the interests of the working masses, and has a significant number of readers in the village" (no. 151/506). The purpose of the St. Petersburg paper, as expressed in a New Year's editorial in

1911, was "the welfare of the fatherland and the enlightenment and development of the people." The papers carried occasional and respectful coverage of meetings of medical assistants, primary school teachers, and agronomists. Enlightenment activities of workers' organizations and adult education programs were covered in greater detail.

The articles on developments in Russian literary culture and, in particular, on the classical writers of the late nineteenth century were so effusive as to leave little doubt that the editors sought to uplift lower-class readers by acquainting them with Russia's literary glory. Half an issue of the paper was devoted to Turgenev on the twenty-fifth anniversary of his death. The editors promised that Turgenev and the other classical writers would soon be known and appreciated throughout Russia, "and glorious will be their names" (no. 56, 1908).

The *Kopeika's* cultural role was also expressed in the premiums offered subscribers, many of which were works of classical Russian literature. Readers who paid a couple of rubles extra in order to receive some of the magazine supplements in 1917 were offered Tolstoy's complete works in fifty-six small volumes, in addition to some light fiction. Subscribers to the Moscow *Kopeika* in 1909, when it was still closely affiliated with the St. Petersburg paper, were promised selections from among one hundred serious works of literature, history, natural science, popular agronomy, or home economy (14 Dec. 1909). One of the *Kopeika* supplements for 1912, the magazine *Volny* (Waves), contained essays on classical Russian writers, a couple of letters by Chekhov, excerpts from Tolstoy's last works, and a note in memory of Pushkin, as well as light stories by Remizov and other contemporary writers.[103]

News very soon became a main selling point of the kopeck newspapers. The editors promised in the first issue of the Moscow edition "to give new masses of people, for whom the large newspapers are unsuitable because of price or language, the possibility of knowing what is happening in the world." To bring world news to a wide circle of readers was an important objective. "All that interests the world," "all that is found in the large newspapers," promised the publishers of the St. Petersburg paper in a 1910 flyer.[104] The same image of the kopeck newspaper of St. Petersburg was presented in advertisements. "The kopeck newspaper satisfies the demands of the most varied strata of society; every reader can find what interests him in the *Gazeta kopeika*, since world life is reflected in all its fullness on its pages," read an announcement in an issue for January 1, 1915. "Subscribe to the Petrograd[105] *Gazeta kopeika*," read a January 2, 1917, advertisement in the paper. "The cheapest and most widely circulated newspaper in Russia. Our own correspondents are everywhere." *Moskovskii listok* had offered its readers the excitement and scandal of local city life, but the editors of the *Kopeika* promised the same excitement and exclusive stories collected over the whole empire and from the world beyond it.

The main subjects covered in the St. Petersburg paper in 1913 were foreign affairs (12 percent of all space), entertainment and serial fiction (11 percent), and police and court cases (8 percent). Domestic politics, working and living conditions, events in the countryside, culture and education, received relatively less coverage. Advertising consumed almost half (43 percent) of the newspaper.[106] On the eve of the February Revolution, the coverage differed somewhat; the emphasis was more on domestic politics and urban life, there were many fewer advertisements, and, of course, there was much news of the war.

During January 1910, the *Kopeika* carried coverage of the English parliamentary elections, Turkish-German relations, events in the Balkans and Manchuria, Austro-Russian relations, prolonged flooding in France, and developments in Persia, as well as other foreign stories. Under the conditions of press supervision after 1905, the editors of the *Kopeika* presented significant information about Russian domestic politics, speeches in the Duma, political positions adopted by various parties, and important legislative and administrative decisions by the government. Coverage of these topics increased in the last year or so of the old regime, when popular interest in domestic politics increased.

Events of international politics—wars, revolutions, treaties, the appearance of new heads of state—were all covered by the kopeck newspapers, particularly as they related to Russia. This was one of the major differences between the St. Petersburg *Kopeika* and earlier papers such as *Moskovskii listok*. Readers of the *Kopeika* were more likely to orient themselves in a world context as Russians than as Muscovites or St. Petersburg residents. One not atypical and somewhat humorous example of the way in which the editors of the St. Petersburg paper reminded readers that they were Russians in a world of many nationalities was a story about deserters during the Russo-Japanese War who had stayed on the eastern border of the empire and were terrorizing the inhabitants of Manchuria. In addition to their destructive activities, the correspondent explained, the former Russian soldiers also served a positive function, that of spreading Russian culture, by teaching the Chinese how to make cabbage soup, set up samovars, and drink vodka (no. 12, 1908). The author of the article was quick to add, however, that the soldiers were unable to settle happily outside of Russia and longed most of all to return to their native villages.

The Russian Empire and the world beyond were portrayed in the kopeck newspapers as a seemingly endless stream of places in which exciting or curious events had taken place. This portrayal, as well as more substantive articles, also helped Russian readers find an identity in a national and world context. "A pauper strikes it rich" (Poltava), "A monstrous suicide" (Vilna), "A wolf savages five peasants in a village near Minsk," "A victim of duty" (about a surgeon who dies of blood poisoning in Kiev), "A fire in a Tambov prison," "Lightning strikes 13 in Berlin" were all headlines or stories that appeared in the St. Petersburg tabloid during May and June of 1910.[107]

Crime and city life remained topics of special interest to readers of the *Kopeika*, and a gory murder, a dramatic police case, or an exciting trial were always covered with great enthusiasm. The St. Petersburg paper had stories in 1909 about the lives of coachmen (no. 176), street artists (no. 328), low life on Ligovskii boulevard (no. 330), the bums' bourse near the Obukhovskii Bridge, where old clothes and shoes were traded (no. 339), and the "pirates" on the Neva river (no. 344).

The Kopeck Novels

Serial fiction was important in the kopeck newspapers, as it had been in *Moskovskii listok*, but the content of the kopeck novels differed markedly from those printed in Pastukhov's newspaper. The world of the kopeck novels was open to energy and enterprise, and even Churkin's Siberian adventures and his designs on a rich peasant's daughter pale beside it. Whereas Churkin's schemes were doomed from the start by his predilection for crime, those of the kopeck heroes seem replete with the possibility of fulfillment. Nothing like these stories can be found either among the literature of colportage or in the earlier newspaper serials.

Readers were offered only one novel at a time in Gorodetskii's paper, unlike Pastukhov's sheet, and that novel appeared in every issue. Perhaps the unsophisticated readers of the *Kopeika* were less able to balance several continuing stories than were those of *Moskovskii listok*. The first kopeck novel was *Scarlet Roses of the East*, which began to appear two months after the first issue. Serialized novels remained a regular part of the newspaper until the end of its existence. Almost nothing is known of the authors of these novels, since the October Revolution cut short the papers' existence and precluded their appearance, and the memoirs that would have made identification possible were never published. Anzimirov, the first editor of the Moscow paper, wrote several of the novels himself. Otherwise the authors of kopeck fiction remain screened behind the pseudonyms they chose at the time, which were reminiscent of those used by provincial actors. Raskatov ("thunderclap"), Gromadov ("huge"), and B. Reutskii were the most prominent authors in the St. Petersburg newspaper.

The novels were presented to the readers as informative and realistic. The editors of the St. Petersburg newspaper claimed in their advertising flyer for 1910 that the "large sensational novels" were distinguished from the incredible detective adventures that were then sweeping the lower-class market by the fact that they were "a reflection of reality."[108] The Kopeck Library of Sensational Novels was described in a 1913 (no. 1662) advertisement in the St. Petersburg paper as containing "novels and tales from Russian life." These claims were not exactly untrue. The serialized novels contained information about places and events in the news, and that was part of their attraction. There was a story set in Turkey at the time of the Young Turk Revolution, and one on the site of the great Messina earthquake. Another was set in the Siberian gold fields, and still others allowed readers to imagine themselves in the new areas of settlement in the Caucasus, at the Baku oil fields, at the front in the Russo-Japanese War, World War I, and finally on the streets of Petrograd during the February Revolution.

The editors could claim that their novels were based on real places, events, and phenomena, but in fact the realism was very similar to that of the detective stories they maligned. Both kinds of popular fiction were imaginative adjuncts to the news items that appeared in the newspaper. The crime journalism and detective fiction complemented each other, and so did journalistic forays into the wide world and the adventure novel.

Adventure, crime, and the career of a bandit hero accounted for nearly 60 percent of the thirty-four novels that appeared in the St. Petersburg paper from its founding through 1917. Most of the rest concerned the supernatural, war, or revolution. Crime, banditry, and adventure were also important in the Moscow newspaper. In addition, the Moscow paper contained stories about revolutionaries of the 1870s, as well as a historical war novel about the defeat of Napoleon and a story about a struggling proletarian artist.

The Bandit Hero Anton Krechet

The St. Petersburg newspaper was associated in the minds of many readers with the hero of a single long adventure, much in the way that Pastukhov's paper had been identified with the bandit Churkin. The feats and adventures of Anton Krechet[109] fascinated readers in over eight hundred issues of the paper from 1909 through 1916.

Krechet is a bandit, but a very different type from the crude and bloodthirsty Churkin. He is much more cultured than Churkin, and, although his class origins are never made clear, he is identified as a natural aristocrat who is taken for a member of the gentry wherever he goes. Like Churkin, however, he has the physical strength that was respected at all levels of society. When asked by the labor activist L. M. Kleinbort why they read the *Kopeika*, factory workers replied, "Because of Anton Krechet."[110] The appeal of Krechet went beyond the factory, however, as one of the most perceptive early Soviet investigators of popular literary taste, M. I. Slukhovskii, concluded.[111] The peasant reader, he suggested, "searches for the description of heroic lives in belles lettres. In the past this group of readers was attracted by Raskatov's book, *Anton Krechet*." Slukhovskii may have overstated the case for Krechet's popularity, and his "peasant reader" was probably a migrant rather than a full-time agriculturalist, but the popularity of the serial was widely recognized.

The novel begins when Krechet gallops up to the porch of a gentry manor house 50 miles from "one of the great Volga cities" and is mistaken for an awaited estate manager by a kindly landowner and his beautiful daughter. They are nervous about reports that a bandit, alleged to be Krechet himself, is raiding their district. Before many issues of the newspaper had elapsed, Krechet collars the villains who have been using his name, and swears love for the landowner's daughter.

The lovers are soon separated, and Krechet, like Churkin, has ample opportunity for additional romance. Unlike Pastukhov's bandit, however, Krechet seeks only a simple and peaceful life free from his pursuers, the evil police agents who are always hot on his trail. Krechet's "sins" are almost all in the past, and as a bandit in spite of himself he is a more positive figure than Churkin. There are bloody feats, but Krechet's victims are usually police spies and detectives, not innocent merchants and peasants. He kills, but only in defense of his freedom. He even goes out of his way occasionally to pursue real criminals and to protect the innocent.

His search for freedom takes him through Western Europe, and then back to Russia and across the whole Empire, in search of an official pardon as a volunteer in the Russo-Japanese War (1904-1905). He outsmarts the Japanese army and wins his pardon. Returning home a hero, Krechet establishes himself and his comrades on an estate in central Russia, where they live like gentry.

Other tales in the St. Petersburg paper closely resembled the Krechet series, but there were also a few detective stories in which the sympathies of the reader were not on the side of the outlaw. *The Lane of Death* (no. 294, 1909) by Reutskii is about a detective's clever pursuit of a psychotic killer, the lord of a Bessarabian estate, whose murders are attributed by superstitious local inhabitants to the supernatural.

The supernatural is the dominant element in some other tales. A rational explanation was considered necessary, but the explanation is often awkwardly grafted onto the story. "In the Devil's Claws" by Raskatov (no. 454, 1909) is such a story. A mysterious villain with power over animals and people carries out obscure machinations with the help of a lovely but spellbound female animal trainer. The hero, a circus strongman and wrestler who gave up the university for the pleasures of the ring, is almost defeated by a local weakling whom the villain has infused with infernal strength. The beautiful animal trainer is freed, the villain's plans are thwarted, and his mysterious plots and murders are explained. But his hypnotic power remains something of a riddle.

Action in exotic places and treasure hunting were the lure of other kopeck serials. In *Scarlet Roses of the East* a harem escape takes place against the backdrop of the Young Turk Revolution (no. 56, 1908), and in "In the Hands of the Avenger" (no. 255, 1909) a heroic Russian sailor finds himself entangled in Italian intrigue during the great Messina earthquake. There were also adventures in Russian settings. An abandoned gypsy child, raised by a kindly Volga steamboat watchman, sets out to find his future and a treasure, and becomes a famous circus acrobat in the course of his wanderings in "The Foundling" by Raskatov (no. 1468, 1912). "Which is better," a passenger asks the gypsy boy, "to live here like a muzhik till death, or to go off on the wide, merry, and free road . . . to live like a lord?" (no. 1486). The same call to adventure echoes in a novel about the newly settled areas of the Caucasus, "Satan's Cliff" (no. 1371, 1912), by P. Gromadov. Practically a manual for day dreaming about migration, the novel begins with Georgii and two friends hiking along the narrow path of a Caucasian mountain, but soon flashes back to the young men, several years earlier, sitting in a St. Petersburg beer hall, sighing about a new life of farming and adventure. The lure of success is also what another young hero has in mind in Raskatov's novel, "The Treasure Hunters" (no. 743, 1910), in which a young man finds love and wealth at the Baku oil fields.

The adventure tales set in the regions of particular interest to readers or in foreign lands in the news were replaced by war novels with the outbreak of World War I, and then by tales of the Revolution. "The Broken Chains," subtitled "A Novel from the Revolution," shows many of the characteristics of the other kopeck novels.[112] There is an old steel mill master worker Stepan Beloiartsev, "well made and strong as an oak," with only a few grey hairs to show his age; his soldier son, Pavel, whose looks indicate a "decisive and forceful character"; workers such as Savelii and Grigorii "with smoky faces" and "phenomenal strength" and the young favorite of the factory, Philipp. On the other side are the double agent Vlasov and the police spy Grishin. This cast has plenty of opportunities to demonstrate traditional virtues and vices during the adventurous days of the February Revolution in dramatic battles that pit workers, soldiers, and Cossacks against officers, spies, and the police—"pharaohs" as they were called.[113] The story ends with the rescue of imprisoned revolutionaries and the destruction of villainous policemen.

The novels that appeared in the Moscow newspaper in 1909 and 1910 were similar to those in the St. Petersburg *Kopeika*, although there was a more political tone to tales such as Anzimirov's "Murk—A Social Novel from Life" (no. 153, 1909). The most remarkable tale in this respect, which seems to prefigure Soviet socialist realism, is "Nikolai Zharov: A Novel from a Worker's Life" by I. A. Danilin. The story is a proletarian romance in the style of Gorky's *Mother*. Zharov is a worker-artist who passes up the love of the factory owner's daughter in order to continue to dedicate his life to his proletarian comrades. He dreams of setting up a mutual fund, and the novel ends with his profession of faith: "Soon, soon, all will belong to labor, labor will be honored, you will become citizens of the country with equal rights" (no. 285/865, 1911).

The kopeck novels were in one respect closer to the more traditional literature of colportage than the novels serialized earlier in the cheap newspapers of the nineteenth century. Aspects of chivalrous stories and fairy tales appear occasionally. *The Broken Chains* begins like a fairy tale with the tsar surrounded by foolish counselors, and the situation worsens until a fool becomes a minister. "Everything is fine, father, everything is all right, father, only have faith in me and listen to me," he exclaims.[114] "And the tsar listened, and the minister fool ruled." When the detective in *The Lane of Death* confronts the mad killer, it is a duel of "knights." When the agronomist Silen in the Moscow serial "Turgid Waves" confesses an affair with another woman, he explains that he was "enchanted" by a women who called him "her knight, her beautiful prince" (no. 193, 1909). Despite these folkloric flourishes, the readers of these novels found themselves in a world that was more up-to-date, urban, and cosmopolitan than that of the lubok tale.

The Readers of the Kopeck Newspapers

The differences between the kopeck newspapers and *Moskovskii listok* are partly explicable purely in terms of the size of their intended readership. With over five times the circulation of *Moskovskii listok* on the eve of World War I, the St. Petersburg *Kopeika* was probably read by a much larger proportion of lower-class readers, although some of the same social groups read both newspapers. This is also true with respect to the Moscow edition of the kopeck newspaper, with three times the circulation of Pastukhov's paper. Whereas Pastukhov thought of janitors and coachmen when he envisioned his lower-class readership, Gorodetskii and Anzimirov more often thought of factory workers, day laborers, and new cadres of rural readers as their audience. The editors of the Moscow paper explained to their readers in the second issue in 1909, for example, that they would produce the Monday edition of the paper, which had to be set on Sunday, at a separate press in order to guarantee workers their Sabbath rest. Similarly, the St. Petersburg editors justified raising the price of the paper to 2 kopecks in 1914, with the explanation that the alternative was to close the paper and put "more than a thousand laboring people" out of work (no. 2164, 1914).

The intention of the editors of the kopeck newspapers to address their papers to the lower-class population of the capital was particularly evident in the "workers' life" column in 1908 and 1909, and in columns such as the one signed by Skitalets. Skitalets, who is not to be confused with the Russian writer who used the same pseudonym, wrote on a variety of subjects, including illness among the lower classes, clinics (no. 674, 1910), poverty and fires in the town of Mogilev (no. 699), and schools for chauffeurs and airplane pilots (no. 712). Skitalets exposed the hard life of the working poor, but he also expressed a work ethic his editor, a self-made man, was likely to appreciate. In July 1910 (no. 702), he complained that whereas in Norway tram riders could be relied upon to pay for their transport voluntarily and without supervision, Russian trams and trains were plagued by a mass of freeloading riders or "hares" (*zaitsy*). This was an indication, he complained, that "Among us almost no one respects his own labor, and the lazybones and good-for-nothings are legion" (no. 702, 1910).

Although the kopeck newspapers had more lower-class readers than *Moskovskii listok*, these readers were in some respects more sophisticated. Whether they were newly literate migrants from the countryside or working people who had grown up in the city, their interests extended beyond the urban environment and their newspaper offered them national and international news. The provision of information about the world had become an essential function for even the cheapest newspapers by the early twentieth century.

Suggestive if inconclusive evidence of the differences and the similarities between the readership of *Moskovskii listok* and the St. Petersburg *Kopeika* is found in their advertisements. Newspaper advertising was important to both papers. A sample comparison of the advertisements appearing in *Moskovskii listok* in early December 1882 with those in *Gazeta kopeika* in a similar period in 1908 and 1913 supports the view that the St. Petersburg kopeck newspaper had a larger proportion of lower-class readers than Pastukhov's publication. Roughly 40 percent of the advertisements in *Kopeika* were for medical treatment, mostly at clinics and almost exclusively for venereal disease. Most of the remaining advertisements in the kopeck newspaper were for staple goods, such as clothes, footwear, and cigarettes. There were also notices, however, of white-collar jobs such as bookkeepers. Training was offered for automobile mechanics and drivers and for careers in the new movie business. Cultural announcements, particularly for printed materials, constituted another significant category of advertisement. These included everything from the nineteenth-century Russian classics to books on the occult and guides to the secrets of love.

Moskovskii listok carried many more advertisements for luxuries than the kopeck newspapers. For example, advertisements in December 1882 touted "elegant underwear," "fashionable muffs," and "little dogs for ladies." The employment and business notices, which included shops for sale and retail packaging materials and other items of use to merchants, were suggestive of the newspaper's favored clientele. So also were announcements of job openings for bookkeepers and governesses. The fact that more advertisements in *Moskovskii listok* seem intended for prosperous readers does not mean that less affluent citizens did not read the paper. We can only conclude that some advertisers used the paper to reach yet another class of readers, while the advertisements for cheaper goods in the *Gazeta kopeika* suggest a mostly lower-class readership.

Except for shop signs and window displays the advertisements in newspapers were probably the first seen by many of the readers. The daily newspapers with their mass circulation were thus the forum for the development of the lively but short-lived Russian advertising industry.

Other Serial Fiction

The success of the popular periodical press contributed to that of another kind of popular literature, the serial adventure story and the installment novel. Both of these were similar to the fiction serialized in the cheap newspapers. They were available along with newspapers at newsstands and railroad kiosks, from street peddlers who displayed their wares in doorways, and from shopkeepers who sold them along with candies, cigarettes, and toys. Some of the serialized adventure stories were self-contained tales of the life of a known fictional hero, most notably a famous detective. Others, such as the installment novels, comprised separate episodes of a single large novel, so that readers with little ready cash could buy and enjoy the novel installment by installment.

The success of the serial novels, like that of the newspapers, depended on a regular readership. This was a street literature much like the journalism of the kopeck press, but without the news and without the constraints of factual accuracy that occasionally limited kopeck journalists. The semblance of fact combined with the freedom of fiction was a characteristic of the literature and a source of its great appeal.

The one significant difference between this serialized fiction and that published in the newspapers was that these stories were usually situated abroad, often in Europe and America, with foreign heroes and heroines. This cosmopolitanism was expressed also in the inclusion of motor cars and other paraphernalia of modernity, and the pace of these stories was even more brisk than that of the newspaper serials.

To contemporaries, the street literature of the early twentieth century was epitomized by the serial detective story, featuring Russian versions of such heroes as Sherlock Holmes, Nat Pinkerton, and Nick Carter. Published as complete adventures in thirty-two or forty-eight pages, and usually sold for 5 to 7 kopecks, each publication contained one story in the continuing cycle of a known hero. The Pinkerton craze, or the *Pinkertonovshchina*, as it was sometimes known, began inauspiciously with the publication of a few stories about Pinkerton and Holmes in 15- and 20-kopeck editions of 5,000 to 10,000 copies in 1907.[115] In 1908 prices fell to 5 and occasionally to 2 and 3 kopecks. The stories sold well, and the size of the editions rose rapidly to 50,000 and 60,000 copies. During 1908 nearly 10 million copies of detective stories were published at 15 kopecks or less. The detective serials declined swiftly after 1908. The number of copies fell by half in 1909 and by considerably more in 1910. In 1911, 1912, and 1913 only a few hundred thousand copies of the serials appeared, and in 1914 there were none at all. There was a revival in 1915, however, and again a substantial number of cheap detective serials appeared on the popular book market.

Pinkerton, Carter, and Holmes were the most popular heroes. There were 6.2 million copies of Pinkerton, 3.1 million of Carter, and 3.9 million of Holmes adventure stories published at 15 kopecks or less from 1907 through 1915. The average size of an edition of a Pinkerton from this period was 21,500 copies, of a Carter 19,300 copies, and of a Holmes only 9,200 copies, a figure that reflects the many unsuccessful as well as successful attempts to sell serials about Holmes.

The stories were adapted from or inspired by foreign originals. The source of greatest richness was the American Nick Carter serial, which was written by a number of different authors and was popular among

American readers from the 1880s to the 1920s. The authors of the American serial drew on many foreign works for their material, including the fiction of Emile Gaboriau and Ponson du Terrail.[116] The Pinkerton stories, however, were apparently of European origin and circulated in France and Germany.[117] The American detective Allan Pinkerton (1819-84) produced such anti-labor novels as *The Molly Maguires and the Detectives* (1877), and his son, A. Frank Pinkerton, wrote detective stories, but they did not create anything like the Russian versions of Nat Pinkerton, the detective. With some justification, a member of the Pinkerton family declined all responsibility for the Russian Pinkertons and charged in a German interview that "Russian hack writers" were "writing fairy tales" and "speculating on my name."[118]

The Russian detective serials diverged sharply from the traditional popular fiction issued by the publishers of *lubochnaia literatura*. Paced even faster than the kopeck novels, the stories depicted their heroes constantly on the move, especially in newsworthy foreign cities. The detectives rushed from trains to automobiles, from steamships to airplanes and balloons. There was movement and excitement everywhere. "Mister Nat Pinkerton?" asks the Cleveland police chief in one of the most popular Russian Pinkerton serials, *Nat Pinkerton, the King of Detectives*. "Is it really you? Five minutes ago I telegraphed you in New York."[119] Another Pinkerton adventure begins with the "Chicago to San Francisco Express" pulling out of the station.[120]

Critics of the detective novel have drawn a distinction between the detective story and the thriller. In the detective novel the lure is the intellectual joy of following the solution to the enigma. In the thriller the reader is drawn on by the excitement of the chase, the hero's peril, and the punishment of the criminal.[121] The thriller requires a less sophisticated reader. To follow the hero through escapades and scrapes is less demanding than to follow the logic of the analytical detective.

The Russian serials are thrillers, but their heroes also solve puzzles, defend the social order against the chaos of crime, and, in cases in which the supernatural is suspected, uphold the natural order of things as well. These last two functions of the adventure story led the French critic Régis Messac to identify the nineteenth-century feuilleton novels by Eugene Sue and others with the popularization of scientific thought.[122]

The adventure *Point of Steel* in the *Nat Pinkerton, the King of Detectives* serial (no. 75, 1916) begins: "Panic! All the police of New York are on alert. The population of the enormous city was gripped by panic." A series of baffling murders has taken place and only Pinkerton is able to explain the crimes and send the villain to the electric chair. Another adventure, *Arrest in the Clouds*, starts: "Nat Pinkerton had already been riding on the express from Chicago to New York for two hours. The great detective had just aided the Chicago police in the capture of several important criminals. He spent in total only a few hours in Chicago, and, in his opinion, the case turned out to be altogether simple, but nevertheless it had caused the local police great concern" (no. 12, 1908).

The Russian detectives do not fit the classic mold of Conan Doyle's Holmes or Poe's Dupin, even when they have the same names. The original Holmes and Dupin spent more energy cracking the puzzle of the crime than the head of the criminal; as Kornei Chukovskii aptly observed in a lecture on the Pinkerton serials in 1908, the Russian version of Pinkerton was usually more eager to pursue and subdue miscreants than to outwit them.[123] Yet some resemblance to the originals remains. The Russian Pinkertons, Carters, and Holmses are private detectives rather than policemen. By choosing such heroes, the Russian authors, translators, and adaptors showed that, in the imaginative realm, they were willing to replace official enforcers of community values with private ones. This turn of thought made the appearance of the private detective in Western European and American popular fiction such an innovation.[124] It was a particularly important sign in the Russian context.

One appeal of the Russian Pinkerton and Carter stories was their Americanness, but the landscape seen in the detectives' constant travels is the kind visible on a map of the world. "The express had already left Lake Michigan behind, and in the distance the waters of Lake Erie could already be seen. Now the train approached the city of Cleveland."[125] An adventure in one of the most popular Nick Carter serials, *Nick Carter, the American Sherlock Holmes*, begins with the detective returning from an uncharacteristic vacation in "sunny Florida, far from the snow and ice of populous New York."[126]

The use of American names and places does not appear to have constrained authors, and the stories often include scenes that are more Russian than American. When a rich businessman, in danger of losing his fortune to a gang of Hudson River pirates, turns to Pinkerton, the detective's first question is one that would have been out of character for the real strike-breaking Pinkerton. "Aren't you treating your people too harshly and don't you pay them too little?" asks the detective.[127] No one who knew anything about the Pinkertons and their agency could have read these lines without a smile, though the question fully keeps with the political climate of post-1905 Russia.

When Nick Carter enters a police station disguised as a rich butcher in the adventure *Ines Navarro the Beautiful Demon*, he hands the officer on duty a card, setting up another very Russian scene. " 'Do you know how to read?' he asked politely. The sergeant was dumbfounded. What impudence! This clown asked him, does he know how to read?"[128] However, when he sees the card with the writing of his superior, "the bearer of this is always allowed to see me at any time of the day or night," he sends for his chief. Similarly, the detective's arrival in New York in January has a Russian ring: "The darkness of night still stood over the enormous city. It was seven A.M., and the dim January morning began to change to a melancholy short day" (no. 5).

Any detective story could be made into a Pinkerton. A minor Pinkerton serial published as a supplement to an installment novel was nothing more than a rough imitation of Poe's "The Murders in Rue Morgue." The Russian story begins: "Bob Ruland, the pupil and chief assistant of the famous detective Nat Pinkerton, sat among old friends, toughened by various marvelous detective adventures, and talked about his teacher."[129] Skipping Poe's remarks about the analytical mind and the ratiocinative detective Dupin, the author of the Russian version goes straight to the Paris streets, with the first demonstration of Pinkerton/ Dupin's powers.

The editors of one of the most popular Pinkerton and Carter serials were particularly anxious to protect their exclusive rights to the distinctive Carter serial covers, which they claimed had been specially prepared for "the Russian edition of Nick Carter and do not have anything in common with the covers of the English and German publications."[130]

Following the success of the first Holmes and Pinkerton serials, a host of imitations appeared. Though sometimes more crudely written than the most successful series and often less popular, these ancillary serials were written to fit the same formula. There were serials in which the famous detectives were brought to Russia or set to work on Russian cases abroad, such as the serial *Nick Carter, the King of Detectives Known to All the World*, whose author also claimed the crown of detection for his hero. Everything is peaceful as Carter, who has just solved a million-dollar case, prepares to return home from England to New York. "Nick Carter stood with his chief assistant Shik on the deck of the steamship St. Paul, which was ready to depart in a quarter of an hour."[131] Immediately, however, Carter spies a ferocious anarchist on a nearby ship and the chase begins. He trails the anarchist to Stockholm, disguises himself as a muzhik, and, singing revolutionary songs and swearing "I am a nihilist from birth," joins the terrorists. He is soon found out, however, and trapped at the anarchists' hideout. "Come in, Mr. Carter," says the anarchist leader "with a diabolical laugh." The anarchists prepare to dump him through a trapdoor into a sewer, but the detective overpowers them and disposes of them instead. "That's the way we deal with such dirty criminals in the United States," he announces.

"Nick defeated all three of his enemies, throwing their bodies into the sewer, which was intended for garbage and all sorts of muck."

A writer named P. Nikitin produced several Holmes serials that were set in Russia and retained some of the characteristics of the original detective team. Nikitin's Holmes and Watson tour the Russian Empire to solve cases that included a gypsy kidnapper in Odessa, a counterfeiter in Vladimir, and pirates on the Black and Azov seas. For Nikitin's Holmes, like Conan Doyle's original, the discovery of a case is a source of delight rather than outrage, as it is for Pinkerton and Carter. " 'No, it is altogether marvelous!' exclaimed Sherlock Holmes, passing me a page of the newspaper. 'Read those comments on the theft of a live person, dear Watson; it will cheer you up and give you a good appetite for dinner.' " So begins *The Secret of Stesha the Gypsy*, one of Nikitin's more violent tales.[132] In the first episode of the series, Nikitin's Holmes solves the case of the Vladimir counterfeiter, who had fabricated a spectre to keep out unwanted guests. Occasionally Nikitin used his serial to express his liberal views, as when his Russified Holmes complains that "the most filthy element of society remained almost without supervision" when the Russian police were busy combatting subversion during the Revolution of 1905. Similarly, while riding down the Volga, his Holmes remarks on the failure of Russians to develop the river's potential wealth. "Yes, my dear Watson, we English could show the Russians what it means to manage such a river."[133]

Besides various incarnations of great foreign detectives, there were serials of purely Russian invention, but they were generally less successful than those starring the international sleuths. In response to interest in Japan generated by Russia's unsuccessful war with that country, there were two Japanese detective serials, *Oka-Shima, the Famous Japanese Detective* (1908) and V. A. Gladkov's *Kio-Hako, the Japanese King of Detectives* (1917). Oka-Shima is described as the half-Russian son of a retired Russian officer and a Japanese woman. He is an adventurer who developed "his remarkable mind through study and travel and is now considered one of the most educated Japanese."[134] Kio-Hako, also an intellect, is a pipe-smoking Holmesian figure who speaks many languages and solves cases as far afield as South Africa, Italy, and China.

Serials with Russian heroes were *I. D. Putilin, the Genius of Russian Detection* (St. Petersburg, 1908) and *Tref, the First Detective in Russia* (St. Petersburg, 1910). Except for the adventures of Putilin, which appeared in eighteen booklets for a total of 383,000 copies, the Russian detectives never gained any substantial readership; neither did the few serials with criminal heroes or heroines, such as *The Unusual Adventures of Kornet Savinno, the Famous Russian Adventurer* (St. Petersburg, n.d.).

Readers and Writers

Readers' preference for serials with foreign detectives paralleled their new curiosity about foreign places. The stories set in foreign countries showed more inventiveness than those situated in Russia, either because of the availability of foreign models or because of the greater skill of their authors.

The only detective author to publish an autobiography, and probably the only one to write one, was V. A. Gladkov, who was both author and publisher of the Kio-Hako series. Gladkov felt compelled to explain his origins after the February Revolution. He identified himself on each issue of his 1917 serial as a wounded army volunteer and recipient of the St. George Cross, but after the Revolution he wished to tell his readers more about himself. He began his autobiography in the fifth issue of the serial with "Comrade reader."[135] What he wished to explain, first of all, was his class. "I am the son of parents a little higher than middle (*srednii*) class," he continued. His mother was of "noble blood," but his father was lower middle class (*meshchanin*) and an upholsterer by profession. The young Gladkov studied briefly at a Moscow gymnasium, and then attended a railroad school, from which he graduated with a certificate as an engineer. He volunteered for the war, was wounded, and began his writing career. He was twenty years old in 1917, a bright young man who appears in a picture in several numbers of the series in a sports jacket, tie, and jaunty cap. His sympathies were patriotic and perhaps liberal. Echoing the nationalism and hope some felt after the February Revolution, Gladkov wrote Easter greetings to his readers in the eighth issue of the series: "I feel a time of such joy is coming, when Russia, spreading its powerful strong wings and soaring over the whole universe, will say a real 'Christ is risen!' " Although Gladkov was perhaps unique in addressing his audience, his interest in readers was probably shared by his fellow authors. Close attention to readers was essential for a writer of the detective serials, since success depended on continual sales.

The detective serials developed as appendages to the daily newspaper. The places and events of the newspaper provided the material for the serials. The authors presented their heroes to the readers as if they were part of the news. "Nat Pinkerton is not an imaginary character," read a statement in bold type on one of the early issues of a popular Pinkerton serial. Pinkerton, the editors explained, is a "man whose name is even now glorified abroad, and especially in America."[136] "In America everyone knows his face; Nick Carter is alive. He is an inspector of the New York secret police and there are daily descriptions of the feats of this man, the greatest American genius, in all American newspapers."[137] V. A. Gladkov not only promoted his Kio-Hako as a real person, he treated him as a press celebrity in the stories. When Kio-Hako arrives in Venice to solve the case of *The Killer's Bloody Handkerchief* in the third issue of his serial, the detective has already been glorified in the newspapers. When he and his assistant appear in the street, they are greeted with cheers by "the simple-hearted Italians: 'Long live the detectives!' " The pretense that the stories were true was a device likely to appeal to un-educated and semi-educated readers who were suspicious of imaginative literature.

Installment Novels

Analogous to the detective serials were the installment novels, a Russian version of the roman-feuilleton, but one in which small portions of the novel were sold separately, each with a brightly colored cover, rather than serialized in a newspaper. The pagination was usually continuous, and the installments were divided wherever the sixteen- or thirty-two-page signature ended, often in the middle of a sentence. The first install-ment was frequently given away free or with the purchase of the second. The first issues were therefore published in very large editions, but the number of copies usually fell steadily as the novel progressed. Novels were sometimes sold in separate parts to a more educated audience in nineteenth-century Russia, but these were usually substantial, relatively complete portions of a story. There were twenty-six popular installment novels in 1908 alone.

The installment novels were no less Western than the detective serials, but their authors borrowed from an older source. The endless adventures and disguises of the heroes, the diabolical schemes of the villains and the grim fate that threatens the heroines are all similar to the narrative pattern elaborated by Eugene Sue and Ponson du Terrail. The installment bandits are constantly changing their disguises. They make speeches stating their noble intentions. The heroines fall into the clutches of villains and escape. Plots rise and fall on improbable riddles of parentage or melodramatic family dramas. Although a bandit is often the central figure of these stories, the allure of a puzzle and its solution is similar to that of the short detective adventure.

The heroes of the installment novels are usually Robin Hood-type robbers, who have been cast out of society through no fault of their own, and who go on to right wrongs and occasionally aid the poor. Typical novels were *The Cave of Leikhveis or 33 Years of Love and Fidelity*

Underground (1909-10) by V. A. Reder; *Robert Gaisler, the Head of the Death Bearers, or a Victim of Blind Justice* (1912), and *The Bandit Son Ataman Vilde and his Daring Band* (1912).

The Cave of Leikhveis was one of the most popular novels. The first installment appeared in 200,000 copies in the fall of 1909, and the seventy-fourth installment was published in 1910 in 65,000 copies. The early installments came out three times a week. Leikhveis is described as a minor nobleman in eighteenth century Wiesbaden. He is charged with a crime, but is guilty only of rescuing his beloved from an arranged marriage. Driven out of respectable court circles, living as a hunted renegade, he dreams of escape to America, but when his hopes are dashed, he becomes a bandit. He battles injustice, helps "the poor and oppressed," and defends women, but the main task confronting him and the lady who marries him, the countess Lora von Bergen, is the struggle with their personal enemies from their hideout in a cave.

The adventures of Gaisler and Vilde are similar to those of Leikhveis. Gaisler, a naive young doctor, is tricked into committing a murder by an evil countess, who pretends that her sister has died of unknown causes and has the unsuspecting Gaisler perform an instant autopsy. After the deed is done, Gaisler escapes to join a gang of forest robbers, becomes their chief, and converts most of the ruffians to good works.

A similar plot unfolds in the Vilde story. The novel begins typically for these works. "Help! Save us! Whip up the horses full speed ahead! Bandits!" shout two frightened aristocratic girls.[138] They are rescued by Hans Vilde, a young forester, who has been raised by their uncle. Vilde loves one of the young girls, but their uncle blasts his hopes of marriage by telling him the terrible secret of his patrimony, that his father was a bandit. Like Gaisler and many other heroes of this type, he then becomes a bandit chieftain.

Although bandit tales were the most numerous among the installment novels, other stories without bandits contained similar plots about heroes who find themselves outcasts. *Anton Petrov or the Bloody Day* (1914) is a story about a young Russian who craves adventure and joins the French Foreign Legion. As a Russian under French officers, fighting against Arabs, he is an outcast, and his efforts to prove himself and to return to his homeland are similar in some respects to the efforts of the bandits to rejoin their societies.

There were other types of installment novels with different kinds of plots. At the time of the Turkish Revolution, for instance, tales set in Turkey could be found among the installment novels as well as in the serialized stories of the kopeck newspapers. There were also adventures of wrestlers, dramas of mistreated and avenged women, stories about the marvels of science, and adventures in the tropics. In addition, some tales were about criminals and detectives, a few of them involving such characters as Holmes and Pinkerton, but most featuring other personalities. There were also stories in which crime itself was the focus of interest. Some of these works were offered to readers under such titles as "the secrets" of St. Petersburg, Odessa, Tomsk, and other cities.

A small but significant number of the installment novels are recognizable translations of familiar foreign works. Mark Twain's *The Prince and the Pauper* (1913) was sold in 1-kopeck installments. Edgar Allen Poe's *The Narrative of A. Gordon Pym* was published by *Gazeta kopeika* with the title *The Unusual Adventures of Arthur Pym* (1910) and sold in 2-kopeck installments in a first printing of 100,000 copies. Eugene Sue's *The Mysteries of Paris* (1910) and *The Wandering Jew* (1910) were both sold in 5-kopeck segments. The novels of Alexandre Dumas were also published, including his *Les Mohicans de Paris. Les Exploits de Rocambole*—the picturesque epic by Ponson du Terrail that had captivated French readers for many years—had circulated widely in Russia from the late nineteenth century. It was republished as an installment novel in 1910 in half a million copies, and parts 57 through 105 appeared in 25,000 copies each, still a sizable edition.

Like the roman-feuilleton, the installment novel belongs to the imaginative world of the newspaper, and the heroes and heroines were presented to their readers as real people. "His name thundered throughout all Germany in the eighteenth century, and whole legends about his feats and deeds passed from mouth to mouth" read a note on the cover of the first issue of *The Cave of Leikhveis*. But history was not the lure. Readers were told further that the cave was covered with the inscriptions of "tourists," and that "the ruling Emperor Wilhelm II himself was interested in the adventures of this remarkable man, and personally had visited the cave of Leikhveis." The author of the novel *The Countess Toiler* explained to her readers in an advertisement for the novel: "Readers of my novel, I have finally yielded after a long spiritual struggle to the request of my friends, to whom my sad fate was partly known, and have published my notes in the form of a novel."[139] "The detective called Hector Grinfeld in our essays is not Sherlock Holmes and is not a mythical person," explained the editors of *The Genius of Evil or the Famous Russian Detective Hector Grinfeld* (1907) by V. Osteral.[140]

This pretense of factuality was assurance to readers that by reading the novels they were acquiring information, much as they did when they read the newspapers. Admiration for "facts," as the American critic Dwight MacDonald has observed, is one of the characteristic qualities of modern popular culture.[141]

Publishers, Distributors, and Readers

The publishers of both the installment novels and the serials were dependent on the success of the cheap newspapers, their readership, and
their distributional networks. The well-established Moscow publishers
of popular literature issued little material of this type, probably because
they were already linked with extensive rural distribution networks and
because their success with existing materials made them wary of taking
chances with a different type of publication. The new fiction was produced primarily by new firms in St. Petersburg, Warsaw, Odessa, and a
few other provincial cities. The first Holmes serial was published by a
minor firm in Warsaw in 1907.[142] N. A. Aleksandrov, a St. Petersburg
publisher who had hitherto produced a little popular fiction, issued the
first mass edition of a Holmes serial in April 1908—in 40,000 copies at
7 kopecks each—*The Dagger of Negus*. He also published the first successful Pinkerton serial, *Nat Pinkerton—the King of Detectives* and the
successful Carter adventures, *Nick Carter—the American Sherlock
Holmes*. Another St. Petersburg firm, Razvlechenie (Entertainment), produced rival editions of detective serials and also the popular *The Cave
of Leikhveis*. Among the most successful publishers of the installment
novels were several Warsaw firms including S. A. Kaufman, R. B. Liubich,
Polza (Use), and Pechatnoe Slovo (Printed Word).

The appearance of the provincial firms in popular publishing indicates
the expansion and decentralization of the industry. This was a result of
the new opportunities inherent in the expansion of the reading public
and from the increased availability of distribution outlets, most notably
kiosks and small shops. The development of new firms in the publishing
of these types of materials runs counter to the trend in lubok literature,
over which Sytin had nearly acquired a monopoly. The installment and
serial novels became popular in the capitals and in other urban areas. A
journalist observed in a pedagogical magazine in 1909 that during that
year "the literature of crime detection" had prevailed over all types of
printed materials at newsstands, in railroad and tram cars, as well as
among pupils and students.[143]

Street sales of detective adventures were substantial. Even in 1915,
long after the rage for these stories had peaked, the Chief Administration
for Press Affairs recorded street sales in St. Petersburg of 288,225 copies
of Nat Pinkertons, 72,380 Nick Carters, and 68,979 Holmeses.[144] A
scruffy peddler of Pinkertons and other cheap publications was shown
in a 1911 (no. 38) photographic essay in *Ogonek*. The peddler, in a beat-
up worker's cap, is kneeling before a motley collection of publications

spread out on a bast mat. "The book peddlers of the capital," reads the caption, "roam the outlying markets and go beyond the Neva embankment with their distinctive portable bookshops." In Moscow, similar sales were observed. One commentator noted the widespread sale of serials and installment novels in the suburbs and small towns surrounding the city, as well as the appearance of impromptu libraries among the owners of small shops and newspaper sellers who rented out these works at a kopeck each.[145] The Warsaw firm of S. A. Kaufman advertised for distributors in *Gazeta kopeika* (no. 852, 1910) under the heading "Newspaper commerce, kiosks, wholesalers, and bookstores." The publisher promised, "It is possible to earn a lot on our publications." Potential distributors were offered sole rights of sale in their cities for best-selling novels (*khodkie romany*), complete stories, and novels divided into a number of parts. The detective serial publisher N. A. Aleksandrov announced on the back cover of one of the early Pinkertons that the serial was available at all newsstands and bookstores and by subscription through the firm's representatives in Moscow, Vilna, Odessa, Ekaterinoslav, Warsaw, and Kiev.[146]

Contemporary observers believed that the detective stories were read by young people, primarily boys, and by workers and other members of the lower classes. This view is probably correct. A few of the stories show the marks of a juvenile literature. The Razvlechenie serial *Indian Chiefs* was described in an advertisement as "suitable for the young" as well as of general interest.[147] Some detectives had young helpers with whom younger readers might be expected to identify. Nevertheless, the majority of the stories seem to have appealed to adults, or at least to young adults. "Hail to Nat Pinkerton, the chief, the ideal and hero of millions," wrote the critic Kornei Chukovskii.[148] The workers were Pinkerton readers, he observed in another prerevolutionary essay. "For a long time I could not believe my eyes when I saw the way the workers were gobbling up Nat Pinkerton."[149] Bookstores in the working-class area of St. Petersburg sold these types of works together with other cheap publications, including *Gazeta kopeika*, and a lesser number of schoolbooks and children's books.[150] "They read Nat Pinkerton and are satisfied with that," complained a trade unionist at a meeting of workers in publishing in 1910.[151]

The serials even trickled into the villages. According to a study of fourteen- and fifteen-year-old St. Petersburg city school children, a fifth of the children who had read detective stories became acquainted with them in the countryside, where they bought them at a railroad station or from returning workers, soldiers, or vacationing gymnasium pupils.[152] In one village the books "went from hand to hand," in the words of a pupil, and were read by the entire literate population, adolescents and adults alike.

The authors of the serial adventures could have few illusions about their readers' sophistication. In response to questions from "numerous" readers, V. A. Gladkov felt compelled to explain why his stories about a Japanese detective were printed in Russian rather than Japanese. "Readers," Gladkov wrote after printing two Japanese words in Russian transliteration, "you will hardly guess the secret of these two words if you wrack your brains for a whole year."[153] To publish both Russian and Japanese versions with facing texts, he added, would be a waste of space.

Readers continued to demand and read the detective serials and installment novels after the Revolution, although their production was halted and the stock of existing works was gradually depleted.[154] A 1924 survey of young Moscow workers revealed that nearly half were acquainted with the stories of Pinkerton and Holmes.[155] Some of this material clearly remained in circulation, and it retained its allure.

In contrast to the lubok tales, the new street literature of detective adventures appealed simultaneously to widely varying levels of readers. The writer and regular columnist in Suvorin's conservative newspaper *Novoe vremia* (New Times), V. V. Rozanov, observed that one could confiscate the forty-eight-page Sherlock Holmes booklets from the children, but then afterwards one would be tempted to sin by reading the booklets oneself until four in the morning.[156] The Soviet writer Marietta Shaginian, who produced a revolutionary version of the serial novel in the early 1920s, recalled nearly sixty years later how, as a twenty-year-old, she had bought the successive issues of the Pinkerton adventures and had read them with satisfaction in the evenings.[157] The novels were popular, she recalled, because they were stimulating. Readers were confronted with a puzzling problem in the first few pages, and they could read on until the problem was solved. The novels also presented a clear image of the struggle between good and evil, and the positive heroes were always certain to bring the evil criminals to justice.[158]

Verbitskaia and the Women's Novels

A final type of popular commercial fiction that had a substantial claim on the imagination of a wide circle of readers in the early twentieth century was the woman's novel, particularly that created by Anastasia Alekseevna Verbitskaia (1861-1928). Verbitskaia, a moderately successful contributor to thick journals, burst noisily onto the Russian literary scene after the Revolution of 1905 with a series of multivolume potboilers. She appealed for attention to emotions and personal fulfillment, and borrowed thoughts from a number of Western European thinkers, including Friedrich Nietzsche and George Sand, among others. Her characters led adventurous lives, and Verbitskaia advocated women's rights at a time when there was a substantial movement for the emancipation of women in Russia.[159] Her works seemed intended for relatively prosperous women, but their attraction was clearly much wider. Chukovskii mocked radicals who believed in proletarian art in 1911 with the observation that the workers went from Pinkerton to Verbitskaia.[160]

Verbitskaia's leap from uncelebrated but respectable mediocrity to clamorous renown began inauspiciously, according to her account, with the publication of her first big novel, *The Spirit of the Times* (1907), at her own expense, on credit.[161] That the novel had not been serialized first in one of the thick journals was unusual; that it nevertheless sold well was still more so.[162] Within a year she brought out the first volume of a second fat book entitled *The Keys to Happiness*. Six volumes appeared between 1908 and 1913, with an average of nearly 35,000 copies each.[163] At this time an edition of over 10,000 was unusual, and even popular respected writers such as M. P. Artsybashev, A. I. Kamenskii, and A. V. Amfiteatrov seldom topped it. When her fame peaked in 1914, more than twenty books had appeared in over half a million copies.[164] So successful was she that an enterprising charlatan who wrote under the pen name of Count Amori was able to sell tens of thousands of his own version of the ending to *The Keys to Happiness*, and also two volumes of a fictitious biography of Verbitskaia herself, entitled *The Amorous Adventures of Madame Verbitskaia*, which also sold very well.[165]

Verbitskaia was distinguished from well-liked serious writers by the air of scandal that surrounded her success and the unmitigated hostility of the educated critics. Maxim Gorky sold better than Verbitskaia at the height of his success, but he enjoyed the respect of an audience that stretched from educated readers and their critics down to a much lower reading public. Verbitskaia's novels were never considered belles lettres. Her success was like that of the sensational English writer, Elinor Glyn (1864-1943),[166] whose *Three Weeks* (1907) created a furor similar to that of *The Keys to Happiness*. Verbitskaia's novels also resembled the works of the late nineteenth-century English romancer Marie Corelli (1855-1924) in their melodramatic tone and the way in which "the public" discovered them for themselves. Corelli also built up a gigantic readership on syrupy romances the critics ridiculed.[167] What distinguished Verbitskaia's work from other types of Russian popular fiction was her presumption that her writing was the equal of serious literature. This assertion, in addition to other characteristics that distinguish her work

FIG. 5. TOP LEFT: Petr Nikolaevich Sharapov, a lubok publisher and furrier for whom I. D. Sytin worked, from *Pol veka dlia knigi* (Moscow: Sytin, 1916). TOP RIGHT: Frontispiece to A. A. Verbitskaia, *To My Reader* (Moscow: Verbitskaia, 1908). CENTER: The cantonal administration building in Gnezdnikov, in which Sytin went to school and where his father worked as a clerk. BOTTOM: I. D. Sytin. From *Pol veka dlia knigi* (Moscow: Sytin, 1916).

155

from the contemporary belles lettres, gives her novels something of the quality of a modern best-seller. In this she was an innovator.

Verbitskaia became a celebrity, and her public stance added to her success. She presented herself to her readers in two volumes of auto-biography, *To My Reader* (1908) and *My Memoirs—Youth, Dreams* (1911), each of which contained several signed pictures of the writer. According to her own account, she resembled her heroines. She was born into a prosperous officer's family in Voronezh, but her father's career faltered and he died while she was in her early teens. The family lived poorly on a country estate, and she and her sister received a secondary education at an institute for girls. Her talent was discovered by a teacher who remarked: "If you decide to write, I admit, something will come of you."[168] Her sudden poverty cost her a suitor, who demanded a dowry of 10,000 rubles.[169]

She and her sister then sought work as governesses. They went to the Moscow Society of Governesses and presented their qualifications, with their blushing and embarrassed mother standing by. Interviews with pro-spective employers meant humiliation before uncultured and insensitive people, and the young Verbitskaia insulted one couple by announcing that she disliked children. At the Society, watching the elderly governesses file by, the young Verbitskaia took fright: "To be a governess for an entire lifetime. Oh God, save me and Shura from this bitter lot. Let it only be a stage on our path" (p. 207). Like so many other figures in the world of popular publishing, Verbitskaia experienced "the struggle for existence," in the contemporary Social Darwinist phrase, and it is no accident that this was a major theme of her work.

The making of careers was the subject of Verbitskaia's three big novels, *The Spirit of the Times* (1907), *The Keys to Happiness* (1908-13), and *The Yoke of Love* (1914). Her heroines are all performing artists. They start out in deprivation, lacking money and lovers. What they have is "talent." Talent is everything in Verbitskaia's world. The talent of the wealthy hero of *The Spirit of the Times*, Toboltsev, carries him from a position as director of an amateur troupe to that of a "rising star" whose place is "in the capital" (1:76). Attention in this novel, set at the time of the 1905 Revolution, then shifts to Katia, a young music teacher, who also has talent and supports a sister and an invalid mother. A series of lucky coincidences lands Katia a minor role in Toboltsev's troupe. Her part is a great success. She is recognized as someone with "surprising talent," and, after a triumphant performance, wins the love of Toboltsev and a million-ruble marriage (1:104).

Through her talent, Mania, the ingénue heroine of *The Keys to Hap-piness*, wins the affections of a fabulously wealthy Jewish magnate who becomes her patron and lover. He takes her to Paris where she realizes her "cherished dream" and becomes the famous "Marian," known and beloved by all Paris. *The Yoke of Love*, the last of Verbitskaia's novels, is also about the realization of talent. Nadezhda, a poor wardrobe seamstress, catches the eye of a famous actress, who thinks she might be "a natural talent." Soon the former seamstress is living in a glittering and exciting world.

Verbitskaia's tales have none of the perilous escapades that distinguish the newspaper serials and some of the installment stories, but the heroines have rivals and enemies who try to thwart their progress. At the top of the ladder are wealth and love. "Never had she seen such luxury even at a distance," thinks Katia, the music teacher, as she enters a luxurious dacha provided for her by her millionaire husband, Toboltsev (1:306). " 'What splendor,' said Mania, stopping in the study before originals by Rembrandt, Dürer, and Van Dyke" in *The Keys to Happiness* (1:52). Emotional fulfillment means love and adventures in love. The heroines sail through triangles and quadrilaterals always to true love—and sometimes also to disaster. Katia's Toboltsev seduces two other women during the course of their romance. Mania drifts back and forth between a cultured and progressive Jewish magnate and a reactionary aristocratic monarchist, who "loved like a savage" (2:42). Nadezhda floats helplessly between a good-for-nothing drunken comedian and a worthy tragedian, and ends up with the wrong actor.

The descriptions of these love affairs seemed scandalous to contemporary readers, perhaps because of Verbitskaia's penchant for characters swept away by blind impersonal desires. Toboltsev is drawn blindly toward the bed of Katia's sister: "He embraced Sonia and again felt—a day dream!—the touch of her breasts, knees, the sleepy smell of her mouth, which constantly intoxicated him" (1:127). Mania likewise falls helplessly into passion: "Ah, to forget oneself, to feel ecstasy, to feel oneself again a goddess on earth" (2:155-56).

Talent's path to a career is also a path to culture. For Verbitskaia's heroines, culture meant knowledge of the great names, familiarity with famous places, and, most of all, the triumph over ignorance. Mania in the *Keys to Happiness* is taken through Europe and Russia by the knowledgeable Jewish magnate Steinbach. In Italy, Steinbach lectures Mania and the reader at length: "Dante was the Homer of Italy" (3:70). In Florence: "As in Greece and Rome the flowering of art here was also connected to political liberation" (3:70). The travel sections extend as much as a hundred pages without respite: "Every day they were in the museum, and in the evening they read Von Fricken's *History of Art*" (3:79). In the travelogues readers glimpse high culture through the eyes and experience of the protagonists. Steinbach takes Mania to the Louvre: "A gloomy four-cornered building spread out before her" (3:209). Scraps of philosophy, dance, the theater, and the world of art all blend into the plots of the novels. "Is she not Desdemona?" wonders Nadezhda in *The Yoke of Love* (p. 231). One can almost feel Verbitskaia's readers trying to retain these snippets, these ersatz capsules of culture. One critic called her works a kind of cultural "department store," in which all manner of interesting things could be found.[170]

Women's emancipation and progressive politics were also part of Verbitskaia's public stance. Before she became famous, she wrote sympathetically and emotionally about the problems of women as writers, schoolteachers, and family members.[171] As a publisher she specialized in translations of foreign novels about the plight of women. In her novels women are urged to liberate themselves and to realize their potential, but men remain the arbiters of their lives. Mania in *The Keys to Happiness* announces that she wishes to be mistress of her fate, but it is a man who says "Very well, I will give you the keys to happiness" (1:107). The Pygmalion-Galatea myth recurs again and again in the novels, as male patrons form the women to their own specifications. "Your soul is clay in my hands, and I am fashioning a beautiful statue from it," says Toboltsev to one of his mistresses (1:148). She urged her women readers to "be themselves," as her sympathetic contemporary biographer explained,[172] but Verbitskaia's personal liberation meant primarily escape from class and from the oppression of poverty, not of men.

Verbitskaia also considered herself a Social Democrat. She participated in the Revolution of 1905 and the "strictly determined aim" of her publishing house, she explained in 1911, was "criticism of the bourgeois order in the West."[173] Her novels are sprinkled with political references.[174] Mania finds seats in a crowded theater for a few haphazardly encountered workers who tell her, "We are not bourgeois; there is no place for us in the theater" (4:158). "I will dance for them," she says to herself. Steinbach sympathizes with the Social Democrats and ultimately gives his land and factory to the peasants, but, like Toboltsev, he remains a spokesman for the self. When Mania considers social action, he comments, "All paths lead to Rome; all roads lead to liberation. Choose your own" (3:200). Mania does just that, abandoning her career to fall at the feet of the Black Hundred's leader and anti-Semite, Nelidov. Political demands and allegiances never force Verbitskaia's protagonists to give up their wealth or social positions. No political message emerges from her writings other than the idea of self-cultivation, which had something in common with the message of the intellectuals involved in the *Landmarks* (*Vekhi*) symposium, who in 1909 urged educated Russians to abandon politics for their own spiritual and cultural pursuits.

Verbitskaia's novels, with their success stories and guidebook culture, revolutionary trappings and fleshy individualism, romantic interludes and morbid melodrama, suggest a particular reading audience. They seem beyond the reach of the lower classes in price and subject, and they have none of the folkloric touches that characterize the lubok literature. They were, at the same time, vulgar and corny compared with serious contemporary works of belles lettres. Although her emphasis on emotions seems to resemble the stress on experience in the writings of some of her more accomplished contemporaries who belonged to the literary movement broadly defined as modernism, Verbitskaia spoke to a different audience for whom the message had a different meaning. To shop girls and others who were bound to work for their daily bread, Verbitskaia's emphasis on feelings did not point so much to self-discovery as to an escape from routine and drudgery. What she created was a surrogate literature for readers who did not attain the level of contemporary belles lettres.

Verbitskaia's critics were not in agreement about the social composition of her readership, but all seemed to include a middling component. A critic in *Russkie vedomosti* (no. 7, 1911) suggested she appealed primarily to girls working in shops and trades. Kornei Chukovskii thought her works were read more widely, but that they showed the taste of barbers, shopkeepers, and servants: "The stamp of their aesthetic is on every work."[175] This is plausible. Her fantasies of upward mobility could appeal to a very wide audience, but her long-winded and naive pronouncements about culture suggest a readership willing to accept such digressions as the price of a little learning on the cheap. Her readers were probably people who had escaped wholly or partially from lower-class origins and had a smattering of education. Such people existed in substantial numbers in the early twentieth century and they made great efforts to obtain positions in industry, in the railroads, and in the service sector as, for example, schoolteachers, midwives, and medical assistants. Their politics were likely to be on the left, and Verbitskaia's radical political speechifying and her ritual praise of socialism may have pleased them. Her hostile remarks about the bourgeoisie may have also struck a sympathetic chord among the "newly arrived."

Verbitskaia's notoriety seems also to have drawn a large audience. In her heyday, she headed the list of most-read authors at libraries and public reading rooms.[176] Her readers were thought to be primarily women. She created heroines with adventuresome lives who did not give a care for children or family, but who in the end suffered enormously for their independence. Readers could enjoy these feats of daring vicariously, and at the same time console themselves for their more prudent and humdrum lives. On finishing a Verbitskaia potboiler, readers could conclude that home and hearth were best, after all. Although Verbitskaia's readers did not have the adventures of her heroines, they also did not have to face the consequences of those adventures, which were invariably ruin and despair.

The antifeminist resolutions to Verbitskaia's novels are so sweeping that they obliterate the positive accomplishments of the heroines in the world outside family and marriage. At a time when it was possible to write very freely about women's emancipation and sexual questions, it seems unlikely that Verbitskaia merely tacked on these endings to make it possible to state the liberated message. Nor does the occasional portrayal of sexual themes appear to explain her success, since such topics were dealt with more explicitly by other authors. It was instead the combination of emancipation and submission that appealed to her readers. The same appeal may account for Verbitskaia's popularity among young Communist women soon after the October Revolution.[177]

Other women writers were able to attract some of Verbitskaia's audience. E. Nagrodskaia's *The Wrath of Dionysius* had a scandalous success much like Verbitskaia's *The Keys to Happiness*. It was published in a tiny first edition of 500 copies in 1910 at 1.50 rubles, and went through nine editions by the end of 1915 in a total of 21,500 copies.[178] Princess O. Bebutova, author of *The Path to a Career* and *Gold Dust*, a two-volume artistic success story in the style of Verbitskaia, was also popular. The first volume of this work appeared in two editions of 10,000 copies each in 1917.[179]

The sale of 20,000 copies of a book by a single author priced at a ruble or more, even when the sales took place over several years, was unusual in early twentieth-century Russia. Despite the hostile reports by liberal critics, these women achieved great popularity. The authoritative newsletter of the Wolf Bookstore reported that during the first ten months of World War I, the women writers—Bebutova, Verbitskaia, Lappo-Danilevskaia, and, to a lesser degree, Nagrodskaia—were selling best of all at the large St. Petersburg bookstores.[180] Since none of these writers was published by important firms, this was a considerable achievement. A peripheral member of this group was the writer of girls' adventure stories, L. A. Charskaia. Charskaia, whose romantic tales were published by the Wolf firm, dabbled in fiction similar to the women's novels, with such works as *Her Majesty Love*, which was published by Kaspari,[181] and her 1913 serialized romance in *Rodina*, "The Power of the Earth."

Other Cheap Fiction

Was there a male equivalent to the women's fiction? There were novels without special interest to women that do seem suitable for a semi-educated audience of either sex—more sophisticated than the lubok readers, but remote from more serious writing. Pazukhin's many novels, some of which were originally serialized in *Moskovskii listok*, were issued separately, and so were novels by feuilletonists such as N. N. Breshko-Breshkovskii, who wrote many adventure stories for *Priroda i liudi*. One of Breshko-Breshkovskii's stories was *The Shame of the Dynasty*, a steamy tale featuring the debauched monk Rasputin. The resourceful Count Amori, who cashed in successfully on Verbitskaia's fame, also wrote many novels that sold well for a ruble or more. Count Amori's ending to Kuprin's novel *Yama* (1913) appeared in 17,000 copies, in three editions. His *The Bloody Track, Secrets of Nevskii Prospect*, and *Secrets of the Japanese Court* were each published in 10,000 copies or more in 1914. He also wrote cheaper tales, including an installment novel entitled *The Criminal Banker* (1913), which sold for 5 kopecks and appeared in a first issue of 50,000 copies; *The Daughter of Wilhelm II* (1914) in 18,000 copies, also at 5 kopecks; and *The Countess-Artist* (1916) in 25,000 copies at 20 kopecks.

A sprinkling of relatively expensive works by anonymous authors appeared in the early twentieth-century catalogues of lubok publishers. In 1910, N. A. Kholmushin listed *Vanka Kain, the Famous Moscow Detective* and *The Terrible Rogue and the Bandit Churkin* (in four parts) for a ruble. A. T. Kuzin offered readers *Makarka the Murderer* and *Vanka Kain* for 1.60 rubles each in 1914. The Moscow publisher A. S. Balashov listed Churkin and Kain stories at 1.20 rubles each in a 1912 catalogue, and A. D. Sazonov offered similar works in a 1914 catalogue. The actual prices of these types of books, however, were apparently lower than those for the women's novels. Sazonov, according to his 1914 catalogue, offered titles to his dealers at one-tenth of their suggested selling price, so that a book with 1.50 rubles printed on the cover could be sold profitably for 25 kopecks. The women's novels, which had larger pages, better paper, and were sold primarily through established bookstores were unlikely to have been offered at such discounts.

Still lower in price, but not more widely distributed, were stories by A. P. Aleksandrovskii and Kh. A. Shukhmin, two authors whose writings were characteristic of some of the more vulgar newsstand materials. These works appeared in large numbers of titles in editions of 5,000 and occasionally as high as 10,000 copies, and were among the few works that had a clearly right-wing tone. Aleksandrovskii, who was published by the patriotic firm of Balashov, produced risqué titles such as *The Wedding Night of a Father and a Daughter* (1910), and *The Unsuccessful Marriage of the Seventeen-Year-Old Katia* (1913). The stories were generally more suggestive than pornographic, and they were also heavily loaded with traditional morality. In *The Unsuccessful Marriage of the Seventeen-Year-Old Katia*, the daughter of a poor government clerk who lives with her widowed mother in a working-class district in Moscow is seduced by the rakish married son of a rich Volga merchant. The seducer's plans for marriage miscarry when his wife's relative spies him in the street, and brings his abandoned wife to the planned wedding. Exposed and humiliated, the villain shoots himself. Katia retreats to a nunnery.

Kh. A. Shukhmin was a successful humorist, a gift he eventually put to use as a war propagandist. Typical of his pre-World War I prose was *How the Devil Stole a Mother-in-Law's Tongue—A True Story of the Twentieth Century* (1913). "As soon as people invented marriage," he begins, "the mother-in-law was also invented."[182] The hero of the story is an unsuccessful young writer, plagued by a rich but unfriendly mother-in-law in whose house he lives. After a number of such affronts, the young man contemplates suicide, but the devil appears and offers to steal the mother-in-law's troublesome tongue. The devil explains that he would like to add the sharp tongue to his instruments of torture. He appears in the guise of a doctor, gets the mother-in-law to stick out her tongue and "with inhuman force, seized it, tore at it, and ripped it out" (p. xiv). Silenced, the mother-in-law realizes the error of her ways, and an angel promises her a new and better tongue. Shukhmin, who was also published by the right-wing firm of Balashov, wrote sentimental and salacious tales in addition to his humorous ones. Later, as a prolific World War I propagandist, Shukhmin produced such fictional and satirical diatribes as *Wilhelm's Journey through the World on the Devil's Tail* (1914) and *Wilhelm in the Sultan's Harem or the Bloody Feast* (1914).

Perhaps the only novels with a male orientation that overlapped with those of Verbitskaia were those by more or less respectable neo-realist writers such as M. P. Artsybashev and A. P. Kamenskii, both of whom wrote about sexual questions and did almost as well as the women writers, largely as a result of the scandal surrounding their works. Male adventure writers such as V. I. Nemirovich-Danchenko and A. V. Amfiteatrov also established a substantial audience.

Information, Ideas, and Entertainment

The development of the popular periodical brought about far-reaching changes in the character of the information, ideas, and entertainment available to the common reader. Periodicals had a wide impact on many aspects of the experience of those ordinary people who were able to obtain them. The appearance of the newspaper and magazine illustrations and the sometimes lurid covers of the installment novels and detective adventure serials was also an important step in the formation of a new popular visual language, just as the popular prose constituted a new language in print. Drawings and photographs of people and places in the news were a lesson in how the world could be presented on a flat surface for people whose only previous exposure to pictorial representation may have been icons, lubok prints, and an occasional shop sign. Even the illustrations that appeared in newspaper advertisements were important, as people learned to interpret various styles of representation. The most colorful of the new popular illustrations were the brightly colored prints produced by the new technique of chromolithography and popularized initially by Marx in *Niva*. The *Niva* bonus pictures were the first serious rivals to the traditional lubok prints among the peasants. The same technique was used to produce the colored cover illustrations for the installment novels and the detective serials, as well as for the lubok tales. The development of the half-tone engraving process that made it possible to reproduce photographs without redrawing also led to dramatic changes in popular visual imagery.[183]

The styles of illustration found in the periodical press in pictures ranged from scenes of exotic places and idealized peasant girls in romantic poses found in *Niva* to more severe drawings and photographs in the early twentieth-century newspapers and magazines. This style in the popular press was contemporaneous with the widespread appreciation and reproduction of the seemingly realistic but also sentimental paintings of the Wanderers school (*Peredvizhniki*). The paintings of these artists were made into *Niva* bonus prints and were later reproduced and sold by the editors of the St. Petersburg *Gazeta kopeika*.

The periodicals, serial detective adventures, and installment stories with their recurrent formulas, familiar plots, and exotic settings provided both information and entertainment for large numbers of Russian readers. The information was often supplemental to the daily newspaper. Sometimes a political message appeared in the stories published after 1905. Usually the bias was vaguely leftist, as in the serials of the Moscow kopeck newspaper and Verbitskaia's novels. More rarely there was a liberal tone, as in P. Nikitin's Holmes series. Occasionally, as in a few of the Nick Carter serials, there was sympathy for struggle against revolution. These scattered political flourishes reveal the writers' sensitivity to the highly politicized atmosphere following the Revolution of 1905. Their tilt toward the left, in contrast to the lubok authors of the late nineteenth century, is indicative of the general shift of public opinion. None of the stories was primarily political, however. Politically motivated writers could find more satisfactory outlets to get across their message than popular literature. Those on the left were served by a variety of legal and illegal publications, ranging from thick journals and the trade union press, to illegal leaflets and pamphlets.

The authors of the serial and periodical literature succeeded even more than those who created the lubok fiction in forming a new language of the imagination that was shared by large numbers of ordinary people, particularly in the cities. The Churkin and Krechet stories became the subjects of some of the earliest popular silent films, and the actors who specialized in playing the bandits made careers out of the roles—E. Petrov-Kraevskii as Churkin and A. Zheliabuzhskii as Krechet.[184] *The Keys to Happiness* was also filmed in 1913 and was one of the longest of the pre-World War I films.[185] Authors such as Pazukhin, Count Amori, and Breshko-Breshkovskii had second careers writing film scenarios and adapting their fiction to the screen.[186] The stories that readers found captivating in print were recreated visually, just as the earlier lubok tales had provided subjects and heroes for the lively colored lubok illustrations.

The main difference between the periodical literature of the newspaper serials and the older lubok booklets of the colporteurs was that for the first time readers were exposed to the sustained influence of the printed word. Readers' imaginations were captured by the newspaper serials at the same time that their interests were engaged in the day-to-day commentary on events at home and abroad. The authors of the newspaper serials could therefore exert a greater influence on the imagination and consciousness of their readers than could the lubok writers. Unlike the lubok booklets, the serials were usually read simultaneously by groups of lower-class readers who shared in the development of the plot, the feats of the heroes and heroines, and in the descriptions of different locales. Readers who did not understand some aspect of the story could ask others among their friends who were likely to be reading the same day's adventure. For this reason, the writers of the newspaper serials could assume greater collective sophistication on the part of their readers than could the lubok authors.

The same continuing influence on readers that made the newspapers the most powerful vehicle for acquainting the ordinary people with the printed word was at work in the success of the serial adventure stories and the installment novels. The authors might have some difficulty beginning with a subject readers knew little or nothing about, but once successfully begun, there was a self-sustaining quality to these works. After reading one detective serial, readers already knew something about the world displayed in other popular detective stories, and the same was true for many of the installment novels. Such stories were important in establishing a popular demand for genres of fiction. Authors were able to address a growing expectation on the part of readers that a work would follow certain general outlines that could be anticipated. In this sense, readers learned to seek out particular types of works.

The serial adventures, and possibly the installment novels as well, may have had a more diverse audience than the newspaper feuilleton. Reports of the popularity of the Pinkertons are suggestive. The Pinkerton craze, which enveloped people on different social levels in the same fantasies, had a modern aspect to it. The diffusion of these publications across class lines meant that certain day dreams, as well as their personification in particular heroes and heroines, were widely shared. The establishment of a popular literature that satisfied readers of different classes is also evinced by the popularity of the novels of Verbitskaia and other women writers. Verbitskaia's vogue was similar to that of the Pinkertons, with the difference that her novels cost more, were more difficult to read, and appealed to a better-heeled audience. Her novels also represented a step toward a new and more homogeneous popular literature that transcended class boundaries.

The development of a corpus of fantasies and information accessible to the new common reader had momentous consequences for the adoption of new attitudes and for the transformation of old ones. By seeking out these new publications and reading them, ordinary people developed a more modern and cosmopolitan orientation toward the world around them. Their receptiveness to the new ideas in popular literature suggests that the ideas were reinforced by other nonliterary experiences in the lives of ordinary people. Some of these changes in attitudes and ideas are explored in the next four chapters.

V

BANDITS: IDEAS

OF FREEDOM AND ORDER

THE NEW popular culture of common literacy developed during a time when the lives of ordinary people were changing. What did these changes mean to lower-class readers? Can we learn anything from the fiction about the development of popular attitudes toward what was constant and what was changing in the lives of ordinary Russians? Why did the readers choose one sort of story instead of another? Is it possible to identify imaginative formulas that are characteristically Russian in the fiction? Or, on the contrary, do we find that the literature is similar to that of other countries? The answers to these questions are the subjects of the next four chapters, each of which is about the evolution of a single broad theme in the fiction.

Four Themes in the Popular Fiction

The themes are freedom and rebellion, national identity, science and superstition, and success. They are prominent in the literature and central to this study's thesis that the Russian common readers began to think of themselves and the world around them in increasingly individualistic and self-conscious terms. The four themes are also prominent in the study of the popular cultures of Western Europe and North America and are therefore suitable for cross-cultural comparisons. In the Russian context, these themes have a special import, since they show the beginnings of precisely the change that Belinsky so desired—the gradual transformation of the Russian muzhik from an ignorant villager bedeviled by superstitions and resigned to a fate of poverty and exploitation, to a citizen of a nation and an individual with opportunities, curiosity, energy, and ambition.

The first theme, freedom and rebellion, is the most important. The image of the rebellious individual was a complex one for Russian popular writers to conceptualize, not so much because censorship precluded portrayal of revolutionary heroes, but because there was no tradition of successful revolt. There was, on the contrary, a great fear of disorder and its consequences, and an acceptance of the need to submit to established authority. The popular writers wrestled with this legacy, and they created heroes who exemplified the tension between freedom and order. Yet Russia was on the verge of one of the major rebellions in history, and the writers also produced stories that reflected and stimulated disrespect for established authority.

The treatment of the second theme, national identity, also evinces the growth of new attitudes. The issue of what it meant to be a citizen of the Russian Empire was a pressing one at a time when traditional religious and political loyalties came under great stress. The popular writers shifted their attention from the tsar and the Orthodox Church as symbols of national pride. In place of tsar and Church, they began to explore the physical and human geography of the empire as definitions of what it meant to be Russian. They pointed out with pride the great expanse of empire. They portrayed the diversity of peoples and showed the place of Great Russians among them. By doing this the popular writers presented their readers with a more complex and more reflective idea of Russianness. As a result, they inadvertently propagated an idea of empire that could survive the fall of the tsar and the state Church.

Science and superstition were subjects of great interest to Russian popular writers and to their readers as well. The transition from an oral to a written culture meant the identification of new sources of authority and the rejection of some old ones. Popular literature is a naive literature, and when the writers addressed questions of science and superstition they left their readers in no doubt about where they stood. They debunked superstitions and encouraged a rational approach to the natural world. They even began to explore the promise of science and technology. On one level, they simply provided the curious with information, but on another they discredited familiar beliefs and demonstrated the power of reasoning.

The last theme is that of success and social mobility, and it is here that a new individuality and self-awareness are most fully apparent. The popular writers presented their readers with upwardly mobile heroes and heroines almost from the time of the emancipation. They made happiness and prosperity the rewards of energy and virtue. They generally disavowed forbearance, a time-honored religious response to poverty and misfortune, and they ignored the ideals of solidarity and social progress promoted by growing numbers of revolutionary activists. Yet, as in the treatment of the themes, the authors expressed a very Russian view of the world, and their success stories differ in very interesting ways from those produced in the United States, for example.

The analysis of these themes is not without difficulties.[1] Russian popular commercial literature was in its infancy during the prerevolutionary period. The themes took shape only gradually and for the most part they never had the consistency of a popular genre such as the American success story or the Western novel. The analysis depends in part on an appreciation of the different types of fiction. The literature of the lubok, the newspaper serials, the detective stories and the installment novels, and the women's fiction all had different audiences with different needs and interests. The lubok fiction had a wide rural readership, and even in the late nineteenth and early twentieth centuries it was the most conservative in most respects. The newspaper serials were directed toward a more urban audience, whose horizons tended to be wider. The detective stories and installment novels also reached a primarily urban readership, but one that was young and therefore likely to adopt new ideas and attitudes. The women's novels, which found favor with a more prosperous readership, reveal a different perspective on the same issues.

Comparisons with Western European and American fiction highlight the Russianness of this literature, as well as its cosmopolitan aspects. The Western European and American popular fiction that most approximates the Russian was that published from the middle of the nineteenth century to the early twentieth. Even though Western Europe and North America had much higher rates of literacy and were far more industrialized at this time than Russia, regular reading of daily newspapers, serialized novels, and other popular fiction became commonplace among ordinary people only in the second half of the nineteenth century. This was partly a result of technical progress and partly due to other causes. Cheap popular newspapers, for example, began to appear in England and France only in the 1860s and 1870s, and this is the time when the first dime novel was published in America.[2] There existed in a sense a common popular culture that was shared by Western Europe and America in the half century before World War I, but Russia, as a poor cousin of more literate neighbors, could borrow little until the end of the period. Whether borrowing from foreign sources, however, or drawing on their own imaginations, Russian popular writers addressed their market, and even in translating foreign novels publishers had to be very choosy in order to satisfy the demands of the new readers.

Rebellious Heroes in Popular Fiction

Bandits were important in lubok and newspaper serial fiction, and popular writers who developed these heroes drew on folklore and history to dramatize longstanding issues in Russian culture. Bandits were the most important protagonists of the installment novels that gained popularity in the early twentieth century, and the private detective, in some ways an analogous figure, was the preeminent hero of the serialized adventure stories that flourished at the same time. The fact that the writers were most successful with these types of characters rather than with other more socially and politically acceptable ones, such as the frontiersman, the explorer, or even the self-sufficient Cossack defender of the border-lands, is evidence of the centrality of the bandit and later the detective in the Russian popular imagination.

The more traditional lubok and newspaper serial tales of bandits and criminals illustrate two fundamental issues in Russian culture. The re-lationship between the individual and society is explored, and society is shown inevitably to be the stronger of the two. The states of freedom and order are juxtaposed and shown to be mutually exclusive. Those who choose freedom must live outside the social order, and they are doomed by their decision. Bandits and criminals are outsiders whose freedom is a challenge to society and order. In their fictional lives and adventures, these characters question what place a self-assertive and re-bellious individual can occupy within or outside society.

The bold outlaws who abandon the social order and eventually return to it, either redeemed or broken, have much in common with the heroes of the monomyth, whose journey to another world and ultimate return to earth is incarnate in many religions, including Christianity. Joseph Campbell has described this cycle of adventure, which is also prevalent in literature, as a progression through rites of passage of separation, initiation, and return.[3] Many stories in Western popular literature follow this pattern,[4] and their Russian counterparts that were written for a less educated audience do as well, with several important differences. Russian bandits and criminals seek readmittance to society on society's terms. Unlike the heroes of the monomyth and classic figures of Western popular culture such as Tarzan, Horatio Alger's Ragged Dick, Ponson du Terrail's Rocambole, or George W. M. Reynolds's Richard Markham, the Russian heroes do not return from their adventures as masters of two worlds or with boons to bestow. They return humbly as ordinary men. Their voyage to an outer world of freedom and adventure does not affirm the value of individual heroism, but instead demonstrates the superiority of society over the individual, even, and particularly, over the extraordinary individual.

Russian outsiders differed from their American, French, and English counterparts in their means of reentry into respectable society. Rocam-bole and Richard Markham, heroes of mid-nineteenth century French and English serial fiction, and Deadwood Dick, the protagonist of Edward

FIG. 6. *Solovei the Bandit* (Moscow: Sytin, 1914).

Wheeler's enormously successful dime novel series, rejoin society by gaining the respect of citizens firmly established in the community. The judgment of the community legitimates their rebellion against an unjust authority in the name of another conception of justice or virtue. For the heroes of Russian popular literature there was no unofficial court of appeal. Only the state and Church had moral authority to pardon the rebellion of the Russian fictional bandits, and they could earn a full pardon by patriotic feats, such as heroism during wartime, or, occasionally, through acts of religious penitence such as pilgrimages. There was no room for legitimate rebellion against the institutions of organized society in the form of the state and the Church.

The authors of Western European nineteenth-century low literature recaptured elements of the ancient adventures of such heroes as Odysseus and Gilgamesh in their writings,[5] and their fiction shares inspiration with the earliest classics of Western thought. Western popular literature is among other things a paean to the adventuresome individual and his deeds of daring, and the heroes who disrupt the order of things can turn to an alternative court of judgment for vindication or praise. The heroes of Russian low literature are still adventurers whose daring and bravado are lauded. The break with the everyday world is still celebrated, but the hero's stature as an independent actor is greatly diminished by the power of the legitimate social order, incarnate in the divinely sanctioned autocrat and the Orthodox Church.

The choice of bandits, rebels, and criminals as heroes of popular stories did not imply an idealization of actual bandits or criminals. Most of the stories, even those based on historical figures, have little relationship to the deeds of real bandits or criminals. Nevertheless, the existence of real bandits and the vocabulary of crime helped to determine that the bandit, rather than some other character, would personify the fictional conflict between freedom and order.

Bandits in Russian Life

Banditry was understood very broadly in Russia, and the notion of a bandit was rich in popular associations.[6] A bandit (*razboinik*) in the last half century of tsarist rule was a violent criminal, someone who carried out armed robbery; but the word had other connotations, implying someone who belonged to a band of rebellious and free people.[7] The bandit was someone whose profession brought him into conflict with the state, and therefore the bandit was a figure with whom the authorities found it difficult to make peace.[8] Punishment for involvement in a gang of bandits in the late nineteenth century was harsh—twelve to fifteen years of hard labor, and in the Caucasus the punishment was death.[9]

Accounts of banditry in Russia go back to the most remote Russian past, when Saint Vladimir advised the Russian bishops to punish the bandits who were multiplying in the land.[10] During the stormy years of Tatar rule, and in the period of the rise of the Muscovite state, there were many opportunities for brave freebooters to make a living from brigandage. Maxim Gorky called the great Novgorod bandit Vasilii Buslaevich, whose stormy, drunken, and expansive character was glorified in the *byliny*, a Russian Siegfried.[11]

The wellsprings of banditry in the fifteenth, sixteenth, seventeenth, and eighteenth centuries were usually the Cossack communities along the southern border of the state, and later in Siberia. The freewheeling, semi-professional peasant soldiers were linked to banditry in their very origins. They were only gradually integrated into the class system and legal order of the autocracy, and continued in ambiguous relation to state authority even in the nineteenth century. Cossacks strategically located their communities in the disorderly and violent border areas, and could prey on either the enemies of Russia and the marauding nomadic peoples, or on the prosperous merchants and official dignitaries whose business took them to areas where the protection of the central authority was weak at best.

The Cossacks produced the great peasant rebel and pretender, Stenka Razin. Razin led his fellow Cossacks and other disgruntled people against the authority of Alexei Mikhailovich, and a century later Emelian Pugachev shook the foundations of Catherine the Great's rule. Less well known but important rebels and pretenders who were associated with mutinous Cossacks were Bolotnikov, an escaped military slave who led a rising during the Time of Troubles in the beginning of the seventeenth century, and K. A. Bulavin, who challenged the authority of Peter the Great in the early eighteenth.

There were also at least four types of bandits active in the late nineteenth and early twentieth-century Russian Empire. The *khunkhuzy* (from "red beards" in Chinese) operated in robber bands in Manchuria and the border areas of the Russian Empire from the middle of the nineteenth century to the middle of the twentieth.[12] The *abreki*, bandits of the northern Caucasus, functioned during the same period. Ordinary Russian bandits, *razboiniki*, flourished throughout the empire in the late nineteenth and early twentieth centuries. In addition, the revolutionary expropriators who held up banks in the last decade of the old regime operated like bandits and were often referred to as such. The Bolshevik and anarchist raids on banks and mail coaches were an important source of funds for both groups, and were often carried out with the aplomb associated with bandit raids. Each of these forms of banditry were portrayed in Russian popular fiction, but the ordinary Russian *razboiniki* were by far the most common in literature, as well as in life.

Banditry as practiced by violent gangs of highwaymen and robbers was probably limited to the countryside and smaller towns, and was more prevalent on the periphery of the empire than in the center. Nevertheless, holdups of merchants and other travelers on the highways of central Russia remained a fact of life throughout the nineteenth and early twentieth centuries.[13] The former chief of the Moscow Investigative Police, General A. F. Koshko, described several early twentieth-century bandits in his memoirs, including Vaska Belous, the chief of a gang that robbed in the environs of Moscow.[14] Vl. Mikhnevich, who studied the criminal population of St. Petersburg in the 1860s and 1870s, concluded that the hardened professional murderers, whom he identified as "bandits of the classical type," did not operate in the cities because police surveillance was strict.[15]

Newspaper readers in the capitals could follow the exploits and downfall of various bandit chieftains in the late nineteenth and early twentieth centuries. Typical of the bandits described in the press was one Semeniuta "who terrorized the district" of Aleksandrinskii in Ekaterinoslav Province in 1910, according to an account in *Russkoe slovo*, Sytin's popular newspaper.[16] This was the very place where Baron Korf had established his model zemstvo school nearly a half century earlier. A similar story appeared under the title "A Gang of Bandits: Letter from Voronezh" in *Nedelia* (The Week) in 1885, the year that Pastukhov's greatly successful fictional bandit Churkin was suppressed.[17]

A close relative of the bandit was the *vor*, a word usually translated as thief or felon, but which referred to criminals in general, including bandits and traitors.[18] Grishka Otrepev, the first False Dmitry, who opposed Boris Godunov and briefly occupied the Russian throne during the Time of Troubles at the beginning of the seventeenth century, was called a *vor*, as was the second False Dmitry, "The Felon of Tushino."[19] So was Vanka Kain, the legendary crook, thief, and bandit of the eighteenth century who briefly abandoned his criminal profession and became a detective, and was widely known in song and in popular stories.

Both thieves and bandits were presumed to have been organized on the basis of the primitive Russian union or guild, the *artel*. This was a means by which off-farm workers in the nineteenth and early twentieth centuries pooled capital and earnings as woodcutters, fishermen, agricultural laborers, and craftsmen. Tramps also sometimes elected an elder and organized themselves on this principle, as did convicts sent to Siberia.[20] Criminals had their distinctive slang, which may have been related to the language of the lubok peddlers.[21] Phrases from the language of the peddlers turned up in songs about bandits and crooks, such as in one about Vanka Kain which appears in P. V. Kireevskii's nineteenth-century song collection.[22]

Real bandits were thus a part of daily life in late nineteenth and early twentieth-century Russia. Few people had actual encounters with bandits, but the journalistic accounts and rumors of incidents placed banditry squarely in real as well as in literary or imaginative life. Popular writers also found the bandit a suitable hero because of the way bandits and criminals were popularly regarded. As the writers sought to invent a sufficiently captivating central character, folklore and history constituted important frames of reference. They found no dominant literary model for the hero of the Russian adventure story, in contrast to the propagators of the American Western who could look back on James Fenimore Cooper's Leatherstocking.[23] The bandit proved so suitable—and the popular writers succeeded in fixing this hero in the popular imagination—partly because the bandit was already a familiar figure in Russian oral culture. Equally important, the bandit was a hero whose adventures conformed both to the peasants' long struggle for freedom and to the traditional view of man's helplessness before the forces of whimsical nature.

The bandit personified rebellion against authority, but it was rebellion doomed to failure. The bandit could not succeed as a bandit. Constrained to choose between punishment and repentance, the bandit became an object of compassion. For writers who needed a hero who was both a victim of a hostile environment and a rebel against it, the bandit was an ideal choice.

Folklore of Banditry and Crime

Popular attitudes toward real acts of banditry were ambivalent. Not surprisingly, peasants were utterly unsympathetic to acts of lawlessness that threatened them directly. People who stole from those within the commune were punished with great dispatch and considerable brutality.[24] Once criminals were sentenced by state authorities for serious crimes, however, the peasants' attitudes toward them changed from anger to pity. "The view of the criminal as a victim of circumstances, as a fallen brother, is widespread among the people," wrote E. I. Iakushkin in the introduction to his 1910 bibliography on Russian common law.[25]

Western observers and Russian commentators alike have described the solicitude of the general population for convicts of all sorts. George

Kennan, in his classic study *Siberia and the Exile System* (1891), described how, as groups of convicts passed through a small village on their way to Siberia, "children and peasant women appeared at doors with their hands full of bread, meat, eggs, and other articles of food."[26] S. V. Maksimov, in his prerevolutionary *Siberia and Penal Servitude*, attributed such alms giving to the belief that charity was a means of personal atonement and a way of pleasing God.[27] The solicitude for the convict was also nourished, Maksimov points out, by the popular belief that "crime is a misfortune and the criminal is an unfortunate person."[28] This belief is composed in part of the traditional fatalism of those with little power to change their lot in life, in part of the Russian Orthodox belief in the holiness of suffering (kenoticism), and in part of the widespread experience of injustice of those at the bottom of the social order.

The traditions of Russian Orthodox Christianity contributed to popular attitudes toward criminals, outcasts, and convicts. The kenotic idea of salvation through suffering and nonresistance to evil is symbolized in the image of the humiliated and outcast Christ. The saints of the Orthodox Church sought to live this doctrine in a life apart marked by self-inflicted suffering and deprivation. The same ideal was expressed by the many holy fools, who astounded foreign travelers in early modern Russia with their self-inflicted suffering and hardship.[29] The criminal crucified on the cross with Jesus and forgiven of his sins was a bandit (*razboinik*), the most dangerous kind of criminal, and not a felon (*vor* or *tat'*).

The experience of serfdom and Russia's class system influenced Russian attitudes toward crime. Among common people, there was little respect for the property of the gentry, the state, and the imperial family. Stealing from state forests or from landowners was often not considered theft.[30] Nor, on occasion, was the taking of grain from the first harvest. Stealing from those outside one's own commune was not regarded by peasants with the same severity as stealing from those within it. The popular dream of a "black repartition," a final division of the lands, was also incompatible with respect for current property rights in land.

The idea that the convicted criminal was an object of pity rather than contempt or loathing may have come from the arbitrariness of Russian justice. People who endured penalties devised by serf owners and corrupt local authorities were likely to see the criminal's treatment by the state in the light of their own experiences. This affected even the gentry, and in Pushkin's story, "Dubrovskii," an honest landowner who loses his property and later his position because of official corruption turns to banditry. This sense of the criminal as victim made the bandit hero a sympathetic figure, and the anticipation of his coming punishment inspired compassion instead of wrath or scorn.

Russian popular songs featured bandits, criminals, outlaws, and rebels. Bandits appear in the oldest historical epics, the byliny, about Kievan Rus and the struggle against the Tatars, as well as in historical songs about events of the seventeenth and eighteenth centuries.[31] Songs about bandits and criminals were sung throughout urban and rural Russia in the nineteenth and early twentieth centuries. Great rebels and outlaws of the past were celebrated, and more contemporary bandits and criminals were treated with wry sympathy. Bandit songs are included in all the great nineteenth-century popular song collections. There were also songs about Cossacks and rebels, who had much in common with bandits but were not always identified as such.

Historical epics about Stenka Razin and other Cossack rebels began as Cossack songs, but by the end of the nineteenth century, they were popular among peasants and workers throughout Russia. In the course of diffusion, the costume of these Cossack heroes changed from the Cossack dress to more European-style clothing.[32] The old Cossack became the main popular champion among the common people, according to the prerevolutionary specialist V. F. Miller. So compelling was his image as a hero that even the heroes of the byliny, such as Ilia Muromets, were made Cossack chiefs, as well as bandits, in some versions.[33] The preeminence of the Cossack and bandit chieftain in the popular imagination was also reflected in entertainments among lower classes in the cities. A common Christmas game that St. Petersburg laborers and factory workers were observed to play in the last third of the nineteenth century involved a chorus singing the classic folk song, "Down Mother Volga." The main character in the game was a Cossack chief armed with a gun and attended by a Cossack captain.[34]

Criminals, thieves, and cheats were equated with bandits and Cossack rebels in the late nineteenth and early twentieth centuries, and songs about these types of lawbreakers supplanted and supplemented the bandit songs during this period. Some investigators argue that these songs in celebration of feats of brigandage are different from both the songs of daring lads (*udalye pesni*), and from the historical songs of peasant rebels, and that they were popular primarily among criminals.[35] Often, however, various types of rebels and outlaws merged into a single composite hero of disorder and freedom, as is apparent in the occasional alliance between the traditional Cossack and bandit hero, Stenka Razin, and Vanka Kain, the semilegendary early eighteenth-century Moscow thief and detective. Razin and Kain appear together, for example, in a song collected in Perm Province, even though Razin lived a century and a half before Kain.[36] One prerevolutionary investigator suggested that these figures were linked together in the memory of the common people because they were thought to have been damned, anathematized, and rejected by heaven and earth alike.[37] Bandits were also identified in apocalyptic dreams with the myth of the redeemer tsar who would regain his rightful place on the throne and bring justice and freedom. Both Razin and Pugachev used this myth to gain adherents. The bandit as imaginary hero in this context personified the yearning for a better world and a kind of anarchistic freedom.[38]

Facts and Fiction of Banditry

Journalistic accounts of bandits' adventures were often similar to fictional serialized bandit stories. An account of banditry on the outskirts of Moscow in 1910 reported in *Russkoe slovo* (no. 87) began: "On Friday at about ten o'clock in the evening on the Izmailovskii road, V. A. Moreek, aged sixty-five, and his twenty-year-old son Ivan were riding in a coach toward their estate, which is located near the Izmailovskii preserve. They had a large sum of money with them. Two dark figures jumped out of the forest, shots rang out, and the cry 'Hands up!' sounded." After a wild chase, the two escaped to Moscow. But for the timely escape, the incident could have been the first installment of a serialized novel in one of the cheaper newspapers. Bandits were not portrayed as heroic in the newspapers, but the language used in reporting cases of banditry and the choice of detail show how closely attuned the journalistic and fictional accounts of bandit exploits were to each other.

The fictional bandits were always associated with the unromantic actuality of lawlessness, as well as with its wider social implications. The best evidence for this is provided in the background of Pastukhov's famous serial in *Moskovskii listok* in the early 1880s, *The Bandit Churkin*. The real Churkin was an unheroic thug and bully. When Pastukhov decided to write the story, he sent his reporter, Giliarovskii, to Churkin's village to gather information about the bandit. Everyone Giliarovskii encountered, according to his colorful account, told him the same story: Vaska Churkin, a former factory worker and drunkard, robbed both strangers and local inhabitants with his gang, stole from storehouses, and went the rounds of local factory owners several times a year extorting money on threat of arson. Churkin was sent to Siberia, escaped, and returned to take up his old ways. According to one account, he was killed by local peasants. In another telling he was poisoned by his wife.

Giliarovskii's picture of Churkin the petty thief and scourge of his region rings true. The area in which Churkin lived was a part of the district of Bogorodskii in Moscow Province known as Guslitsa. It was a spot where the three provinces of Moscow, Vladimir, and Riazan came together. The district of Bogorodskii was a center of textile production, but Guslitsa itself stood apart from the more prosperous factory villages. It was a swampy forested area, 55 miles from the city of Moscow. Two well-traveled roads passed through it, and there was more than a fair share of taverns. According to a columnist in *Moskovskii listok*, Guslitsa was economically depressed in the early 1880s, with factory production declining and local plants closed. Peasants turned to traditional hop raising or went off to the other factory centers nearby (no. 87, 1882). Guslitsa was also a cultural center for the Old Believers. There were many holy places and secret monasteries for the dissidents, and these were patronized by Old Believer factory owners. A commentator in the Orthodox Church's missionary publication, *Bratskoe slovo* (Fraternal Word), complained in 1884 that the area was almost completely populated by Old Believers.[39] "From Guslitsa came Old Believer priests, Scripture buffs, readers, and from here, according to legend, ought to come the antichrist," wrote A. L. Peregudov, in his early Soviet memoir about the area.[40] Old Believer retreats persisted there through the years of war and revolution and into the second decade of Soviet power.

In Churkin's time Guslitsa was a hotbed of petty lawlessness. Tramps, vagrants, and ruffians armed with oak staves roamed freely in the forest; so did holy wanderers in black cassocks, with sacks of religious books on their backs and iron hats on their heads to protect them from the oak staves. In the center of the area was the Spaso-Preobrazhenskii Guslitskii Monastery, which was founded after the emancipation to counter the influence of the dissidents. Horse stealing, cockfights, counterfeiting, and dealing in false passports and moonshine were part of life in this corner of Moscow Province. According to Peregudov, the inhabitants were known as swindlers and cheats by the popular saying of their neighbors: "It is difficult to believe a Gusliak; he swears five times and cheats ten."[41] A steady stream of convicts, both criminals and Old Believers, flowed from Guslitsa to Siberia.

This was the center of dissidence and disorder in which Churkin grew up. Like many of his fellows, he found employment at a dye works, where he eventually attained the position of dye master, but he quarreled with his employers. Whether he rebelled against oppression and injustice at the plant or got into trouble for drinking, he ended up in jail, fled, and became a "bandit." So he lived from the time of the emancipation until his capture and death about twenty years later. In banditry and flight he crossed Russia to Siberia and returned. The lore of Churkin—the songs and legends about him initiated or at least encouraged by Pastukhov's serialized novel—outlasted the old regime.

Vaska Churkin was not the only criminal in his family, and the details of the trial of his brother Stepan were published in the "News from the Moscow Circuit Court" column of *Moskovskii listok* in April 1882 (nos. 103-106). Stepan Churkin identified himself in court as Vasilii's brother. He was described as stocky, above average height, "with long black hair combed back, and a thick black beard that adds to his solid appearance." With him were two others—one, a large fellow, and the other "a puny peasant." In answering questions, Stepan Churkin identified himself as an Old Believer, and one may assume that his brother was also. The charges against them were indicative of the kinds of brutish crimes committed by the Churkin brothers: (1) In May 1879, the Bogorodskii police received reports that a gang of four or five armed ruffians was operating in the forest, including Stepan Churkin and his brother Vasilii, who had murdered the village elder Peter Kirov and fled from the Bogorodskii prison. The Churkins had been seen by another village elder who met them and was informed that if he told anyone, he would end up like Peter Kirov; (2) in May the merchant's son Ivan Gusev met Vasilii Churkin and several unknown persons in the forest near the village of Barskoi (Churkin's home); they threatened him with a revolver, demanded that his father pay them a hundred rubles, and warned him against telling anyone; (3) on May 11 the two Churkins and a third person stopped the peasant Peter Shchepetkov and threatened him, whereupon he gave them 50 rubles; (4) Stepan Churkin was recognized and captured by peasants on May 25. He fired three shots at them and had a false passport. His accomplice escaped but was captured on the same day.

Details of the Churkins' previous offenses came out in the trial. Stepan Churkin had fled from Siberia, where he had been sent into exile, and when he was subsequently recaptured and tried in July 1877, he was sentenced to flogging and then to hard labor. A Bogorodskii policeman testified that beginning in 1873 measures were taken to capture Churkin, and a troop of thirty-two peasants was organized to look for the Churkins, but "nothing came of it, since the peasants were afraid of the bandit, because he demanded money and threatened to kill them if they refused" (no. 104). The appearance of the Churkins again in this area, according to the policeman, created a panic among the local peasants. Vasilii Churkin, he explained, had already fled the authorities twice, once from a convoy when he was on his way to Siberia, and a second time from prison after the murder of the elder Peter Kirov. Shchepetkov apparently went to the police, who suggested that he help them set an ambush for the Churkins. When he was asked about this in court he refused to answer: "The witness fell silent and in great agitation began to drum loudly on his cap, and the court was temporarily adjourned" (no. 105).

The description of the capture of Stepan Churkin and his comrade shows the famous brothers as petty ruffians and bunglers for whom local peasants had little sympathy. According to Prokofii Kranov, one of the peasants who captured him:

It was a Sunday, at two in the afternoon. We're sitting by ourselves at the window, when suddenly I see two people, one of them with a red beard. Titov says to me: "These are not good people." "Why not?" "The beard isn't right." When they come up to us we see that it's Churkin. I say to my comrade, "Let's give them a fright," and I cry out: "Churkin! Makhalkin," that's the way he was called. He turns around and goes off. We ring the bell and go after them. On the road, running, Stepan throws off his coat and I pick it up, and there's lead in the pocket. Meanwhile, we all go on, and then a shepherd runs toward Churkin. We cry: "Hold him," and he, Churkin, stretches out his hand with the pistol and that fellow goes off to the side and Churkin goes on until he is into the bog up to his neck. Then we caught him. The other went off and was caught on the same day. (No. 106)

The capture of Stepan Churkin involved forty peasants. According to the Bogorodskii policeman, Stepan Churkin told them that his brother Vasilii was hiding in Vladimir Province, but he was not captured there. "In 1880," the policeman testified, "I received the news that Vasilii Churkin had died" (no. 104).

Pastukhov did not present his readers with the real Churkin, but he did not stray so far from the truth as to create a Robin Hood. Giliarovskii claimed that when he told Pastukhov that Churkin was a hooligan and petty thief, the editor became excited and shouted at him, "They are slandering him."[42] Churkin, as Pastukhov portrayed him, was not an angel or defender of the poor. He differed from the real Churkin primarily in the scale of his activities, and in the larger implications of his criminality.

The Churkin of *Moskovskii listok* is described as "solidly built, broad shouldered, and as quick in his movements as a tiger."[43] Like the real Churkin, he is a dye factory worker who earns a good salary but wishes to have still more, takes to theft, and loses his job. On the surface he is described as bloodthirsty and unromantic. He moves from nasty petty crime to grand schemes. His crimes mount over hundreds of pages until he is murdering freely and stealing thousands of rubles from prosperous merchants and cattle dealers.

Churkin does not stay long in the Moscow region. He flees to Siberia and opens a tavern with the proceeds of his criminal activities. He poses as a prosperous merchant while traveling in search of merchants to rob. He has love affairs and would-be love affairs, and abandons his wife and daughters. After staging his own mock funeral to fool the police, he heads home to Guslitsa. When he reaches home his spirits rise briefly at the

FIG. 7. The bandit Churkin, seated by a fire with his wife and child; his henchman Osip stands beside them. They have made camp on the way to Siberia. From N. I. Pastukhov, *The Bandit Churkin*, part 1 (Moscow, 1883), facing page 210.

sight of his native forest and village, but his sudden death ends any dreams of reconciliation and new adventures.

Churkin is no defender of the common folk. True to the character of the real bandit, the fictional Churkin is more likely to murder a poor peasant for his horse than to alleviate his poverty. In one incident Churkin and his comrade meet a simple and utterly inoffensive peasant on the road, and strangle him with his own belt. Churkin slyly ingratiates himself with the local peasants in the Siberian village where he has his bar by giving them vodka and an occasional ruble, but the reader is assured that he feels nothing but contempt for them. When he does hand out money, it is with the clearly calculated objective of buying friends. The only instance in the entire novel when Churkin sympathizes with a peasant is when early in the serial he forbids his gang from taking the boots from a poor wayfarer (p. 24). No factory workers appear in the novel, and Churkin's only lower-class allies are a few shepherds. His true comrades are other criminals—"berries off the same bush"—but they usually share his murderous inclinations, and he and his accomplice kill many of them.

Churkin also has a side more calculated to win sympathy. He mocks the authorities with bravado. After a jailbreak, accomplished with the help of his crafty wife, Churkin appears in disguise before the governor of Moscow, offering information about his own whereabouts. When the police hunt him, his shepherds—"his secret police"—keep him informed, and he slips through the hands of the police. Pastukhov's Churkin and other Russian fictional bandits do not defend the oppressed or attract attention with bold attacks on property. Their appeal lies instead in their doomed struggle for personal freedom.

The bandit story in popular fiction is a Russian myth about the contradiction between freedom and the orderly world, and the individual's imperative to choose between them. This rather than the desire for revenge against the bosses seems to explain why workers may have thought Churkin "a good bandit" and "a daring fellow," as one worker recalled.[44] The bandit stands for freedom, and in the stories he leads a life of perpetual feast and unchecked passions. He is independent and lives in a brotherhood of outcasts, but in the devil's domain. The divine order requires acceptance of honest toil, deprivation, and self-control, and the bandit stands outside this order. The rewards of living an orderly life are the support of family and community, and the cost is submission to authority. The dichotomy between freedom and the orderly world of work and family is complete, and the individual must choose either the free but demonic or the constrained but divine life. The choice is tragic because in the world of God there is no escape from toil and submission, but the price of freedom is damnation. The good things of the divinely sanctioned life preclude freedom, and freedom itself is a condition that cannot be sustained.

The opposition between freedom and the orderly world, and the need to sacrifice the former to gain the latter, is understandable in the context of the long Russian experience with autocratic rule and various forms of bondage.

The World of the Damned

The authors of the bandit stories created a fictional milieu in which the conflict between freedom and the orderly world was acted out in many different settings. The association of bandits with the world of the devil was expressed by their love of lightning, thunder, and storms, by frequent companionship of witches, sorcerers, and wizards, and by occasional deals with the devil himself. Ermak, the sixteenth-century conqueror of Siberia and one of the most popular protagonists of historical lubok tales, appears in a story by V. Shmitanovskii, *Ermak, or the Conquest of the Siberian Kingdom* (1858), amid peals of thunder and flashes of lightning. The bandits' dancing campfire on the banks of the Volga and their uproarious feast after looting a river boat all bespeak their tie with the demonic. In an 1877 tale, *Stenka Razin, the Bandits' Ataman*, a wizard appears in the bandits' camp, foretells their capture and death, and vanishes,[45] In Misha Evstigneev's three-part tale, *The Witch from Beyond the Dnieper, or the Solovei Bandit*, and in the anonymous *The Witch and the Black Raven, or Terrifying Nights Beyond the Dnieper*, published by Konovalova in 1912, bandits turn to witches to enhance their powers.[46] The idea that banditry was sin and linked with forces of supernatural evil helped to establish the opposition between the bandit's world and that of ordinary God-fearing people.

The popular writers were usually unwilling to include supernatural elements in their stories in a straightforward way, and the demonic context of banditry was most often implied rather than directly stated. Bandits were sometimes dressed in demonic regalia in order to frighten their victims, as in Volgin's story, *The Fatal Secret* (Moscow, 1897). The hero of this story learns that his father was a bandit who frightened people by dressing as a corpse. The son laments that his father's crimes turned him in fact into an evil fiend, and he donates all the ill-gotten wealth to churches and a monastery.

Churkin is also linked with the world of the devil. Churkin loves storms, and during one terrifying tempest he shouts at each roll of thunder and flash of lightning, "That's what I love, once again, that's the way" (pp. 193-96). The sense that demonic forces follow him wherever he goes is implicit in the fears of the canton elder's lovely daughter, Stepanida, whom he wants to marry. She sees him all covered with blood in a dream, and later others think that she has been bewitched. Even Churkin's loyal shepherds symbolize his association with the forces of evil, since shepherds were frequently thought to possess secret powers.[47] At one point Churkin and his henchman Osip are called "Our heroes of the dark kingdom" (p. 235). The link between banditry and the demonic is only hinted in the kopeck serials. Krechet visits with a mysterious gypsy at one point, and at another he goes to an island alleged to be haunted.

The World of the Feast

Scenes of lavish feasting recur in the bandit stories, and bandits are associated with the feast (*pir*) throughout lubok stories. The sagging table heaped with food and wine symbolizes the bandit's rejection of self-denial and moderation of personal desires. Such a table is described in *Kondrashka Bulavin, Who Was a Rebel in the Reign of the Emperor Peter I*, an anonymous tale that appeared in a fourth edition in 1849 and in a shortened version in 1874.[48] "On it stood many tasty dishes and flasks. Whole barrels of foreign wine rested on the benches. About fifteen people feasted at the table, wholeheartedly working on roast game and enormous pies" (2:5). After looting a Volga river boat, Shmitanovskii's Ermak and his gang drag their booty into the forest. "There the feasting began. Barrels of wine buried in the ground were torn open in a wink, and a large wooden ladle went from hand to hand among the feasters. Their merriness doubled when each had drunk half a ladleful, and various songs, dances, and conversations began."[49]

Pastukhov's Churkin also feasts. While detachments of peasants armed with oak staves comb the forests in search of him, the bandit and his cronies celebrate in a graveyard with friendly villagers. There are "pretty girls and young married women," and Churkin himself is not averse to singing a song. There is "plenty of wine and beer, and so many spice cakes and nuts that there was no place to put them" (p. 32). The Churkin story is punctuated by feasting and carousing, including a rousing scene at Churkin's fake death and burial.

The first Krechet novel contains few scenes of feasting, but readers are informed that in their hideaway, the Wolf's Lair, Krechet and his gang "held mad orgies" (p. 79). In order to escape from prison, Krechet hypnotizes his guards with tales of the life of the feast, "a sea of wine, and

FIG. 8. *The Lion-Hearted Ataman* (Moscow: Sytin, 1914).

185

women half naked in voluptuous dances" (p. 213). As the story gets underway, so does the life of sensual abandon. The feast is then developed to include a more comprehensive life of ease, with travel, fine clothes, and impressive equipages, including first-class rail cars. Krechet can live flamboyantly, without a care for money, because he has found a treasure, and does not have to depend on robbery.

The life of the feast is openly compared to the life of toil and responsibility. Before Kuzma becomes a bandit in V. Volin's 1901 story, *Ataman Kuzma Roshchin*, he considers working for a merchant. A fellow he meets on the Volga River counsels him instead to form a gang. "What do you get for your working? Through summer and half of fall you work like a good horse, and when winter comes you are no use to anyone, and it's 'Get going—don't ask me where!' " (pp. 32-33). The opposition between the world of work and another world of freedom and merrymaking is found in Russian oral culture, and had a place in Russia's cultural past.[50] Both Ivan the Terrible and Peter the Great appointed mock tsars and commanded them to create a temporary carnival, a laughable merry world that was a topsy-turvy version of the strict world of order.[51] These rituals of early modern Russia are consistent with the tension between freedom and order expressed in the bandit stories. Both the Churkin and Krechet serials contain scenes of carnival-like mockery, in which readers are allowed some laughs at the expense of the servants of order.

The bandits are not shown to enjoy widespread support of the populace, and they have few friends. Churkin is protected only by shepherds, whom he is always careful to reward. Krechet has only a few loyal henchmen to aid him. The bandits appeal to readers' sympathies, however, by their mockery of authority rather than through their sympathy for the common people. It is perhaps only in this sense that the Russian fictional bandits can be considered "social bandits," in the phrase of Eric Hobsbawm; that is, bandits striving for social justice.[52]

World of Violence and Bloodshed

The Russian fictional bandits little resemble noble champions of the people's honor and livelihood. Nor do they steal from the rich to give to the poor. In perhaps the only case of a Robin-Hood-type lubok bandit, Evstigneev's *The Daring Bandit*, the charity proves misguided. Evstigneev's hero befriends a poor peasant family and serves as godfather to a newborn son, but the ungrateful peasant informs on the bandit, who then unceremoniously murders him.[53]

The bandit's realm is not that of justice and equality. Instead, the bandits inhabit a world of violent, confusing, and horrifying chaos where people have been turned into beasts that prey on each other. Although the life of the feast has obvious appeal, it is inseparable from the ruthless violence and carnage that result when orderly ways are abandoned. In an 1877 anonymous tale, Stenka Razin and his comrades are described celebrating on the banks of the Volga River. "It was enough to glance at the insolent expressions on their faces, on their broad knives, boar spears, guns, and bludgeons to judge the beastly occupation of this crowd."[54] When Pugachev moved on the town of Orenburg in *The Love of a Cossack* (1863),

The villians did not spare either sex or age. They took babes from the embraces of their desperate mothers and killed them. The old went as the young; elders were tormented to death. Innocent virgins were given up to the stormy crowd with evil joy for violation. The holy temples of God were defiled and destroyed and nothing was considered holy. Hell itself smiled on the acts of its favorite.[55]

Churkin and his vicious henchman Osip leave a trail of smashed skulls from the town of Bogorodsk to Irbit and back, along with spectacular fires and innocent cries for help. This makes Churkin and the other lubok bandits curious heroes. Although Churkin's contempt for the peasantry may have appealed to some urban readers, there is no corresponding sympathy for city folk. Churkin even kills the coachman who drove him and his family to Siberia. His henchman Osip, even more hard-hearted than Churkin, feels pity "for the first time in his life, not for men but for beasts," when he and Churkin slaughter the horses from the dead coachman's sledge to make the murder look like robbery. In place of the promise of social justice are carefully drawn scenes in which Churkin and Osip watch their victims and plot their downfall. In these instances, the threat that the bandit's world poses to the world of order is chillingly portrayed. For example, the lovely Stepanida has spurned Churkin's love, and while she and her chosen husband go about their peaceful domestic life, Churkin and Osip lurk in the shadows outside their house, plotting their murder. The planned murders are intended as Churkin's personal vengeance on those who have thwarted him. Pastukhov portrays the scene without sympathy for Churkin, observing merely that "Hatred burned deep in his bloodthirsty soul" (p. 382).

Krechet is a more sympathetic character than Churkin, but he also lives in a world of unbridled savagery. He is forced to kill to defend his freedom, and he does so again and again. One man is thrown to a wolf pack, and another has his skull smashed. When Krechet wants to return home to his mother's funeral, he has some of his henchmen stage a riot to divert the police. His command is translated into fires, looting, and wanton destruction.

Much of the violence in the Krechet novels is directed against women, and this perhaps appealed to readers uncomfortable with the loosening of traditional family ties and with the novelty and confusion that increasing geographic and social mobility brought to relations between the sexes. The association of banditry with violent domination of women is implicit in the feasting and battle scenes in many stories, but in the first of the Krechet novels the theme is more explicit. Krechet has spurned his old girlfriend, Maria, who is red-haired and "insatiable in love and hate." Maria is an enemy who cannot be ignored, and much of the plot involves Maria's attempted revenge against Krechet. Krechet's chosen, Nina, is a passive woman who has studied at a women's institute, plays the piano, and "values her honor dearer than life." Throughout the tale, Nina and other passive women are frequently attacked and threatened by villains, some of whom are rival bandits, and some evil landowners, counts, and others. Krechet regularly rescues Nina and occasionally pitches in to save other innocent women. The cycle of threatened violence and rescue may have satisfied fantasies of sexual power and bolstered Krechet as a positive hero. These scenes also symbolize the vulnerability of women unprotected by family and community, and suggest the possibilities of license and abuse inherent in the free life of the bandit.

World of Isolation and Freedom

The bandit's freedom from the bonds and responsibilities of life in society also brings isolation from the comforts of family and community. The fictional bandits are condemned to an orphan's life, with comrades in crime serving as a poor substitute for true kin. With no ties to family or society, the bandit roams homeless over vast territories. Churkin's coworkers in a textile factory, in a lubok version of Pastukhov's story, ask him where he will go when he is fired, and he replies, "Where the wind walks; yes, where one is free as a bird."[56] In a Stenka Razin tale, after a marriage proposal is refused, Stenka rides out into the steppe in despair. "Yes, I am now a homeless wanderer," he says, alone with the wind and the wild beasts.[57]

The imagery of the Razin story is very similar to that of trials of saints in the wilderness in saints' lives. Despite their sinful lives, there is an aura of martyrdom and almost saintliness in the isolation of some of these outcast heroes, even though their suffering is never sufficient in itself to win their redemption. While his comrades feast, the noble bandit of Ivin's tale *Brynsk Forest, a Story of the Sixteenth Century* (1900), sits in his hut. "He understood that he had neither parents nor a betrothed who ardently loved him. He sat sadly and let his head sink, the orphan-ataman."[58] Misha Evstigneev's bandit hero in *The Witch from Beyond the Dnieper, or Solovei the Bandit* (1868) laments, "I would willingly exchange the life of a bandit for an honest family life."[59] Churkin is likewise a solitary figure, who loves to be by himself in the forest. He is the comrade and brother only of other criminals, all of whom prove untrustworthy and murderous like himself. Churkin is further isolated as an Old Believer, separated from what the Orthodox considered the true community of the faithful. To confirm his status as an outsider, throughout most of the novel he travels under a fake Turkish passport.

Krechet is also identified by the classic marks of the outsider. At one point he poses as an Old Believer, and later he also claims to be a Turkish citizen. After he has earned his pardon through service, his isolation ends: "Krechet returned to the camp and the military family met him in a warm and friendly way, as a man who could be counted among them by right."[60]

The positive side of the bandit's isolation was his freedom. Churkin sings of the delights of freedom and of his love of the forest depths. Churkin's favorite song, into which he poured "his whole spirit," is about freedom. The refrain is: "I love you, mother nature, free spirit, free freedom (*volia-vol'naia*). For you I am ready to endure everything. I love only the carefree life (*zhizn' razdol'naia*)" (p. 73). Similarly Krechet refuses to give himself up to the authorities—even though he recognizes his guilt—because he cannot stand the thought of being behind bars.

The carefully drawn isolation of the bandits in these stories made the heroes' need to return to the community apparent. Their power and freedom are shown to be no substitute for the truly valuable acceptance by family and society. They can threaten society temporarily, but society has an even stronger defense, and that is the bandit's ultimate need to rejoin the community. Tales of the bandit as outcast hero excited the rebellious imagination of lower-class readers, but ultimately confirmed the existing order.

The Bandit's Dilemma: Repentance or Punishment

The central dilemma of the bandit heroes is personal, not social. The bandit is preoccupied with the personal questions of sin, redemption, and punishment. Bandits and their personal experiences with sin and repentance appear in two revealing legends collected by the great nine-teenth-century folklorist, A. N. Afanasev.[61] In the first, a peasant youth finds a pot of gold but hears a voice warning him not to take it. He heeds the warning, but returns to his find a second and third time. The third time the voice tells him that if he wants the gold, he must first go home and sin with his mother, his sister, and his godmother. The mother, when told of these events, is enthusiastic. She provides the liquor and they all sin. Then she sends him back for the gold. The son, however, is seized with remorse over what he has done, and takes to the open road without the gold. He spends the rest of his life atoning for his sins, and his only reward is an honest burial.

In a second variant of this story, a shepherd commits the same sins, and is told to water three birch logs until they become trees. Only two grow, and the hermit tells him that his last sin will be forgiven when a flock of black sheep turns white. While tending the sheep, the shepherd meets a bandit singing merrily. The bandit explains that the more people he kills at night, the higher his spirits are in the day. The shepherd is outraged and kills the bandit. He returns to his flock to find that it has turned white. The hermit explains that the peasant community prayed for him in gratitude for deliverance from the murderous bandit. In each of these folk tales, the banditry is only a symbol of the protagonist's moral alienation from his community, and his central problem is how to atone for his transgressions.

Redemption

Bandits in the lubok fiction have chosen to leave society or have been forced out of it, and their central problem is how to return to the community. The Russian lubok bandit stories have the singular characteristic that the bandit heroes usually attain redemption in the form of a state pardon granted in recognition of patriotic acts. They can choose whether to seek redemption through state service or accept the only alternative—solitary death and humiliation.

The twin resolutions of the bandit formula may seem designed to please the state censors, but such a view would be mistaken. The censors could demand that fictional miscreants be punished, but they were hardly responsible for the proliferation of such stories. Presumably, if the formula had not been popular, authors would have written about something else. Nor does it seem likely that the censors' preferences explain the appearance of stories with the redemption variant. This more powerful and frequent resolution had much in common with the Muscovite religious tradition and seems to have had deep popular roots. Those who fought for the Muscovite rulers were portrayed during this period as holy warriors, and warfare itself became a well-worn path to sainthood. The idea of redemption was also in accord with the notion of the divinely anointed tsar, against whom rebellion was sacrilege.

The two main variants of the lubok bandit story can be represented by a list of narrative functions that the protagonist fulfills, in accordance with the methodology developed by V. Propp, in his *Morphology of the Folktale*, and used by Will Wright in *Sixguns and Society*.[62] In the first variant, the functions are as follows:

The Redeemed Bandit
1. The bandit shows himself to be a self-assertive and superior individual.
2. The bandit manifests his opposition to authority.
3. He feasts and enjoys his freedom.
4. He suffers, feels remorse, or receives a warning.
5. He seeks pardon through state service.
6. He is pardoned and all his sins are forgiven.
7. He dies a hero, or becomes an ordinary but honorable person.

An alternative plot is that of the doomed rebel, and in this plot the functions are as follows:

The Doomed Bandit
1. The bandit shows himself to be a self-assertive and superior individual.
2. The bandit manifests his opposition to authority.
3. He feasts and enjoys his freedom.
4. He suffers, feels remorse, or receives a warning.
5. He ignores the opportunity for pardon.
6. He continues to live the life of the feast.
7. He is either captured and executed, or killed in battle.

In neither variant of the bandit story is it important whether the bandit took to outlawry because of a wrong done to him. This distinguishes these Russian stories from myriad other bandit tales in which the crucial definition of the bandit hero is of a man who, like Robin Hood, suffers some personal injustice, goes on to seek personal revenge, and in the process battles against injustice more generally.[63] The Russian bandits lack the righteousness of other rebellious heroes, even when they are victims of injustice, because by becoming a bandit they join with the devil. They enter the demonic world of freedom and disorder in which it is impossible to live for very long. Pardon or death are their only alternatives. The key to pardon is state service, and service washes away all sins. The only meaningful freedom that the bandit has is to choose whether to seek redemption through state service or to die an outlaw's death.

The moral of the bandit story, particularly in the redemption variant, is one that disarms the rebellious individual. Only the state authorities can grant moral as well as legal pardon to criminals and bandits. According to this formula, the state has a monopoly on virtue and patriotism. There are no legitimate alternative ways to serve the community or nation. The traditional peasant belief in the good tsar who is led astray or betrayed by evil advisers could be used to justify rebellion.[64] However, the sense that freedom is ephemeral and that society can always crush its opponents is a powerful argument in favor of the established order. The belief in the inevitable triumph of the established order over the insurgent individual was always conservative.

There are many examples of fictional bandits who chose redemption through state service. One of the most popular bandit heroes was Ermak, the late seventeenth-century conqueror of Siberia. S. Sipovskii, a Soviet specialist, reported in 1929 that there were fifty lubok works and stories about Ermak, and that interest in him grew in the late nineteenth and early twentieth centuries.[65] Ermak was a rebel Cossack and bandit chieftain who was sometimes confused with Stenka Razin in folklore.[66] According to the accounts of his life that were retold in lubok fiction, he embarked on his conquest of Siberia in order to please the tsar and win a pardon for his past crimes of banditry. In Shmitanovskii's early tale, *Ermak, or the Conquest of the Siberian Kingdom* (1858), Ermak is seen at the outset standing aside from his feasting comrades, tormented by moral anguish over his sinful life as a bandit. He worries about "the future unhappiness that sooner or later ought to be his lot if he does not repent" (1863, 1:12).

Ermak and a comrade explain that they became bandits inadvertently, through no fault of their own. This does not absolve them of guilt, in contrast to the non-Russian bandits of the Robin Hood type, for whom there is no sin in banditry and no need to seek pardon. Ermak and his comrade gather a great band of outlaws and set out to conquer Siberia. "We would give it to the Russian tsar, and he would forgive our earlier villainies. Then we would be happy" (1:57-58). In the course of the conquest, they kill many of the native people, who are referred to as Tatars but are reported to be Moslem. After the conquest, Ermak's comrade returns to the capital and is pardoned and rewarded. He brings the good news to Ermak, but the redeemed bandit is ambushed by a Tatar chieftain and dies a martyr's death.

The Stenka Razin stories follow the second plot, that of the bandit who does not seek a pardon and perishes in ignominy. In the anonymous *Stenka Razin, an Ataman of the Bandits in the Reign of Aleksei Mikhailovich* (1865), Razin is described as a poor orphan who is taken in, along with his sister, by an old Cossack. The sister is ruined by the son of the local cossack chief, and Stenka kills him and takes to the forest as a bandit. Even though he has been forced into banditry, he does not choose to give it up. The tsar has him captured, brought to Moscow in chains, and beheaded.[67] In another Stenka Razin story, published in 1877, the bandit does feel a presentiment of his impending capture and death, but he still does not repent and perishes.[68] In both cases, the bandits deserve their punishment, and in the 1865 tale, Razin recognizes this himself. "I am guilty before God and before you, good people, forgive me," he exclaims before putting his head down on the executioner's block.[69]

The two alternative plots appear simultaneously in some stories, as one bandit repents and turns in an unrepentant one to receive a pardon. A tale about K. Bulavin, the leader of a Cossack uprising against Peter the Great, first published in 1849, is of this type. Bulavin is betrayed in the story by members of his gang, one of whom addresses the heavens with the words, "Your ways are inscrutable, Lord. Through storms and destruction you lead the way to bright and joyful days. From a criminal you have made me true to my great tsar, who is blessed by God."[70]

Adventures of ordinary bandits were more common among lubok themes than were those of historical rebels. In about half of these stories, the hero repents and seeks pardon through national service, and in the remainder the rebel is doomed and perishes. The hero of a late nineteenth-century tale by Ivin gives a classic speech of the repentant bandit:

Long have our names been terrifying in the area of Brynsk forest. Long have we been considered damned in the Orthodox churches. Long has the Moscow tsar hunted us and put a price on our heads. For a long, long time we have been doomed to a terrible and shameful death, and therefore I ask you, comrades, is it not better that we leave our shameful trade forever and try, if even in a small way, to expiate our guilt before the tsar? Isn't it better for us to attack the heathen Crimeans, to stand up for the Orthodox faith, for the motherland, and the tsar father, and afterwards to give ourselves up and beg forgiveness from the tsar and busy ourselves with honest work?[71]

In *A Bolt from the Blue*, an anonymous story published by Gubanov in Kiev in 1904, the hero is sent to prison for an accidental killing, escapes, and redeems himself by heroism in the Russo-Turkish War of 1877-78.[72]

Makarka the Murderer (1909) is a story of fierce class hatred, but even Makarka who hates all nobles loves the tsar and is redeemed by patriotism. Makarka declares war on the local nobility after his sister is abducted and killed by a lecherous lord. No Robin Hood, he embarks on a frenzy of revenge, killing not only noblemen, but also their women and children. He then learns of the Napoleonic War and heads for Moscow "to work for our Mother Russia, for Orthodoxy." When the war ends, his identity is discovered, and he is sentenced to death for banditry despite his patriotic service. A girl of noble birth takes pity on him and gives him poison, however, so that he is spared the indignity of public execution. Even though he is not pardoned, Makarka's death is honorable. "The Lord did not permit the humiliation of a man who served his neighbor in his own way, and who risked his life so many times to save his fatherland."[73]

The Redemptions of Churkin and Krechet

The Churkin story conforms well to the formulaic bandit plot through the first four functions, at which point the bandit feels remorse for his crimes. Churkin was not allowed to seek redemption through service, however, nor did he die the death of the doomed rebel, because the fateful oak branch ordered by the censor brought his adventures to an abrupt end. At the time of his demise, Churkin was stricken with remorse and loneliness in his isolation from his native villagers and family. He had not yet, however, made the decision to fight the tsar's enemies in order to redeem himself. His procrastination could well have resulted in his capture in his native village, if the oak branch had not simplified Pastukhov's task of resolving the story.

The Churkin story nevertheless contains elements suggestive of the redemption formula. After settling in Siberia, Churkin becomes homesick for his native Guslitsa, which as a center of the Old Belief is called "that Palestine within Russia" (p. 878). Planning his return to Guslitsa, Churkin stages a mock funeral and burial for himself to fool the police who were closing in on him.

The funeral scene is a macabre presentiment of Churkin's coming demise. His journey home to Guslitsa/Palestine is marked by threatening dreams and bad omens. When he reaches Guslitsa, he is recognized by villagers despite his crude wig and false beard, and they refuse him sanctuary. "He must hide from people like some kind of beast" (p. 1349). His shepherds urge him to see his parents, but he refuses, emphasizing his isolation, calling himself "a slice cut from the loaf" (p. 1374). He is thus alone and rejected when he meets the oak branch.

The sense of foreboding during Churkin's trip home suggests that Pastukhov did not intend to have Churkin redeem himself. The author kept his options open, however, since Churkin thinks of going to Kishinev or perhaps settling in Turkey until his crimes are forgotten. The Russian-

Turkish border was tense, and opportunities for heroism could have been developed. Among Churkin's lubok adventures that appeared separately from the newspaper serial is one in which the bandit is captured, publicly whipped, and then sent into the Crimean War as a common soldier.[74] After the war he fights rebellious tribesmen in the Caucasus, and then returns happily to Guslitsa.

The Krechet story conforms closely to the redemption formula typified by the Ermak tale. Repentance and the search for the redemption begin almost at the start of the serial. When we are introduced to Krechet, he is already an outlaw. His mother and his sentimental wife Nina urge him to give up his evil ways. Krechet has many adventures before the path to redemption becomes clear. When the Russo-Japanese War breaks out, he manages a long and treacherous journey to the front, where he receives a medal for bravery. He confesses his identity to a stern general, who agrees to intercede for him. The promise of redemption is suffused with religious imagery: "The gloom that surrounded him" was dispersed by a "brilliant and radiant" light in the distance, and a new path opened before him; and "There was a singing in his soul, and for the first time in many long years he looked on life as a participant and not as a persecuted outcast."[75] Krechet returns to battle, is wounded, and is taken to a camp hospital, where he again meets his beloved Nina, who is serving as a nurse. The Krechet story continues for several more volumes after his pardon. He rejoins society by settling with his wife, child, and a couple of loyal gang members on an estate in European Russia. He raises a son who fights the Germans, instead of the Tatars, Turks, or Japanese, and who defends innocent women against lecherous landowners and villains.

The Contrasting Western Adventure Formula

The difference between the Russian and Western European or American treatment of the fictional bandit or outcast hero is interestingly conveyed in the tale behind Alexandre Dumas' popular feuilleton novel, *The Count of Monte-Christo*. The true story that inspired Dumas closely followed the formula of the Russian doomed-bandit story: A young man's buddies decided to play a practical joke and denounced him to Napoleon III's political police on the eve of his wedding.[76] The joke resulted in seven years of prison for the would-be bridegroom. After his release, the wronged man returned to kill the pranksters, but was in turn killed by one of his former comrades who had opposed the prank. The man's vengeance was his attempt to attain personal justice from an unjust

FIG. 9. The first appearance of Anton Krechet, the hero of the *Gazeta kopeika* serial. The illustration is taken from the separate edition of the story: M. Raskatov, *Anton Krechet* (St. Petersburg: Kopeika, 1909), p. 7.

society. In that sense his actions were legitimate, but however legitimate his motivation, he sought recourse outside the law and therefore perished.

As Dumas reconstructed the story, the Count of Monte-Christo successfully sees to the punishment of those who wronged him, and goes on to do a rash of good deeds. At the end of the story he is unbowed and unrepentant and sails off for new challenges, like the archetypical Western adventurer that he is. The fictional count differed from the fictional Russian outlaws, even though the hapless bridegroom's story fit the formula of the Russian bandit tales.

Dumas' tale, like many other Western popular stories, is formed to accommodate a hero whose powers far surpass those of ordinary people. Western superheroes such as the three musketeers, whose adventures could be endless because they were infallible,[77] were more suitable popular literary figures than Russian characters such as Churkin and Krechet, who ultimately had to face up to their personal failings and whose adventures were therefore finite.

The importance of the state as the arbiter of the bandit's fate in these stories contrasts sharply with equivalent Western European and American fiction. One of the most popular American heroes was Edward L. Wheeler's Deadwood Dick. The series of his adventures went through many editions in the Beadle Frontier Library after it first appeared in 1879-85. The character of Deadwood Dick is developed cumulatively, even though each of the dime novels contained a complete adventure. Zane Grey created a more modern version of the same sort of hero in his *Riders of the Purple Sage* (1912), which is still in print. Two equally popular English serial tales, which first appeared considerably earlier, were Pierce Egan Jr.'s *Robin Hood and Little John or the Merry Men of Sherwood Forest* (1840) and G.W.M. Reynolds' *The Mysteries of London* (1844-46). Egan's *Robin Hood* sold many thousands of copies in separate installments. It was frequently republished, widely imitated, and published abroad.[78] Reynolds was one of the founders of the English popular press and claimed a circulation of 40,000 copies a week for his lengthy tale of crime, misfortune, and success.[79] French counterparts to these stories include Eugene Sue's immensely popular *Mysteries of Paris*; Ponson du Terrail's many-volume serial fable of crime and intrigue, *Rocambole*, which began to appear in the 1850s; and the serial novels of Emile Gaboriau (1835-73). All three French authors reached a wide lower-class reading public with their feuilletons. Ponson du Terrail and Gaboriau both wrote for *Le Petit Journal*, which was perhaps the first French newspaper designed particularly for the lower classes.[80]

The English, French, and American stories feature outcasts and outlaws, yet the problem of pardon and reentry into society is quite different for these characters than it is for the Russian heroes. In the Western European and American tales, society is weak and the hero must act the part of a private enforcer of morality and justice. Deadwood Dick is driven to outlawry by injustice, when an evil guardian seizes his inheritance and then tries to kill him. Since he has received no justice from the courts, "Nothing remained for me to do but to fight in my own way," he announces in the first issue of the serial.[81] Pursuing justice for himself, he attains it for others. This makes him a stand-in for the responsible citizen who sees to it that right wins out, despite the shortcomings of government and society. The life of Zane Grey's hero, Lassiter, is similar. He gives up his career as a Texas ranger and becomes a gunman after his sister is abducted by a Mormon preacher. His black guns symbolize his identity as an outlaw, but they are also a means of administering personal justice. "Gun-packing in the West since the Civil War," he explains, "has growed into a kind of moral law."[82]

Pierce Egan Jr.'s Robin Hood is a similar character. He defends the good people of Nottingham while England is misgoverned and Nottingham is oppressed by the evil Baron Fitz Alwine and his sheriff. Eugene Sue's mysterious Prince Rodolphe is an incognito dispenser of justice in a weak society in *The Mysteries of Paris*. In Ponson du Terrail's *Rocambole*, a variety of free-lance defenders of the virtuous successfully foil the evil schemes of villains, until Rocambole, himself a determined miscreant from childhood, reforms and becomes the chief defender of wronged and victimized innocents. In Gaboriau's enormously popular serial of the adventures of Lecoq, the private champion of justice in an imperfect society is replaced by a professional detective. Lecoq, however, does not represent a state system that assures justice. He is more like Sherlock Holmes than Lestrade, and when he is in difficulty he turns not to his superiors in the police department, but to an amateur *éminence grise*, who invariably puts him on the right track.

Russian outlaws did on occasion do good deeds, but these actions were parenthetical to their main occupation, which was resolution of the personal conflict between the need for freedom and the need to regain a place in society. When Western European and American outlaws decided to return to society, they sought pardon—not from the state or some other representative of official authority, but from the community of their fellow citizens. Deadwood Dick does not turn himself in to the sheriff. Instead he walks into the town saloon and announces, "I have come here to Eureka to lead an honest existence, and be a citizen among you."[83] Vigilante justice was one expression of the citizens' power in the American Western novel.[84] The selective rejection of legally constituted public authority was another. Zane Grey's hero, Lassiter, shoots his enemy, the Mormon preacher, while the latter is sitting as presiding judge of the local court. According to the literary conventions of the genre, Lassiter's action is a legitimate expression of the moral authority of the private citizen. Private individuals rarely acquired such authority in the Russian fiction, and if they broke the law they had to look to the state and not the community for forgiveness. The Russian means of redemption through one heroic act of patriotism or state service was consistent with the Orthodox path to absolution, but the American heroes were judged by their cumulative record of good works performed despite their outlaw status. The Russians can, in general, earn a pardon through one loyal act of patriotism for the state, but the American hero must prove himself worthy in the eyes of the community. The Russian act of repentance and redemption conforms to the logic of a society in which all political authority stems from a monarch; the American's self-assertion and appeal to the community bespeak democratic vistas.

Egan's Robin Hood is like Deadwood Dick and Lassiter in his personal assumption of moral authority. Formally he is an outlaw, but to the people of Nottingham he is a benefactor whom they support against his enemies, the legally constituted authorities in the persons of Baron Fitz Alwine and the sheriff. When Richard the Lion-Hearted returns from the crusades to depose his wicked brother John, Robin Hood helps him. However, it is not for this act that the king pardons his crimes of outlawry, but because he "succoured those who needed aid" in the king's absence.[85] Later Richard dies and John returns to power. Robin Hood again takes to the forest, but he retains his place in society despite his official designation as an outlaw.

In Reynolds' *The Mysteries of London*, an erring brother confesses his crimes to his relatives and friends assembled at his deathbed, and he is pardoned by them.[86] Ponson du Terrail's heroine, Baccarat, atones for her former life of crime and debauchery in hundreds of pages of good deeds. Her pardon comes from heaven, but it is expressed in the proposal of marriage from a Russian count. The proposal marks her formal reacceptance by the honest and law-abiding community.[87] Rocambole himself is also morally reborn in the series when, after ten years in prison, his heart is touched by "an honest sentiment."[88] He agrees to help an unjustly condemned fellow prisoner right a wrong done to two orphan girls. Rocambole's future pardon comes from heaven but his path to it is through good deeds done to his fellow men. When he saves a convict from the guillotine, he identifies himself as "a man whom God may perhaps pardon one day."[89] When he has succeeded in restoring to the orphans their fortune and well being, he contemplates suicide. His suicide is averted by those he has helped, however, and they tell him that his good deeds have won him a pardon in heaven. He is no longer a bandit, and he has won his way back into society without the help of the authorities.

The problem of reentry into society seems less acute for outlaws and criminals in the Western European and American stories, precisely because the outlaw's allegiance to a code of unofficial justice is shared by the community in which he operates. This alone frequently makes his separation less complete. When the Western European or American outlaw decides to rejoin respected society, he presents his record of sins and good deeds directly to the community for judgment. The Russian bandit, on the contrary, must seek pardon either from the tsar or his representative. There is no unofficial code of justice that the authorities might violate. There is no recognition of a code above the authorities or independent from them. The power of the tsar and, through him, the authorities, dwarfs all and inhibits the creation of heroes such as those that dominated English, French, and American popular fiction.

The Popular Crime Story

A new kind of crime story, in which the criminal's primary relationship was to the community rather than to the state, gained popularity in the early twentieth century. In this respect the criminal story differed from the bandit tale, although early prototypes of the criminal protagonists had many of the characteristics of the bandit. The first and most renowned of the lubok criminals was Ivan Osipov, the eighteenth-century rascal better known as Vanka Kain.[90] Kain's life included stints as a thief, a robber, a bandit, a detective, and a convict, and made him the ideal subject for a criminal adventure story. Kain was among a select group of outlaws whose names became familiar to the general populace. He was perhaps the author of an autobiography, and probably wrote songs about his adventures and feats. The pioneer lubok writer Matvei Komarov used Kain's life to create the Russian criminal novel.[91]

Early accounts of Kain's life have many of the elements of the typical bandit tale, and the facts of his life appear consistent with the conventions of bandit fiction. Kain was born into a serf family in the province of Moscow in 1714 or 1718. His owner was a merchant, and at the age of thirteen Kain was sent to Moscow to work in the owner's shop. According to his autobiography, he was poorly treated and began to steal. He joined with local thieves and ran off to lead a life of crime, eventually ending up in a gang of Volga bandits. When he tired of this life, he offered his services to the chief of the dreaded Investigations Chancellery (*Sysknoi prikaz*), the headquarters of which was known as a place of torture, imprisonment, and execution.

At this point in his career, Kain's name appears in official documents, and his nineteenth-century biographer, G. Esipov, was able to reconstruct his adventures. Kain gave the chief of the Investigations Chancellery a written statement of his regret for his past crimes, and volunteered to work at catching thieves. He began that very night and rounded up thirty-two crooks, including his former collaborator. His night's work earned him the title "Kain the Informer," and his power within official circles grew. He was poorly paid for his services, however, and turned to extortion, which he managed from his new house in the Kitai Gorod section of central Moscow. There he ran his own court, complete with thugs and hangmen. His misdeeds were eventually brought to light, and he was beaten, branded, and sentenced to perpetual servitude in Siberia, where he is alleged to have written his autobiography and songs.

Kain's name was so well known in the nineteenth century that it was occasionally used by popular authors who wanted to signify a criminal hero. V. F. Potapov's *Vanka Kain, a Russian Tale in Verse* (1859) is about a smith who turns to crime, and the story has nothing to do with the real Vanka Kain; neither does the Kain who appears as a criminal in one of the serial novels of the Moscow *Kopeika* entitled "Tempest" (197/551, 1910).

The stories based on Kain's life are interesting because they show a gradual shift away from the bandit formula to a different kind of crime story. Three versions of Kain's life are: (1) Matvei Komarov's late eighteenth-century tale, *The Detailed and True History of Two Crooks, the First Being the Glorious Russian Criminal, Bandit, and Moscow Detective of Times Past Vanka Kain with All His Investigations, His Mad Cap Wedding, Various Funny Songs, and His Portrait; the second, the French Thief Cartouche and His Comrades*; (2) Misha Evstigneev's *Vanka Kain, a Collection of Stories from the Life of the Courageous Criminal, Detective and Bandit* (1869); and (3) the anonymous serial, *The Adventures of Vanka Kain*, which appeared in ten issues in 1918 in Moscow and was one of the last works of popular commercial fiction published in Russia.[92]

Komarov claimed to have heard the adventures directly from Kain in 1755, while the latter was in prison. His Kain is an energetic and self-assertive hero who, like the bandit heroes, overcomes difficulties by ingenuity and bravado. He is a positive figure who turns to crime because of bad influences, a poor education, and the difficulties of serfdom. For Kain, a serf, freedom is the central problem. He runs away from his master "knowing that freedom is the best thing on earth, and that under the yoke of servitude even virtuous people are not all happy" (p. 6). He embarks on a merry life of robbery and theft and ridicules the authorities when they hold him between escapes. He goes to the Volga, but when he tires of the dangers of the criminal existence, he returns to Moscow to start a new career. His motive, however, is not remorse, and in this he differs from the bandit heroes. Rather, he seeks a change of scene and different working conditions, which he finds as a detective and thief catcher. He does not give up his criminal ways, and he is eventually caught and punished.

Komarov's story contains elements of the bandit tale, such as the descriptions of the life of ease and feasting and the mockery when Kain steals a priest's clothing, but the world of disorder is different from that of the bandit stories. There is no model of order to which Kain's criminal world can be contrasted. Everyone steals in this story, and when Kain leaves his master for a free life of crime, he does not reject a proper and orderly existence. Policemen commit crimes, and everyone takes what he wants and lives according to passions with few inhibitions.

The story was later reorganized by subsequent authors to fit the emerging conventions of the bandit tale. In Evstigneev's telling, Kain's disorderly sinful life is clearly contrasted to that of orderly and law-abiding people. Kain's master is portrayed as a kindhearted merchant who takes Kain into service out of generosity. The future criminal's family members are identified as cobblers, not serfs. A debauched and villainous father sets him on the path of crime. In this version, Kain never feels remorse or gives up his life of crime, and in this respect Evstigneev's and Komarov's renditions differ from both the redemption and doomed-bandit formulas.

Kain's service to the authorities begins when a high official decides to impress a visiting English lord with the superior skills of Russian thieves. Kain is released from jail to serve as patriotic thief and succeeds in robbing the English gentleman. The official is so pleased that he makes Kain a detective, and puts him in charge of pursuing criminals. The new detective is not so discriminating in his choice, however, and continues to rob both crooks and honest people. Kain's identity as a detective is almost insignificant in this story. The only arrest he makes is that of his former girlfriend, who has thrown him over. She turns against him as soon as she is brought in, and the two are justly punished. His fate is that of the doomed bandit, despite his service.

Several small touches in Evstigneev's story are reminiscent of the bandit tale. The story opens with a terrible storm, during which Kain's drunken father curses horribly, and his dying mother fears for Kain's lost soul. Kain's outcast status is communicated with the information that he was forced to live in the northern Europeans' settlement (*Nemetskaia slo-boda*), and with the hint that "Many say he was not a Russian" (p. 54). After he begins his life of crime, Kain, his friend, and girlfriend live a merry life of freedom and debauchery.

The 1918 Kain serial retains elements of the bandit story, but the importance of the state has been reduced. The anonymous author begins with Kain bemoaning his sentence of hard labor: "And so, good-bye freedom, that gift of God that Vanka prized more than anything else on earth."[93] Like Churkin, Kain is known and respected by both the criminals and the authorities. He soon escapes from prison and heads back to his native forests, where he is in his own element. In the second installment, Kain is in the Siberian town of Irbit, the place of Churkin's refuge, but Kain's adventures, in this telling, more resemble Anton Krechet's. Kain's family refuses to give him refuge. Fellow villagers do not turn him in, because, according to the author, informing was considered despicable in Siberia and the Urals. He is pursued everywhere, however, and is denied a peaceful life.

In the classic bandit tale, the hero at this point learns of a war or some other service that he can perform for the tsar. In the Kain story, the criminal hears that a rich merchant has offered a reward of 10,000 rubles to the person who can solve the case of a big robbery in the forest.

The detective who solves crimes that threaten society is a more modern and independent character than the bandit who seeks only to reenter the society he once rejected. The early twentieth-century Russian detectives in this mold include the heroes of installment adventures, such as Sherlock Holmes, Nat Pinkerton, and Nick Carter. Vanka Kain solves the case by outwitting the peasant bandits who committed the robbery. After he collects his reward, Kain begs the intercession of the merchant in regaining a place in respectable society. He is pardoned, and his new place in society is expressed by his marriage to a peasant girl.

After his pardon, Kain becomes a detective, but most of his adventures occur when he foils his enemies among criminals or protects society from various disasters. For example, he rescues the passengers of a train when a mad engineer threatens to destroy it. He saves a girl from being thrown off a bridge, and puts a child murderess out of business. Kain is a sinner, like other Russian outlaw heroes, but he is redeemed through service to the community rather than to the tsar or the state.

Another crime story that diverged from the bandit tale, and suggested the appearance of a more modern formula, was M. D. Klefortov's *Sonka of the Golden Hand* (1903). The story was based on the life of Sonia Bliuvshtein, a criminal more famous in her day than Churkin. When

Anton Chekhov went to visit the penal colony at Sakhalin, one of the prisoners he sought out was the famous Sonka.

In Klefortov's story Sonka grows up in wretched poverty, but she is ambitious, talented, and aspiring: "She had a kind of hellish strength of will."[94] She marries a rich man, has a child, and goes abroad, but soon leaves her family to wander and return to Russia. When she is apprehended, she defends her life of thievery by claiming that she served the poor. The public applauds her at her trial, and when she is sent to the penal colony at Sakhalin, her fellow inmates treat her with respect. Her self-justification and support from several alternative communities make Klefortov's Sonka a more successful and hopeful rebel than the traditional bandits, even though her social service is never spelled out in the story. She expresses her defiance of the authorities, and her appeal to another alternative authority, in her song, which concludes:

> But sometime the people will know
> that I did not steal for myself
> but for those who suffer,
> who are oppressed by want,
> who die from hunger,
> who are compelled to steal by need.
> Then, truly, everyone will say:
> Yes, let her be blessed. (Pp. 17-18)

Sonka is not a Robin Hood, however, and she is no social bandit. She repents her life of crime and dies in the Sakhalin clinic, dreaming of her daughter. She has no means of atonement, but she is attended by a kindly physician, a representative of civil society.

Crime stories is which the criminal's absolution came from other than official quarters were numerous in the late nineteenth and early twentieth centuries. Many appeared before the abolition of prepublication censorship after 1905, as did Klefortov's story. In Pazukhin's melodramatic tale, *So It Was Fated to Be* (1898), a guilty merchant recognizes his crime and atones by making a pilgrimage, as does an evil cook in *The Lady Bandit Solovei* (1904) by Foma Balagur.

A kopeck novel about the February Revolution, *Broken Chains*, appeared in the St. Petersburg paper soon after the event and showed many of the characteristics of the new crime novel.[95] The hero, Beloiartsev, rebels against the tsar and urges his fellow soldiers not to fire on protesting workers. He is arrested and sentenced to death, but he is saved by the intervention and support of the community, in the form of his comrades. At the end of the novel he is seen marching down the avenue, a soldier among other soldiers. It is no longer the state that dispenses justice or determines his fate.

The substitution of the community for the state in the salvation of outcast heroes in stories such as *Sonka of the Golden Hand* and *Broken Chains* represents an important shift in thinking, bringing these Russian stories closer to French, English, and American fiction. The portrayal of the community as the victim of crime and the community as an authority capable of pardoning the criminal suggests the existence of a shared code of conduct, which could be violated by the criminal and upheld by the community. The idea of the existence of such a code is a step in the development of a sense of law, and, by implication, a limit on the sphere of authority granted to the tsar.

These changes came about long after the actuality of Russian legality had begun to change. The judicial reform of 1864 was a corollary to the emancipation of the serfs. The establishment of independent courts and the growth of the legal profession led to a heightened sense of legality among educated Russians, even if the autocracy was unwilling to adjust to the implicit limitations of its prerogatives.[96] The fact that evidence of a new perspective on crime and law should appear in the popular literature a half century after the court statutes is hardly surprising. The legal reforms had an impact on the whole population, even though the peasants were insulated from their operation in certain cases by the existence of special peasant courts. Popular Russian perspectives on the criminal remained distinctive in some respects, however. Most interestingly, the Russian writers did not generally portray either a dangerous underclass or vicious master criminals who threatened society as a whole. Images of a dangerous underclass were prominent in the feuilleton novels of such authors as Eugene Sue, Ponson du Terrail, and G.W.M. Reynolds. Villains so pernicious that they could only be destroyed appear throughout the Western European fiction as well as in the American.[97] One of the effects of the feuilleton crime novel, according to Michel Foucault, was to distance criminals from society and therefore to make their punishment easier to accept.[98] The fact that this distancing did not take place in the Russian fiction as much as in the Western European may suggest a hesitation to abandon the idea of redemption. In any case, the Russian authors did not find the idea of the poor and deprived very threatening. The bandit and criminal protagonists had several symbolic meanings, but they did not generally symbolize a menacing underclass.

The greatest contrast between the Russian popular fiction and the contemporaneous Western European and American was in the fate of the adventuresome hero. The reformed Russian outlaws returned to their community without their powers or understanding greatly enhanced by

Fig. 10. Drozov, *Before Execution: Innocent Judged Guilty* (Moscow, 1914).

their adventures. In this they differed from many of their American and Western European counterparts. Tarzan returned from the jungle to prove himself the master of civilized society. The strength forged in the jungle did not appear to affect his manners adversely. Ponson du Terrail's protagonists, Rocambole and Baccarat, gain in stature after they atone for their sins. Richard Markham, the hero of G.W.M. Reynolds' *Mysteries of London*, marries an Italian princess and becomes a kind of democratic king in Italy. All of these outcasts return to society with enhanced power and authority. The Russians do not. Their return to society is predicated upon recognition of their rightful place. That place was not miserable or contemptible, but it held none of the grandeur of the bandit's life.

All popular fiction is the stuff of daydreams, but Russian daydreams are held in check by rules that do not govern French, English, or American popular literature. The constraints on individual rebellion and initiative, as expressed in the literature of banditry and crime in the late imperial period, were great. Individuals were restrained in the imagination of popular writers of both lubok fiction and newspaper serials by the certainty that they were weaker than the political authority and the social order of their communities. Freedom lay outside that order, but it was a doomed freedom. The strong individual was inspired to sample that freedom, but in order to survive he had to return to the community.

The bandit as a symbol of freedom gained by living beyond the limits of organized society resembles in some respects the image of the frontiersman in American popular literature.[99] Frontiersmen such as Kit Carson were portrayed as noble and pure, however, and the presumption was often maintained that their way of life was superior to a civilized one, even if their world was violent. There was never such a presumption in the Russian fiction, and the bandit's world, as well as his freedom, was always illegitimate. Writing on their theme, the Russian popular authors conveyed a conservative and traditional message to their readers. Yet the reading of bandit stories was also a way for ordinary people to explore ideas of freedom and rebellion. The popularity of the bandit tales may therefore signify a growing interest in these ideas among ordinary people, even though the ideas are discredited according to the formula of the stories.

Rebellion and Freedom Recast—Private Detectives

New images of the free and independent individual began to appear in popular commercial fiction as war and revolution threatened the foundations of Russian society. The ideas of freedom and order prevalent in the lubok and newspaper tales of banditry are absent from the detective stories and installment novels that flooded the cheap publishing market after the Revolution of 1905. The authors of this fiction spurned the striking imbalance between an impregnable society and state on one hand, and a doomed although rebellious individual hero on the other. In its place, they created what was a new type of protagonist for Russian readers, the private detective. The private detective was a hero of order and his appearance in Russian popular literature signifies the diffusion of a new sense of order, one in which the private community had an increased stake.[100]

The private detective is a defender of civil society and not the state. He is stronger than the official representatives of order, and it is to him, rather than to the authorities, that society must look for security. The detective serves society, but he does so from the outside, on his own terms, and at society's insistence. Pinkerton, Carter, and Holmes were all foreigners, and many of the detective stories were set in foreign countries. This distance may have made readers more willing to accept the idea that the state and society could be helpless before lawless elements, and would have to seek the services of these extraordinary individuals. The criminals whom the detectives confront are too powerful for ordinary officials to subdue. Dr. Kvartz, "the criminal scientist," is so clever that even Nick Carter sometimes falls victim to his shenanigans.[101] In one such instance, the director of a New York prison appeals to Carter for help in the case of a mysterious phantom who is terrorizing both guards and prisoners. Carter asks if the demon "turned out to be stronger than the prison authorities."[102] The prison director's answer is "absolutely." The private detective is, par excellence, that individual to whom society must look for assistance. He alone is the master of the knowledge and prowess necessary to rout the professional criminal. Regarding the bungling police detectives, Carter remarks in another story, "Such idiots call themselves detectives."[103]

The detective installments show a weakening of the classic dichotomy between freedom and order. The detectives are heroes who have some of the opportunities that go with freedom and the life of the feast, but they also enjoy the benefits of life in legitimate society. Because they are such powerful figures, the detectives can traverse the hitherto impermeable barrier between freedom and order. Enjoying the fruits of freedom, justified in their independence, they are blessed rather than damned. Their initiative and individuality is a boon to society. Vanka Kain in the 1918 detective adventure lives the high life of the outsider, but he has a family and the respect of society.

FIG. 11. *Nat Pinkerton, the King of the Detectives* (Petrograd: Razvlechenie, 1915).

CHAPTER V

Rebellion and Freedom Recast—Bandits

The weakening of traditional attitudes toward the rebellious individual is also apparent in the installment novels. Here for the first time appear genuine Robin Hood-type heroes who fight against a corrupt authority, with justice and a community of honest people on their side. These heroes, who are also usually foreigners, do not have to choose between bowing their heads before the representatives of the state or losing them. Robert Gaisler, a bandit chieftain, is introduced on the first page of an installment novel as "a people's hero."[104] His innocence is clear at the outset of the story, and once driven beyond the law he defends helpless people, unlike Churkin and the lubok bandits. When a poor old woman is almost run down by a fancy coach, Gaisler forces the aristocratic passenger to give her a large sum of money (p. 172). Even Krechet, who occasionally rescues damsels in distress, never champions the cause of the poor in this way. Ataman Vilde, another one of the installment bandits, is likewise counterposed to a social order that has lost its legitimacy.[105] So is Franz Lerman, also a hero of an installment novel.[106] Both are driven to banditry against their will, but once they become bandits, justice is on their side. Their fate is sweeter than that of the lubok bandits, who are grateful to receive a pardon. Like Gaisler, who settles happily in America with his beloved, they are not forced to accept the social order they challenged.

The reformulation of these classic Russian social dilemmas is also apparent in other installment novels. The bandit was so natural a hero for Russian popular writers that bandit protagonists were grafted on to several historical tales, such as *Garibaldi—The Bloody Adventures of the Dreaded Ataman of the Bandits* (1902), one of the earliest installment novels. The young aristocratic Garibaldi returns home to discover the death of his father at the hands of his stepmother and her lover. He kills the murderers and flees. He joins a bandit gang, dons a mask, rescues old men and children, and performs other praiseworthy feats.[107] The hero of *The Secrets of Napoleon or the State Traitor Joseph Boianovskii* (1908) is also driven to banditry, in his case because he is unjustly accused of treason. None of these outlaws commits recognizable crimes, and they have no cause to feel remorse. The device of banditry is used because the heroes must be shown to be outsiders, and the classic Russian outsider is the bandit.

These characters are like the rebellious outsiders found in other popular literatures. The fact that they are innocent of any crimes, although branded criminals, is all important. One of their functions is to allow the rebellious and self-assertive individual to triumph in the face of an unjust and vulnerable social order.

Old Mentalities and New

The popular writers who presented rebellious and self-assertive individuals and who broke down the imaginary dichotomy between freedom and order offered what was for ordinary Russian people a radically new way of looking at the world. According to contemporary observers, the readers of the detective adventures and the installment novels were primarily urban teen-agers and young adults. These are the very people one would expect to be among the first in the lower classes to manifest a new mentality. This shift in thinking accompanied actual changes in the pattern of daily life. Ordinary people did become more open in their opposition to the tsarist order in the late nineteenth and early twentieth centuries, judging from the scale and frequency of conflict. The spontaneous and often hopeless outbursts of the past gradually gave way to more focused opposition, particularly in labor disputes, in which workers increasingly engaged in strikes and made political demands. The world of the riot was very much that of the freedom found in the lubok bandit tales and newspaper serials. The dream of a foredoomed, but nevertheless satisfying outburst of anarchistic violence against the authorities, the wealthy, or the totality of organized society in the name of that all-encompassing freedom gradually faded from the pages of the popular fiction. In its place appeared new images of the relationship between the rebellious individual and the official representatives of order, and the balance no longer tilted so heavily against the former. The dissemination of new ways of thinking about the individual and society in popular stories accompanied changes in thinking on the part of those who read them. Each reinforced the other.

Labor historians have puzzled over the question of when, if ever, the spontaneous violence of the prerevolutionary working class gave way to disciplined political action.[108] The evidence in the popular literature is very strong for the view that the new ways of thinking found a hearing among lower-class readers only in the early twentieth century, and then predominantly among the young adults of the cities. Only after the Revolution of 1905 had weakened the perceived power of tsarist authority in the minds of the lower classes did lower-class readers find in fiction a preponderance of protagonists who were able to enjoy freedom without paying a terrible price for rebellion. At the same time, society began to replace the state as a source of legitimate authority in the literature. The abolition of prepublication censorship after the Revolution of 1905 may have encouraged writers to treat rebellious heroes more sympathetically, but it is unlikely to have stimulated them to write detective stories. The production of both the detective stories and the installment novels required a break with earlier patterns of thinking among the writers who wrote them and the readers who read them.

The fact that the new heroes were primarily foreigners, and that the works themselves were in some cases rough translations, implies that the transition to new ways of thinking was only partial. Popular writers used foreign models to imagine the new types of heroes and situations, and readers found it easier to accept new ways of thinking in a foreign setting. The new sense of the individual, as well as the less pessimistic vision of freedom, were late arrivals, however, and the dominant attitude toward these issues remained the earlier one, as expressed in the lubok works and newspaper serials.

The themes of the outcast individual and the conflict between freedom and the orderly world were not exclusive to the domain of popular literature in Russia during this period. The popular stories on these themes differed from those of belles lettres of the prerevolutionary period not only in the quality of writing and inspiration that separates art from artifact; writers of belles lettres generally treated the theme of the rebellious outsider and the conflict between freedom and order with a richness and ambivalence that does not appear in the popular works. The paths of acceptable behavior were much narrower in popular literature than in belles lettres. Dostoevsky explored the limits and confines of the human community in *Crime and Punishment, The Devils, The House of the Dead,* and in other works. Tolstoy wrote many stories about heroes who could find no peace outside of a community of universal love. The problem reappeared as a theme in early Soviet literature. Ostap Bender, the heroic con man of Ilf and Petrov's novels, roams the Soviet countryside much like a comical version of Churkin, even down to his Turkish citizenship and his dream of a flight to the south. The problem of the criminal outsider or rebel is also a subject that Leonid Leonov explores in *The Thief* and *The Badgers.* The rebellious heroes of Russian belles lettres are crushed by the existing social order, as are many of their popular counterparts. Something of the almost mythical force they confront can be seen in the prerevolutionary popular literature.

The treatment of freedom and order and the exploration of the ideas personified in the bandit and criminal protagonists may have been important to the audience for popular literature in part because the familiar structure of rural life was breaking down. Bandit stories, with their message that meaningful life can be found only in the community, probably answered both the desires and fears engendered by the increased independence that came with opportunity.

The early twentieth century detectives and installment bandits represented a more complete affirmation of the energetic outsider than anything hitherto available to Russian lower-class readers. The popularity of these stories, the cheapest commercial reading material sold, attests to the genesis of a new and more Western understanding of freedom and the role of the individual among the literate common people of prerevolutionary Russia.

VI

NATIONALISM AND NATIONAL

IDENTITY

Tsarist Russia was a sprawling multinational empire, and in the nineteenth century the question of national identity was an important one in both political and cultural life. The survival of the empire after the October Revolution may have depended at least in part on popular notions among Great Russians that the empire had value to them and not only to the deposed autocracy.[1] We know little about the popular conception of what it meant to be Russian in premodern Russia, but the early lubok tales suggest that the Orthodox Church, and, to a lesser extent, the tsar were the foremost emblems of Russianness throughout much of the nineteenth century. These two symbols of nationality recur in the early stories and their treatment by the authors implies that to be Russian was to be loyal to the tsar and faithful to the Orthodox Church. Yet by the late nineteenth century, the tsarist state was one of the most archaic political structures in Europe. Educated Russians influenced by Western ideas and culture sought new ideas of Russianness. The spread of education and secular thinking influenced all classes, as did social and geographic mobility. Contact with new groups led to expanded aspirations and stimulated curiosity. Participation in and knowledge of war had a similar effect, and there were many lubok war stories in which national identity was a central issue. Improvements in the technology and scope of communications also expanded people's understanding of the geographic and political setting in which they lived. It was no longer enough to know the name of one's village, neighboring villages, and the nearest big market town. People wanted to learn more about their surroundings, and it became easier for them to acquire the information. The breakdown of the insularity of the village encouraged people to think of themselves in relation to a larger world, and to ponder what it meant to be Russian within that world.

A quest for the definition of Russianness was shared by Russians of all cultural levels. For readers of higher literature, the question was one primarily of what constituted the substance of Russian national identity, as opposed to that of a foreign nation or people. For many readers of popular literature, the concept of national identity, itself, was new. Peasant loyalties were primarily to family, village, tsar, and Church, and the concept of a nation of peoples with shared loyalties was not well developed. Yet as peasants acquired some secular education and spatial mobility, and as the army was modernized and based on general male conscription, the traditional relation of the individual to the tsar and Church ceased to anchor common people firmly amidst the changes around them. The exploration of the idea of national identity and its prominence in the popular fiction shows that this was an issue for many of the most successful authors, and one that remained in flux throughout the period.

The oldest ideas of Russianness have an artificial and brittle quality when contrasted with the more instinctive national feelings of many other European peoples.[2] The Russian sense of national identity based on tsar and Church had something in common with American patriotism, even though the latter was a democratic rather than an autocratic creed and there was no official American state religion.[3] Many European peoples were culturally relatively homogeneous and lived in compact geographic configurations. Both of these factors contributed to the formation of a stable sense of identity with a larger group defined by culture, geography, and ethnicity even before the concept of nation was of much relevance. For these peoples, the development of a national identity followed rather directly from its precursors.

In neither Russia nor America were the foundations of a coherent national consciousness so strong. Russian settlements were dispersed geographically across a huge continent, much of which was shared with peoples of different languages and religions. The Russian Empire had expanded rapidly in recent times and included within its boundaries an extremely diverse mix of national minorities. Borders were still contested in many places, and the loyalties of minorities incorporated into the empire by conquest were logically a matter of conjecture. In addition, the empire, extending from Europe to Asia, and stretching its muscles in both directions, was too "Asiatic" and "Oriental" to be fully accepted as a member of the European family of nations, but, at the same time, educated Russians rejected cultural affiliation with the Orient. For these reasons, the question of what it meant to be a Russian in a world of peoples of different nationalities was a major cultural issue that pervaded much of Russian letters, and it was certainly prominent in popular literature.

One statement of a definition of Russianness is offered in lubok stories in which an outsider, defined either by religion or nationality, undergoes a rite and is recognized as a member of the Russian community. The formal process of becoming Russian by either swearing allegiance to the tsar, converting to Orthodox Christianity, or both is described in a few lubok tales. The heroes of these stories are Great Russians, and those who become Russian are usually members of groups who are later added to the empire. This was the most primitive and unreflective idea of national identity found in the popular fiction. The non-Russians, even when they converted to Christianity, were not shown to adopt a new set of values that changed their behavior. The more profound meaning of Russianness or non-Russianness was not examined in this early naive literature, but the conversion to Orthodoxy signaled the change in status from alien to Russian. The lack of reflectiveness is consistent with the literary simplicity of the early tales in which neither character nor motivation is developed with subtlety or depth.

A second and more reflective idea of national identity appears more frequently in the lubok tales and also in the newspaper serials and women's novels. These are not stories about becoming Russian but about what it means to be a Great Russian among the various peoples of the empire.

The third and most modern vision of a Russian national identity was expressed frequently in all the varieties of popular fiction during the late nineteenth and early twentieth centuries. This was the portrayal of the empire as a geographic entity. Descriptions of specific places figure prominently in the fiction from this period, and the focus of attention shifted during the last two decades of the old regime from central Russia to the border regions and Siberia. In stories set in the far reaches of the empire, authors appealed to a curiosity about place that increased with the geographic mobility of lower-class readers. At the same time, they presented a vision of Russia defined not by the cultural and political life of the capitals, but by the diversity of landscapes and peoples and the sheer size of the empire.

The newer notions of Russianness shared some common elements with the idea of national identity already established in the United States, but the Russian popular writers paid little attention to the kinds of public values and civic virtues associated with American national identity in the late nineteenth and early twentieth centuries. Considering the political character of late Imperial Russia, it is not surprising that the emerging popular conception of national identity included only a rudimentary concept of citizenship, with its attendant rights and obligations.

The most dramatic feature of the new Russian sense of national identity evident in the popular literature is a growing cosmopolitanism. The negative stereotypes that predominate in the lubok fiction and signify long-established suspicions of foreigners do not appear often in the more modern types of popular literature. On the contrary, Western Europeans, Americans, and even Japanese heroes are prominent in the early twentieth-century fiction.

The traditional emblems of Russianness began to lose their power in the late nineteenth and early twentieth centuries. The susceptibility of Russian soldiers to radical slogans during World War I and the revolutions of 1905 and 1917 are evidence of this. The new ideas of Russianness that filtered into the popular milieux were less coherent than the old symbols, and also less exclusive. Xenophobic attitudes toward foreigners found in the early popular literature are less common in the late imperial period. The popular literature in which the issue of national identity figures prominently during the early twentieth century is often cosmopolitan, and there is little reference to either the tsar or the Orthodox Church.

Early Ideas of Russianness

In the old form of Russian national identity, the Orthodox Church and the God-appointed tsar comprised the fulcrum for both political authority and Russianness. The expansion of the empire and its long consolidation until well into the second half of the nineteenth century took place under the dual banners of Orthodoxy and autocracy. The nearly theocratic tsar was officially promoted as a divine legatee on earth, and was called "batiushka," or father, a term of endearment also used for the village priest. The bureaucratic monarchy in fact became more secular in the eighteenth and nineteenth centuries, but the theocratic authority of the tsar and the assertion of the tsar's omnipotence remained fundamental to the political integration of classes and peoples within the empire. That the common people, including serfs, felt a personal bond of loyalty to the tsar was evident in their willingness to petition for redress of grievances, even when the very act of petitioning was a punishable crime. In appealing to the tsar for justice, they expressed their belief in his link to a divine order in which justice prevailed over the imperfect laws of this world. Personal loyalty to the tsar was something in which people of ethnic, religious, and linguistic diversity might share.

Orthodoxy was a more exclusive bond of empire than was autocracy, since it held little attraction to people of different religions. Orthodoxy also distanced Russians from the Catholics in Poland, Muslims in the Crimea and Central Asia, Christians of the Caucasus, Jews in various places, and native peoples of the Far East whom tsarist authorities sought to incorporate into the empire. Yet it was a powerful bond among the Orthodox.

The dual emblem of tsar and Church retained its effectiveness for the Great Russian and Ukrainian peasant populations long after it lost meaning for the increasingly secularized educated elite. The authors of Russian popular fiction were influenced by the secular nationalism of educated Russia, but they also stood close to the earlier ideas of Russianness. When they wrote about historical subjects or wars, they expressed their own often confused national feelings about what it meant to be Russian, as well as their mistrust of certain nationalities inside the empire and fears of foreigners beyond its borders. Their confusion was, in a sense, justifiable. When Georgians or Crimean Tatars were incorporated into the Russian Empire, did they become Russians who did not speak the Russian language? If not, they remained Georgians or Tatars whose loyalties were first to their own peoples, and some of whom would leave the empire at the first opportunity. There was no supra-ethnic concept of nation or empire to which diverse peoples could be attracted with a modicum of voluntarism. Yet the empire did include diverse peoples, and was expanding to include even more. The issue of what bound the empire, besides the tsar's armies, was explored implicitly in much of the popular fiction.

Swearing allegiance to the tsar is shown to be a means of assimilation and acceptance for non-Russian nationalities in some lubok tales. A grudging allegiance, if maintained, earned a guarded acceptance. An allegiance granted enthusiastically and based on recognition of Russians as stronger, cleverer, smarter, or more heroic people than one's own earned the character even more sympathetic treatment within the story. If the non-Russian went further and converted to Orthodoxy, he or she was accepted as equal to Russians in the story, and intermarriage was possible. Of the many peoples portrayed in the fiction, only the Jews appear to have been completely excluded from these possible routes to assimilation, suggesting perhaps the influence of both popular anti-Semitism and official policy.

The fusion of the tsar and Orthodoxy into one symbol of Russianness was expressed in several stories. In a broadside from the Crimean War, Nicholas' well-known phrase, "Understand and submit, O Nations, for God is with us," is rendered as "Understand heathens, understand and submit, for God is with us."[4] The hero of Ivin's bandit story *Brynsk Forest* urges his followers to fight "for the Orthodox faith, for the motherland, and the tsar father."[5] Heroes in Volgin's tales, *Those Who Pray to God and Serve the Tsar Will Not Go Astray* and *Corpse Without a Coffin*, pray, "Lord, thank you for giving me the chance to spill my blood on the field of battle for tsar and fatherland," and ask for a blessing "in the holy task of standing in the ranks of Russian soldiers" during the Russo-Turkish War of 1877-78.[6]

Personal service to a particular tsar is described in only a few of the stories, but in these the intimate relationship between the tsar and individual peasants or soldiers is coupled with the idea of the tsar as a symbol of Russianness. Several stories of this type about Peter are Evstigneev's *Anecdotes and Legends about Peter the Great, the First Emperor of the Russian Land, and about his Love for the State* (1873); *Tales of the Tsar Father Peter the Great and How He and His Stalwart Soldiers Fought the Enemy* (1892); and *The Legend of How the Soldier Saved the Life of Peter the Great from Death at the Hands of Bandits*, which appeared in many editions from the 1840s until 1917.[7] In these stories Peter is variously portrayed as a model of self-sacrifice and hard work, a generous man grateful for the unknowing service of a loyal soldier, and a valiant leader in battle. In each, the tsar is shown to know the common people and to be attentive to their needs. A noticeable characteristic of the popular fiction of the late tsarist era is that the tsar hardly ever appears in heroic form. The glorious deeds of historic tsars were a common theme of folklore, and in this respect, as in others, folklore and popular literature differed. In popular literature repentant bandits and foreigners who were won over to the Russian cause might swear loyalty to the tsar, but the tsar is more important as a passive focus of allegiance than as an active leader of soldiers in conquest. This point is made rather clearly by the surfeit of lubok tales about Ermak, the conqueror of Siberia, and the paucity of tales about his tsar, Ivan the Terrible. The lubok authors preferred Ermak as the protagonist for their tales and relegated Ivan to an abstract role as the symbol of nationality that Ermak serves.[8]

The idea of Russianness defined by personal loyalty and service to the tsar was strongly expressed in Ivin's tale, *The Gypsy Avenger*, a story set in the thirteenth century that has almost nothing to do with gypsies. The country is under the Tatar yoke, and Tatars raid and loot. The hero of the story is Stanislav, a Lithuanian prince, who has come to offer his services to Grand Prince Alexander Nevskii in the fight against the Tatars. Stanislav treats Alexander as his natural superior and is grateful when the Russian Grand Prince appoints him Prince of Pskov. The authors of the lubok tales always use the term *Russkii* for Russian, which implies Great Russian, rather than *Rossiiskii*, which refers to all citizens of the empire. The word Muscovite, which would be historically correct in some tales, is almost never used.

Stanislav swears by the Russian pagan god Perun, and when he arrives the Pskovites initially refuse to be ruled by the Lithuanian "barbarian."

The authority of Alexander prevails, however. Stanislav takes the oath to defend Pskov, joins the Orthodox Church, and marries the daughter of Prince Dmitry, who has succeeded Alexander. In Lithuania, Stanislav is now considered a traitor, but in Russia he is a loyal defender of the realm. "He was a threat to enemies, and did not even spare his former kin, the predatory Lithuanians."[9] Ivin concludes, "Impartial history named him a hero, but the Church canonized him in order to immortalize his good deeds." In this story, the grand princes of Russia take the place of the tsar, who has yet to make his historical appearance. Loyalty to the princes and conversion to Orthodoxy assure Stanislav a place equal to that of ethnic Russians.

Russification through conversion to Orthodoxy is important particularly in stories involving interaction with peoples of the Muslim East. A common theme of these stories is romance between an Oriental and a Russian suitor or bride, conversion of the lover to Orthodoxy, and flight of the young couple to Russia.

Ivin combined this plot with that of personal service to the tsar in his story *Iapancha*, a tale of the conquest of Kazan by Ivan the Terrible. The Tatar prince Iapancha is the hero of the cavalry of Kazan, but he has fallen in love with a Russian captive. Natasha would seem objectively to be in the weaker position, since she is a prisoner in the court of the khan, but she adamantly refuses to convert to Islam in order to marry Iapancha: "Don't think, lord, that the daughter of a Russian boyar could betray her faith, her fatherland, and the customs of her fathers."[10] So it is Iapancha who does precisely that, and converts to Orthodoxy. Even after his conversion, Iapancha continues to defend the city, but he is sentenced to death by the Tatar khan. His new faith gives him strength to meet death honorably and with confidence that he and Natasha will be together in the hereafter, but the two are saved when the Russians blow up the city walls with mines.

Natasha and Iapancha make their way to the Russian camp, where Iapancha is brought to Ivan the Terrible, and swears his loyalty to the tsar: "Lord, I fulfilled my duty to the fatherland. I stuck with it as long as my conscience allowed. But now I resolutely belong to you, as the true tsar and defender of unfortunates. I want to be a Christian and your subject" (p. 93). Iapancha's conversion is important not only because his soul is saved, but also because it signals his new loyalty to the "Russian" side. His conversion is more a national than a religious experience.

The national, rather than religious, emphasis in some conversion stories is reinforced by the physical flight or transport of the converts to Russian territory. In Ivin's tale, *The Bandit Churkin, a Captive of the Circassians* (1885), a Circassian girl is discovered on the battlefield by Russian troops

ЯПАНЧА
ТАТАРГКІЙ НАѢЗДНИКЪ

FIG. 12. I. S. Ivin (pseud. Kassirov), *Iapancha, the Tatar Horseman*
(Moscow: Sytin, 1916). Courtesy of the John G. White Collection of the
Cleveland Public Library.

and is christened. In Lunin's *In Chains Among the Chinese* (1910), a Chinese girl falls in love with a captured Russian sailor. She converts to Christianity, but is killed when the two attempt to escape.[11] Escape to Russia and marriage to a Russian does not change the nationality of the characters, but it does presage their eventual assimilation into Russian society.

A very early story on the theme of captivity and conversion that may have served as a model for the later tales is N. Zriakhov's *The Battle of the Russians with the Kabardinians or the Beautiful Mohammedan Dying on the Grave of Her Husband* (1843). This story, which was retold in a number of lubok editions, takes place in the Caucasus, where Russian soldiers are battling the Circassians, who are led by a "Prince Uzbek." A wounded Russian is captured and is offered the hand of the prince's daughter if he will convert to Islam. Andrei's faith and loyalty prove to be stronger than that of the princess Selima, and she is the one who converts. Selima announces her decision with the words, "I suppose from your explanations that your religion is much superior to ours."[12] Andrei completes the princess's conversion by teaching her the Russian language, songs, and dances. When Andrei is freed in an exchange of prisoners, Selima flees to the Russian camp, and the two return to his family estate. Selima, now Sophia, has a child. Andrei's wounds do not heal, and when he dies, Selima expires of a broken heart on his grave. The child remains as a symbol of the entry of the Circassians into the empire dominated by the Great Russians. Selima's father, Prince Uzbek, has become reconciled to the marriage, and he instructs his son and heir to respect and love Christians, and "in particular Russians, who are not only glorious for their victories in the whole world, but also for their good deeds" (p. 128).

Denationalization: Seduction and Captivity

The traditional idea of Russianness as belief in Orthodoxy and service to the tsar emphasized the capital as the geographic focus of patriotic feeling. Those fighting or serving on the far borders of the empire among enemies and nonbelievers were in danger of losing their Russianness. They carried their faith and loyalty like holy relics of nationality. Just as outsiders could become Russian by adopting Orthodoxy and swearing allegiance to the tsar, Russians who were tempted either by foreign delights or torments to waver in their faith were lost and cut off from everything Russian. Under this conception of Russianness, there could be no expatriates, only apostates.

The fear of losing one's nationality was expressed most commonly with respect to the peoples of the Moslem world, reflecting Russian historical experience with wars and raiding bands of nomads. Moslem culture was the major alternative to Russian culture in many border areas, and it is not surprising that Islam was perceived as the main opponent. The almost morbid fear and fascination with which the sensual allure and barbaric cruelty of Eastern societies are portrayed in this literature, however, suggests that these societies were perceived as more than a military threat. It is as if the Russianness of the stories' heroes was not securely welded to their persons and could loosen in the face of temptation or torture.

The possibility of being seduced into treason is raised in the 1854 version of the tale of the Kabardinians. If the hero, Andrei, gives in to Selima's pleading, he will be cursed as a traitor by his parents and his conscience, but he is nonetheless torn. His friend who has come to liberate him urges his immediate escape: "You have now become the prisoner of your feelings and desires, and you forget the holy debt of nature. Drowning in a river of the pleasures of love, you do not wish to swim to the shore of salvation."[13] The hero of the 1893 version is similarly tempted by the pleasures of the Orient. In this story the pleasures include not only the beautiful Circassian lady, but also dancing boys who scandalize Andrei but delight the other guests.

The lure of apostasy is not only sensual, but also material. The Russian heroes who are being courted by their captors live better in captivity than they do in their homeland. The enslaved hero of Lunin's *Slavery among the Asiatics* is made the chief clerk of his rich master, and other heroes are similarly dressed well and treated honorably, at least during the attempt to win their loyalties. The Japanese use both a carrot and stick approach on Krechet, the hero of the kopeck newspaper serial, threatening him with torture and offering him wine, food, and beautiful women if he will voluntarily forsake his homeland (no. 1351, 1912).

A nightmarish image of captivity coupled with temptation and seduction is Gogol's theme in his popular novel *Taras Bulba*, and the same idea is developed in the lubok version of this tale, *The Adventures of the Cossack Ataman Urvan* (1901). A Tatar woman lures a young Cossack into a besieged Polish city in order to see a beautiful Polish lady. The Cossack finds himself, as in Gogol's original, in a Catholic church, face to face with a priest, who, according to the author, is as hated a person as a Jew. The Cossack is seduced by the beauty of the Catholic lady and falls into her embrace: "And the Cossack was lost. He was lost to all Cossacks. He will see no more either the Dnieper region, nor his father's farms, nor the Church of God."[14] The words are Gogol's, but they are also in this case true to the sense of the bowdlerized lubok version.

Neither the English nor the French popular literary tradition manifests such a fear of losing one's nationality as that expressed so clearly in the Russian tradition. The closest thing to the Russian phenomenon may be the American fear of losing one's national identity in Europe. This represents a suspicion of the cultivated world rather than the wilds, however.

Heroes and heroines are captured by the enemies of Russia in many of the lubok tales. The fear of captivity and enslavement by nonbelievers is almost as old as Russian literature, if we are to believe the Igor tale, the hero of which is the first in a long line of Russian champions to undergo the anguish and temptations of captivity. The hero of Volgin's *Corpse without a Coffin* thinks, "Better that they kill me than to be in the hands of these cursed Muslim nonbelievers."[15] Even if he could escape his captors, his prospects would be poor "among vicious enemies, all of whom felt a terrible hatred for every Russian." Fear of captivity is largely a fear of helplessness, slavery, and permanent separation from Russia. The hero of Lunin's tale *Slavery among the Asiatics*, in which the practice of slavery among Central Asian peoples is portrayed with considerable accuracy, is fortunate enough to be sold to a friendly Khiva merchant and farmer. If he had been kept by the Turkmen who captured him, his lot would have been perpetual slavery, despite the fact that Islamic law dictated eventual manumission. Both Krechet and Nina suffer in captivity—she at the hands of the Chinese bandits who kidnap her, and he when he is captured by the Japanese.

The fear of captivity at the hands of one's enemies was for the most part associated with Islamic peoples, but in a few of the women's novels set before and during World War I, the apprehension was experienced by Russians in Germany. The family of the heroine in Bebutova's long novel, *The Barbarians of the Twentieth Century* (1915), is caught in Germany when war is declared, and they find themselves in the same terrifying plight as did earlier captives of the Islamic peoples. In this case the captives are women, and rape and dishonor await them when they are placed at the mercy of an evil German officer. Their German servants are delighted at the fall in fortune of the Russians, and a maid tells her Russian mistress, "You will be our slaves, and we will be your masters."[16] Another Russian family faces the same horrors when they are trapped in Berlin in Charskaia's novel *Her Majesty Love*. As they try to get to the railroad station, angry crowds surge around their automobile, blocking their path and shouting, "Down with Russia! Death to it!"[17] The Russian men are taken off the train to prison, and the women are threatened and abused by German soldiers and officers, just as in Bebutova's novel. The authors of these stories emphasize the vulnerability and peril of Russians away from the protection of their homeland.

The almost ritualistic statement that it is better to be killed than taken captive was sometimes difficult even for the authors to explain. In Pa-

FIG. 13. V. Volgin, *A Prisoner of the Turks* (Moscow: Sytin, 1914).

zukhin's novel about the Crimean War, *Russia in Arms* (1892), the hero fears captivity more than death, but his reasons seem almost petty. He thinks not about dishonor or torture, but about bad food and poor medical care at the hands of the British and French, and cries, "No, no! Better death."[18] Pazukhin attempted to bolster his hero's motivation by including newspaper reports about how bad conditions of the Russian prisoners actually were.

The captivity theme may have had roots in Russia's historical past, in the subjugation of Russians by the Mongols, and in enslavement by foreigners through abduction or capture during war. It may have been important for other than historical reasons, since it was so common in the fiction. These stories were about national identity rather than about the experience of bondage. If the stories were about the plight of the enslaved, there would have been tales about Russians enslaved by Russians, since this phenomenon was not uncommon in Russia's past.[19] There are no such stories in the popular literature, suggesting that the appeal of the captive tale was in its treatment of the tension between Russianness and foreignness.

The position of the captive was rich in psychological appeal and in dramatic potential that could be developed in fiction. For Orthodox Christians acceptance of a foreign culture, particularly an Islamic one, meant apostasy and damnation. Yet these cultures in their richness and differentness were fascinating and enticing. The captive was in a foreign culture, but, as long as he held out, not of that culture. His determination to maintain his Russianness gave readers a perspective from which to view what was exotic and attractive, yet taboo in the foreign culture. Many of the stories have a sexual subtheme, as the captive is tempted by a foreign seductress, or, if the Russian is a woman, sexually violated by a foreign man in a position of power. In the captive stories, one sees a sense of Russianness defined in relation to particular foreign cultures that were both alluring and threatening. The real threat was not that of living in captivity, but of losing one's nationality by succumbing to the temptations or weakening under harsh or generous treatment in a foreign land. This fear is different from that of being separated from friends, family, and familiar culture and is hard to understand except as evidence of a deeply felt insecurity about national identity.

Minorities of the Empire

Members of the many minority groups in these stories usually look up to the Great Russians with whom they come into contact as superior people with powers greater even than those of the most valiant and accomplished native person. The unquestioned superiority of the Russians in the stories symbolized the place that authors of popular fiction accorded minority peoples within the empire. As long as minority peoples willingly recognized Russians as representatives of a higher culture and expressed a desire to join that culture, they could enter Russian society roughly equal to those born into the culture. The authors, however, show little recognition of minority cultures as different from but equal to Russian culture. The relative ease with which individual minority people achieve high status within Russian society in these stories indicates a degree of cultural tolerance and pluralism, but those who succeed in Russian society do so because they are willing to enter on that society's terms.

The paternalism on the part of Russians and the rather abject admiration on the part of minority people are developed in a number of stories. The bandit hero Anton Krechet, in the *Gazeta kopeika* serial,[20] meets Manchurian hunters in the taiga on his way to fight in the Russo-Japanese War, and, to their astonishment, strangles a tiger with his bare hands (no. 1284, 1912). Georgii, the hero of another kopeck serial, "Satan's Cliff," earns the admiration of native Georgians in the Caucasus by doctoring their ills and those of their animals. He also rescues some of them from Tatar bandits. As a result, "The whole neighboring population of the mountain knew Georgii and strove to express their love and respect for him by one or another means" (no. 1385). The paternalistic relationship between the Russians and the Georgians is idealized: "The warm feelings of these simple poor people, honest and industrious, but ignorant and helpless, touched Georgii to the depths of his heart and sparked in him the unremitting wish to serve them to his last strength" (no. 1385). This relationship is cemented when Georgii marries a Georgian princess. Even though she is a princess, she feels herself inferior to Georgii because she does "not even know how to speak Russian."

In a story of the cultural assimilation of a gypsy, "The Foundling" (1912), also a *Gazeta kopeika* serial, a gypsy boy is adopted by a Russian watchman at an obscure river settlement. The gypsy sets out in search of the secret of his origins but returns to his adopted Russian family. In the course of his quest he has found a treasure, and he offers it to his Russian foster father. The authors of these tales show protagonists of foreign or minority origins who choose to join Russian families, rather than remain in their native cultures. The minority characters' desire for approval and acceptance from the Great Russians engaged the sympathies of the Great Russian readers.

There is little development of the idea of pan-Slav unity in this fiction. Poles were described in a few of the stories—usually as friends of Russia—unless the stories were set in a period of struggle between the two countries. Foma Balagur explains in one of his tales that Poles were closest to the Russians among the Slavs. "The life of the Poles was bad then when they were not yet subjects of Russia and comprised a separate kingdom among themselves."[21] The authors of these stories considered the Ukrainians subjects of Russia without any claims to national independence. E. Grebenka wrote of the accession of the Ukraine: "In 1654 the struggle for the faith in Little Russia ended happily with its adherence to Russia. The people began to rest easy."[22] When the Ukrainians were mentioned specifically as an ethnic group, it was as defenders of the southern borders of Russia, or they were stereotyped as likable, thick-headed clowns. In one of Evstigneev's dialogues, a Ukrainian wants to buy pig fat and asks for hair grease instead, which, he finds, smells worse than the lard they make at home.[23] In another, a general finds that a good-natured Ukrainian peasant, a *khokhol*,[24] has been assigned to him as an orderly. The fellow's entire face is obscured by his enormous moustaches and sideburns. He cannot remember the name of his regiment and has difficulty making himself understood in Russian. The general does not lose patience but remarks good humoredly, "It is not your fault you are not a fellow from Iaroslavl" (p. 79).

Nationalities that did not fit into the paternalistic image of the Russian family of peoples were portrayed in negative terms. Individuals who tried to block the conversion of Moslems to Christianity, who obstructed the friendship between Russians and various non-Russian peoples, or who clung to religions and cultures antithetical to assimilation in an empire in which Russian culture dominated were treated as enemies. The Christian Georgians and the Muslim Caucasian mountain peoples were generally accorded a predisposition toward friendship with Russians, but the 1854 version of the Kabardinian tale features an evil Circassian named Tamerlane who opposes the Russian hero. A similar figure appears in the 1893 version of the tale.

Tatars were presented as the most dangerous and terrible of peoples within the empire, testifying to the long historical memory of the popular writers. In Suvorov's popular history of the Russian Empire the Tatars are presented as fearful and powerful: "Out of the Asiatic steppe there surged into Russia the Tatars, the remnants of whom you have probably seen. These people were terrible; they were ferocious in appearance and pitied no one. Neither rivers nor mountains nor dark forests could stop them."[25] Balagur describes the destructive frenzy of a Tatar invasion in *The Terrible Death of the Fierce Tatar*: "The Tatars burned the village, stole the peasants' goods, and slaughtered the inhabitants or caught them with lassos."[26] Evstigneev also wrote of the Tatar invasion in his story *The Terrible Treasure or the Tatar Prisoner*: "The Tatar's lash threatened everyone. No one could call his wife his own, his daughter a daughter, his son a son. The Russian man was a slave, and it was as if he had nothing."²⁷ Shmitanovskii included episodes of hand-to-hand combat with the Tatars in his story of Ermak's conquest of Siberia, and as the Tatars leap into the fray, they shout, "Allah! Allah!"

Tatars usually appear as objects of scorn or low-dealing cheats in stories set in the late nineteenth and early twentieth centuries. In a collection of humorous stories by Evstigneev, a Russian nobleman refuses to hire a Tatar named Abdul Khan as his coachman, saying facetiously that "khan" means prince, and he does not need a prince to drive his coach.²⁸ In "The Devil's Cliff" a Tatar youth challenges Georgii, the Russian hero, to a horse race, the winner of which is to keep the loser's horse. When the Tatar loses, he kills his horse, demonstrating both his barbaric cruelty and his unwillingness to honor his agreement.²⁹ Later in the tale, the hero kills some Tatar bandits who have attacked an Armenian and his daughter. Even a dead Tatar can be terrifying: the shaved crown of the corpse gleamed in the moonlight, and "its eyes stuck out of their sockets, dead, glassy, and bulging, and in them was reflected the flickering flame of the match" (no. 1388).

Ivin's Prince Iapancha was presented more favorably than other Tatars, since he converted to Christianity, recognized the authority of the tsar, and married a Russian. This may reflect a friendly attitude toward the Tatars of Kazan, who accepted Russian rule more readily after their conquest than did the Crimean Tatars, but it may simply suggest respect for a prince who joined the Russians.

Turkmen were presented in much the same way as the Tatars, although they do not appear as frequently. Lunin's hero in *Slavery among the Asiatics* is appalled to see Turkmen dragging poor captives behind their horses.³⁰ In another story, the predatory Turkmen are contrasted to the peaceable settled Uzbeks: "The Turkmen are great predators. Robbery comprises their profession even at the present time, but the Uzbeks are a peaceful enough people."³¹

Neither gypsies nor Jews appear frequently in the lubok literature, but both are more evident in the periodical fiction. The lubok image of the gypsy is unsympathetic, but that in the serial stories is generally positive. This later view perhaps reflects a trickling down of the gypsy's image from high culture, where he often was portrayed as a kind of noble savage. The gypsies in Ivin's *The Gypsy Avenger* are akin to the Tatars. The horse-trading, fortunetelling gypsy appears in several stories.³² In contrast, the gypsies in the kopeck serial novel *The Alley of Death* are primitive but innocent people. They are ignorant, passionate, and easily manipulated by the Russian characters, but there is nothing evil about

FIG. 14. V. A. Lunin (Kukel), *Slavery among the Asiatics* (Moscow, 1914).

them. The gypsy hero of "The Foundling" is a positive character who marries a Russian and wins the affection of his adopted Russian father. Sherlock Holmes helps out a beautiful and sympathetically drawn gypsy girl in one of Nikitin's adventures of Holmes in Russia.[33] In the kopeck novel "Satan's Cliff," however, evil gypsies plot to steal an Armenian girl with the intention of mutilating her and selling her to professional beggars. Their plan is foiled by the timely arrival of the Russian hero. In this story, the Russian is presented as the force for order among minority peoples who, without his restraining hand, would prey on each other.

In contrast to the mixed portrayal of gypsies in this literature, Jews are almost uniformly negative characters. Jews appear in only a few of the lubok tales, but they turn up in some of the serial novels, particularly those published in Pastukhov's *Moskovskii listok*, although not in his story *The Bandit Churkin*. They are usually portrayed as greedy, boastful, and treacherous when they appear in popular fiction, and their manners and speech make them seem ridiculous. Their image is often that of Judas, the enemy of Christendom. The negative portrayal of Jews in popular fiction echoed both their unfavorable treatment in Russian belles lettres and popular prejudices. Nikolai Gogol's work contains strongly drawn anti-Semitic stereotypes, and his works were frequently published in lubok editions. According to one critic writing in 1917, traces of Gogol's unflattering characterization of Jews can be found even in the works of Chekhov.[34]

The lubok writer Misha Evstigneev, who belonged to the tradition of popular humor on which Chekhov would later draw, produced a number of anti-Semitic sketches. In one of them, two crafty Jews from Smolensk discuss whether or not it is proper to do business on the Sabbath, and they then devise all sorts of subterfuges for this purpose.[35] An equally comical but more sinister Jew appears in the 1893 version of the tale about the Kabardinians. A Jew brings the Circassian princess to her Cossack lover and then sells information about her illicit activities to her father. An equally unpleasant Jew, "dressed luxuriously, but without any taste," squeezes a Russian nobleman in Lunin's tale, *Times Past*. His face reveals his Oriental origins.[36] An extreme example of anti-Semitism in a lubok tale is found in *The Adventures of the Cossack Ataman Urvan*. This tale contains a favorable description of a pogrom, and its anonymous author opines that Jews as a people should be driven out of Russia, or, better still, dumped in the river. The author bewails the suffering of the Ukraine: "Yids filled it like cockroaches in a dark cottage, sucking the blood of our people living there."[37]

The images of Jews in Pastukhov's *Moskovskii listok* reflected the anti-

Semitic editorial policy of the newspaper. The hero of Pazukhin's novel "Velvet Ladies" berates his girlfriend for abandoning him for a Jew: "I think you are bewitched by this dwarf, this alien, and you will cease to love him. Tania, I may be no beauty, and I may be no wonderful bridegroom, but I am all the same a Russian. I have an honest name, honest labor, and I love you."[38]

Jews appear no more than a couple of times in the kopeck serials, but their image is unflattering. This is surprising given the fact that the St. Petersburg paper had a Jewish editor. The Judas image was modernized in these cases, and Jews were portrayed as police spies. A particularly noxious character of this sort appears in the Krechet series, and tracks down the Russian hero in France. Like the Jew in the story about the Kabardinians, he is smug and contemptuous of others. Krechet eventually loses patience with him, and kills him, along with two of his cronies.[39]

Verbitskaia's best-selling *The Keys to Happiness* contains much about Jews and attitudes toward Jews and is a rare example of the sympathetic portrayal of them in the popular fiction. Steinbach, a Jewish millionaire from the Ukraine, is the heroine's lover and benefactor. He takes her to Europe and educates her. He is handsome and refined and donates money to good causes, but Mania is constantly reminded of his Jewishness. She wants to forget that he is a Jew and to dissociate him from the dirty and ragged Jews of the region. Despite her affection for Steinbach, Mania turns to the cold, reactionary, anti-Semitic Russian nobleman, Nelidov. Nelidov condemns Steinbach with the observation, "His millions are the sweat and blood of our people. He is a Yid . . . and with that all is said."[40] Nelidov is in debt to Steinbach and fears that his estate will be forfeited to the Jew, and that "a dirty insolent Jew" will sleep in his ancestral bed. Verbitskaia expressed a sympathy for Jews that was fashionable in liberal circles; but she also presented perfectly acceptable and interesting characters such as Nelidov who hated Jews.

Despite such innovations as the creation of the Jewish police spy, anti-Semitic stereotypes did not gain hold in either the detective adventures or the installment novels. At a time when officially sponsored anti-Semitism was rife, it is noteworthy that authors of the detective adventures and installment novels did not for the most part make anti-Semitism a characteristic of their fiction. Other themes appear to have been more important to the authors and their readers. The readership of the detective adventures and installment novels was concentrated among the young people of the cities, and the suggestion that anti-Semitism was either uninteresting or unappealing to this group is perhaps significant. The only story with an anti-Semitic bias that appeared in either type of fiction was published in the Ukraine in a small edition.[41] Also indicative of these changing views was the fact that Klefortov in his early twentieth-century criminal tale did not even bother to identify Sonka of the Golden Hand as a Jewess and he never gave his readers her last name, which was Bliuvshtein.

Images of Foreigners

Two types of foreigners appear in this literature, Westerners and non-Westerners. The non-Westerners were seen mainly as military antagonists and were dangerous, but they were culturally inferior. People from the West could usually be fooled by the Russians, but their admiration and esteem was sought after and could often be attained by some remarkable feat. Most of the interaction of Russian heroes and heroines with foreigners in these stories is structured by the image of the ferocious but primitive non-Western peoples and the haughty but foolish Westerner.

War usually meant war with the Muslim East in the popular fiction. War that did not involve the Muslim East was hard to imagine, even after the Russo-Japanese War of 1904-1905. In one story, an old man warns his grandson about the impending war that became World War I, and the youth replies, "What kind of war can there be when all the Muslim nonbelievers are lounging around the stove?"[42] Turks appeared frequently as captors of Russians and as a people of both beastly cruelty and natural indolence and debauchery. When the hero of Volgin's *Turkish Prisoner* falls on the battlefield, he sees "the beastly face of the janissary moving toward him."[43] In *The Russian Strongman*, Ali Baba, the Turkish champion, is said to have "a bestial face" and "a hairy chest."[44] The same Turks are easily ensnared by female beauty and particularly favor Russian, or non-Turkish, women. The villain in Lunin's *The Female Slave or Three Weeks in a Harem* promises to dismiss his whole harem and submit to the fancies of the Bulgarian beauty he has abducted.[45]

This stereotype of the Turks came into full bloom in the commercial propaganda of World War I, such as Shukhmin's *The Turkish Devil* (1915) and *Turkish Amusements or the Mohammedan Bestialities* (1915). In the second of these stories, the sultan is shown lying in bed reading his official correspondence, throwing away anything that does not pertain to the harem.[46]

Arabs and blacks appear infrequently in the popular fiction; but when they do, they are described as primitive peoples, with characteristics common to the non-Western foreigners. A black man in Gladkov's Japanese detective series is portrayed in such outrageous terms as to appear absurd to the modern reader. The hero regains consciousness to see before him "a black skin with mad burning eyes and foam on his half-closed mouth. He was a typical Negro."[47]

Fig. 15. *A Bolt from the Blue: A Story from the Last Russo-Turkish War* (Kiev: Gubanov, 1904).

With the shift in attention eastward during and after the war with Japan in 1904-1905, Chinese and Japanese characters appear with greater frequency in the literature. The Chinese are portrayed as treacherous and cowardly and are uniformly hostile to the Russians. Krechet loses his way in the taiga, and some Chinese men demand money in exchange for directions. Krechet snaps, "You are greedy like all your kin, and dishonorable as well."[48] The real enemies in the Krechet serial are the Chinese bandits, the *khunkhuzy*, who capture Nina. Much of Krechet's energy is spent outwitting these bandits and not fighting the Japanese, with whom Russia was then at war.

The Japanese are portrayed with a mixture of respect, hostility, and fascination, perhaps as a result of the impression of the Russian defeat in the Russo-Japanese War. A Japanese circus wrestler is more sympathetically drawn than are either the Turkish or black wrestlers.[49] Japanese officers and soldiers are formidable opponents, and a teen-aged Japanese aristocrat captured by Krechet proves to be a model of nobility. The boy is honorable and joins with Krechet in pursuit of the Chinese *khunkhuzy* who have kidnapped Nina.[50]

The hostility mixed with contempt expressed for the Chinese, and the grudging respect for the Japanese, are both explicable in historical terms. Russian contacts with the Chinese were relatively harmonious from the establishment of relations in the seventeenth century until the 1840s, when Russian statesmen were able increasingly to exploit the weakness of the Chinese. Thereafter, the powerlessness of China could easily have given rise to Russian contempt. Russo-Japanese relations developed only in the mid-nineteenth century, and they were relatively pacific until the construction of the trans-Siberian railroad in the 1890s. Since that time Japan proved a resolute opponent of Russia, and the image of the Japanese in popular fiction was drawn in the aftermath of the Russo-Japanese War, from which Japan emerged the victor.

Foreigners from the West are treated much differently than are the dangerous Turks and Tatars, and the contrast between the image of the Westerner in the popular literature and that expressed in the literature of educated Russia in the postemancipation era is striking. Whereas educated Russians either admired the West for its economic and technological superiority or counterpoised a particularly Russian spirituality to the supposed moral poverty of Western material prosperity, the popular writers expressed a good-natured condescension toward the Westerner. Their confidence derived perhaps from their closeness to an Orthodox tradition that was as self-assured in dealing with errant Christians as with the infidel. In addition, the popular writers had not been abroad and had little conception of what superior Western technology meant in practice. The Westerners they saw were, for the most part, out of their own element in a strange land where they knew little of the language and customs. They were in many respects less adept at handling the problems of daily life than was the simplest and most humble Russian. The parochial experience and world view of many of the popular writers and their readers allowed them to view the foreigner from the West with humor and condescension.

Westerners appear in the early lubok stories primarily as the butt of jokes. Matvei Komarov wrote his late eighteenth-century adventures of Vanka Kain with the tongue-in-cheek purpose of demonstrating that Russia had adventurers and rascals as remarkable as those of Western Europe.[51] Foreigners do not figure in Komarov's story, but they do in Evstigneev's 1869 version. In this telling, Kain begins his career of thievery at the behest of a high Russian official, who wants to show a visitor that Russian crooks are "no dumber than the English."[52] Kain steals the visiting Englishman's money, watch, and even his buttons and medals and earns the praise both of the Russian official and the English victim. In *Oh Those Iaroslavites! What a Fine Folk!* (Moscow, 1868), an anonymous lubok tale that went through many editions, a sausage-eating German loses his money and his pants to a clever Russian dog. The author invites the reader to chuckle and enjoy the good fortune of the dog's master.[53]

Whereas the Russian heroes of lubok literature made fools of Western foreigners, the protagonists of the kopeck serials and women's novels earn their admiration. The authors of this fiction created cartoonlike scenes in which Russians show their superior strength, talent, and wit. Klefertov's Sonka of the Golden Hand achieves renown abroad by setting up a school for thieves in London. When Krechet arrives in France, he immediately becomes the patron of the village in which he settles; he easily passes for a Frenchman, and the villagers elect him to the town council. The hero of *The Russian Strongman*, an installment novel published in 1909, challenges the reigning German champion with, "I am a Russian";[54] the Russian's attractive appearance and marvelous athletic skill soon win him glory. In another installment novel, a Russian hero accepts a most dangerous assignment for the French Foreign Legion: "The Russian went to save the Frenchmen";[55] he proves himself a hero and is made a noncommissioned officer.

In the women's novels, intended for a more sophisticated audience, Russian women win fame and glory abroad through the performing arts. In Bebutova's novel *Gold Dust*, the heroine is a Russian singer whose talent, voice, beauty, and dress completely eclipse the other singers.[56] Verbitskaia's heroine in *The Keys to Happiness* is a famous Russian dancer who enraptures all of Paris.

Characters of individual Western nationalities do not appear frequently enough for clear stereotypes to be discernible. Characters identified as Germans are the most common, but "German" was also used as a generic term for all Westerners. The Germans are not sympathetic characters, but neither are they particularly evil, except in stories set during the war years. A boorish cigar-smoking German disturbs passengers on a train in one of Evstigneev's humorous sketches, and domineering and arrogant Germans turn up in Pazukhin's 1892 novel *Russia in Arms*, as well as in the World War I stories.

The French and Italians do not fare much better than the Germans. They are portrayed occasionally in the kopeck serials as weak characters easily bettered by the stronger and more forceful Russian heroes. A superstitious Italian circus director needs help from a courageous Russian strongman in the serial "In the Devil's Claws" (1909). Krechet fights a duel with a jealous Frenchman, who cuts a pathetic figure next to the majestic Russian. Krechet's French sidekick, Rigo, addresses him as "your worship," a telling note that seems to sum up the wishful image of the relationship between Russians and Westerners in this fiction.

When compared to foreigners in this fiction, Russians are portrayed as braver, tougher, and, in the case of men, more able to suffer pain and violence in battle. The trait most often stressed is courage. The fearlessness of the Russian soldier was the theme of a number of stories based on folk tales about soldiers who drive out demons from houses and castles.[57] The theme of the courage of the Russian soldier is predictably developed in the commercial propaganda from World War I. The foreigners, on the other hand, are softer, weaker, sybaritic, and richer, and they often outnumber their Russian opponents. The relationship between Russians and foreigners was usually an adversary one, except in stories in which the foreigners are assimilated into Russian families.

The negative treatment of foreigners in the popular literature is not surprising, since suspicion of foreigners is one of the traits most commonly noted by Western travelers to Russia since the earliest times. The installment novels and detective serials break with this tradition, and in this respect they are a remarkable departure from the popular literary tradition.

No Longer a Nation Apart

Readers of the early twentieth century installment novels and detective serials were invited to admire foreigners, just as educated Russians had been admiring Western Europeans and Americans for nearly a century.

When the popular writers invited their readers to applaud the foreign heroes, however, there was little of the ambivalence that characterized educated attitudes toward the West. The foreign heroes were simply marvelous in the way of all the heroes of popular fiction.

For Russian readers to view non-Orthodox Europeans and Americans as people in their own right, rather than as alien unbelievers, was a break with a historic tradition of religious exclusiveness that extended into the distant past. With the diminution of this view, ordinary Russians were influenced by the conclusions, if not the thought, of the Renaissance and Enlightenment that had reached educated Russians in the course of the nineteenth century. This new perception of the rest of the world was a logical extension of secularization and the gradual lessening of the Church's hold on the Orthodox population. When Russian readers followed the adventures in stories such as *Richard Gilderbrant—the Victor of the Gang of the Invisible Hand*, or *Garribaldi—The Bloody Adventures of the Dread Bandit Ataman*, or *Nick Carter—The American Sherlock Holmes*, they identified with people who seemed like themselves, except that they were heroes who lived in faraway and seemingly exotic places.

In the prefaces to these stories, the authors often informed their readers that the heroes were famous in their own countries, and that Russians should therefore be interested in their deeds. Commercial writers were necessarily close to their audiences and often mixed in the same milieu as their readers. That they could present foreigners in this way is evidence of a retreat from the image of the world bifurcated into Russians and others that pervades the nineteenth-century stories. The message found repeatedly in the installment tales and detective adventures is that these Germans, Italians, Frenchmen, and Americans are people just like you and me. In fact, some of the foreigners behave suspiciously like Russians, suggesting that their Russian creators were not well acquainted with actual foreign ways of living, but the lack of authenticity is irrelevant. Neither is it important whether the stories were rough translations or retelling of foreign tales, or if they were Russian originals. The impact and significance of the stories was the same. When Carter and Pinkerton performed their feats, they became heroes to their readers. When Holmes comes to Russia in P. Nikitin's original Russian serial, it is simply as a great investigator, and there is no conflict between the English detective and his Russian clients. An extreme example of the new and more cosmopolitan thinking about Russians and foreigners is seen in the Japanese detective serials. The author of the Kio-Hako series, Gladkov, makes a great show of his friendship with the famous Japanese detective and claims that the tales come from their correspondence. The anonymous author of the Oka-Shima serial recommends his series to readers because "crimes occur in all countries of the world," and "Japan, thanks to its recent successes, has interested the whole world."[58]

Sometimes the authors were able to present foreign heroes as superior to their Russian equivalents because their very foreignness freed them from certain constraints within Russian society. This was particularly true in the case of the bandit heroes of the installment novels, whose rebellion and outlawry were often easier to justify when the lawful authorities were foreign rather than Russian. Right could be fully on the side of such foreign rebels as Antonio Porro without threatening the legitimacy of tsarist political authority. Thus when Porro, in the installment novel *Antonio Porro—the Dread Avenger* leaps from a crowd to rescue a carpenter trapped on a burning bell tower, he is presented as a fully righteous individual, a true hero to the whole community. When the carpenter recognizes his deliverer as the famous bandit, Porro asks, "And now will you denounce me to the police?"[59] The carpenter answers, "I am no betrayer," and when the two descend to safety, the crowd hails the bandit's feat with "cries of joy." There is no dark shadow of guilt over the hero, and he has no grave crimes to repent.

The sharp distinction between Russians and foreigners in popular fiction had blurred. This distinction had set the Russian fiction apart from equivalent English, French, and American works that appeared as late as the 1870s. Foreigners mingle freely with the native citizens in the fiction of writers such as Eugene Sue, Ponson du Terrail, Gaboriau, Reynolds, and even Edward Wheeler. Later in the nineteenth century, however, English popular literature became more nationalistic, and so, one suspects, did that of the rest of Western Europe and the United States.

Russian popular literature, however, was moving in a contrary direction, becoming more, not less, cosmopolitan. At a time when Conan Doyle's Sherlock Holmes was turning his attention to protecting England from various pernicious and criminal foreigners, Russian lower-class readers were delighting in the feats of English, American, German, French, Italian, and Japanese heroes. This did not mean that there was no international fare for the Western European and American common readers or that Russian readers were more cosmopolitan. The trend was different, however. The exclusiveness that had been so characteristic of Russian culture for hundreds of years was beginning to fracture with the experience of ordinary people living in a more cosmopolitan and mobile world. In the installment novels and detective serials observed to be popular among the younger readers of the cities, the invisible barriers between Russians and foreigners seem to have dissolved, making these stories the most Westernized and cosmopolitan literature yet to gain popularity among ordinary Russian people.

FIG. 16. *Antonio Porro, the Dread Avenger*, no. 14 (Warsaw: Liubich, 1914).

A New Popular Vision of Empire

As secular thinking and mass education spread in the latter half of the nineteenth century, pride in the glory and breadth of the Russian lands supplemented the cultural symbols of tsar and Church in popular literature. This change was particularly apparent in the newspaper serials. In placing their characters in the steppe and taiga, writers of popular literature encouraged a territorial view of Russianness emphasizing a mighty empire.

The view of Russia as a large and beautiful land of diversity and contrast was present in high culture by the end of the eighteenth century. Karamzin wrote in this way about Russia in his history, which was published in the first decade of the nineteenth century. The later incorporation of these ideas into popular literature is evident in a comparison of early and late versions of the Kabardinian tale. In neither Zriakhov's original nor the anonymous 1854 version is there anything attractive about the Circassian lands besides their women. On the contrary, Zriakhov treats the high mountain air as a bothersome impediment to Russian troops eager to crush their enemies for "the glory of God and the Russian tsar."[60] The border between the Russian Caucasus and the Circassian lands is "the rapid and terrible river Terek." The primitive wilderness of the lands of the Kabardinians is contrasted to the civilized landscape of Russia across the border. When Selima imagines Russia she says, "If I had the power and freedom I would go with you to your fatherland, which ought to be more beautiful than our wild mountains and crags, filled with predatory beasts and birds of prey."[61] The anonymous author of the 1854 edition abandons the mountains entirely and sets his battle in a forest. In this story the land of the Kabardinians is no more than a place to escape as soon as possible.

The anonymous author of the 1893 version of the story begins with a dedicatory poem on the theme of Russia as the third Rome. The victory of the Russian troops over the Circassians is presented as a glorious step in the expansion of the empire. The story also has a preface explaining the completion of the actual conquest of the Caucasus, which took place more than two decades after the original story was written. In this version the area is seen as beautiful and rich. "There are many medicinal salts in the Caucasian mountains, and within them are gold, silver, copper, salt, and coal. Oaks, beech, pear, and apple trees grow in the valleys, and at the foot of the mountains there are pomegranates, wild oranges, chestnuts, and grapes."[62] The newly conquered land has become a garden of plenty.

In this later version, Andrei's idea of his homeland encompasses new lands, such as the Circassian mountains. "Holy Orthodox Mother Russia," he sighs in a virtual hymn to the Russian land. "Everything in holy Russia is dear to us; her sons are equally pleasing. Steppe and forest, standing grain and full threshing floor, thatched cottages and cart trains, the village dance (*khorovod*) and the Christmas games, the playful fairy tale and the inspiring word of our native writers, the chivalrous feats of our glorious soldiers and the monuments of antiquity, the standing crosses of our innumerable temples and the holy graves of our ancestors."[63] Nothing is missing from this picture except the autocracy and the Orthodox Church.

The theme of the beauty and expanse of the Russian land was also developed by V. Suvorov, the lubok historian, in his thirty-two-page commercial historical primer, *How the Russian Kingdom Was Formed* (1898). Suvorov describes ancient Russia as a land "covered with age-old oaks, among which great rivers flowed on four sides, carrying their water into four seas: the northern [White], the Black, the Caspian, and the Baltic."[64] According to Suvorov's account, when Riurik, the legendary Varangian founder of the Russian state, sent his envoys to seek the "Greek Kingdom" in the south, they reached Kiev and found "such a beautiful and rich country as they had never seen."[65]

The expanse of Russia, particularly the unfolding of the empire to the south, is described in stories such as Lunin's *Slavery among the Asiatics*, in which a sailor recounts his adventures on the Caspian and describes life along the Volga and among steppe nomads.[66] The sense of proprietorship over a rich land threatened by rapacious neighbors was expressed in *The Adventures of the Cossack Ataman Urvan* (1901), the lubok version of *Taras Bulba*. The story begins with a description of the struggle of the Ukrainian Cossacks against the enemies of Russia: "It was necessary for the people living there to stand up for their native land and to preserve it from the invasion of wild hordes of Tatars, regiments of Poles, and the insatiable Jews."[67]

Later lubok stories, unlike the earlier ones, often began with concrete identification of a place and description of the landscape. The bandit story *Vasil Chumak* begins with the rhetorical query, "Who does not know Little Russia, that marvelous region?"[68] Volgin begins the bandit story *Ataman Kuzma Roshchin* with "The Volga is the greatest river in the Russian Empire."[69]

There is still more attention paid to descriptions of locations in the newspaper serials. Churkin's saga is replete with stops in places of interest to Russian readers, even though Pastukhov was more eloquent in description of Churkin's bloody adventures than with scenery. Pazukhin's story *In the Whirlwind of Life* (1912) begins with "On a cold rainy fall evening an automobile rushed along the Iaroslavl highway from the village of Malaia Mishch to Moscow."[70] More important as a catalogue of Russian places for Russian readers were the kopeck serials, which ranged widely over the whole of the empire to its most remote corners. From Bessarabia to the Caucasus to the oil fields of Baku and the Siberian taiga and the Far East, the kopeck readers could follow the outline of the empire. P. Stravopolskii's "King of the Taiga" was advertised with the announcement that he had traveled widely in Siberia and had experienced life among the gold prospectors firsthand. His novel was set in a string of settlements stretching "from the bank of the holy sea [Baikal] to the mountains."[71] Raskatov's serial "Satan's Cliff" opens with "In the first days of April 189–, three young people with the appearance of neither hunters nor prospectors forced their way along one of the mountain gorges of the Caucasus, overgrown with age-old plane trees" (no. 1371, 1912). This southern region is described as one so rich that a stick poked in the ground will begin to grow.

Anton Krechet also lived in a broad empire that belonged to Russians. When he heads for the front in the Russo-Japanese War, Krechet crosses "the spine of the Urals" and sees "shining smooth as a mirror the emerald surface of cold Baikal."[72] "Along the narrow iron rails, across granite crests, through dense wilds, along great Siberian rivers, through tunnels fixed in the rock face of the mountains, he flew on and on."

Many of the installment novels and detective adventure stories were set abroad and so did not feature Russian geography. In some of the women's novels by Verbitskaia and others, descriptions of Russian landscapes are prominent. The romance with Russia as a geographic entity is particularly accentuated in stories in which characters cross a border in or out of Russia. Krechet and Nina leave Russia in a marvelous airship flying toward France, where they hope to build a new life. When they cross the border, however, they feel sadness rather than joy. "Tears shone in Krechet's eyes. 'The border,' he said. 'Russia is behind us.' " Both Nina and Krechet vow to return (no. 715, 1910). When Krechet does return, pursued by a whole trainload of foreign detectives, he crosses the border and falls to kiss the ground. " 'Russia,' he whispered. 'We are saved' " (no. 991, 1911).

The Russian fascination with Siberia, the Caucasus, and other regions into which settlers came resembles American interest in the frontier as a place open to energy and initiative.[73] Russians who felt constrained in the developed heartland of their country also moved toward the outlying territories in search of freedom and independence. Yet the Russian popular vision was more restricted than the American. The Russian writers presented the territories of settlement as exotic and exciting, but they never held them up to their readers as better than Moscow or St. Petersburg. American popular writers played with the idea of the superiority of the West over the East and the frontier over settled life. There were no Russian tenderfoots to illuminate the contrast between an inept newcomer and a knowledgeable master of the frontier. No newly arrived Russian defers to an established settler as does the narrator of *The Virginian* (1902), Owen Wister's classic Western.[74] Georgii, the hero of the kopeck serial "Satan's Cliff," is the only settler in the Russian popular fiction who has to learn how to operate in a new environment, but his skills are never measured against those of more experienced Great Russians and he soon outpaces the natives without difficulty.

The outlying regions of Russia were portrayed as a less friendly environment than the American popular writers' frontier. American writers often showed the landscape of the frontier to be strikingly beautiful and sometimes endowed it with great serenity.[75] Untamed nature in the Russian fiction, on the contrary, frequently seems threatening. Wild places are never a refuge for the Russian heroes, except for the bandits who hide temporarily in forests. Russian adventurers seldom supposed themselves to be in Eden, as Americans in pristine landscapes often did. The Russians never exclaim, "Do not let us ever go away from here!" as does Owen Wister's heroine in a remote valley.[76] The Russians are also more closely tied to home and community, and they cannot move on to a new place as easily as do Americans. They are more bound to the familiar, and they often return home. When they do not, they are nevertheless concerned about establishing ties in a community. Their adventures are evidence of an increasing individualism in the context of Russian traditions, even if they are not at all eager to "go it alone," as Americans in fiction often do.

The shift in thinking about national identity evident in the popular fiction of the last two decades of the old regime was linked to a general change in outlook. The ideas propagated in the literature represented a more individualistic form of national identity than the earlier loyalty to the tsar and the Orthodox Church—and a freer one. To be truly Russian in the earlier sense was to accept the political authority of the tsar and the spiritual authority of the Church. In practical terms this meant obedience to the local officials and priests who represented the autocracy and Orthodoxy.

The newer idea of Russianness allowed the common people to distance themselves somewhat from the political authority of the old regime. Obligations to Church and state still remained, but they no longer served as the primary expression of national identity. The emphasis on the enormity and diversity of the empire required a more complex and reflective conception of the interrelations among the peoples who comprised it than did the traditional linear relation between the tsar and his subjects. Moreover, under the old conception of nationality, the common Russian was last in the pecking order. In the newer view, the most humble Great Russian was invited to think of himself as generously assisting the smaller and culturally backward nationalities that comprised the empire. This provided a sense of pride and status congruent psychologically with the other changes that were part of the greater geographic and economic mobility of common Great Russians at the end of the nineteenth century. This sense of nationality was also one that could survive the collapse of the autocracy and motivate Great Russians to fight to maintain the empire during the chaos of revolution and civil war.

VII

SCIENCE AND SUPERSTITION

Belief in the supernatural was still widespread in rural Western Europe in the eighteenth and nineteenth centuries, and presumably the less literate Russian peasant was even more superstitious than his counterpart in the West.[1] Yet the commercial popular writers who served an audience of peasants and those not far removed from their roots in the peasantry urged their readers to reject superstition and approach daily life with rationality and a respect for scientific explanations. In their treatment of science and superstition, the writers contributed to the flow of new and more modern ideas that was reaching common readers.

Belief in witches, sorcerers, devils, sprites, and folk healers was pervasive in rural Russia even after secularization had diminished the hold that the supernatural exerted in much of Western Europe. Vladimir Dal identified six kinds of popular superstition prevalent among Great Russian peasants in the second half of the nineteenth century.[2] These included remnants of pagan religious beliefs, superstitions that explained natural phenomena, those based on only partially understood causation of events experienced and observed, allegories and folk wisdom, miscellaneous superstitions, and those used by charlatans to fool the gullible. There were more than forty names for devils and sprites in Dal's time. Demonic evil and its agents on earth—witches, sorcerers, and the dead—were thought to intrude constantly into daily life, and the powers of darkness were even thought to be able to penetrate the sanctuary of churches.[3] The devils were thought to be so powerful on Easter night that peasants feared to venture outside their cottages.[4] Sorcerers (*koldun, koldun'ia*) were greatly feared. They could be either men or women, and, in S. V. Maksimov's metaphor, they were the oak that held firm in the storm of time that swept other superstitions away.[5] The sorcerer could put damning spells and the evil eye on victims. Faith in sorcerers diminished in the industrial areas and their environs in the late nineteenth century but remained strong throughout most of rural Russia.

Witches were another source of worry for the superstitious. Those thought to be witches (*ved'my*) were always women—sometimes young widows. Among Great Russian peasants, witches were not always distinguished from sorcerers, although witches were invariably women and thought to have tails and to cavort with devils. The local faith healer (*znakhar, znakharka*) was closely associated in popular perceptions with witches and sorcerers. These people openly interceded with the world of the supernatural and derived some of their living from this traffic in spells and charms, and by the accounts of some observers were thought to perpetuate fear of the supernatural.[6] They claimed to find lost objects and foretell the future. In their role as healers, they dispensed various herbal remedies. Although sorcerers and witches were feared and hated, the popular judgment on healers was more ambivalent, as was the perception of their place in the world of the supernatural. They were thought to be able to communicate with powers of darkness, but, at the same time, often began their cures with a prayer and the sign of the cross.

Anthropologists and others who have studied primitive societies in which superstitious beliefs remain strong have found that these beliefs serve as a personal and moral explanation for misfortune and disaster.[7] Superstition also tends to reinforce the status quo, since those who break with traditional norms fear that supernatural retribution will follow.

Writers of Russian popular fiction were well aware of the conservative power of superstition, and they took as their conscious task the unmasking of these archaic beliefs. Because many writers were themselves of common background, they knew the role that belief in sorcerers, witches, devils, and folk healers played in the lives of the common people. Yet because the writers had, for the most part, educated themselves enough to have gained some intellectual distance from their origins, they felt a duty to enlighten their less well-educated readers and free them from superstitions that limited their understanding of the modern world. Some writers approached this task with humor by poking fun at devils and other potentially frightening specters. Other authors painstakingly presented rational explanations for seemingly supernatural events. The message in every case was that supernatural forces of evil had no power over the lives of people who ceased to believe in them, and that ordinary people need not surrender control over their own lives to devils or their agents on earth. In debunking the supernatural, the popular authors of the newspaper serials and detective stories communicated a high regard for science and its potential accomplishments. They also revealed a budding fascination with technology and new-fangled gadgets.

All of the lubok tales were at a very low level of sophistication, and none were genuine works of popular science. The lubok writers did not communicate much about the scientific method, nor did they impart an understanding of how science differs from magic. But in their limited task of combatting superstition, the popular writers made an important contribution to promoting a more modern outlook among common readers.

Schoolteachers, doctors and medical assistants from the zemstvos and other institutions, agronomists, and priests would probably have rejected the idea that they were allied with the popular writers. Their interests not infrequently converged, however, in the fight against superstition. N. A. Rubakin maintained a voluminous correspondence with educated people and organizers working in villages, and many complained that popular superstitions made their work more difficult. One correspondent, probably an activist in the Socialist Revolutionary Party, wrote from the province of Tver in central Russia, a region in which literacy was high and industrial development was considerable. He had organized a study group of peasants during 1905, and, using materials sent by Rubakin, led as many as forty people in readings of the works of Gorky, Andreev, and other progressive writers. In 1907, however, he wrote that a sorceress had appeared in the village, and that the peasants blamed all their woes on the poor woman. "The peasants all believe in devils and won't listen to a word," he complained. The organizer concluded his letter with the observation that he wanted to write a popular pamphlet against the belief in sorcerers, and he hoped that Rubakin would help him.[8] The organizer thought of the sponsored literature as the appropriate forum for his proposed tract, but popular commercial writers were already turning out stories on the same theme.

With popular belief in superstition so strong, it is not surprising that writers made the question of the supernatural a subject of their fiction. What is surprising is that they presented such an unambiguous demonstration that the supernatural did not exist, rather than pandering to what would seem to be popular beliefs. By attacking or at least rejecting superstition, the writers carried out their own self-conceived mission as enlighteners, but they also satisfied readers. Commercial works debunking superstition would not have appeared in such numbers and for so long had they not found a ready readership. The buyers and readers of this literature must have sympathized with and been intrigued by this treatment of the supernatural. Perhaps the literate were the least likely to believe in witches and demons, even though they lived in a world in which popular superstition was common. They may have identified with the heroes in the stories who frequently point out to lesser characters the absurdity of their superstitious beliefs.

A number of lubok stories had titles that implied the supernatural, when, in fact, they had little or nothing to do with devils or witches. The suggestiveness of the titles testifies to the allure that the supernatural had for readers, since it was the title and cover picture that enticed the buyer. The absence of superstition in the content of the story constituted a kind of trick on the reader in which the reader cooperated, and served as a rather different approach to debunking superstition.

Fig. 17. *The Witch and Solovei the Bandit* (Moscow: Sytin, 1890). Courtesy of the John G. White Collection of the Cleveland Public Library.

One tale of this sort is Balagur's *The Devil in a Basket*, in which the devil turns out to be demon drink. The story begins with the admonition that "every literate person ought to know that no witches, wood sprites, or sorcerers exist." The tale is a simple one about a prosperous old man, a former soldier, who is brought low by a fondness for vodka, which he packs in a basket on the pretense that he will go fishing or mushrooming.[9] Similar stories appear among those by A. Aleksandrovskii, a writer who occasionally wrote risqué tales issued in a somewhat more expensive format than the usual lubok booklet. His *The Ghost of His Wife from beyond the Grave Gave Him No Peace for Twenty Years* (1912) turns out to be a mundane story, fully consistent with the natural world.[10] Similarly, in the 1918 version of the adventures of Vanka Kain, one of the installments has a picture of an evil looking crone on the cover, but she turns out to be a simple murderess instead of a witch.[11]

Unmasking Superstition

The more sophisticated readers in Victorian England were secure in their understanding of the rational world and were titillated by the suggestion in ghost stories and occult tales that another dimension existed. Russian popular writers could not afford subtleties or doubts on this point. Tales in which people who claimed supernatural powers were unmasked, or in which the superstitious were shown to be fools, were common in Russian publications, and seeing such figures brought low was apparently a source of satisfaction and amusement for readers.

Lubok writers who mocked the superstitious sometimes played on the theme of Christianity versus paganism. Foma Balagur's *A Story of How One Peasant Woman Fooled a Hundred Muzhiks* is of this type.[12] Balagur told his readers that sorcerers and folk healers were the successors of crafty pagan priests who had fooled the common people before the arrival of Christianity, and that belief in their powers dated from the time when people had "neither the light of the teaching of the holy Orthodox faith, nor the light of literacy or any kind of education" (p. 3). Balagur also pointed out that the sorcerers' positions were very profitable for them, both materially and because they enjoyed the respect of the community.

This picture of popular superstitiousness as a legacy of the ignorant and pagan past is important because it places both the Orthodox priest and the schoolteacher in the ranks of those who oppose superstition. Rationality and the Orthodox religion were generally assumed to be allied against superstition. In only a very few stories is the clash purely between the religious and the superstitious. These tales echo an older polarity between paganism and Christianity, and the element of secular rationalism is left out. In one such story, *A Victim of Superstition* (Moscow, 1910), a peasant goes to a sorceress for help in locating his lost bullocks, instead of relying on his priest's promised prayers to Saint Seraphim Sarovskii. On his way to the sorceress, the peasant is thrown from his horse and killed. His wife ruefully concludes that it was the work of the devil, and that "if he had only listened to the advice of our priest, Father Andrei, then he would be alive, and, for praying to the saints, God would have sent us more than he took away."[13] It could be argued that this story represents an effort to substitute officially sanctioned Orthodox superstition for its unacceptable pagan precursor, rather than an attempt to fight all superstition. The moral of the story, however, is clearly that consultations with sorceresses can lead to no good.

Orthodoxy and rationality were usually assumed to work together in combatting superstition. Orthodoxy provided a positive belief in the supernatural that was not, in this context, inconsistent with scientific and rational thinking. Secular rationalism provided the knowledge and understanding needed to strip superstitiousness—the negative and non-Orthodox belief in the supernatural—of its powers.

Religion and superstition clearly were not equated in the lubok tales, nor was atheism considered a necessary concomitant to the rational world view. Balagur advised his readers, with respect to the superstitious in their midst, that "It is about time to bring such people to their senses, and, further, for them to speak with literate people, best of all with their parish priests or with the rural schoolteachers about their stupid beliefs in folk healers and sorcerers."[14]

Some authors explained superstition simply as foolishness. In Ivin's *A Devil's Nest* (Moscow, 1889), a fisherman announces the appearance of a devil in the river, and after several further sightings and the loss of some laundry from the river bank, the peasants conclude that they do, indeed, have a devil. They consider turning to the authorities for help, but instead send the three bravest villagers out in a boat to find the devil and drive it away. What they find is a hawklike bird that has sunk its talons into a pike, and in its drowned state it is hauled through the water on the back of the fish. They put their "devil" in a sack, and dump it before the terrified villagers. The villagers' fright turns to chagrin: "They were so unexpectedly deceived in their expectations that they were even shamed and vexed, as a grown-up is vexed when deceived by a clever little child."[15]

Some stories combined straightforward preaching with didactic tales. The anonymous author of *The Sorcerer, Folk Healer, and Black Cat* (1899) told readers that superstition was a pagan remnant and a result of ignorance about the natural world. When monsters were born or comets appeared, he wrote, people feared disasters and saw these events as punishment for sins. "So the superstitious people frightened themselves and others, not understanding that such phenomena can be very easily explained. They happened and happen simply and according to the laws of nature, just as there is day and night, winter and summer."[16] The author does not provide scientific understanding, but offers the assertion that rational explanations do exist. He continues to relate a tale in which an escaped convict masquerades as a sorcerer and deceives gullible village women.

The best example of the eagerness of lubok writers to combat superstition is the way in which Ivin rewrote Turgenev's story, "Bezhin Meadow." In Turgenev's tale the hunter-narrator gets lost, encounters some peasant boys sitting around a campfire, and listens to their marvelous tales of sprites, water nymphs, devils, and the dead. Ivin's story is called *The House Sprite Makes Mischief* and was published by Gubanov in 1889. It is based on Turgenev's text but differs markedly from the original in the treatment of the supernatural element of the story. Ivin retains the tales of the supernatural and some of the descriptions of nature, but he makes the tellers of the tales superannuated peasants in order to show that such superstitions are outmoded.[17] He destroys the artistic value of Turgenev's story, but he gives the text a new educational purpose. He heightens the suggestion of the supernatural by touches such as the new title, and by changing the time in which the story takes place from July to Easter and adding additional supernatural phenomena. He also adds two characters, a foolish believer in tales and a rational skeptic who rolls his tobacco in newspaper and derides such beliefs. The skeptic has the last word: "You old men are respected, but you are complete fools. Have you lived a century and learned nothing?"[18] He offers drunkenness and too much attention to the babbling of women as explanations for the sightings of sprites and the like: "All this is stupidity and rot, I say, and nothing more." He urges people to believe their own eyes rather than what they hear, and most listeners are convinced. Only a few old men cling to their superstitions.

The line between the commercial lubok tale in which superstitions were derided and the works of popular science had blurred by the early twentieth century. An interesting example is K. Palilov's *Devilish Delusion*,[19] a thirty-two-page lubok booklet published by Sytin in 1914. There is no indication that this story was intended for other than the regular commercial channels of distribution, and its cover does not distinguish it from other lubok booklets with which it was sold. Yet the painstaking scientific explanations for apparently mysterious phenomena

Fig. 18. K. Palilov, *A Devilish Delusion* (Moscow: Sytin, 1914).

253

are equivalent to those found in some of the more successful popularizations of science.

The story is set in the Caucasus, where the narrator is presumably on military service. His Cossack companion tells him about a swampy ravine that is haunted. A friend who slept in the ravine was set upon by a wood sprite, then saw his double, and heard his own words thrown back at him. The narrator rejects these superstitions and leads his Cossack companion through the explanation that swamp gas caused the weight on his friend's shoulder (i.e., the wood sprite), the double was only a shadow, and the voices only echoes. The explanation is laboriously explicit:

"Do you know what a gas is?"

"No, how could I know this?"

"Well, every body or object can be either in a solid form, like a stone, or in liquid form, as, for example, water, or in a gaseous form, like air."

The Cossack kept silent. It was evident that he did not quite understand all of this.

"Take, for example, ice," I continued. "It is hard when it forms, then it becomes liquid, and if the water boils, it turns into steam—that is, into gaseous form."

The narrator then explains how gas is produced from rotting vegetation, and that the gas made the Cossack groggy. The echo is explained as an analogy to waves on a river or lake. The Cossack is gradually convinced in this fashion that there is a rational explanation for everything that has happened.

Upon reaching their destination, the narrator ruminates on how "everything is beautiful, natural, and reasonable in nature," although there are still "many dark sides" to human life. He concludes with the prediction, echoing the radical critics of the 1860s, that science will ensure the eradication of superstition and mystery. "This great force of science will unmask all sorcerers, house sprites, and wood sprites, and a new generation of people will speak about them as the sad delusions of the past. This time will surely come soon." It is typical of these stories that the superstitious are portrayed as characters with whom the reader would not choose to identify: children, servants, foolish women, members of various nationalities, and others who are shown to be weak, gullible, or out of date.

Rational Heroes

A variant of the story in which superstitions are debunked is that in which a hero or heroine who personifies rationality triumphs over ignorance and evil, and engages the admiration of the reader. Stories of this type appeared soon after the emancipation, even before the big commercial lubok firms became established. Nester Oko's 1868 story, *The Secrets and Death of a Sorcerer*, is about a widely feared charlatan who doctors the sick, advises the lovelorn, and finds "lost" horses that his accomplice has conveniently stolen.[20] He is destroyed by a local nobleman, "a great admirer of natural science," who sets out to entrap him. With a policeman secreted nearby, the sorcerer is invited to the nobleman's house and confronted with an electrical show that includes moving walls, lightning and thunder, an animated figure of death, miscellaneous devils, and finally Satan himself, "with moveable jaws and eyes burning with electric sparks" (p. 102). The terrified charlatan confesses his crimes, and he and his confederates are locked up by the policeman. The author concludes with the observation that "many deeply suspicious peasant women were still frightened of him, and even some men," but the nobleman was thought to have taken over some of his powers. This story has the characteristic alliance of education (the nobleman) and science (electricity) unmasking a charlatan who has claimed supernatural powers. It is also characteristically vague about how electricity could have produced the remarkable effects described. Science in this case is close to magic, but all the same the force that produced the effects is named and is shown to be controlled by a human being without supernatural intercession. The charlatan's ignorance leads to his downfall.

The popular prototype of the rational hero in Russian folklore was not the enlightened nobleman but the common soldier returning home from service in the prereform army. Brave and devout soldiers in folklore exorcise devils, and they also appear occasionally in similar roles in lubok tales. In Volgin's folkloric tale, *A Night at Satan's, a Tale of Enchantment* (1883), a returning soldier frees a prince's house from devils and wins himself a prosperous retirement.[21] In another story that became one of the most popular lubok tales, a common soldier meets Peter the Great when the latter is hunting incognito in the forest and has lost his way. The two take shelter in the hut of a witchlike crone, and are set upon in the night by her bandit sons. The soldier saves Peter, and, in this story, the bandits are undone in part by their superstitious beliefs when they conclude that the soldier is a ghost.[22]

Bandits and criminals, as well as soldiers, were rational protagonists in the lubok stories, and sometimes also in folklore. As rogues who lived by their wits, these characters could not afford to be superstitious, and, instead, used the fears of the gullible to their own advantage. In *Iashka the Thief—the Brass Buckle, a Popular Humorous Story* (1896), Iashka becomes a thief, marries a bandit's daughter, and then decides to return to an honest life in the village. The bandits agree to let him go and keep

200 rubles if he can prevent them from stealing his pig. Iashka succeeds by dressing as a devil and frightening them off. When they learn that they have been tricked, the bandits say, "Yes, you know how to fool people worse than a devil. You are a sorcerer, Iashka." Iashka counters, "I am not a sorcerer at all but your pupil and son-in-law, and now an honest man who doesn't want to give up 200 rubles for nothing, because I am not stupid."[23] The hero's rationality allows him to triumph over a larger number of presumably accomplished but superstitious thieves.

Such rational heroes were most common in the newspaper serials and other periodical fiction. Churkin, Pastukhov's bandit hero, is unfazed by the terrors of the supernatural. One of his enemies goes to a sorceress for help in locating Churkin and his sidekick, Osip. The two calmly follow him to the hut, and watch through the window while the rival seeks to enlist the powers of the occult against them. The sorceress has all the proper equipment, including a black cat and a black rooster, but all the same, she is shown to possess no special powers. She happens to see Churkin at the window and so is able to tell his rival where Churkin is. When the rival leaves the hut, Osip kills him, and he and Churkin burn the sorceress in her house, despite her plaintive cries for mercy. The rival's attempt to use supernatural powers has been his undoing, and the sorceress not only is powerless to affect anyone else's life, but she cannot even save her own.

Churkin has no faith in folk healers, either. When he wants to arrange his own fake funeral, he calls in the local healer, Aunt Aksinia, with confidence that she will not be able to distinguish a live body from a dead one. Pastukhov elaborated on Aunt Aksinia's medical talents: "If some of her patients recovered, then it happened not because she cured them, but because the illness went away by itself. Many went to the grave from her drugs" (p. 1124).

The heroes of the serials in the kopeck newspapers also demonstrated a lack of belief in the supernatural, but they aped educated Russia in accepting a dash of hypnotism and even spiritualism. In the story "In the Devil's Claws," the circus wrestler, Masanov, is shown to be educated when we are informed that he has given up the university for the circus ring. He faces a villainous enemy who uses a poisonous snake and hypnotism to achieve his ends. The circus director, an Italian, is superstitious and fears that the villain is "someone with a tail." Masanov believes his enemy to be mundane rather than diabolical, and he triumphs in the end (no. 497, 1909).

Anton Krechet, the hero of the kopeck serials, also uses hypnotism—in one case, to rescue innocent people from a gang of ruffians. When those he has saved stare at him in admiration and amazement, Krechet responds, "Don't look at me so confusedly. Or do you really think I am a wizard or a magician? Now there are no wizards and magicians—my strength is hypnotism."[24] Some of the rescued have never heard of such a thing, but Krechet the progressive observes that "there has to be a first time for everything."

Occasionally a hero must use the gullibility of others in order to help them, but the reader is clearly informed that a stratagem is being employed. In one of the St. Petersburg serials Georgii, a former railroad engineer, has settled in a Caucasian village and become a benefactor of the region. In order to help a worried Armenian merchant find his lost son, Georgii poses as a sorcerer, much to the father's terror (no. 1391, 1912). A judicial investigator in the serial *The Valley of Death* (1909), uses a similar tactic in interrogating gypsies suspected of murder: "I am a sorcerer," he affirms. "I know everything, and nothing can be hidden."[25]

The Russian detectives who thrived in the installment adventure stories were not practitioners of the scientific method like Sherlock Holmes or Gaboriau's Lecoq, but they were rational heroes who used logical analysis along with the occasional heavy fist. The Pinkerton story, *The Black Monk*, is improbably set in a castle in Bridgeport, Connecticut. A mad Jesuit has frightened people away and local residents fear that supernatural evil is at work. Pinkerton catches the Jesuit and brings him before the castle's owner. "You see, Mr. Rogers," he calmly explains, "this is the most ordinary scoundrel who will now explain to us the motives for his acts."[26] The servants of the castle quake in terror before the black-cloaked monk, but they calm down when convinced that they are dealing with a common criminal. A character in another Pinkerton adventure mocks "stupid people" who believe in the supernatural.[27] Similarly, an escaped convict posing as a ghost frightens people in P. Nikitin's series of Sherlock Holmes' adventures in Russia. Holmes and Watson are called in by a merchant, who assures them that since he was educated abroad and finished university, "it follows that I do not believe in devilry."[28]

Régis Messac has observed in his classic work, *Le "Detective Novel" et l'Influence de la Pensée Scientifique* (Paris, 1929), that the difference between the ordinary feuilleton novel of the mid-nineteenth century and the modern detective story is the presence of the deductive investigator. It is this that distinguishes the labyrinthine intrigues of Ponson du Terrail's picaresque hero Rocambole from the cases solved by Gaboriau's, and later Conan Doyle's, heroes. Gaboriau's famous fictional detective, Lecoq (1869), reasons deductively, testing theories as he follows a chain of evidence.[29] Lecoq belongs in the company of Poe's Dupin and Conan Doyle's Holmes as a ratiocinative detective. These brainy fellows were more refined than the heroes of the American dime novels, such as Nick

Carter, and more intellectual than the Russian detectives, who excel in brawn and bravado. The American Nick Carters often solve their cases by physical prowess and skills of observation rather than through scientific logic, and in this respect they resemble the Russian heroes. Messac called this method "wood craft" rather than detection; it is the technique of Natty Bumppo more than that of Dupin.[30]

In contrast to Lecoq and Holmes, both of whom have real scientific credentials, neither the Russian Pinkertons and Carters nor the detectives of the American dime novel are men of science. Holmes is an expert chemist, and Lecoq worked for an astronomer before taking up detection. The Russian detective heroes rely less on science and technology than Holmes, Lecoq, or, for that matter, the American Nick Carter, who is at least capable of checking a corpse's dental records. They fall somewhere between Messac's categories of the hero of the feuilleton and the scientific investigator.

Use of Humor to Promote Rationality

In some of the stories in which superstition is derided, devils and sorcerers become farcical figures only slightly less ridiculous than those who believe in them. In *The Appearance of the Devil with Horns and Claws in Petersburg, a Description Prepared from Rumors and Talk Spread in Recent Days* (1868), two lower-middle-class rascals decide to augment their dwindling resources by dressing as the devil and holding up passersby. All goes well until a sturdy merchant grabs the devil and holds him until the police arrive. The final chapter is entitled "The Devil Behind Bars."[31] Another story of this type that appeared in the 1860s was Evstigneev's *The Spider and the Folk Healer* (Moscow, 1867), in which a quick-witted charlatan convinces a merchant obsessed with a spider that he has been freed of his nemesis.[32] The reader can see that the healer is a quack and has the last laugh on the gullible merchant.

In some stories the humorous intent is so obvious that even the most naive reader could not fail to see the point. Stories of this type were published first for urban readers in the 1860s, and at the end of the nineteenth century they appeared for rural readers as well. In Evstigneev's 1868 farce *The Devil in a Jar of Pomade, a Joke for Shrovetide* the hero buys a jar of hair restorer to improve his chances of marrying favorably. He opens the jar only to find it full of a mass of devils. He catches one and wonders whether to sell it to the zoo or to a museum, but is finally convinced to let the devil work as his matchmaker.[33] In an early twentieth-century humorous story, M. Zotov's *How a Master from the Putilov and Mytishchensk Plants Taught the Devil to Operate a Lathe* (Moscow,

1910), the devil gets bored in hell and decides to settle on earth. He is found by some workers, cleaned up, and set to work at the lathe, where he finds that "he sweated like he never sweated in hell."[34] This is not an anticapitalist story, but rather one suggesting that the workers were tough and spirited enough to have a laugh on the devil himself.

Sorcerers were seldom farcical figures in the popular literature, perhaps because they were still feared. The reader is usually informed that a lubok tale in which a sorcerer possesses magical power is a fairy tale (*skazka* or *volshebnaia povest'*) or a legend (*predanie* or *legenda*). Since unexperienced peasant readers read very literally and made a clear distinction between fairy tales and "truth," this *caveat lector* was quite important. Volgin's tale *The Wizard and the Knight* (1911) was subtitled "a fairy tale."[35] Lunin wrote an introduction to one of his tales of this sort, and explained that fairy tales were fantasies, and that the reader of his book, "already forewarned in advance against its probability," would "burst out laughing."[36] Ivin began his story *The Struggle Between the Devil and a Woman* (Moscow, 1897) with the rambling caveat, "This incidence deserves no credence, but it ought to be true, because it was told to me by my deceased grandma, who herself heard it from grandpa, and my grandpa was the sort of man who always loved to joke."[37] These kinds of introductions set a light tone to the story for readers sophisticated enough not to need the warning, but they also alerted the more credulous to suspend their belief.

Science and Scientists

The lubok writers frequently attacked superstition, but they did not often hail science or scientists as an alternative authority. The presentation of science is more common in the periodical literature of the early twentieth century. The authors of the kopeck serials demonstrated a firm belief in science as a weapon against human ignorance and a tool for progress. Yet even they communicated little of the substance of scientific inquiry, both because their readers were probably not well enough educated to follow scientific arguments, and because, one suspects, the writers themselves had a very primitive understanding of what science was about. Science is often invoked when the reader is asked to accept something marvelous and mysterious without the aid of superstitious belief. In this sense, the popular literature might be considered antiscientific, since the use of science is more akin to magic than to logic.

Nevertheless, the consistent promotion of rationality and the communication of a kind of respect and awe for the mysterious knowledge called science that is clearly evident in the periodical literature makes the label "antiscientific" unfair. Perhaps the literature was protoscientific. Readers whose scientific understanding did not advance well beyond the level evident in the popular stories could not serve as a public able to discern the slow processes of real scientific inquiry from the quick returns and inflated claims of pseudoscience. Public support for real science, however, also had to be based on a wide audience weaned from superstition and committed to a world view based on rational inquiry. In this function popular commercial literature succeeded, even though it was scorned by educators.

An early example of this questionable invocation of science occurs in Nester Oko's tale, discussed above, in which a nobleman uses electricity to frighten a purported sorcerer into confessing his crimes. The electrical display produced for the undoing of the ignorant sorcerer appears to rival the effects seen in any present-day carnival chamber of horrors. The description was undoubtedly an embellishment of Oko's primitive understanding of what electricity could do, and the story contains no explanation of how these frightening effects could be achieved. It is enough for Oko to say that electricity, and not the devil, is responsible, and he then has license to create as marvelous and fantastic a scene as he wishes.

The use of hypnotism in more than a few of the kopeck novels entails a similar questionable use of science. The rational hero or villain's ability to hypnotize individuals or whole groups of people is suspiciously similar to the sorcerer's ability to cast a spell. Yet hypnotism is modern and "scientific," and thus a legitimate weapon in the writer's arsenal against superstition. Hypnotism gives the hero tremendous power over enemies, and no hero who had at his disposal only the techniques of true science would have such power. Anton Krechet's ability to hypnotize whole groups of people instantaneously is to actual hypnosis what Oko's electrical display was to the feeble current of his day. Yet both were based on a large enough grain of scientific truth to satisfy the writers and convince readers that science, and not the supernatural, was at work.

Andrei Tiazheloispytannyi (Prokhorov) invokes science in justification of his tale, *The Tormenting Feats of the Terrible Man-Eating Sea Monster, a Dangerous Merciless Bandit or a Sea Devil* (Odessa, 1910). He concludes, "There are still many more sea monsters about which I could write more stories, but ignorant people do not believe them and take them for fairy tales, even though scientists themselves know from science that monsters exist."[38] Perhaps in light of the fascination with the Loch Ness Monster and Bigfoot in our own time, we should not judge Tiazheloispytannyi too harshly.

Medicine was one area in which the lubok authors invoked science. The modern medicine of the day was usually treated in the lubok stories with respect but with little drama. This is not surprising, since the literature predates the possibility of miracle cures that came later with more advanced medical research and wonder drugs. Doctors were figures of authority, and readers were urged to turn to doctors not because medicine guaranteed a cure, but because the local healer was as likely to aggravate as to assuage the condition. The lubok writers' condemnation of folk healers was almost a moral position, since use of the healers tended to be associated with belief in the supernatural.

The increasing authority of doctors in the chronological development of the fiction is evident in three versions of the Kabardinian tale. In both Zriakhov's 1842 and the anonymous 1854 tellings, the wounded hero is treated by a skillful healer from among the Kabardinians. Zriakhov goes so far as to praise the healer's medicines and ointments as superior to those of the Europeans (part 1, p. 29). After Andrei returns to Russia, his health deteriorates. Even the most skillful surgeons have given up hope and have "named the day and hour of his death," but the healer of the Kabardinians arrives and is able to prolong his life for a short time. In the 1854 version, the healer is not clearly distinguished from a doctor, and is said to command a "profound knowledge of the doctor's art" (p. 21).

The anonymous author of the 1893 version clearly wants his readers to differentiate between a folk healer and a scientific doctor. He writes of the folk healer:

Such self-taught individuals are encountered among all peoples, especially in the lower class. Among us they are known by the names of folk healers, sorcerers, and fortunetellers, and so forth. . . . Truly, one cannot compare the self-taught folk healers with learned doctors. The advantage ought always to stand with the latter, since scientific knowledge stands higher than personal experience not supported by science. The learned doctor ought to enjoy great confidence, compared with the folk healer.[39]

Balagur also signals the growing popular respect for doctors in a 1912 story about an ambitious young man who makes the mistake of taking his ills to a healer. His nose begins to rot, and he realizes his mistake too late to save it: "He remained forever a deformed noseless monster, as if in punishment for the fact that he did not go to a doctor in good time."[40]

The prestige of doctors in popular literature was consistent with the expansion of public and private health care in postemancipation Russia.[41] Zemstvo doctors and other medical personnel tried to convince the common people of the efficacy of modern medicine, and their image in the popular fiction is evidence of their success. The medical assistants and midwives who were often more important than doctors in providing care to rural communities were largely ignored. The lubok authors appreciated the difference between a physician and a feldsher. As Balagur put it in the story cited above, his hero's mistake was "forgetting that good people from the village go to the city for treatment" (p. 73). The physician was a symbol for them of the link between science and practical life.

The power of science and scientists was explored more fully in several of the serial novels. Some of the kopeck writers made a curious invocation of the doctor and "scientific" medicine to justify stories bordering on the occult, just as they used "science" to support fantastic twists in other stories. Several of these stories were subtitled "Notes of a Psychiatrist"; the fledgling "science" of psychiatry was mentioned to give a rational explanation for highly suspect developments in the plot. Nevertheless, figures of science are revered in such stories. In the kopeck serial *The Valley of Death*, a series of murders takes place, and a lady faints before each of the killings. "Simple people" have superstitious explanations for her strange behavior, but a doctor explains, "Science, in my person, thinks the explanation is different. Evidently Vera Borisovna has very sharp senses, as is often the case with hysterical women, and detects phenomena that are inaccessible to the ordinary mortal" (p. 85).

In one of the Krechet episodes the magical flavor of popular science is developed very clearly when Krechet strikes up an acquaintanceship with a scientist. The scientist frightens people away from his laboratory by projecting pictures with a magic lantern on a screen suspended between two trees. Peasants who see the pictures think they are ghosts and devils, and flee. The scientist's appearance and personality are suggestive of wizardry. He is dark complexioned and wizened, and, like Jules Verne's Captain Nemo, he is obsessed with science both for its own sake and as a vehicle for attaining personal power. He lives in complete isolation, dreaming of the wealth and power that will follow from success in his experiments. "Money! Money!" he expostulates in a fit of exasperation. "Let me have some of it now, and in half a year millions will already be at my feet, and I will be the most powerful man in the world" (no. 624, 1910). He is very bookish, and his lab is heaped with weighty tomes—something readers were likely to associate more with black magic than with early twentieth-century science.

Yet for all his oddity, the scientist has a strong positive side. His dream is to build an airship in which one can ride as comfortably as in a train. Krechet praises the invention and provides the scientist with some needed funds. The serial appeared in the St. Petersburg newspaper during "Aviation Week" in 1910, and the difference between the primitive airplanes demonstrated in the sky over the city and the scientist's remarkable airship was enough to make the story science fiction. Krechet and his comrades work with the scientist for several months, at the end of which the airship rises into the night sky like a gigantic bird. They all drink champagne to the honor of the man whose genius "tamed the air to his will" (no. 675). The treatment of science and the scientist in this story communicates more awe than scientific understanding, but the scientist is shown, for all of his weirdness, to be working both for the hero and for the general good.

The only hero who comes close to being a man of science himself is Georgii, the assistant railroad engineer who settles in the Caucasus in "Satan's Cliff." Georgii is knowledgeable about technology because of his training with machines, but he also knows enough veterinary and human medicine to earn the respect of the local inhabitants. He comes upon a peasant about to put a wounded colt out of its misery and buys the animal for a ruble. He takes the animal back to his farm, gets his medical kit, and washes the wound with a special solution. "After this Georgii made up some strong-smelling ointment and spread it over the wound" (no. 1384, 1912). The horse gradually recovers, and Georgii keeps away the flies, since "in some places in the wound, worms had hatched from the eggs laid by the flies" (no. 1385, 1912). The former owner of the young horse is amazed at the animal's recovery, and Georgii's reputation spreads. Sick animals, and soon sick people, are brought to him for treatment. The reader is then informed that the former railroad engineer had originally taken a course in veterinary medicine in St. Petersburg. In treating people, Georgii was "guided by his own life experience with such means as castor oil and quinine." The author quickly adds that the illnesses of the local people were restricted to belly aches, colds, and minor cuts, and "Sometimes they came with eye ailments, and these Georgii cured quickly with simple zinc drops."

Education and science were often linked in the kopeck novels, and several contain powerful figures identified as men of science or technology. The leader of a band of gold seekers in P. Stavropolskii's kopeck serial "The King of the Taiga" is "a man with great education, especially technical" (no. 1195, 1910). In N. Tolstoy's "The Tsars of the World, a Fantastic Novel of the End of the Twentieth Century," a specialist in electricity invents a force that can explode mines and destroy fortresses from a great distance.[42]

One of the Moscow *Kopeika* serials written by the paper's editor, V. A. Anzimirov, features a self-taught Cossack student of science named Titov. Titov was trained as a steel worker, but studied widely on his own the subjects of "higher mathematics (for a better understanding of physics, which he loved better than all the sciences), natural science, history, and philosophy (in order to understand the meaning of life), languages (in order to read the best thoughts of human genius in the original), drafting and drawing (in order to illustrate all that struck him . . .)" (no. 31/386, 1910). This passage is interesting because it shows that the image of a well-educated person that was communicated to readers at this time included and even gave primacy to scientific learning. Ivin presented a similar figure in his story, *Where Do We Find Our Happiness?*, an odd tale that appeared in only one edition.[43] The hero is a scholar, inventor, and engineer, but his creations are never described.

The masters of scientific knowledge are positive figures in almost every case. One of the few negative examples in the serials is of a doctor at a philanthropic clinic who fails to treat properly the illness of the proletarian hero, and is dismissed as a "horse doctor."[44] The hero is treated correctly at another clinic, and so the image of doctors as a group is not challenged. One of the Nick Carter serials, however, features a mad and malevolent scientist named Doctor Kvartz. He is a doctor and a surgeon, as well as a master of almost all sciences and languages. Carter proves to be a match for the man, but neither the nature of science nor the image of the scientist is called into question.[45]

The confidence in science expressed in this literature is sometimes paired with an admiration for and fascination with technology. The interests in technology and mobility are combined in the many stories that feature modern means of transportation. The hero of *Oh Those Iaroslavites! What a Fine Folk!* (St. Petersburg, 1868) rides a train and earns his fare by helping the stoker and carrying baggage. Even when he is walking, he stays close to the tracks, and all of his good fortune is linked with the railroad and the stations.[46] Evstigneev wrote a number of humorous tales about incidents on railroads, and this theme turns up in other lubok stories as well. The heroes of the twentieth-century serial fiction are not limited to railroads, but also travel on airships, steamships, balloons, and even in a stolen Japanese submarine.[47]

Gadgets and equipment are part of the incidental props of a number of the serials. Georgii, the Caucasian settler, wants to buy a camera so that he can send pictures of his farm back to friends in St. Petersburg.[48] In another story, spies signal with electric flashlights and colored glass.[49] In still another, adventures take place around the oil drilling equipment in Baku.[50]

The Contrast with Western European and American Fiction

Despite the interest in technology shown in the stories, there is an absence of the literature of science fiction and tinkering that was so well developed at that time for popular American audiences. Among late nineteenth-century American dime novels are stories such as Edward S. Ellis' *The Huge Hunter, or the Steam Man of the Prairies* (no. 271 in Beadle's Half-Dime Library, 1882), in which a boy-inventor builds a robot that takes him and some of his friends across the country at "railroad speed."[51] More than a hundred utopian novels were published in America during the last quarter century before World War I, and a fascination with technology was central to many of them.[52] This kind of literature was less prevalent in Russia than in America. Nor was there a Russian Jules Verne or an H. G. Wells. The works of these writers circulated in Russia in translation but were not adapted for the lowest level of the reading public, perhaps because of a more limited experience with new technology by both writers and readers. There was also little evidence of popular interest in electricity in the Russian fiction, probably for the same reason.

The treatment of science and superstition in Russian popular literature highlights a clear difference between it and nineteenth-century European and American popular literature. The unmasking of devils, witches, sorcerers, and folk healers was not a theme of import in the English and French popular literature of the nineteenth century, although it was, to a degree, in the American. In the works of American and Western European writers such as Edward L. Wheeler, Pierce Egan, Jr., G.W.M. Reynolds, Eugene Sue, Ponson du Terrail, E. Gaboriau, and others with an audience analogous to that of the Russian serial fiction writers, the treatment of the supernatural differs markedly from Russian low literature. The supernatural world does not enter into the stories of Ponson du Terrail or Gaboriau. In Rocambole's adventures, non-Europeans, such as an Indian woman, or ignorant servants are superstitious, but superstition is entirely incidental to the main events. Religion, however, is accepted as a natural and integral part of the lives of positive heroes and heroines.

Colporteurs in mid-nineteenth-century France circulated works of the occult, black magic, and divination, some of them of ancient origins.[53] However, stories debunking superstition that were so prevalent in Russia were nonexistent among the French. The occasional popular diatribe against such books probably originated in educated circles. Popular French authors, publishers, and distributors apparently did not feel either compelled by conscience or tempted by profits to lecture their readers about superstitious beliefs. French readers either accepted these books on the occult at face value, or they read them with a wink, but they seem to have formed their own judgment without much critical guidance.

English certainty about the rational character of the world was sufficient to support a literature that titillated readers with exploration of the shadowy dimension. Gothic fiction may have lost some of its appeal with the expansion of the popular press toward the end of the first half of the nineteenth century,[54] but the Victorian period was the heyday of the English ghost story. Some of the best spine tinglers were published in popular periodicals such as Dickens' *Household Words* and *All the Year Round*. Ghost stories may not have reached the lowest level of readership, but tales such as James Malcolm Rymer's (1804-1882) *Varney the Vampire* (1847), and Reynolds' *Wagner the Wehr-Wolf* (1846), which was published in his own *Reynolds' Magazine*, certainly did. In the first, a vampire roams the English countryside, terrorizing good people and adding to the vampire population. In the second, a despairing old man is offered the Faustian bargain of youth, wealth, and power in exchange for four hours service a month as a werewolf. There is a scene in *Wagner* that is exactly opposite its equivalent in the Russian stories. A coolly rational judge sentences Wagner to die at sunset despite the reservations of his more superstitious colleagues. The judge declares, "The moment is now at hand when a monstrous and ridiculous superstition . . . shall be annihilated forever."[55] Much to the judge's presumed surprise, Wagner bursts from the dungeon as a terrifying monster at the appointed hour and tramples the judge to death.

The heroes, and not just the weak-minded, see ghosts in Pierce Egan, Jr.'s, *Robin Hood*: " 'Almighty Heaven! Look there,' suddenly cried Little John, pointing to the trunk of the tree. A figure of a female, a thin, pale, misty shadow it was—a ghastly, ghostly thing—stood looking on them."[56] No equivalent passages appear in the Russian literature unless they are prefaced by the announcement that the story is a fairy tale, or are followed by a rational explanation. English readers apparently were able to take this fantasy in stride and enjoy it.

Old-fashioned oracles and books of dream interpretation appeared in the lubok literature of the nineteenth and early twentieth centuries, but they never comprised a significant proportion of the whole. An audience for other occult literature did develop in Russia; but these readers were prosperous and overlapped little with the readership of the lubok and kopeck stories. A few lubok publishers advertised guidebooks to black and white magic, but these works were priced at a ruble or more—well beyond the reach of the common reader. Advertisements for these books appeared in the kopeck newspapers, but again at higher prices than lower-class readers were likely to pay. Other literature on the occult that was available was also relatively expensive.

Common in Russian stories, and also popular in England and America, was the tale in which an elaborately constructed and seemingly supernatural plot is, at the end, shown to have a rational explanation. The Holmes stories such as "The Sussex Vampire," "The Devil's Foot," and

The Hound of the Baskervilles are of this type. Similar stories occasionally appear in the Deadwood Dick series. The principal characters do not put much credence in supernatural explanations, however, either in the Holmes or the Deadwood Dick stories. They wait rather patiently until the rational explanation is slowly revealed to them, and it is the reader who carries the full weight of the supernatural implications. In the Russian stories, all characters except the hero generally assume supernatural explanations and then are convinced otherwise as the story unfolds.

Two curious kopeck novels with occult overtones appeared in 1910 and 1911 and suggest that the treatment of the supernatural was about to undergo a change. The novels represent a break with past treatment of the supernatural in popular literature, but were perhaps inspired more by the fascination with the occult that swept educated Russia at this time than by changing attitudes toward the supernatural among the lower classes. In Raskatov's "The Evil Spell" (1911), a gang of crooks seems to have supernatural powers, and the story ends ambiguously, leaving readers uncertain about the crooks' ability to cast spells. Reutskii's *One or Two* (1910) features a séance in which the evil spirit of a medieval Arab philosopher is conjured and mysterious deaths follow. This story, like others by Reutskii, is subtitled "Notes of a Psychiatrist," but psychiatry does not provide a rational explanation in this case.

The women's writers did not explore the supernatural, but Verbitskaia revealed the gap that separated her from the lubok authors when she had her heroine, Mania, believe "in everything: the witch, the devil, and the mermaid."[57] The authors of the new movement of literary modernism often portrayed demonic characters in their works, and Verbitskaia wanted to identify her heroine with this fashionable literary milieu.

The presentation of science and superstition in the lubok tales, the newspaper serials, and the installment adventures exemplifies the function of the popular commercial fiction in the encouragement and legitimation of new attitudes. Superstition was the anchor for a whole system of peasant beliefs, and when popular writers denounced it they encouraged their readers to develop more rational views of the world. Yet the very emphasis on debunking reveals the low level of the Russian common readers compared to those in the United States and Western Europe. Questions about the supernatural were still alive for lower-class Russian readers, and a repudiation of demons was still called for. Sophisticated British, French, and American readers—as well as more educated Russian readers—could on the other hand, simply derive a thrill from the mock fear inspired by visitations from the other world.

The primitive notion of science expressed by some of the Russian popular writers also contributed, in a limited way, to the diffusion of more modern perceptions of the world. At the low level of popular literature, occasional attempts to demonstrate the marvels of technology or to enthrone something called science in the place of familiar popular beliefs may have meant no more than the replacement of one vague and mysterious explanation or phenomenon with another. The establishment of rational and secular heroes, among whom were men of science, and the debunking of popular superstitions were, however, important indicators of the Russian common reader's more modern outlook.

Popular superstitions still flourished in late imperial Russia, but a reading of the popular fiction suggests that belief in the power of supernatural forces and in magical remedies for human ills was probably diminishing. Keith Thomas has argued convincingly in *Religion and the Decline of Magic* that the crucial factor in the decline of magic and the widespread dissemination of a more scientific and rational approach to the natural world in seventeenth-century England was the growth of a notion of self-help in both the religious and economic sense.[58] People who felt that their success or failure depended primarily on their own efforts were, in his view, less likely to seek supernatural assistance. The idea of self-help in the context of postemancipation Russia meant increased economic opportunities for people of the lower classes and their greater assertiveness in directing their lives. The question of success and social mobility was an important theme in popular literature, and this is the subject of the next chapter.

VIII

SUCCESS

THE READERS of Russian popular fiction in the last half century of the old regime were people with aspirations. Changes in the technology of transportation, new economic opportunities, and a greater fluidity in social structure made it possible for individuals born into the peasantry to contemplate alternatives to life within their native villages. Those who had already made the transition to the city could see the diversity of urban work and living conditions and picture themselves moving upward from their humble origins. Change and mobility were on people's minds, and those who stayed home were affected as much as those who packed up and left. Many readers of popular literature were first-generation literate, and in the very act of learning to read they had expressed a desire for a life different from that of their parents.

With an audience of people aspiring to better lives, it would be strange indeed if writers of popular literature did not respond with stories about success and failure, as popular writers had done elsewhere.[1] In fact, the questions of what constitutes success, who achieves it, and why they succeed in doing so are prominent in popular literature throughout the period from the emancipation to the Revolution.

Commercial popular literature in general reflected the reality that those who built themselves significantly better lives frequently left their villages. In only a few of the commercial stories, in contrast to the sponsored literature, is success to be found in a happy peasant community. In taking their characters out of the village, writers faced a problem that their mobile readers also confronted. Since the seventeenth century, Russian society had been divided into legally sanctioned and hereditary castes. This formal structure, together with the table of ranks that had been instituted by Peter the Great, was weakening in the second half of the nineteenth century. Déclassé gentry were almost as common as upstart peasants, such as the former serf who tried to help out the bankrupt gentry family in Chekhov's play, *The Cherry Orchard*. The importance of the merchant class, the most mobile of the old class groupings, declined as peasant entrepreneurs and others gained footholds in many areas of commerce. The formal class groupings still existed, however, and were accorded a certain legitimacy bred of familiarity. The idea of a peasant attaining the status of a businessman was more remarkable than the same mobility would have been in a less stratified society. These official class categories served more, in the late nineteenth century, to mark rather than inhibit mobility, but they presented popular writers with an additional task both in plotting their characters' upward progress and in justifying it.

Success was an important theme in the popular literature because the literature developed when barriers to economic mobility for the common people were diminishing. It is remarkable that popular images of success developed so much later in Russia than in Western Europe and America, but it would have been more remarkable had a vivid popular imagery of success existed much before the emancipation of the serfs. Until that time the lives of the common people were sharply restricted by the system of hereditary castes and by the backwardness of the economy.

Folk Tales as Precursors of the Success Stories

Russian folk tales include numerous stories of virtuous heroes and heroines rewarded for their courage, honesty, loyalty, or simply for their virtue. In many, worthy commoners succeed by earning the hand of a prince or a princess in marriage. In some, brave soldiers drive demons from castles and perform other feats, for which they are rewarded by rich patrons. The popular commercial printed literature of success differs from its oral precursors in the greater verisimilitude of the plotting and characterization. It is no longer sufficient to identify characters as a nobleman, a rich merchant, a beautiful peasant girl, or a handsome prince. The characters of the print literature are endowed with individual traits with which readers can identify. Nor do they live in "far-away kingdoms" and "far-away lands," but they reside in villages or cities of the real world. Unless the reader was well forewarned that what followed was a "fairy tale," writers were constrained to present stories that could actually have happened. At the same time, the authors had to present events that were infrequent in real people's lives, so that they were a focus of longing rather than a chronicle of daily experience.

The earliest lubok success stories were not celebrations of success, but cautionary tales about the perils of aspiring too high or living above one's station. Before lubok fiction reached a substantial lower-class audience, writers such as A. A. Orlov and V. F. Potapov wrote about merchants' sons who failed to preserve their fathers' wealth. These prodigals chose the life of the dandy rather than that of the hard-working, honest, and abstemious merchant, and that was their undoing. A peasant version of this kind of story was P. Tatarinov's *Fomushka in Piter* [St. Petersburg], *or Wealth Is No Help to a Stupid Son* (1852). Fomushka is a clever and literate young peasant, popular with the village girls. He ignores his dying father's advice to avoid the city, and takes his inheritance of 6,000 rubles to St. Petersburg. He dreams that there "in a year he would be Foma the merchant!" In less than a year he is fleeced of his fortune and is glad to return to the countryside. The story concludes with the admonition, "Don't sit in someone else's sled," which is a popular saying as well as the title of a play by Ostrovskii.[2]

Ivin wrote a cautionary tale entitled *A Family Sin* about a poor soldier's daughter, Nastia, who likes to read and becomes too cultured for her village companions. She marries the son of the village smith but finds him crude and unfeeling. Soon after they marry, the husband opens a shop, but it does not succeed. When their child is stillborn, Nastia becomes despondent and throws herself into the river. She is rescued by her husband, and, after this dramatic act, the village women regret their meanness toward her. The husband gives up his shop and takes a farm, and the community accepts Nastia. Both husband and wife have given up their aspirations for something better than the life of the ordinary peasant, and after their sacrifice, they achieve a kind of happiness. This tale was published rather late, in 1889, and is unusual for its treatment of success at that time.[3] Writers of commercial lubok fiction very rarely portrayed farming as a route to success or happiness. To most, success meant escape from the laborious life associated with both peasant farming and unskilled urban factory work.

The lubok authors presented a surprisingly mundane and unflamboyant vision of success, perhaps in conformity with their readers' expectations about truth and verisimilitude in print. The newspaper serial writers had a more urban and sophisticated audience, and gave their imaginations freer rein, as did the women's writers and some of the authors of the cheap early twentieth-century fiction.

Images of Success

The image of success expressed in the lubok tales combined elements of material and personal success with fame and public recognition. Material success meant attaining wealth and a comfortable life, usually in the city. Personal success depended on a happy marriage, often followed by the birth of a son. Both material and personal success were important in the lubok fiction, but full public recognition of material success was sometimes downplayed. The lubok authors' unwillingness to celebrate material success wholeheartedly was probably due to a concern about antagonizing the community by calling undue attention to one's good fortune.

Fame was an important aspect of success in the newspaper serials, the women's fiction, and in the more expensive popular works. The protagonists of the newspaper serials on occasion concealed their good fortune, but the heroes of the installment adventures and the heroines of the women's novels gloried in public acclaim. In the installment novels fame was gained by feats of the sort reported in the popular newspapers: deeds of daring or crime, or, alternatively, success in combatting crime. Fame in the women's novels and the other cheap turn-of-the-century fiction came, for the most part, from talent in the world of letters or the performing arts.

Among the stories having the theme of success, several paths recur frequently enough to be identified as patterns. One clear avenue to success was that of finding a patron who owned a shop or enterprise, being taken into his family, and eventually marrying his daughter. The authors of these stories combined both material and familial success, since the hero ended up well established both in business and at home. Of the stories that treated the theme of success, about a fifth featured adoption by a patron.

The adoption plot had a basis in reality. In nineteenth-century Russia, merchants frequently picked out capable young men from among their employees, took them into their houses, trained them to manage the business, sponsored them in their own activities, and picked brides for them. This was a career path known to popular authors from within their own industry. Sytin owed his rise to the patronage of Sharapov, and was adopted by the old man. Shataev may have had a similar experience. He was a distant relative of the Kholmushin family and was trained to run their business, a position he kept for most of his life. Merchants made this decision not only when they had no capable heir, but also occasionally when they had the wealth and ambition to raise their sons as gentry.[4] The patron on a smaller scale was a familiar figure to peasants in their own lives, and even at local markets peasants were likely to find patrons among the merchants with whom they dealt who might lend them money or let them buy on credit.

The idea of going to live in a family of distant relatives or even of nonrelated people also owed something to the history of the Russian peasant family. With the formation of the extended family in the seventeenth century, old and impoverished serfs and orphans were on occasion compelled by their owners to live with others for economic reasons.[5] A story that is true to the patronage model in every respect is

FIG. 19. V. A. Lunin (pseud. Kukel), *Rejected Love, or the Widow's Revenge* (Moscow: Konovalov, 1914).

273

Foma Balagur's *Petia Chimney Sweep, Dirty in Body, Clean in Soul* (1904). Petia is a poor orphan cared for by a good but impecunious woman. By gathering mushrooms and berries, sewing, and selling small handicrafts, the woman manages to feed Petia and send him to primary school, but her eyesight fails, and she can no longer work. A friend from a neighboring village, where men make their livelihood as chimney sweeps in Moscow and St. Petersburg, offers to take Petia on as an apprentice. Petia works diligently, cleans himself up every day, and puts on fresh clothes. One day he happens upon a wallet containing 500 rubles and some financial papers. He follows his aunt's advice and tracks down the owner to return it. The owner turns out to be a rich self-made stove manufacturer, who, conveniently enough, has a daughter. The stove maker presses Petia to accept a third of the money, which is his legal due as the finder, and only reluctantly does Petia agree. They go to a restaurant, and Petia does not drink alcohol with his meal, thus further winning the good opinion of the stove maker. He is offered a job and soon becomes the stove maker's trusted assistant. Both he and his aunt are invited to live in the stove maker's home, and before long he has married the boss's daughter and established a family of his own.[6]

A story of patronage that deviates slightly from the model is *The Young Bandit Ataman "Storm"* (1913) by an anonymous author. The hero is a poor boy of clerical origins who makes a precarious living as a church singer, earning 15 rubles a month. He has the courage and good luck to rescue a merchant from bandits. The merchant thanks him by handing him a purse with 5,000 rubles in it. The hero, however, catches the eye of the merchant's daughter and returns the purse. Within six months he has married the daughter. He inherits the merchant's two bookshops, and is shown many years later telling the story of his success with some relish, seated in an armchair, smoking a cigar, and with his daughter, who attends a gymnasium, at his side. In this story, the man was not adopted into the family prior to the marriage, nor was he first trained in the business, but he nevertheless succeeds through the good offices of his patron.[7]

In a third variant of the patronage story, a young man is adopted, and his patron arranges his wedding, but he does not marry the boss's daughter. This happens in Lunin's tale, *Masha the Orphan or the Sober Lovelace* (1901). Here, as in over a third of the stories, the protagonist is a woman. A resourceful widow with three small children takes a job at a rural factory. Her daughters grow up to be beautiful, and the widow must fend off the advances of the boorish factory administrator and his sons. The administrator takes a dislike to her son, Serezha, who then leaves the factory for a job at a city shop. He is an excellent salesman, and his new boss soon adopts him and helps him settle his whole family in the city. Thanks to the boss's generosity, Serezha is able to marry his girlfriend. He becomes the shopkeeper's chief assistant and is soon sponsored in his own business.[8]

Heroes and heroines who succeed in these stories are shown at work in a number of walks of life, but it is perhaps not surprising that the work done by most of the readers, rural farm work or unskilled urban factory work, was not part of the picture of success. A city job or the ownership of a shop or enterprise is a sign of success in nearly a third of the stories. Andrei, in the early lubok classic that was republished many times, *Oh Those Iaroslavites! What a Fine Folk!* becomes a *buffetchik* (bartender or manager of a snack shop) at the St. Petersburg Hotel Razdole (Horn of Plenty). From this position, he can return in triumph to his native village and carry the most desirable girl back to the city as his wife.[9] In Lunin's story *Put Your Hopes in God, but Try Hard Not to Fail*, success comes in the form of a job as a cabby, with an assistant to lighten the work.[10]

Proprietorship of a shop or a bar was a clear kind of success for lower-class inhabitants of both the city and countryside. The clever heroine of Evstigneev's tale, *A Nose at 10,000* (1897), is a poor seamstress betrothed to an equally poor employee of a tea shop. The two are too poor to marry. She attends a masquerade and is approached by a would-be seducer, a rich merchant's son in search of a fling. She wins his affection, and has him furnish her with a shop in order to convince his father that she is a respectable match. As soon as the shop is in her own name, she throws over the inexperienced rich paramour and settles down to a happy life with her old boyfriend.[11]

The hero of one of Aleksandrovskii's early twentieth-century tales, *The Unexpected Meeting of a Husband with His Wife after a Twenty-Five-Year Separation* (1912), also ends up as a prosperous property owner. When the story opens the hero has just married a lively widow and is the proprietor of a tea shop. She flirts with other men, however, and when he turns to drink she drives him from the shop. He finds work as a janitor and saves his money until he has enough to open first one beer hall, then another, and then an inn. One day a rich gentleman rents a suite at his inn, and among the servants' passports he sees the name of his wife. She approaches him eagerly but is rebuffed.[12]

The vision of success often seen in the stories of *Moskovskii listok* was close to that of the lubok patronage tales. Most of the wealth that came to the heroes of these stories originated in the pockets of old-fashioned Moscow merchants. In Pastukhov's long serial, Churkin aspires to marry an elder's daughter, but the man who is shown to win her hand works for a merchant and inherits all his boss's wealth. Churkin puzzles in astonishment over "how the former merchant's assistant could become a capitalist so quickly" (p. 642). In Pazukhin's serial "What Will Be Will Be," which appeared in *Moskovskii listok* in 1892, wealth is again a merchant's legacy. The money has been willed to a merchant's illegitimate daughter, but a treacherous assistant appropriates the money instead. A hotel servant is instrumental in directing the inheritance to its rightful heir. Fate then favors the good servant when he finds the wallet of another merchant and returns it to receive a large reward. With the money he fulfills a lifelong dream and buys an orchard.

Writers of lubok fiction and some of the authors of the newspaper serials represented success as an association with a rich patron or employment at a desirable job in the city. Other authors, particularly of the newspaper serials, did not limit their characters to such prosaic and modest images of success, and instead put them on the track of buried treasure and vast stores of loot. The treasure theme has deep roots in Russian folklore, as in that of other cultures. Heroes in Russian folk tales find or steal treasure almost as frequently as they marry princesses. Maxim Gorky complained, perhaps unjustly, that a predilection for quick riches made the Russian laborer a poor worker. He pointed to a parallel in folklore with the comment that the Russian worker had little enthusiasm for the irksome process of labor, and hoped instead "to build temples and castles in three days." If this could not be done, Gorky continued, "he throws the task over." Gorky made his comments in a testimonial to I. D. Sytin, whom he hailed as a model of enterprise and initiative.[13]

The dream of easy money appears frequently in both the *Moskovskii listok* and kopeck serials. Often the search for treasure is woven into an adventure story. Finding a treasure allows the hero to live on a scale more lavish than even that of a rich merchant. Treasure allows Krechet to live like a gentleman throughout his years on the run, and even to play the philanthropist. The gypsy hero in "The Foundling," another kopeck serial, leaves his adoptive home on the Dnieper to seek his fortune and unravel the secret of his origins. A mysterious talisman left him by his mother arouses his curiosity, and when a steamboat passenger asks him, "What's best, to live here till death like a muzhik, or to go off on the wide merry free road . . . and live like a lord?" he takes up the challenge of the quest (no. 1486, 1912). After a series of adventures, he finds the fortune associated with his talisman. His success is complete when he marries the daughter in his adoptive family.

The pauper hero of the kopeck serial "The Treasure Hunters," who is too poor to win the hand of the daughter of a rich shopkeeper in a mining town on the steppe, sets off into the barren wastelands to look for treasure, since, the author tells us, "to attain position and wealth step by step, to scrimp and save kopeck after kopeck, to heap up enough capital to satisfy Shchukin [the girl's father]—for that one would have to spend half a lifetime" (no. 764, 1910). The hero prefers to look for treasure, and he finds some. With treasure in hand, he obtains permission to marry the shopkeeper's daughter.

A more industrious path to wealth is indicated by Raskatov in his 1912 St. Petersburg kopeck serial "Satan's Cliff," but here, too, treasure caps the heroes' efforts and completes their triumph. Three friends in St. Petersburg meet in a beer hall and dream about how nice it would be "if they were suddenly made rich and free by magic" (no. 1372). They decide to pool their skills and resources to buy a farm in the south where "you can do what you want to and be your own boss" (no. 1375). After two and a half years of scrimping, they have earned the necessary 700 rubles and move south. They buy a farm and work hard for several years setting it up; they sell their first tobacco crop for 2,000 rubles, and that, together with their other earnings, constitutes a substantial income. But, as if this believable and attainable success were not enough for the reader, the three also find a treasure, which the rightful owner, a Georgian princess, gladly shares with them.

Public recognition and fame are elements of success that have various degrees of importance in different stories. Ivin gave a singular and rather moralistic twist to the question of fame in his story, *Where Do We Find Our Happiness?* The story is told in the form of a fairy tale. Two brothers attend their dying father, who gives them a magic ring and instructs them to roll it and follow it wherever it goes: they would find happiness where it stops. They do as they are told and the ring comes to rest before a substantial farmhouse in a large village. The two brothers sign on as hired hands, and the younger one soon finds a treasure in the garden. He marries the farmer's daughter, they have a son, and he is happy. The elder brother, however, is not satisfied with his lot and seeks a more dramatic fulfillment.[14] He has read all the books in the local school library, and goes to the city, where he becomes a learned man and an inventor and a builder. When he walks through the streets, people take off their hats to him, and after he dies they pray for his eternal rest and happiness. Ivin concludes, "This means that our true happiness is to be found in striving for learning, and in doing useful and good things for the people" (p. 36). Public recognition of the elder brother's contribution to the common good is a substitute for personal, familial, and material happiness. The brother's fame is treated as a well-deserved compensation for his effort and is not shown to be central to his motivation.

A very different kind of recognition is found in the women's novels of the early twentieth century, and also occasionally in the newspaper serials: the fame and adulation of stardom that are often achieved in one of the arts. Writers who presented their characters as stars before whom "all of Paris fell to its knees" tapped into the strong wish of many readers to be known and admired and escape their relatively unmarked lives in the big anonymous city. This fantasy probably appealed to adolescent girls chafing under middle-class restraints or on isolated estates, and to less fortunate working-class girls with grandiose dreams.

The fact that fame was most often achieved in the arts may have been a result of Russian attitudes toward wealth gained from business or commerce. Money from these sources, although clearly sought after by those who had the opportunity, was regarded with ambivalence or hostility by much of Russian society, both because it was not old, established wealth and because commerce and industry were associated with the exploitation of others. The artist, on the other hand, was considered free of conventions, obligations, and greedy dealings. Money came to these people not because they consciously set out to amass it, but rather incidentally—because the adoring crowds wanted to reward their talents. Therefore, talent, unlike entrepreneurial skills, justified fame and glory.

Contrasting attitudes toward art and industry are seen in Pazukhin's serial in *Moskovskii listok*, "The Millionaire's Daughter." A villainous son tries to cheat his brother out of an inheritance, but his attempt is foiled by an artist. For this act the artist wins the love of an heiress; but when he proposes marriage, she hesitates, feeling she is inferior despite her great wealth. "You are strong and powerful, a knight," she replies, "and a wide field of activity lies before you. Who am I but a poor humble girl, a merchant's daughter" (no. 241, 1893).

Success in the arts may have figured so prominently in this literature because many of the readers were women, and the performing arts were one of the few arenas in which women could distinguish themselves independently at this time. Success in the world of art was Verbitskaia's stock in trade, and her works were known to appeal mostly to women. Mania, the heroine of *The Keys to Happiness*, is a half orphan living in bourgeois penury with a mad mother, and she dreams that "art will make her free" (1:152). The reader knows that this means freedom from want and from the need to labor, freedom to travel and to live independently and adventurously. Mania's artistic talent also frees her from moral conventions, and she is able to enter the world of art as the mistress of Steinbach, her wealthy patron. Steinbach sponsors her in Paris, where she is trained for the stage with the best teachers. Mania rhapsodizes, "Oh to be something! A poet, a sculptor, an artist, an individual. To open the world of one's fantasy! To give people joy, to create one's own world" (4:209). After she achieves success on the stage, "a broad path opened before Maria Sergeevna. Glory, the love of the public, independence, creativity" (4:220).

The struggle for artistic success is also the theme of Verbitskaia's *The Yoke of Love*. The heroine is Nadezhda, a poor orphan who finds success on the stage, where she makes her debut as Ophelia. "She is no longer Nadia Shubeikina, a poor Moscow trades girl who challenged life and did not wish to accept her grim lot. She is the daughter of a courtier, born at the court, here in Denmark under the lowering sky" (p. 29). Nadezhda achieves artistic success and fame, but no personal happiness.

The hero of Verbitskaia's first novel, *The Spirit of the Times*, is also transformed by artistic success. Toboltsev comes from a rich Old Believer family, but his riches cannot compare to the success he achieves when he is recognized as the "rising star" of an amateur theater group. His fame is assured and his place is said to be "in the capital" (1:76). In the lubok stories, the ability to get to the capital on the strength of one's talents would be success enough in itself. Toboltsev could clearly have moved to the capital any time he wished, but here the capital serves as the epitome of the world of art.

Verbitskaia's novels appeared at a time when writers and artisans were becoming the great heroes of Russian popular journalism. Maxim Gorky's struggles upward from poverty and squalor were well known, and he became a model for aspiring artists and writers. The doings of writers such as Gorky—their romances, summer outings, holidays, and off-the-cuff comments on issues of the day—were reported in detail in the press. One of the popular magazines even featured a cover picture of the writer Kuprin in his dressing gown, "after swimming."[15]

Many of the writers of popular fiction outfitted their characters in elaborate costumes, and the fantasy of dress can be seen as an expression of aspirations for success and upward mobility. Even for readers who had no concrete plans for self-betterment, dressing up was an escape from the monotony of the working life, and readers apparently cared about the details of costume. The transitory character of elaborate dress was apparent even within the context of the stories. In one sense, elegant clothes represented a hopeless serf's dream of success; but in another, clothing did increasingly make the man in the last few decades of the old regime, and therefore the urge to dress up stemmed from a more realistic desire for mobility. By the late nineteenth century, gentry were ceasing to list rank on their calling cards,[16] and as the formal system of hereditary castes and civil ranks broke down, dress became an important indication of status. At the same time, workers and other lower-class urban inhabitants had more discretionary income to spend on clothing than their peasant parents had had, and soon urban costumes appeared in the villages, often causing a stir.

The heroes of the early lubok tales wore fantastic costumes that were unlikely to be seen anywhere except in the imaginations of the popular writers. In the later lubok stories, the styles of the gentry predominate, and they in turn give way to merchant dress. Heroes in the newspaper serials often wore European suits. Bulavin, who led a revolt against Peter the Great, appears in the 1849 version of *Kondrashka Bulavin* dressed as if he is headed for a carnival, with a gold belt and a tall beaver hat studded with pearls.[17] Volgin's lion-hearted ataman wears a sail-blue kaftan, with velvet trousers, high boots, and a red shirt.[18] Churkin, on the other hand, arrives at a village feast the very picture of a dashing village lad who has been to the city and returned, sporting a red calico shirt, a blue fitted coat, wide velveteen trousers, long goatskin boots, and a small felt hat bedecked with peacock feathers (p. 31). Later, Churkin wants to pass for a merchant and dresses the part; but Osip, looking like a peasant in his short sheepskin jacket, has difficulty playing this role and is told in a bar not to sit in the merchants' section. In a subsequent scene, however, they both pass for merchants. Then Osip also acquires a merchant's long coat and exclaims to Churkin, "Now I will be like a merchant, and you will see how they honor me" (p. 1002).

Krechet is a different kind of hero, and he wears clothes with ease to fit any part he chooses to play. He is introduced as dressed in "an elegant summer suit" (p. 8), but he can also pass for a simple peasant or stride through the taiga with the best of the Mongol hunters. He is a natural aristocrat. He is not interested in passing for gentry, but he recognizes the importance of dressing up. When his son comes home after graduating from gymnasium, Krechet puts on a frock coat, and his two trusted henchmen go off to town to buy themselves ties.

Qualities for Success

Russian popular authors stressed the qualities necessary for success. Pluck, energy, and resourcefulness in the face of obstacles count for much in the lubok tales. Many of the heroes and heroines who attain their goals are shown to have been severely tested along the way. Andrei, the hero of *Oh Those Iaroslavites!* is shown at the outset struggling against the force of a terrible storm: "It is nighttime in such a blizzard that you can't see your hand in front of your face. Head bowed, a young fellow of 22 or 23 trudges along a country road with a knapsack on his back."[19]

Another hero, in Lunin's *A Good Comrade*, walks 200 miles to get to Moscow and have his chance at a job. Women such as Varvara in Lunin's *Place Your Hopes in God, but Try Hard Not to Fail* work hard to put their children on the road to success. Another strong woman of this type is Lunin's heroine in *Masha the Orphan*. Even though she is weak, pregnant, and homeless, she gets a job and provides for her family, including Masha.[20]

Some of the characters in the serial fiction were shown to scrimp and save as they move toward success. Paradoxically, it is not the self-denial that ultimately assures their fulfillment, but rather it serves as a justification for the lucky break that fate gives them. Kolobrodov, the good hotel servant in Pazukhin's "What Will Be Will Be," remarks that he lived in "dirty and cramped quarters" even though he wanted "to live like a human being" (no. 69, 1892). He saves with the hope of buying an orchard, but it is not until he is lucky enough to find a merchant's wallet and receives a generous reward for returning it that he can realize his dream. One has the impression that his total earned savings had been insignificant compared to the needed sum. Klokochev, a good merchant in another of Pazukhin's tales, is widely respected for his honesty, his old-fashioned life style, and his religiosity. He is said to have worked his way up in the world, starting with "a kopeck" and a cart. His break came in Siberia when he came into a good deal on a bundle of furs and several tons of pine nuts.[21] Similarly, Georgii and his comrades in the kopeck serial "Satan's Cliff" save to buy their farm in the Caucasus, but they also find buried treasure. Verbitskaia's heroines forego current pleasures for future artistic success. Katia, in *The Spirit of the Times*, supports an invalid mother by teaching at a women's institute. When her musical talent is discovered, her teacher tells her, "Work. You have a great future before you. Who knows?" (1:88). In fact, each of Verbitskaia's heroines must work hard to develop the talents that lead to artistic success and fame.

More important even than perseverance and self-denial in the quest for success in the lubok tales is education and love of reading. These were also qualities that marked an individual for better things in the traditional saints' lives. "Study, son, and you will become someone," says the widowed mother of the hero in *The Young Bandit Ataman "Storm"* (pp. v-vi). It is the desire to go to school and learn to read that sets an orphan on the road to success as a shopkeeper in P. S. Kuklin's *The Sensible and Industrious Son of the Present Times, Left an Orphan in Infancy* (1883). The hero is sent to live with an uncle and asks to go to school. School is followed by learning a trade and going to war, but literacy was the first step. The orphan begins to give reading lessons to his neighbors.[22] Similarly, in Lunin's *The Foundling or a Fortunate Meeting*, the hero gains his boss's attention by staying behind with a book while the other apprentices play.[23] Some of the retold fairy tales that had little to do with success show literate heroes. In Suvorov's *The Tale of Ivan the Tsar's Son, the Firebird, and the Grey Wolf*, published by Sytin in 1910, literacy is used to distinguish the hero from his brothers. "Usually the older two brothers only feasted, pranced about on horses, and chased pretty girls, but Ivan the Tsar's son sat peacefully, read books, and did his sums."[24]

Education is also important in the newspaper serials, but here it means more than a few years of primary school. Kolobrodov, the good hotel servant who buys an orchard in Pazukhin's "What Will Be Will Be," was born a peasant but accumulated a home library of forty books. "He had the complete Old Testament in modern Russian translation, the Gospels, some other books of spiritual content, and then Pushkin in a cheap edition, Koltsov, Nekrasov, . . ." and others, including works of history.[25] Tania, the ambitious heroine of Pazukhin's "Velvet Ladies," is sent to a private school instead of the parish school. She is forced to withdraw when the family shop is destroyed by fire, but continues to read books and learns from them about "a completely different life."[26] The heroine of Pazukhin's "In the Claws of Cupidity" is not only literate, but also works as an assistant librarian in Moscow. She meets her future husband, who happens to be rich, when he comes to the library to borrow a book.[27]

Education in the kopeck serials usually means relatively advanced education, such as that of Krechet, or the engineer Migunon in Raskatov's "The Gold Seekers." In the Moscow edition there were characters such as Silin, a former student and schoolteacher, and Nikolai Zharov, the proletarian artist who spends a period of enforced idleness during a serious illness reading books and hoping to get into an art school.[28]

Love of learning was a character trait of the heroes in the old saints' lives; but unlike the saints, the protagonists of the popular tales seek education for concrete practical aims. Education differentiates the heroes of popular stories from ordinary people just as the saints were shown to be different and special because of their diligence in learning. The knowledge learned from books added to the aura of holiness associated with the saints, however, whereas for the secular popular heroes education is primarily a means for material advancement.

Intelligence is inherent in the heroes' predilection for reading and schooling. In order to succeed, characters need to use their wits and imagination, but guile leads to success in only a few of the stories. Nevertheless, contrary to Russian folk tales, the popular commercial literature shows no golden path for a good-hearted Ivan-the-fool: naive and blundering heroes simply do not succeed in these stories.

Talent was especially important as a personal quality for success in the more urban fiction of the twentieth century and in the women's literature, but it counted for little in the world of the lubok writers. Talent occasionally figured in the kopeck novels, as in "The Foundling," in which the hero shows his abilities as a circus acrobat. It is in the women's stories that talent reigns supreme as both the foundation and justification for success. In the case of each of Verbitskaia's heroines, talent and its recognition by a rich patron who can support its development lifts a poor but deserving girl out of obscurity and into fame and fortune.

A story of mobility achieved through talent that had both literary merit and popular appeal was Maxim Gorky's memoir. His autobiography was serialized in I. D. Sytin's newspaper *Russkoe slovo* in late 1913 and was an instant success. *Russkoe slovo* had a daily circulation of 325,700 copies in 1913, and 619,500 copies in 1914.[29] Gorky's *Childhood* began to appear in November 1913 and continued into 1914. Excerpts of the second part, *Among People*, appeared in 1915. The fact that the astute Sytin published Gorky's work for a reading public that must have approached several million indicates the extent to which artists and writers had captured the imagination of Russian readers.

Gorky's autobiography contains so many of the elements of the popular success formula that it is difficult not to see it as a more literary variant of the popular stories. Like many lubok heroes, Gorky began life as an orphan, or at least as a half orphan. The first words of the memoir announce his father's death. His grandfather is also an orphan, and he tells the young Gorky his story of becoming a master craftsman and head of a guild. The prized worker at the grandfather's dye works, Gypsy, is another orphan, and the grandfather avows that Gypsy will become rich one day. Young Gorky's protector in his struggle to make his way in the world is an elderly woman, his grandmother, and in this, too, he resembles many of the lubok heroes. Gorky also has patrons, but they lend him books instead of offering their daughters to him.

The achievement of success is a recurring theme in the memoir, and the young Gorky considers various paths toward that goal. In the second volume he works briefly in a shop, and he discusses, with a fellow worker at the Nizhnii-Novgorod Fair, the possibility of achieving success through a prosperous marriage. Gorky ultimately rejects all practical and materialistic alternatives and chooses the path of books and learning. The novel is replete with hints about what not to do while perfecting oneself for a career as a writer. Since his readers already knew the end of the story, there was no doubt that Gorky's path was the correct one.

Gorky's use of talent as a motive force toward success is similar to Verbitskaia's. For modern readers who revere Gorky and revile or ignore Verbitskaia, the comparison of the two is little short of sacrilegious. It is true that Gorky's autobiography is incomparably more pleasurable to read than are Verbitskaia's pretentious romances. Both the autobiography and the women's novels, however, are stories of success structured around talent and its discovery, and readers responded enthusiastically to this common element in both. Recognition of Gorky's talent is a theme of the memoir from the beginning. From the time when a kindly adult asks him to write down stories about his grandma, to the bishop's surprise visit to his primary school, Gorky's gift sets him apart from his fellows. The reader is made to understand that despite the young Gorky's pranks, he does well in school. His progress in learning to read is an important part of the narrative, and in this the autobiography resembles the lubok success stories. Gorky, in fact, relates that he read lubok literature as a child, but he does not praise the booklets in his memoir. His autobiography differs from Verbitskaia's tales in that the success and recognition he achieved in the field of literature are not presented with the hyperbole used by Verbitskaia.

The suggestion that the tremendous appeal of Gorky's memoir was due in part to its affinity to the popular success story does not impugn its literary merit.[30] With his autobiography Gorky recaptured his place as one of the most popular writers of Russia for a very wide public of educated and semieducated readers, a position he had lost in the period after 1905 when he turned to more modernist themes.

The Russian popular authors' eagerness to stress the virtues of education and reading sets their stories apart from the contemporaneous English, French, and American popular fiction. No attention at all is paid to this subject in the stories of Sue, Ponson du Terrail, Gaboriau, Reynolds, or Wheeler. In fact, there is even an occasional comment to the contrary. When the young Lecoq, who later became Gaboriau's famous detective, finds himself an orphan without an inheritance, the only legacy he has is his education. This does not help him at all initially: "He envied the lot of those who, with a trade at their fingertips, could boldly enter the office of any manufacturer and say, 'I would like to work.' "[31] He eventually finds a job with an astronomer; but that comes to nothing, and his thoughts turn to crime. When the astronomer dismisses Lecoq with the admonition that he would make either a famous crook or a great detective, Lecoq chooses the latter and finds his métier. In the Deadwood Dick serial, overeducated Europeans, particularly English gentlemen, are shown to be inferior to the rough-and-ready Americans. Protagonists in American popular literature fear overcultivation and effeteness, and they value "down home" common sense. Protagonists in the Russian literature value education and fear ignorance.

The belief in the value of literacy and education in achieving success that was communicated to readers of Russian popular literature may have in part reflected the writers' conviction that they owed their own success to literary training. It may also have been the case that in Russia, where popular literacy was much lower than in Western Europe or America, the rewards to those with basic reading skills were higher. Certainly the idea of what constituted an adequate education differed among Russian, European, and American popular authors. The writers of American, English, and French popular literature were, for the most part, much better educated than their Russian counterparts, and literacy and a smattering of primary schooling did not amount to much in their world. What constituted a useful education in their view was more likely to be beyond the reach and experience of their readers, however. For Russian writers, who were much closer to their audience in social origins and experience, literacy did seem to make a difference, and they were eager to praise its virtues.

Justifications for Success

Success as presented by the authors of Russian popular literature was clearly desirable, but its attainment was not celebrated unequivocally. Both the definition of success and the ambiguity regarding its achievement reflect the peasant origins of many of the writers and most of the readers of popular Russian fiction in this period. Even though the village was less isolated in this period than in earlier times, the village and family were still primary in the daily lives of peasants. The decision to seek success in a path not cleared by parental footsteps necessarily meant rejection of family and village. This was not the case when peasants left the village temporarily for seasonal labor, but this pattern of migrant labor was considered simply a variant of village life, and not a clean break.

Peasant attitudes toward wealth were formed over the course of generations in a village economy, which was relatively closed and in which economic growth was slow, if discernible at all. Under these conditions, anyone who got rich seemed to do so at the expense of some other person in the village. This view of wealth in a peasant community was not unique to the Russian village. Mexican villagers in the mid-twentieth century similarly considered the village economy to be a closed zero sum game, in which wealth could only be redistributed and seldom created.[32] The Russian village economy in the second half of the nineteenth century was in fact not closed, but traditional attitudes toward wealth remained strong enough to form an admixture with newer attitudes in the stories.

Achievement of wealth in the traditional village setting was therefore associated with either rejection or exploitation of the community, or both. The ambiguity surrounding new wealth in a community in which everyone knew everyone else meant that the successful person had to use some or all of his new resources to placate the community.[33] The successful person might also conceal signs of prosperity and live like other villagers in order not to incur his neighbors' jealousy.

Newly prosperous Russian villagers were most likely expected to share their wealth with their communities. Until the Stolypin reforms of 1906-10, the village was a corporate community, with collective responsibility for financial obligations to the state and some responsibility for the welfare of its poorer residents. The Russian village in the latter half of the nineteenth century did not totally stifle individual enterprise and initiative, however, nor was the economic welfare of villagers determined totally within the perimeters of the community. The attitudes of both popular writers and their readers toward success were colored by the historical traditions of the communal village economy.

Suspicion of commerce and business and the contrasting belief in the moral superiority of agricultural and physical labor can be explained by these traditional views of wealth. Yet for most people, remaining in agriculture meant a continuation of the same daily toil, and commerce and other morally dubious urban employment at least held out a hope for quick riches. Success thus had both the flavor and the allure of the forbidden fruit, and Russian popular literature reflected this ambiguity in a number of ways.[34] Because success was not an uncomplicated achievement, the triumphs of the heroes and heroines in the popular stories could not simply be presented and celebrated: they also had to be justified, sometimes in rather subtle ways.

Many of the heroes and heroines of Russian popular literature of this period were orphans. Their lack of ties to family and community allowed them to succeed without violating traditional obligations to parents left behind in the village. Orphans were peripheral members of the community, and hence did not have to share their good fortune with the collective, although many chose to do so in a token generosity—more to demonstrate their wealth than to spread it.

The orphan was useful as a literary device, but the prevalence of these children in the literature also reflected their plenitude in real life during this period.[35] There was probably an increase in illegitimacy in the post-emancipation period with the influx of rural inhabitants into the cities, and the plight of orphans was clearly evident in daily life. The loss of either or both parents through death or abandonment made a child an orphan in the Russian understanding.

The idea that the orphan must make his way without the support of the village community—and sometimes even face its opposition—is evident in Ivin's story, *The Secret of Starotiagovsk* (1892). Both the hero and his girlfriend are poor orphans living in the village. Amid the mockery of the entire village, the hero sets off to Moscow to seek his fortune. He succeeds all the same in finding a job, and saves money for his marriage.[36]

If one person's good fortune is assumed to come from another's misfortune, one way to justify success is to show that the loser deserved to be parted from his wealth. Popular writers used a variety of stratagems to distance readers from the losers in their tales. Evstigneev, in *Masha's a Fine Girl, but Not Our Girl* (1871), a story that prefigures the humor of the young Chekhov, made the victims too ridiculous to pity and the swindler too sympathetic to blame. Masha is a young Moscow hat maker. Her boyfriend is a "retoucher of photographs," and their joint earnings are insufficient for them to marry. Their fortunes change when Masha is approached by a would-be seducer, and is coached by another hat girl on how to enrich herself at his expense. As the comic plot develops, Masha is jointly courted by the short and fat Nil Vasilevich and his tall and thin neighbor, Klim Klimovich, each unknown to the other. When her finances are in order, she sets the wedding day, and both would-be grooms arrive to face each other and the newly married Masha and her retoucher of photographs. The two spurned suitors retire to count their losses and renew their friendship over vodka, black bread, and mushrooms.[37] The moral of the story appears to be that fools and their money are soon parted, and rightly so.

The loser in F. I. Kuzma's *Oh Those Iaroslavites! What a Fine Folk!* is not a fool but a foreigner, and this status places him clearly outside the circle of those with whom the reader feels sympathy. The story enjoyed great popularity and went through at least twenty editions between 1868 and 1908.[38] Its hero is Andrei, a poor village orphan who wants to marry the village elder's daughter. The elder is unwilling to consider so unprepossessing a suitor, and Andrei sets off amid the jeers of the villagers to seek his fortune in St. Petersburg. He does a number of good deeds on his way, one of which is to save the life of an injured dog he finds along the railroad tracks. The dog is adept at fetching objects, and to test Andrei's claims of the dog's talents, a passing German traveler throws a silver ruble by the roadside and bets Andrei that the dog will not find it. The dog disappears for hours, and Andrei gives him up for lost. The next day Andrei is already on the outskirts of St. Petersburg when the dog reappears with the German traveler's trousers in its mouth. When Andrei inspects the trousers, he finds not only the original silver ruble, but a purse with 700 rubles. The German who had pocketed the ruble lost not only his windfall, but also his entire capital and his pants. Andrei is able to use the 700 rubles to establish himself as a bartender (*buffetchik*) at a fashionable Petersburg hotel. He returns to his village with both money and a good position in the city, and the elder is only too willing to bless Andrei's marriage.

Earlier in the story Andrei had found a pittance that belonged to a widow, and, although he was sorely tempted to keep the money, he obeyed his conscience and returned it to her. He feels no compunction about keeping the foreigner's money, however, and the reader shares his happiness at his good fortune. Since the German is an outsider, the reader need not condemn Andrei for keeping the 700 rubles.

Success was sometimes presented and justified as a reward for patient suffering, and this idea has roots in the Russian religious tradition of kenoticism. Heroes and heroines in a few stories gain from the magnitude of their grief and their passivity in meeting it. The hero of Lunin's *Guiltless but Guilty, or a Prayer to God is Never Lost* (1895) is a young orphan who serves humbly and faithfully in a business firm until he is wrongfully charged with theft. He is convicted and sent into exile, and his wife and child suffer, but he does nothing to change what he perceives to be his fate. "The Lord, who is perhaps sending me this trial, will surely help me in the future," he thinks. "Who can know His holy will and whether He does not arrange everything for the best?"[39] His passive response to suffering justifies the good fortune that awaits him. He thrives in exile, and when the real thief is discovered, he is offered his old job back at the princely salary of 1,000 rubles a month. His daughter is soon married to the boss's son.

Another device that popular authors used upon occasion to justify success was the Oliver Twist solution, in which a hero or heroine regains a proper position that he or she had been wrongfully denied. Lunin wrote several stories of this sort, and was possibly of gentry origins himself. The hero of *The Foundling or a Fortunate Meeting* (1898) is sent off with other orphans to a village to be cared for by foster parents. The parents were paid 3 rubles a month, a common practice that the zemstvo often funded. The boy stands out in the village for his love of learning, and his foster father decides to send him at the age of ten to Moscow, since he understands nothing of peasant life. He works for six years as an apprentice in a metal-working shop until a chance encounter with an aristocratic lady restores him to his proper place in life. She happens to see his gold necklace and recognizes him as the son she was forced to give up in a period of ruin and misfortune.

The ways in which the successful person related to his or her community and, in particular, how newly acquired wealth was used were as important in justification of success as was the path to prosperity. The anthropologist George M. Foster observed in his study of Mexican villagers of the 1940s that inhabitants of developing peasant societies are often torn between two contradictory goals. These are "material success and security, and the nonmaterial desire to be thought well of and to insure one's spiritual future."[40] A person who acquired new wealth was thus obligated to share it with the rest of the community. Lubok writers recognized the legitimacy of the community's claims on new wealth when they portrayed the deserving rich as people who did not scorn their less fortunate friends and neighbors. The self-made stove maker, the patron of *Peter Chimney Sweep*, is a model of the image of the good merchant. His strict piety, also associated with some of the Moscow industrialists, may have owed something to Old Believer codes of behavior: "Syroezhkin was among those people who made their mark for themselves by their own hard labor. . . . Despite his riches, Kondratii Ivanovich did not forget his village, visiting it sometimes and marrying a girl from it, whom he was not ashamed to bring to Moscow and settle in his house" (p. 22). Similarly, Kuklin's hero in *A Sensible and Industrious Son* "does not forget God and the poor." He also marries a peasant girl, although all the merchants offer him their daughters. Moreover, "he did not love wealth."[41]

The stories also contain images of illegitimate and improperly used wealth, the possessor of which neglects his obligations to religion and the community. In Aleksandrovskii's *Hunger Tsar* an evil kulak squeezes his starving fellow villagers, all the time planning an escape to the city. He has contempt for the uneducated muzhiks of his village and is preoccupied with getting rich.[42] The protagonist of the anonymous *The Merry Days of the Merchant Pillager-Devourer* (1917) announces, "For money I am ready to do anything."[43] Many such grasping and selfish characters are negatively portrayed in the newspaper serials in *Moskovskii listok*.

Some of the cautionary tales about the dangers of aspiring too high also carry the message to remember the community and religious duties. The hero of Volgin's *The Drowned Woman*, unlike the model merchants of *Peter Chimney Sweep* and *A Sensible and Industrious Son*, is unwilling to marry the village girl who loves him. He falls for a woman beyond his station, is rejected, and both he and the village girl take their lives.[44]

The obligation to share with the community and the desire to remain part of the community explain the hero or heroine's peculiar response to wealth in several of the stories. Wealth is not used for luxurious or even moderately comfortable living; instead, the heroes who become rich but continue to live in their former style are implicitly presented for emulation. The poor suitor in the kopeck novel "The Treasure Hunters" finds a treasure and wins the girl of his choice, but he continues to live as if he had no wealth: "Rumors spread that I sought and found a treasure. The whole town learned of it, but many, in particular those who knew me well, noticed my humble life and wondered where the treasure was" (no. 834, 1910). Anton Krechet also finds a treasure and considers living the high life with "hundreds of servants," but he soon gives up the idea. He claims later that he never cared much for wealth, nor made much effort to attain it (no. 674, 1910).

Popular writers did not always depict heroes eager to placate their communities. The striving for wealth or success in some stories creates intense rivalry and animosity between the hero and his community, whether urban or rural. The hero of Lunin's *Guiltless but Guilty* is disliked by all of his colleagues, and they try to drive him from the office. The schoolteacher in *The Factory Beauty* is the enemy of all the factory clerks, and he must even hire a bodyguard when he goes out at night. Ivin's orphan hero in *The Secret of Starotiagovsk* and Andrei in *Oh Those Iaroslavites!* are both spurned by their fellow villagers, and this makes their marriages more difficult.

The atmosphere presented in many of these stories is one of animosity bordering on paranoia, in which the hero must make his way against the obstructions and malevolence of his rivals. Krechet announces at the beginning of his adventures that "The world in which I live has its own struggle for self-esteem. There is the same thirst for power that is everywhere" (no. 379, 1909). Many of Verbitskaia's characters are surrounded by enemies plotting their downfall. At the Parisian dance studio Mania's fellow students dislike her, and her relations with them are those "between the crowd and talent" (4:14). Nadezhda, in *The Yoke of Love*, is plagued by relentless rivals, who eventually saw through the boards on her stage bed in an attempt to injure her. Success beckons her, but "will she master it, alone, without friends and protectors, surrounded by intrigues, envy, and prejudice?" (p. 27). The attention to rivalry and the ill-wishes of jealous onlookers probably reflects the authors' experiences in raising themselves from the milieu of their origins, as much or more than the experiences of their readers, most of whom did not come so far from the social class of their childhoods.

The popular writers preached a Russian gospel of success and praised individual achievement by effort, energy, skill, and talent, but they did not entirely banish fate from participation in their stories. The retention of an element of fatalism may be related to the sense of rivalry and occasional paranoia in the stories. Neither the readers nor writers were ready to accept the idea that man makes himself in this world, and that success or failure is entirely in the power of the individual to determine. Those who did not achieve their ambitions could attribute their failure either to human machinations or to the intervention of fate.

The idea that individuals control their destinies is sometimes opposed to belief in the action of fate or God in distinguishing modern and traditional values.[45] By retaining an element of fatalism in the stories, writers made it easier for readers to accept the grandiose triumphs of the heroes and heroines without feeling ashamed of their own much more modest successes or even failures. Chance and friendly providence count for a great deal in the stories. The hero of *The Young Bandit Ataman "Storm"* announces, "And happiness often depends on blind chance" (p. vii). When the orphans of the story *For the Rich a Feast, for the Poor the Open Road* are adopted by rich patrons, the author observes, "Evidently, fate took pity on them."[46] Lunin asks in *The Foundling*, "What is one to do if fate is a mother to some and a stepmother to others?" (p. 7). Later in the same story he comments, "One person knows how to attend to his own well-being and is happy. Another considers himself unhappy because he does not live the way he wants. Finally, a third lives deliberately to the detriment of his own well-being, but considers fate the reason for all adversity and need" (p. 7). In short, people are responsible for their lives, but some get a better start than others.

Fate is also important in many of the kopeck novels. An exception is "Satan's Cliff," the only one in which the success theme is tied exclusively to personal responsibility. While Georgii and his friends work on their farm in the Caucasus, their comrades in St. Petersburg write to them. One dreams of joining them, and another is resigned that his "clumsy mug" will never fit into a better life: "Evidently such is my fate. I will die at factory work" (no. 1383, 1912). A third one laughs at them and pictures their coming failure and hungry days. Georgii attributes their success to energy and initiative: "Three years ago we thought up this project, and all three of us saved 700 rubles. Look! Now we are already our own bosses, and soon we'll be rich" (no. 1409, 1912). Georgii remembers the good deeds he has done in the past, and in passing attributes some of their success to a reward for virtue. But he also pronounces, "A man makes his own fate."

Verbitskaia develops a theme close to a Russian work ethic, but her successes always depend on talent as well as work. Verbitskaia's audience included middle-class readers, and both the writer and her readers were probably more confident of their abilities to form their lives and more satisfied with the results of their efforts. Upon Mania's triumph as a dancer, Verbitskaia observes: "You say that she is the darling of fate, the chosen one? Yes, but it is not talent alone that gives us strength in the struggle with life. Only labor conquers it. Persistent labor and faith in one's god. That god is art" (4:220). Katia, in *The Spirit of the Times*, also keeps herself to a stern work ethic, and expects the same of others. She meets a beggar woman with a child and chastises her, "Why don't you work? You are healthy, young, and strong. Aren't you ashamed?" (1:86). Verbitskaia's stories also show the interest in Social Darwinism current at the time. Steinbach, the magnate and patron in *The Keys to Happiness*, remarks, "The struggle for existence refers to the experience of the most capable, not the best" (2:119).

The theme of success in the Russian stories can be compared briefly to that in Western European and American works. The world of the French feuilleton novel in the second and third quarters of the nineteenth century has some of the attributes of the zero-sum society so prevalent in much of the Russian popular fiction. The flow of intrigue in Sue's *Mysteries of Paris* and Ponson du Terrail's *Rocambole* suggests a society in which a loser is paired with each winner. This idea was reinforced in Sue's case by vaguely socialistic views and a concern for the laboring poor, who were perceived to be trapped in their poverty.[47] The Rocambole epic does contain some characters who achieve prosperity through their own efforts, such as Leon Rolland, an artisan who becomes a prosperous factory owner (4:400). Gaboriau retains in his fiction the atmosphere of labyrinthine intrigue characteristic of the feuilleton novel, but also shows more forcefully the potential for making one's own fortune through pluck and work. One of the heroines of *Other People's Money* contributes to the family upkeep and funds a profligate brother by taking in sewing. She tells her fiancé that if she were a man, she would want to start as an orphan with no one and nothing, and through her own will, intelligence, daring, and labor make something of herself.[48] Remarks such as this imply a low opinion of the working poor and an acceptance of the existing distribution of income.

Reynolds' *The Mysteries of London* carries a similar message. Two brothers seek their fortunes. One takes the low road, and the other shuns crooked deals, even though he soon loses his inheritance. In the end, though, the virtuous one succeeds and marries an Italian princess. Reynolds concludes that the energetic and industrious can succeed by sticking to the straight and narrow. For him, English society often operates in such a way that the deserving are rewarded for both their efforts and their virtue (2:424). The same message is promoted in Horatio Alger's many American success stories. The hero of his *Strong and Steady*, for example, sets out on his own when his prosperous father loses the family fortune through speculation and dies. At the conclusion of the book the young go-getter has already begun to earn his fortune.

The American Deadwood Dick serial offers a most striking contrast to the Russian stories. The Deadwood series includes many tales of success. There are boom towns, thriving settlements, businessmen flush with capital, and trappers and scouts who win and lose fortunes in the fur business. One story in which success forms the main plot is *Jack Hoyle's Lead or the Road to Fortune*. Jack is a young orphan who has been swindled out of his inheritance by his father's crooked partner. He starts out with nothing, but vows to make a great fortune. Jack is unlike the Horatio Alger heroes, who show implausible honesty and catch the favorable eye of their superiors.[49] Jack does some sharp dealing, including selling farm cats as "celebrated Belgian mousers." He also does more serious buying and selling, and finally makes his fortune in oil and gold.

Unlike the Russian heroes, Jack shows no compunction about displaying and enjoying his wealth. The author ends with, "Here we leave Jack and his wife enjoying themselves on the wealth that Jack's industry had accumulated. Long may he and all other boys of his stamp live and prosper."[50] Jack appears to feel none of the ambivalence associated with material success that his Russian counterparts do. The English and French heroes are also more comfortable with their well-deserved wealth than are the Russian, and the deeds that lead to their success often win the acclaim of the community.

When the popular writers wrote about success they helped their readers develop new ways of thinking about earning a livelihood, planning for the future, and making a career, and also about setting goals, seeking satisfaction, and developing aspirations. The attention to geographic mobility, education, and the qualities of perseverance, pluck, initiative, and a willingness to try something new was likely to be important to people who were learning to cope with new opportunities and new demands. The demonstration in the stories that success was earned and deserved should have helped readers accept the rapid social mobility they saw around them, even if they did not take part in it. Such stories served to legitimize emerging patterns of wealth and status and to strip the legitimacy from the old hierarchy of social classes. Among the many different justifications for wealth given in these stories, birth and status are rarely mentioned.

Nevertheless, the authors were unwilling to accept great extremes of wealth and poverty wholeheartedly. The heroes and heroines do not seek lives of luxury and splendor but only a middling and comfortable prosperity. There is very little picaresque spirit of adventure in these stories, almost no humor, and few scenes of good cheer. The unwillingness of the authors to allow their protagonists to enjoy the full material fruits of their efforts may come not only from a peasant's sensitivity to new wealth and suspicion of its origins, but perhaps also from a concern with justice and equality. The authors told their readers that energy and initiative were rewarded, but they did not often show the concomitant proposition that poverty was the result of indolence or passivity. Even the moderate gains of the protagonists are achieved at the cost of much sacrifice and painful exertion.

The popular authors presented a world in which success was achieved in the marketplace and measured largely by materialistic standards. The authors of women's fiction and those who wrote some of the more expensive booklets in the early twentieth century seemed ambivalent about this image of success. When they portrayed accomplishment in the arts as a kind of public service that justified great rewards, they presented an alternative idea of how rewards should be distributed in society. Their readers were likely to be somewhat more educated and more prosperous than those of the other types of fiction and therefore more aware of the socialist critique of capitalism. These authors appealed to this concern, which some of them shared. On the question of the legitimacy or illegitimacy of material wealth, the views of educated and semi-educated Russians on the one hand and the newly literate on the other appear to have diverged in the last years of the old regime. This divergence is part of the larger difference in values between the common reader and the educators and propagandists who produced the special printed materials intended for this audience.

IX

THE EDUCATED RESPONSE:

LITERATURE FOR THE

PEOPLE

CRITICS, pedagogues, propagandists, and others concerned with popular education greeted the new literature with a combination of disdain and dismay. Their opinions were probably widely shared by the educated elite and also by the semi-educated, who constituted an important minority in Russian society. Slightly over a million people had attended but not necessarily graduated from a higher or secondary institution, according to the census of 1897, and they comprised 5 percent of the literate.[1] Since Russian secondary schools took pupils after only three or four years of primary schooling, these were not highly educated people. Even those with an incomplete secondary education, however, often had enough literary experience to remove them from the main audience for popular literature.

The educated observers' antipathy for the new popular culture of common literacy stemmed from two general concerns. First, the appearance of the commercial literature signified a kind of cultural diversity that was new for Russia, and educated and semi-educated people found it difficult to accept. The symbols and forms of cultural expression became increasingly diverse, and there was a perceived divergence between high and low culture. These changes can be seen as the natural consequence of the shift to a more modern and complex society, as Emile Durkheim pointed out in his *Elementary Forms of Religious Life*. Increased cultural diversity was apparent throughout Europe in the nineteenth century, although the responses of educated minorities differed in different countries.[2] Many educated Russians were committed to a conception of cultural order according to which the lower classes would share in a culture common to all Russians. This culture would be created by educated Russians but would be accessible to all. The proper goals of literacy and education were to enable people of lower-class origins to share in this general culture. The desired character of the general culture differed among educated Russians of different political persuasions, but most were committed to a concept of cultural unity. The development of an autonomous popular commercial literature was inconsistent with these notions of harmony.

The second complaint against the popular literature concerned its content. Russians strongly believed that what one reads influences one's character and personality. Thus educated Russians who condemned popular commercial literature feared that it would hasten the deterioration in the values and character of the lower classes. They also resented its competition with the propagandistic and educational materials they favored.

Popular commercial literature was a literature of the marketplace, and its rejection by educated Russians was due most generally to their reluctance to allow the market to arbitrate or influence cultural life. They feared that values expressed and propagated through the market might not be the "right" ones. They did not welcome the evidence that common people had ambitions to improve their lives, and that these ambitions were most often individualistic and materialistic. The popular conceptions of success expressed in the literature were unsettling both to defenders of the traditional Russian social structure and to proponents of radical visions of an egalitarian society. Moreover, there is little evidence either in the literature or from other sources that common people understood or shared the reluctance of educated Russians to allow the market to serve cultural demands. The record of popular literature and its reception suggests that the values of common people were more consistent with the growth of a market economy in Russia in the late nineteenth and early twentieth centuries than were those of their more educated compatriots. The debate about popular literature thus had wide implications not only about Russian literary life, but also about political and economic life.

Educated Russians' rejection of popular commercial literature led some of them to become active in an effort to create and distribute an alternative literature among the lower classes in the cities and countryside. The motives of activists in sponsoring a "people's literature" were similar to those of educators who promoted primary schooling. Educated activists, philanthropists, Church and state officials, and political propagandists produced a considerable body of noncommercial publications designed to carry their values to the common reader. Because they distrusted the literary marketplace, they relied on subsidies and other nonmarket incentives to reach readers.

The broad issues presented in commercial publications were those that were on the minds of many newly literate Russians. The authors and publishers of noncommercial alternative literatures frequently addressed the same concerns, but in doing so they sought to promote a particular view that often diverged from that found in the commercial publications. The treatment of themes such as freedom and order, national identity, science and superstition, and success differed among the competing groups of educated Russians who produced sponsored literatures, but they had a common distaste for the values communicated through the commercial literature.

These activists apparently had little success in influencing the attitudes of the common people: they were not able to turn readers away from the popular commercial literature. The strongly felt and well-articulated suspicion of the market as a mechanism for communication between writers and readers, however, had a significant effect on the future development of Russian culture in the Soviet era, as did nonmarket ideals about what popular culture should be. These proved particularly attractive to schoolteachers and other upwardly mobile people of common origins who stood on the lower rungs of the ladder of success.

When the producers of edifying or instructive publications pitted their products against the wares of the magnates of popular culture, two characteristically Russian literary worlds contended. The choice might be between a chapbook tale of worldly success and an authorized saint's life; between a fictionalized attack on superstition and a pamphlet on personal hygiene; between a chivalric adventure and a story by Tolstoy or Turgenev; or between a bandit saga serialized in a kopeck newspaper and a trade union weekly with songs of social struggle. Not only were the contestants characteristically Russian, but so was the outcome. Whereas in Western Europe and North America the sponsored publications gradually gave way to a continually evolving popular commercial culture, in Russia it was the commercial product that vanished, censored out of existence after 1917 by a generation of revolutionary administrators determined to create a world in which such things had no place. The hostility of the revolutionaries toward frivolous reading, their suspicion of the common people's literary taste, and their certainty of the importance of literature in the transformation of man were shared by a wide circle of their contemporaries in the prerevolutionary era.

The commercial and noncommercial literature for the common reader differed in content and purpose, in method of distribution, and in who paid for the final product. The sponsored product generally reached its reader through an intermediate purchaser—usually an institution involved in mass education—instead of the market. Sometimes groups that disagreed about much else would agree about the kinds of books peasants should read, and they would share the cost of distributing such literature. Thus, works published by the Orthodox Church or by a state-supported institution would often find willing purchasers among the activists in provincial government and in philanthropic organizations. Educators and interested organizations also ordered specific works from commercial publishers, and distributed them either free or at a subsidized price. In addition to distributing literature directly to the urban and rural lower classes, the Church, the state, and various philanthropic organizations provided publications to libraries, schools, parishes, and other organizations under their jurisdiction. The institutions of mass education comprised a large market, lucrative enough to induce commercial publishers to produce the works they sought, causing the noncommercial publishers of sponsored literature to decline in the late nineteenth and early twentieth centuries.

Critics of popular literature were often animated by mutually exclusive visions of the Russia of the future, yet they shared a belief that the popular commercial literature of the marketplace was harmful and should be supplanted by a more wholesome alternative. Some worried about the violence and bloodshed portrayed in the tales; some complained of salacious passages; and others worried about harmful superstitions. Each critic faulted the exclusion from commercial literature of his particular message, but many critics expressed a common concern about what they called the "cynicism" of the commercial literature. By cynicism they meant the popular authors' appeals to worldly desires and materialistic daydreams, and the presentation of the attainment of earthly delights by fair means and foul. Criticism from clerics, state bureaucrats, Westernizers, the populists, liberal enlighteners, and Marxists varied in intensity and with time, but most were united in the view that the lower-class reader and the market could not be left alone to determine the literary fare of "the reader from the people."

Advocates of a special literature for the people were often moved by two seemingly contradictory ideals. They thought of "the people" as a separate cultural and moral entity, and, in general, wanted to preserve the popular qualities that remained untainted by modern life. At the same time, however, they deplored that same separation as a hindrance to the unity of values and culture they sought to promote for all Russians. The apparent contradiction was resolved in the idea of a literacy limited and restricted to a sponsored people's literature. As long as they read primarily the works specially provided to them, the common people could share in the best of the literary culture of educated Russia while retaining their traditional virtues and remaining protected from a variety of divisive and harmful influences, including the materialism of urban life.

The idea of a special people's literature was ultimately rejected, even by the authorities, since it proved impossible to isolate "the people" as a particular group. The notion of a restricted literacy continued to live on, however, in the ideal of a new common culture that was to be shared by all who could read. The dream that the newly literate common people could and would absorb what was best in Russian and world culture—and in this way fulfill that hoary dream of merging with the intelligentsia—had great allure for educated Russians. It also satisfied many of the upwardly mobile people of common origins who were known as "intelligentsia from the people." For these people, too, the idea of an easily identifiable cultural minimum that they could master was enormously attractive. The glorification of the names of the great Russian writers of the nineteenth century and some from the twentieth also satisfied the need to develop a sense of national identity that did not depend on the tsar or the Orthodox Church.[3] The widespread adoption of the classics of Russian literature and their authors as emblems of national identity was a victory for radical and liberal publicists and a defeat for tsarist authorities, who had long considered Russian belles lettres subversive. For many educated Russians the classics seemed to typify the kind of reading matter that could serve as a bridge between the common people and themselves.

Official Responses: Ideas and Censorship

The earliest and most complete vision of limited popular literacy was that of a religious literacy consisting of the ability to read Scripture and the works of the Church fathers written in Church Slavonic. This vision was widely held by educated Russians both within and outside the Church and state hierarchies in the first half of the nineteenth century. The official view of secular reading during the reign of Nicholas I (1825-55) was stated by the tsar's Minister of Education, S. S. Uvarov, in 1834, when, in response to requests "from many people" to permit the publication of Russian equivalents to the English *Penny Magazine* and the German *Heller Mag*, he asked the Main Censorship Department, "Is it useful to allow the introduction and implantation here of this type of cheap literature that has the aim and immediate consequence of acting upon the lower-class reading public?"[4] The Censorship Department answered that this secular literature and the very idea of secular influence on the common people was incompatible, politically and otherwise, "with our existing order." To this judgment Nicholas affixed the addendum, "Completely true. By no means allow."

Other influential people in Nicholas' reign took a similar view. It was affirmed in an official pronouncement of the Ministry of Education at the end of Nicholas' rule that only religious works should be published for the common reader, since "books of spiritual content bolster the simple people's faith and hope in holy Providence for new labor and for the benign bearing of all types of privation, whereas secular books only . . . lead them away from their work and try their patience."[5] Religious works were understood to be exclusively those written in Church Slavonic. The view of the Church was even more restrictive.[6] A churchman of the time argued successfully against publication in the vernacular of one of the more popular saint's lives, *St. Nicholas the Miracle Worker*, on the grounds that changes in the Church Slavonic text could be interpreted by the common people as changes in the faith.[7]

The official attitudes of Church and state officials toward popular commercial publications depended largely on their perceptions of the possibilities of producing an alternative literature. Confidence in the effectiveness of Church publications persisted well into the 1870s, and Church officials viewed the commercial publications as unnecessary and undesirable. During the 1880s and 1890s officials became more concerned about the circulation of liberal and radical publications and concomitantly more tolerant of the commercial product. By the early twentieth century, state and Church authorities had come to accept the positive value of Russian belles lettres and secular literature, including some popular science, and the commercial tales and pictures were again criticized in official publications, although their production on a large scale was permitted.

The changing position of the state authorities with respect to the literature of the lubok was reflected in regulations governing the movement of the peddlers. In 1865 the Ministry of Internal Affairs sharply restricted the activities of lubok sellers, who after that needed permission from the authorities in each locale they entered. These rules were changed in July 1881, and the peddlers were allowed to obtain permits where they lived. In justification for this leniency, the Main Administration for Publication Affairs issued a circular in which the authorities explained that the old rules had inhibited trade in popular literature. "Since the printed works sold by the merchants of the Moscow firms of Manukhin, Abramov, Morozov, and others really comprise, so to speak, the age-old historical property of the people, and cannot in their essence inspire misgivings comparable to those of other works, their circulation among the people has not caused and is not causing any harmful consequences," read the Administration's circular.[8] The faith of the authorities in the natural piety and patriotism of the peasantry was also expressed in the 1880s by K. P.

Pobedonostsev, the influential procurator of the Holy Synod and adviser to Alexander III, when he suggested that the common people could be relied upon to choose heroes valued for "an ideal of strength, virtue, and holiness," such as would be shown in an official saint's life.[9]

Many churchmen undoubtedly shared the Chief Procurator of the Synod's faith in the traditions of the common people, but critics in clerical journals sometimes linked lubok literature with religious dissidence and secular influence. One observer in *Missionerskoe obozrenie* (The Missionary Survey) in 1904 argued that since peasants who turned to sectarianism were raised in a superstitious atmosphere and enjoyed the "nonsensical and charlatanish gibberish" of the popular tales, the fantastic element in this literature must be culpable in reinforcing religious dissidence.[10] Some churchmen blamed literacy in general. "Literacy by itself in the hands of the ignorant only increases the possibilities of mistakes and error" read a statement of the 1851 Synod, which was quoted with approval in an editorial of the official Church school journal at the end of the 1890s.[11] A village priest discovered peasant children reading *Bova Korolevich*, *Eruslan*, "*Milord* Itself," and stories by Tolstoy, and commented, "Such reading undoubtedly brings harm to the children and acts destructively on their morals," but he was consoled by the observation that their parents preferred "Godly books."[12] A clerical correspondent wrote in 1875 that it was better to give the people nothing than to give them "not only useless, but positively harmful books, pictures, and the like." He continued with the prediction that if such material was not withdrawn from the market, the result would be "to ruin the people's taste and further coarsen their morals."[13]

Religious leaders were worried about revolutionary propaganda, and for this reason—as well as to encourage correct religious instruction among the populace—they supported and produced officially sanctioned noncommercial publications. The Minister of Education warned in 1875 of the revolutionary threat accompanying the populist movement, and an observer in the magazine *Pravoslavnoe obozrenie* (Orthodox Survey) commented that "people's literature" was an important counter to the radical publications. He distinguished publications that were vapid or of low quality from those in which "the people would find for themselves, in lively and artistic exposition, correctly Christian and positive scientific answers to all those questions that cannot help but interest the common person as a Christian and as a human being."[14]

The state's response to the new popular culture was twofold. State officials could publish favored materials, and they could also use the regulatory and censorial powers to restrict publication and distribution of works they considered harmful. The provision of alternative literature and regulation of undesirable works were mutually reinforcing efforts to mold the opinions and reading habits of the common people. The clerical censor was responsible for all works touching on religion. These were to be examined from the standpoint of religious teaching, state order, morality, and proper language.[15] The Church also had a monopoly on the publication of works entrusted to it, although it permitted private publishers to issue such materials, particularly in the last third of the nineteenth century. The civil censor, according to rules issued in 1865, was responsible for scrutinizing works of less than ten signatures. Books of more than ten signatures were freed from prepublication censorship after that date. Most works intended for a popular audience were less than ten signatures, and hence remained subject to censorship until 1905, when prepublication censorship for all works was rescinded. The civil censors were under the authority of the Main Administration for Press Affairs, which was part of the Ministry of the Interior.

There were also pedagogical censors. The main pedagogical censor, the Scholastic Committee of the Ministry of Education, was established in the course of government attempts to centralize control over schooling in the early nineteenth century. It gained responsibility for school books, pedagogical literature, and other pedagogical questions in 1856, and in 1867 became responsible for selecting appropriate printed materials for the common people. An analogous organ of the Church, the Scholastic Committee under the Synod, was responsible for approving books for the educational network under Church control. In addition, a Committee on the Organization and Education of Troops, formed in the 1860s, specified the books that were to be allowed in the army.[16] A similar committee was established for the navy much later. In this way, regulation of the distribution of printed materials supplemented the censorship procedures.

The effect of censorship on the selection of works published is hard to measure, but a record remains of works intended for the common reader that were refused the censor's stamp or were withdrawn from circulation. The poet Nekrasov attempted unsuccessfully in 1862 to publish a series of books for the newly literate, including his own poems.[17] The firm Posrednik, with which both Leo Tolstoy and I. D. Sytin were involved at one time, enjoyed regular conflicts with the censor, and in the 1880s and 1890s several of Tolstoy's morally instructive tales were rejected.[18] Saltykov-Shchedrin's writings were also disliked by the censors.[19] In the early twentieth century, the works of the writers who published in *Znanie* (Knowledge) were often rejected by the pedagogical censor.[20] In 1907 the thriving publishing firm Don Speech was closed down entirely. In each case, however, the kinds of books the censor had prohibited appeared on the market later. Censorship eased in the early twentieth century, becoming much less efficient as the quantity of popular reading matter increased. Nekrasov's works were widely available in cheap editions by the early twentieth century, as were Tolstoy's stories, and some of the publications formerly carried by Don Speech were taken up by other publishers. Censorship in these cases delayed but did not completely halt publication of works found objectionable by the censor.

Censorship and government control of the publishing industry had the effect of restricting and narrowing the endeavors of private activists in mass education, some of whom could do little more than distribute approved texts. It also affected the price structure of the book market. Publishers whose works appeared on lists of books approved for libraries and public readings could command higher prices than similar works not on the approved lists.[21] Books and pamphlets that passed the censor but were restricted to smaller editions than the commercial publisher would have printed sold for higher prices than they would have in an unregulated market.

State censorship was also exercised through control over distribution, but here, too, there was a gradual retreat. The Special Section of the Scholastic Committee under the Ministry of Education was responsible for determining which texts were suitable for reading aloud to common audiences, and which should go to primary and secondary school libraries. In 1869, soon after the committee was founded, it issued a short list of approved texts, and this short list was the practical guide to public readings from 1869 until the last decade of the century, when new questions and demands led to modifications in the list and in its function, and raised broad questions about the regulation of the common reader's access to printed materials.

The censors and regulators monitored both popular commercial literature and the works produced by private philanthropic organizations and individuals. The authorities were concerned with revolutionary propaganda, but, in addition, they were quite apprehensive about the effect of any secular literature on the common readers—and this, until the last quarter of the century, included the works of Russian classic writers. The official retreat from censorship of literature for the common reader is evident from the changes in lists of works approved for reading aloud in public auditoriums and at schools. The 1869 list of works for public readings[22] included patriotic and religious texts, with a few entries of belles lettres and popular science. Among the spiritual works were saints' lives, including the popular *Nicholas the Miracle Worker*, as well as titles such as *The Christian Feat of the Soldier*. Most of the historical works were patriotic tales of military victories, such as *The Feats of Russian*

Troops in the Turkish War of 1877-78. The one piece about foreign lands and peoples was *Holland and the Dutch.* Of the 137 entries, 25 were works of belles lettres, including Gogol's *Taras Bulba,* and Pushkin's "Poltava," *The Captain's Daughter,* and *Tales of Ilya Muromets.* The list included some hagiographic biographies, such as *The Self-taught Mechanic K. P. Klubin.* There were several short pieces on topics of natural science, such as thunder, birds, and snow.

The list was modified in the early 1890s to include a few additional works of Russian belles lettres, more popular science, and the 800 titles already approved for primary school libraries. In addition, publications of the Standing Commission on Public Readings in St. Petersburg, a semi-official organization, were approved for readings in other cities. A break in official policy came in 1901, when the Ministry of Education issued a catalogue of 2,868 titles for public readings. Of these over a third were belles lettres. Religious works comprised a quarter and the rest were primarily history, geography, and natural science.[23] Restrictions on what could be read aloud to the common people were finally lifted in 1906, when permission was granted to read publicly all works that were not prohibited for general circulation by the censor, but local authorities still monitored the selections.[24]

The relaxation of official wariness toward the classics of Russian belles lettres was also apparent in the change in composition of the lists drawn up by the Synod and the Ministry of Education of the works permitted in primary school libraries. The first school library list was issued in 1864 and contained few works by classical writers, with the exception of Tolstoy's stories and primers for the people. In 1913 the works of many classical and contemporary writers were on the list.[25] An unwilling witness to the relaxation of restrictions on literary materials, the head of the Scholastic Committee of the Ministry of Education, A. I. Georgievskii, explained in his 1902 history of the Scholastic Committee that among the books for the people were properly included "the common national literature intended for all classes of society and the population," as well as "a special literature intended exclusively for children, and for the simple, little-educated, and little-developed common people."[26] Georgievskii expressed the opinion that the special literature for the common reader should be enriched by works from a shared national literature, but he continued to feel that Russian belles lettres should be treated with caution.[27]

The failure of the censors was both an intellectual and practical one. Educated Russians agreed that the people should be protected from the destructive influence of harmful literature. They disagreed on what particular works were harmful, and on whether it was necessary to create a special separate literature for the people or to ease the integration of the people into a broader Russian literary audience. There was increasing difficulty, however, in deciding who "the people" were. As geographical and social mobility increased toward the turn of the century, the job of selective censorship for the people became even more confounding, and the censors candidly expressed their confusion about the nature of that aspect of their work. In order to insulate the common people from the literary marketplace, they had to decide who the common people were and how to identify them. This proved an insurmountable difficulty.

A proposal to establish special surveillance over materials published for the young and for the common people was considered and rejected in 1865, even though the tsar approved it. Officials of the Main Administration for Press Affairs found the proposal impractical because there were too many publications and because Russia was too big to institute a system of stamping books to be sold by colporteurs and at fairs, as was the practice in France.[28] The idea of a special censor for people's books was considered again in 1899, and it was rejected for the same reasons.

The process of compiling and modifying the lists of books permitted for circulation among the common readers also revealed a lack of clarity on the part of the officials charged with the task. The confusion became apparent in the discussion prompted by the rapid development of free reading rooms, which were founded by philanthropic individuals, institutions, and organizations, first in the capitals and then in the countryside. The Special Section of the Scholastic Committee of the Ministry of Education was charged with their supervision and with determining what books should be in the libraries and who should be allowed to use them. According to Georgievskii's account, the committee members were unable to reconcile the contradiction between the official view of "the people" and the more complicated reality. The committee members considered it their charge to devise a policy to protect "the people" from potentially harmful reading matter, but, like the censors before them, they were unable to figure out who "the people" were.

When the Pushkin Reading Room received a large shipment of books in 1897, D. A. Tolstoy, the Minister of Internal Affairs, suggested that only those approved by the Special Section of the Scholastic Committee could be accepted, since workmen and other ordinary people were among those who used the reading room.[29] The mayor of St. Petersburg, V. I. Likhachev, argued, however, that since city folk could get all sorts of books at public libraries for a small fee it was inappropriate to restrict them in this case. The members of the Special Section then suggested that the reading rooms of the capital be upgraded to the status of public libraries, and that the common people and minors should be barred from using them. The Ministry of Education balked at this suggestion because "it is not always possible to distinguish the simple people, minors, and pupils by external appearance." The reading rooms were placed under the authority of the Special Section in 1890 but the catalogue was expanded.

The discussion related by Georgievskii reveals the confusion of many of those officially charged with protecting the common reader from harmful literature. Clearly, had they chosen to, they could easily have restricted admittance to the libraries and reading rooms by any number of criteria. The problem was not that they lacked the means to protect people from harmful reading experiences; they were unsure of the identity of the people they were charged to protect, or whether there were gradations of common readers, and whether material harmful to some unsophisticated readers might be useful to others.

By the time Georgievskii finished his book in 1902, the question of the purpose of the reading rooms and the identity of the "simple people" who were to use them had degenerated into muddle. A prominent official, P. A. Annin, suggested that the simple people were not only the members of the lower classes with low levels of intellectual development, but also those with more education who maintained "a condition of life and occupation peculiar to the lower classes."[30] Clearly none of these definitions of the purpose or target of censorship could serve as a basis for a coherent and consistent policy.

Publication and sponsorship of materials for the common reader by the Church was substantial during the last decades of the nineteenth century and the first decades of the twentieth. The first Church publications for popular distribution were the Scriptures and books for church services. In the last years of his reign, Alexander I authorized some Russian admirers of the English Religious Tracts Society and the Great Britain and Foreign Bible Society to publish their own and translated religious works. Hundreds of thousands of copies of morally instructive works and Scripture were published. After his death, the project gradually faltered, though efforts continued during the first decade of Nicholas's reign. Nearly 350,000 copies were published by the Synod for the Great Britain and Foreign Bible Society between 1828 and 1854, and approximately 10.5 million in the fifty years that followed.[31] The Synod also published for other religious institutions, including Church parish schools, the Society to Spread Scripture in Russia, and the St. Petersburg Boroditskii Brotherhood.

The Scriptures, lives of the saints, and church service books were the primary publications of the Church in the mid-1880s. The three works issued in the largest editions in 1885 were *Lives of St. Cyril and Methodius*, the New Testament in Slavonic, and the New Testament in facing Russian and Slavonic, as shown in Table 7.

Synod publishing for the Church school system began in 1883, when more than one-third of the 55,000 rubles provided by the state for Church schools was assigned for school books. In that year the decision was taken to supply Church parish schools with books and to publish special texts for this purpose.[32] The first Church publications for the schools were largely religious, though there were also a few primers for learning Russian, in addition to Church Slavonic. In 1889 the Church made it compulsory for parish schools to use the texts it published, and in 1891 this ruling was extended to include literacy schools, which had come under clerical control. The publishing activities of the School Council of the Synod, the organization responsible for school books, increased rapidly, and in 1893, under the Council's authority, a Publishing Committee was established to oversee the sale and printing of texts and school aids for the parish and literacy schools and also of books for extracurricular reading. In 1900 the function of the Committee broadened to include publication of books for people's libraries and reading rooms. At this time the Procurator of the Synod was made a "member-editor" of the Publishing Committee, an indication of the importance of this program in state policy. The support of the state was also manifest in the increasing funds allotted to publishing out of the rapidly growing state subsidies to the parish schools. The primarily religious publications of the School

TABLE 7. Publications of St. Petersburg and Moscow Synod Presses in 1885

Titles	Copies
St. Petersburg	
Lives of St. Cyril and Methodius	371,000
The New Testament, Slavonic	100,000
The New Testament, facing Russian and Slavonic	100,000
Short prayer book, Russian	115,000
The Gospels, Slavonic	59,000
The Gospels, Russian	50,000
The Gospels, facing Russian and Slavonic	30,000
The Gospels, four parts	25,000
Psalter, Slavonic	40,000
Psalter, Russian	20,000
Moscow	
Psalter, Slavonic	30.000
Book of Hours	40,000

Source: A. A. Bakhtiarov, *Istoriia knigi na Rusi* (St. Petersburg, 1890), p. 239.

Council increased from twenty titles in 4 million copies in 1891-94 to 137 titles in 20.2 million copies in 1900-1908.[33]

The official and semiofficial religious literature for the common people also included didactic and sometimes political publications. There were tracts about pilgrimages to the Holy Land and the Orthodox Monastery at Mount Athos in Greece. Tiny, easily portable booklets were published for pilgrims in the late nineteenth and early twentieth centuries, with titles such as *Time Flies in Days and Nights as if on Wings, How Pleasing to God is Childish Simplicity,* and *The Orthodox Christian's Path to the Heavenly City,* which counseled humility, fear of God, love for one's neighbor, and reading of spiritual books, and warned against malice, pride, judging others, theft, greed, lechery, and foul language.[34]

Typical of the clerical publications were the *Troitskie* and *Afonskie Sheets.* The *Troitskie Sheets* were published, according to the Synod report for 1884, "to provide the simple Russian people with edifying reading, and thus to promote their religious and moral education and enlightenment."[35] Over 76 million copies of these leaflets were published between 1879 and 1897. The 1903 series of leaflets included many narrative tales about St. Saraphim Sarovskii, who was the object of an official cult. There were also leaflets praising the simple hardworking life, such as *No Person is Lost if He Believes in the Church of Christ,* which is about a rich man's son who drinks up his wealth but finds peace through faith, feeds his family by doing manual labor, and even saves up enough to educate his sons.[36] There was also an attack on "the false prophet Leo Tolstoy," and a tribute to the "sufferer for the faith, tsar, and fatherland," Metropolitan Joseph of Astrakhan, who met martyrdom at the hands of the peasant rebel Stenka Razin.[37] The *Afonskii Sheets* were more polemical, at least according to the 1913 series. The reader of these tracts was instructed that "the family is the basis of the state," that "state authority was established by God," and that "outside the Orthodox Church there is no salvation for man."[38]

The clerical authors went beyond traditional religious writings to impart warnings against theft and against trying to avenge injustice. Crime was repaid by grief and heartbreak in their tales, and only God had the right to judge.[39] The proper response to hardship and misfortune was patience and humility, as in the story *Maxim the Rich or the Judgment of God* (1895), in which Ivan and Evdokiia, who know how to bear misfortune, are tested and rewarded.[40] The evil Polish lord in Galicia, where they live, casts eyes on Evdokiia, orders her to work in his home, and conspires to have Ivan jailed for theft. The two humbly bear their grief and, in the course of time, are rewarded for leaving the judgment to God. Their reward takes the form of their son Maxim's prosperity.

Maxim was born while his father was in jail. He grows up, goes into the army, and serves abroad. He proves a sober and intelligent fellow, and while others drink he learns about agriculture. When he returns home he plants an orchard and prospers. Although he dresses in simple clothes, everyone calls him Maxim the rich. There are two lessons in Maxim's success. He is prosperous, but he is content to remain a peasant; he does not try to leave his station in life. Even though Maxim achieved success through his own efforts, his abilities and achievement were the Lord's reward to the patient and long-suffering father.

The authors of the clerical tales also stressed friendly relations between rich and poor, based on charity from above and gratitude from below. In "Akulia," a story by Klara Lukashevich, whose works were published by the Synod Scholastic Committee, an orphaned peasant girl, driven from the house of her brother, heads for St. Petersburg in search of work.[41] She bears no grudge. Hired as a servant by a mean shopkeeper, she proves unaccustomed to the work, is mistreated, falsely accused of theft, and dismissed. Hired again by an equally nasty owner of furnished flats, Akulia refuses to steal, as the other employees do, and eventually falls sick after being sent out repeatedly for cigarettes without a coat. Following a stint in a charity ward, she finds herself on the street, pale and weak. Trusting her good instincts, she goes to a church to pray. There a kindly gentry lady takes pity on her, and in contrast to bourgeois employers offers her money, which she refuses. The lady takes her in, feeds her, and cares for her. Akulia becomes the helper of her benefactress, who herself cares for two orphaned granddaughters. The girls teach Akulia to read and write, but her benefactress dies, and the girls are taken by distant relatives and sent to institutes. By now an accomplished servant, Akulia gets an excellent new position, and the story ends with her saving money, keeping contact with her beloved young ladies, and all three dreaming of living together some day in the future.

The true heroes and heroines in the religious stories are those who are self-sacrificing and have faith. This is again demonstrated in another tale by Lukashevich, "The Signalman," the story of a railroad worker who prevents a train wreck, though he thinks he must sacrifice the life of his child to do so.[42] The child is miraculously saved, but the signalman falls sick and is cared for by the grateful railroad management. Whereas the heroes and heroines of the commercial fiction made their way up the social ladder by energy, initiative, education, and sometimes good luck, those in the literature sponsored by the Church were rewarded solely for their moral virtue. Material success was not an acceptable aspiration, although it could be attained as a reward for virtue.

Another contrast between the clerical tales and the commercial alternative was in the treatment of the supernatural. In the commercial tales, apparently supernatural phenomena were shown consistently to be un-mysterious or at least scientifically explicable. In the clerical works, un-likely events were proof of divine intervention in the affairs of men. A 1913 tale in the *Afonskie Sheets* was about a rich wool merchant named Raev, who lived near a monastery not far from Tver. He mocked the faith and the holy martyrs of the monastery, and despite ominous por-tents, he did not mend his ways. He met an unhappy end when he tumbled out of a boat and sank rapidly to the bottom. The tale concluded, "The unexpected and clearly unnatural death of Raev made a strong impression on his friends and relatives, and Christians saw evidence of the punish-ment of God for the abuses of the holy faith and the Church of Christ."[43]

Clerical publicists emphasized traditional moral and religious stric-tures. For them Orthodoxy and the tsar were the preeminent emblems of Russian national identity; but toward the end of the nineteenth century they turned to broader and more secular ideals of Russianness, as had the authors of commercial popular literature. Increased tolerance by the Church of some types of secular literature led to support for publications such as the Parish Library, a series of inexpensive booklets published in close alliance with the Church in the late nineteenth and early twentieth centuries. The editor of the series was a member of the Synod Publishing Commission, and the series received some Church aid.[44] The editors explained the purpose of the series in a statement on the back cover of the first books: "Our humble aim is to use from our rich literature all that is useful and worthy of the literate reader." From 1898 to 1902, seventy-two titles were issued in the series in a million and a half copies, and less than a fifth of the titles were religious. Works of belles lettres and history outnumbered religious texts. Some of the works of nineteenth-century authors appeared in the series, including those of Gogol and Pushkin, both with critical and biographical commentaries.

When they turned to the great figures of nineteenth century Russian literature, the clerical publicists followed in the footsteps of educators and enlightenment activists, but the churchmen portrayed the writers as defenders of the faith. The reader learned from *Nikolai Vasilevich Gogol, His Life and Literary Activities with Examples from His Works* (1896) that Gogol's career as a writer and his service to Russia were achieved through divine guidance. The editor of the collection, P. Smirnokovskii, wrote that although Gogol wished to serve Russia as an official, "an invisible hand ordered the matter, so that he was bound in any case to take up the pen."[45] As for Gogol's irreverent satirical eye, the editor explained that "revealing the various dark sides of the Russian man, he fervently loved him and Russia, and not only loved them! . . . he believed in their strength, and in the fact that this strength will develop with time, and the Russian man will stand before the whole world, powerful in body and spirit."[46] The treatment of Pushkin was more muted. The editor wrote, "The religious direction of Pushkin grew and grew from year to year. In this way, in the last years of his life, he came to an awareness of those main 'principles' on which the well-being of our fatherland is founded. These are the love of the fatherland and the tsar, religion, and nationality; that is, the knowledge of the spirit of one's people."[47]

The churchmen's increasing appreciation that popular reading could not be so sharply restricted showed also in the publications of the School Council and the Publishing Committee of the Synod. Three-quarters of the works published in 1891-94 were religious, and most of the rest were short primers, but by 1900-1909, works of literature, history, and popular science constituted a quarter of Church school publications. Another third were school texts. Between 1891 and 1909 the publication of secular school readers increased, as did that of patriotic historical works.[48] In the following decade a few works by eighteenth and early nineteenth-century writers, such as Zhukovskii, Fonvizin, and Zagoskin, were included among Church school publications. The nineteenth-century classics were notably absent from the list, but some of these appeared in the Parish Library with Church support.

State-Sponsored Publications

The ideological symbiosis of the autocracy and the Orthodox Church was expressed in the literary policies of the state, in encouragement and contributions to Church efforts, and in state publishing activities for the people. Although less active than the Church, state authorities produced and subsidized periodicals, booklets for public readings, and war propaganda that added to the growing body of reading material for the common people. The state authorities' main concern with popular literature was prophylactic: they sought to prevent the moral and political corruption of the peasantry and urban lower classes.

The power to censor and regulate gave the state an advantage in any publishing activity it chose to enter, and the advantage was resented by many private participants in mass education. One liberal critic complained at the turn of the century that many educated people had wanted to publish a newspaper for the common reader, "but before private people and social organizations were given the possibility of going to the people with a newspaper adapted to their demands, the government itself made the first attempt."[49] The government attempt was the relatively successful periodical for peasants, *Selskii vestnik* (Rural Herald, 1881-1917). The paper began as a weekly and sold for two rubles a year through the mail, or for a ruble if received through the local cantonal authorities. It was published as a supplement for the official *Pravitelstvennyi vestnik* (Governmental Herald), and contained columns of practical agricultural advice, information on national and international affairs, and questions and answers based on peasant letters. Of the 30,000 copies printed in 1889, half were sent free to cantonal authorities and many of the rest were probably channeled in the same direction.[50] Paid subscriptions rose to 35,000 in 1893, increased in the period of the Russo-Japanese War, fell somewhat afterwards, and rose again during World War I when the paper became a daily and circulation rose to nearly 87,000 paid subscribers. At that time over 16,000 copies were distributed free of charge.[51] The paper was always heavily subsidized and the government lost money on every issue, even at the height of the paper's success during the Russo-Japanese War.[52]

Selskii vestnik was intended as an instrument of local administration as well as propaganda. It was a means whereby local rural authorities and literate peasants could be informed about government decisions that related to them. The existence of the paper meant that peasants who went to the cantonal administration to solve a problem, or village elders who went there on business, were likely to find a newspaper to read. According to A. S. Prugavin, *Selskii vestnik* was the fourth most popular newspaper among peasants of Moscow Province in 1883, with twenty-seven subscriptions, and, according to a survey of schoolteachers, it was the most popular among peasants in Novgorod Province, with thirty-three subscriptions in 1884-85.[53]

Similar to *Selskii vestnik* were the publications of several official commissions established in the 1870s to oversee public readings intended to divert the lower classes of the capitals from drink, and to improve their morals.[54] The first commission was established in St. Petersburg in November 1871 under the authority of the War Ministry and on the premises of the Pedagogical Museum in Solianoi Gorodok. The second, the Standing Commission for Popular Readings, which served as the central authority over all public readings, was founded a year later under the Ministry of Education.[55] A third and semi-official commission was established in Moscow in 1874 and was associated with the Society for the Spread of Useful Books. Both Petersburg commissions began to publish immediately, and the one in Moscow began in 1884-85; by 1889 they had published more than three hundred titles. The average size of editions for the Standing Commission's works was ten thousand copies, and by 1887 it had published over one hundred titles. By that accounting, the total output of the three commissions must have approached three million booklets by 1889.[56] Belles lettres made up a comparatively small portion of the commissions' lists. Many of the works issued were religious or informational, with titles such as *About the Crimea* and *About Thunder*. The two works of literature published by the commission were patriotic ones: Pushkin's epic poem "Poltava," and Gogol's *Taras Bulba*. The first was retold in prose, and the second in an abridged version. Also included were historical patriotic texts on famous Russians, such as Peter the Great, Lomonosov, and Suvorov, as well as religious works, such as *About God as the Highest Spirit* and *Woman Inside Christianity and Outside It*. The Commissions required that only their works be read at public readings, and not until the turn of the century were these rules relaxed.[57]

The educated observers did not rate the quality of these books very highly. One critical observer commented after reviewing the publications of the Standing Commission of Public Readings that he had expected to find works of known Russian writers, scholars, and men of science, but instead "it appeared that we had arrived in a society completely unknown to us."[58] He felt these books were condescending, trite, and full of grammatical errors. Unlike the authors of the rival lubok tales, however, the writers who produced these works were well paid: they received 50 rubles for an accepted manuscript, and 150 rubles upon publication. The fee amounted to about 30 kopecks a line, which was much more than well-known writers received for publication in major journals.[59]

Government officials also attempted to influence the experience of the common people with books and reading through activities of another semi-official organization, the Trusteeship of The People's Temperance. The Trusteeship was funded by the treasury out of the proceeds of the state liquor monopoly and operated a wide network of libraries, houses of culture, and public readings from 1895 to 1917. The Trusteeship functioned at the provincial and district levels. The membership consisted of representatives of the state, Church, and local governmental bureaucracies, in addition to nonvoting members who donated their time but did not participate in policy matters. In 1904 there were 22,664 regular members and 15,436 nonvoting members of the Trusteeship, most of whom were officials, landowners, landcaptains, clerics, and military officers.[60]

The activities of the Trusteeship reflected the increased official tolerance at the turn of the century for the common reader's exposure to Russian classics and the special publications of the intelligentsia. The official summary of the activities of the Trusteeship for 1911 contains a list of titles recommended to local committees including those published by I. I.

Gorbunov-Posadov, the follower of Tolstoy who continued to operate the publishing firm of Posrednik after Tolstoy left. In the 1904 and 1907 *Explanatory Guide to Books for Reading* published by the Trusteeship, the recommended titles were primarily belles lettres, popular science, agronomy, and geography. In the 1907 guide, belles lettres were grouped into three categories: those describing "the life of the people and all kinds of toilers"; works of well-known Russian writers, "namely, Griboedov, Ostrovskii, L. N. Tolstoy, and A. P. Chekhov"; and works of foreign authors.[61] State authorities did not yet accept the classics and other works of belles lettres as appropriate reading matter for the common people to the extent that the compilers of the Trusteeship's lists did. The Trusteeship was an officially approved and supported organization, however, and its recommendations reflected the softening of official opposition to the dissemination of belles lettres and the classics. The state authorities continued to publish a wide variety of religious and patriotic propaganda, though they no longer did so at the exclusion of all other literature.

Both the state and the commercial publishers produced books for soldiers, and about wars and campaigns. During wartime the state actively encouraged colporteurs and urban book peddlers to maintain a large supply of patriotic broadsides and stories. During the Russo-Turkish War of 1877-78, lubok prints proclaimed in song, "We are ready to die for the tsar and for Russia," and depicted notable heroes, as was done during the War of 1812 and the Crimean War.[62] In the cities, "flying sheets" circulated with much the same message. One pictured Turkish regiments entering a Russian mill and reemerging as messy flour.[63] Similar works appeared in much greater quantities during the Russo-Japanese War of 1904-1905 and World War I. A lubok sheet from the Russo-Japanese War entitled "The Cossack's Breakfast" depicted an enormous Cossack devouring a Japanese soldier, and the reader could sing an accompanying song that included such lines as "I'll tear your hide with my teeth."[64] During the First World War polychrome posters replaced the old lubok lithographs, and carried such titles as "The Cruelties of Turks and Kurds Against Christians" (1915); "I Myself Will Appear to You" (Christ visiting a wounded Russian soldier, 1914-15); and "The Heroic Action of the Cossack Kuzma Kriuchkov" (shown killing eleven German cavalrymen, 1915).

The symbiosis of state and private patriotic publishing was exemplified by the firm of Sytin, which issued 2.7 million portraits of the imperial family in 1899 and 3.4 million in 1909.[65] Sytin claimed in January 1914 to have published 3.8 million copies of books and pamphlets devoted to the 300th anniversary of the Romanov dynasty in 1913, and 350,000 copies of works associated with the hundred-year jubilee of the defeat of Napoleon in 1912.[66]

An important source of state-sponsored publications for the military in the late nineteenth and early twentieth centuries was the firm of V. A. Berezovskii, which was founded in 1879. Operating as an official supplier for the army, Berezovskii was able to sell vast quantities of military propaganda, instructional materials, and other works to the state for use in regimental libraries and in training programs at prices considerably higher than those charged by commercial publishers for comparable products.[67] There were hundreds of titles in its "Soldiers' Library," in which heroic soldiers slaughtered their adversaries and won St. George crosses, or proved themselves remarkable in peacetime situations.

Readers of Berezovskii's publications were admonished to respect authority and obey superiors, as were readers of all publications sponsored by the state and Church. Andrei Lovkach, the protagonist of a 1904 story, disobeys his mother, proves to be a poor soldier, and is later undone by his own sloppiness. His unloaded gun fails to protect him, and he is eaten by wolves in a forest.[68] Bezpalov, an orphan who has made good in the army, courts an equally grim fate in *At Liberty* (1897) when he rejects the advice of his commanding officer to reenlist. Instead, he listens to a former tramp who regales him with the delights of a "free" life in the capital. He is soon reduced to begging, but fortunately he meets his former commander, who allows him to return to the regiment. "Well, I said the city was not for you," the officer quips.[69] The presentation of a kind of freedom that leads to disaster is similar to the message found in the traditional bandit tales, but the picture of a hero undone by his own initiative diverges sharply from the values expressed in almost all the commercial fiction and particularly in the success stories.

One of Berezovskii's objectives was to motivate Russian soldiers, and his authors stressed loyalty to the tsar and the Church. His early twentieth-century publications show some of the same tendencies, however, that appeared in the popular commercial literature. The soldiers in his stories fight primarily for their homeland and dear ones, and they are not Orthodox warriors. The Japanese are not identified as non-Christians in tales from the Russo-Japanese War of 1904-1905, but rather as "swine" and "slant-eyed devils."[70]

Berezovskii's publications also contained variants of the idea of a family of peoples under Great Russian hegemony. The hero of the story *All People Are of God* (1899) is a noncommissioned officer distressed to find himself burdened with a Tatar draftee.[71] The Tatar proves himself a good chap, however, and the officer is glad of his company. Jews are portrayed negatively, as in the lubok tales and in the late nineteenth-century serials published in *Moskovskii listok*. For example, in a typical tale from the Russo-Japanese War by S. Severnyi, Russian soldiers are endangered by a treacherous Jew who thinks only of money.[72]

The sharpest divergence between the values found in the Church and state-sponsored publications and those of the market was in the treatment of mobility. Worldly success was not a suitable objective in Berezovskii's publications or in other official materials. *Antip and Semen* (1899) is a story of two rivals and is set in early nineteenth-century Russia. Antip, the son of a village elder, buys his freedom, marries the local beauty, and becomes a millionaire through some dubious dealing. Semen, the local orphan, is drafted and becomes a noncommissioned officer. He is wounded at Borodino and pensioned off. Of the two, the poor Semen is content and honorable. The wealthy Antip is miserable and does not have the respect of the community. When Semen dies, Tsar Nicholas I sees the soldier's cap on his coffin and personally pays tribute to the old soldier. Antip, in contrast, lies on his deathbed and prays that his sins be forgiven. The lesson is not only that dishonesty does not pay, but that enterprise and wealth are suspect, though service and more moderate goals are not. This was a very different lesson than that found in the commercial publications. Even here, however, education was praised: "Of course, education does not ruin anyone, and Antip's children became better, thanks to it."[73]

The willingness of state and Church publicists to allow a modicum of social mobility did not preclude their advocacy of a fully traditional response to hardship and suffering. "Do Good and Good will Result" was the title of a story in the officially favored magazine *Chtenie dlia soldat* (Reading for Soldiers) in 1901.[74] The story is set in a prosperous village, but the reader is reminded that to some fate is "worse than an evil stepmother." The wealth of the hard-working and devout peasant Vasilii Lunev is swept away in a series of disasters culminating in a fire. Faith is not insurance against suffering, the author of the tale observes, since "he who loves God is also tested."[75] Vasilii rebuilds his cottage and struggles to feed his family, and he does not forget God or blame him. He prays every Sunday and places his hopes on a son named Mitia, whom he sends to school. Mitia is diligent and serious, and fortune again seems to smile on the family, but Mitia falls in love with the daughter of a rich peasant who prefers a more prosperous suitor. Fortunately for Mitia, the Russo-Turkish War commences, and both he and his rival are called to the colors. Mitia distinguishes himself and writes home of his triumphs. The whole village gathers to hear a letter in which he tells of rescuing the company commander and being made a noncommissioned officer. Hearing of his feats in the cause of liberating the brother Slavs from the

Moslem yoke, the father of his beloved relents, and when Mitia returns, with his arm in a sling and a St. George cross on his chest, a joyful marriage is celebrated. The reward is not his, however, but his father's, as in the story *Maxim the Rich*, and Vasilii concludes that the saying "Do good and good will result" is true, and "sooner or later God rewards a hundredfold."[76] Since the reason for Mitia's prosperity is his father's piety, what might have been a success story similar to the commercial tales becomes instead a lesson in traditional values.

Unofficial Responses

The Church and the state as institutions might be expected to be concerned with the piety and patriotism of the common people, and to act on this concern by providing appropriate reading material. What motivated the many private citizens working with philanthropic societies and other unofficial organizations of mass education to contribute their efforts and resources to promote a particular literature for lower-class readers? The answer lies in the perception on the part of many educated Russians that they had a moral obligation to influence and contribute to the cultural development of the newly literate and to the widely shared belief that Russian literature could serve as a bridge between classes. Educated Russians of different political persuasions looked to different literatures, but they shared a common belief that a "proper" literature was a necessary beacon to guide the Russian peasant along an as yet dimly perceived path out of generations of serfdom and backwardness.

The attitude that animated many educated Russians in their relations with the common people may be described as "culturism," a term that has been applied to China, but that, when its meaning is modified in some dimensions, can be fruitfully borrowed. Edwin O. Reischauer and John K. Fairbank explain: "By it we mean to suggest that in the Chinese view the significant unit was really the whole civilization rather than the narrower political unit of a nation within a larger cultural whole."[77] The concept of the nation, although very much alive in late nineteenth-century Russia, was associated in the minds of many educated people—and especially those who considered themselves members of the intelligentsia— with a retrograde political order counterposed to their own ideals. Loyalty to the tsar and identification with the Orthodox Church, the traditional emblems of Russian nationality, had become unacceptable to many Westernized Russians as a basis for citizenship in the course of the nineteenth century. For these people national identity became secondary to a cultural identity based on the ideals of the radical and liberal critics of the nineteenth century that was shared by members of the intelligentsia or "society."

The notion of a cultural rather than a political or religious identity was particularly attractive to the upwardly mobile people of common origins. Organizations of self-educated people flourished in the early twentieth century, and many of these people identified themselves as members of the "intelligentsia from the people." Magazines such as *Vestnik znaniia* (Herald of Learning, 1903-18) and *Novyi zhurnal* (New Magazine, 1908-17) were typical expressions of this movement, although there were many different types of organizations and publications.[78] Readers of these publications worked in many different professions— from schoolteachers and bookkeepers to railroad employees and telegraph operators—and were united in a search for learning and culture. They wanted to consider themselves educated, but with no more than a few years of formal schooling they were confused by a profusion of ideas and information. They were drawn to science as universal knowledge and to classical Russian literature as a source of national pride. They also wanted to share their learning, such as it was, with the lower classes. The cultural idea of national identity seemed tailored to fit the needs of these people, and their publications were full of articles about the great figures of Russian and world culture.

Whereas Chinese culturism upheld the established order, Russian culturism condemned it. The term "culture" was conceived in the broadest sense of shared values, but these values were expressed primarily through the Russian literary tradition, which consisted of a pantheon of respected authors and critics and of the judgment that the true function of belles lettres was to illuminate social reality and transform readers. The terms *kulturtreger* and *kulturnik* were both used to describe educated Russians who participated in popular education, but both seem too narrow and value-laden to be fully descriptive. Culturism is a more neutral and informative concept combining both the sense of values and mission in the Russian context.

The intelligentsia also shared a sense of indebtedness to the people, and felt morally obligated to alleviate their suffering. The debt could be discharged by leading the peasantry out of backwardness. This construction of the relationship between the educated and the uneducated was reinforced by the social and occupational experience of many educated Russians, who were professionally engaged in education, health, local government, communications, or other noncommercial sectors of the economy and considered their activities "cultural work" to improve the lot of the common people. With the combination of the perceived debt to the people and the belief in the transforming power of literature, it was natural that these educated Russians would be highly concerned about the quality and content of the literature reaching the newly literate.

Efforts to mold the literary taste of the common reader were also an expression of a more fundamental desire to bring the common people into a consensus of values shared by educated Russians, or to create a new consensus incorporating the values of the common people. The effort to promote such a consensus can be understood as analogous to efforts to inculcate modern concepts of nationality elsewhere, with the important distinction that in Russia this citizenship was limited to an identification with the intelligentsia, in opposition to established political and clerical authority. Success in this endeavor would both discharge the intelligentsia's debt to the people and close the gap between the common people and the rest of Russian society.

Many educated Russians who participated in cultural work found the idea of a Russia divided between an educated minority and a mass of illiterate and unschooled peasants distressing and dangerous. Although this image of a sharp dichotomy began to lose its verisimilitude in the course of the nineteenth century, especially after the emancipation of the serfs in 1861, the continuing small size of the industrial and commercial bourgeoisie, the meagerness of the intermediate social groups, the increasing but still low level of general education, and the persisting legal and social discrimination against the peasantry lent substance to it, as did the peasant violence associated with the 1905 Revolution. Moreover, the experience of exposure to the more advanced societies of Western Europe reinforced the educated Russians' awareness of the relative backwardness of their country, and encouraged them to view the common people as an undifferentiated and remote entity. The image of the dichotomy persisted almost equally among those who identified themselves with the intelligentsia and those who sought to distance themselves from it. Even the sharpest critics of the Westernized positivist intelligentsia in the early twentieth century clung to what was by then an outmoded caricature of Russian society.[79]

The perceived cleft provoked a dream of cultural unity. Hopes for a totalistic resolution of the division between the intelligentsia and the people animated Russian intellectuals of both Westernizer and Slavophile perspectives. Whether the new unified culture was to be the cosmopolitan stuff of the industrialized West or was to come from within Russia, the dream had a captivating simplicity. Whether the emphasis was on the dissemination of a superior culture from educated Russia to the people, or on the generation of a true "people's culture" from within the peasantry and proletariat assisted by the intelligentsia, the popularity of commercial low literature appeared an insufferable obstacle to the millennial solution.

This yearning for cultural wholeness was evident in one of the earliest unofficial discussions of the consequences and potential inherent in common literacy, the four volumes of diverse comments published in the 1840s by the Imperial Moscow Agricultural Society, *About the Spread of Literacy Among the Whole People in Russia on a Religious Moral Basis*. The works were dedicated by the publishers to the Russian Orthodox clergy.[80] The work contained a discussion of the significance of literacy, and also information about the accomplishments of enlightened nobles such as Prince D. V. Golitsyn, president of the Society, who ordered instruction in reading and church singing for peasant boys on his estate, with the explanation that "this softens the coarseness of the heart and attracts people to the church."

To those who organized the compendium, literacy was seen as a means to uphold good morals and to prevent the corruption that, in their view, was spreading among the common people with the development of the market economy and factory production. The antidote to social decay they suggested was "moral-religious literacy" based on a knowledge of Church Slavonic, and a shared religious culture that connected the present day with the earliest period of Russian history. "There was a time," one commentator wrote, "when the Russian people were educated in one common people's school." "In this school," he continued, "all studied together, from the great princes and royal tsars, the spiritual authorities and the boyars, down to the simple people."[81]

To spread religious literacy among the common people, the authors of the commentary suggested use of The Book of Hours, the Church primer, and the Psalter in Church Slavonic. These books would provide a "library for practical Christian life." The authors of the compendium contrasted the spiritual texts with the undesirable secular literature, read either for entertainment or for relief from idleness and boredom. The undesirable reading material was lubok literature, which was then beginning to appear in the sacks of peddlers on their rounds through the countryside.

The attractiveness of the ideal of cultural wholeness owed something to the overall structure of Russian historical development. Without either a well-defined classical heritage or a renaissance, which could illuminate it and set off the Middle Ages from the secular culture and concerns of the modern world, educated Russians looked back directly to the relative cultural harmony of the premodern period and compared it to their own experience in a time when industrialization, urbanization, and rural development were dissolving traditional social and community ties. The

perceived contrast was very sharp, as shown by the comments of contributors to the Moscow Agricultural Society compendium about the
implications of popular literacy.

The noncommercial sponsored literature for the common people represented a minimum of shared values and served perhaps as a kind of
surrogate for a compulsory primary school curriculum that would extend
beyond instruction in the three R's. Such a curriculum was never instituted in prerevolutionary Russia; but the efforts to create a literature for
the common reader, and to establish some agreement on the kinds of
books the newly literate should read and which authors they should
revere, was an analogous step toward national cultural integration. The
people to benefit primarily from such integration were not likely to be
the common people, who were the targets of so much effort, but rather
the so-called "intelligentsia from the people," who had the energy and
incentive to master a certain amount of learning.

Educated Russians who thought about the reading habits of the common people in the late nineteenth and early twentieth centuries generally
held a variant of one of two basic perspectives on the peasantry and the
common people. Either they idealized the innate virtues of the folk, or
they denigrated popular mores and argued that the common people
needed to replace traditions born in backwardness and superstition with
new attitudes and values conducive to progress. The dichotomy in the
two viewpoints became apparent in the Slavophile and Westernizer de-
bates of the second quarter of the nineteenth century. It recurred in the
arguments between populists and liberals in the last third of the century,
and was recapitulated in the disputes among Marxists about proletarian
culture before and after the October Revolution. Adherents of both views
wanted the emergent literary culture of the common people to be strictly
contained. Both perspectives converged on a total vision of the culture
of the common people that denied the diversity and the natural com-
plexity of the literary culture growing out of the developmental process.
In that respect, both tended toward a kind of antimodernism, in which
the confusing divisions of the industrial era were challenged in the name
of simpler ideals.

Implicit in the hostility to popular commercial literature was the assumption that the muzhik was not competent to choose his own reading
material. The conscience and guidance of the *intelligent* was to substitute
for a consciousness and initiative the common man lacked. Culturist
intellectuals of all shades of opinion viewed the common people as prisoners of circumstances beyond their control. Their purchase of lubok
literature was explained either by the dearth of suitable alternatives, or
by the action of external forces that prevented a correct choice. Early

observers leaned toward the former explanation. This was the view of the pioneer publisher of "people's books," A. F. Pogosskii, as well as that of Dostoevsky. "A year or two more," wrote Pogosskii in 1863, "and every literate boy will laugh at the merchant who offers him something about some kind of frightful witch, Bova Korolevich, Eruslan Lazarevich, and similar village idiots."[82] Dostoevsky wrote on the eve of the emancipation, "The people will forget *The Beautiful Mohammedan* for my books."[83] Both Dostoevsky and Pogosskii dreamed of the emergence of a new unified culture based on the common people's appreciation of good literature. When this appreciation did not manifest itself in the marketplace, educated activists first emphasized the failure of the intelligentsia to make the proper reading matter available, and then became convinced that systematic barriers blocked the literature the people deserved and wanted. The barriers were thought to result from censorship, the greed and self-interest of the booksellers and publishers, and the capitalist system itself.

Slavophile and Populist Perspectives

The early commentators on popular literature who leaned toward populism were generally optimistic about peasant preferences. If the peasants chose lubok literature, there was no reason to suppose they would not be equally delighted with an adequate substitute. This was the view of Leo Tolstoy, who was engaged in producing books for the common people in the 1880s. Tolstoy began his involvement with popular literature by condemning those who sought to bring the word of educated Russia to the people: "If the people want to read *The English Milord*, then what right do we have to complain about that."[84] He hoped, however, that the people would create a worthy literature for themselves. When this did not happen, he became convinced that selected intellectuals should and could participate in the development of a literature for the people. He expressed his vision to a visitor who came to Iasnaia Poliana in 1886. New schools were raising the number of new readers to millions, he said. "And these millions of Russian literates stand before us like hungry little blackbirds, with open mouths. Give us intellectual food. . . . Deliver us from all these lubok Eruslan Lazareviches, Milord Georgs, and other food of the market."[85]

A. S. Prugavin (1852-1918-19), a pioneer in the study of lubok literature and a radical populist in the early 1870s, believed that peasants bought the lubok books because they had no choice. He took a dim view of this literature and distinguished between a legitimate popular literary culture and a corrupt commercial interloper. As a populist he identified the counterfeit culture as urban and the true culture as rural. He distinguished a peasant lubok literature from city works he called "Nikolskii Market literature," after the area in Moscow where many of the popular publishers were located. "What a sea of vulgarity, superstition, prejudice, and ignorance of all types" came from these publishers, he complained.[86] This sea, he feared, was rapidly submerging true folk literature in "the influence of the factory, the barracks, the lower middle class or the servants, the tavern, and the petit press."[87] He appealed to the intelligentsia "to take all measures to paralyze at the root this corrupting influence that can be carried by ignorant speculators, who have grasped the petit press in their hands."[88] The legitimate lubok publishers, he felt, had outlived their usefulness.

The fear among the populists that the purity of the common reader would be sullied by the literary product of the marketplace was expressed most sharply by the socialist writer, S. A. Rappoport (1863-1920), who used the pen name of An-skii. He was the author of a well-known play, *The Dybbuk*. Writing in *Essays About People's Literature* (1894), Rappoport suggested that the influence of the peasants who had left the countryside for the city explained many of the negative aspects of popular literature. These "renegades," he argued, were transforming lubok literature into a "renegade literature."[89] Only the popular literature that predated Peter the Great spoke to true peasant needs, he felt, and that literature was primarily a foreign import. The post-Petrine literature of the lubok had, in his view, no moral value. Worse still, he felt, was the city literature of the Nikolskii Market, to which he relegated *Milord Georg*, the first rivulet of "this dirty stream." The message of the works, in his view, was "extreme cynicism, not covered by even the usual fig leaf of banal morality. The aim of life is debauchery and riches."[90]

Rappoport ascribed the success of lubok literature and its destructive character to the capitalist system. The lubok writers, he complained, took up literature "exclusively from need, and look on writing as a trade, not seeing in it either art or a moral task." The publishers, who were "governed exclusively by the profit motive," issued only what would sell.[91] As a result, the peasants got trash to read. Even when confronted by the vogue of Pinkerton novels, Rappoport continued to argue, as late as 1913, that Russia could escape Western Europe's literary fate and develop a healthy mass literature before the taste of the common people was ruined by commercial fare.[92]

A more moderate expression of populist protectiveness toward the common reader was that of the Kharkov circle of schoolteachers led by Kh. D. Alchevskaia, who published three surveys of popular reading material entitled *What to Read to the People* (1884, 1887, 1906). Alchevskaia devoted herself to popular education with an almost religious fervor. Her father had opposed her education and prevented her from attending school. She educated herself, made a prosperous marriage, and decided to use her energies and financial means to make education available to women less fortunate than she. She began teaching at a women's Sunday school in Kharkov in 1862. When the school was closed by the authorities, she continued teaching her pupils illegally in her home. The Kharkov school again functioned legally in 1870, after she became a certified schoolteacher, and she opened a second school in the village of Alekseev in Ekaterinoslav Province, where her husband owned an estate.

Not only did Alchevskaia want to teach, she also wanted to study her pupils to find out what they liked to read and how different texts affected them. She evaluated texts for their suitability for peasants and lower-class urban readers, and published her findings in her compendium, *What to Read to the People*. After the first volume appeared in 1884, she began to study the readers themselves.[93] Alchevskaia's method was to read the texts aloud, note the response, elicit additional comments, and then enter into discussion with her pupils. In the discussions, she and her teachers sought to teach humanitarian values, which they understood in Tolstoyan terms, and respect for the written word, while widening the intellectual horizons of their pupils. They tried to demonstrate that the reader from the people could appreciate the best in belles lettres, and they denied the need for a special people's literature. They shared with the populists, however, a belief in the purity of the peasant. Fairy tales, they felt, represented the people's treasure of moral ideas and expressed the belief "that truth always triumphs," in contrast to "cynical rakish factory songs."[94] They found some lubok works acceptable if the moral message was clear and the heroes chaste and noble, such as in one version of *The Battle between the Russians and the Kabardinians*. When the moral message was not evident, they were quick to condemn the work, as in the case of *Milord Georg*, the popularity of which Alchevskaia attributed to the taste of the "factory people infected with the cynicism of the city."[95]

The populist critics came to believe, as did some other *intelligenty*, that the literature of the lubok was the work of commercial profiteers who left the common people with no alternative. The lubok publishers, in this view, engaged in speculation on the people's ignorance and corrupted the muzhik instead of inspiring him and informing him about life. They assumed that if given a choice, the people would choose more elevated reading matter. To the commercial literature of the lubok, poisoned by urban influence, they counterpoised an ideal literature to be created by the altruistic intelligentsia. This literature would draw on the best in belles lettres and would help the common people realize their ethical and cultural potential. The censure of popular commercial literature was also an appeal for their own substitute and for the presentation of the selected works of worthy authors to the common reader in special editions, in libraries, and in public readings.

Westernizer and Liberal Perspectives

Liberals and the Westernizers regarded popular literature from a different perspective. Instead of fearing urban influence, they welcomed it. Some were willing to accept commercial popular literature as an unavoidable phase in the breakdown of peasant culture, but they assumed that the literature of the lubok would be followed by good books that would integrate the common people into a unified high culture. When this did not seem to take place, they offered explanations that reduced the ordinary reader to the status of victim rather than participant. He was the victim of scheming publishers, of wily distributors, of a whole system of commercial relations, or even of the intelligentsia that failed to provide him with an acceptable alternative to commercial literature.

This was the viewpoint of Belinsky, who wavered between the belief that readers might move from the English Milord to the world of great literature, to complaints that trash such as *The Adventures of Bova Korolevich* "only dirties their minds."[96] Belinsky held the intelligentsia responsible for a failure to provide common people with suitable reading matter, and for forcing them to slake their thirst for reading at such "dirty pools."[97] The utilitarian concerns of the critics of the mid-nineteenth century were not brought sharply into focus on the popular commercial literature then still in its infancy; but they established a critical tradition in which utility in promoting progress was the standard, and by this standard many subsequent observers condemned commercial popular literature.

The nineteenth century enlightener's case against the literature of the lubok was most sharply stated by the educator E. Nekrasova in her essay *Popular Books for Reading in the Twenty-Five Year Battle with Lubok Publications*, first published in the 1880s. In criticizing lubok literature for its lack of positive moral value, for its "naked cynicism," for the way it converted the printed word into "nonsense," and for its failure to uplift the reader, Nekrasova was close to Rappoport and Prugavin. Unlike the populists, however, she blamed the peasants for the quality of the lubok tales, which she felt appealed to "the coarse undiscriminating taste" of the "coarse uneducated reader."[98] This did not legitimize the lubok in her estimation. Since a demand for the lubok existed, it was all the more important, in her view, to stop its circulation. "It is not necessary to ask what they like in the present development of their taste," but instead, to study "their lives, conditions, and interests," and come up with a suitable alternative literature.

Even the respectability and recognition that Sytin won did not legitimize the popular lubok literature he published. When he was honored on the fiftieth anniversary of his publishing activities, most contributors to his anniversary symposium praised him as a traditional enlightener, and ignored or down-played the commercial side of his enterprise.[99] To the distributor of people's books, A. Kalmykova, he was a person who sold lubok literature from commercial necessity, while his soul "burned with the wish" to publish better books. To the critic Ovsianiko-Kulikovskii, Sytin was one of those "ideological publishers," for whom "commercial enterprise" was social service.[100] Only the critic S. Vengerov, who hailed him as a "self-made man," to use the English phrase, and perhaps Maxim Gorky, who identified him as a man who found the meaning of life in work, indicated acceptance of Sytin the businessman.

Although most articulators of the culturist idea condemned the official system of Church and state censorship, with its authorized lists of books permitted in people's libraries and at public readings, they unwittingly justified the need for the existence of just such a system in their arguments against popular commercial literature. Their differences with the authorities were often not about the need to protect the common reader from the dangers of diversity, but rather about the composition of the lists.

The views of N. A. Rubakin (1862-1946), another important figure in the production and study of books for the common reader, illustrated the dilemma of many moderates and of some on the left. Rubakin commented on an enormous range of subjects, but concentrated his efforts on the study of books and their readers. He compiled bibliographies, offered advice to those seeking self-education, and wrote works of popular science. He was influential in shaping the attitudes of thousands of educators and schoolteachers toward books and proper reading for the lower classes, who supported him enthusiastically. Between 1889 and 1915 he corresponded with 11,000 people, many of whom were self-educated workers.[101] From 1889 to 1928 over 20 million copies of his books were printed, and he became a phenomenon on the book market. He bargained with editors for the rights to publish his advice-to-readers column, and sold his literary properties for a large sum after he moved to Switzerland in 1907. In 1919 and 1920, the Soviet of Workers' and

Soldiers' Deputies published twenty-two of his books and brochures in 1.42 million copies.

Rubakin, like many associated with the Socialist Revolutionary Party, stood somewhere between populism and Marxism.[102] His dream of a revival of rural life made him closer to the more moderate Marxists, but his advocacy of the dissemination of Western learning made him remote from them. He believed that the common people wanted knowledge, that new kinds of enlightened readers were appearing, and that books were a key instrument in the transformation of Russians as individuals and as members of society. His belief that peasants and workers wanted good books was documented in his *Study of the Russian Reading Public* (1895). Here he described the progress of lower-class readers from Bova to Pushkin, and he identified the appearance of new worker and peasant readers. He felt that worker readers were on a level nearly equal to that of the *intelligent*, but that peasant readers were a more modern variant of the traditional village devotee of Scripture. He expected that a new literature by poets and writers from the people would be produced, and that it would express "the grief and joys of their class."[103]

Rubakin was also an active propagandist of belles lettres and popular science, however, and he praised educated book peddlers "to whom it is not money that is dear, but books, and not even books, but ideas."[104] He elaborated his view in the introductory essay to the 1911 edition of his three-volume bibliography, *Among Books*, in which he addressed himself particularly to librarians and booksellers.[105] Rubakin believed in the force of books to uplift the common reader, and he was torn between the desire to discourage the distribution of certain kinds of popular commercial literature and a more tolerant respect for literary diversity. He favored diversity, but not without some ambivalence.

Rubakin felt that no special belles lettres were necessary for the common reader. He expected that the true book would always win over the false, and argued that "the real friends of enlightenment have never been afraid and never will be afraid of books that contain ideas and views unlike their own." He spoke against the exclusion of "unsympathetic tendencies" of thought from libraries. His belief in the importance of books was so strong, however, that he felt it imperative that new readers develop a proper orientation toward particular books, and he proposed evaluative standards. He recommended that scientific books be judged according to whether or not they were "true." Books about normative issues were to be judged according to whose interests they served. Books that, in his opinion, expressed reactionary and anachronistic views or that evaluated life from the standpoint of the exploiting classes did not meet with his approval. He felt that the works of "the most outstanding and talented reactionaries" should be included in large general libraries (containing 20,000 or more titles), but should be excluded from smaller collections. In Rubakin's view, the purpose of these libraries was not to spread ideas that "had lived out their time," or were being disseminated by the police. Only readers who had developed a critical judgment were prepared for these works, he felt. Rubakin did not want libraries to conceal books from readers, but he felt that small libraries should exclude books that would not be useful for the "unprepared" reader.

Rubakin's effort to make the literature of educated Russia more accessible to the common people was part of a general trend in the early twentieth century. In a symposium dedicated to Sytin in 1916, B. Syromiatnikov summed up the growing consensus against a special literature exclusively for the common people and expressed the hope for a cultural unity that would encompass all classes. He condemned the "false currency" of people's literature and "the separation of culture into culture for the lord and culture for the common people" as a "shameful anachronism."[106]

Syromiatnikov perceived the classics of nineteenth-century Russia as the literature that could link the reading publics of educated and lower-class Russian readers. The classics were meaningful to readers with varying levels of critical experience and were accessible to a wide audience. Syromiatnikov quoted Nekrasov's earlier hope that "Belinsky and Gogol, and not the stupid Milord will be brought from the market," and added, "The book will come alive, and . . . the populace itself will reach out 'to Belinsky and Gogol' and to the good book of popular science. . . ."

Marxist Perspectives

The moderate educators' confidence in the accessibility and intrinsic worth of nineteenth-century belles lettres and popular science to the common reader was shared by some Russian Marxists. Although the Marxists stressed class conflict, and therefore rejected the idea of cultural unity in the present, the idea of an all-embracing common culture had a place in their vision of a perfect society. Marx and Engels did not offer their followers a consistent prescription for the literature of the future, or even for the literature to be read by the proletariat in the capitalist era, but they encouraged a utilitarian approach to literature similar to critics such as Belinsky, Dobroliubov, Pisarev, and Chernyshevsky.[107] Russian Marxists who tried to define proletarian culture were heirs to a Russian critical tradition that stressed the moral value of literature as well as its mimetic function. When they considered the question of the workers' reading, they divided in a way similar to that of populists and liberals. While some were willing to grant the usefulness of Russian literature, others wished to jettison it in favor of an entirely new people's literature they thought was in the making.

Criticism of popular commercial literature was always an argument in favor of sponsored alternatives, and the clearer the image of the alternative, the stronger was the complaint against the commercial product that interfered with its acceptance. The idea of a proletarian literary culture in the era of capitalism provided such an image. The vision of a new workers' literature that would superannuate the class-bound literatures of gentry and bourgeois Russia appeared as early as the mid-1880s. G. V. Plekhanov suggested in a censored preface to a literary reader for workers that the literature of educated Russia could have only a limited appeal to the proletariat. "You ought to have your own poetry, your own songs, your own verses," he maintained.[108]

The idea of proletarian culture as distinct from the culture of educated Russia was expressed most forcefully by A. A. Bogdanov, a one-time Bolshevik who left the party and became the theorist of the proletarian culture movement after the October Revolution. Bogdanov described literature as the organizer of collective consciousness in his 1911 essay, *The Cultural Tasks of Our Time*, and called for a literature to inspire the victory of the collective.[109] In condemning the individualism of the old intelligentsia, Bogdanov came close to dispensing with the culture of educated Russia entirely. The new culture would be created not by those from the upper classes, but by a new intelligentsia from the proletariat. Similar ideas were voiced elsewhere in the Bolshevik press.[110] Reminiscent of populist hopes for the peasantry, these visions foundered on the workers' preference for commercial publications.

The Menshevik A. N. Potresov differed with the advocates of proletarian culture. In an argument with the Bolsheviks he suggested that the workers would have to absorb the general culture of the civilized world instead of developing a separate culture of their own.[111] Popular literature was criticized from a similar perspective by L. M. Kleinbort, one of the most perceptive observers of the prerevolutionary working class. Kleinbort, in a series of essays—many of them published after 1905 in the Menshevik-dominated *Sovremennyi mir* (Contemporary World)—described the emergence of the working-class intelligentsia he expected to acquire the cultural heritage of educated Russia. He contrasted the backward, less conscious, still countrified workers, trapped in "the kingdom of the *Kopeika*," with the more enlightened workers involved in educational and cultural programs.[112] Although he expected this "grey uncultured stratum" to vanish, he worried about the influence of the kopeck press on it. He complained that the kopeck newspaper had become a great capitalist business by satisfying the demands of those workers. Drawn instinctively to the paper, they sought to escape their cares in boulevard novels and sensational stories. Instead of providing information about reality, Kleinbort charged, the *Kopeika* kept the worker in the dark: "It lets him forget, though for a moment, his unbearable position."[113] A true working-class paper should have the opposite effect. The less conscious workers were doomed to read the *Kopeika* nevertheless, he felt, so long as the penal conditions of labor persisted.[114]

Trade union journalists also condemned the *Kopeika* for dulling workers' political perceptions and for displacing their more serious publications. In doing so, they repeated educators' long standing complaints against popular commercial literature, and they drew on a fund of already circulating ideas about proletarian culture and the workers' moral superiority. They also tended to reject the market as a legitimate means for satisfying readers' tastes. The *Kopeika* was damned first of all as commercial speculation at the workers' expense. "The tragedy of contemporary art and culture," wrote one trade unionist, "is that the capitalist character of production makes the instrument of culture, science, and aesthetics only a means of personal enrichment."[115] Publishers, who hungered for profit and cared little for the intellectual and moral needs of their readers, seduced the common reader with cheap goods, in this view. Reading the boulevard press was a vice like alcoholism, complained one labor journalist;[116] the *Kopeika* was habit forming and dangerous, suggested another. The enticed worker developed a "lasting taste for its dirty gruel," and lost interest in "all that is pure, clear, and lacks the smell of scandal and drunken brawls."[117]

The Search for Cultural Unity

Those who condemned popular commercial literature blamed the censorship, the commercial system, the booksellers and publishers, and even the spoiled taste of the reader. Such criticism implied the need for further efforts to promote the beneficial alternative, and, if these were not successful, the need for censorship. Prugavin insisted that since the lubok publishers no longer served the needs of the common reader, "the important business of providing the people with intellectual nourishment should be taken from their hands and put into the hands of the intelligentsia."[118] E. Nekrasova insisted that "all thinking Russia" recognized the need to curtail lubok literature and to let the intelligentsia publish and distribute the books intended for the common reader.[119] The way she hoped this would happen was for *intelligenty* to become capitalists in the publishing business, but her appeal had more authoritarian implications. M. O. Menshikov, one of the ablest conservative publicists at the time of the Revolution, warned in the newspaper *Novoe vremia* (New Times) on February 23, 1917: "The people do not need books in general, but good books; for bad books, like rotten provisions, are transformed from food into deadly poison." "Better that five or six separate, fully approved publications should circulate among the people than thousands of foolish ones," wrote a clerical correspondent who shared Menshikov's sentiments.[120] The Kharkov schoolteacher, Alchevskaia, was also willing to deal summarily with books that threatened the purity of the people, such as *Milord Georg*. "We would sincerely like books of this sort to be removed from circulation," she wrote in 1887.[121] So vehement was the hue and cry against booksellers at the height of the early twentieth-century craze for Pinkerton novels that their trade association magazine issued an unsigned rejoinder: "The bookseller is a businessman. He stocks and sells the article that goes briskly."[122]

Fear of the *Kopeika* led the editors of the trade union paper *Nashe pechatnoe delo* (Our Printed Matter) to threaten that "The daily poisoning of the worker masses by various *kopeiki* has begun to call forth an ever stronger protest from advanced workers."[123] "We must throw over the 'sheets' and the 'kopecks' and read a workers' newspaper every day," affirmed *Vestnik prikazchika* (The Shop Assistant's Herald) in 1913.[124] "Hands off, sirs, for the workers' business can be managed only by the workers themselves," wrote the editors of *Edinstvo* (Unity).[125] In 1908 the Central Bureau of Trade Unions refused to provide *Gazeta kopeika* with information, and urged workers not to serve as worker correspondents for it.

Lenin shared the concerns of those who condemned the commercial press. He urged the liberation of writers from "the money bag," and literature from "shopkeeper literary relations" in his 1905 essay, "Party Organization and Party Literature."[126] Although most concerned with the outlets for political propaganda, Lenin echoed moderate proponents of the culturist idea in advocating control over "the publishing houses and distribution centers, bookstores and reading rooms, libraries and various bookselling establishments." Only a stress on narrow party control distinguished Lenin on this issue.

Labor journalists urged workers to read trade union periodicals, Marxist works on social questions, and the few slim volumes of proletarian literature that had appeared; but they also promoted, as did Lenin on occasion, the reading of the Russian classics and the works of contemporary writers associated with realism, such as Gorky, Andreev, Korolenko, and Kuprin. "The thinking workers will meet in the person of V. G. Korolenko," wrote a columnist in *Novoe pechatnoe delo* (New Printed Matter), "the writer-citizen as a fighter for truth."[127] The metal workers' newspaper *Nash put* (Our Path) hailed Tolstoy as a "defender of the oppressed," a critic of inequality, and a writer who would live in the memories of Russian workers.[128] Social critics such as Belinsky were also given front-page treatment in this trade union paper.[129] Although some trade unionists dreamed of a workers' literature and a workers' art, most found utility in the classical literary tradition.

The new century brought increased diversity for all levels of society, but old attitudes toward popular literature persisted. They were reinforced by the increasing politicization of public life. Few among the educated Russians involved in the new party politics of the early twentieth century or in the intense intellectual life of that period, and few among the new intelligentsia of schoolteachers and others of common origins would have disagreed with Prugavin's pleas that the baudy lubok prints that fouled the imagination of the people be replaced by reproductions of realistic paintings by Repin, Vereshchagin, Kramskoi, Surikov, and others that encouraged social consciousness.[130] So wide was the agreement about these cultural symbols by the early twentieth century that Prugavin's hopes were fulfilled not only by idealistic activists and schoolteachers, but also by the editors of the Kopeck newspaper of St. Petersburg. Subscribers to the newspaper in 1908 and 1910 were offered reproductions of famous pictures by the very artists Prugavin mentioned.[131] The expectation that the common reader should find a social and political message in what he read was widely shared, and by the early twentieth century a consensus existed among a spectrum of educated Russians from Church and state authorities to Bolsheviks that a minimum of classical Russian belles lettres and some form of popular science should occupy an important place in the reading of the common people.

The culturist ideal was rejected by a few moderate intellectuals associated with literary modernism, the innovative movement in European belles lettres that began with symbolism and lost its momentum after the avant-garde experiments of the 1920s and 1930s. The modernist writers created a literature that was almost by definition too complex for the common reader, since understanding their works presupposed an appreciation for innovation and experimentation in language and subject. The acceptance of its legitimacy as literature put the culturist ideal in jeopardy, since it meant recognizing a special literature for an educated elite and therefore the division of the reading public.

Among the few intellectuals inclined to accept the new popular culture as the logical result of social and economic change were, not surprisingly, people associated with this literary movement. Kornei Chukovskii, one of the most perceptive liberal critics in the prerevolutionary period and later a major figure in Soviet literary life, identified the new popular culture as inevitable although regrettable. He stereotyped the reader of the commercial literature as a new mass man, "a microcephalic reader," for whom "happiness is a silver ruble."[132] A. S. Izgoev, an influential liberal journalist, likewise pointed to the success of the Pinkerton novels and the gutter press as the sad but unavoidable result of the poor taste of the lower classes.[133]

The nearly unanimous condemnation of the commercial popular literature was among the motivations that stirred activists of various political persuasions to produce and distribute an alternative literature for the common reader.

Unofficial Publications for the People

Although the unofficial publishers for the people divided along traditional lines between those who stressed the importance of the peasantry and those who saw only backwardness in rural Russia, there were striking similarities in the materials they wished to promote. Most shared a firm belief in the importance of popular science for the common reader, and they expressed an idea of national identity that also set them apart from the official publicists. In these respects they were closer to their commercial rivals.

Most educated activists shared a cultural idea of national identity that was linked with the great works of Russian literature. In the minds of these educators and propagandists, Pushkin, Lermontov, Gogol, Dostoevsky, Tolstoy, Chekhov, and a few other nineteenth- and early twentieth-century writers stood for what was best and noblest in educated Russia. When they emphasized the importance of Russian literature as an emblem of Russianness, they wished to forge a new sense of national consciousness as an alternative to popular identification with the tsar and the Orthodox Church. In commercial popular literature, too, the emphasis on the tsar and Church as symbols of nationality declined, but the new treatment of nationality found there was oriented more toward geography and ethnicity than toward culture.

The concept of Russianness as a cultural identification with the works of the great nineteenth-century writers was shared by "the new intelligentsia." These people sought a minimal sophistication that would give them a sense of identity as Russians and would certify their modest success. The primary-school teachers figured prominently among them, and the enthusiasm of these people for the classics made selections from the works of classical Russian writers the most important sponsored printed material for the common reader.

The influence of educated Russians was probably most powerfully felt among this group. When the editors of the magazine *Vestnik znaniia* (Herald of Learning), which catered to the new intelligentsia, asked their readers in 1910 to identify the most important people in science and literature, the names most commonly listed included Tolstoy, Turgenev, Dostoevsky, Gogol, Chekhov, Gorky, Andreev, Darwin, Hegel, and Marx.[134]

The list represented a level of learning accessible to primary-school teachers and others with no more than a few years of postprimary education. The semi-educated might not be able to read what these authors wrote, but they could aspire to gain some familiarity with their names and the ideas and works associated with them. The identification of a minimum of learning was an important step in the development of popular education inside and outside the primary school.

Despite the emphasis on science and new concepts of nationality, there was a fundamentally conservative streak in much of the unofficial people's literature. The notion of alliance between the educated *intelligenty* and the common people was implicit in the idea of the Russian classics as the proper reading for the newly literate. So was the idea that "the people" would remain "the people," whether peasants or workers, despite their literacy and reading. For revolutionaries the alliance was to overturn the established order, but they had little impact on the common reader until the early twentieth century. For most unofficial publicists, on the contrary, the alliance tended to legitimize existing stratification. Although they did not usually go so far as to urge their readers to forego all material aspirations, they looked askance at the dream of upward mobility. For revolutionaries, as for the official propagandists, wealth and personal achievement gained within the context of the market were suspect. This was the most important difference between the unofficial publishers for the people and their commercial rivals. The former were less sympathetic to upward mobility in a market economy than the latter.

One of the pioneer publishers with a Westernizing outlook was A. F. Pogosskii, the editor of magazines such as *Soldatskaia beseda* (Soldier's Discussion) and *Narodnaia beseda* (People's Discussion), who also worked on *Chtenie soldata* (The Soldier's Reading) in the 1850s.[135] He was one of the founders of the St. Petersburg Literacy Committee. His publications were not unlike efforts by other concerned *intelligenty* who, as early as the 1840s, had tried to make good reading material cheaply available. Pogosskii's magazines were too expensive for the peasant or lower-class urban reader, and his periodicals were primarily of interest to educators. He appealed, unsuccessfully, to lubok publishers to abandon their usual product and issue works of great Russian writers, such as Turgenev and Gogol.

Despite his belief that the common people could read belles lettres, Pogosskii also wrote and published his own stories based on his experiences as a noncommissioned officer. Although he was more skillful and imaginative than most contemporary authors of special people's books, he preached traditional moral lessons, and, as a result, tsarist authorities circulated some of his tales in the army until the Revolution.[136] In one of Pogosskii's typical tales the reader is encouraged to accept his station in life. "Grandpa Nazarych" appeared at the time of the emancipation.[137] Nazarych is a serf sent off to fight against Napoleon. He earns three medals and is eventually made a noncommissioned officer, although he refuses the honor for a long time out of humility. Loved and respected by his officers and fellow soldiers, he cannot bear to retire and serves until a doctor tells him he is too old. He returns home after a forty-year absence and finds no relatives, but his kindly former master gives him a post as forester. When he can no longer do this work, his employer gives him the forester's cottage in which he has been living, and five acres in return for his loyal service. "It's all mine!" Nazarych exclaims, but then catches himself.[138] "A sin, a sin!" he whispered. "Any pride is a sin." In the course of his years as a forester, Nazarych shelters an abandoned pregnant woman who proves to be a distant relative, and when she dies he has a grandson to look after. He saves for the future of the child, but then gives his savings to a needy couple. The couple later proves willing and able to help him by taking in the child should Nazarych die. The lesson of this story was conservative and morally exemplary.

Pogosskii's heroes stood for traditional morality, but they sometimes also battled against superstition and ignorance. In the story "Soldier's Beer," a passing soldier visits a wedding at which a local herb doctor and "sorcerer" threatens the company. The soldier calls the sorcerer a fake. "All wisdom is given by God, for the purpose of helping poor and ignorant people, and there is nothing frightening in it," he exclaims.[139] The sorcerer challenges the soldier to drink a tankard of beer on which he has put a spell. The soldier crosses himself and drinks. Undaunted, he challenges the sorcerer to drink a tankard himself. The soldier secretly puts tobacco in the sorcerer's beer, and the sorcerer confesses, when he is unable to finish it, that his powers are a sham. He is later identified as a horse thief and hangs himself.

Another early example of the attempt to package traditional homilies and respect for the logic of science was the monthly *Gramotei* (Literate

Person), published by I. N. Kushnerev in the 1860s and 1870s. In article after article in this magazine, the reader was shown that to be literate meant to recognize the value of science, agronomy, medicine, technology, and progress: thunder was not the sound of the prophet Elijah's chariot, as was commonly believed;[140] there was no need to fear graveyards and the dead;[141] and "The literate person knows from books what's what and does not let himself get hoodwinked by superstitious stories," reads one characteristic text.[142] Scientists and inventors were heroes to emulate.

The same magazine, however, contained stories warning the common reader not to try to outdo his fellows or to aspire to a position above his station. The 1868 tale "Dodger," set in the late pre-emancipation period, is a good example.[143] The villain of the story is a promising young man named Pavel, who is almost a model of the talented and aspiring worker. Pavel, the reader is informed, was never a part of peasant society, and is among those peasants who pay quitrent and do not farm. His parents have high hopes for him and send him out to become a weaver. Diligent and hardworking, he shuns the lighthearted company of his fellows. He attracts the attention of the foreman and is pointed out as an example to others. He is a "natural economist," however, and is soon consumed by a love for money. He collects a small horde in a chest, adding to it by stealing company goods and selling them to a shopkeeper. He is also literate: he reads religious books, convinced that his sins will be forgiven. Looking prosperous and accomplished, Pavel returns to his home village and convinces the village elder to let him marry his daughter and to help him and his future bride purchase their freedom. The elder helps him find a position as an assistant to a factory owner at a good salary. Pavel continues to steal, however, and he and his wife dream of entering the merchant class. In time, Pavel's boss discovers his thieving, but by then he has salted away enough to open his own Moscow shop. As he leaves the factory, his boss asks him, "Aren't you afraid of almighty God?"[144] Although no divine retribution comes to pass in the tale, the intimation is that Pavel will not escape punishment, and that both ambition and thieving are sins, with the effort to satisfy ambition leading directly to sin.

Similar in content to works published by Kushnerev were certain periodicals of the 1860s and 1870s, such as *Russkii rabochii* (Russian Worker), whose announced intention was to give the common reader entertainment, "advice for a correct and honest life," and "examples for emulation."[145] A critic in *Otechestvennye zapiski* (Notes of the Fatherland) observed that, despite certain differences, publications of this sort were "all striving to teach the people farming, to destroy drunkenness

336

and laziness, to entertain them with jokes, and to portray Europe as Russophobe and Slav hating and us as ideal people, and so forth."[146]

Works of this type were also published by philanthropic organizations such as the Society for the Dissemination of Useful Books, which was founded in 1861 and issued its works in over two million copies in the first twenty-five years of its existence.[147] The Society published works of popular science suggestive of a Westernizing idea of people's literature, as well as moralistic tales apparently designed to encourage the peasants in the retention of simple virtues. This was the message of such works as *Truthful Peter* (St. Petersburg, 1878) and *Labor Feeds and Laziness Ruins* (7th ed., 1877).[148] In *Truthful Peter* a boy kills his master's cat, but he tells the truth and is rewarded for his honesty. His behavior is held as an example to others. In *Labor Feeds and Laziness Ruins* two apprentices serve the same master; one is diligent and hard working, and the other is lazy. The diligent lad marries a shopkeeper's daughter, and the lazybones ends up in prison. Similar moralistic fables were published frequently in the 1870s, 1880s, and early 1890s.

The firm Posrednik (Intermediary) was the first and perhaps the only venture in sponsored books for the people to reach a mass audience through the commercial distribution system. It began in 1884 as a joint endeavor of Tolstoy and Chertkov, in cooperation with the young publisher I. D. Sytin. Tolstoy and Chertkov prepared the texts and Sytin published and distributed them. Posrednik represented the culmination of earlier efforts to create a special peasant literature, but it was also a departure from those efforts. It signaled the growing tendency of many to consider the works of major writers the most effective and proper alternative to commercial low literature, and served as a bridge between the literary efforts of those who sought moral improvement and those who sought cultural enlightenment. The efforts of the Posrednik publishers can be placed in the populist tradition, and had much in common with the work of Pogosskii and other pioneers of publishing for the people. The mission of Posrednik, according to the editors, was to produce "the best content at the cheapest price," and the best content was "as near as possible to the teaching of Christ."[149] "Literature is inseparable from life" read the statement of the editors in 1894. "Each literary work is a moral or immoral act of its author, and therefore the question of what to write is identical with the question of how to live."[150]

The Posrednik product was an attempt to combine the format and appeal of the lubok with the moral message of the editors. Most typical of Posrednik books were the didactic tales of Tolstoy, such as *Where Love is God Is* and the peasant stories of Tolstoy's protégé, S. T. Semenov. Tolstoy exalted the wisdom of peasants in his tales; but the wisdom he praised came from their understanding of moral issues rather than from knowledge of either the culture of educated Russia or of the material world. He advocated his philosophy of pacificism, simplicity, and humility in stories about how to live a proper life.

The rejection of the values of the marketplace characteristic of Posrednik publications under Tolstoy's influence was epitomized by Tolstoy's fable, "How a Little Devil Redeemed a Hunk of Bread." The story is about a devil who steals bread from a poor peasant, but is outraged when the peasant does not begrudge his loss; rather, the peasant concludes that whoever took the bread probably needed the food more than he. The devil plots revenge for the peasant's altruism. He teaches him to plant grain in swampy land in a dry year and on a hill in a wet year. The peasant prospers while others go hungry, and he soon begins to distill alcohol with his surplus grain. His soul is lost, the devil explains, not because of the alcohol, but because of the surplus. The use of the supernatural to make the point underlines the difference between these tales and their commercial counterparts.

Semenov wrote more down-to-earth tales than Tolstoy, but he also aimed to instruct. He warned readers of the perils of the city and of materialism in such tales as *Happiness is Not in Money* and *A Good Life*. Nekrasova complained that such works discouraged readers from an active involvement in life by teaching to "Resign yourself, be humble, be patient, do not oppose evil, turn away from riches, prefer physical labor."[151]

Posrednik's *Proverbs for Everyday* (1887) began with "To live is to serve God" and "Man is not born for himself," but the book also contained practical suggestions about farming and finding work during the winter. For example, learning a winter craft that could be performed at home was better than going to the city and risking corruption, according to the advice for January. This was the booklet in which Tolstoy inveighed against superstition and offered a thousand rubles to any sorcerer who could harm him with a spell.[152]

Few great writers besides Tolstoy were published by Posrednik, since the editors sought works that conveyed a Tolstoyan message. Of the first fifty titles, thirteen were by Tolstoy. The dissemination by Posrednik of carefully selected works of belles lettres and the success of the enterprise encouraged other efforts to bring the literature of educated Russia into the experience of the common people.

Posrednik published more than 12 million copies in the first four years of its existence, and distributed 8 million copies of books issued by other culturist organizations.[153] The secret of Posrednik's success was the merger of the genius of Tolstoy with that of Sytin. Sytin had developed

Fig. 20. *Proverbs for Every Day* (Moscow: Posrednik [Intermediary],
1887).

a network of peddlers for his own extensive publishing operations, which eventually became the largest in Russia. The peddlers carried the Posrednik books along with Sytin's regular lubok publications. Both Tolstoy and Sytin ceased to be actively involved in Posrednik toward the end of the century, but the firm continued to thrive under the management of I. I. Gorbunov-Posadov from 1897 until 1917.[154] According to the back cover of one of the Posrednik publications, more than a thousand titles were published between 1885 and 1908, and most were priced at less than five kopecks.[155] By 1908 Posrednik was publishing on many subjects, including lives of saints, popular medicine, temperance, agronomy, and vegetarianism, as well as stories by Tolstoy; the firm ranked fifth in Russia by number of copies published (1.7 million), and sixth by the value of sales operations.[156] According to the 1906 catalogue, the firm's offerings were sharply divided among the small booklets, such as Tolstoy's stories that sold for as little as a kopeck and a half, the tales of peasant life by Semenov and others for three kopecks, and more expensive works, such as *The Thoughts of Mazzini* and *Christianity and International Peace*. The firm published a broader selection of works over time, but the basic ideological perspective established in the 1880s and early 1890s was retained.

The success of Posrednik after its separation from the Sytin firm was very likely due to its popularity among those who purchased for libraries, schools, and other institutions of mass education. By 1906, Gorbunov-Posadov could claim ten prizes from such organizations as the St. Petersburg and Moscow literacy societies and various zemstvo committees.[157]

Other publishers soon followed the lead of Posrednik. The most important of the projects stimulated by Posrednik were those of the editors of the magazines *Russkoe bogatstvo* (Russian Wealth) and *Russkaia mysl* (Russian Thought). Like the editors of Posrednik, the editors of these publications were committed to the idea of a special literature for the people. The editors of the *Russkoe bogatstvo* series, for example, sought to provide illustrations of "virtue, vice, merit, and shortcomings in the private and social life of the peasantry."[158] The firm's publications had titles such as *Don't Throw Good Money after Bad* and *How the Peasant Peter Guzhov Acquired Money in Moscow*. These stories illustrated the idea that city life was an inferno of vice and temptation. The peasant family of Peter Guzhov was destroyed when a son went to Moscow to work, was corrupted by city ways, and unwittingly lured the rest of the family to the capital and to their doom.[159]

Revolutionary populists also frequently stressed the virtues of rural life in the booklets they produced for the peasants, but in addition they were concerned with explaining social and economic causes of poverty.[160] Censorship proved an effective barrier to the distribution of their publications, but the works were probably not flashy enough to win an audience on the open market. They might have found a substantial readership, however, through the intercession of sympathetic teachers and educators. Tracts written in the style of folklore, such as *The Clever Trick* and *The Story of a Kopeck*, circulated among a very small audience and had little significance outside revolutionary circles. The special people's literatures of a populist inspiration, whether radical or moderate, like the works of Semenov, were never genuinely popular, even though works of this type continued to appear in the early twentieth century.

The alternatives to publications with a special message for the common reader were generally belles lettres and popular science. The earliest attempts to publish belles lettres for the people date from the early 1870s, when the Pskov landowner Fan-der-flit and his co-editor, A. Kochetov, founded "The People's Edition" to provide the common people with works of worthy writers.[161] The booklets sold at prices ranging from 6 to 35 kopecks, too high for the individual peasant purchaser. Some respectable commercial firms began to publish "people's editions" in the 1870s and 1880s, most notably that of A. S. Suvorin, the editor of a conservative St. Petersburg daily. By 1895, 3.8 million copies of books in Suvorin's series, "The Inexpensive Library," had been sold, including works of Russian and foreign authors, as well as translations of Latin and Greek classics.[162] The prices were too high for lower-class readers (25 kopecks), so the books probably went to school libraries and other institutional repositories.

V. N. Marakuev was another private publisher whose work exemplified the efforts of idealistic private individuals to reach the common people with good Russian and foreign literature. He decided to "go to the people, to the masses of the people," as he put it in 1884, "with literature and science" to liberate them "from superstition" and to provide them with what is "true in our literature."[163] He felt that the literature presented to the people should be selected to be "positive in the sense of a positive type, . . . a positive Russian idea."[164] Marakuev's series began to appear in 1882, and included translations of Dickens and Shakespeare, as well as selections from Russian literature. He failed to convince colporteurs to sell his works and thus had to distribute them himself.[165]

The effort to spread belles lettres and popular science among the common people was furthered by the work of several private committees on literacy and education, and by the activity of the district and provincial zemstvo organizations. The St. Petersburg Literacy Committee (1861-95) was organized to support primary schooling, to publish books for the people, and to gather information related to these activities. Leo Tolstoy and I. S. Turgenev, as well as other representatives of Russian intellectual life such as A. F. Pogosskii, participated. By 1865 the committee had 528 members, and by 1895 membership had risen to 1,025.[166] The committee published nearly two million copies between 1880 and 1895.[167] The last years of its existence were quite active ones and provoked the ire of the authorities, who placed it under the control of the Ministry of Education in November 1895; it was reorganized and renamed the St. Petersburg Literacy Society. Six hundred members left in protest.[168] The Moscow Literacy Committee (1845-95), which was engaged in similar activities, was closed at the same time. The Kharkov Society for Spreading Literacy Among the People (1869-191?) apparently did not suffer the same fate.

The St. Petersburg committee favored works of belles lettres in its selection of titles for publication rather than special creations for the people, except in the area of popular science. The first books it published in the 1880s were works of Pushkin, Gogol, Lermontov, Shevchenko, and other noted writers. An initial attempt to publish selections from the Gospels was rebuffed by the Synod.[169] In the 1890s the committee shifted its selections to more contemporary writers, including Korolenko, Garshin, and other lesser-known authors, who described rural life in clear critical tones. The committee's publications were exclusively secular, and stories such as Garshin's "Four Days" and Korolenko's "Murderer" contrasted sharply with more patriotic and benign visions of Russian life presented in official and semiofficial works. "Faithful to the worldly truths of life at the end of the nineteenth century," wrote the committee's historian, "the publications of the committee sketch before us the painful picture of the material needs of the simple people, . . . their struggle, . . . and the conditions of their reality."[170] Commenting on the publications of the former St. Petersburg Literacy Society in 1895, a reviewer in the Church school magazine complained that with few exceptions the committee's publications were depressing. Peasant family life as described in the committee's works was a picture of "complete depravity and licentiousness."[171]

Zemstvo publishing activity was similar to that of the literacy committees. Zemstvos published primarily informational works, classics, and other belles lettres, rather than spiritual and moralistic texts. Zemstvo activists were drawn into publishing by their culturist ideals and by the opportunities to satisfy the needs of zemstvo educational institutions for books. Regulations limited zemstvo publishing activities and resulted in the preponderance of works communicating practical economic information, since production of these works conformed with the legal man-

FIG. 21. N. V. Gogol, *The Fair at Sorochintsii* (St. Petersburg: St. Petersburg Literacy Society, 1909).

343

date of the zemstvos. Eleven zemstvos had their own printing presses by 1904.[172] The most significant of their periodicals was the *Viatka Agricultural and Cottage Industry Newspaper*. Founded in 1894 as a biweekly, the Viatka paper soon became a weekly for the captive subscribership of the zemstvo schools and libraries within the province. In 1898 the paper had a circulation of 5,000 copies, distributed free of charge primarily to schools and libraries. At first the paper contained mainly information about agriculture, but later it expanded to include articles about natural science, belles lettres, and subjects of general interest. Short stories by contemporary writers, such as Korolenko and Mamin-Sibiriak, also appeared in the paper. Other zemstvos attempted, without much success, to publish periodicals for the common people, and some also published informative pamphlets, but this was on a moderate scale.

A leader in the publication of popular science and other educational materials was F. F. Pavlenkov (1839-1900), a radical activist of the 1860s who subsequently turned his attention to cultural work. He published schoolbooks, works of Russian and foreign authors, and three very successful series, "The Popular Science Library for the People" (1890-1913), "The Library of Useful Knowledge" (1890-96), and "The Lives of Significant People" (1890-1915). Pavlenkov's books were generally too expensive for individual peasants or workers. Several books in his "Illustrated Pushkin Library," however, sold for as little as 2 kopecks, and a few stories in the "Illustrated Gogol Library" cost 3 and 4 kopecks.

Despite close observation by the censor, Pavlenkov was able to create and market profitably an extensive body of popular instructional and literary material that was very much in accordance with his culturist vision and his understanding of the kind of information that should be widely disseminated among the common people. His series "Lives of Significant People" included works on religious figures, state leaders and national heroes, scholars and scientists, philosophers, philanthropists and educators, explorers, inventors, writers, artists, musicians, and actors. The selection reflected Pavlenkov's valuation of who was a significant person. Of the 198 biographies available in 1910, almost one-third were writers, and half of these were Russian writers. The presentations were occasionally rather tendentious. For instance, the author of the booklet *N. V. Gogol* (1910), A. N. Annenskaia, tried to reconcile Gogol's unwelcome conservative political and religious pronouncements with his social service as a writer. "As a thinker and a moralist," she explained, "Gogol stood lower than the foremost people of his time, but from his early years he was animated by a noble striving to benefit society and a lively sympathy for human suffering."[173]

The dreams of Pavlenko, Rubakin, and others of a mass of serious publications for the common people were partially realized during the period of the Revolution of 1905 and afterward, when the ending of prepublication censorship made possible the appearance of many new types of publications. One of the most active new publishing firms was Don Speech, which issued 12 million copies, primarily works of belles lettres, between 1903 and 1907.[174] The firm specialized in the shorter works of realist writers who demonstrated social commitment, such as Andreev, Korolenko, Gorky, and Kuprin. Works selected by the firm, like those chosen earlier by the St. Petersburg Literacy Committee, tended toward a critical perspective on Russian life. As the educator N. Malinovskii observed, they illustrated the vast extent "of the people's poverty, ignorance, and brutality."[175] Don Speech was closed in 1907, and other new companies that published during the same period such as Znanie (Knowledge), the Viatka Company, and Prosveshchenie (Enlightenment) were either shut down, as was the Viatka Company, or failed. Books in the realistic style that were favored by these firms, however, continued to be produced by more commercial firms, such as that of Sytin.

The final years of the old regime, the period of war and revolution stretching from the first years of the century to 1917, brought significant changes in the character of the publications for the people. Over the course of the last decade and a half of the nineteenth century and the first dozen years of the twentieth, an enormous quantity of books was published for the common reader by commercial and noncommercial presses for distribution through the educational network. There was a gradual shift away from the publication of special people's books by noncommercial enterprises, however, and enlightenment activists increasingly relied on commercial firms to supply them with printed material they found acceptable for the common reader. As early as 1890 the educator Ia. Abramov observed that since "the same works published by the St. Petersburg Literacy Committee, or at least the same types of works, are published by private and even lubok publishers, the Committee is naturally driven from the book market."[176] His comments were perhaps premature, but many of the special publications for the people that flourished in the late nineteenth century ceased to be important in the twentieth, particularly after the 1905 Revolution. Although the St. Petersburg and Moscow literacy committees were reorganized in 1896, they never regained their earlier importance.[177] The large culturist firms such as Posrednik and Polza (Use) continued to expand in the post 1905 period, but they did not keep pace with their more commercial competitors. The firm of Sytin, the largest in Russia, was by 1909 publishing 3.2 million textbooks, almost five times the number it had published in 1899, and had increased its share of the growing textbook market.[178] One zemstvo commentator observed in 1904, "One can say with certainty that the Moscow zemstvo school cannot get by without such great publishing firms of Petersburg as Poluboiarinov, Lukovnikov, and Uchebnyi Magazin, just as the Petersburg schools cannot get by without Dumnov, D. Tikhomirov, K. Tikhomirov, and Sytin."[179] A new kind of commercial book market had formed. By 1909 Sytin was producing well over a third of all religious reading matter and people's books—a category that included lubok works—issued in Russia, as well as religious texts intended for distribution through the Church school network.[180] Even patriotic material came primarily from private firms such as Sytin's. In 1909 the firm issued 1.4 million portraits of the tsar and members of the royal family—an increase from 900,000 in 1899. A glance at the Sytin catalogue for 1914 shows the wide variety of educational works, cheap editions of Russian classics, and publications in series such as "The Popular Religious Library" that comprised part of the regular production of the large commercial publishing firm.

A dramatic change in the kinds of unofficial sponsored materials for the common reader in the last years of the old regime was the increase in more narrowly political texts and the decline in the traditional enlightenment works. The Revolution of 1905 and its aftermath brought a flood of literature on political and social questions. Rubakin estimated that in the two or three years of the revolutionary period nearly 60 million "progressive" political pamphlets, as well as a mass of other pamphlets, were released. By his calculation, the political pamphlets consisted of 24 million copies of materials associated with the Socialist Revolutionary Party, 26 million copies of Social Democratic works, and 8 to 10 million copies of anarchist publications.[181] The Wolf Bookstore catalogue listed 1,699 brochures, of which 250 were Socialist Revolutionary, 426 Kadet, 70 anarchist, and 953 Social Democratic works. In 1906 the Kadet publishing house, Narodnoe pravo, issued over 700,000 booklets at 5 kopecks or less. These works were sold through sympathetic bookstores and by local party committees.[182] Among the political materials were many new party periodicals, but none of them achieved anything approaching the circulation of the big commercial dailies after 1905, partly because of the limits imposed by the censors. The autocracy's success in crushing the Revolution of 1905 put an end to radical pamphleteering until 1917, when another flood of such materials appeared.

Distribution Networks for Sponsored Publications

The same motivations that led people to become active in the publication of sponsored works of popular literature encouraged participation in programs and institutions of adult education that served to distribute sponsored materials to their intended audience. The Church, the state, and competing groups of private citizens used a wide variety of means for this purpose. For the state and the Church, the parish clergy, local officials, the military, employees of the Trusteeship of the People's Temperance, and members of a number of conservative and religious organizations served as bearers of the message. For "society," as liberal educated Russians liked to refer to themselves, the conduits were the zemstvos, private organizations such as the literacy committees, Sunday schools, and other educational institutions permitted by the government.

The so-called "new intelligentsia" also served as a vital conduit of printed material to the common reader. Trade unions and cooperatives became an important source of books and periodicals for ordinary people in the early twentieth century, and these organizations were likely to have been staffed at the lower levels by people with little education. So were local libraries. There were 13,000 "people's libraries" in the empire in 1911, according to the school census taken in that year.[183] There were also factory libraries, urban public libraries and reading rooms, and libraries associated with trade unions, cooperatives, and other voluntary organizations. In addition, institutions such as "houses of culture" and "people's universities," which were supported by public and private funds, also provided some of these services, and radical activists participated when they could.

Public readings were the most important forum for presentation of the printed word to common people, and readings were held in the major cities in the late nineteenth century and throughout the countryside in the early twentieth. Public readings were first held at a few urban locations in 1869; in 1876 readings were permitted in provincial capitals, and in the 1890s readings from a restricted list of texts were allowed in the countryside. Rules issued in 1901 facilitated readings at primary schools, and this became a common supplementary activity of teachers and a popular form of public entertainment in rural areas. A magic lantern show was usually part of the program by the 1890s. Readings were organized by private individuals, teachers, and priests, or they were sponsored by various philanthropic and educational organizations, such as the commissions on public reading and the Trusteeship of the People's Temperance. There were roughly 200,000 public readings at over 15,000 primary schools in 1910 alone.[184]

An army of enlighteners was needed to staff these institutions and to carry out their functions. Many people who participated in these activities understood book distribution to be more than the physical task of transporting the book to the reader. The book had to be properly presented and interpreted, and its lessons pointed out. Activists who held this view considered themselves to be engaged in dissemination of the process of reading and of the particular message of the work, and they did not feel that they could trust the peddlers or urban book vendors to fulfill this important task.

Schoolteachers, priests, and others whose work put them in direct contact with the common people and who were highly educated were especially active in the effort to distribute books and interpret their meanings. Many of these people lent books to readers or simply gave them as gifts. Significant numbers of books owned by peasants in the late 1880s in three primarily agricultural villages in Voronezh Province, near the Don River, were received as gifts, according to lists submitted to Prugavin in 1889. In one village, many of whose inhabitants produced handicrafts or engaged in off-farm labor, a third of the seventy-seven books found were gifts. In a second village, gifts accounted for eleven of seventy-one books, but only three of these derived from the clergy. In a third village, there were nearly two hundred books, of which about twenty were described as gifts. The sources of the gifts were not identified, but more than half were secular titles, primarily schoolbooks.[185] The informal distribution of books as gifts and by lending can only have increased in the early twentieth century, as inexpensive books became increasingly available. A pedagogical author in 1905 observed that "enterprising people" and "lovers of reading" were buying books especially to give to peasants to read, in some cases free of charge, and in others for a fee of a few kopecks a month.[186] According to one early twentieth-century study of 13,074 books in peasant possession, 26 percent were gifts, 5 percent were purchased from churches and monasteries, another 5 percent were purchased from zemstvo book centers, 31 percent were bought in villages from peddlers or at fairs, and 24 percent were purchased in cities or outside the province.[187]

The well-educated activists who distributed the printed material were financially independent and could act according to their ideological convictions in their dealings with the common people, whether in the countryside or in the cities. The lower-level cultural workers were more dependent on the people with whom they worked, and therefore were more responsive to local demand. A financially independent activist could try to press a favorite work on an unwilling or unenthusiastic group of readers, but the local schoolteacher or parish priest was more likely to consider both ideological convictions and local preferences in order to strengthen the prestige of the printed word and of the local church or school. Teachers also wished to demonstrate the importance of the secular word. The questions that should be answered in people's literature, according to one teacher who wrote Rubakin, were: "What is the universe?

What is the world in general? What is man in particular? . . . How must and should humanity live?"[188]

Teachers were natural intermediaries between educated Russia and the common people, and also the most evident distributors of the printed word. Their status in the community was linked to their success in demonstrating the value of literacy, the usefulness of books, and their own authority over a kind of knowledge that many of the parents of their pupils and potential pupils did not yet possess. The precarious position of teachers in the countryside, their dependence on community support, their need to maintain enrollments and to guide their students successfully through the examination provided ample incentives for them to distribute books, even when the school had no library. Although the private sale of books by schoolteachers was illegal in the schools under the authority of the Ministry of Education until 1904, many of them sold books anyway.[189] A parish schoolteacher from Riazan Province who corresponded with Rubakin described a police search-and-seizure of his stock of books at the turn of the century. The raid netted works by the realist writers Korolenko and Garshin, and by the radical critics Dobroliubov and Belinsky.[190]

As cheap editions of works of Russian literature and popular science became increasingly available, teachers could more easily provide their communities with books. "Many teachers, fulfilling the requests of pupils, adolescents, and adult peasants, have to buy books of their own choice during trips to the city," wrote a commentator in a symposium published by a pedagogical journal in 1911.[191] "This phenomenon is noted not only in remote places," he continued, "but even in the comparatively cultured settlements near Moscow."

Popular science and the Russian classics were emphasized in the secular distribution of printed material because these were the works the rank and file of enlighteners felt the ordinary people should read. The early twentieth-century experience of the Saratov Men's Sunday School shows the prevalence of these kinds of works in the adult education programs. Much of the secular instruction at the Saratov school was organized around "explanatory readings." For the semiliterates, readings were presented on the themes: how people live now, how people lived before, where people live, about peoples and states, and about Russia. The readings included geography and history, popular science, and literature. Literature was used to provide information about the world and society. About two-thirds of the books borrowed from the library were works of Russian belles lettres, primarily those of Gorky, Tolstoy, Korolenko, Chekhov, Dostoevsky, Gogol, and Pushkin. Readings for the Easter holiday included Nekrasov, Chekhov, and Nikitin. Among the pamphlets read by the semiliterate group, the one on Russian literature was the most popular. The students' response to works of popular science was described graphically in the school's annual report for 1905:

It was interesting to see the confused faces of the pupils when the teacher turned to them with unexpected questions, such as "Why does the moon wane?" The question hits simple people on the head like a hammer. The most terrifying thing about these questions is that they are natural and spontaneous. The pupil was embarrassed because he was shocked to realize that such a natural question had never come into his head.[192]

Teachers' comments suggest that popular science could be difficult to present to peasant listeners. A teacher in St. Petersburg Province remarked in 1887 that natural science texts had no success with either children or adults. The listeners complained, "Again those butterflies! We are fed up."[193] Teachers could present popular science more successfully when a practical demonstration of the worth of the information was possible. For example, when the horses of a village in Vologda Province were threatened by anthrax in 1909, the teacher had no trouble gathering the peasants together for a reading about the disease and its proper treatment.[194] Readings about public health and hygiene were often conducted by feldshers or doctors rather than schoolteachers. After the Revolution of 1905, medical lecturers traveled widely with brochures and slides.[195]

In the early twentieth century, even officially sponsored readings, such as those under the auspices of the Trusteeship of the People's Temperance, featured a mixture of popular science and Russian classics. By 1905 most of the texts used in the Moscow readings sponsored by the Trusteeship were works of literature. According to the 1905 report, at 119 Trusteeship readings in that year, half the titles were literary, 30 percent were scientific, and only 20 percent were religious.[196] Literary texts were chosen by the Trusteeship to emphasize patriotism and military heroism. Some works of the classics were included, however, and the authors of the Trusteeship's 1904 Moscow report explained, "The Commission strives to support interest in the timeless untendentious artistic creations of the classical writers of the Russian land: Gogol, Pushkin, Tolstoy, Turgenev, and others."[197]

The increasing emphasis on Russian writers as symbols of national pride was also evident in special literary evenings. Prugavin described a literary evening for villagers in the late 1880s that included singing and reading from the works of Pushkin, Nekrasov, and Turgenev, as well as a short commentary on Peter the Great.[198] At a reading in a Church school in 1902, writers were compared to priests: "Talented writers also perform a great service to the people in the matter of moral development.

They awaken and develop in us the best feelings for truth, goodness, and beauty."[199]

Revolutionaries found that the same sorts of materials were also suitable for their purposes, if properly interpreted. N. K. Krupskaia taught at the Smolensk evening classes for workers from 1891 through 1895, and she conducted a more secular and politically structured program than did the other teachers. In her memoir, Krupskaia describes her reaction when a worker showed her a book, *The Trials of the Virgin*. "How much fanaticism was in this book," she observed. "On how much ignorance was this book based, and, at the same time, how inventively and emotionally was it written!"[200] According to her account, Krupskaia discussed the book with the worker, changed his choice of reading material, and even influenced his son. She used a combination of popular science and works of belles lettres to get her views across to her students. When pupils asked for *Vasilii Churkin*, she gave them Dostoevsky's *Memoirs from the House of the Dead* or *Oliver Twist*.

The popular education movement lost something of its élan in the early twentieth century. Enthusiasm for organized public readings declined as literacy increased and cheap books, brochures, and periodicals became more widely available. Public readings retained their popular appeal primarily in the more backward areas where schools were few and contacts with the book distribution system rare. When the literate common people could purchase printed materials and read them at home at leisure, or when the illiterate could listen to their children or friends read texts of their own choosing, public readings by educators lost their appeal. The informal gatherings of friends drew on a long tradition of group reading and respect for public readers. Printed materials were more abundant in the countryside at this time than in the past, but the available copies still served many readers. A newspaper could be read more quickly by twenty people if one of them read it aloud than if each had a go at it individually.

Informal readings were held widely during World War I. The Moscow Literacy Society organized a special commission in 1915 to help supply rural Russia with newspapers. A teacher from Chernigov Province wrote that peasants formed circles for reading the newspapers.[201] Another account told of a "Reading Cottage" in a village in Penza Province in 1916, in which twenty to thirty people gathered daily to hear the priest and literate peasants read newspapers and the works of Gogol and Tolstoy. Many of the listeners were the wives of soldiers. The provincial zemstvo supplied the reading cottage with maps and brochures.[202] "The contemporary village lives a transformed life," wrote one teacher at this time. "The particularity of this transformation is the peasants' thirst for the printed word."[203]

The common readers' increasing command of literacy was a tribute both to their own efforts and to those of the enlightenment activists and schoolteachers. Cultural activists were not, for the most part, satisfied that the common people had learned the lessons they taught about what and how to read, but there was little they could do about it in the first years of the twentieth century. A new reading public had appeared, and its presence was felt at every level of Russian cultural and intellectual life.

EPILOGUE

LITERACY is one of the building blocks of modern social life, but the skills of reading and writing are significant only when they are used. Since tsarist authorities never made primary education compulsory and probably lacked the power to do so effectively, the decision of ordinary people to become literate was predicated on their understanding of its potential usefulness. The fact that in the late nineteenth century nearly three-quarters of the children in the Russian Empire entered primary school and over half continued into the second year suggests that parents and children did indeed find the skill useful.

In a society with a low level of formal education, literacy could be maintained and developed only through reading. The existence of cheap popular reading material was a prerequisite for the spread of literacy in Russia. Such material had to be of a sort that the newly literate were eager and able to read. In the Russian case, the market proved an effective means for identifying and satisfying the demand of the common reader. Ordinary people showed their preference for commercial popular literature by spending their hard-earned and very few rubles to obtain it. What was extraordinary about Russian popular commercial literature in contrast to Western European and American was its peasant character. Written for peasants and former peasants by people who were close to their world and concerns, it served these often first-generation readers with information and ideas they could readily absorb as they sought to make sense of the changing world around them. To create such a literature, popular writers had to develop a new language for ordinary people, with a shared if limited vocabulary and a common stock of clichés, symbols, and ideas. The establishment of this language of popular communication meant that many ordinary people were able to receive and exchange information through the printed word for the first time. The popular commercial materials in particular contained a fund of shared information that ordinary people could seek out as they needed it. To peasants and former peasants with new expectations and unfamiliar problems to solve, reading about fanciful characters and situations was a crude but simple way of acquiring useful ideas and symbols. The treatment of themes such as national identity, science and superstition, success and mobility, and crime and rebellion answered popular demand and reflected changes in attitudes among those who made up the new reading public.

Popular literature also had a preservative role, and the common reader could find old and familiar truths refurbished. The new in these materials, however, gradually displaced the old and opened the way for new behavior. The early twentieth century was a time of rebellion, and in the popular literature the crushed or penitent rebel gave way to the alternative image of a strong outsider who could solve the problems of society better than the official representatives of order. The existence of new forms of popular communication was one of the differences between the effective popular revolts of the early twentieth century and the doomed peasant rebellions of the past. Popular communication through the printed word facilitated the cumulative build-up of rebellious ideas and the spread of disaffection. The oldest and most serviceable weapon in the ideological arsenal of the autocracy—loyalty to tsar and Church—rusted rapidly when exposed to the atmosphere of change evident in the new commercial popular literature.

Tsarist officials made a conscious decision in the second half of the nineteenth century to promote schooling and to permit popular commercial publishers and authors and a wide variety of private activists to produce and distribute their wares. At the same time, the hesitation of the authorities and the restrictiveness of the official policies stand out, as do the often futile propaganda efforts of the state and the Church. The authorities had come to believe that widespread peasant illiteracy was incompatible with modern industrial and military power, but they wanted to promote literacy and reading in a way that did not threaten longstanding popular beliefs about the tsar and the Church. On this basis, they first permitted the zemstvos to operate schools for peasants, then supported the Church school system to counteract zemstvo activities, and finally sought to gather the reins of primary schooling in their own hands.

The process of development was more spontaneous in the area of publishing than in schooling. This was probably crucial, since only the commercial publishers were able to speak effectively to popular demand. The significance of the commercial system for the production and distribution of popular reading material became apparent after the October Revolution when Soviet authorities took over the publishing industry and the press, destroyed the marketing network of peddlers and small shops, pulped the existing stocks of cheap commercial publications, and then found it difficult to produce printed material of their own that ordinary people could and would read.

The dominant trend in the popular culture of the prerevolutionary era was toward the development of values similar to those found elsewhere in the industrialized world. The producers and distributors of sponsored materials generally accelerated this process. The direction of the sponsored and commercial efforts diverged most sharply in one area: the acceptance of the promise of the market economy. For the commercial writers the allure of individual mobility and success—the escape from a squalid lower-class life into bourgeois comfort—was one of the most effective themes for satisfying customers. To the sponsors of the noncommercial materials, it was a dangerous chimera that misled the lower classes or threatened the stability or appropriate development of society.

Speculation about an inherently Russian pattern of development that predetermined the shape of Soviet society often rests on the premise that Russia was unique either in its popular culture or in its social structure. Each country is in many respects unique, but the social structure of Russia in the last half century of the old regime was rapidly becoming more like that of the West, and so was its popular culture. What clearly distinguished Russia was a strongly felt, clearly formulated, and widely held antipathy to the functioning of the market economy. This was perhaps a transitional response to the dislocations and stress of rapid development by the more articulate members of society. In the cultural sphere it was expressed by scorn for the market as a mechanism for dissemination of the printed word, objection to cultural diversity and elitism exemplified by the appearance of both popular culture and literary modernism, and distaste for the values of individualism and material ambition displayed in commercial popular literature. It is certainly possible to explain this antipathy by reference to the remnants of a premodern social structure, the pace of economic and social change, or even older cultural traditions. The evidence of this study, however, suggests that insofar as the opposition to the values of the market economy, to increasing individualism, and to the idea of personal success was manifest in Russian culture, it did not appear primarily among the newly literate common people, but rather among other social groups.

The newly literate consumers of lubok publications and the cheap periodicals presumably had no complaint with the commercial enterprise of popular literature. The opposition to this aspect of the market economy, however, was not restricted to a small circle of radical *intelligenty*. It is sometimes argued that the narrow pursuit of an ideological mirage on the part of the intelligentsia plunged Russia into revolution and ultimately set the course for the development of Soviet society. Repugnance for the values of the market as they were expressed in the popular literature was not limited to the intelligentsia, but seems to have extended to the middle ranks of Russian society, including such people as school-teachers, priests, civil servants, and technicians in industry, agriculture, and local government. For the semi-educated generally, and for those engaged in popular education in particular, the notion of a common heritage in which all could share was an important alternative to the popular culture.

Condemnation is clearly neither censorship nor prohibition, but the diatribes against popular commercial literature during the prerevolutionary period showed both an intolerance for the cultural diversity characteristic of modern industrial society and a telling lack of respect for the preferences of the lower classes. The Bolsheviks had the active support of only a minority of educated people in their program to remake Russia, but both revolutionary and nonrevolutionary Russians who participated in cultural life often shared a conviction that cultural choices could be curtailed in the name of high ideals. The literature of the lubok and the popular commercial periodicals were prime targets of this unofficial censure. So was literary modernism—the elite and esoteric belles lettres that also belied hopes for a unified culture in which all could share.

Popular commercial literature was useful to the newly literate common readers in understanding the modern world. It contained information that was not readily available elsewhere to the lower classes. Its authors spun dreams of material success and individual advancement embellished with much fable and fancy. The repudiation of this literature and the market values it contained by educated and semi-educated people stemmed from a wider hostility toward the market system, with its attendant inequality and strife. Those who found the literature of the lubok and the commercial periodicals most pernicious saw them as obstacles on the path to a brighter future for all Russians. To deny the common people the right to pick and choose what to read and to restrict the information available to them, however, was to limit their freedom and to add new barriers to the inequalities of education and social status. To ban the new dreams of the market economy from the popular milieu also meant to unhitch at least part of the train of cultural development that had carried many ordinary people into a world of more modern thought and imagination.

BIBLIOGRAPHICAL ESSAY

AND DISCUSSION OF SOURCES

THIS ESSAY is designed to assist those who wish to pursue further the study of Russian prerevolutionary popular literature. My purpose is to provide the specialist with additional information about the sources and methodology I have used. When I began this study I had very few clues to either the location of published materials or the existence of archives that might prove helpful. As I pursued the subject, however, I identified an increasing number of sources, some of which I used fully and others which I neglected. I have made reference to a wide variety of publications in the footnotes, and I will not cite these a second time here. Works of a general and theoretical character are cited in the notes to the Introduction, as are studies of Russian popular literature published after 1917. Prerevolutionary investigations are discussed in Chapter 9.

Information pertinent to this subject is preserved in a number of archives. Archives that I consulted for specific pieces of information are cited in the notes. The only archive I explored extensively was that of N. A. Rubakin—a gigantic collection including correspondence, autobiographies of popular writers, responses to surveys on popular reading and much other relevant material. It is located in the Manuscript Division of the Lenin Library in Moscow (fond 358), and the holdings are described in *Zapiski Otdela rukopisei, Gosudarstvennaia Ordena Lenina biblioteka SSSR imeni V. I. Lenina* (Moscow, 1963). I was fortunately allowed to consult the list of holdings and to order what I wanted from this collection, which contained more information than I could absorb.

My greatest difficulty was to locate and study the popular literature itself. Neither the names of the authors nor the titles of the popular works are usually listed in the general catalogues of Soviet libraries. The cheap periodicals, such as the kopeck newspapers, were also difficult to find when I began my work but are now more readily available. Research in Soviet libraries was further complicated by regulations prohibiting the xeroxing or microfilming of all fiction. The Joseph Regenstein Library of the University of Chicago, however, was able to purchase copies of many works.

I located and used two substantial Soviet collections, those of the Saltykov-Shchedrin Library in Leningrad and of the Lenin Library in Moscow. The Leningrad catalogue proved the most valuable and contains, by my count, 1,529 titles of works of popular fiction, many of which are listed in multiple editions. The catalogue fills twelve file drawers. The entries are divided by subject, but in a very rough and incomplete fashion. Religious lubok titles, which I did not consult, are not in this catalogue but are listed elsewhere in the subject catalogue under the heading "History of Religion. Atheism." Books about black magic, dream interpretation, and other such subjects are also found under this entry. Almanacs, letter-writing guides, and similar works are listed separately elsewhere in the library.

The card files of the popular literature collection are coded, but the code is apparently from the prerevolutionary period and not a current means of identification. The drawers have the following contents (by number):

1. Eighteenth- and nineteenth-century fiction.
2. Fiction, 1896-1917, by author.
3. Crime fiction, plays, lubok versions of Russian and foreign belles lettres.
4. Lubok versions of oral literature.
5. Lubok historical and false historical works.
6. Lubok songbooks, organized by type of song.
7. Lubok songbooks, organized by title.
8. Couplets, anecdotes, satire and humor.
9. Conditionally designated lubok titles (primarily crime stories) and some enlightenment literature for the people, organized by subject.
10. Enlightenment literature for the people, organized by subject.
11. Enlightenment literature for the people.
12. Enlightenment literature for the people.

The Moscow catalogue is part of the special systematic catalogue of the Lenin Library. It contains 727 titles of lubok fiction, by my count, and these were mixed with enlightenment works. Some of the titles are grouped under headings that include fiction, crime, fairy tales and legends, lubok versions of Russian and foreign works, drama, and humor.

Significant holdings outside the Soviet Union include those of the John G. White Department of Folklore, Orientalia, and Chess at the Cleveland Public Library, which contains over a hundred lubok titles. Many of these are songbooks. The titles are listed in the *Catalogue of Folklore, Folklife, and Folksongs* (Boston: G. K. Hall, 1978), pp. 343-48, published by the Cleveland Public Library, with an introduction by the head of the John G. White Collection, Alice N. Loranth. The University of Chicago has a large and growing collection of microfilms and original publications based on the materials I have used.

In order to pose the questions I wished to ask, I had to code and count these materials, since the subject headings in the library catalogues were generally not suitable for my purposes. The "fiction" category was too broad, for example, and that for lubok versions of works of belles lettres was too incomplete to be useful. I coded all titles of popular commercial fiction listed in the two catalogues. Each work was given a subject code, a date of first publication, a date of last publication, and a note on the number of editions. The few works that appeared in many editions over a long period of time were listed in all their editions. Some folk tales and chivalric stories, for example, were listed in all editions so that their popularity could be traced over time. I broke the coded information down into editions published each year, so that a title that, according to my listing, appeared five times between 1865 and 1874 would be counted as appearing in one edition every two years during that period, even if in fact it appeared three times in 1865 and once in 1874. Since most titles had a life of no more than a decade or so and were republished frequently, if at all, this did not seem to me a significant problem. The holdings of the Leningrad and Moscow collections were similar, and I merged the two data sets. The number and percentages of lubok titles on different subjects are described in Tables 8 and 9.

In order to check the representativeness of my sample, I compared my subject headings for the 1890s with the relatively complete listing of lubok titles available in bookshops in 1892 and 1893 compiled by the Moscow Literacy Committee. The results, which are shown in Table 10, suggest that my sample included roughly two-thirds of all editions published in the 1890s, and that it corresponded reasonably well to the subjects at the beginning of the decade.

The most frequently republished lubok titles included fairy tales and chivalrous stories. The frequency with which these titles appeared is described in Tables 11, 12, and 13.

The only subject heading in the library catalogues that I used extensively was the historical one. Despite my difficulties in identifying the subjects of some stories, I found this part of the Leningrad catalogue helpful in determining which historical subjects were most popular. The importance of some subjects, such as Peter the Great, was perhaps understated in the catalogue because some stories are excluded arbitrarily

Table 8. Subjects of Lubok Editions
(in number of editions)

Subjects	1820-49	1850s	1860s	1870s	1880s	1890s	1900s	1910s	All
Folk	74	89	138	179	210	274	191	207	1,362
Chivalry	88	23	76	127	113	143	105	108	783
Instr.	18	5	11	16	21	39	31	33	174
Merchants	20	5	4	3	1	12	12	14	71
Travel	4	6	12	31	22	50	56	55	236
Humor	11	13	21	56	21	28	54	102	306
War	10	20	13	46	54	78	85	232	538
History	39	16	19	32	47	100	100	146	499
Bandits	3	4	28	37	33	60	58	78	301
Crime	13	3	8	9	11	22	129	237	431
Science	10	7	18	27	27	68	61	135	353
Romance	7	4	2	15	27	84	71	267	478
Rom./Crime	0	0	0	0	0	1	8	61	70
Other	7	0	0	2	8	22	33	75	147
Unknown	10	8	14	16	19	83	48	149	347
Total	314	203	364	596	614	1,064	1,042	1,899	6,096

Sources: This table is based on all editions catalogued in the Lenin Library in Moscow and the Saltykov-Shchedrin Library in Leningrad. Rom./Crime refers to stories in which both romance and crime were indicated in the title.

TABLE 9. Subjects of Lubok Editions
(in percentages)

Subjects	1820-49	1850s	1860s	1870s	1880s	1890s	1900s	1910s	All
Folk	24	44	38	30	34	26	18	11	22
Chivalry	28	11	21	21	18	13	10	6	13
Instr.	6	2	3	3	3	4	3	2	3
Merchants	6	2	1	1	0	1	1	1	1
Travel	1	3	3	5	4	5	5	3	4
Humor	4	6	6	9	3	3	5	5	5
War	3	10	4	8	3	7	8	12	9
History	12	8	5	5	9	9	10	8	8
Bandits	1	2	8	6	5	6	6	4	5
Crime	4	1	2	2	2	2	12	12	7
Science	3	3	5	5	4	6	6	7	6
Romance	2	2	1	3	4	8	7	14	8
Rom./Crime	0	0	0	0	0	0	1	3	1
Other	2	0	0	0	1	2	3	4	2
Unknown	3	4	4	3	3	8	5	8	6
Total	99	98	101	101	98	99	100	100	100

Sources: This table is based on all editions catalogued in the Lenin Library in Moscow and the Saltykov-Shchedrin Library in Leningrad. Rom./Crime refers to stories in which both romance and crime were indicated in the title. Totals may not equal 100 due to rounding-off.

361

TABLE 10. Library Catalogues Compared with Moscow
Literacy Committee Lists

Subjects	Library Cat.	(in%)	Literacy Comm.	(in %)
Folk	274	(26)	98	(31)
Chivalry	143	(13)	20	(6)
Instr.	39	(4)	20	(6)
Merchants	12	(1)	2	(1)
Travel	50	(5)	8	(3)
Humor	28	(3)	16	(5)
War	78	(7)	25	(8)
History	100	(9)	36	(12)
Bandits	60	(6)	9	(3)
Crime	22	(2)	16	(5)
Science	68	(6)	24	(4)
Romance	84	(8)	14	(4)
Rom./Crime	1	(0)	0	(0)
Other	22	(2)	24	(8)
Unknown	83	(8)	1	(0)
Total	1,064	(100)	313	(100)

Sources: In this table I compare all titles and editions published in the 1890s and found in the catalogues of the Saltykov-Schedrin and Lenin libraries with those lubok works identified in 1892 and 1893 by the Moscow Literacy Committee and listed in their *Obzor knig dlia narodnogo chteniia i narodnykh kartin 1892* (Moscow, 1893) and *Obzor Knig 1893* (Moscow, 1894).

as "pseudo-historical." The results of my coding of the titles listed in the catalogue are contained in Table 14.

The newspapers were in some respects easier to work with than the lubok tales, since none of the material was missing. The quantity was such, however, that I had to be very selective. For this reason, I concentrated on the kopeck newspapers, whose early twentieth-century success was widely discussed at the time, and I read all the fiction published in the St. Petersburg edition and most of what appeared in the Moscow paper. The allocation of space in the St. Petersburg edition is indicated in Table 15, and the themes of the novels published in the two newspapers are shown in Table 16.

The detective stories and installment novels have suffered most from the wear and tear of time in the Soviet collections, and I was only able to read a limited number of these stories. Information about them is shown in Tables 17, 18, and 19.

The composition of the installment novels published between 1907 and 1914 is shown in Table 20.

The sample of lubok tales that I read in order to study the development

TABLE 11. Most Republished Lubok Titles, 1870-1917
(in number of editions)

Stories	1870s	1880s	1890s	1900s	1910s	Total
Bova	33	27	26	12	32	159
Eruslan	20	19	29	20	28	142
Ivan and Firebird	15	20	30	23	20	125
Humpbacked Horse	9	12	26	18	22	99
Milord Georg	16	12	16	8	10	89
Frantsyl	15	15	18	8	12	86
Guak	15	12	12	14	9	86
Lion and Tsar's Son	7	18	16	9	20	75
Ivan the Knight	6	4	16	12	10	55
Ilia Muromets	7	3	11	13	14	54
Russ. and Kabardinians	10	3	14	4	11	43
Soldier Iashka	7	3	11	13	14	35
Ensign Sword Belt	4	7	9	14	34	0
Soldier Saved Peter	1	1	6	7	12	34
Total Number Editions	161	153	238	170	228	1,116

Source: This table is based on the catalogue of the Saltykov-Shchedrin Library. I have not included characters such as the witch Baba Iaga, who was the subject of many different types of stories.

of the four themes was necessarily selective. Many if not most of the titles listed in the catalogues no longer exist, so I had to read those I could find rather than take a sample from the catalogue. The popularity of the stories about banditry and crime, which are discussed in Chapter 5, is evident from Tables 8 and 9, which also reflect some interest in stories about science.

Similar information is not available about stories with themes on national identity and success. The original publication dates for the stories I used were rarely available, but the date of the surviving edition is nevertheless significant. Stories on these themes were usually short-lived, since the subject matter changed so rapidly, and the fact that a particular story was published in a given year indicates that the ideas it contained were in some sense current. The decades in which the lubok titles discussed in Chapters 6 and 8 were published are shown in Tables 21 and 22.

I attempted to quantify the development of the different themes as I worked with the stories. In some cases, the results were helpful and

TABLE 12. Editions of Five Fairy Tales

Decade	Number of Editions	% of all Lubok Editions
1820-49	6	2
1850s	15	7
1860s	41	11
1870s	44	7
1880s	57	9
1890s	99	9
1900s	75	7
1910s	86	5
Total	423	5

Source: This table is based on the editions of *Ivan the Tsar's Son and the Firebird*, *The Little Humpbacked Horse*, *Ivan the Knight*, *Ilia Muromtsev*, and *The Lion Who Raised the Tsar's Son* that are listed in the catalogue of the Saltykov-Shchedrin Library in Leningrad.

TABLE 13. Editions of Five Chivalrous Tales

Decades	Number of Editions	% of All Lubok Editions
1820-49	44	14
1850s	17	9
1860s	55	15
1870s	99	17
1880s	85	14
1890s	101	9
1900s	62	6
1910s	91	5
Total	554	9

Source: This table contains editions of the five most popular lubok chivalric tales listed in the catalogue of the Saltykov-Shchedrin Library. The tales are those featuring the adventures of Bova, Eruslan, Milord, Frantsyl, and Guak.

TABLE 14. Historical Lubok Tales

Subject	1820-49	1850s	1860s	1870s	1880s	1890s	1900s	1910s	Total
Ermak	0	2	4	5	4	7	8	7	37
Bandits	0	3	0	4	4	1	6	18	36
Peter	1	1	0	0	1	2	7	17	29
Ivan IV	1	1	0	0	1	0	1	1	5
Other tsars	0	0	0	0	0	5	2	6	12
Religious	4	4	1	4	3	4	4	1	25
Pre-14th c.	6	1	0	5	2	10	4	0	28
14th-17th c.	0	0	0	0	0	9	5	6	20
R-Turk. War	0	0	0	0	3	7	10	11	31
Nap. War	1	0	1	0	1	1	0	3	6
Other Wars	1	4	1	1	3	10	6	31	57
Other	0	8	1	2	8	13	9	34	75

Source: Catalogue of historical lubok tales in the Saltykov-Shchedrin Library

TABLE 15. Content of St. Petersburg *Kopeika*
(allotment of space per issue in percentages)

Subject	1913	1917
Foreign affairs	12	10
Domestic politics	4	8
Workers and urban life	5	9
Peasant and rural life	1	0
Culture and education	5	5
Entertainment and fiction	11	13
Police, law, crime	8	3
News briefs	9	9
Religion	1	1
Army/WWI	0	17
Advertisements	43	24
Other	1	1
Total space	100	100

Source: Gazeta kopeika, January 4-10, 1913, and January 4-10, 1917.

TABLE 16. Themes of Kopeck Novels

Themes	SPB *Kopeika* (1908-17)	M *Kopeika* (1909-10)
Bandits	7	1
Crime	6	2
Adventure	8	1
Supernatural	4	0
War	7	1
Revolution	2	3
Other	0	1
Total	34	9

revealing, and in others less so. The extent of interest in different nationalities in the lubok fiction is shown in Table 23. The number of stories in which Russians are taken captive by the non-Western peoples is shown in Table 24.

This sort of analysis proved particularly useful in the chapter on success. The types of success the protagonists sought are shown in Table 25, and the means they used to achieve it are shown in Table 26.

TABLE 17. Detective Serials
(in number of copies, in thousands)

Heroes	1907	1908	1909	1910	1911	1912	1913	1914	1915	Total
Pinkerton	55	3,706	1,042	246	72	243	229	0	575	6,168
Carter	0	1,558	884	98	72	92	82	0	280	3,066
American*	0	365	53	0	0	0	0	0	0	418
Holmes	47	2,141	934	81	60	162	157	0	291	3,873
Lister	0	0	605	124	72	0	0	0	335	1,136
Women	0	451	7	0	0	0	0	0	0	458
Russian	0	400	542	45	0	0	0	0	0	987
Other	0	1,314	891	715	0	31	0	0	0	2,951
Total	102	9,935	4,958	1,309	276	528	468	0	1,481	19,057

*American heroes other than Pinkerton and Carter.
Source: Detective adventures listed at 15 kopecks or less in Knizhnaia letopis' (1907-15).

TABLE 18. Number of Installments per Detective Serial

Heroes	1907	1908	1909	1910	1911	1912	1913	1914	1915	Total
Pinkerton	6	123	49	15	6	16	28	0	46	289
Carter	0	54	51	7	6	8	9	0	24	159
American*	0	23	6	0	0	0	0	0	0	29
Holmes	9	218	61	6	5	14	21	0	25	359
Lister	0	0	48	8	6	0	0	0	18	80
Women	0	40	2	0	0	0	0	0	0	42
Russian	0	20	31	13	0	0	0	0	0	64
Other	0	102	120	25	0	7	0	0	0	254
Total	15	580	368	74	23	45	58	0	113	1,276

*American heroes other than Pinkerton and Carter.
Source: Detective adventures listed at 15 kopecks or less in Knizhnaia letopis' (1907-15).

TABLE 19. Size of Editions of Detective Serials
(in thousands of copies)

Heroes	1907	1908	1909	1910	1911	1912	1913	1914	1915
Pinkerton	9	30	21	16	12	15	8	0	13
Carter	0	29	17	14	12	12	11	0	12
American*	0	16	9	0	0	0	0	0	0
Holmes	5	10	15	14	12	12	8	0	12
Lister	0	0	13	13	12	0	0	0	19
Women	0	11	4	0	0	0	0	0	0
Russian	0	20	18	4	0	0	0	0	0
Other	0	13	7	29	0	4	0	0	0
All	7	17	14	13	12	12	8	0	13

*American heroes other than Pinkerton and Carter.
Source: Knizhnaia letopis' (1907-15).

TABLE 20. Themes of Installment Novels
(in numbers of titles)

Theme	1907	1908	1909	1910	1911	1912	1913	1914	Total
Crime & Detection	2	7	5	9	9	4	4	2	42
Bandits	0	7	10	9	4	11	4	2	48
Women	0	4	2	11	11	8	3	1	40
Other	0	6	3	10	5	5	5	2	36
Adventure	0	1	1	3	1	0	0	0	6
Foreign Classics	0	1	0	5	1	0	0	1	8
Totals	2	26	21	47	30	27	16	8	170

Note: Novels published over two years or more are counted in each year that they were published.
Source: Knizhnaia letopis' (1907-14).

TABLE 21. Decades in Which Lubok Stories about National
Identity Were Published

Decade	No. of Stories	Decade	No. of Stories
1840s	2	1880s	2
1850s	3	1890s	13
1860s	1	1900s	8
1870s	2	1910s	24
		Total	55

TABLE 22. Decades in Which Lubok Success Stories Were Published

Decade	No. of Stories	Decade	No. of Stories
1850s	1	1890s	17
1860s	3	1900s	10
1870s	1	1910s	21
1880s	2	Total	55

TABLE 23. Nationalities Appearing in Lubok Tales

Nationalities	Number of Titles	Nationalities	Number of Titles
Turks	13	Uzbeks	2
Germans	13	Georgians	2
Tatars	12	Gypsies	2
Poles	8	Bulgarians	2
Circassians	6	Ukrainians	2
Jews	4	Armenians	1
W. Europeans	4	Chinese	1
Lithuanians	3	Persians	1
Turkmen	2		

Note: Taken from fifty-five lubok tales with national-identity themes.

TABLE 24. Lubok Stories about Captivity

	Non-West	West	Other	Total
Captivity	16	1	0	17
No captivity	13	24	1	38
Total	29	25	1	55

TABLE 25. Types of Success in Sample of Lubok Stories

Success	No. of Stories
Peasant farming	1
Money in the village	4
Rural job or rural trade	3
City job or city trade	8
Adoption by a patron	9
Owning a shop or enterprise	6
Fame or artistic success	3
A good marriage	7
Regaining position as gentry	3
Money in the city	1
Total	45

Note: It was not possible to identify the type of success sought in some stories in which the protagonist failed.

TABLE 26. Means to Success in Sample of Lubok Stories

Means	No. of Stories
Education and Reading	15
Work and/or Pluck	7
Cleverness or Guile	4
Talent	1
Suffering and Patience	4
Luck and/or Honesty	3
Total	34

Note: The means to success are considered only in those stories in which the hero or heroine attains his or her objectives.

NOTES

Frequently cited works in the Notes can be identified by the following abbreviations:

EZh	Ezhemesiachnyi zhurnal	RSH	Russkaia shkola
IKMV	Izvestiia knizhnykh magazinov t-va M. O. Vol'f	RV	Russkii vestnik
		S	Strannik
ISSSR	Istoriia SSSR	SL	Sovremennaia letopis'
IV	Istoricheskii vestnik	SM	Sovremennyi mir
KL	Knizhnaia letopis'	SO	Sovremennoe obozrenie
KV	Knizhnyi vestnik	SV	Severnyi vestnik
MB	Mir Bozhii	SZN	Saratovskaia zemskaia nedelia
NO	Narodnoe obrazovanie	TsGALI	Tsentral'nyi gosudarstvennyi arkhiv literatury i isskustva SSSR
NSh	Narodnaia shkola		
NP	Nash put'		
NPDE	Nashe pechatnoe delo	TsV	Tserkovnyi vestnik
NoPD	Novoe pechatnoe delo	UiSh	Uchitel' i shkola
O	Obrazovanie	VE	Vestnik Evropy
OZ	Otechestvennye zapiski	VK	Vestnik kooperatsii
PO	Provoslavnoe obozrenie	VNU	Vestnik narodnogo uchitelia
PS	Pravoslavnyi sobesednik	VS	Voennyi sbornik
RB	Russkoe bogatstvo	VV	Vestnik vospitaniia
RM	Russkaia mysl'	VZ	Vestnik znaniia
RNU	Russkii narodnyi uchitel'	ZhMNP	Zhurnal Ministerstva Narodnogo Prosveshcheniia
RO	Russkoe obozrenie		

INTRODUCTION

1. These changes in material life during the nineteenth and early twentieth centuries are charted in the remarkable maps of the *Russkii istoriko-etnografi-cheskii atlas "Russkie"* (Moscow, 1963).

2. There are many studies about how to measure and define literacy, and much argument about what literacy signifies. The discussion has shifted from arguments about literacy rates and the evidence for literacy to consideration of the context in which the skill was practiced. A broad-ranging discussion of current historical issues is found in *Literacy in Historical Perspective*, ed. Daniel P. Resnick (Washington, D.C.: Library of Congress, 1982). Harvey Graff's *Literacy in History: An Interdisciplinary Research Bibliography* (New York: Greenwood Press, 1981) is an excellent systematic bibliography. Other similarly useful works include

Literacy in Traditional Societies, ed. Jack R. Goody (Cambridge, Eng.: Cambridge University Press, 1969); L. Stone, "Literacy and Education in England, 1640-1900," *Past and Present*, no. 42 (1969), pp. 69-139; F. Furet and J. Ozouf, *Lire et écrire: L'Alphabétisation des Français de Calvin à Jules Ferry* (Paris: Editions de Minuit, 1977).

3. There are many contemporary theories about how literacy spreads, why people attend school, and the effects of schooling. An excellent summary of these diverse approaches is John E. Craig, "The Expansion of Education," *Review of Research in Education*, vol. 9 (1981), pp. 151-213. The theory that proved most useful to me in understanding the prerevolutionary Russian case is the theory of human capital, which perceives education as an investment in people. It is applied particularly in the section on literacy and schooling but was useful for this entire study. Classic works in this area are T. W. Schultz, "Investment in Human Capital," *American Economic Review*, no. 51 (1961), and *Transforming Traditional Agriculture* (New Haven, Conn.: Yale University Press, 1964), and Gary S. Becker, *Human Capital* (New York: Columbia University Press for NBER, 1964). Evidence that the spread of literacy depends in part on consumer demand and perceived benefits is found in David F. Mitch, "The Spread of Literacy in Nineteenth Century England," Ph.D. diss., University of Chicago, 1982. Other works that proved particularly stimulating include Carlo M. Cipolla, *Literacy and Development in the West* (Harmondsworth, Eng.: Penguin, 1969); *Education and Economic Development*, ed. C. A. Anderson and Mary Jane Bowman (Chicago: Aldine Publishing Co., 1963); Richard Hoggart, *The Uses of Literacy: Changing Patterns in English Mass Culture* (Harmondsworth, Eng.: Penguin, 1958); *Schooling and Society*, ed. L. Stone (Baltimore: Johns Hopkins University Press, 1976).

The view that literacy leads necessarily to modernization of the personality, presented in works such as A. Inkeles and D. Smith, *Becoming Modern: Individual Change in Six Developing Countries* (Cambridge, Mass.: Harvard University Press, 1974), has been challenged by other scholars. See, for example, Harvey J. Graff, *The Literacy Myth* (New York: Academic Press, 1979); Thomas W. Laqueur, "Toward a Cultural Ecology of Literacy in England, 1600-1850," in *Literacy in Historical Perspective*, ed. D. Resnick, pp. 43-58; and David Cressy, "The Environment for Literacy," pp. 23-42, in the same volume.

4. There is a vast literature about popular literature and popular fiction. The discussion by John G. Cawelti in his *Adventure, Mystery, and Romance* (Chicago: University of Chicago Press, 1976) was very helpful to me, and the book contains an extensive bibliography. Other works I relied on for a general orientation include Richard D. Altick, *The English Common Reader* (Chicago: University of Chicago Press, 1957); Joseph Campbell, *Hero with a Thousand Faces* (Cleveland: Meridian, 1956); Umberto Eco, *The Role of the Reader* (Bloomington: Indiana University Press, 1979); Eugen Weber, *Peasants into Frenchmen* (Stanford, Calif.: Stanford University Press, 1976); Theodore Zeldin, *France 1848-1945: Taste and Corruption* (Oxford, Eng.: Oxford University Press, 1977); Henry Nash Smith, *The American West as Symbol and Myth* (Cambridge, Mass.:

Harvard University Press, 1950); Peter Burke, *Popular Culture in Early Modern Europe* (London: Maurice Temple Smith, 1978); Robert Mandrou, *De la culture populaire aux 17e et 18e siècles* (Paris: Stock, 1964); Neil Harris, "Iconography and Intellectual History: The Half-Tone Effect," in *New Directions in American Intellectual History*, ed. John Higham and Paul Conkin (Baltimore: Johns Hopkins University Press, 1979); Leo Lowenthal, *Literature, Popular Culture, and Society* (Englewood Cliffs, N.J.: Prentice-Hall, 1961). Other works that I found helpful are cited throughout the book.

5. A useful statement of the case for a sociology of popular literature and an example of its practice is Wendy Griswold's "American Character and the American Novel: An Expansion of Reflection Theory in the Sociology of Literature," *American Journal of Sociology*, vol. 86, no. 4 (1981), pp. 740-65. A discussion of theories of popular culture is contained in Patrick Brantlinger, *Bread and Circuses: Theories of Mass Culture as Social Decay* (Ithaca, N.Y.: Cornell University Press, 1984). For a statement of the Marxist perspective from which folklore rather than popular literature, seems the true expression of popular consciousness, see Arnold Hauser, *The Sociology of Art*, trans. Kenneth J. Northcott (Chicago: University of Chicago Press, 1982).

6. As Charles A. Ruud argues in *Fighting Words: Imperial Censorship and the Russian Press, 1804-1906* (Toronto: University of Toronto Press, 1982), censorship was of declining importance in the late nineteenth and early twentieth centuries.

7. The list of works in this area since the 1920s is very short, and the emphasis is on the archaic rather than the modern forms of popular fiction. Two pioneering studies, one about early chivalrous tales and the other about literature as an institution at the beginning of the nineteenth century, are V. Shklovskii, *Matvei Komarov—zhitel' goroda Moskvy* (Moscow, 1929), and T. Gritz, V. Trenin, and M. Nikitin, *Slovesnost' i kommertsiia* (Moscow, 1929). There are several other studies of the chivalrous tales, including V. D. Kuz'mina, *Rytsarskii roman na Rusi* (Moscow, 1964); L. N. Pushkarev, *Skazka o Eruslane Lazareviche* (Moscow, 1980); Gary Cox, "Fairy-Tale Plots and Contemporary Heroes in Early Russian Prose Fiction," *Slavic Review*, vol. 39, no. 1 (March 1980), pp. 85-96; T. N. Apsit, "Povest' o Frantsele Venetsiane i ee chitateli," in *Rukopisnaia traditsiia XVI-XIX vv. na vostoke Rossii* (Moscow: Nauka, 1983), pp. 126-30. N. M. Zorkaia's *Na rubezhe stoletii: u istokov massovogo iskusstva v Rossii, 1900-1910* (Moscow: Nauka, 1976) is a fascinating study of early twentieth-century mass culture in Russia; it includes popular literature but the emphasis is on silent film. An excellent description of the Russian chapbooks is A. V. Blium, "Russkaia lubochnaia kniga vtoroi poloviny xix veka," in *Kniga: Issledovaniia i materialy*, vol. 42 (Moscow, 1981), pp. 94-114. I discuss varieties of Russian popular literature in "Readers and Reading at the End of the Tsarist Era," in *Literature and Society in Imperial Russia, 1800-1914*, ed. William Mills Todd III (Stanford, Calif.: Stanford University Press, 1978), pp. 97-150, 282-91, and in "The Kopeck Novels of Early Twentieth Century Russia," *Journal of Popular Culture*, vol. 13,

no. 1 (1979), pp. 85-97. Contemporary studies of Russian popular literature are cited in the appropriate sections of the book.

CHAPTER I

1. "Zametki," *PO* (November 1863), pp. 157-59.

2. *Vseobshchaia perepis' naseleniia Rossiiskoi Imperii 1897 g.—obshchii svod po Imperii rezul'tatov razrabotki dannykh*, vol. 1 (St. Petersburg, 1905), p. 39.

3. A. G. Rashin, "Gramotnost' i narodnoe obrazovanie v Rossii v XIX i nachale XX v.," *Istoricheskie zapiski*, vol. 37 (1951), p. 50.

4. A. G. Rashin, *Naselenie Rossii za 100 let* (Moscow, 1956), p. 304.

5. Ibid., p. 295.

6. *Pervaia vseobshchaia perepis' naseleniia Rossiiskoi Imperii 1897 g.*, vol. 24 (St. Petersburg, 1905), p. 67, and vol. 6 (St. Petersburg, 1904), part 2, p. 37.

7. D. Erde, *Negramotnost' i bor'ba s nei* (Sevastopol', 1926), p. 193; Tsentral'noe statisticheskoe upravlenie, *Gramotnost' v Rossii* (Moscow, 1922), pp. 10-11, 29.

8. On the Kiselev reforms I have relied on N. M. Druzhinin, *Gosudarstvennye krest'iane i reforma P. D. Kiseleva*, vol. 2 (Moscow, 1958).

9. P. A. Zaionchkovskii, *Provedenie v zhizn' krest'ianskoi reformy 1861 g.* (Moscow, 1958), provides figures on the number of copies printed.

10. *Krest'ianskoe dvizhenie v 1861 godu posle otmeny krepostnogo prava*, ed. E. A. Morokhovets (Moscow-Leningrad, 1949), pp. 43, 51, 76.

11. *Krest'ianskoe dvizhenie v 1861 godu*, pp. 66, 109.

12. Ibid., p. 312.

13. *Velikaia reforma*, ed. A. I. Iakovlev et al., vol. 5 (Moscow, 1911), p. 173.

14. *Krest'ianskoe dvizhenie v Rossii v 1861-1869 gg.*, ed. L. M. Ivanov (Moscow, 1964), p. 66.

15. "Zametki," *PO*, no. 1 (1862), p. 12.

16. V. Iakovenko, "Chto dumaet o gramotnosti i narodnoi shkole krest'ianin Kromskogo uezda," *SV*, no. 5 (1888), p. 59.

17. *RNU*, no. 12 (1880), p. 32.

18. V. Ivanovich, "Referaty i melkie soobshcheniia," *VV*, no. 7 (1903), p. 116.

19. V. S. Dokunin, "O vliianii zakona 14 iiunia 1910," *UiSh*, nos. 11-12 (1914).

20. "Zametki," *PO*, no. 1 (1862), p. 139.

21. Theodore W. Schultz, *Transforming Traditional Agriculture*, pp. 175-206, and John W. Mellor, *The Economics of Agricultural Development* (Ithaca, N.Y.: Cornell University Press, 1966), p. 352.

22. Iakovenko, "Chto dumaet," pp. 59-60.

23. N. Astyrev, "Ocherki byta naseleniia vostochnoi Sibiri," *RM*, no. 8 (1890), p. 33.

24. N. Valentinov, "Provodnik kooperatsii," *VK*, no. 1 (1911), p. 53.

25. Rybnikov, *Kustarnaia promyshlennost' i sbyt kustarnykh izdelii* (Moscow, 1913), pp. 15-23.

26. V. V. Petrov, "Ob otnoshenii naroda k gramotnosti," in *Voprosy narodnogo obrazovaniia v Moskovskoi gubernii*, vol. 3 (Moscow, 1900), pp. 4-5.

27. Iv. Ozerov, *Na bor'bu s narodnoi t'moi* (Moscow, 1907), p. 6; I. I. Ianzhul, A. I. Chupov, and I. N. Ianzhul, *Ekonomicheskaia otsenka narodnogo obrazovaniia* (St. Petersburg, 1891), p. 80.

28. Ianzhul et el., *Ekonomicheskaia otsenka*, p. 80.

29. *Vseobshchaia perepis'—obshchii svod*, vol. 1, p. 85.

30. Cited in A. G. Rashin, *Formirovanie rabochego klassa Rossii* (Moscow, 1958), pp. 164-67.

31. Arcadius Kahan, "Determinants of the Incidence of Literacy in Rural Nineteenth Century Russia," in *Education and Economic Development*, ed. Anderson and Bowman, p. 302.

32. L. M. Ivanov, "O soslovno-klassovoi strukture gorodov kapitalisticheskoi Rossii," in *Problemy sotsial'no-ekonomicheskoi istorii Rossii*, ed. L. M. Ivanov et al. (Moscow, 1971), pp. 323-29.

33. Rashin, *Naselenie*, p. 323.

34. Barbara A. Anderson, *Internal Migration During Modernization in Late Nineteenth-Century Russia* (Princeton, N.J.: Princeton University Press, 1980), pp. 96-100; Joseph Bradley, "Patterns of Peasant Migration," *Russian History*, no. 1 (1979), p. 38.

35. Petrov, "Ob otnoshenii naroda k gramotnosti," p. 6; I. P. Bogolepov, *Gramotnost' sredi detei shkol'nogo vozrasta v Moskovskom i Mozhaiskom uezdakh Moskovskoi gubernii* (Moscow, 1894), p. 64; V. V. Petrov, "Ob otnoshenii naroda k gramotnosti," VV, no. 4 (1900), pp. 130-31.

36. Kahan, "Determinants of the Incidence of Literacy," p. 301; K. Muromskii, *Byt i nuzhdy torgo-promyshlennykh sluzhashchikh* (Moscow, 1906), pp. 5-6.

37. Muromskii, *Byt' i nuzhdy*, p. 9.

38. N. Rybnikov, *Derevenskii shkol'nik i ego idealy* (Moscow, 1916), p. 115.

39. Bogolepov, *Gramotnost'*, p. 64.

40. Petrov, *Voprosy narodnogo obrazovanniia*, vol. 3, pp. 9-10.

41. Rashin, *Formirovanie rabochego klassa*, p. 584.

42. I. M. Koz'minykh-Lanin, *Gramotnost' i zarabotki fabrichno-zavodskikh rabochikh Moskovskoi gubernii* (Moscow, 1912); Ianzhul et al., *Ekonomicheskaia otsenka*, pp. 65, 71.

43. Rashin, *Formirovanie rabochego klassa*, p. 584.

44. Robert Eugene Johnson, *Peasant and Proletarian: The Working Class of Moscow in the Late Nineteenth Century* (New Brunswick, N.J.: Rutgers University Press, 1979).

45. Rubakin archive 5/1. The archive of N. A. Rubakin, educator, bibliophile, and scholar, is located in the Manuscript Section of the Lenin Library (fond 358). The archive contains materials collected by Rubakin and others about the cultural experience of peasants and other common people in the late nineteenth and early twentieth centuries. Sometimes the document pages are unnumbered, and in that case I cite, as I do here, only by carton/folder.

46. Rubakin archive 20/11, p. 1.

47. *Aperçu des chemins de fer Russes*, vol. 1, part 1 (Brussels, 1898), p. 199.

48. J. N. Westwood, *A History of Russian Railways* (London: Allen and Unwin, 1964), p. 304.

49. I. M. Pushkareva, *Zheleznodorozhniki* (Moscow, 1975), pp. 46, 51.

50. S. Semenov, "Derevnia vo vremia voiny," *EZh*, no. 3 (1915), p. 67.

51. A. A. Kaufman, *Obshchina, pereselenie, statistika* (Moscow, 1915), p. 168.

52. *Pereselenie i zemleustroistvo za Uralom v 1906-10 gg. i otchet po pereseleniiu i zemleustroistvu za 1910 god* (St. Petersburg, 1911), p. 2. Separate volumes are listed here as *Pereselenie* by year.

53. *Priamur'e. Fakty, tsifry, nabliudeniia sobrannye na Dal'nem Vostoke sotrudnikami obshchezemskoi organizatsii* (Moscow, 1909), p. 110.

54. *Pereselenie* (St. Petersburg, 1911), pp. 2-8, for these and the following figures.

55. Donald Treadgold, *The Great Siberian Migration* (Princeton, N.J.: Princeton University Press, 1957), pp. 239-52.

56. Kaufman, *Sbornik*, p. 168.

57. Pereselencheskoe Upravlenie, *Spravochnaia knizhka dlia khodokov i pereselentsev na 1911 god* (St. Petersburg, 1911).

58. *Pereselenie* (Petrograd, 1914), p. 10.

59. The picture is printed in *Pereselenie* (St. Petersburg, 1911), p. 32.

60. The pictures discussed are printed in the volumes of *Pereselenie* published in 1911, p. 23; 1915, p. 14; and 1914, p. 10.

61. A. A. Kaufman, *Po novym mestam* (St. Petersburg, 1905), p. 107.

62. Ibid., p. 46.

63. Ibid., p. 23.

64. Anderson, *Internal Migration*, pp. 138-39. The literacy of migrants from Poltava in 1900 was only 10 percent, according to the publication of the provincial zemstvo's statistical bureau: Statisticheskoe biuro Poltavskogo Gubernskogo Zemstva, *Pereseleniia iz Poltavskoi Gubernii s 1861 goda po 1 Ianvaria 1901 goda*, vol. 2 (Poltava, 1905), p. 107.

65. P. A. Zaionchkovskii, *Voennye reformy 1860-1870 v Rossii* (Moscow, 1952), p. 18.

66. Ibid., pp. 18-19, 21.

67. Ibid., p. 308.

68. V. Patrakov, "O gramotnosti nizhnikh chinov," *VS*, no. 5 (1870), p. 53.

69. P. Bobrovskii, "Vzgliad na gramotnost'," *VS*, no. 3 (1871), pp. 85-86.

70. Ibid., p. 44.

71. *Statisticheskie svedeniia po nachal'nomu obrazovaniiu v Rossiiskoi Imperii*, vol. 2 (St. Petersburg, 1900), pp. 274-77.

72. L. G. Protasov, "Klassovyi sostav soldat russkoi armii pered oktiabrem," *ISSSR*, no. 1 (1977), pp. 45-46.

73. Patrakov, "O gramotnosti," *VS*, no. 9 (1870), p. 54.

74. "Iz zapisnoi knizhki redaktsii," *VS* (May 1892), p. 35.

75. Rediger, "Unter-ofitserskii vopros," *VS*, no. 3 (1880), p. 152.

76. V. Datsevits, "Neskol'ko slov o vospitanii," *VS*, no. 11 (1880), p. 92.

77. Butovskii, "Shkola gramotnosti," *VS*, no. 6 (1886), p. 303.

78. Butovskii, "Vospitatel'nye zadachi komandira," *VS*, no. 12 (1884), pp. 281-82.

79. Butovskii, "O kazarmennoi nravstvennosti," *VS*, no. 1 (1883), p. 126.

80. Rubakin archive 18/9, p. 3.

81. "Kritika," *NSh*, no. 11 (1874), p. 58.

82. Petrov, "Ob otnoshenii naroda k gramotnosti," p. 35.

83. Petrov, "Ob otnoshenii naroda k gramotnosti," in *Voprosy narodnogo obrazovaniia*, vol. 3, p. 5.

84. N. Bunakov, "Sel'skaia shkola i narodnaia zhizn'," *RNU*, no. 2 (1890), p. 35.

85. Vasilii Mikhailovskii, *Nachal'noe obuchenie pravoslavnoi very* (St. Petersburg, 1880), p. 23.

86. "Voronezhskie pis'ma," *PO*, no. 9 (1862), p. 13.

87. *RNU*, no. 3 (1903), p. 48.

88. *RNU*, no. 4 (1890), p. 62.

89. Sv. F. Bogorodskii, "Pouchenie k poselianam o gramotnosti," *S*, no. 1 (1867), p. 28.

90. Mikhailovskii, *Nachal'noe obuchenie*, p. 6.

91. Rubakin archive 5/1, p. 45.

92. *VV*, no. 5 (1896), pp. 78-79.

93. On restricted literacy, see Jack Goody, "Restricted Literacy in Northern Ghana," in his *Literacy in Traditional Societies*, and Sylvia Scribner and Michael Cole, *The Psychology of Literacy* (Cambridge, Mass.: Harvard University Press, 1981).

94. *TsV*, no. 46 (1899), p. 1624.

95. "Nachal'noe narodnoe uchilishche," *RNU*, no. 3 (1894), p. 180.

96. N. F. Bunakov, *Sel'skaia shkola i narodnaia zhizn'* (St. Petersburg, 1906), p. 8.

97. *Sbornik statisticheskikh svedenii po Moskovskoi gubernii*, vol. 9 (1884), pp. 144-45.

98. Pokrovskii, "Mnenie sel'skogo zakonouchitelia," *NO*, no. 2 (1912), p. 155.

99. V. I. Isevich-Borodaevskaia, *Bor'ba za veru. Istoriko-bytovye ocherki i obzor zakonodatel'stva po staroobriadchestvu i sektanstvu v ego posledovatel'nom razvitii* (St. Petersburg, 1912), p. 309.

100. M. Gor'kii, *Sobranie sochinenii*, vol. 13 (Moscow, 1951), pp. 284-85.

101. V. N. Vitevskii, *Raskol v Ural'skom Voiske, otnoshenie k nemu dukhovnoi i voennograzhdanskoi vlasti v kontse xviii i v xix vv.* (Kazan', 1878), p. 58.

102. See *Sel'sko-khoziaistvennyi i ekonomicheskii byt staroobriadtsev po dannym ankety 1909 goda* (Moscow, 1910), pp. 201-202.

103. Quoted in A. S. Prugavin, *Staroobriadchestvo vo vtoroi polovine xix veka* (Moscow, 1904), p. 106.

104. "Neskol'ko slov o molokanakh," *OZ*, no. 6 (1870), p. 296.

105. Iasevich-Borodaevskaia, *Bor'ba za veru*, p. 60.

106. Frederic C. Conybeare, *Russian Dissenters*, Harvard Theological Studies, no. 10 (New York: Russell and Russell, 1962), pp. 239-49; A. I. Klibanov, *Istoriia religioznogo sektanstva v Rossii* (Moscow, 1965), p. 147; *Vseobshchaia perepis'—obshchii svod*, vol. 2, pp. 74-75.

107. I. Belliustin, "Eshche o dvizheniiakh v raskole," *RV*, no. 6 (1865), pp. 766-67.

108. See William L. Blackwell, "The Old Believers and the Rise of Private Industrial Enterprise in Early Nineteenth-Century Moscow," in *Russian Economic Development from Peter the Great to Stalin*, ed. William L. Blackwell (New York: Franklin Watts, 1974), pp. 137-58.

109. Rubakin archive 6/7.

110. Rubakin archive 5/13, p. 71.

111. Gleb Uspenskii, *Polnoe sobranie sochinenii*, vol. 6 (Kiev, 1903), pp. 19-20.

112. "Novye priznaki v nashei literature," *OZ*, no. 3 (1878), pp. 264-65.

113. A. Engel'gardt, "Iz derevni," *OZ*, no. 3 (1878), pp. 6-7.

114. See Kh. Podborovskii, "Voprosy russko-iaponskoi voiny v sovremennoi derevne," *VZ*, no. 11 (1904), pp. 105-20.

115. Rubakin archive 274/41.

116. Rubakin archive 13/12.

117. *Rus'*, no. 64 (1904), clipping in Rubakin archive 32/3.

118. Rubakin archive 7/12.

119. Boris Frommett, "Vliianie voiny na obshchestvennuiu i umstvennuiu zhizn' derevni," *Zhizn' dlia vsekh*, no. 2 (1915), p. 283.

120. V. Iv, "Osvobozhdaiushchaiasia derevnia," *VV*, nos. 4-5 (1917), p. 137.

121. *UiSh*, nos. 15-16 (1915), p. 80.

122. Frommett, "Vlianie voiny," p. 284.

123. *EZh*, no. 2 (1915), p. 124.

124. Rubakin archive 5/4.

125. Rubakin archive 20/11.

126. N. F. Bunakov, *O domashnikh shkolakh gramotnosti* (St. Petersburg, 1885), p. 20.

127. Iakovenko, "Chto dumaet," p. 61.

128. A. Gartvig, "Soznana li naseleniem potrebnost' vo vseobshchem obuchenii?" *RSh*, no. 4 (1895), p. 136.

129. P. Shesternik, "Sel'skie shkol'nye biblioteki," *RNU*, no. 2 (1891), p. 34.

130. B. V. Bank, *Izuchenie chitatelei v Rossii (xix v.)* (Moscow, 1969).

131. The results of Rubakin's survey are preserved in his archive together with the replies to Prugavin's questionnaires.

132. Jeffrey Brooks, "Studies of the Reader in the 1920s," *Russian History*, nos. 2-3 (1982), pp. 187-202.

133. "Ped. khronika," *RSH*, nos. 5-6 (1894), p. 352.

134. V. Iv, "Osvobozhdaiushchaiasia derevnia," p. 144.

135. N. F. Bunakov, "Sel'skaia shkola i narodnaia zhizn'," *RNU*, no. 11 (1890), p. 377.

136. "Neskol'ko slov k voprosu o tom, chto chitat' narodu," *RNU*, no. 1 (1887), p. 6.

137. *RNU*, no. 2 (1890), p. 18.

138. See Goody, "Restricted Literacy in Northern Ghana," and Weber, *Peasants*, p. 25.

139. S. A. Rappoport (An-skii), *Narod i kniga* (Moscow, 1914), p. 67.

140. *Massovyi chitatel' i kniga*, ed. N. D. Rybnikov (Moscow, 1925), p. 14.

141. M. A. Smushkova, *Pervye itogi izucheniia chitatelia* (Moscow-Leningrad, 1926), p. 14.

142. M. I. Slukhovskii, *Kniga i derevnia* (Moscow-Leningrad, 1928), p. 30.

143. Kh. D. Alchevskaia, *Chto chitat' narodu*, vol. 1 (Kharkov, 1884), pp. 296, 314.

144. V. Iv, "Osvobozhdaiushchaiasia derevnia," p. 148.

145. Slukhovskii, *Kniga i derevnia*, pp. 110-11.

146. B. Bank and A. Vilenkin, *Krestianskaia molodezh' i kniga* (Moscow-Leningrad, 1929), p. 58.

147. *Massovyi chitatel'*, pp. 69-70.

148. Brooks, "Readers and Reading," pp. 140-43; N. A. Rubakin, *Etiudy o russkoi chitaiushchei publike* (St. Petersburg, 1895), pp. 192-207.

149. L. M. Kleinbort, *Ocherki rabochei intelligentsii*, vol. 1 (Petrograd, 1923), p. 66. The essays were originally published in prerevolutionary journals.

150. Moskovskii gubernskii sovet profsoiuzov. Kul'totdel, *Chto chitaiut vzroslye rabochie i sluzhashchie po belletristike* (Moscow, 1928), p. 30; *Massovyi chitatel' i kniga*, p. 9.

151. Kleinbort, *Ocherki*, vol. 1, p. 69.

CHAPTER II

1. I discuss this issue at greater length in my essay, "The Zemstvos and the Education of the People," in *The Zemstvo in Russia: An Experiment in Local Self-Government*, ed. Terence Emmons and Wayne S. Vucinich (Cambridge, Eng.: Cambridge University Press, 1981), pp. 242-78. Ben Eklof also reached this conclusion in "Schooling and Literacy in Late Imperial Russia," in *Literacy in Historical Perspective*, ed. D. Resnick, pp. 105-28.

2. A. S. Prugavin, *Zaprosy naroda i obiazannosti intelligentsii v oblasti prosveshcheniia i vospitaniia* (St. Petersburg, 1895), pp. 48-49.

3. *RNU*, nos. 6-7 (1899), pp. 120-28.

4. L. N. Tolstoi, *Pol'noe sobranie sochinenii*, vol. 8 (Moscow, 1936) p. 133.

5. Rubakin archive 5/15.

6. Prugavin, *Zaprosy*, pp. 10-12; N. V. Chekhov, "Khronika narodnogo obrazovaniia v Rossii. Narodnoe obrazovanie u staroobriadtsev," *RSH*, no. 10 (1909), p. 48.

7. I. Korneenko, "Kakoe znachenie imeet nachal'naia shkola," *Strannik* (August 1894), p. 482.

8. Brooks, "The Zemstvo and the Education of the People"; Ben Ekloff, "Peasant Sloth Reconsidered," *Journal of Social History*, vol. 14, no. 3 (1982).

9. N. A. Korf, *Russkaia nachal'naia shkola*, 6th ed. (St. Petersburg, 1879).

10. *Statisticheskii vremennik*, 3rd series, vol. 1, pp. 294-95, xxxii.

11. Boris Veselovskii, *Istoriia zemstva za sorok let*, vol. 1 (St. Petersburg, 1909), p. 472.

12. *Istoricheskii ocherk razvitiia tserkovnykh shkol* (St. Petersburg, 1909), p. 6.

13. S. A. Rachinskii, *Zametki o sel'skikh shkolakh* (St. Petersburg, 1882), p. 44.

14. *Istoricheskii ocherk razvitiia tserkovnykh shkol*, p. 60.

15. *Nachal'nye uchilishcha vedomstva Ministerstva narodnogo prosveshcheniia v 1914 godu* (Petrograd, 1916), prilozhenie, pp. vi-ix.

16. I discuss these and the following calculations in more detail in "The Zemstvo and the Education of the People."

17. *Pervyi Obshchezemskii s"ezd po statistike narodnogo obrazovaniia 1913 goda. Doklady* (Khar'kov, 1913), p. 249.

18. The method used to derive these probabilities was to distribute the school children by grade, according to data in the 1911 school census for numbers of children in years 1, 2-3, 4-5. Drop-out rates for the first year were used to separate years 2-3. Since the census did not contain information for individual years 4-5, I arbitrarily assumed that 70 percent of these pupils were in the fourth year and 30 percent in the fifth. The likelihood that any child who began school would attend for a given number of years was derived from the data on the percentage of all school-aged children (ages 7-14) in school by the construction of a matrix in which the rows add up to the proportion of children of a given age in school, and the columns add up to the proportion of children aged 7-14 who attended school for a given number of years. The calculations are explained more fully in my essay, "The Zemstvo and the Education of the People," pp. 269-73.

19. *Trudy mestnykh komitetov o nuzhdakh sel'skokhoziaistvennoi promyshlennosti, Arkhangel'skaia guberniia*, vol. 1 (St. Petersburg, 1903), p. 251.

20. P. A. Vikhliaev, *Ekonomicheskie usloviia narodnogo obrazovaniia v Moskovskoi gubernii* (Moscow, 1910), pp. 26-27. He cites I. P. Bogolepov.

21. "Mysl' sel'skogo sviashchennika," *S*, no. 3 (1864), p. 33.

22. *Trudy mestnykh komitetov. Astrakhanskaia guberniia*, vol. 2 (St. Petersburg, 1903), pp. 114-15.

23. "O vliianii zakona 14 iiunia 1910 na narodnoe obrazovanie," *UiSh*, nos. 11-12 (1914), p. 42.

24. Andrei Gartvig, "Soznana li naseleniem potrebnost' vo vseobshchem obuchenii?" *RSh*, no. 4 (1895), p. 150.

25. V. V. Petrov, "Ob otnoshenii naroda k gramotnosti," *VV*, no. 4 (1900), pp. 135-36.

26. Vikhliaev, *Ekonomicheskie usloviia*, pp. 33-37.

27. "Zametki," *PO*, no. 1 (1862), p. 14.

28. *Istoriia rabochikh Leningrada*, vol. 1, ed. S. N. Bank et al. (Leningrad, 1972), pp. 134-35; Reginald E. Zelnik, *Labor and Society in Tsarist Russia* (Stanford, Calif.: Stanford University Press, 1978) pp. 37-41.

29. Vikhliaev, *Ekonomicheskie usloviia*, p. 37.

30. Ibid., p. 250.

31. *Usloviia byta rabochikh v dorevoliutsionnoi Rossii*, ed. N. K. Druzhinin (Moscow, 1958), pp. 7-9.

32. *Odnodnevnaia perepis'*, vol. 1, pp. 6-7.

33. Ibid., pp. 4-5.

34. A. S. Prugavin, *Zakony i spravochnye svedeniia po nachal'nomu narodnomu obrazovaniiu*, 1st ed. (St. Petersburg, 1898), pp. 25, 270.

35. V. Debel', "Krest'ianskie vol'nye shkoly gramotnosti v Tverskoi gubernii," *RSh*, no. 6 (1890), pp. 135-38.

36. A. S. Prugavin, *Raskol-sektantstvo, materialy dlia izucheniia religiozno-bytovykh dvizhenii russkogo naroda* (Moscow, 1887), p. 245.

37. Prugavin, *Zakony i spravochnye svedeniia po nachal'nomu narodnomu obrazovaniiu*, 2nd ed. (St. Petersburg, 1904), pp. 138-39.

38. *Istoricheskii ocherk razvitiia tserkovnykh shkol*, pp. 148-49.

39. E. A. Zviagintsev, in *Narodnaia zhizn' i shkola*, vol. 2 (Moscow, 1913), pp. 3-29, summarizes most of these studies.

40. Ibid., p. 16.

41. *Odnodnevnaia perepis'*, vol. 1, pp. 6-7.

42. "Kak prepodavat' Zakon Bozhii," *NO*, no. 1 (1914), pp. 29-30; *Iz materialov s"ezda inspektorov narodnykh uchilishch Smolenskoi gubernii*, p. 73.

43. N. V. Chekhov, "Na poroge v shkolu i iz shkoly," *VNU*, no. 10 (1911), p. 25.

44. Petrov, "Chemu uchat," pp. 68-69; A. Anastasiev, "Obuchenie v nachal'-nykh shkolakh," *ZhMNP*, no. 6 (1905), p. 24.

45. *RNU*, no. 12 (1886), p. 607.

46. V. Charnolushii, "Voprosy narodnogo obrazovaniia na pervom obshche-zemskom s"ezde," *RSh*, no. 12 (1911), p. 90; "Pervyi obshchezemskii s"ezd po narodnomu obrazovaniiu," *VV*, no. 6 (1911), p. 109.

47. Zviagintsev, *Narodnaia zhizn'*, pp. 18-19.

48. N. Sokolov, "Iz dnevnika uezdnogo nabliudatelia," *NO*, no. 9 (1897), p. 33.

49. Chekhov, "Na poroge," p. 24.

50. N. Strakhov, "Zadachi i priemy obucheniia chteniiu," *NO*, no. 10 (1897), pp. 13-19.

51. Korf, *Russkaia nachal'naia shkola*, p. 67, and *Trudy 1-go Vserossiiskogo s"ezda*, vol. 1 (Petrograd, 1915), p. 142.

52. Korf, *Russkaia nachal'naia shkola*, p. 62.

53. K. Ushinskii, *Detskii mir i khrestomatiia*, 2nd ed. (St. Petersburg, 1861), pp. iv-vi; includes preface to the first edition.

54. Ibid., p. 16.

55. F. Zharov, "Estestvoznanie," *VNU*, no. 4 (1910), p. 17.

56. A. Baranov, *Kniga dlia klassnogo chteniia, primenennaia k obucheniiu rodnomu iazyku v nachal'nykh shkolakh, 2 i 3 god obucheniia,* 72nd ed. (Moscow, 1915).

57. N. Bunakov, *Azbuka i uroki chteniia i pis'ma,* 100th ed. (Petrograd, 1916), pp. 31, 35.

58. *Trudy 1-go Vserossiiskogo s"ezda,* vol. 1 (Petrograd, 1915), p. 42.

59. A. Baranov, *Dobrye semena,* 34th ed., vol. 2 (Moscow, 1915), p. 147.

60. D. I. Tikhomirov, *Veshnie vskhody. Tret'ia i chetvertaia kniga dlia chteniia* (Moscow, 1911), p. 74.

61. I. Gorbunov-Posadov, *Krasnoe solnyshko. Pervaia kniga dlia chteniia* (Moscow, 1906), pp. 6-7.

62. See, for example, the writing assignment, "Home is Better," in A. Anastasiev, *Narodnaia shkola. Rukovodstvo dlia uchitelei i uchitel'nits,* 7th ed., vol. 2 (Moscow, 1910), p. 373.

63. Bunakov, *Azbuka,* p. 5.

64. Tikhomirov, *Veshnie vskhody,* pp. 271-95.

65. N. A. Korf, *Nash drug,* 19th ed. (St. Petersburg, 1908), pp. 180-83, and (St. Petersburg, 1871), pp. 308-309.

66. V. and E. Vakhterov, *Mir v rasskazakh dlia detei,* part 3 (Moscow, 1912), pp. 102, 127.

67. Ibid., p. 277.

68. Baranov, *Kniga dlia klassnogo chteniia,* p. 147.

69. N. A. Rybnikov, *Aftobiografii rabochikh i ikh izuchenie* (Moscow-Leningrad, 1930), p. 51.

70. Ibid.

71. Chekhov, "Na poroge," p. 29.

72. *Trudy 1-go Vserossiiskogo s"ezda,* vol. 1, pp. 152-56; Chekhov, "Na poroge," pp. 3-36.

73. F. Kuli, "Krest'ianskie deti," *NO,* no. 1 (1912), p. 21.

74. Rybnikov, *Derevenskii shkol'nik i ego idealy,* pp. 104-22.

75. A. Mirnyi, "V nauku," *NO,* no. 8 (1897), pp. 51-54.

76. Ibid.

77. "V zashchitu gorodskikh uchilishch'," *RNU,* nos. 8-9 (1892), p. 92.

78. *NO,* no. 4 (1904).

79. I. Pokrovskii, "Mnenie sel'skogo zakonouchitelia," *NO,* no. 2 (1912), p. 155.

80. V. Charnoluskii, "Voprosy narodnogo obrazovaniia," *RSh,* no. 9 (1911), p. 62.

81. Chekhov, "Na poroge," p. 36.

82. *Trudy 1-go Vserossiiskogo s"ezda,* vol. 2, pp. 315-18, and "Referaty i melkie soobshcheniia," *VV,* no. 8 (1901), p. 71.

83. *Trudy 1-go Vserossiiskogo s"ezda,* vol. 1, pp. 26-36.

84. F. Ch., "Referaty," *VV,* no. 8 (1901), p. 74.

85. V. Stremlianov, "Khuliganstvo i uchitel'," *UiSh,* nos. 11-12, p. 57, and

Pervyi Obshchezemskii s"ezd po narodnomu obrazovaniiu 1911 goda. Doklady, vol. 1 (Moscow, 1911), p. 164.

86. These observations are based on data compiled from *Spravochnaia kniga Vestnika znaniia na 1911 god* (St. Petersburg, 1911), pp. 322-97.

CHAPTER III

1. M. V. Muratov, *Knizhnoe delo v Rossii v XIX i XX v.* (Moscow-Leningrad, 1931), pp. 203-205.

2. *Ezhegodnik. Obzor knig dlia narodnogo chteniia v 1892* (Moscow, 1893), pp. 36-37; and *Ezhegodnik. Obzor knig dlia narodnogo chteniia v 1894* (Moscow, 1895), pp. 38-39.

3. *Statistika proizvedenii pechati v Rossii v 1910 godu* (St. Petersburg, 1911), p. 72.

4. Muratov, *Knizhnoe delo v Rossii*, pp. 303-305.

5. N. Snegirev, *Lubochnye kartinki russkogo naroda v moskovskom mire* (Moscow, 1861), pp. 5-6.

6. D. N. Rovinskii, *Russkie narodnye kartinki*, book 1, vol. 23, in *Sbornik Otdeleniia russkogo iazyka i slovesnosti Imperatorskoi Akademii nauk* (St. Petersburg, 1881), p. iii.

7. Ibid.

8. N. I. Pastukhov, *Ocherki i rasskazy "starogo znakomogo"* (Moscow, 1879), p. 46.

9. I. A. Golyshev, *Sobranie sochinenii*, vol. 1, part 1 (St. Petersburg, 1889), p. 11.

10. A. A. Fedorov-Davydov, *K voprosu o sotsiologicheskom izuchenii starorusskogo lubka*, Institut arkheologii i iskusstvoznaniia (Moscow, 1927), p. 99.

11. F. Iezbery, *Vserossiiskii muzei, ili sobranie predmetov, kasaiushchikhsia poznaniia Russkoi Imperii* (Warsaw, 1879), p. 78.

12. *Ezhegodnik. Obzor knig v 1893* (Moscow, 1895), pp. 252-54.

13. *Tovarishchestvo pechataniia izdatel'stva i knizhnoi torgovli I. D. Sytina* (Moscow, 1910), p. vi.

14. Rovinskii, *Russkie narodnye kartinki*, book 5, vol. 27, pp. 31-35, and Golyshev, *Sobranie sochinenii*, vol. 1, pp. 4-5.

15. Rovinskii, *Russkie narodnye kartinki*, book 5, vol. 27, pp. 34-35.

16. E. Gollerbakh, *Istoriia graviury i litografii v Rossii* (Moscow-Petrograd, 1923), p. 32.

17. Golyshev, *Sobranie sochinenii*, vol. 1, p. 14.

18. Peter C. Marzio, *The Democratic Art* (Boston: David R. Godine, 1979), pp. 69-88, 176-211.

19. M. Chernokov, *Knizhniki* (Leningrad, 1933).

20. *KV*, nos. 6-7 (1891), p. 266.

21. N. Rubakin, "Knizhnyi potok," *RM*, no. 12 (1903), p. 166.

22. The sample consisted of all titles that appeared in *Knizhnaia letopis'* in the third week in June, the fourth week in August, the first week in October, and

the second week in December, and were published by the large commercial publishers.

23. *Skazka o Ivan-bogatyre, o prekrasnoi supruge ego Svetlane i o zlom volshebnike Karachune* (Kiev, 1900).

24. *Narodnye russkie skazki A. N. Afanas'eva v trekh tomakh*, ed. V. Ia. Propp (Moscow, 1957), nos. 267-69, vol. 2, pp. 329-37.

25. N. Andreev, "Ischezaiushchaia literatura," *Kazanskii bibliofil*, no. 2 (Kazan', 1921), p. 9.

26. *Kupecheskaia doch' Vasilisa Prekrasnaia* (Sytin: Moscow, 1915), and Afanas'ev, *Narodnye russkie*, vol. 1, pp. 159-65.

27. I. S. Ivin (Kassirov), *Il'ia Muromets, naibol'shii bogatyr' kievskii vo vremena sv. kniazia Vladimira* (Kiev, 1899).

28. V. D. Kuz'mina, *Rytsarskii roman na Rusi* (Moscow, 1964), and L. N. Pushkarev, *Skazka o Eruslane Lazareviche* (Moscow, 1980).

29. Pushkarev, *Skazka*, p. 58.

30. This count is based on Kuz'mina for Bova, Pushkarev for Eruslan, and my count of the other titles, which is described in the Bibliographical Essay.

31. Boris and Iurii Sokolov, *Skazki i pesni Belozerskogo kraia* (Moscow, 1915), pp. 206-209, 213.

32. Kuz'mina, *Rytsarskii roman*, pp. 41, 85.

33. *Povest' o prikliuchenii angliiskogo Milorda Georga* (Moscow, 1901) is a 108-page version and *Povest' o prikliuchenii angliiskogo Milorda Georga* (Moscow, 1890) is 180 pages long.

34. *Povest' o prikliucheniiakh angliiskogo Milorda Georga* (Moscow, 1896) is a 32-page version.

35. *Slavnyi bogatyr' Antipka. Rasskaz iz derevenskoi zhizni* (Moscow, 1914).

36. V. A. Lunin (Kukel'), *Babushka Marfa ili za Bogom molitva, a za tsarem sluzhba nikogda ne propadaet* (Moscow, 1899).

37. F. K. Shalaev, *Novoe puteshestvie na lipovoi mashine s odnim rublem za 1,000 verst'* (St. Petersburg, 1874). The number of editions is given in the 1903 edition of the story.

38. *Soldat Iashka* (Moscow, 1868).

39. M. Evstigneev, *Anekdoty i predaniia o Petre Velikom* (Moscow, 1873).

40. *Predanie o tom, kak soldat spas zhizn' Petra Velikogo ot smerti u razboinikov* (Moscow, 1890). There are thirty-four editions of this story listed in the regular catalogue of the Saltykov-Shchedrin Library.

41. Lunin (Kukel'), *Shikarnaia zhena* (Moscow, 1901).

42. Lunin (Kukel'), *Fabrichnaia krasavitsa* (Moscow, 1897).

43. V. Shklovskii, *Matvei Komarov, zhitel' goroda Moskvy* (Leningrad, 1929).

44. Maksim Gor'kii, *Sobranie sochinenii*, vol. 31 (Moscow, 1951), p. 330.

45. A. K. Nesterov and M. Evstigneev, *Panorama tolkuchago rynka*, vol. 2 (St. Petersburg, 1858).

46. *Vagon tret'ego klassa—veselye stseny* (Moscow, 1868); *Iskusstvo zhit' na chuzhoi schet v Moskve* (Moscow, 1868).

47. M. Evstigneev, *Udaloi razboinik* (Moscow, 1869).

48. Prugavin, *Zaprosy*, p. 402.

49. V. Suvorov, *Ocherki istorii russko-turetskoi voiny* (Moscow, 1877).

50. Prugavin, *Zaprosy*, p. 402.

51. *Ezhegodnik. Obzor knig dlia narodnogo chteniia i narodnykh kartin* (Moscow, 1895), p. 27.

52. Rubakin archive 232/1, p. 14, and I. F. Masanov, *Slovar' psevdonimov* (Moscow, 1957), p. 205.

53. Ivin (Kassirov), *Iumoristicheskii al'bom s karikaturami* (Moscow, 1878), p. 1.

54. Ivin (Kassirov), *Prikliucheniia russkogo riadovogo soldata vozvrashchavshegosia s voiny* (Moscow, 1878).

55. Rubakin archive 232/1, p. 4.

56. Ivin (Kassirov), "Kratkaia avtobiografiia" (1892), Rubakin archive 20/11.

57. Ibid.

58. *Budil'nik; Razvlechenie.*

59. Rubakin archive 232/1.

60. M. I. Ozhegov, *Moia zhizn' i pesni dlia naroda* (Moscow, 1901), pp. 1-34, contains a brief autobiography on which I also rely for the following account.

61. *Literaturnaia gazeta*, no. 36 (August 20, 1930), p. 4.

62. N. P. Izergina, *Pisateli v Viatke* (Kirov, 1977), pp. 159-64.

63. *Kirovskaia pravda*, no. 196 (August 18, 1960), p. 4.

64. Rubakin archive 232/1, p. 1.

65. Rubakin archive 20/11. The list does not appear in the archive, and he probably never sent it.

66. Ivin (Kassirov), *Pesni rodiny, stikhotvoreniia 1877-93* (Moscow, 1893), p. 194.

67. Ibid., p. 137.

68. Ibid., pp. 94-95.

69. Rubakin archive 20/12, p. 3.

70. L. N. Tolstoi, *Polnoe sobranie sochinenii*, vol. 50 (Moscow, 1952), p. 30.

71. Rubakin archive 20/11.

72. "O narodno-lubochnoi literature," part 2, *RO*, no. 10 (1893), p. 785.

73. Rubakin archive 20/11, p. 4.

74. Rubakin archive 232/1.

75. Ivin (Kassirov), *Pesni rodiny*, pp. 24-25.

76. Rubakin archive 232/1, p. 12.

77. Ivin (Kassirov), *Pesni rodiny*, p. 197.

78. Rubakin archive 5/13, p. 5.

79. Rubakin archive 5/13, p. 53.

80. Rubakin archive 232/1, p. 14.

81. Ozhegov, *Moia zhizn'*, p. 6. He was a member of the Surikov circle of self-taught writers at one time.

82. Rubakin archive 21/18, pp. 1-30.

83. Rubakin archive 21/19.

84. Lunin (Kukel'), *Nuzhda skachet* (Moscow, 1912), p. 6.

85. *The Reader in the Text: Essays and Interpretation*, ed. Susan R. Suleiman and Inge Crossman (Princeton, N.J.: Princeton University Press, 1980), and Wayne Booth, *The Rhetoric of Fiction* (Chicago: University of Chicago Press, 1961).

86. See T. Grits, V. Trenin, and M. Nikitin, *Slovesnost' i kommertsiia* (Moscow, 1929).

87. A. V. Blium, "Russkaia lubochnaia kniga," p. 97.

88. B. P. Orlov, *Poligraficheskaia promyshlennost' Moskvy* (Moscow, 1953).

89. Ibid., p. 127, and M. N. Kufaev, *Istoriia russkoi knigi v xix veke* (Leningrad, 1927), pp. 171-73, 216-19, 319.

90. N. A Leikin, *Apraksintsy* (St. Petersburg, 1904).

91. N. I. Sveshnikov, *Vospominaniia propashchego cheloveka* (Moscow-Leningrad, 1930), pp. 367-68.

92. Ibid., pp. 379-80.

93. *Vystavka proizvedenii pechati za 1908 god*, p. 38, lists only five titles for 1908.

94. *Katalog knizhnoi torgovli N. I. Kholmushina* (Moscow, 191?).

95. F. Belorusa, *Karpatskie razboiniki* (St. Petersburg, 1890).

96. *Ezhegodnik. Obzor knig 1892* (Moscow, 1893), p. 3.

97. I. A. Belousov, *Literaturnaia Moskva* (Moscow, 1926), p. 29.

98. *KV*, nos. 6-7 (1898), p. 723.

99. *KV*, no. 6 (1890), pp. 246-48.

100. *Sankt-Peterburgskie vedomosti*, no. 10 (January 11, 1909); clipping in Rubakin archive 38/7.

101. F. Dukhovnikov and N. Khovanskii, "O razvitii knizhnoi torgovli v Saratove," in *Saratovskii krai: istoricheskie ocherki, vospominaniia, materialy*, vol. 1 (Saratov, 1893), p. 346.

102. Prugavin, *Zaprosy*, p. 301.

103. *Zhizn' dlia knigi* (Moscow, 1962), pp. 21-23.

104. E. A. Dinershtein, *I. D. Sytin* (Moscow, 1983), p. 8.

105. *Zhizn' dlia knigi*, p. 20.

106. Prugavin, *Zaprosy*, pp. 284-85.

107. *Ezhegodnik 1892* (Moscow, 1893), p. 27.

108. Belousov, *Literaturnaia Moskva*, p. 31.

109. Prugavin, *Zaprosy*, pp. 286-88.

110. Ibid., p. 288.

111. M. N. Kufaev, *Istoriia knigi v XIX veke* (Leningrad, 1927), p. 202.

112. *Pol veka dlia knigi. Literaturno-khudozhestvennyi sbornik posviashchennyi piatidesiatiletiiu izdatel'skoi deiatel'nosti I. D. Sytina* (Moscow, 1916), pp. 3-28.

113. Ibid., p. 387.

114. *Ocherk izdatel'skoi deiatel'nosti T-va I. D. Sytina* (Moscow, 1911), p. vi.

115. F. Dukhovnikov and N. Khovanskii, "O razvitii knizhnoi torgovli," pp. 345-46.

116. *Katalog knizhnoi i kartinnoi torgovli I. D. Sytina i K*° (Moscow, 1888).

117. *Katalog knizhnoi torgovli naslednitsy P. N. Sharapova, O. V. Luzinoi* (Moscow, 1887).

118. *Knigoizdatel'stvo I. D. Sytina* (Moscow, 1900).

119. *Katalog knizhnoi i kartinnoi torgovli A. D. Sazonova* (Moscow, 1899).

120. B. P. Orlov, *Poligraficheskaia promyshlennost'*, pp. 247-48.

121. *Otchet o khode torgovli v Nizhegorodskoi iarmarke 1915 goda*, ed. S. V. Speranskii (Moscow, 1916), pp. 299-300.

122. Belousov, *Literaturnaia Moskva*, pp. 49-50.

123. Ibid., p. 50.

124. I. A Golyshev, "Kartinnoe i knizhnoe narodnoe proizvodstvo," *Russkaia starina*, no. 3 (1886), p. 714.

125. Sveshnikov, *Vospominaniia*, pp. 380-81.

126. Ivan Zabelin, *Istoriia goroda Moskvy*, vol. 1 (Moscow, 1905), pp. 637-51.

127. *KV*, nos. 3-6 (1860), p. 37.

128. P. Petrov, "Sukharevskii knizhnyi torg v Moskve," *Bibliograficheskie izvestiia*, no. 3-4 (1915), pp. 114-19.

129. *Ocherki istorii Leningrada*, vol. 3, ed. B. M. Kochakov (Moscow-Leningrad, 1956), p. 588.

130. A. A. Bakhtiarov, *Istoriia knigi na Rusi* (St. Petersburg, 1890), p. 263.

131. Andreev, "Ischezaiushchaia literatura," p. 3.

132. Ibid., p. 3.

133. Bakhtiarov, *Istoriia knigi*, p. 263.

134. Ibid., p. 264.

135. A. S. Prugavin, *Zaprosy naroda*, 1st ed. (Moscow, 1890), p. 153. All other references are to the expanded second edition that appeared in 1895.

136. N. Tikhonravov, "Ofeni," in *Vladimirskii sbornik* (Moscow, 1857), pp. 22-23, and N. Trokhimovskii, "Ofeni," *RV*, no. 6 (1866), pp. 560-61.

137. In Vladimir, Shuiskii, Muromskii, Kovrovskii, Viaznikovskii, Gorokhovetskii, and Sudogodskii uezds; in Moscow, Serpukhovskii, and Podol'skii uezds; and in Tula Aleksinskii uezd.

138. Ia. E. Vodarskii, *Promyshlennye seleniia Tsentral'noi Rossii* (Moscow, 1972), p. 190.

139. Ibid., pp. 192-93.

140. Prugavin, *Zaprosy*, p. 326.

141. S. Ia. Elpat'evskii, *Vospominaniia za 50 let* (Leningrad, 1929), p. 192.

142. Trokhimovskii, "Ofeni," pp. 571-672. See also *Voennostatisticheskii sbornik*, vol. 4, ed. N. N. Obruchev (St. Petersburg, 1871), pp. 532-33. He gives the estimate of 5,000 in 1867, excluding *khodebshchiki; VV*, no. 7 (1903), p. 111.

143. Prugavin, *Zaprosy*, p. 289.

144. N. Rubakin, "Kakimi sposobami rasprostraniat' knigi na Rusi," *O*, no. 2 (1901), pp. 89-90.

145. *VV*, no. 7 (1903), p. 112.

146. Rubakin, "Kakimi sposobami," p. 23.

147. Ibid., p. 84.

148. "Knizhnaia torgovlia," *KV*, no. 16 (1860), p. 183.

149. Golyshev, "Kartinnoe i knizhnoe," p. 708.

150. V. Denisov, *Voina i lubok* (Petrograd, 1916), p. 14.

151. M. Gor'kii, *Polnoe sobranie sochinenii*, vol. 3 (Moscow, 1969), pp. 195-96.

152. Prugavin, *Zaprosy*, p. 371.

153. "Ofenskii promysel vo Vladimirskoi gubernii," *Vestnik Vladimirskogo gubernskogo zemstva*, no. 22 (1900), pp. 16, 36.

154. *Spravochnaia knizhka po bibliotechnomu delu, knizhnoi torgovle i izdatel'stvu*, ed. V. I. Charnoluskii (Petrograd, 1914), pp. 68-93.

155. Muratov, *Knizhnoe delo v Rossii*, pp. 153-54, 183-84. A. A. Govorov, *Istoriia knizhnoi torgovli v SSSR* (Moscow, 1976), p. 233.

156. A. Smirnov, "Chto chitaiut v derevne," *RM*, no. 7 (1903), p. 113.

157. Rubakin archive 6/15, p. 15.

158. *Ezhegodnik vneshkol'nogo obrazovaniia*, ed. V. I. Charnoluskii (St. Petersburg, 1910), p. 263.

159. Tikhonravov, "Ofeni," pp. 22-23.

160. Golyshev, "Kartinnoe i knizhnoe," p. 708, and I. D. Sytin, "O torgovle narodnymi knigami v raznos," in *Trudy pervogo s"ezda russkikh deiatelei po pechatnomu delu v S. Peterburge, 5-12 aprelia 1895 g.* (St. Petersburg, 1896), pp. 18-19.

161. *Ezhegodnik Ministerstva finansov* (1870-1913); see also B. N. Mironov, *Vnutrennii rynok Rossii vo vtoroi polovine XVIII-pervoi polovine XIX v.* (Leningrad, 1981), p. 177. Mironov gives a figure for peddlers who traveled by foot.

162. A. Engel'gart, "Iz derevni," *OZ*, no. 3 (1878), p. 11.

163. *O*, no. 3 (1901), p. 24.

164. Konstantin Konichev, *Russkii samorodok* (Leningrad, 1966), pp. 3-6.

165. M. I. Slukhovskii, *Kniga i derevnia* (Moscow-Leningrad, 1928), p. 152.

166. Ibid., p. 152.

167. G. Gavrilov (a peasant correspondent) in *Bednota*, no. 1241 (June 14, 1922).

CHAPTER IV

1. A. I. Nazarov, *Oktiabr' i kniga* (Moscow, 1968), p. 227.

2. *Rasprostranenie pechati v dorevoliutsionnoi Rossii i v Sovetskom Soiuze* (Moscow, 1967), pp. 15-16, 28-29.

3. Govorov, *Istoriia knizhnoi torgovli*, p. 178, and *KV*, no. 49 (1903), p. 1572.

4. Rubakin archive 12/16.

5. *KL*, no. 1 (1907), p. 19; no. 6 (1907), p. 27.

6. *KL*, no. 1 (1907), p. 19.

7. *Moskva v ee proshlom i nastoiashchem*, vol. 12 (Moscow, 1912), p. 16.

8. "Reklamisty izdateli," *O*, no. 3 (March 1900), pp. 30-36.

9. E. Tsyperovich, "Reklama," *SM*, no. 1 (1911), pp. 203-204.

10. Ruud, *Fighting Words*.

11. *Rasprostranenie pechati*, pp. 15-16, and B. I. Esin, "Materialy k istorii gazetnogo dela v Rossii," *Vestnik Moskovskogo universiteta. Zhurnalistika*, no. 4 (1967), pp. 85-86, and no. 2 (1969), pp. 80-81.

12. *Niva*, no. 53 (1894), pp. 22-23.

13. Jeffrey Brooks, "Russian Nationalism and Russian Literature," in *Nation and Ideology: Essays in Honor of Wayne S. Vucinich*, ed. Ivo Banac, John G. Ackerman, and Roman Szporluk (Boulder, Colo.: East European Quarterly Monographs, 1981), pp. 315-34. See also Chapter 8.

14. *Niva*, no. 49 (1912), p. 979.

15. *Niva*, no. 15 (1900).

16. *Niva*, no. 52 (1889), p. 1353.

17. *Niva*, no. 53 (1894), jubilee appendix, p. 23; K. Konichev, *Russkii samorodok* (Leningrad, 1966), p. 27; *KV*, no. 6 (1903), p. 180.

18. A. Bakhtiarov, *Slugi pechati* (St. Petersburg, 1893), p. 116.

19. Konichev, *Russkii samorodok*, p. 27.

20. Vas. Iv. Nemirovich-Danchenko, *Na kladbishchakh (Vospominaniia)* (Revel', 1921), pp. 44-45.

21. *Rodina*, no. 1 (1879).

22. *Ogonek*, no. 2 (1913).

23. "A. A. Kaspari," *Naborshchik i pechatnyi mir*, no. 157 (1913), p. 655.

24. *Rodina*, no. (1913), pp. ii-iii.

25. *Ogonek*, no. 50 (1910), no. 52 (1912), no. 50 (1914).

26. N. G. Malykhin, *Ocherki po istorii knigoizdatel'skogo dela v SSSR* (Moscow, 1965), p. 233.

27. A. Admiral'skii and S. Belov, *Rytsar' knigi* (Leningrad, 1970), p. 10.

28. See *Priroda i liudi*, no. 52 (1914), twenty-fifth anniversary issue, and *Mir prikliuchenii*, no. 12 (1914), fifth anniversary issue.

29. See B. P. Baluev, *Politicheskaia reaktsiia 80-x godov XIX veka i russkaia zhurnalistika* (Moscow, 1971), for an interesting discussion of the new journalism.

30. Cited in *Novyi kolos*, no. 2 (1917), p. 34.

31. *Polveka dlia knig*, p. 405.

32. "Nekrolog," *RM*, no. 9 (1911), p. 44.

33. *Moskovskie vedomosti*, no. 174 (July 30, 1911).

34. Ibid.

35. Ivan Belousov, "Vospominaniia," in *Segodnia—Al'manakh khudozhestvennoi literatury, kritiki i iskusstva*, no. 1 (1922), pp. 11-14.

36. N. Pastukhov, *Stikhotvoreniia* (Moscow, 1862), p. 23.

37. Ibid., p. 27.

38. Ibid., p. 40.

39. Belousov, "Vospominaniia," pp. 11-12.

40. *Moskovskie vedomosti*, no. 174 (July 30, 1911).

41. V. A. Giliarovskii, "Moskovskie gazety v 80-kh gg," *Byloe*, no. 6 (1925), pp. 119-30.

42. V. M. Shevliakov, "Originaly i chudaki," *IV*, no. 11 (1913), p. 521.

43. Giliarovskii, "Moskovskie gazety," p. 120.

44. Aleksandr Chekhov, "Zapiski reportera," *IV* (July 1907), p. 71.

45. Vl. Giliarovskii, *Sochineniia v chetyrekh tomakh*, vol. 3 (Moscow, 1967), p. 100.

46. K. Reshetov, *K novoi zhizni* (Moscow, 1928), p. 117.

47. Shevliakov, "Originaly," pp. 528-29.

48. A. P. Chekhov, *Polnoe sobranie sochinenii i pisem*, vol. 16 (Moscow, 1979), p. 156.

49. Shevliakov, "Originaly," p. 529.

50. Belousov, "Vospominaniia," p. 112.

51. Giliarovskii, *Sochineniia*, pp. 133-36.

52. Shevliakov, "Originaly," pp. 524-25.

53. N. Pastukhov, *Ocherki i rasskazy* (Moscow, 1879).

54. Giliarovskii, "Moskovskie gazety," p. 123.

55. *Po sledam minuvshego* (Moscow, 1948), p. 30.

56. A. P. Kugel', *Literaturnye vospominaniia 1882-1896* (Petrograd-Moscow, 1923), pp. 109-14.

57. Ibid.

58. Giliarovskii, *Sochineniia*, pp. 109-15.

59. N. I. Pastukhov, *Razboinik Churkin. Narodnoe skazanie* (Moscow, 1883-84). I quote from the separate edition of the tale, which was published in five parts soon after the corresponding section of the serial appeared. The pagination is sequential. Parts 4 and 5 have an 1884 publication date even though they were actually published in 1885, after the novel was finished. The illustrations in these parts were approved by the censor in June 1885.

60. Giliarovskii, *Sochineniia*, p. 115.

61. Shevliakov, "Originaly," pp. 521-22.

62. The article is reprinted in *Russkii vestnik*, no. 2 (1884), pp. 905-909.

63. *Literaturnoe nasledstvo*, vol. 22/24 (Moscow, 1935), p. 514.

64. Chekhov, *Sochineniia*, vol. 16, p. 52.

65. Ibid., p. 143.

66. Belousov, "Vospominaniia," pp. 113-14.

67. *Russkaia ballada*, ed. V. I. Chernyshev (Leningrad, 1936), pp. 368-69, 471-72. The citation in the notes is to an article in *Russkie vedomosti* (no. 21, 1888).

68. Belousov, "Vospominaniia," p. 113.

69. Shevliakov, "Originaly," p. 529.

70. Prugavin, *Zaprosy*, p. 403.

71. Giliarovskii, "Moskovskie gazety," p. 123.

72. Giliarovskii, *Sochineniia*, pp. 79-81.

73. Giliarovskii, "Moskovskie gazety," p. 123.

74. A. Pazukhin, *Chudaki nashego veka* (Moscow, 1901), p. 51.

75. V. Lobanov, *Stoleshniki Diadi Giliaia* (Moscow, 1972), p. 34.

76. Giliarovskii, *Sochineniia*, p. 99.

77. A. Chekhov, *Polnoe sobranie sochinenii i pisem*, vol. 1 (Moscow, 1975), pp. 93, 552.

78. *Sbornik statisticheskikh svedenii po Moskovskoi gubernii, narodnoe obrazovanie*, vol. 9 (Moscow, 1884), pp. 150-51. This was followed by *Russkie vedomosti* (32), *Sovremenye novosti* (31), *Sel'skii vestnik* (27), and *Niva* (22).

79. I. A. Belousov, "Ushedshaia Moskva," in *Ushedshaia Moskva* (Moscow, 1964), p. 394.

80. *IKMV*, no. 9 (1911), p. 234.

81. Muromskii, *Byt i nuzhdy*, p. 13.

82. Ibid., pp. 15-16.

83. Orlov, *Poligraficheskaia promyshlennost'*, pp. 14-19.

84. Giliarovskii, *Sochineniia*, p. 6; *Zhurnalistika*, no. 2 (1969), p. 79.

85. L. N. Beliaeva et al., *Bibliografiia periodicheskikh izdanii Rossii 1901-1916*, vol. 2 (Leningrad, 1959), p. 358.

86. Belousov, "Vospominaniia," p. 112.

87. Kugel', *Literaturnye vospominaniia*, pp. 110-16.

88. *Den'*, no. 160 (June 17, 1913).

89. *Den'*, no. 45 (March 10, 1918). This is the main source for Gorodetskii's life.

90. V. A. Svirskii, *Istoriia moei zhizni* (Moscow, 1947), p. 522.

91. N. A. Anzimirov, *Kramol'niki* (Moscow, 1907).

92. *Derevenskaia gazeta 1909-15*. See his *Moi malen'kie skazki* (Moscow, 1911).

93. *Den'*, no. 160 (June 17, 1913), and *Moskovskaia gazeta kopeika*, no. 1 (April 20, 1909).

94. *Tovarishchestvo izdatel'skogo dela "Kopeika"* (St. Petersburg, 1910); *Gazeta kopeika* (June 19, 1913).

95. I am grateful to Louise McReynolds for making this information available to me. According to A. Z. Okorokov, *Oktiabr' i krakh russkoi burzhuaznoi pressy* (Moscow, 1970), p. 55, however, the paper's prerevolutionary circulation reached a million. The correspondents of the Moscow zemstvo in 1915 identified *Kopeika* as the third most popular newspaper in the villages of Moscow Province. See *Novyi kolos*, no. 2 (1917), p. 34.

96. *Polveka knig*, p. 504; Okorokov, *Krakh*, p. 55.

97. See *Russkoe slovo*, no. 204 (September 3, 1916).

98. V. A. Katanian, *Maiakovskii-khudozhnik* (Moscow, 1963), pp. 54-57.

99. Beliaeva, *Bibliografiia*, p. 369; *Trudovaia kopeika*, no. 20 (1912).

100. *Russkoe slovo*, no. 117 (May 23, 1912).

101. *Moskovskaia gazeta kopeika*, no. 59 (1909).

102. See coverage for October 3, 1913, and October 29, 1913.

103. *Volny*, nos. 1-4 (1912).

104. *Tovarishchestvo izdatel'skogo dela "Kopeika"* (St. Petersburg, 1910).

105. St. Petersburg was renamed Petrograd during World War I.

106. These figures and the following are based on one week of the newspaper, January, nos. 4-10, 1913, and 1917.

107. May 1, 1910; May 13, 1910 (no. 650); May 2, 1910 (no. 639); June 1, 1910 (no. 669); June 28, 1910 (no. 695); June 30, 1910 (no. 697).

108. *Tovarishchestvo izd. dela "Kopeika,"* p. 2.

109. The word *krechet* means gyrfalcon, but the surname was probably common enough so that readers did not immediately think of this meaning.

110. Kleinbort, *Ocherki,* p. 13.

111. Slukhovskii, *Kniga,* p. 30.

112. The novel was not completed in the newspaper. I use the separate edition, M. Raskatov, *Porvannye tsepi* (Petrograd, 1917).

113. *Faraon* was commonly used as a derogatory term for the police.

114. Raskatov, *Porvannye tsepi,* p. 5.

115. These and all other figures unless otherwise noted are based on the listings in *Knizhnaia letopis'*. Detective fiction was given a separate subject heading in 1908, but the decision of what to include under this heading was arbitrary and erratic. I have therefore recalculated the totals for different types of stories from the individual listings. See also the bibliographical essay.

116. Edmund Pearson, *Dime Novels or Following an Old Trail in Popular Literature* (1929; reprint, Port Washington, N.Y., 1968), p. 212.

117. See "Pinkertonovshchina" in *Literaturnaia entsiklopediia* (Leningrad, 1929), and N. Tasin, "Bul'varnyi roman vo Frantsii," *SM,* no. 9 (1913), p. 204.

118. Cited in "Nat Pinkerton o sebe," in *Sinii zhurnal,* no. 42 (October, 1913).

119. *Nat Pinkerton—korol' syshchikov. Arest v oblakakh,* no. 12 (St. Petersburg, 1907-1909).

120. Ibid.; *Giena v poezdakh "Ekspress,"* no. 9 (reprint, Riga, 1924).

121. A. E. Murch, *The Development of the Detective Novel* (New York: Philosophical Library, 1968), pp. 140-41; Howard Haycraft draws a similar distinction in his *Murder for Pleasure* (New York, 1968), p. 83.

122. Régis Messac, *Le "Detective Novel" et l'influence de la pensée scientifique* (Paris: Librairie Ancienne Honore Champion, 1929).

123. Kornei Chukovskii, "Nat Pinkerton i sovremennaia literatura," in *Kniga o sovremennykh pisateliakh* (St. Petersburg, 1914), pp. 22-72.

124. Ian Ousby, *Bloodhounds of Heaven* (Cambridge, Mass.: Harvard University Press, 1976), p. 141.

125. *Nat Pinkerton—korol',* no. 12.

126. *Nik Karter—amerikanskii Sherlok Kholms, Ines Navarro prekrasnyi demon,* no. 5 (Petrograd, 1915-16).

127. *Nat Pinkerton—korol'. Piraty Gudzonovoi reki,* no. 8 (reprint, Riga, 1924).

128. *Nik Karter—amerikanskii Sherlok,* no. 5.

129. The stories are printed as a supplement to Viktor fon Fal'k, *Tainy Napoleona ili gosudarstvennyi izmennik Iosif Boianovskii,* no. 1 (Warsaw, 1908).

130. *Nat Pinkerton—korol',* no. 25.

131. *Nik Karter—korol' vsemirno-izvestnykh syshchikov. Vo vlasti terroristov,* no. 1 (Warsaw, n.d.).

132. P. Nikitin, *Noveishie prikliucheniia Sherloka Kholmsa v Rossii. Taina tsyganki Steshi,* no. 4 (Moscow, 1908).

133. Nikitin, *Noveishie prikliucheniia. Neulovimaia shaika,* no. 9; *Zakoldovannyi most,* no. 15.

134. *Oka-Shima, znamenityi iaponskii syshchik,* no. 1 (Khar'kov, 1908).

135. V. A. Gladkov, *Kio-Khako, iaponskii korol' syshchikov,* no. 7 (Moscow, 1917).

136. *Nat Pinkerton—korol',* no. 12.

137. *Nik Karter—amerikanskii Sherlok,* no. 1.

138. Gvido Fel's, *Razboinichii syn, ataman Vil'de* (Warsaw, 1912).

139. *Antonio Porro* (Warsaw, n.d.), no. 14.

140. V. Osteral, *Genii zla ili znamenityi russkii syshchik Gektor Grinfel'd,* no. 3 (Ekaterinoslav, 1907).

141. Dwight MacDonald, *Against the American Grain* (New York: Random House, 1952), p. 393.

142. *Knizhnaia letopis'* (1907), listing number 7381.

143. N. Verigin, "Literatura syska v otsenke uchenikov srednikh klassov gimnazii," *Pedagogicheskii sbornik,* no. 10 (1906), p. 288.

144. Tsentral'nyi gosudarstvennyi istoricheskii arkhiv SSSR, fond 776 (Chief Administration for Press Affairs), op. 9, delo 37, p. 3. I thank Louise McReynolds for making this information available to me.

145. *Moskva v ee proshlom i nastoiashchem,* vol. 12 (Moscow, 1912), p. 15.

146. *Nat Pinkerton—korol',* no. 37.

147. *Indeiskie vozhdi,* no. 6 (St. Petersburg, 1908).

148. Chukovskii, *Kniga o sovremennykh pisateliakh,* p. 55.

149. Ibid., p. 16.

150. P. Zhulev, "Rodnaia kartinka," *Voprosy narodnogo obrazovaniia,* nos. 14-15 (November-December 1913), pp. 54-58.

151. *Russkoe slovo,* no. 140 (1910).

152. A. Suvorovskii, "Nat Pinkerton v detskom ponimanii," *Vestnik vospitaniia,* no. 1 (1909), pp. 157-58; see also the report in *Nedelia Vestnika Znaniia,* no. 28 (1911), p. 7.

153. Gladkov, *Kio-Khako,* no. 5.

154. G. I. Porshnev, *Revoliutsiia i kul'tura naroda* (Irkutsk, 1917), p. 66.

155. "Chitaiushchaia rabochaia molodezh' Moskvy," *Krasnyi bibliotekar',* no. 8 (August 1924), pp. 38-45.

156. V. V. Rozanov, *Opavshie list'ia* (St. Petersburg, 1913), p. 341.

157. Marietta Shaginian, *Chelovek i vremiia. Istoriia chelovecheskogo stanovleniia* (Moscow, 1980), pp. 4-6.

158. Ibid., pp. 405-408.

159. Richard Stites, *The Women's Liberation Movement in Russia* (Princeton, N.J.: Princeton University Press, 1978).

160. *Rech'* (February 21, 1911).

161. See her comments in the preface to her *Kryl'ia vzmakhnuli!* (Moscow, 1918); see also V. Dadonov, *A. Verbitskaia i ee romany* "Kliuchi schastia" i "Dukh vremeni" (Moscow, 1911).

162. *Knizhnaia letopis'*, October 27, 1907, lists vol. 1 in 7,000 copies, but it does not offer a reliable listing of her books. The second volume is listed for the first time only as a second edition on February 29, 1909. Verbitskaia regularly lists the *tirage* of her various works on the last page of each new publication, and I have used these lists where indicated because there are gaps in the *Knizhnaia letopis'* listing. On the last page of *Kliuchi schast'ia*, vol. 1 (Moscow, 1910), she claims that *Dukh vremeni* (Moscow, 1908) had a tirage of 35,000 copies. By 1914, on the last page of *Igo liubvi*, she raises this to 51,000 copies. This is the last such list I found, and the tirage of *Igo liubvi* is not given and this work is not listed in *Knizhnaia letopis'*.

163. *Knizhnaia letopis'* lists vol. 1, December 1908, as 10,608 copies, and February 14, 1909, as 15,000 copies; vol. 2, October 10, 1909, as 15,000 copies, and March 6, 1910, as 25,000 copies. In 1914, in *Igo liubvi*, she lists the second edition of vol. 1 as 25,000 copies and the other volumes as follows: 3 (44,000); 4 (25,000); 5 (30,000); 6 (30,000).

164. From her list in *Igo liubvi* (Moscow, 1914).

165. Graf Amori, *Pobezhdennye* (Moscow, 1914); *Liubovnye pokhozhdeniia M-me Verbitskoi*, vols. 1 and 2 (Moscow, 1914).

166. On Glyn, see Anthony Glyn, *Elinor Glyn: A Biography* (New York, 1955).

167. On Corelli, see Thomas F. G. Coates and R. S. Warren Bell, *Marie Corelli the Writer and the Woman* (London, 1903); Eileen Bigland, *Marie Corelli the Woman and the Legend* (London, 1953).

168. A. Verbitskaia, *Moemu chitateliu*, vol. 1 (Moscow, 1908), p. 338.

169. A. Verbitskaia, *Moi vospominaniia*, vol. 2 (Moscow, 1911), p. 9.

170. *Russkie vedomosti*, no. 7 (1911).

171. See *Po novomu—roman uchitel'nitsy* (Moscow, 1905), originally printed in *Obrazovanie* (1902), and *Vecherinka*, which is reprinted with it and was originally printed in *Russkoe bogatstvo* in 1902.

172. Dadonov, *Verbitskaia*, p. 177.

173. Verbitskaia's preface to Leona Frap'e, *Ogon'ki* (Moscow, 1911), p. 5.

174. Dadonov, in *Verbitskaia*, pp. 70-71, blames politics for her hostile reception from liberal critics.

175. K. Chukovskii, *Kniga o sovremennykh pisateliakh* (St. Petersburg, 1914), p. 9.

176. Kleinbort, "Maksim Gor'kii i chitatel' iz nizov," *VE*, no. 12 (1913), p. 171.

177. M. A. Smushkova, *Pervye itogi izucheniia chitatelia* (Moscow-Leningrad, 1926), p. 8; see also G. I. Porshnev, *Revoliutsiia i kul'tura naroda* (Irkutsk, 1917), p. 66.

178. E. A. Nagrodskaia, *Gnev Dionisa* (St. Petersburg, 1910).

179. O. G. Bebutova, *Puti k kar'ere* (Petrograd, 1917), and *Zolotaia pyl'* (Petrograd, 1917).

180. *IKMK*, no. 7 (1915), p. 105.

181. L. A. Charskaia, *Ee velichestvo Liubov'* (Petrograd, 1915).

182. Shukhmin, *O tom, kak chert ukral iazyk u teshchi* (Moscow, 1913), p. iii.

183. Harris, "Iconography and Intellectual History," pp. 196-211.

184. N. A. Lebedev, *Ocherk istorii kino SSSR. Nemoe kino*, 2nd ed. (Moscow, 1965), p. 53.

185. B. S. Likhachev, *Kino v Rossii (1896-1926)*, part 1, 1896-1913 (Leningrad, 1927), p. 196.

186. Lebedev, *Ocherk istorii kino*, p. 53.

CHAPTER V

1. The method of analysis and the composition of samples of stories considered in chapters 5, 6, 7, and 8 are discussed in the bibliographical essay.

2. Altick, *The English Common Reader*, pp. 294, 355; Zeldin, *Taste and Corruption*, p. 178.

3. Campbell, *Hero With a Thousand Faces*.

4. My comparison is exclusively with English, French, and American popular fiction, which represent a clear alternative pattern. Students of German popular literature will note some interesting parallels with the Russian.

5. Paul Zweig, *The Adventurer* (New York: Basic Books, 1974), pp. 13-14, 126-27.

6. See, for example, N. Aristov, *Ob istoricheskom znachenii russkikh razboinichikh pesen* (Voronezh, 1875); I. I. Illiustrov, *Zhizn' russkogo naroda v ego poslovitsakh i pogovorkakh*, 3rd ed. (Moscow, 1915), p. 278; and numerous portrayals of bandits in A. N. Afanasov, *Narodnye russkie skazki*, ed. V. Ia. Propp (Moscow, 1957). See also discussions of bandits in Yuri Glazov, " 'Thieves' in the USSR—A Social Phenomenon," *Survey*, no. 1 (98) (Winter 1976), pp. 141-56; and Valerii Chalidze, *Criminal Russia* (New York: Random House, 1977).

7. *Tolkovyi slovar' zhivogo velikorusskogo iazyka Vladimira Dalia*, vol. 3 (St. Petersburg, 1907), pp. 1473-74; *Ulozhenie o nakazaniiakh ugolovnykh i ispravitel'nykh 1885 goda*, 18th ed., published by N. S. Tagantsev (Petrograd, 1916), p. 1043.

8. V. Sergeevich, *Lektsii i issledovaniia po drevnei istorii russkogo prava* (St. Petersburg, 1910), pp. 420, 431-35, 449-50.

9. *Ulozhenie o nakazaniakh*, pp. 1041-49, articles 1627-36, and p. 638, article 922; *Entsiklopedicheskii slovar'*, Brokgauz-Efron, vol. 26 (St. Petersburg, 1899), p. 110.

10. Aristov, *Ob istoricheskom znachenii russkikh*, p. 3.

11. Cited in V. Propp, *Russkii geroicheskii epos*, 2nd ed. (Moscow, 1958), p. 443.

12. These were predominantly ethnic Chinese despite the name *khunkhuzy*, or "red beards."

13. See S V. Maksimov, *Sibir' i katorga* (St. Petersburg, 1900), p. 246; See also E. N. Tarnovskii, "Dvizhenie prestupnosti v Rossiiskoi imperii za 1899-1908," *Zhurnal Ministerstva Iustitsii*, no. 9 (1909), pp. 66-70; S. S. Ostroumov, *Prestupnost' i ee prichiny v do revoliutsionnoi Rossii* (Moscow, 1960, 1980); *Otchet po glavnomu tiuremnomu upravleniiu za 1913 god*, part 2 (Petrograd, 1914), appendix, p. 33.

14. A. F. Koshko, *Ocherki ugolovnogo mira tsarskoi Rossii* (Paris, 1926), pp. 181-92, and A. de Kochko, *Scènes du monde criminel russe* (Paris, 1929), pp. 171-85.

15. V. Mikhnevich, *Iazvy Peterburga: Opyt istoriko-statisticheskogo issledovaniia nravstvennosti stolichnogo naseleniia* (St. Petersburg, 1886), p. 141.

16. *Russkoe slovo*, nos. 101, 255 (1910).

17. *Nedelia*, no. 50 (1885), pp. 1774-76.

18. V. Dal', *Tolkovyi slovar' zhivogo velikorusskogo iazyka*, vol. 1 (1903; Paris: Librarie des cinq continents, 1954), p. 595, and Chalidze, *Criminal Russia*, p. 4.

19. Dal', *Tolkovyi slovar'*, p. 595.

20. E. I. Iakushkin, *Obychnoe pravo, materialy dlia bibliografii obychnogo prava*, vol. 4 (Moscow, 1909), p. 62.

21. See S. V. Maksimov, *Sibir' i katorga* (Moscow, 1900), pp. 160-70, for a discussion of the relation between criminal slang and the language of *ofeni*.

22. *Pesni sobrannye P. V. Kireevskim*, vol. 9, ed. P. A. Bessonov (Moscow, 1872), pp. 35-36, and notes.

23. John G. Cawelti, *The Six-Gun Mystique* (Bowling Green, Ohio: Bowling Green Popular Press, 1970), p. 34.

24. E. I. Iakushkin, *Obychnoe pravo*, vol. 1 (Moscow, 1910), pp. xvii-xix, and Chalidze, *Criminal Russia*, pp. 11-16.

25. Iakushkin, *Obychnoe pravo*, p. xix.

26. George Kennan, *Siberia and the Exile System*, vol. 1 (London, 1891), p. 401-402.

27. S. V. Maksimov, *Sibir' i katorga* (St. Petersburg, 1900), p. 6.

28. Ibid., p. 17.

29. George P. Fedotov, *The Russian Religious Mind*, vols. 1 and 2 (Cambridge, Mass.: Harvard University Press, 1946, 1966).

30. Iakushkin, *Obychnoe pravo*, pp. xx-xxi; Chalidze, *Criminal Russia*, pp. 4-7.

31. See *Pesni sobrannye P. V. Kireevskim*, vols. 5-10 (Moscow, 1863-74); A. I. Sobolevskii, *Velikorusskie narodnye pesni*, vols. 6-7 (St. Petersburg, 1900, 1902); and V. F. Miller, *Pesni sobrannye P. N. Rybnikovym*, 2nd ed., vols. 1-3 (Moscow, 1909-10).

32. *Fol'klor krest'ianskoi voiny 1773-1775* (Leningrad, 1973), pp. 68-69.

33. Vsevolod Miller, *Ocherki russkoi narodnoi slovesnosti. Byliny*, vol. 2 (Moscow, 1910), pp. 327-58, and vol. 3 (Moscow-Leningrad, 1924), pp. 254-68.

34. Vl. Mikhnevich, *Istoricheskie etiudy russkoi zhizni*, vol. 2 (St. Petersburg, 1882), pp. 423-29.

35. T. M. Akimova, "O zhanrovoi prirode russkikh udalykh pesen," *Russkii fol'klor*, no. 5 (1960), pp. 183-218.

36. *Pesni sobrannye P. V. Kireevskim*, vol. 7 (Moscow, 1868), pp. 138-39.

37. D. L. Mordovtsev, *Van'ka Kain. Istoricheskii ocherk* (St. Petersburg, 1897), p. 8; idem, *Politicheskie dvizheniia russkogo naroda*, vols. 1 and 2 (Moscow, 1871); idem, *Samozvantsy i ponizovaia vol'nitsa*, 2nd ed., vols. 1 and 2 (St. Petersburg, 1886).

38. K. V. Chistov, *Russkie narodnye sotsial'no-utopicheskie legendy* (Moscow, 1967), pp. 24-36; Eric Hobsbawm, *Bandits*, 2nd rev. ed. (New York: Pantheon, 1981), p. 30; Daniel Field, *Rebels in the Name of the Tsar* (Boston: Houghton Mifflin, 1976), pp. 31-32; Haruki Wada, "The Inner World of Russian Peasants," *Annals of the Institute of Social Science*, University of Tokyo, no. 20 (1979).

39. "Iz Guslits," *Bratskoe slovo*, no. 2 (1884), p. 81.

40. A. L. Peregudov, "Guslitsa," *Novyi mir* (June 1927), pp. 194-201.

41. Ibid., p. 194.

42. Giliarovskii, *Sochineniia*, p. 114.

43. Pastukhov, *Razboinik Churkin*, pp. 2-3.

44. S. Reshetov, *K novoi zhnzni* (Moscow-Leningrad, 1926), p. 8.

45. *Sten'ka Razin, ataman razboinikov* (Moscow, 1877).

46. M. Evstigneev, *Ved'ma iz-za Dnepra, ili razboinik Solovei* (Moscow, 1868), and *Ved'ma i chernyi voron, ili strashnye nochi za Dneprom* (Moscow, 1912).

47. S. V. Maksimov, *Nechistaia nevedomaia i krestnaia sila* (St. Petersburg, 1903), pp. 193-96.

48. *Kondrashka Bulavin, buntovshchik byvshii v tsarstvovanie imperatora Petra I*, vols. 1 and 2 (Moscow, 1849).

49. V. Ia. Shmitanovskii, *Ermak, ili pokorenie sibirskogo tsarstva*, vol. 1 (Moscow, 1863), pp. 11-12.

50. A. I. Klibanov, *Narodnaia sotsial'naia utopiia v Rossii. Period feodalizma* (Moscow, 1977), pp. 9-34, and Chistov, *Russkie narodnye*, pp. 237-340.

51. D. S. Likhachev and A. M. Panchenko, *"Smekhovoi mir" drevnei Rusi* (Moscow, 1976).

52. Hobsbawm, *Bandits*.

53. M. Evstigneev, *Udaloi razboinik* (Moscow, 1869).

54. *Sten'ka Razin, ataman razboinikov* (1877).

55. *Liubov' kazaka, ili pogibel' Emel'ki Pugacheva* (Moscow, 1863), p. 20.

56. K. S. N-va, *Razboinik Churkin. Narodnoe skazanie* (Moscow, 1884), p. 8.

57. S. I. Glebov, *Zhizn' i kazn' Sten'ki Razina volzhskogo atamana* (St. Petersburg, 1912), p. 29.

58. Ivin (Kassirov), *Brynskii les, povest' XVI stoletiia* (Moscow, 1900), p. 20.

59. Evstigneev, *Ved'ma iz-za Dnepra*, p. 15.

60. M. Raskatov, *Na avanpostakh* (St. Petersburg, n.d.), p. 85.

61. A. N. Afanas'ev, *Narodnye russkie legendy* (Moscow, 1914), pp. 194-281.

62. V. Propp, *The Morphology of the Folktale*, trans. Lawrence Scott, 2nd rev. ed. American Folklore Society Bibliographical and Special Series, no. 9 (Austin:

University of Texas Press, 1968), and Will Wright, *Sixguns and Society, A Structural Study of the Western* (Berkeley: University of California Press, 1975).

63. This idea is developed in Hobsbawm, *Bandits*, and Ralph A. Austin, "Social Bandits and Other Heroic Criminals: Western Models of Resistance and their Relevance for Africa," in Donald Crummey, ed., *Rebellion and Social Protest in Africa.*

64. Wada, "The Inner World of Russian Peasants," and Field, *Rebels in the Name of the Tsar.*

65. S. Sipovskii, in *Sibirskaia sovetskaia entsiklopediia*, vol. 1 (Novosibirsk, 1929), p. 900. My count from the historical lubok catalogue of the Saltykov-Shchedrin Public Library turned up thirty-seven titles about Ermak, in contrast to twenty-nine for Peter the Great, the second most popular figure in historical lubok fiction. See the bibliographical essay.

66. R. G. Skrynnikov, *Sibirskaia ekspeditsiia Ermaka* (Moscow, 1982), p. 49.

67. *Sten'ka Razin, razboinichii ataman byvshii v tsarstvovanie tsaria Alekseia Mikhailovicha* (Moscow, 1865).

68. *Sten'ka Razin, ataman razboinikov* (1877).

69. *Sten'ka Razin* (1865), p. 35.

70. *Kondrashka Bulavin*, (1849), vol. 2, p. 77.

71. Ivin (Kassirov), *Brynskii les* (Moscow, 1900), pp. 96-97.

72. *Buria v stoiachikh vodakh: povest' iz poslednei russko-turetskoi voiny* (Kiev, 1904).

73. Don Bocharo, *Makarka dushegub, istinnoe proisshestvie* (Moscow, 1909), p. xvi.

74. I. S. Ivin (Kassirov), *Razboinik Churkin v plenu u cherkesov* (Moscow, 1885).

75. Raskatov, *Na avanpostakh*, p. 85.

76. Michael Ross, *Alexandre Dumas* (London: David and Charles, 1981), pp. 202-206.

77. Umberto Eco, *The Role of the Reader*, pp. 107-24.

78. *The Penny Dreadful*, ed. Peter Haining (London: Victor Gollancz Ltd., 1976), pp. 50-51.

79. Louis James, *Fiction for the Working Man, 1830-1850* (London: Oxford University Press, 1963), p. 165.

80. Zeldin, *Taste and Corruption*, pp. 178-80.

81. Edward L. Wheeler, *Deadwood Dick Library*, vol. 1, no. 1, *Deadwood Dick, Prince of the Road* (reprint, Cleveland: Arthur Westbrook Co., 1889), p. 30.

82. Zane Grey, *Riders of the Purple Sage* (New York: Pocket Books, 1980), p. 147.

83. Wheeler, *Deadwood Dick Library*, vol. 1, no. 6, *Death Face, the Detective.*

84. See, for example, the hanging of a rustler in Owen Wister's western novel, *The Virginian* (1902; New York: Pocket Books, 1977).

85. Pierce Egan, Jr., *Robin Hood and Little John or the Merry Men of Sherwood Forest* (London: W. S. Johnson, 1850), p. 263; other Robin Hood stories also

follow this pattern. See, for example, Howard Pyle's classic, *The Merry Adventures of Robin Hood* (1883; New York: Charles Scribner's Sons, 1946).

86. G.W.M. Reynolds, *The Mysteries of London*, vol. 2 (London, 1846), p. 442.

87. Ponson du Terrail, *Rocambole, les drames de Paris. Le Club des valets-de-coeur*, vol. 3 (Monaco: Editions du Rocher, 1964), p. 567.

88. Ponson du Terrail, *La Resurrection de Rocambole. Le Bagne de Toulon*, vol. 1 (Paris: E. Dentu, 1867), p. 152.

89. Ibid., p. 305.

90. The main historical source for Kain's life is G. Esipov's "Van'ka Kain," in *Os'mnadtsatyi vek, istoricheskii sbornik*, vol. 3, ed. Petr Bartenev (Moscow, 1869), pp. 280-342, which is based on the available state archives relating to Kain. D. L. Mordovtsev, *Van'ka Kain, Istoricheskii ocherk* (St. Petersburg, 1897), and V. V. Sipovskii, *Iz istorii russkogo romana XVIII-go veka (Van'ka Kain)* (St. Petersburg, 1902), also contain important information.

91. Shklovskii, *Matvei Komarov*, pp. 33-76, and also Sipovskii, *Iz istorii russkogo romana*. Kain's autobiography is printed in Grigorii Knizhnik, *Zhizn' Van'ki Kaina im samim rasskazannaia* (St. Petersburg, 1859).

92. M. Komarov, *Obstoiatel'nye i vernye istorii dvukh moshennikov pervogo rossiiskogo slavnogo vora, razboinika i byvshego moskovskogo syshchika Van'ki Kaina so vsemi ego syskami, rozyskami, sumasbrodnoiu svadboiu i raznymi zabavnymi ego pesniami vtorogo frantsuzskogo moshennika Kartusha i ego sotovarishchei* (Moscow: A. Reshetnikov, 1794); Misha Evstigneev, *Van'ka Kain. Sobranie predanii iz zhizni otvazhnogo vora, syshchika i razboinika* (Moscow, 1869); and *Pokhozhdeniia syshchika Van'ki Kaina* (Moscow, 1918), issues 1-12.

93. *Pokhozhdeniia syshchika Van'ki Kaina*, no. 1 (Moscow, 1918), p. 1.

94. M. D. Klefortov, *Son'ka Zolotaia ruchka* (Odessa, 1903), p. 5.

95. I cite the book version. M. Raskatov, *Porvannye tsepi* (Petrograd, 1917).

96. Richard S. Wortman, *The Development of a Russian Legal Consciousness* (Chicago: University of Chicago Press, 1976), pp. 243-89.

97. David Brion Davis, *Homicide in American Fiction, 1798-1860* (Ithaca, N.Y.: Cornell University Press, 1957), pp. 84-143, 210-36; Louis Chevalier, *Laboring Classes and Dangerous Classes in Paris During the First Half of the Nineteenth Century*, trans. Frank Jellinek (Princeton, N.J.: Princeton University Press, 1981), p. 394.

98. Michel Foucault, *Discipline and Punish*, trans. Alan Sheridan (New York: Pantheon, 1977), pp. 286-87.

99. Smith, *Virgin Land*, pp. 81-89.

100. There is a large and growing literature on the detective story. See, for example, Ousby, *Blood Hounds*; Cawelti, *Adventure, Mystery, and Romance*; and Stephen Knight, *Form and Ideology in Crime Fiction* (Bloomington: Indiana University Press, 1980).

101. *Nik Karter—Amerikanskii Sherlok Kholms*, no. 9, *Doktor Kvarts—prestupnyi uchenyi*, p. 2.

102. *Tainstvennye prikliucheniia amerikanskogo syshchika Nik Kartera* (Petrograd, 1916; Riga, 192?), p. 99; this is an undated Riga reprint from the 1920s.

103. Ibid., p. 10.

104. *Robert Gaisler* (Warsaw, 1912), p. 1.

105. Fel's, *Razboinichii syn, ataman Vil'de.*

106. *Ataman razboinikov Frants Lerman* (Kazan, 1918).

107. *Garibal'di. Krovavye prikliucheniia groznogo atamana razboinikov* (Odessa, 1902).

108. See, for example, Daniel R. Brower, "Labor Violence in the Late Nineteenth Century," with comments by Robert E. Johnson, Ronald Grigor Suny, and Diane Koenker, *Slavic Review* (Fall 1982), pp. 417-53.

CHAPTER VI

1. Zbigniew Brzezinski, "Tragic Dilemmas of Soviet World Power," *Encounter*, no. 4 (December 1983), pp. 10-17.

2. Hans Kohn, *The Idea of Nationalism* (New York: Macmillan, 1946); Karl W. Deutsch, *Nationalism and Social Communication* (New York: MIT and John Wiley, 1953); and Carlton J. Hayes, *Essays on Nationalism* (New York: Macmillan, 1926).

3. Arthur Mann, *The One and the Many: Reflections on the American Identity* (Chicago: University of Chicago Press, 1979).

4. *I nasha denezhka ne shcherbata!* (Moscow, 1854), p. 5.

5. Ivin (Kassirov), *Brynskii les*, p. 97.

6. V. Volgin, *Za bogom molitva, a za tsarem sluzhba ne propadut* (Moscow, 1904), p. 4; idem, *Mertvets bez groba* (Moscow, 1910), p. 7.

7. Evstigneev, *Anekdoty i predaniia o Petre Velikom*; V. Ia. Shmitanovskii, *Predanie o tom, kak soldat spas zhizn' Petra Velikogo*; Diadia Fedor, *Rasskazy o tsare-batiushke Petre Velikom, kak on s svoimi molodtsami soldatami protiv supostatov voeval* (St. Petersburg, 1897).

8. I discuss this in "From Folklore to Popular Literature: A Changing View of the Autocrat and the Empire," forthcoming in *Russian History.*

9. Ivin (Kassirov), *Tsygan mstitel', ili prestupnik po nevole* (Moscow, 1915), p. 88.

10. Ivin (Kassirov), *Iapancha, tatarskii naezdnik* (Moscow, 1915), p. 54.

11. Lunin (Kukel'), *V tsepiakh u kitaitsev* (Moscow, 1910).

12. N. Zriakhov, *Bitva russkikh s kabardintsami, ili prekrasnaia magometanka umiraiushchaia na grobe svoego supruga*, vols. 1 and 2, 3rd ed. (Moscow, 1843), vol. 1, p. 106.

13. *Bitva russkikh s kabardintsami* (Moscow, 1854). p. 67.

14. *Prikliucheniia kazatskogo atamana Urvana* (Kiev, 1901), p. 55.

15. Volgin, *Mertvets bez groba*, p. 16.

16. O. G. Bebutova, *Varvary XX veka*, vol. 2 (Petrograd, 1915), p. 214.

17. Charskaia, *Ee velichestvo*, p. 101.

18. A. M. Pazukhin, *Opolchennaia Rossiia* (Moscow, 1892), p. 315.

19. Richard Hellie, *Slavery in Russia, 1450-1725* (Chicago: University of Chicago Press, 1982).

20. All references to kopeck novels are to those in the St. Petersburg edition of the newspaper unless otherwise noted.

21. Foma Balagur, *Gol' na vydumki khitra* (Moscow, 1904), p. 4.

22. E. Grebenka, *Nezhinskii polkovnik Zolotarenko* (Iaroslavl', 1915). p. 3.

23. M. Evstigneev, *Stseny iz narodnogo byta raznykh stran i obshchestv* (Moscow, 1872).

24. A derogatory term for a Ukrainian, from top knot or tuft of hair.

25. V. Suvorov, *Kak zachalos' russkoe tsarstvo* (Moscow, 1898), p. 14.

26. F. Balagur, *Uzhasnaia smert' svirepogo tatarina* (Moscow, 1898), p. 16.

27. M. Evstigneev, *Strashnyi klad, ili Tatarskaia plennitsa* (Moscow, 1884), p. 32.

28. Evstigneev, *Stseny*, p. 80.

29. *Gazeta kopeika*, no. 1386 (1912).

30. Lunin (Kukel'), *Nevol'nichestvo u asiatov* (Moscow, 1898).

31. Lunin (Kukel'), *Balovnitsa, ili v dikie stepi khochu!* (Moscow, 1912), p. 83.

32. See, for example, Evstigneev's *Stseny*, pp. 70-78.

33. P. Nikitin, *Noveishie prikliucheniia Sherloka Kholmsa v Rossii. Taina tsyganki Steshi*, no. 4.

34. B. Gorev, "Russian Literature and the Jews," in V. Lvov-Rogachevskii, *A History of Russian Jewish Literature*, ed. and trans. Arthur Levin (Ann Arbor: Ardis, 1979), p. 17, 24-25.

35. Evstigneev, *Stseny*, p. 144.

36. Lunin (Kukel'), *Byloe vremia* (Moscow, 1903), p. 38.

37. *Prikliucheniia kazatskogo atamana Urvana*, p. 3.

38. *Moskovskii listok*, no. 312 (1893).

39. M. Raskatov, *Na chuzbine* (St. Petersburg, 1914), p. 50.

40. Verbitskaia, *Kliuchi schast'ia*, vol. 2, p. 30.

41. Osteral, *Genii zla*.

42. Kh. Shukhmin, *Slavnyi podvig donskogo kazaka Koz'my Kriuchkova* (Moscow, 1914), p. viii. Traditional Russian stoves had a place over them on which one could warm oneself.

43. V. Volgin, *Turetskii plennik* (Moscow, 1909), p. 11.

44. *Russkii bogatyr'* (Moscow, 1919), p. 17.

45. Lunin (Kukel'), *Nevol'nitsa ili tri nedeli v gareme* (Moscow, 1892), p. 62.

46. *Turetski d'iavol* (Moscow, 1915), and *Turetskie zabavy* (Moscow, 1915).

47. Gladkov, *Kio-khako*, no. 5, p. 6.

48. M. Raskatov, *Poslednii peregon* (Petersburg, 1918), p. 46.

49. *Russkii bogatyr'*, p. 17.

50. Raskatov, *Na chuzhbine*, p. 27.

51. M. Komarov, *Obstoiatel'nye i vernye istorii dvukh moshennikov*, p. iii.

52. Evstigneev, *Van'ka Kain*, p. 35.

53. *Ai da Iaroslavtsy! Vot tak narodets!* (St. Petersburg, 1868), p. 15.

54. *Russkii bogatyr'*, p. 25.

55. *Andrei Petrov—krovavyi den'* (Warsaw, 1914), p. 8.

56. *Zolotaia pyl'*, p. 11.

57. See, for example, I. V. Krylov, *Strannye i chudnye prikliucheniia otstavnogo soldata Arkhipa Sergeevicha. Starinnoe russkoe predanie* (Moscow, 1844), pp. xiii-xiv.

58. *Oka-shima*, p. 1.

59. *Antonio Porro, groznyi mstitel'*, no. 14 (St. Petersburg, n.d.), p. 422.

60. Zriakhov, *Bitva*, vol. 1, p. 4.

61. Ibid., vol. 2, p. 69.

62. *Bitva russkikh s kabardintsami ili prekrasnaia magometanka, umiraiu-shchaia na grobe svoego muzha* (Moscow, 1893), p. 5-6.

63. Ibid., p. 71.

64. Suvorov, *Kak zachalos' russkoe tsarstvo*, pp. 3-4.

65. Ibid., p. 7.

66. Lunin (Kukel'), *Nevol'nichestvo*.

67. *Prikliucheniia kazatskogo atamana Urvana*, p. 3.

68. N. A. Il'shevich', *Znamenityi razboinik i grabitel' "Vasil' Chumak"* (Odessa, 1904).

69. V. Volgin, *Ataman Kuz'ma Roshchin* (Moscow, 1901), p. 3.

70. A. M. Pazukhin, *V vikhre zhizni* (Moscow, 1912), p. 3.

71. *Gazeta kopeika*, no. 1185 (1911).

72. Raskatov, *Na avanpostakh* (Petrograd, n.d.), p. 31.

73. Smith, *The American West as Symbol and Myth*.

74. Wister, *The Virginian*, p. 49.

75. See, for example, ibid., p. 101, and Grey, *Riders of the Purple Sage*, p. 163.

76. Wister, *The Virginian*, p. 355.

CHAPTER VII

1. See, for example, Keith Thomas, *Religion and the Decline of Magic* (New York: Scribner, 1971); James Obelkevish, *Religion and Rural Society* (Oxford, Eng.: Oxford University Press, 1976); Eugen Weber, *Peasants*; and Robert W. Malcolmson, *Life and Labour in England, 1700-1780* (New York: St. Martins, 1981), pp. 86-92.

2. V. Dal', *Polnoe sobranie sochinenii*, vol. 10 (Moscow-St. Petersburg, 1898), pp. 294-95.

3. S. V. Maksimov, *Nechistaia, nevedomaia i krestnaia sila* (St. Petersburg, 1903), p. 3-48.

4. Ibid., pp. 410-11.

5. Ibid., p. 109.

6. *Ogonek*, no. 43 (1908).

7. Most of these studies have been conducted in Africa. See, for example, M. G. Warwick, *Sorcery in its Social Setting, A Study of the Northern Rhodesian Cewa* (Manchester, Eng.: Manchester University Press, 1965, 1970); John Middleton

and E. H. Winter, eds., *Witchcraft and Sorcery in East Africa* (London: Routledge and Kegan Paul, 1963); and E. E. Evans-Pritchard, *Witchcraft (Oracles and Magic) Among the Azande* (Oxford, Eng.: Clarendon Press, 1937).

8. Rubakin archive 274/41.

9. F. Balagur, *Chert v lukoshke* (Moscow, 1904).

10. A. Aleksandrovskii, *Dvadtsat' let ne davala pokoia ten' zheny iz za mogily* (Moscow, 1912).

11. *Pokhozhdeniia syschika Van'ki Kaina*, no. 9 (1918).

12. F. Balagur, *Rasskaz o tom, kak odna baba sotniu muzhikov obmanula* (Moscow, 1912).

13. L. G. Strel'chenko, *Zhertva sueveriia, rasskaz iz malorossiiskoi zhizni* (Moscow, 1910), p. xi.

14. Balagur, *Rasskaz o tom*, p. 9.

15. Ivin (Kassirov), *Chertovo gnezdo* (Moscow, 1889), p. 34.

16. *Koldun, znakhar', charodei, i chernaia koshka* (Moscow, 1899), p. 7.

17. Ivin (Kassirov), *Domovoi prokazit* (Moscow, 1889).

18. Ibid., p. 31.

19. K. Palilov, *D'iavol'skoe navazhdenie* (Moscow, 1914).

20. Nester Oko, *Tainy i smert' kolduna* (St. Petersburg, 1868).

21. V. Volgin, *Noch' u satany—Volshebnaia povest'* (Moscow, 1883).

22. *Predanie, o tom kak soldat spas zhizn' Petra Velikogo* (Kiev, 1895).

23. *Vor Iashka—Mednaia priazhka. Narodnyi shutochnyi rasskaz* (Kiev, 1896), p. 40.

24. M. Raskatov, *Anton Krechet*, (St. Petersburg, 1909), p. 40.

25. B. Reutskii, *Ushchel'e smerti*, 5th ed. (St. Petersburg, 1917), p. 124.

26. *Nat Pinkerton—korol' syshchikov*, no. 37, *Chernyi monakh* (St. Petersburg, 1907-1909).

27. *Nat Pinkerton—korol' syshchikov*, no. 25, *Chernye shariki*, p. 27.

28. Nikitin, *Noveishie prikliucheniia Sherloka Kholmsa v Rossii. Taina Nizhegorodskogo glavnogo doma*, p. 4.

29. Messac points out, however, that Gaboriau was confused about the difference between deductive and inductive reasoning, even though his detective seemed to manage well enough. See Messac, *Le "Detective Novel,"* pp. 507-508.

30. Messac, *Le "Detective Novel,"* pp. 570, 579.

31. *Poiavlenie cherta s rogami i kogtiami v Peterburge* (St. Petersburg, 1868).

32. M. Evstigneev, *Pauk i znakhar'* (Moscow, 1867).

33. M. Evstigneev, *Chert v pomadnoi banke* (Moscow, 1868).

34. M. Zotov, *Kak masterovoi putilovskogo i mytishchenskogo zavoda obuchal cherta na tokarnom stanke* (Moscow, 1910).

35. V. Volgin, *Charodei i rytsar'. Volshebnaia povest'* (Moscow, 1911).

36. Lunin (Kukel'), *O molodom rytsare Sarmae i korolevskoi docheri Blanke* (Moscow, 1897), p. 3.

37. Ivin (Kassirov), *Bor'ba mezhdu chertom i zhenshchinoi* (Moscow, 1897), p. 4.

38. A. V. Prokhorov (Andrei Tiazheloispytannyi), *Vozmutitel'nye pokho-zhdeniia strashnogo morskogo chudovishcha* (Odessa, 1910), p. 8.

39. *Bitva* (1893), pp. 89, 90.

40. Balagur, *Rasskaz o tom*, p. 88.

41. See Samuel C. Ramer, "The Zemstvo and Public Health," in *The Zemstvo in Russia, An Experiment in Local Self-Government*, ed. T. Emmons and Wayne S. Vucinich, pp. 295-307, and Nancy Mandelker Frieden, *Russian Physicians in an Era of Reform and Revolution, 1856-1905* (Princeton, N.J.: Princeton University Press, 1981). Nancy Frieden concludes (pp. 201-28) that—improbably in my view—on the basis of the physicians' own complaints, they failed to gain in status.

42. Serialized in Moscow *Kopeika*, no. 92/447 (1910). A complete run of the newspaper including these numbers was not available at either the Saltykov-Shchedrin or the Lenin libraries.

43. Ivin (Kassirov), *V chem nashe schast'e* (Moscow, 1893).

44. *Kopeika*, no. 251/817 (1911).

45. *Nik Karter—Amerikanskii Sherlok*, no. 9, *Doktor Kvartz*.

46. *Ai da Iaroslavtsy! Vot tak narodets!* (St. Petersburg, 1868).

47. Raskatov, *Poslednii peregon*, p. 175.

48. *Gazeta kopeika*, no. 1383 (1912).

49. *Gazeta kopeika*, no. 1270 (1913).

50. *Gazeta kopeika*, nos. 745-751 (1910).

51. Edward S. Ellis, *The Huge Hunter, or The Steam Man of the Prairies* (no. 271 in Beadle's Half-Dime Library, 1882), reprinted in *Eight Dime Novels*, ed. E. F. Bleiler (New York: Dover, 1974), pp. 107-22.

52. Neil Harris, "Utopian Fiction and Its Discontents," in *Uprooted Americans*, ed. Richard L. Bushman et al. (Boston: Little Brown, 1979), pp. 211-44.

53. Charles Nisard, *Histoire des Livres Populaires*, vols. 1 and 2 (Paris, 1864; reprint, New York: Burt Franklin, n.d.), vol. 1, pp. 122-215.

54. Louis James, *Fiction for the Working Man, 1830-50* (1963; Middlesex England: Penguin, 1974), pp. 72-73.

55. Reynolds, *Wagner the Wehr-Wolf*, p. 67.

56. Egan, *Robin Hood*, p. 48.

57. Verbitskaia, *Kliuchi schast'ia*, vol. 1, p. 46.

58. Thomas, *Religion and the Decline of Magic*.

CHAPTER VIII

1. John G. Cawelti, *Apostles of the Self-Made Man: Changing Concepts of Success in America* (Chicago: University of Chicago Press, 1965).

2. P. Tatarinov, *Fomushka v Pitere ili glupomu synu ne v pomoshch' bogatstvo* (St. Petersburg, 1852).

3. Ivin (Kassirov), *Semeinyi grekh* (Moscow, 1889).

4. Alfred J. Reiber discusses these practices in his study, *Merchants and En-*

trepreneurs in Imperial Russia (Chapel Hill: University of North Carolina Press, 1982), p. 26.

5. Hellie, *Slavery in Russia*, pp. 705-706.

6. Foma Balagur, *Petia trubochist, soboi cheren', dushoi chist'* (Moscow, 1904).

7. *Molodoi razboinik ataman "Buria"* (Moscow, 1913).

8. Lunin (Kukel'), *Masha sirota ili tregubyi volokita* (Kiev, 1901).

9. *Ai da Iaroslavtsy!* The first publisher of this tale, F. I. Kuzma, was probably its author.

10. Lunin (Kukel'), *Na Boga nadeisia, a sam ne ploshai* (Moscow, 1898).

11. M. Evstigneev, *Nos v desiat' tysiach* (Moscow, 1897).

12. A. Aleksandrovskii, *Neozhidannaia vstrecha muzha s zhenoi posle dvadtsatiletnei razluki* (Moscow, 1912).

13. *Polveka dlia knig*, p. 29.

14. Ivin (Kassirov), *V chem nashe schast'e*.

15. *Sinii zhurnal*, no. 28 (1913).

16. L. E. Shepelev, *Otmenennye istorii chiny, zvaniia i tituly v Rossiiskoi Imperii* (Leningrad, 1977).

17. *Kondrashka Bulavin*, vol. 2, p. 5.

18. V. Volgin, *Ataman L'vinoe Serdtse* (Moscow, 1908), p. 35.

19. *Ai da Iaroslavtsy!*, p. 3.

20. Lunin (Kukel'), *Masha-sirota* (Kiev, 1901).

21. A. M. Pazukhin, *Tak bylo suzhdeno. Golubka Mania* (Moscow, 1897), p. 240. (The two titles were published together.)

22. P. S. Kuklin, *Blagorazumnyi i trudoliubivyi syn tekushchikh vremen, ostavshiisia sirotoi v mladenchestve* (Moscow, 1883).

23. Lunin (Kukel'), *Naidenysh, ili schastlivaia vstrecha* (Moscow, 1898).

24. V. Suvorov, *Skazke ob Ivane-Tsareviche, zhar-ptitse i serom volke* (Moscow, 1910), p. 8.

25. *Moskovskii listok*, no. 102 (1892).

26. *Moskovskii listok*, no. 259 (1893).

27. *Moskovskii listok*, no. 52 (1882).

28. *Moskovskaia gazeta kopeika*, no. 116 (1909), and no. 251/817 (1910).

29. *Polveka dlia knig*, pp. 4-5.

30. Erik H. Erikson pointed out in his *Childhood and Society* (New York: Norton, 1963) some of the qualities that make Gorky's memoir a success story, such as a Protestant morality and a struggle against temptation, but he considered the narrator a protorevolutionary.

31. Gaboriau, *Lecoq*, p. 12.

32. George M. Foster, *Traditional Cultures and the Impact of Technological Change* (New York: Harper and Row, 1962), pp. 51-53. I am grateful to Bernard Cohn for bringing this and other work in this area to my attention.

33. See F. G. Bailey, "Debate, Compromise, and Change," in F. G. Bailey, ed., *Debate and Compromise* (Oxford, Eng.: Basil Blackwell, 1973).

34. Many of the attitudes toward wealth discussed above are common to peasant societies, and not particular to nineteenth-century rural Russia. See, for

example, Robert Redfield, *Peasant Society and Culture* (Chicago: University of Chicago Press, 1954); Foster, *Traditional Cultures*; and William C. Rau, "The Tacit Conventions of the Modernity School," *Amercian Sociological Review*, vol. 45, no. 2 (April, 1980).

35. David Ransel, "Abandonment and Fosterage," in *The Family in Imperial Russia*, ed. David Ransel (Urbana: University of Illinois Press, 1978).

36. Ivin (Kassirov), *Starotiagovskaia taina* (Moscow, 1892).

37. M. Evstigneev, *Khorosha Masha, da ne nasha* (Moscow, 1871).

38. Twenty editions are identified in the Saltykov-Shchedrin Library catalogue.

39. Lunin (Kukel'), *Bez viny vinovatyi, ili za Bogom molitva nikogda ne propadaet* (Moscow, 1895), p. 36.

40. George M. Foster, *Empire's Children, The People of Tzintzuntzan* (Mexico: Smithsonian Institution Institute of Social Anthropology, publication no. 6, 1948). p. 288.

41. Kuklin, *Blagorazumnyi i trudoliubivyi syn*, p. 17.

42. Aleksandrovskii, *Tsar' golod* (Moscow, 1910), p. 41.

43. *Veselye dni kuptsa Marodera-Zhivoglotova* (Moscow, 1917), p. 5.

44. V. Volgin, *Utoplennitsa* (Moscow, 1916).

45. Rau, "Tacit Conventions of the Modernity School," p. 248.

46. *Bogatyi v piru* (Moscow, 1890), p. 32.

47. Louis Chevalier, *Laboring Classes and Dangerous Classes*, trans. Frank Jellinek (Princeton, N.J.: Princeton University Press, 1981), pp. 403-408.

48. Gaboriau, *Other People's Money*, pp. 255-56.

49. Gary Scharnhorst, *Horatio Alger, Jr.* (Boston: Twayne Publishers, 1980), pp. 117-39.

50. *Jack Hoyle's Lead or the Road to Fortune*, Deadwood Dick Library, vol. 3, no. 28.

CHAPTER IX

1. *Vseobshchaia perepis'—Obshchii svod*, vol. 1, pp. 188-89, 190-95, 198.

2. Burke, *Popular Culture in Early Modern Europe*.

3. I discuss this in "Russian Nationalism and Russian Literature," pp. 315-34.

4. A. Kotovich, *Dukhovnaia tsenzura v Rossii (1799-1855)* (St. Petersburg, 1909), pp. 300-302.

5. Ibid., p. 309.

6. Gregory L. Freeze, *The Parish Clergy in Nineteenth-Century Russia* (Princeton, N.J.: Princeton University Press, 1983), pp. 42-48.

7. Kotovich, *Dukhovnaia tsenzura*, pp. 302-304.

8. The circular is reprinted in *Spravochnaia knizhka po bibliotechnomu delu, knizhnoi torgovle i izdatel'stvu*, ed. V. N. Charnoluskii (Petrograd, 1914), pp. 77-79.

9. K. P. Pobedonostsev, *Moskovskii sbornik* (Moscow, 1901), p. 168-69.

10. *MO* (1904), p. 187.

11. "Vysokoe prizvanie pravoslavnogo dukhovenstva," *NO*, no. 5 (1897), p. 2.

12. *TsV*, no. 33 (1887), p. 532.

13. G-v, "Sovremennoe obozrenie," *PO*, no. 1 (1875).

14. Z., "Sovremennoe obozrenie," *PO*, no. 11 (1875), p. 585.

15. Kotovich, *Dukhovnaia tsenzura*.

16. *Voennaia Entsiklopediia*, vol. 13 (St. Petersburg, 1913), pp. 77-78.

17. A. A. Govorov, *Istoriia knizhnoi torgovli v SSSR* (Moscow, 1976), p. 194.

18. L. N. Tolstoi, *Polnoe sobranie sochinenii*, vol. 25 (Moscow, 1937), pp. 665-738 (commentary), and S. Semenov, "Vospominaniia L. N. Tolstogo," *VE*, no. 4 (1908), p. 25. A. V. Blium, "Izdatel'stvo 'Posrednik' i ego chitateli," in *Istoriia russkogo chitatelia*, vol. 3, ed. I. E. Barenbaum (Leningrad, 1979), pp. 72-74.

19. A. V. Blium, "Pedagogicheskaia tsenzura o Shchedrine," in *Saltykov-Shchedrin 1826-1976. Stat'i materialy, bibliografiia* (Leningrad, 1976), pp. 360-64.

20. A. V. Blum, "Iz istorii massovogo chteniia 'Znanievskoi literatury'," in *Istoriia russkogo chitatelia*, vol. 2 (Lenningrad, 1976), pp. 92-99.

21. O. Kaidanova, "Nasha deshevaia literatura," *O*, no. 5 (1905), p. 163.

22. V. Vakhterov, "Narodnye chteniia," *RSh*, no. 11 (1896), pp. 141-49, reprints the 1877 list and the 1890 and 1894 modifications.

23. N. Tulupov, "Narodnye chteniia," *RSh*, no. 4 (1902), pp. 1-2.

24. *Narodnaia entsiklopediia*, vol. 10 (Moscow, 1910), pp. 188-89.

25. *Katalog knig i periodicheskikh izdanii dopushchennykh v uchenicheskie biblioteki nashikh uchebnykh zavedenii* (St. Petersburg, 1913).

26. A. I. Georgievskii, *K istorii Uchenogo komiteta Ministerstva narodnogo prosveshcheniia* (St. Petersburg, 1902), pp. 156-57.

27. Ibid., p. 185.

28. A. I. Georgievskii, *K istorii*, pp. 41-58.

29. Ibid., pp. 148-50.

30. Ibid., p. 197.

31. William Canton, *History of the British and Foreign Bible Society*, vol. 5 (London: The British and Foreign Bible Society, 1910), p. 66; James Moulton Roe, *The British and Foreign Bible Society, 1905-1954* (London: The British and Foreign Bible Society, 1965), p. 64.

32. *Istoricheskii ocherk razvitiia tserkovnykh shkol za istekshee dvadtsatipiatilet let (1884-1909)* (St. Petersburg, 1909), pp. 545-68, lists School Council publications.

33. Ibid., pp. 562-68.

34. These were printed on the Russkaia Afonskaia Tipografiia in 1912, 1912, and 1902, respectively. Such publications and the pilgrimages are discussed by Theofanis George Stavrou in *Russian Interests in Palestine, 1882-1914* (Thessaloniki: Institute for Balkan Studies, 1963).

35. *Vsepoddanneishii otchet ober-prokurora Sviateishogo Sinoda K. Pobedonostseva za 1884* (St. Petersburg, 1886), pp. 84-86.

36. *Net propashchego cheloveka esli verit on v tserkov' khristovu, Troitskie listki,* no. 27 (1903).

37. *Troitskie listki,* no. 130 (1903), and no. 149 (1903).

38. *Afonskie listki,* no. 2 (1913), pp. 9-12, 25-28, 53-56.

39. See A. N. Sevast'ianov, "Greshnyi zarabotok," *Narodnaia chital'nia* (October 1907); P. Shul'gin, *Noch'iu,* a free supplement to *Chital'nia narodnoi shkoly* (St. Petersburg, 1903).

40. Ioann Naumovich, *Maksim-Bogach, ili sud Bozhii* (Moscow, 1895).

41. K. Lukashevich, *Na zhiznennom puti* (St. Petersburg, n.d.).

42. K. Lukashevich, *Iz zhizni. Tri rasskaza* (St. Petersburg, 191?).

43. *Afonskie listki,* no. 2 (1913), pp. 61-64.

44. *Istoricheskii ocherk razvitiia tserkovnykh shkol,* p. 558.

45. *Nikolai Vasil'evich Gogol'. Ego zhizn' i literaturnaia deiatel' nost',* vol. 1, ed. P. Smirnokovskii (St. Petersburg, 1898), pp. 8-9.

46. Ibid., vol. 2, p. 254.

47. *A. S. Pushkin. S ego biografiei i ob"iasnitel'nymi stat'iami A. Falonova,* vol. 1, 3rd ed. (St. Petersburg, 1898), pp. 41-42.

48. *Istoricheskii ocherk razvitiia tserkovnykh shkol,* pp. 562-68.

49. A. Ashevskii, "Gazeta v derevne," *MB,* no. 9 (1899), p. 3.

50. I. S. Vertinskii, *Gazeta v Rossii i SSSR* (Moscow, 1931), p. 3.

51. B. Aref'ev, "Chitatel' narodnoi gazety," *RB,* no. 12 (1898), pp. 26-33; *KV,* nos. 25-26 (1915), pp. 5-6.

52. James H. Krukones, "To the People: The Russian Government and the Newspaper *Sel'skii vestnik* ('Village Herald'), 1881-1917" (Ph.D. diss., University of Wisconsin, 1983), pp. 95, 265, 294.

53. *Moskovskii listok, Russkie vedomosti,* and *Sovremennye izvestiia* were more popular. See Prugavin, *Zaprosy,* pp. 211-12.

54. E. Nekrasova, *Narodnye knigi dlia chteniia v ikh 25-letnei bor'be s lubochnymi izdaniiami* (Viatka, 1902), pp. 32-38.

55. According to one account, the Standing Commission was established on the initiative of the Petersburg police chief, Trepov, who wrote to Alexander II and stressed the importance of providing moral and religious lectures for the common people. Alexander II agreed, but he stressed the need for caution and close surveillance. Representatives of the Ministries of Internal Affairs, War, and Education, as well as Trepov and Alexander II's aide-de-camp Isakov served on the committee. I have not seen the published account of the Commission, but it is cited in *Vospitanie i obuchenie,* no. 8 (August 1887), pp. 194-95.

56. S. A. Rappoport (An-skii), *Ocherki narodnoi literatury* (St. Petersburg, 1894), p. 58.

57. Charnoluskii, "Chastnaia initsiativa v dele narodnogo obrazovaniia," *RSh,* no. 9 (1909), p. 47.

58. M. N. Popov, "Vred ili pol'za," *Delo,* no. 3 (1873), p. 56.

59. Ibid., pp. 82-85.

60. Glavnoe upravlenie neokladnykh sborov i kazennoi prodazhi pitei, *Po-*

pechitel'stva o narodnoi trezvosti v 1905 godu, vol. 4 (St. Petersburg, 1908), pp. 8-9.

61. *Tolkovyi ukazatel' knig dlia chteniia*, vol. 2 (Moscow, 1907), p. 5; also *Tolkovyi ukazatel' knig dlia chteniia*, vol. 1 (Moscow, 1904).

62. See Catalogue, F. Iezbery, *Vserossiiskii muzei ili sobranie predmetov*, pp. 87-89.

63. I. S. Vertinskii, *Gazeta v Rossii i SSSR XVI-XX vv.* (Moscow, 1931), p. 58.

64. I. Belokonskii, "Lubochnaia literatura o iaponsko-russkoi voine," *O*, no. 7 (1904), p. 110.

65. *Tovarishchestvo I. D. Sytina* (1910), p. vi.

66. The claim was contained in a request for permission to publish a history of the house of Romanov under the title "Three Centuries." *TsGALI*, fond 1788, 1/1, p. 2.

67. See his catalogue, Komissioner voenno-uchebnykh zavedenii V. A. Berezovskii, *Katalog sklada knig i uchebnykh posobii dlia voisk* (Petrograd, 1915).

68. A. K. Vasil'kovskii, *Andrei Lovkach* (St. Petersburg, 1904).

69. A. K. Vasil'kovskii, *Na vole* (St. Petersburg, 1897), p. 23.

70. S. Severnyi, *V peredovoi derevne* (St. Petersburg, 1912), and S. Severnyi, *V plenu u plenykh* (St. Petersburg, 1912).

71. A. K. Vasil'kovskii, *Vse liudi bozhii* (St. Petersburg, 1899).

72. S. Severnyi, *Na sapernykh rabotakh* (St. Petersburg, n.d.).

73. A. K. Vasil'kovskii, *Antip i Semen* (St. Petersburg, 1899), p. 19.

74. *Chtenie dlia soldat*, no. 1 (1901).

75. Ibid., p. 164.

76. Ibid., p. 178.

77. Edwin O. Reischauer and John K. Fairbank, *East Asia: The Great Tradition* (Boston, 1960), p. 293.

78. I discuss this group and these publications in "Popular Philistinism and the Course of Russian Modernism," forthcoming from Stanford University Press in a volume edited by Saul Morson.

79. See the symposium *Vekhi*, 2nd ed. (Moscow, 1909), and Jeffrey Brooks, "*Vekhi* and the *Vekhi* Dispute," *Survey*, no. 1 (86) (Winter 1973), pp. 21-50.

80. *O vsenarodnom rasprostranenii gramotnosti v Rossii na religiozno-nravstvennom osnovanii*, vols. 1-4 (1846; Moscow, 1849).

81. Ibid., vol. 1, p. 23.

82. Quoted in Nekrasova, *Narodnye knigi*, pp. 14-15.

83. F. M. Dostoevskii, *Polnoe sobranie sochinenii*, vol. 9 (St. Petersburg, 1891), p. 138.

84. Tolstoi, *Polnoe sobranie sochinenii*, vol. 8 (1936), pp. 364, 112, 132, 340-41.

85. G. P. Danilevskii, "Poezdka v Iasnuiu Polianu," *IV*, no. 23 (1886), p. 539.

86. Prugavin, *Zaprosy*, p. 300.

87. Ibid., p. 396.

88. Ibid., pp. 399-400.

89. Rappoport (An-skii), *Ocherki narodnoi literatury*, pp. 14-15, 42-43.

90. Ibid., pp. 39, 40.

91. Ibid., pp. 42-43.

92. S. A. Rappoport (An-skii), *Narod i kniga* (Moscow, 1913), p. 41.

93. D. M. Lekarenkom, "Iz istorii izucheniia chitatelia v dorevoliutsionnoi Rossii," in *Moskovskii gosudarstvennyi bibliotechnyi institut. Trudy Instituta* (Moscow, 1938), pp. 104-106.

94. Kh. D. Alchevskaia, *Chto chitat' narodu*, vol. 1 (St. Petersburg, 1884), pp. 248, 347, 459.

95. Alchevskaia, *Chto chitat'*, vol. 2 (1887), pp. 548-49, 551-53.

96. V. G. Belinskii, *Polnoe sobranie sochinenii*, vol. 8 (Moscow, 1955), pp. 154-55.

97. Ibid., vol. 3, p. 210.

98. Nekrasova, *Narodnye knigi*, p. 7.

99. *Pol veka*, pp. 341, 29-32.

100. Ibid., pp. 97, 125-26, 92.

101. A. Rubakin, *Rubakin (Lotsman knizhnogo moria)* (Moscow, 1967), pp. 5-7.

102. Alfred Erich Senn, *Nicholas Rubakin, A Life for Books* (Newton, Mass.: Oriental Research Partners, 1977), p. 19.

103. N. Rubakin, "Novye vremena—novye vlianiia," *RM*, no. 7 (1905), p. 126.

104. N. Rubakin, *Knigonosha* (St. Petersburg, 1906), p. 30.

105. N. A. Rubakin, *Sredi knig*, vol. 1 (Moscow, 1911), pp. 31-32, 146-53, 191.

106. *Pol veka*, pp. 237-39.

107. Peter Demetz, *Marx, Engels, and the Poets* (Chicago: University of Chicago Press, 1967).

108. G. V. Plekhanov, *Iskusstvo i literatura* (Moscow, 1948), p. 485.

109. A. Bogdanov, *Kul'turnye zadachi nashego vremeni* (Moscow, 1911), p. 76.

110. N. Surin, "Proletarskaia kul'tura v likvidatorskom osveshchenii," *Prosveshchenie*, no. 2 (1914), pp. 91-103; A. V. Lunacharskii, "Pis'ma o proletarskoi literature," *Bor'ba*, no. 1 (February 22, 1914), pp. 23-24.

111. V. L. L'vov-Rogachevskii, *Ocherki proletarskoi literatury* (Moscow-Leningrad, 192?), pp. 45-64.

112. Kleinbort, *Ocherki*, pp. 13-14.

113. Ibid., pp. 25-26.

114. Ibid., p. 25.

115. Kvadrat, "Deshevaia gazeta i kinematograf," *Pechatnoe delo*, no. 11 (1909).

116. Metalliat, "K kharakteristike nastroenii v rabochei srede," *Nadezhda*, no. 2 (September 26, 1908).

117. Martin Malyi, "Pressa i rabochie," *Nadezhda*, no. 2 (September 26, 1908).

118. Prugavin, *Zaprosy*, p. 41.

119. Nekrasova, *Narodnye knigi*, p. 60.

120. Z., "Sovremennoe obozrenie," *PO* (October-November 1875), pp. 586, 588.

121. Alchevskaia, *Chto chitat'*, vol. 1 (1884), p. 59; see also pp. 72-73, 277.

122. *KV*, no. 27 (1908), p. 225.

123. *Nashe pechatnoe delo*, no. 7 (July 18, 1913).

124. *Vestnik prikazchika*, no. 10 (October 29, 1913).

125. *Edinstvo*, no. 9 (September 18, 1909).

126. *V. I. Lenin o literature i iskusstve* (Moscow, 1967), pp. 86-90.

127. *Novoe pechatnoe delo*, no. 7 (July 18, 1913).

128. *NP*, no. 10 (1910).

129. *NP*, no. 18 (1911).

130. Prugavin, *Zaprosy*, p. 365.

131. *Al'bom kopeiki* (St. Petersburg, 1908); see advertisement in *Volny*, nos. 1-4 (1912).

132. Jeffrey Brooks, "The Young Kornei Chukovsky," *The Russian Review*, vol. 33, no. 1 (January 1974), pp. 50-62.

133. A. S. Izgoev, "Vospitanie demokratii," *RM*, no. 7 (1909), pp. 202-208.

134. A. A. Nikolaev, *Khleba i sveta* (St. Petersburg, 1910), pp. 27, 86-87.

135. Nekrasova, *Narodnye knigi*, p. 18.

136. Several of his stories appear in Berezovskii's 1915 catalogue, pp. 329-30. His respected position in educated society, however, separates him from official circles.

137. A. Pogosskii, *Povesti i rasskasy*, part 1, book 1 (St. Petersburg, 1866).

138. Ibid., p. 44.

139. Ibid., part 2, book 2, p. 16.

140. *Gramotei*, no. 1 (1866), p. 120.

141. Ibid., no. 3 (1867), p. 144.

142. Ibid., no. 5 (1862), p. 34.

143. Ibid., no. 5 (1862), pp. 114-58.

144. Ibid., p. 151.

145. "Novye priznaki v nashei literature," *OZ*, no. 8 (1878), p. 276.

146. Ibid., p. 302.

147. Nekrasova, *Narodnye knigi*, p. 26.

148. Alchevskaia, *Chto chitat'*, vol. 1, p. 253, provides a summary of both works.

149. Nekrasova, *Narodnye knigi*, pp. 60-61.

150. *Zadachi redaktsii Posrednika* (Moscow, 1894), pp. 5-6.

151. Nekrasova, *Narodnye knigi*, p. 72.

152. *Poslovitsy na kazhdyi den'* (Moscow, 1887).

153. *Pol veka*, p. 115.

154. O. Kaidonova, *Ocherki po istorii narodnogo obrazovaniia v Rossii i SSSR*, vol. 1 (Canada?, 1938), pp. 388-96.

155. *Bezuboinoe pitanie ili vegetarianstvo* (Moscow, 1908).

156. *KV*, no. 26 (1909), pp. 314, 316.

157. Katalog izdanii knigoizdatel'stva "Posrednik" i "Svobodnogo Vospitaniia" (Moscow, 1906), p. 1.

158. Alchevskaia, *Chto chitat'*, vol. 2 (1889), p. 149.

159. The plots are summarized in Alchevskaia, *Chto chitat'*, vol. 3 (1906), pp. 151-52.

160. See V. G. Bazanov, *Russkie revoliutsionnye demokraty i narodoznanie* (Leningrad, 1974), and *Agitatsionnaia literatura russkikh revoliutsionnykh narodnikov*, ed. V. G. Bazanov (Leningrad, 1970).

161. Nekrasova, *Narodnye knigi*, p. 18.

162. L. N. Pavlenkov, "Proshloe i nastoiashchee pechatnogo dela v Rossii," *IV*, nos. 5-6 (1895), p. 868.

163. V. N. Marakuev, *Chto chital i chitaet russkii narod* (Moscow, 1886), pp. 1-4, 14-15.

164. Ibid., p. 3.

165. Nekrasova, *Narodnye knigi*, p. 45.

166. *Ocherki istorii shkoly i pedagogicheskoi mysli narodov SSSR: Vtoraia polovina XIX v.*, ed. A. I. Piskunov (Moscow, 1976), pp. 354-55.

167. D. D. Protopopov, *Istoriia S. Peterburgskogo komiteta gramotnosti* (St. Petersburg, 1898), pp. 226-27.

168. *Ocherki istorii shkoly*, p. 355.

169. Protopopov, *Istoriia*, p. 204. The books the committee published are listed in this study.

170. Ibid., p. 226.

171. "Kritika i bibliografiia," *NO*, no. 3 (1897), p. 55.

172. *SZN*, no. 8 (1904), p. 90.

173. A. N. Annenskaia, *N. V. Gogol'* (St. Petersburg, 1910), p. 76.

174. Kaidonova, *Ocherki*, vol. 1, p. 13.

175. N. Malinovskii, "Deshevye obshchedostupnye knigi," *RM*, no. 6 (1905), p. 405.

176. Ia. Abramov, "Ocherki chastnoi initsiativy v dele narodnogo obrazovaniia v Rossii," *RSh*, no. 8 (1890), pp. 117-18.

177. N. Rubakin, "Knizhnyi potok,"*RM*, no. 12 (1903), p. 177.

178. *Tovarishchestvo pechataniia izdatel'stva i knizhnoi torgovli Sytina*, p. vi.

179. V. Sytin, "Knizhnye sklady i knizhnaia torgovlia v zemskoi Rossii," *SZN*, no. 9 (1904), p. 83.

180. Ibid., p. vi.

181. N. Rubakin, "Knizhnyi priliv i knizhnyi otliv," *SM*, no. 12 (1909), pp. 9-12.

182. *KV*, no. 42 (1906), pp. 1013-16.

183. *Odnodnevnaia perepis'*, vol. 16, part 2, p. 181.

184. Ibid., pp. 2-3.

185. Rubakin archive 6/16 and 6/17.

186. "Melkie soobshcheniia," *VV*, nos. 7-8 (1905).

187. A. A. Nikolaev, "Kniga v sovremennoi russkoi derevne," *VZ*, no. 8 (1904), p. 171.

188. Rubakin archive 5/3, p. 2.

189. "Pedagogicheskaia khronika," *RSh*, no. 3 (1913), p. 79.

190. Rubakin archive 262/36, p. 29.

191. *Shkola, zemstvo i uchitel'*, ed. E. A. Zviagintsev (Moscow, 1911), p. 90.

192. "Otchet Saratovskoi muzhskoi voskresnoi shkoly," *SZN*, no. 2 (1905), p. 30.

193. Rubakin archive 5/26.

194. Perekati-pole, "Dnevnik narodnogo uchitelia," *RSh*, no. 10 (1909), pp. 73-79.

195. V. V. Korsakov, "O prosveshchenii i vospitanii derevni," *VV*, no. 3 (1917), pp. 160-76.

196. *Popechitel'stva v 1905. Otchet po S. Petersburgskomu popechitel'stvu*, p. 31.

197. *Popechitel'stva v 1904. Izvlechenie iz otcheta Moskovskogo stolichnogo popechitelstva*, p. 33.

198. Prugavin, *Zaprosy*, p. 160.

199. "Izvestiia, soobshcheniia i zametki," *NO*, nos. 6-7 (1902), p. 85.

200. N. K. Krupskaia, *O bibliotechnom dele* (Moscow, 1957), pp. 30-31.

201. "Gazeta v derevne," *VV*, no. 4 (1916), p. 178.

202. *IKMV*, no. 3 (1916), pp. 42-43.

203. "Gazeta v derevne," *VV*, no. 4 (1916), p. 178.

BIBLIOGRAPHY OF RUSSIAN
POPULAR COMMERCIAL LITERATURE

THE FOLLOWING is an alphabetical listing of all the works of popular literature in all the editions I consulted for this study, with the exception of works found solely in periodicals. The call numbers of titles in Soviet libraries are given in parentheses when available. L stands for the Saltykov-Shchedrin Public Library in Leningrad and M for the Lenin Library in Moscow. The L and M are prefixes that I have added and are not part of the Soviet call numbers. The call numbers in the Lenin Library consist of a capital letter of the Roman alphabet followed by two numbers, one placed over the other. I add the prefix M, separate the letter from the numbers, and divide the numbers by a slash rather than a horizontal line. Therefore, for example, the call number U followed by 3 over 4 (U¾ appears as (MU 3/4). Titles and editions listed in the Soviet subject catalogues are frequently unavailable, and I give the call numbers only for editions I have seen. No locations are given for the women's novels, since these are easily located in the United States and the Soviet Union.

Titles or editions found at the Joseph Regenstein Library at the University of Chicago (UC), the Harper Collection of the University of Chicago (UCH), the Cleveland Public Library (CPL), the University of Illinois at Urbana (UIU), or the New York Public Library (NYP) are identified only when these are the original works consulted or if there is a question about the existence of a Soviet original. The reason for this decision is that American microform collection of this material will grow, whereas the Soviet collections probably will not. Many of the titles listed in this bibliography are available on microfilm at the Joseph Regenstein Library of the University of Chicago.

Ai da Iaroslavtsy! Vot tak narodets! Pravdivyi rasskaz o tom, kak odin iaroslavets prishel peshkom v Piter, nadul cherta, odurachil nemtsa, sdelalsia bufetchikom i zhenilsia na starostikhinoi dochke. St. Petersburg: Kuz'ma, 1868, 16 pages (L18.234.4.5); St. Petersburg: Kholmushin, 1908, 84 pages (L34.52.7.1058); the 1908 edition also includes poems of the peasant F. K. Shelaev and another story, *Lipovaia mashina.*

Aleksandrovskii, A. P. *Dvadtsat' let ne davala pokoia ten' zheny iz za mogily.* Moscow: Balashov, 1912, 16 pages (L18.256.9.134).

———. *Kak devki sozhgli parnia v pechke (sviatochnyi rasskaz).* Moscow: Balashov, 1911, 16 pages (L37.37.11.32).

Aleksandrovskii, A. P. *Kak muzh el po nocham v mogile svoiu zhenu.* Moscow: Balashov, 1914, 16 pages (L40.23.7.436).

———. *Kak muzhik cherta obmanul.* Moscow: Balashov, 1914, 16 pages (L37.54.8.362).

———. *Katorzhnik za monastyrskoi stenoi.* Moscow: Balashov, 1911, 48 pages (L20.88.8.177).

———. *Katorzhnik sorok raz zhenatyi.* Moscow: Balashov, 1910, 48 pages (L20.106.8.482).

———. *Krovavoe nasledstvo.* Moscow: Balashov, 1912 (L37.37.11.431).

———. *Molodoi razboinik ataman "Buria."* Moscow: Balashov, 1913, 16 pages (L43.16.9.405).

———. *Neozhidannaia vstrecha muzha s zhenoi posle dvadtsatiletnei razluki.* Moscow: Balashov, 1912, 16 pages (L37.44.10.175).

———. *Neudavshaiasia svad'ba 17-ti-letnei Kati.* Moscow: Balashov, 1913, 48 pages (L20.43.9.9).

———. *Pod rodnym krovom cherez 30 let katorgi.* Moscow: Balashov, 1910, 48 pages (L34.87.1.88).

———. *Polnochnyi uzhas na kladbishche u mogil'nogo kresta.* Moscow: Balashov, 1910, 48 pages (L34.87.5.550).

———. *Poslednii potselui nevesty.* Moscow: Balashov, 1912, 48 pages (L20.92.8.195).

———. *Rokovaia noch' krasavitsy Parashi.* Moscow: Balashov, 1914, 47 pages (L40.3.7.262).

———. *Roman lakeia s gornichnoi Feklushei.* Moscow: Balashov, 1911, 46 pages (L20.84.8.347).

———. *Smert' novobrachnykh u khrama pod nozhom mstitelia.* Moscow: Balashov, 1911, 48 pages (L20.43.9.115).

———. *Smertnyi boi tserkovnogo storozha s mertvetsom.* Moscow: Balashov, 1911, 16 pages (L37.45.10.228).

———. *Sorok let v mogile. Ten' Napoleona na kremlevskikh stenakh.* Moscow: Balashov, 1911, 48 pages (L20.84.8.315).

———. *S togo sveta zhena.* Moscow: Balashov, 1910, 48 pages (L18.337.2.158).

———. *Tainstvennaia sluzhba v polnoch' v pokinutom khrame.* Moscow: Balashov, 1910, 16 pages (L34.48.8.584).

———. *Tainy moskovskikh bul'varnykh allei.* Moscow: Balashov, 1911 (L20.92.8.925); 1913, 48 pages (L20.46.9.297).

———. *Tri mertvetsa(!) samoubiitsy v gostiakh u d'iachka.* Moscow: Balashov, 1910, 47 pages (L18.337.2.306).

———. *Tri zhertvy pod toporom zlodeia.* Moscow: Balashov, 1910, 47 pages (L18.142.4.75).

———. *Tsar' golod.* Moscow: Filatov, 1910, 46 pages (L20.106.8.487).

———. *Uzhasnoe zlodeianie bliz odinokoi zabytoi mogily.* Moscow: Balashov, 1910, 48 pages (L34.87.1.82).

———. *Vechnyi ukor ubiitse.* Moscow: Balashov, 1910, 48 pages (L34.87.6.727).

———. *V ob"iatiiakh liubvi na lozhe smerti.* Moscow: Balashov, 1911, 48 pages (L20.92.8.228).

———. *V puchine voln na volosok ot smerti.* Moscow: Balashov, 1913, 48 pages (L20.43.9.636).

Amori, Graf. *Pobezhdennye.* Moscow, 1914.

———. *Liubovnye pokhozhdeniia M-me Verbitskoi.* 2 vols. Moscow, 1914.

Amur v iubke. Moscow: Aparin, 1914 (L43.23.9.118).

Andrei Petrov—krovavyi den'. No. 3. Warsaw: Liubich, 1914, 29 pages (L20.109.9.8.3).

Antonio Porro, groznyi mstitel'. No. 14. Warsaw: Kaufman, n.d. (UC).

Antropov, R. S. (Roman Dobrogo, pseud.). *Genii russkogo syska I. D. Putilin.* No. 1. St. Petersburg: Belianskii, 1908 (L66-4/12837).

Ataman-Kol'tso, ili posol'stvo k tsariu Ioannu Groznomu. Moscow: Sazonov, 1899, 107 pages (MW 262/606).

Ataman Kondrashka Bulavin, buntovshchik v tsarstvovanie imperatora Petra I. Moscow: Abramov, 1874, 36 pages (MA 131/452).

Ataman Kondrashka Bulavin. Rasskaz iz vremen tsarstvovaniia imperatora Petra I. Moscow: Sytin, 1914, 32 pages (MU 247/1304).

Ataman L'vinoe Serdtse, ili chary volshebnika Sezama. Moscow: Sytin, 1914, 36 pages (L40.14.7.156).

Ataman razboinikov Frants Lerman. Nos. 1-4. Kazan: Kaufman, 1918 (L37.67.1.209/1-4).

Ataman Sten'ka Razin. Petrograd: Kholmushin, 1915, 192 pages (UC).

Azef i Sherlok Kholms. No. 1. St. Petersburg: Nyrkin, 1909, 32 pages (L34.82.4.818).

Balagur, F. *Barynia s ukhvatom, a barin s ukhvatkoi.* Moscow: Sazonov, 1900, 32 pages (L20.62.7.243).

———. *Chert i svintsovye orekhi.* Moscow: Sharapov, 1902, 36 pages (L34.83.8.658).

———. *Chert v lukoshke.* Moscow: Sazonov, 1910 (L34.48.8.541).

———. *Churilko—ob"edalo, kakikh ne byvalo.* Moscow: Sazonov, 1908, 24 pages (L34.84.3.1278).

———. *Geroiskii podvig N. I. Polzunkova. Rasskaz iz russko-turetskoi voiny.* Moscow: Sharapov, 1914 (UC).

———. *Gol' na vydumki khitra. Rasskaz o tom, kak odnogo bedniaka prostaia igolka snachala vyuchila, potom vyruchila.* Moscow: Sazonov, 1904, 32 pages (34.83.4.1112/1-3).

———. *Khrabryi voin Portupei-Praporshchik. Iz poslednei russko-turetskoi voiny.* Moscow: Bel'tsov, 96 pages, 1914 (L43.19.9.183).

———. *Lesnoe chudovishche. Fantasticheskaia skazka.* Moscow: Anisimov, 1897, 36 pages (L20.96.5.332).

———. *Petia trubochist, soboi cheren', duchoi chist'.* Moscow: Sazonov, 1904, 32 pages (L34.83.4.1112/1).

———. *Rasskaz o tom, kak odna baba sotniu muzhikov obmanula.* Moscow: Sazonov, 1912, 90 pages (L37.45.10.86).

Balagur, F. *Solov'ikha—razboinitsa. Rasskaz iz narodnogo byta.* Moscow: Sazonov, 1904, 32 pages (L34.83.4.1112/3).

———. *Uzhasnaia smert' svirepogo tatarina.* Moscow: Sazonov, 1898, 32 pages (MA 245/424).

———. *Zhenushka—zolotoe donyshko.* Moscow: Sazonov, 1910, 24 pages (L34.48.8.564).

Bar-kov. *Akh, kak sladko mne.* Moscow: Lomonosov, 1912, 16 pages (L43.12.9.391).

———. *Rasskaz Luki Medovogo pro zhizn' veseluiu.* Moscow: Lomonosov, 1910, 16 pages (L37.37.11.239).

———. *Tainy bul'varnykh allei.* Moscow, 1911 (L37.44.10.406).

Batrak. *Ot nuzhdy pod poezdy.* Moscow: Balashov, 1913, 16 pages (L43.12.9.351).

Bebutova, O. *Puti k kar'ere.* Petrograd, 1917.

———. *Varvary XX veka.* 2 vols. Petrograd, 1915.

———. *Zolotaia pyl'.* Petrograd, 1915.

Belorusa, F. *Karpatskie razboiniki.* St. Petersburg: Kuzin, 1890, 100 pages (MA 171/1154).

Bitva russkikh s kabardintsami ili prekrasnaia magometanka, umiraiushchaia na grobe svoego muzha. 2 vols. Moscow: Sytin, 1893, 108 and 108 pages (L38.55.2.63-1-2).

Bitva russkikh s kabardintsami ili prekrasnaia zemira, umiraiushchaia na mogile svoego druga. 2 vols. Moscow, 1854, 79 and 106 pages (L18.262.3.20).

Bobyl-Vasiutka. Povest' iz fabrichnogo byta. Moscow: Presnov, 1874, 108 pages (MD 6/265).

Bocharo, Don. *Makarka-dushegub.* Moscow: Bel'tsov, 1909, 16 pages (MR 445/266).

———. *Van'ka Kain na khitrovom rynke.* Moscow: Maksimov, 1906, 16 pages (L34.48.8.248).

Bogatyi v piru, a bednyi v miru. Moscow: Sytin, 1890, 36 pages (MA 203/478; L18.294.4.127).

Boisia Boga i Bog tebia ne zabudet. Moscow: Konovalov, 1899, 32 pages (MS 33/317).

Boisia ne boisia, a sud'by ne minovat'. Rasskaz iz kupecheskogo byta. Moscow: Sytin, 1891, 36 pages (MA 203/557).

Bosforskaia zmeia i tsarevich-rybak s vizantiiskoi tsarevnoi (skazanie). Moscow: Sytin, 1914, 36 pages (UC).

Buinitskii. *Ermak, zavoevatel' Sibiri,* Moscow: Manukhin, 1867, 69 pages (L18.232.6.164).

Buria v stoiachikh vodakh: povest' iz poslednei russko-turetskoi voiny. Kiev: Gubanov, 1904, 108 pages (UC).

Bystritskii, S. I. *"Chelovek zver'" ili Abdul Krovopivets, ataman razboinikov.* Kiev: Gubanov, 1910, 149 pages (L38.65.4.36).

Charskaia, L. A. *Ee velichestvo liubov'.* Petrograd, 1915.

Chmyrev, N. A. *Ataman volzhskikh razboinikov Ermak, kniaz sibirskii. Istori-*

cheskii roman iz vremen Ioanna Groznogo. 4 vols. Moscow: Presnov, 1881-84, 95, 100, 100, and 95 pages (L18.140.6.57).

———. *Gromily. Roman iz byta moskovskikh vorov i moshennikov.* 2 vols. Moscow: Ioganson, 1884, 162 and 124 pages (L18.151.4.31).

Demon soblaznitel' ili chelovek bez serdtsa. Moscow, 1838, 62 pages (MW 35/426).

Dobronravov, N. E. *Strashnaia ved'ma za Dneprom.* Moscow: Sazonov, 1914, 90 pages (L18.268.8.157).

———. *Zakoldovannyi klad.* Moscow: Sazonov, 1912, 88 pages (L43.14.9.73).

Drozov. *Pered kazn'iu nevinno-osuzhdennogo.* Moscow: Sytin, 1914, 96 pages (UC).

Dvenadtsat' brat'ev lebedei. Skazka. Moscow: Sytin, 1914, 36 pages (UC).

Emel'ka Pugachev i Khlopusha. Razboiniki i buntovshchiki. 3 vols. Moscow: Manukhin, 1870, 86, 73, and 92 pages (MF 77/87).

Evno Azev (anarhist-syshchik). Neobychnainye pokhozhdeniia velikogo provokatora. Nos. 1-2. St. Petersburg: Mikhailov, 1909 (L.34.50.7.966).

Evstigneev, M. E. *Anekdoty i predaniia o Petre Velikom, pervom imperatore zemli russkoi i o ego liubvi k gosudarstvu.* Moscow: Manukhin, 1873, 90 pages (UC).

———. *Anna Ivanovna, pod prazdnik. Anekdot.* Moscow: Manukhin, 1870, 36 pages (MR 451/289).

———. *Chert v pomadnoi banke (ne vru, seichas provalit'sia!). Shutka k maslianitse.* Moscow: Gaz. Russki, 1868, 3 plus 4 pages (ME 83/45).

———. *Chto znachit russkaia dubinka v rukakh krepkogo parnia dlia turka. Pesni s Dunaia.* Moscow: Vil'de, 1877, 8 pages (MM 143/38).

———. *Eshche konduktor zheleznykh dorog. Novye zabavnye rasskazy i stseny na poezde.* Moscow: Manukhin, 1869, 16 pages (ME 80/1024).

———. *Fonar' (prodelki temnykh liudei). Veselyi rasskaz.* Moscow: Gaz. Russkii, 1867, 70 pages (MA 126/274).

———. *Govoriashchaia vorona i ee slushateli. Uveselitel'nyi rasskaz.* Moscow: Tipografiia Pochtovgo Departmenta, 1867, 16 pages (ME 80/387).

———. *Iskusstvo zhit' na chuchoi schet v Moskve.* Moscow: Gaz. Russkii, 1868, 30 pages (ME 82/445).

———. *Khorosha Masha, da ne nasha. Veselyi rasskaz.* Moscow: Manukhin, 1871, 35 pages (ME 79/91).

———. *Konduktor zheleznykh dorog. Zabavnye rasskazy i stseny na poezde.* Moscow: Manukhin, 1869, 16 pages (ME 80/1073).

———. *Kroshka-igoshka, skazka o bezrukom i beznogom chude.* Moscow: Manukhin, 1870 (UC).

———. *Moskva v pamiatnikh Russkoi stariny.* Moscow: Morozov, 1880, 15 pages (MU 252/342).

———. *Moskovskie berlogi i nochuiushchii Moskvich (velikopostnaia erunda).* Moscow: Manukhin, 1870, 35 pages (ME 9/153).

———. *Mstitel'.* Moscow: Manukhin, 1870, 144 pages (MF 77/80).

Evstigneev, M. E. *Nos v desiat' tysiach. Veselyi rasskaz.* Moscow: Manukhin, 1897, 36 pages (MA 219/665).

———. *Pauk i znakhar', s legkii sposob pomeshat'sia.* Moscow: Gaz. Russkii, 1867, 72 pages (ME 80/609).

———. *Strashnyi klad, ili tatarskaia plennitsa.* 2 vols. Moscow: Sytin, 1884, 120 and 95 pages (MT 5/517).

———. *Stseny iz narodnogo byta raznykh stran i obshchestv.* Moscow: Presnov, 1872 (MD 18/365).

———. *Tsirul'nik. Veselyi rasskaz.* Moscow: Manukhin, 1878, 35 pages (MU 419/97).

———. *Udaloi razboinik. Skazka.* Moscow: Manukhin, 1869, 16 pages (MF 55/176).

———. *Vagon tret'ego klassa. Veselye stseny.* Moscow: Mamontov, 1868, 30 pages (ME 82/294).

———. *Van'ka Kain. Sobranie predanii iz zhizni otvazhnogo vora, syshchika i razboinika.* Moscow: Manukhin, 1869 (UC).

———. *Ved'ma iz-za Dnepra, ili razboinik solovei.* 3 vols. Moscow: Manukhin, 1863 (MT 100/98); 1868 (UC).

———. *Verneishee lekarstvo ot p'ianstva.* Moscow: Pogodin, 1871, 34 pages (MU 394/788).

———. *Vor Iashka—Mednaia priazhka. Narodnyi shutovyi rasskaz.* Moscow: Manukhin, 1868, 36 pages (ME 82/819); Moscow, 1883, 108 pages, bound with *Lesnoi bes. Narodnaia skazka* (MA 213/1811).

———. *Zhizn' i prikliucheniia Pana Tvardovskogo.* Moscow: Vil'de, 1901, 36 pages (UC).

Fal'k, Viktor fon. *Tainy Napoleona ili gosudarstvennyi izmennik Iosif Boianovskii.* Nos. 1-52 complete. Warsaw: Levinson, 1908, 755 pages (MW 287/170).

Fedor, Diadia. *Rasskazy o tsare-batiushke Petre Velikom, kak on so svoimi molodtsami soldatami protiv supostatov voeval.* St. Petersburg: Kholmushin, 1897, 32 pages (MA 219/875).

Fel's, Gvido. *Razboinichii syn, ataman Vil'de i ego udalaia shaika.* Nos. 1-7. Warsaw: Kaufman, 1912, 957 pages (MW 287/180).

Garibal'di. Krovavye prikliucheniia groznogo atamana razboinikov, ili razbitaia liubov' tainstvennoi ital'ianki. Nos. 1-3. Odessa: Kn. Mag. Roga, 1902, 108 pages (MG 84/130).

Giliarov, A. P. *Kak chert provel noch' v plenu u novobrachnykh.* Moscow: Filatov, 1916, 16 pages (L37.37.11.468).

Gladkov, V. A. *Kio-Khako, iaponskii korol' syshchikov.* Nos. 1, 3-8. Moscow: Pravdivost', 1917 (MW 288/33).

Glebov, S. I. *Belyi general ili istoricheskoe proiskhozhdenie.* St. Petersburg: Kholmushin, 1900, 95 pages (CPL).

———. *Grishka Otrep'ev i smutnoe vremia na Moskve.* St. Petersburg: Kholmushin, 1900, 89 pages (ME 93/429).

———. *Zhizn' i kazn' Sten'ki Razina (volzhskogo atamana).* St. Petersburg:

Korpusnov, 1911, 160 pages (MF 122/520); St. Petersburg: Kholmushin, 1912, 152 pages (UC).

Golokhvastov, K. K. *Abrek, ili rodovaia mest'. Povest' iz vremeni zavoevaniia Kavkaza.* St. Petersburg: Kuzin, 1899, 96 pages (MW 303/342).

———. *Ali Pasha Skitariiskii. Istoricheskaia povest' iz vremeni vostaniia slavian protiv turetskogo vladychestva.* St. Petersburg: Kuzin, 1893, 96 pages (MA 248/382).

———. *Ataman Vas'ka Us. Rasskaz iz epokhi bunta Sten'ki Razina.* St. Petersburg: Kholmushin, 1900, 96 pages (ME 93/432).

———. *Maliuta Skuratov ili zlaia oprichnina.* St. Petersburg: Kholmushin, 1900, 95 pages (ME 93/438).

———. *"Orel," pervyi russkii korabl'. Rasskaz iz epokhi bunta Sten'ki Razina.* St. Petersburg: Kholmushin, 1900, 93 pages (MW 262/585).

Grebenka, E. *Nezhinskii polkovnik Zolotarenko. Istoricheskaia byl'.* Iaroslavl': Nekrasov, 1915 (UCH).

Guak ili nepreoborimaia vernost'. Moscow: Sharapov, 1877, 2 vols., 86 and 70 pages (L18.237.3.48); Moscow: Morozov, 1882, 146 pages (UC); Moscow: Sytin, 1911 (34.103.5.138); Moscow: Konovalov, 1916 (34.103.5.138).

Guliai russkaia shashka po turetskoi shashenitse! Moscow, 1878, 7 pages (MM 143/38).

Il'shevich, N. A. *Znamenityi razboinik i grabitel' "Vasil' Chumak" (Nochi prikliucheniia i strakha).* Odessa: Poliatus, 1904, 40 pages (MM 109/1049).

I nasha denezhka ne shcherbata! Rasskaz muzhika, serogo armiachka. Moscow: Evreinov, 1854, 12 pages (MM 69/267).

Indeiskie vozhdi. No. 6. St. Petersburg: Razvlechenie, 1908, 32 pages (NYP).

Istoriia izvestnogo pluta Van'ki Kaina, samim rasskazannaia. Moscow: Semen, 1865, 32 pages (L18.30.3.90).

Istoriia o khrabrom rytsare Frantsyle Ventsiane i o prekrasnoi korolevne Rentsyvene. Moscow, 1789, 245 pages (L18.261.4.18); Moscow: Presnov, 1893, 107 pages (L18.270.5.213); Moscow: Sharapov, 1888, 35 pages (L18.276.3.35); Moscow: Sytin, 1892, 107 pages (UC); Moscow: Sytin, 1899, 30 pages (UC); Moscow: Sytin, 1902, 32 pages (L18.333.3.300); Moscow: Konovalov, 1912, 108 pages (L37.43.10.1260); Moscow: Sytin, 1915 (UC); Moscow: Sytin, 1917, 96 pages (L37.76.181).

Istoriia o petukhakh. Moscow: Sytin, 1914, 36 pages (UC).

Ivin, I. S. (I. S. Kassirov, pseud.). *Bor'ba mezhdu chertom i zhenshchinoi.* Moscow: Sharapov, 1879, 36 pages (L18.133.5.15).

———. *Brynskii les. Povest' XVI stoletiia.* Moscow: Sytin, 1891, 108 pages (L34.50.8.626); Moscow: Sytin, 1900 (UC).

———. *Chert v duple. Narodnoe predanie.* Moscow: Gubanov, 1893, 345 pages (UC).

———. *Chertovo gnezdo.* Moscow: Abramov, 1889, 36 pages (L18.197.3.3); Moscow: Konovalov, 1912, 24 pages (UC).

———. *Domovoi prokazit.* Moscow: Gubanov, 1889, 36 pages (L18.197.3.6/1).

Ivin, I. S. *Iapancha, tatarskii naezdnik.* Moscow, 1892. (L18.207.6.451/1); 1898 (L20.99.5.217); Moscow: Sytin, 1915, 96 pages (UC).

———. *Il'ia Muromets, naibol'shii bogatyr' Kievskii vo vremena Sv. Kniazia Vladimira.* Kiev: Gubanov, 1899, 105 pages (UC).

———. *Krasavitsa monakhinia.* Moscow: Sharapov, 1886, 35 pages (L18.320.2.540).

———. *Narodnaia skazka ob Ivane Tsareviche, zhar-ptitse i serom volke.* Moscow: Sytin, 1896, 107 pages (L20.83.4.48).

———. *Narodnoe skazanie ob Ivane Tsareviche, zhar-ptitse i serom volke.* Moscow: Gubanov, 1891, 108 pages (L18.207.5.388).

———. *O molodom rytsare Sarmae i korolevskoi docheri Blanke. Shazka.* Moscow: Konovalov, 1897, 107 pages (L20.96.6.297).

———. *Ot liubvi do viselitsy. Rasskaz iz byta masterovykh.* Moscow: Sytin, 1893, 36 pages (L18.163.1.203/2).

———. *Pesni rodiny. Stikhotvoreniia I. S. Ivina (1877-1893).* Moscow: Vil'de, 1893, 2 plus 206 pages (L18.176.5.16).

———. *Pokhozhdeniia tainstvennoi polumaski "Krovavaia lapa," predvoditelia shaiki piratov v rimskikh katakombakh.* Moscow: Sharapov, 1886, 179 pages (L18.256.1.33).

———. *Polnaia skazka o sil'nom, slavnom i khrabrom Vitiaze Bove Koroleviche.* Moscow: Sytin, 1918, 95 pages (L37.74.6.5).

———. *Polnoe narodnoe skazanie o sil'nom, moguchem i khrabrom bogatyre Eruslane Lazareviche i o prekrasnoi supruge ego Anastasii Vakhrameevne.* Moscow: Gubanov, 1891, 108 pages (L18.207.4.70); Moscow: Gubanov, 1896 (UC); 1918 (L37.67.1.584).

———. *Prikliucheniia russkogo riadovogo soldata vozvrashchavshchegosia s voiny.* Moscow: Orekhov, 1878, 31 pages (L18.133.2.45; MS 45/375).

———. *Prokliatyi gorshok ili prokazy d'iavola. Skazka.* Moscow: Sharapov, 1885, 36 pages (L18.209.1.55); Moscow: Sharapov, 1889, 36 pages (UC).

———. *Raek.* Moscow: Orekhov, 1878, 10 pages (L18.233.1.50; MM 143/38).

———. *Razboinik Churkin ili krovavaia rasplata.* Moscow: Sharapov, 1885, 144 pages (L18.218.5.344).

———. *Razbonik Churkin v plenu u Cherkesov (narodnoe predanie).* Moscow: Gubanov, 1885, 143 pages (L18.217.5.110); 1892 (UC).

———. *Semeinyi grekh.* Moscow: A. V. Vil'de, 1889, 105 pages (L20.58.7.249).

———. *Skazka o khrabrom voine Praporshchike-Protupei.* Moscow: Sytin, 1892, 36 pages (UC); Moscow: Sytin, 1900, 30 pages (L20.58.1.520).

———. *Skazka o sil'nom i slavnom Vitiaze Eruslane Lazareviche, o ego khrabrosti i o nevoobrazimoi krasote suprugi ego Anastasii Vakhrameevny.* Moscow: Sytin, 1914, 96 pages (L18.228.10.413).

———. *Starotiagovskaia taina.* Moscow: Morozov, 1892, 36 pages (L18.181.3.253; MA 207/467).

———. *Tsygan' mstitel, ili prestupnik po nevole.* Moscow: Bel'tsov, 1915, 88 pages (UC).

———. *V chem nashe schast'e.* Moscow: Gubanov, 1887, 36 pages (L18.198.5.322); 1893 (UC).

———. *Ved'ma ili strashnaia noch' za Dneprom.* Moscow: Gubanov, 1894, 108 pages (L18.262.7.266).

———. *Vodianoi dedushka i krest'ianskii syn.* Moscow: Sharapov, 1887, 36 pages (L18.320.6.449).

———. *V plenu u cherkesov.* Moscow: Gubanov, 1892, 143 pages (L18.188.3.53).

———. *Zakoldovannyi zamok ili neschastnaia tsarevna.* Moscow: Sharapov, 1889, 36 pages (L18.279.1.68).

Kaftyrev, Semen. *Egorushka-prostak, parenek ne tumanak; mudrenoi nauke uchilsia, schastlivoi zhizni dobilsia.* Moscow: Sytin, 1914 (UC).

Kak russkii mal'chik zabral v plen 300 nemtsev. Moscow: Balshov, 1914 (UCH).

Kholostok, Doktor. *Kak auknetsia, tak otklinetsia.* Moscow: Presnov, 1876, 31 pages (W 298/429).

Klefortov, M. D. *Son'ka "Zolotaia Ruchka." Pokhozhdeniia znamenitoi vorovki-ubiitsy i ee prebyvanie na Sakhaline.* Odessa: Poliatus, 1903, 32 pages (MA 287/714).

Koldun, znakhar' i charodei Chernaia Koshka. Moscow: Sazonov, 1899, 107 pages (MW 301/460).

Knizhnik, Grigorii. *Zhizn' Van'ki Kaina im samim rasskazannaia.* St. Petersburg, 1859, 92 pages (L18.7.3.222).

Kolomiitsev, N. *Bubnovyi kozyr' ili Ivanushka Durachok. Skazka v stikhakh.* St. Petersburg, 1836, 69 pages (L18.145.2.239).

Komarov, M. *Obstoiatel'nye i vernye istorii dvukh moshennikov: pervogo rossiiskogo slavnogo vora, razboinika i byvshego moskovskogo syshchika Van'ki Kaina so vsemi ego syskami, rozyskami, sumasbrodnoiu svad'boiu, zabavnymi raznymi ego pesniami i portretom ego, vtorogo frantsuzskogo moshennika Kartusha i ego sotovarishchei.* St. Petersburg, 1779, 10 plus 232 pages (L18.241.3.58); Moscow: Reshetnikov, 1794, 398 pages (L18.19.7.10); 1793 (L38.79.8.45); 1815 (L18.30.3.60); 1830 (L18.10.3.324); 1859 (L18.7.3.222).

Kondrashka Bulavin—buntovshchik, byvshii v tsarstvovanie imperatora Petra I. 2 vols. Moscow: Smirnov, 1849, 87 and 88 pages (MF 107/57).

Krasavets-ataman Kartush. Moscow: Bel'tsov, 1912, 287 pages (L37.34.8.38).

Kritskii, P. *Geroicheskaia bor'ba Serbov s Turkami na Kosovom Pole.* Iaroslavl': Nekrasov, 1914 (NYP).

Krylov, I. V. *Strannye i chudnye prikliucheniia otstavnogo soldata Arkhipa Sergeicha (starinnoe russkoe predanie).* Moscow: Stepanov, 1844, 120 pages (L18.265.5.11); Moscow: Zhivarev, 1897, 144 pages (L18.283.5.59).

K. S. N-va. *Razboinik Churkin. Narodnoe skazanie.* Moscow: Morozov, 1884, 106 pages (MT 27/651).

Kuklin, P. S. *Blagorazumnyi i trudoliubivyi syn tekushchikh vremen, ostavshiisia sirotoi v mladenchestve. Rasskaz (v stikhakh) iz krest'ianskogo byta.* Moscow: Sytin, 1883, 34 pages (L18.163.1.179); Moscow: Sytin, 1900 (L20.59.6.3).

Kupecheskaia doch' Vasilisa Prekrasnaia. Narodnaia skazka. Moscow: Sytin, 1914, 31 pages (L34.82.5.495); 1915 (UC).

Kupets Aksenov. Moscow: Sazonov, 1907, 96 pages (L34.45.10.218).

Kuzin, S. *Perst bozhii ili zlodeiskoe ubiistvo v lesu.* St. Petersburg: Kuzin, 1892, 95 pages (MA 171/1134). The book also includes "Polnoch'."

Lebedev, P. V. *Vstrecha dvukh priiatelei, sleduiushchikh na puti iz Titovki v Titovku.* Moscow: Kuznetsov, 1870, 16 pages (L18.232.6.281).

Liubov kazaka, ili pogibel' Emel'ki Pugacheva. Moscow: Glushov, 1863, 36 pages (MA 125/17).

Lunin, V. A. (Kukel', pseud.). *Babushka Marfa, ili za Bogom molitva, a za tsarem sluzhba nikogda ne propadaet.* Moscow: Konovalov, 1899, 107 pages (L18.229.1.40).

———. *Balovnitsa, ili v dikie stepi khochu!* Moscow: Konovalov, 1912, 108 pages (L18.256.9.32).

———. *Batiushka volia.* Moscow, Gubanov, 1892, 107 pages (L18.181.6.60).

———. *Beda za bedoi.* Moscow: Vil'de, 1897, 32 pages (L20.97.5.318).

———. *Bez viny vinovatyi ili za Bogom molitva nikogda ne propadaet.* Moscow: M. E. Konovalov, 1895, 108 pages (L18.265.8.91).

———. *Bludnomu synu ne v prok bogatstvo.* Moscow: Vil'de, 1897, 31 pages (L20.98.5.77).

———. *Bog ne bez milosti.* Moscow: Vil'de, 1897, 32 pages (L20.98.5.84).

———. *Brak po raschetu.* Moscow: Gubanov, 1897, 107 pages (L20.96.6.278).

———. *Byloe vremia.* Moscow: Konovalov, 1903, 192 pages (L38.27.9.26).

———. *Dikarka.* Moscow: Vil'de, 1897, 32 pages (L20.97.5.297).

———. *Dobryi tovarishch.* Moscow: Vil'de, 1897, 32 pages (L20.97.5.313).

———. *Dolg platezhom krasen.* Moscow: Vil'de, 1897, 32 pages (L20.97.5.320).

———. *Dve sirotki ili dela davno minuvshikh dnei.* Moscow: Gubanov, 1893, 108 pages (L18.257.8.13).

———. *Dve sopernitsy.* Moscow: Vil'de, 1897, 32 pages (L20.97.5.335).

———. *Fabrichnaia krasavitsa.* Moscow: Vil'de, 1897, 32 pages (L20.98.5.81).

———. *Gor'kaia dolia.* Moscow: Vil'de, 1897, 32 pages (L20.97.5.324).

———. *Istoriia o l'vitse, vospitavshei tsarskogo syna.* Moscow: Konovalov, 1908, 108 pages (L38.74.1.40).

———. *Karaul! Svakhi odoleli.* Moscow: Ansimirov, 1897, 32 pages (L20.96.6.246).

———. *Korabl' mertvetsov.* Moscow: Sazonov, 1908, 24 pages (L34.84.3.1314).

———. *Lesnoe chudovishche. Fantasticheskaia skazka.* Moscow: Anisimov, 1897, 36 pages (L20.96.5.332).

———. *Likhaia tsyganka.* Moscow: Vil'de, 1897, 32 pages (L20.97.5.334).

———. *Maliutka.* Moscow: Gubanov, 1895, 108 pages (L18.260.8.86).

———. *Masha-sirota, ili tregubyi volokita.* Klev: Gubanov, 1901, 108 pages (L34.5.4.14).

———. *Na Boga nadeisia, a sam ne ploshai.* Moscow: Anisimov, 1898, 35 pages (L20.97.5.472).

————. *Naidenysh, ili schastlivaia vstrecha.* Moscow: Konovalov, 1898, 108 pages (L18.265.8.430).

————. *Na Kavkaze.* Moscow: Vil'de, 1897, 31 pages (L20.97.5.301).

————. *Na meste prestupleniia.* Moscow: Konovalov, 1901, 108 pages (L34.38.2.22).

————. *Na musul'manskom kladbishche.* Moscow: Vil'de, 1897, 32 pages (L20.97.5.325).

————. *Ne byvat' by schast'iu, da neschast'e pomoglo.* Moscow: Vil'de, 1897, 32 pages (L20.97.5.319).

————. *Neozhidanno i negadanno.* Moscow: Konovalov, 1895, 107 pages (L18.265.8.78).

————. *Neskromnaia svakha.* Moscow: Vil'de, 1909, 24 pages (L34.48.8.386); Moscow: Sazonov, 1911, 24 pages (L37.37.11.629).

————. *Nevol'nichestvo u aziatov.* Moscow: Konovalov, 1898, 108 pages (L20.99.4.155); Moscow: Sytin, 1914, 96 pages (UC).

————. *Nevol'nitsa, ili tri nedeli v gareme.* Moscow: Gubanov, 1892, 107 pages (L18.181.6.218); Moscow: Sytin, 1914, 96 pages (UC).

————. *Nuzhda skachet, nuzhda pliashet, nuzhda pesenki poet.* Moscow: Konovalov, 1912, 108 pages (L37.43.10.1179).

————. *O molodom rytsare Sarmae i korolevskoi docheri Blanke. Skazka.* Moscow: Konovalov, 1897, 107 pages (L20.96.6.297).

————. *Ot bogatstva da po miru.* Moscow: Anisimov, 1897, 36 pages (L20.96.5.329).

————. *Otchego proiskhodit porcha ili nedug ot lukavogo i kak izbavit'sia ot nee.* Moscow: Konovalov, 1898, 32 pages (L18.265.8.440).

————. *Otvergnutaia liubov' ili mest' vdovushki.* Moscow: Konovalov, 1895, 107 pages (L18.265.8.25); Moscow: Konovalov, 1914, 107 pages (UC).

————. *Pokinutyi turchenok.* Moscow: Gubanov, 1893, 105 pages (L18.181.6.217).

————. *Predanie o vospitanii tsarskogo syna l'vitseiu.* Moscow: Orekhov, 1879, 36 pages (L18.238.5.208).

————. *Rokovaia svakha.* Moscow: Gubanov, 1894, 36 pages (L18.262.7.313).

————. *Semeinyi razdel ili ot bogatstva da po miru.* Moscow: Filatov, 1909, 24 pages (L37.44.10.258).

————. *Shikarnaia zhena.* Moscow: Konovalov, 1901, 108 pages (L34.38.2.21).

————. *Skol'ko voru ne vorovat' a petli ne minovat'.* Moscow: Konovalov, 1907, 108 pages (L38.35.4.64).

————. *Skuptsy.* Moscow: Vil'de, 1897, 32 pages (L20.97.5.326).

————. *V burnuiu osenniuiu noch'.* Moscow: Anisimov, 1897, 36 pages (L20.96.5.324).

————. *Vorozheia.* Moscow: Gubanov, 1893, 36 pages (L18.231.6.56).

————. *Vot, chto sluchaetsia poroi.* Moscow, 1897, 32 pages (20.97.5.322).

————. *V plenu u liudoedov.* Moscow: Sazonov, 1908, 24 pages (L34.84.3.1607).

Lunin, V. A. *V tsepliakh u Kitaitsev*. Moscow: Konovalov, 1910, 108 pages (L34.48.8.589).

———. *V zolotoi kletke*. Moscow: Vil'de, 1897, 32 pages (L20.98.5.76).

———. *Vzryv turetskogo korablia i sem' dnei v plenu u turok*. Moscow: Anisimov, 1897, 35 pages (20.96.5.331).

———. *Zakoldovannyi klad*. Moscow: Gubanov, 1899, 121 pages (L20.58.7.9).

———. *Za minutu do smerti ili prevratnosti sud'by*. Moscow: Gubanov, 1897, 108 pages (L20.98.5.153).

———. *Zhertva neschastnoi liubvi*. Moscow: Vil'de, 1897, 32 pages (L20.97.5.306).

———. *Zhivaia pokoinitsa, ili mest' starogo revnivtsa*. Moscow: Gubanov, 1909, 107 pages (L20.98.5.364).

———. *Znatnyi podvig novgorodskogo kuptsa Igolkina*. Moscow: Anisimov, 1898, 36 pages (L20.97.5.414).

Maksimov, M. M. *Moskovskie tainy. Rasskaz syshchika*. Parts 1-10, Moscow: Glushkov, 1862 (MN 31/193).

———. *Nizhegorodskie bezobraziia. Rasskazy syshchika o temnykh delakh i skandal na iarmarke*. Moscow: Smirnov, 1869 (ME 66/221).

Marusia otravilas'. Sbornik liubimykh narodnykh pesen. Moscow: Nekrasov, 1915, 16 pages (UC).

Masha ili chudnyi son. Moscow: Meier, 1866, 18 pages (ME 59/452).

Mikhei, Diadia. *Ivan Lasun*. Moscow: Sazonov, 1913, 16 pages (UC).

Mironov, N. P. *Bitva russkikh s kabardintsami*. 2 vols. Moscow: Sharapov, 1882, 107 and 107 pages (MW 288/51).

———. *Dneprovskaia rusalka*. Moscow: Sharapov, 1874, 35 pages (L18.237.4.24).

———. *Okhota pushche nevoli*. Moscow: Glushkov, 1874, 35 pages (L18.237.4.101).

———. *Zavetnaia taina, ili doch' prestupnogo ottsa*. Moscow: Sharapov, 1886, 70 pages (L18.209.3.336).

Molchanov. *Narodnaia russkaia skazka o tom, kak Antipka Balalaiku nechaianno slomal*. St. Petersburg: Shataev, 1873, 31 pages (L18.167.3.210).

Molodoi razboinik ataman "Buria." Moscow: Balashov, 1913, 16 pages (L43.16.9.405).

Muromskii les. Roman iz vremen tsarstvovaniia Petra Pervogo. Moscow: Manukhin, 1888, 140 pages (CPL).

Nagrodskaia, E. *Gnev Dionisa*. St. Petersburg, 1910.

Nat Pinkerton—korol' syshchikov. 2nd ed. Nos. 1-114 incomplete. Petrograd: Razvlechenie, 1915-17 (L280.109.9.40); no. 75 (MR 432/902).

Nat Pinkerton—korol' syshchikov. Nos. 8, 9. 12, 25, 37. St. Petersburg: Aleksandrov, 1907-1909 (L38.65.8.23).

Neobychainye pokhozhdeniia 10-letnego syshchika Garri Dzhonsona. No. 1. Moscow, 1910 (MW 287/50).

Neobyknovennye pokhozhdeniia korneta Savinno. No. 1. St. Petersburg: Mil'shtein, 19??, 16 pages (MW 287/9).

Nesterov, A. K. *Voina kukharki s barynei, ili nashla kosa na kamen'*. St. Petersburg, 1866 (L18.232.6.92).

———. *Tainy i smert' kolduna (s natury)*. St. Petersburg, 1868, 108 pages (L18.232.6.175).

Nesterov, A. K., and M. Evstigneev. *Panorama tolkuchego rynka*. 2 vols. St. Petersburg, 1868, 16 and 16 pages (L18.232.2.99).

Nikitin, P. *Noveishie prikliucheniia Sherloka Kholmsa v Rossii*. Nos. 2, 4, 7, 9, 13-16. Moscow: Syshchik, 1908 (MW 287/1).

———. *Sverkh-syshchik. Iz polsednikh prikliuchenii Sherloka Kholmsa v Rossii*. Moscow: Poplavskii, 1900, 287 pages (MU 16/164).

Nik Karter—amerikanskii Sherlok Kholms. Nos. 9-90, incomplete. St. Petersburg, 1908-10 (L19.124.4.132); nos. 5. 9, 52 (L20.109.9.39).

Nik Karter—korol' vsemirno-izvestnykh syshchikov. No. 1. Warsaw: Liubich, 1908, 32 pages (L38.77.1.2073).

Nizhegorodskie bezobraziia. Rasskazy syshchika o temnykh delakh na iarmarke. Moscow: Maksimov, 1869, 136 pages (ME 66/221).

Noch' u Satany. Moscow: Sytin, 1883, 36 pages (UC).

Novye pesni "Ermak." Moscow: Balashov, 1911, 16 pages (UC).

Novye voennye pesni. Geroi kazak, Kruchkov. Moscow: Balashov, 1915 (UCH).

Oka-Shima, znamenityi iaponskii syshchik. No. 1. Khar'kov: Tsederbaum, 1908, 32 pages (MW 288/28).

Oko, Nester. *Tainy i smert' kolduna (s natury)*. St. Petersburg: Tipografiia Pochtovogo departamenta, 1868, 108 pages (L18.232.6.175).

Orlov, A. A. *Anna, kupecheskaia doch', ili Barkhatnyi ridikiul' iz galantereinogo riadu*. Moscow, 1832, 57 pages (L18.232.1.216).

———. *Iskatel' nevest po serdtsu, ili svakhiny predlozheniia*. Moscow: Kirilov, 1839, 33 pages (L18.232.5.200).

———. *Kupecheskaia lavka, zapertaia synom posle smerti roditelia svoego, i rech', proiznesennaia pri trogatel'nom proshchanii riadovichei s kupecheskim synom, vykhodiashchim iz pustoi lavki*. Moscow: Gubernskaia tipografiia, 1833, 39 pages (L18.232.1.209).

———. *Razgul'e kupecheskikh synkov v Mar'inoi Roshche, ili povalivai! Nashi guliaiut!* Moscow: Tipografiia Lazaretnogo Instituta, 1842, 26 pages (L18.232.2.179).

Osteral, V. *Genii zla ili znamenityi russkii syshchik Gektor Grinfel'd*. Nos. 1-15, incomplete. Ekaterinoslav: Iuzhno-Russkoe Knigoizdatel'stvo, 1907, 272 pages (MW 287/137).

Ottolengui, P. *Znamenityi syshchik Birnes—zagadka kto prestupnik*. No. 1. Petrograd: Gosudarstvennaia tipograpfiia, 1918, 31 pages (L17.146.7.13).

Ozhegov, M. I. *Margarita. Pesennik*. Kiev: Gubanov, 1903, 108 pages (L38.74.8.6).

———. *Moia zhizn' i pesni dlia naroda*. Moscow: Filatov, 1901, 96 pages (UC).

———. *Pesennik. Molodetskaia kruchina*. Moscow: Gubanov, 1896, 142 pages (UC).

Ozhegov, M. I. *Pesni v dukhe naroda moego kraia.* Moscow: Filatov, 1901, 94 pages (UC).

———. *Pesni i stikhotvoreniia M. I. Ozhegova, samouchki pisatelia-krest'ianina.* Vol. 2. Moscow: Filatov, 1901, 94 pages (UC).

———. *Poteriala ia kolechko. Pesennik.* Moscow: Gubanov, 1898, 108 pages (UC).

Palilov, K. *D'iavol'skoe navazhdenie.* Moscow: Sytin, 1914, 36 pages (UC).

Pastukhov, N. I. *Ocherki i rasskazy.* Moscow, 1879 (UC).

———. *Piteinaia kontora. Komediia.* Moscow: Smirnov, 1862, 48 pages (UC).

———. *Razboinik Churkin. Narodnoe skazanie.* Moscow: Pastukhov, 1883-84, 1,388 pages, last 5 pages numbered incorrectly as 1684-1688 (UC); Moscow: Pastukhov, 1908 (MP 8/163).

———. *Stikhotvoreniia.* Moscow: Smirnov, 1862, 42 pages (UC).

Pazukhin, A. M. *Ataman L'vinoe Serdtse.* Moscow, 1914 (UIU).

———. *Chudaki nashego veka.* Moscow, 1901 (UIU).

———. *Drama na Volge.* Moscow, 1898 (UIU).

———. *Na rubezhe veka.* Moscow, 1900 (UIU).

———. *Opolchennaia Rossiia.* Moscow: Gaz. Novosti Dnia, 1892, 662 pages (UIU).

———. *Ot skuki v zhenskie ruki.* n.p., n.d., 36 pages (MA 176/750).

———. *Tak bylo suzhdeno.* Moscow, 1901, printed together with *Golubka Mania* (NUP).

———. *Vokrug trona.* Moscow: Lambert, 1917, 147 pages (UC).

———. *V vikhre zhizni.* Moscow, 1912.

———. *Zloba dnia.* Moscow, 1883 (UIU).

Pazukhin, N. M. *Bezumnyi.* Moscow: Gubanov, 1889, 72 pages (L18.197.3.277).

———. *Ermak—pokoritel' Sibirii. Istoricheskii roman iz vremen Ioanna Groznogo.* Moscow: Vil'de, 1885 (L18.241.3.26).

Peterburgskie kolduny i koldun'i. Moscow: Manukhin, 1868, 36 pages (ME 82/457).

Peterburgskie trushchoby. St. Petersburg: Kholmushin, 1908 (L37.20.2.19); St. Petersburg: Kholmushin, 1910, 288 pages (L37.20.2.19).

Permiakov, Egor. *Amurchik.* Moscow: Ianshin, 1883, 13 pages (MW 287/787).

Poiavlenie cherta s rogami i kogtiami v Peterburge. Opisanie sostavlennoe po slukham i tolkam rasprostranivshimsia v poslednie dni. St. Petersburg: Shtauf, 1868, 16 pages (ME 82/432).

Pokhozhdeniia syshchika Van'ki Kaina. Nos. 1-10. Moscow: Artel' Knizhnik, 1918; nos. 2-4, 7-10 (L37.60.6.53); no. 1 (MW 287/41).

Pokhozhdeniia znamenitoi avantiuristki Marii Tarnovskoi ili zhenshchina-d'iavol'. Nos. 1-10. Odessa: Otdykh, 1910 (MW 288/29).

Poselianin, E. *Geroi i podvizhniki likholet'ia XVII veka.* Moscow: Sytin, 1913, 48 pages (UC).

Pospelov, A. *Grishka Otrep'ev.* 2 vols. Moscow: Stepanov, 1844, 40 and 32 pages (L18.232.3.24).

Potapov, V. F. *Alesha Popovich, ili kievskie ved'my na shabashe. Volshebnaia skazka.* 2 vols. Moscow: Stepanov, 1848, 34 and 20 pages (L18.146.2.217).

———. *Andrei Besstrashnyi, invalid Petra Velikogo ili za Bogom molitva, a za tsarem sluzhba ne propadaiut!* Moscow: Gubanov, 1894 (L18.241.6.85/3); vol. 2, Moscow: Volkov, 1851, 52 pages (L18.228.3.28).

———. *Chudesa v reshetke ili pokhozhdenie kupecheskikh synov s kupecheskimi prikaschikami na Nizhegorodskoi Iarmarke.* Moscow: Manukhin, 1866, 144 pages (L18.143.2.39).

———. *Ivan Velikii ili tainstvennaia iurodivaia.* Vol. 1. Moscow: Volkov, 1857 (UC).

———. *Marfa Vasil'evna, tret'ia supruga Ioanna Groznogo.* 2 vols. Moscow: Universitetskaia tipografiia, 1845-46, 120 and 151 pages (L18.257.5.14); Manukhin, 1887 (L18.313.2.7).

———. *Marina Roshcha i sokol'niki, ili skazanie o tom, kak molodye kupchikhi propuskaiut, skvoz butylku ottsovskie denezhki (v stikhakh).* Moscow: Smirnov, 1846 (L18.146.2.237).

———. *Pokhozhdenie Ersha Ershovicha Shchetinina. Russkaia skazka.* Moscow, 1860 (L18.146.6.35); Moscow, 1897, 36 pages (L34.50.8.565).

———. *Raskol'niki. Istoricheskii roman.* Moscow: Smirnov, 1846 (L18.258.5.29); Moscow, 1891, 4 plus 101 pages (CPL).

———. *Solovei razboinik.* Moscow: Sytin, 1909 (L34.50.8.105).

———. *Van'ka Kain. Russkaia skazka.* Moscow, 1847, 48 pages (L18.146.2.215).

———. *Vechnyi zhid. Parodiia.* Moscow: Smirnov, 1846 (UC).

Povest' o prikliuchenii angliiskogo Milorda Georga. Moscow: Reshetnikov, 1799, 408 pages (L18.227.5.27); Moscow: Sharapov, 1880, 215 pages (L18.253.7.9); Moscow: Gubanov, 1892, 108 pages (L18.289.6.11-2); Moscow: Gubanov, 1893, 216 pages (UC); Moscow: Vil'de, 1896, 32 pages (L20.96.3.98); Moscow: Konovalov, 1901, 108 pages (L34.38.2.6); Moscow: Konovalov, 1914, 108 pages (UC); Moscow: Sytin, 1915, 107 pages (L40.10.7.316).

Predanie o tom, kak soldat spas zhizn' Petra Velikogo ot smerti u razboinikov. Kiev: Gubanov, 1895, 90 pages (MA 158/854). This is an anonymous version of a story by V. Ia. Shmitanovskii.

Prikliucheniia kazatskogo atamana Urvana. Kiev: Gubanov, 1901, 108 pages (MW 106/802).

Prokhodimets. *Druz'ia-tovarishchi do groba.* Moscow: Balashov, 1909, 16 pages (UC).

———. *Iz-pod ventsa v tiur'mu.* Moscow: Balashov, 1913, 16 pages (L20.40.9.735).

———. *Marfushka syshchik.* Moscow: Balashov, 1909, 16 pages (L34.82.6.1179).

Prokhorov, A. V. (Tiazheloispytannyi, Andrei, pseud.). *Strashnye vozmutitel'nye pokhozhdeniia neulovimogo razboinika Zelim-Khana ili tainy kavkazskikh peshcher.* Odessa, 1912 (MW 287/145).

Prokhorov, A. V. *Vozmutitel'nye pokhozhdeniia strashnogo morskogo chudovishcha, liudoeda opasnogo besposhchadnogo khishchnogo razboinika.* Odessa, 1910 (L37.37.11.711).

Prokliatie satany ili v krovavom tumane. Nos. 1-78, incomplete. 1917 (MW 481/24).

Rachkov, A. F. *Prikliucheniia strel'tsa, ili tri dikoviny kuptsa. Narodnaia skazka.* Moscow: Sytin, 1914, 36 pages (UC).

Raskatov, M. *Anton Krechet. Roman-byl' iz sovremennoi zhizni.* St. Petersburg: Kopeika, 1909, 240 pages (UC); 4th ed., St. Petersburg: Kopeika, 1911 (L66-8/1271).

———. *Na avanpostakh.* Petrograd: Kopeika, n.d. (UC).

———. *Na chuzhbine.* St. Petersburg: Kopeika, 1912 (UC).

———. *Porvannye tsepi (iz dnei revoliutsii).* Petrograd: Kopeika, 1917 (UC).

———. *Poslednii peregon.* St. Petersburg: Kopeika, 1913, 116 pages (L66-8/985).

———. *V vodovorote (Anton Krechet).* St. Petersburg: Kopeika, 1914, 143 pages (L66-8/984).

Razboinik-svat. Ermak Timofeevich. Moscow: Morozov, 1881, 36 pages (UC).

Reder, V. A. *Peshchera Leikhteisa ili trinadtsat' let liubvi i vernosti pod zemleiu.* Nos. 1-74, incomplete. St. Petersburg: Razvlechenie, 1909-10 (L19.124.2.27).

Reutskii, B. *Odin ili dvoe.* St. Petersburg: Kopeika, 1910 (UC).

———. *Ushchel'e smerti.* St. Petersburg: Kopeika, 1909 (UC).

Richard Gil'derbrant, pobeditel' shaiki "nevidimaia ruka." Nos. 1-8. Warsaw, 1914, 128 pages (MW 287/135).

Robert Gaisler, glava smertonostsev ili zhertva slepoi spravedlivosti. Nos. 1-80. Warsaw: Pol'za, 1912, 1,272 pages (MW 481/5).

Russkii bogatyr'-Korol' bortsov. Sensatsionnyi roman iz zhizni bortsov. No. 1. Moscow: Bel'tsov, 1909, 32 pages (MW 287/153).

Russkii Pinkerton, syshchik Trailin. No. 1. Petrograd: Biblioteka dlia razvlechenii, 1918, 24 pages (MW 287/200; L37.60.4.58).

Safonov, M. A. *Buria v stoiachikh vodakh.* Moscow: Balashov, 1911, 48 pages (L20.88.8.181).

———. *Chert vo vlasti u moshennikov.* Moscow: Balashov, 1911 (L43.13.9.88).

———. *Gde d'iavol bessilen, tam baba sil'na.* Moscow, 1911, 16 pages (L18.283.9.38).

Sam-va, Evg. *Ataman Kol'tso ili posol'stvo k tsariu Ioannu Groznomu.* Moscow: Bel'tsov, 1911, 84 pages (CPL).

Sbornik noveishikh pesen i romansov "Ermak Timofeevich." St. Petersburg: Kholmushin, 1903, 96 pages (CPL).

Senigov, I. *Iaroslav Mudryi.* Moscow: Sytin, 1904 (UC).

Shalaev, F. K. *Novoe puteshestvie na lipovoi mashine s odnim rublem za 1000 verst.* St. Petersburg: Shataev, 1874, 36 pages (L18.237.4.268); St. Petersburg: Kholmushin, 1903, 32 pages (L34.48.6.1084).

Shipulinskii, O. *Akhmetka (Rasskaz ranenogo praporshchika o voine s nemtsami).* Iaroslavl': Nekrasov, 1915 (UCH).

Shmitanovskii, V. Ia. *Ermak ili pokorenie sibirskogo tsarstva. Istoricheskaia povest'*. 2 vols. Moscow: Smirnov, 1863, 70 and 72 pages (UC).

————. *Predanie o tom, kak soldat spas zhizn' Petra Velikogo ot smerti u razboinikov*. Moscow: Sytin, 1890, 72 pages (CPL).

————. *Prokliatyi dom ili kartezhnyi igrok*. 2 vols. Moscow: Smirnov, 1860 (UC); Moscow: Manukhin, 1882, 72 pages (L18.241.6.291).

————. *Solovei razboinik*. Moscow: Sharapov, 1872 (L18.167.3.63); Moscow, 1909 (34.50.8.105).

Shukhmin, Kh. A. *Bal s liubovnymi prikliucheniiami i pozharom*. Moscow, 1913, 16 pages (L40.18.9.515).

————. *Bezprosvetnaia zhizn'*. Moscow: Filatov, 1915, 48 pages (L37.58.5.33).

————. *Bezvremennaia smert', ili liubimtsy publiki*. Moscow, 1915, 48 pages (L37.56.4.358).

————. *Burnyi den'*. Moscow: Balashov, 1914, 16 pages (L40.14.7.180).

————. *Chert, obol'stitel' kupchikh*. Moscow: Balashov, 1914, 16 pages (L37.54.8.468).

————. *Kandaly bogatstva, ili tainstvennyi klad*. Moscow: Balashov, 1914, 48 pages (L37.55.6.2.43).

————. *Na golodnom polozhenii, ili pogonia za millionerom*. Moscow: Balashov, 1914, 16 pages (L37.54.8.491).

————. *O tom, kak chert ukral iazyk u teshchi*. Moscow: Balashov, 1913, 16 pages (L43.15.9.415).

————. *Pod razryvami shrapnelei ili neobyknovennyi starik*. Moscow: Balashov, 1915, 16 pages (UCH).

————. *Puteshestvie okhotnoriadskogo kuptsa na komete*. Moscow: Balashov, 1913 (L43.15.9.418).

————. *Puteshestvie po svetu Vil'gel'ma na khvoste u cherta*. Moscow, 1914 (UCH).

————. *Rokovoe venchal'noe kol'tso*. Moscow: Balashov, 1911, 48 pages (L20.88.8.165).

————. *Slavnyi podvig donskogo kazaka Koz'my Kriuchkova*. Moscow: Balashov, 1914, 16 pages (UCH).

————. *Son kupal'shchiny*. Moscow: Sharapov, 1910, 16 pages (L34.48.8.533).

————. *Tainy bul'varnykh nomerov*. Moscow, 1910, 16 pages (L34.82.4.1121).

————. *Turetskie zabavy ili magometkiny zverstva*. Moscow: Balashov, 1915, 16 pages (UCH).

————. *Turetskii d'iavol, smerti i vozvrati*. Moscow, 1915 (UCH).

————. *Vdovii perepolokh*. Moscow, 1913, 16 pages (L37.58.8.124).

————. *Voina 1914 i geroiskii podvig Maksima Kashevarova*. Moscow: Balashov, 1914 (UCH).

————. *V rukakh krovopiitsev ili dvesti tysiach za spasenie*. Moscow, 1914, 16 pages (L43.23.9.288).

Shvartsberg, M. L. *Artem Omrosiants, groza Kavkaza*. No. 2. Moscow, 1912, 15 pages (L40.20.9.37).

Skazanie o tom, kak soldat spas Petra Velikogo. Moscow: Sytin, 1890, 107 pages (MA 185/1086).

Skazka ob Ivane Bogatyre, o prekrasnoi supruge ego Svetlane i o zlom volshebnike Karachune. Moscow: Morozov, 1899 (L20.58.7.161); Kiev: Gubanov, 1900, 108 pages (UC).

Skazka o khrabrom voine, Praporshchike Portupei. 2 vols. Moscow: Sharapov, 1880, 36 and 36 pages (L18.134.4.159); Moscow, 1892 (UC); Moscow: Sytin, 1917, 96 pages (L37.61.6.71); Moscow: Sytin, 1918, 95 pages (L34.102.8.82).

Skazka o slavnom i khrabrom bogatyre Bove Koroleviche. Moscow: Reshetnikov, 1819, 84 pages (L18.229.4.21); Moscow: Ponomarev, 1881, 36 pages (L18.241.6.103); Moscow: Sazonov, 1894, 32 pages (UC); Moscow: Sytin, 1898, 36 pages (L20.98.5.39); Moscow: Sazonov, 1910 (L34.48.8.537); Moscow: Sytin, 1916, 36 pages (L37.74.6.5); Moscow: Sazonov, 1917, 71 pages (L20.97.5.118); Moscow: Sytin, 1918, 95 pages (L37.74.6.5).

Skazka o slavnom i sil'nom vitiaze Eruslane Lazareviche. Moscow: Reshetnikov, 1820, 60 pages (L18.257.5.13); Moscow: Sytin, 1890, 36 pages (L18.294.4.141); Moscow: Konovalov, 1899, 128 pages (L20.60.7.12); Moscow: Sazonov, 1904, 32 pages (L18.259.9.309).

Skazka pro atamana razboinikov Khvata i pro Nadezhdu dvorianskuiu doch'. St. Petersburg: Arngol'd, 1870, 36 pages (L18.170.2.48).

Slavnyi bogatyr' Antipka. Rasskaz iz derevenskoi zhizni. Moscow: Sytin, 1888, 36 pages (MU 269/146); 1914 (UC).

Slavnyi podvig donskogo kazaka Kuz'my Kriuchkova. Moscow, 1914 (UCH).

Soldat Iashka. Russkaia narodnaia skazka. Moscow: Presnov, 1868, 28 pages (ME 82/1046).

Soldatskie skazki. Iaroslavl': Nekrasov, 191? (UCH).

Solovei razboinik. Russkaia skazka. Moscow: Sytin, 1890, 35 pages (L18.304.1.30); Moscow: Sytin, 1914, 36 pages (UC).

Sten'ka Razin, ataman razboinikov. Moscow: Sharapov, 1877, 35 pages (MW 298/402).

Sten'ka Razin, ataman razboinikov. Moscow: Smirnov, 1865, 60 pages (ME 55/343).

Sten'ka Razin, razboinichii ataman byvshii v tsarstvovanie tsaria Alekseia Mikhailovicha. Moscow: Semen, 1865, 36 pages (ME 58/698).

Strashnaia koldun'ia ili zhivaia pokoinitsa. No. 1. Moscow: Filatov, 1905, 16 pages (UC).

Strashnaia noch' ili neobyknovenno chudesnye prikliucheniia donskogo kazaka v gorakh Kavkaza. St. Petersburg: Transhel', 1892, 29 pages (L18.207.4.507).

Strel'chenko, L. G. *Sirotskaia dolia.* Moscow: Filatov, 1904, 32 pages (L34.82.8.1397).

———. *Zhertva sueveriia.* Moscow: Konovalov, 1908, 16 pages (MW 302/272); Moscow, 1910, 16 pages (L37.44.10.505).

Suvorov, V. *Kak zachalos' russkoe tsarstvo. Istoricheskie rasskazy deda svoim vnukam.* Moscow, 1898 (UC).

———. *Ocherki istorii russko-turetskoi voiny*. Moscow: Rodzevich, 1877 (ME 74/627).

———. *Skazka ob Ivane-Tsareviche, zhar-ptitse i serom volke*. Moscow: Sytin, 1910 (UC).

Taina zolota ili bankir katorzhnikov. Kiev: Gubanov, 1900, 108 pages, adapted from French (*MW 106/809*).

Tainstvennye prikliucheniia amerikanskogo syshchika Nik Kartera. Petrograd: Kholmushin, 1916, 160 pages (MW 34/449).

Tainy Krivogo-Roga. No. 1. Krivyi rog, 1910, 30 pages (MW 288/30).

Tainy sestry miloserdiia ili beglyi katorzhnik. Nos. 2-28. Warsaw: Kaufman, 1911-12 (MW 481/10).

Tatarinov, P. P. *Boltovnia peterburgskogo zevaki ili progulka po dacham*. St. Petersburg, 1856, 35 pages (L18.150.2.570).

———. *Fomushka v Pitere, ili glupomu synu ne v pomoshch bogatstvo*. St. Petersburg: Veimar, 1852, 3 plus 33 pages, (L18.146.2.109); St. Petersburg: Kholmushin, 1894 (L18.279.1.509/3).

———. *Peterburgskaia kukharka ili prikliuchenie na pesniakh*. St. Petersburg: Kholmushin, 1899, 32 pages (MU 281/652).

T. S-v. *Permskie lesa ili zhizn' i prikliucheniia lesnogo brodiagi*. Moscow, 1890, 96 pages (CPL).

Tubin, V. A. *Noveishii polnyi russkii pesennik. Ermak*. Moscow: Sazonov, 1903, 107 pages (L34.83.5.104).

Ul'ianov, A. *Kak sobaka zagryzla nemtsa*. Iaroslavl': Nekrasov, 1915 (UCH).

———. *Liubov' sil'nee vrazhdy*. Iaroslavl': Nekrasov, 1915 (UCH).

———. *Opasnaia razvedka*. Iaroslavl': Nekrasov, 1915 (UCH).

———. *V plenu—iz rasskazov uchastnikov voiny 1914 goda*. Iaroslavl': Nekrasov, 1915 (NYP).

Vasilisa Prekrasnaia, kupecheskaia doch'. Moscow: Sytin, 1915, 16 pages (UC).

Vasin, N. *V svetluiu noch' na "Mandzhurke."* Moscow: Sytin, 1904, 36 pages (UC).

———. *Zabolel v pokhode*. Moscow: Sytin, 1904, 36 pages (UC).

Ved'ma i chernyi voron, ili strashnye nochi za Dneprom. Povest' iz narodnykh predanii. Moscow: Konovalova, 1912 (L37.44.10.24).

Verbitskaia, A. A. *Dukh vremeni*. 2 vols. Moscow, 1907-1909.

———. *Igo liubvi*. Moscow, 1914.

———. *Kliuchi schast'ia*. 6 vols. Moscow, 1908-14.

———. *Kryl'ia vzmakhnuli*. Moscow, 1918.

———. *Moemu chitateliu*. Moscow, 1908.

———. *Moi vospominaniia*. Moscow, 1911.

———. *Po novomu—roman uchitel'nitsy*. Moscow, 1905.

Veselye dni kuptsa Morodera-Zhivoglotova v moskovskikh trushchobakh. Moscow: Bel'tsev, 1917, 7 pages (MW 35/107; L34.104.8.252).

Vladmirov, N. *Andrei-Rotozei ili dash' sebe voliu, spustish' i ottsovskuiu doliu*. St. Petersburg: Kholmushin, 1892, 13 pages (L18.188.3.391). The book also includes *Vot tak Panfil, molodchina: ili uchenie svet, a neuchenie t'ma*, pp. 14-28, and *Skazka pro Senno durachka i prokolduna starichka*, pp. 31-64.

Vl. D-N. *Ubiistvo na sadovoi*. Nos. 1-5. St. Petersburg, 1903 (MW 287/31).

Volgin, V. *Ataman Kuz'ma Roshchin*. Moscow: Konovalov, 1901, 108 pages (L34.38.2.18).

———. *Ataman L'vinoe Serdtse*. Moscow: Konovalov, 1908, 108 pages (L38.74.1.32).

———. *Charodei i rytsar'. Volshebnaia povest'*. Moscow, 1911, 32 pages (L37.44.10.34).

———. *Mertvets bez groba*. Moscow: Sytin, 1893, 35 pages (L18.297.3.338/2); 1904 (L34.52.4.673).

———. *Noch' u satany. Volshebnaia povest'*. Moscow: Sytin, 1883, 36 pages (L18.151.6.339).

———. *Rokovaia taina*. Moscow: Vil'de, 1897, 32 pages (UC).

———. *Strashnaia noch'*. Moscow: Sytin, 1886, 35 pages (L18.171.6.15); 1883 (UC).

———. *Teliach'e serdtse. Veselyi rasskaz*. Moscow: Sytin, 1886, 36 pages (L18.198.5.331); Moscow: Vil'de, 1896, 36 pages (L20.96.6.369).

———. *Turetskii plennik*. Moscow: Sytin, 1886 (L18.198.5.267); Moscow: Sytin, 1909, 32 pages (UC); Moscow: Sytin, 1914, 32 pages (UC).

———. *Ubiistvo na reke Sheksne*. Moscow: Sytin, 1884, 36 pages (L18.146.7.122).

———. *Utoplennitsa*. Moscow: Sytin, 1898 (L20.48.5.83); Moscow, 1916, 32 pages (L37.62.9.199).

———. *Za bogom molitva, a za tsarem sluzhba ne propadut. Istoricheskaia povest' iz vremen Petra Velikogo*. Moscow: Sytin, 1900, 72 pages (L34.82.5.602); Moscow: Sytin, 1904, 64 pages (UC).

Volny krovi. Nos. 1-5. Moscow, 1911 (L19.124.4.57).

Vor Iashka—Mednaia priazhka. Narodnyi shutochnyi rasskaz. Kiev: Gubanov, 1896, 108 pages (MA 213/1811).

Vozdushnyi pirat—prikliucheniia tainstvennogo cheloveka v maske, pokoritelia vozdushnogo tsarstva. Nos. 1-69, incomplete. Warsaw: Liubich, 1912-13 (L19.124.4.152).

V. S. . . . . v. *Kniaz' Zolotoi. Povest' iz vremen tsaria Ioanna Groznogo*. Moscow, 1890, 96 pages (CPL).

Zadneprovskaia ved'ma i strashnyi ataman razboinikov. Moscow: Konovalov, 1913, 108 pages (L43.16.9.118).

Zhena s kaprizom. Zabavnyi rasskaz iz kupecheskogo byta. Moscow: Orekhov, 1882 (MA 218/2022).

Zhenikh iz okhotnogo riada. Zabavnyi rasskaz. Moscow: Konovalov, 1896, 32 pages (MA 238/2058).

Zhenushka zolotoe donyshko. Rasskaz iz narodnogo byta. Moscow, 1910, 24 pages (L34.48.8.564).

Zhidovka. Moscow: Gubanov, 1898, 108 pages (ME 98/438).

Zloi volshebnik-charodei Chernomor i khrabyi vitiaz' Ruslan. Moscow: Konovalov, 1914, 108 pages (UC).

Zotov, M. *Agashin grekh.* Moscow: Lomonosov, 1909, 32 pages (L34.50.7.1279).

————. *Bez menia menia zhenili.* Moscow: Lomonosov, 1911, 16 pages (L43.12.9.294).

————. *Bosiak Sem'ianin dvadtsatogo veka.* Moscow: Filatov, 1905, 8 pages (L34.50.4.578).

————. *Buria v stoiachikh vodakh.* Moscow: Sharapov, 1910, 16 pages (L37.37.11.682).

————. *Geroi moskovskikh trushchob: Aleshka Proidi-Svet i Nastia Gor'kaia.* Moscow: Lomonosov, 1908, 16 pages (L34.48.8.314).

————. *Gore ot zheny.* Moscow: Lomonosov, 1909, 32 pages (L34.50.7.1281).

————. *Kak masterovoi Putilovskogo i Mytishchenskogo zavoda obuchal cherta na tokarnom stanke.* Moscow: Maksimov, 1910, 16 pages (L18.277.8.107).

————. *Kak muzh prodal zhenu s dvumia porosiatami.* Moscow: Lomonosov, 1910, 16 pages (L34.82.3.694).

————. *Poslednie minuty pered kazn'iu.* Moscow: Lomonosov, 1909, 32 pages (L34.50.7.1277).

————. *Priezd deputata Vas'ki Levogo v derevniu.* Moscow: Lomonosov, 1910, 16 pages (L34.82.3.817).

————. *Prikliuchenie s Azefom v Peterburgskikh trushchobakh.* Moscow: Balashov, 1909, 16 pages (L37.37.11.244).

————. *Rabotnichki, Bozhii narod.* Moscow: Lomonosov, 1909, 32 pages (L34.50.7.1282).

————. *Rasskaz Mani.* Moscow: Sharapov, 1911, 30 pages (L43.12.9.737).

————. *V. Moskvu iz Pitera po shpalam.* Moscow: Balashov, 1911, 16 pages (L37.41.10.125).

————. *Zloi razluchnik.* Moscow: Filatov, 1909, 31 pages (L43.12.9.616).

Zriakhov, N. *Bitva russkikh s kabardintsami.* Moscow: 1843 (UC); Moscow, 1879 (L18.133.5.305).

INDEX

LIBRARY OF CONGRESS CATALOGING IN PUBLICATION DATA

Brooks, Jeffrey, 1942-
When Russia learned to read.

Bibliography: p.
Includes index.
1. Books and reading—Soviet Union—History. 2. Literacy—Soviet Union—History. 3. Popular literature—Soviet Union—History and criticism. 4. Soviet Union—Popular culture. I. Title.

Z1003.5.S62B76 1985   028'.9'0947   85-42677
ISBN 0-691-05450-9
ISBN 0-691-00821-3 (pbk.)